College Physics

Second Custom Edition for Phys 100 at the University of British Columbia

Taken from:

College Physics: A Strategic Approach
by Randall D. Knight, Brian Jones, and Stuart Field

The Earth System, Second Edition
by Lee R. Kump, James F. Kasting, and Robert G. Crane

Custom Publishing
New York Boston San Francisco
London Toronto Sydney Tokyo Singapore Madrid
Mexico City Munich Paris Cape Town Hong Kong Montreal

Cover Art: Courtesy of Photodisc/Getty Images.

Taken from:

College Physics: A Strategic Approach
by Randall D. Knight, Brian Jones, and Stuart Field
Copyright © 2007 by Pearson Education, Inc.
Published by Addison Wesley
San Francisco, California 94111

The Earth System, Second Edition
by Lee R. Kump, James F. Kasting, and Robert G. Crane
Copyright © 2004, 1999 by Pearson Education, Inc.
Published by Prentice Hall
Upper Saddle River, New Jersey 07458

Printed in Canada

10 9 8 7 6 5 4 3 2 1

2009460087

MH

Please visit our web site at www.pearsoncustom.com

Pearson
Custom Publishing
is a division of

www.pearsonhighered.com

ISBN 10: 0-558-31136-9
ISBN 13: 978-0-558-31136-0

Contents

The Preface, Chapters 1-9, the Appendix, the Answers and the Index were taken from *College Physics: A Strategic Approach*, by Randall D. Knight, Brian Jones, and Stuart Field. Chapter 10 was taken from *The Earth System*, Second Edition by Lee R. Kump, James F. Kasting, and Robert G. Crane.

Preface to the Student

The most incomprehensible thing about the universe is that it is comprehensible.
—Albert Einstein

If you are taking a course for which this book is assigned, you probably aren't a physics major or an engineering major. It's likely that you aren't majoring in a physical science. So why are you taking physics?

It's almost certain that you are taking physics because you are majoring in a discipline that requires it. Someone, somewhere, has decided that it's important for you to take this course. And they are right. There is a lot you can learn from physics, even if you don't plan to be a physicist. We regularly hear from doctors, physical therapists, biologists and others that physics was one of the most interesting and valuable courses they took in college.

So, what can you expect to learn in this course? Let's start by talking about what physics is. Physics is a way of thinking about the physical aspects of nature. Physics is not about "facts." It's far more focused on discovering *relationships* between facts and the *patterns* that exist in nature than on learning facts for their own sake. Our emphasis will be on thinking and reasoning. We are going to look for patterns and relationships in nature, develop the logic that relates different ideas, and search for the reasons *why* things happen as they do.

(a) Pendulum clock

Once we've figured out a pattern, a set of relationships, we'll look at applications to see where this understanding takes us. Let's look at an example. Part (a) of the figure shows an early mechanical clock. The clock uses a *pendulum,* a mass suspended by a thin rod free to pivot about its end, as its timekeeping element. When you study oscillatory motion, you will learn about the motion of a pendulum. You'll learn that the *period* of its motion, the time for one swing, doesn't depend on the amplitude, the size of the swing. This makes a pendulum the ideal centerpiece of a clock.

But there are other systems that look like pendulums too. The gibbon in part (b) of the figure is moving through the trees by swinging from successive handholds. The gibbon's mass is suspended below a point about which it is free to pivot, so the gibbon's motion can be understood as pendulum motion. You can then use your knowledge of pendulums to describe the motion, explaining, for example, why this gibbon is raising its feet as it swings.

(b) Gibbon locomotion

Like any subject, physics is best learned by doing. "Doing physics" in this course means solving problems, applying what you have learned to answer questions at the end of the chapter. When you are given a homework assignment, you may find yourself tempted to simply solve the problems by thumbing through the text looking for a formula that seems like it will work. This isn't how to do physics; if it was, whoever required you to take this course wouldn't bother. The folks who designed your major want you to learn to *reason,* not to "plug and chug." Whatever you end up studying or doing for a career, this ability will serve you well. And that's why someone, somewhere, wants you to take physics.

How do you learn to reason in this way? There's no single strategy for studying physics that will work for all students, but we can make some suggestions that will certainly help:

- **Read each chapter *before* it is discussed in class.** Class attendance is much less effective if you have not prepared. When you first read a chapter, focus on learning new vocabulary, definitions, and notation. You won't understand what's being discussed or how the ideas are being used if you don't know what the terms and symbols mean.
- **Participate actively in class.** Take notes, ask and answer questions, take part in discussion groups. There is ample scientific evidence that *active participation* is far more effective for learning science than is passive listening.
- **After class, go back for a careful rereading of the chapter.** In your second reading, pay close attention to the details and the worked examples. Look for the *logic* behind each example, not just at what formula is being used. We have a three-step process by which we solve all of the worked examples in the text. Most chapters have detailed Problem-Solving Strategies to help you see how to apply this procedure to particular topics, and Tactics Boxes that explain specific steps in your analysis.
- **Apply what you have learned to the homework problems at the end of each chapter.** By following the techniques of the worked examples, applying the tactics and problem-solving strategies, you'll learn how to apply the knowledge you are gaining. In short, you'll learn to reason like a physicist.
- **Form a study group with two or three classmates.** There's good evidence that students who study regularly with a group do better than the rugged individualists who try to go it alone.
- **ActivPhysics OnLine**™ (www.aw-bc.com/knightjonesfield) provides a comprehensive library of more than 420 tried and tested *ActivPhysics* applets. In addition, it provides a suite of highly regarded applet-based tutorials developed by education pioneers Professors Alan Van Heuvelen and Paul D'Alessandris. The *ActivPhysics* icons that appear throughout the book direct students to specific interactive exercises that complement the textbook discussion.

  The online exercises are designed to encourage students to confront misconceptions, reason qualitatively about physical processes, experiment quantitatively, and learn to think critically. They cover all topics from mechanics to electricity and magnetism and from optics to modern physics. The highly acclaimed *ActivPhysics OnLine* companion workbooks (see Student Supplements) help students work through complex concepts and understand them more clearly. More than 220 applets from the *ActivPhysics OnLine* library are also available on the Instructor *Media Manager CD-ROMs*.

And we have one final suggestion. As you read the book, take part in class, and work through problems, step back every now and then to appreciate the big picture. You are going to study topics that range from motions in the solar system to the electrical signals in the nervous system that let you order your hand to turn the pages of this book. You will learn quantitative methods to calculate things such as how far a car will move as it brakes to a stop and how to build a solenoid for an MRI machine. It's a remarkable breadth of topics and techniques that is based on a very compact set of organizing principles. It's quite remarkable, really, well worthy of your study.

Now, let's get down to work.

1 CONCEPTS OF MOTION AND MATHEMATICAL BACKGROUND

As this snowboarder moves in a graceful arc through the air, the direction of his motion, and the distance between each of his positions and the next, is constantly changing. What language should we use to describe this motion?

Looking Ahead ▶▶

The goal of Chapter 1 is to introduce the fundamental concepts of motion and to review the related basic mathematical principles. In this chapter you will learn to:

▶ Draw and interpret motion diagrams.

▶ Apply the particle model of motion.

▶ Describe motion in terms of distance, displacement, time, and velocity.

▶ Express quantities with appropriate units and the correct number of significant figures.

▶ Describe motion using vectors, and learn how to add vectors.

▶ Understand how different physical quantities can often be expressed using the same mathematical form.

Socrates: *The nature of motion appears to be the question with which we begin.*
Plato, 375 BCE

The universe in which we live is one of change and motion. This snowboarder was clearly in motion in the series of photos that make up the image. In the course of a day you probably walk, run, bicycle, or drive your car, all forms of motion. The clock hands are moving inexorably forward as you read this text. The pages of this book may look quite still, but a microscopic view would reveal jostling atoms and whirling electrons. The stars look as permanent as anything, yet the astronomer's telescope reveals them to be ceaselessly moving within galaxies that rotate and orbit yet other galaxies.

Motion is a theme that will appear in one form or another throughout this entire book. Although we all have intuition about motion, based on our experiences, some of the important aspects of motion turn out to be rather subtle. So rather than jumping immediately into a lot of mathematics and calculations, this first chapter focuses on *visualizing* motion and becoming familiar with the *concepts* needed to describe a moving object. We will use mathematical ideas when needed, because they increase the precision of our thoughts, but we will defer actual calculations until Chapter 2. Our goal is to lay the foundations for understanding motion.

The quest to understand motion dates to antiquity. The ancient Babylonians, Chinese, and Greeks were especially interested in the celestial motions of the night sky. The Greek philosopher and scientist Aristotle wrote extensively about

1

the nature of moving objects. However, our modern understanding of motion did not begin until Galileo (1564–1642) first formulated the concepts of motion in mathematical terms. And it took Newton (1642–1727) to put the concepts of motion on a firm and rigorous footing. This connection between motion and mathematics was the breakthrough that allowed the growth of the science of physics.

One key difference between physics and other sciences is how we set up and solve problems. We'll often use a two-step process to solve motion problems. The first step is to develop a simplified representation of the motion so that key elements stand out. For example, the above photo allows us to observe the position of the snowboarder at several successive times. It is precisely by considering this sort of picture of motion that we will begin our study of this topic. The second step is to analyze the motion with the language of mathematics. The process of putting numbers on nature is often the most challenging aspect of the problems you will solve. In this chapter, we will explore the steps in this process as we introduce the basic concepts of motion.

1.1 Motion: A First Look

As a starting point, let's define **motion** as the change of an object's position or orientation with time. Examples of motion are easy to list. Bicycles, baseballs, cars, airplanes, and rockets are all objects that move. The path along which an object moves, which might be a straight line or might be curved, is called the object's **trajectory.**

Figure 1.1 shows four basic types of motion that we will study in this book. In this chapter, we will start with the first type of motion in the figure, motion along a straight line. In later chapters, we will learn about circular motion, which is the motion of an object along a circular path; projectile motion, the motion of an object through the air; and rotational motion, the spinning of an object about an axis.

Straight-line motion

Circular motion

Projectile motion

Rotational motion

FIGURE 1.1 Four basic types of motion.

The fundamental question we want to ask is: What *concepts* are needed to give a full and accurate description of motion?

Making a Motion Diagram

An easy way to study motion is to record a video of a moving object. A video camera takes images at a fixed rate, typically 30 images every second. Each separate image is called a *frame*. As an example, Figure 1.2 shows a few frames from a video of a car going past. Not surprisingly, the car is in a somewhat different position in each frame.

Suppose we now edit the video, layering the frames on top of each other, and then look at the final result. We end up with the picture in Figure 1.3. This composite image, showing an object's position at several *equally spaced instants of time,* is called a **motion diagram.** As simple as motion diagrams seem, they will turn out to be powerful tools for analyzing motion.

NOTE ▶ It's important to keep the camera in a *fixed position* as the object moves by. Don't "pan" it to track the moving object. ◀

Now let's take our camera out into the world and make a few motion diagrams. The following table illustrates how a motion diagram shows important features of different kinds of motion.

FIGURE 1.2 Several frames from the video of a car.

The same amount of time elapses between each image and the next.

FIGURE 1.3 A motion diagram of the car shows all the frames simultaneously.

Examples of motion diagrams

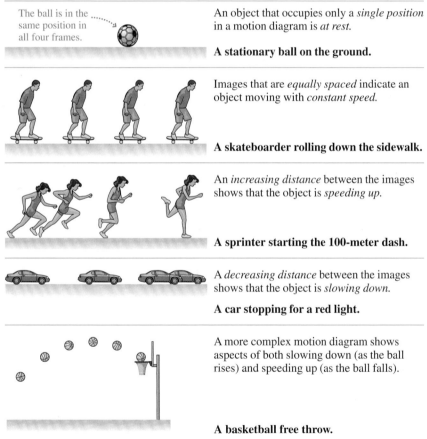

The ball is in the same position in all four frames.

An object that occupies only a *single position* in a motion diagram is *at rest*.

A stationary ball on the ground.

Images that are *equally spaced* indicate an object moving with *constant speed*.

A skateboarder rolling down the sidewalk.

An *increasing distance* between the images shows that the object is *speeding up*.

A sprinter starting the 100-meter dash.

A *decreasing distance* between the images shows that the object is *slowing down*.

A car stopping for a red light.

A more complex motion diagram shows aspects of both slowing down (as the ball rises) and speeding up (as the ball falls).

A basketball free throw.

We have defined several concepts (at rest, constant speed, speeding up, and slowing down) in terms of how the moving object appears in a motion diagram. These are called **operational definitions,** meaning that the concepts are defined in terms of a particular procedure or operation performed by the investigator. For example, we could answer the question "Is the airplane speeding up?" by checking whether or not the images in the plane's motion diagram are getting farther apart. Many of the concepts in physics will be introduced as operational definitions. This reminds us that physics is an experimental science.

STOP TO THINK 1.1 Which car is going faster, A or B? Assume there are equal intervals of time between the frames of both videos.

Car A   Car B

NOTE ▶ Each chapter in this textbook will have several *Stop to Think* questions. These questions are designed to see if you've understood the basic ideas that have been presented. The answers are given at the end of the chapter, but you should make a serious effort to think about these questions before turning to the answers. If you answer correctly, and are sure of your answer rather than just guessing, you can proceed to the next section with confidence. But if you answer incorrectly, it would be wise to reread the preceding sections carefully before proceeding onward. ◀

The Particle Model

For many objects, such as cars and rockets, the motion of the object *as a whole* is not influenced by the "details" of the object's size and shape. To describe the object's motion, all we really need to keep track of is the motion of a single point: You could imagine looking at the motion of a dot painted on the side of the object.

In fact, for the purposes of analyzing the motion, we can often consider the object *as if* it were just a single point, without size or shape. We can also treat the object *as if* all of its mass were concentrated into this single point. An object that can be represented as a mass at a single point in space is called a **particle.** A particle has no size, no shape, and no distinction between top and bottom or between front and back.

If we treat an object as a particle, we can represent the object in each frame of a motion diagram as a simple dot rather than having to draw a full picture. Figure 1.4 shows how much simpler motion diagrams appear when the object is represented as a particle. Note that the dots have been numbered 0, 1, 2, . . . to tell the sequence in which the frames were exposed. These diagrams are more abstract than the pictures, but they are easier to draw and they still convey our full understanding of the object's motion.

Treating an object as a particle is, of course, a simplification of reality. Such a simplification is called a **model.** Models allow us to focus on the important aspects of a phenomenon by excluding those aspects that play only a minor role. The **particle model** of motion is a simplification in which we treat a moving object as if all of its mass were concentrated at a single point. This might seem like an oversimplification, but if all we are concerned with is the motion of an object, it may not be. Using the particle model may allow us to see connections that are very important. Consider the motion of the two objects shown in Figure 1.5. These two very different objects have exactly the same motion diagram! As we will see, all objects falling under the influence of gravity move in exactly the same manner if no other forces act. The simplification of the particle model has revealed something about the physics that underlies both of these situations.

Not all motions can be reduced to the motion of a single point. Consider a rotating gear. The center of the gear doesn't move at all, and each tooth on the gear is moving in a different direction. Rotational motion is qualitatively different from motion along a line, and we'll need to go beyond the particle model later when we study rotational motion.

(a) Motion diagram of a car stopping

(b) Same motion diagram using the particle model

The same amount of time elapses between each frame and the next.

Numbers show the order in which the frames were taken.

A single dot is used to represent the object.

FIGURE 1.4 Simplifying a motion diagram using the particle model.

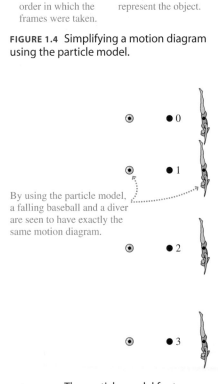

By using the particle model, a falling baseball and a diver are seen to have exactly the same motion diagram.

FIGURE 1.5 The particle model for two falling objects.

<table>
<tr><td>**STOP TO THINK 1.2**</td></tr>
</table>

	A.	B.	C.
	0 ●	0 ●	0 ●
	1 ●		
	2 ●	1 ●	
			1 ●
	3 ●	2 ●	2 ●
		3 ●	3 ●
	4 ●		4 ●
		4 ●	
	5 ●	5 ●	5 ●

STOP TO THINK 1.2 Three motion diagrams are shown. Which is a dust particle settling to the floor at constant speed, which is a ball dropped from the roof of a building, and which is a descending rocket slowing to make a soft landing on Mars?

1.2 Position and Time: Putting Numbers on Nature

To develop our understanding of motion further, we need to be able to make quantitative measurements. That is, we need to use numbers. As we look at a motion diagram, it would be useful to know where the object is (its *position*) and when the object was at that position (the *time*). We'll start by considering the motion of an object that can move only along a straight line. Examples of this **one-dimensional** or "1D" motion would be a bicyclist moving along the road, a train moving on a long straight track, or an elevator moving up and down a shaft.

Position and Coordinate Systems

Suppose you are driving along a long, straight country road, as in Figure 1.6, and your friend calls and asks where you are. You might reply that you are four miles east of the post office, and your friend would then know just where you were. Your location at a particular instant in time (when your friend phoned) is called your **position.** Notice that to know your position along the road, your friend needed three pieces of information. First, you had to give her a reference point (the post office) from which all distances are to be measured. We call this fixed reference point the **origin.** Second, she needed to know how far you were from that reference point or origin—in this case, four miles. Finally, she needed to know which side of the origin you were on: You could be four miles to the west of it, or four miles to the east.

We will need these same three pieces of information in order to specify any object's position along a line. We first choose our origin, from which we measure the position of the object. The position of the origin is arbitrary, and we are free to place it where we like. Usually, however, there are certain points (such as the well-known post office) that are more convenient choices than others.

In order to specify how far our object is from the origin, we lay down an imaginary axis along the line of the object's motion. Like a ruler, this axis is marked off in equally spaced divisions of distance, perhaps in inches, meters, or miles, depending on the problem at hand. We place the zero mark of this ruler at the origin, allowing us to locate the position of our object by reading the ruler mark where the object is.

Finally, we need to be able to specify which side of the origin our object is on. To do this, we imagine the axis extending from one side of the origin with increasing, positive markings; on the other side, the axis is marked with increasing *negative* numbers. By reporting the position as either a positive or a negative number, we know on what side of the origin the object is.

These elements—an origin and an axis marked in both the positive and negative directions—can be used to unambiguously locate the position of an object. We call this a **coordinate system.** We will use coordinate systems throughout this

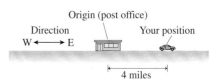

FIGURE 1.6 Describing your position.

Sometimes measurements have a very natural origin. This snow depth gauge has its origin set at road level.

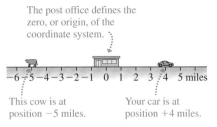

The post office defines the zero, or origin, of the coordinate system.

This cow is at position −5 miles.

Your car is at position +4 miles.

FIGURE 1.7 The coordinate system used to describe objects along a country road.

book, and we will soon develop coordinate systems that can be used to describe the position of objects moving in more complex ways than just along a line. Figure 1.7 shows a coordinate system that can be used to locate various objects along the country road discussed earlier.

Although our coordinate system works well for describing the positions of objects located along the axis, our notation is somewhat cumbersome. We need to keep saying things like "the car is at position +4 miles." A better notation, and one that will become particularly important when we study motion in two dimensions, is to use a symbol such as x or y to represent the position along the axis. Then we can say "the cow is at $x = −5$ miles." The symbol that represents a position along an axis is called a **coordinate.** The introduction of symbols to represent positions (and, later, velocities and accelerations) also allows us to work with these quantities mathematically.

Figure 1.8 shows how we would set up a coordinate system for a sprinter running a 50-meter race (we use the standard symbol "m" for meters). For horizontal motion like this we usually use the coordinate x to represent the position.

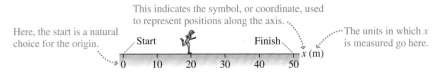

This indicates the symbol, or coordinate, used to represent positions along the axis.

Here, the start is a natural choice for the origin.

The units in which x is measured go here.

FIGURE 1.8 A coordinate system for a 50-meter race.

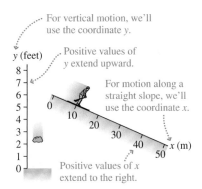

For vertical motion, we'll use the coordinate y.

Positive values of y extend upward.

For motion along a straight slope, we'll use the coordinate x.

Positive values of x extend to the right.

FIGURE 1.9 Examples of one-dimensional motion.

Motion along a straight line need not be horizontal. As shown in Figure 1.9, a rock falling vertically downward and a skier skiing down a straight slope are also examples of straight-line or one-dimensional motion.

Time

The pictures in Figure 1.9 show the position of an object at just one instant of time. But a full motion diagram represents how an object moves as time progresses. So far, we have labeled the dots in a motion diagram by the numbers 0, 1, 2, . . . to indicate the order in which the frames were exposed. But to fully describe the motion, we need to indicate the *time,* as read off a clock or a stopwatch, at which each frame of a video was made. This is important, as we can see from the motion diagram of a stopping car in Figure 1.10. If the frames were taken one second apart, this motion diagram shows a leisurely stop; if 1/10 of a second apart, it represents a screeching halt.

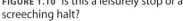

FIGURE 1.10 Is this a leisurely stop or a screeching halt?

For a complete motion diagram, we thus need to label each frame with its corresponding time (symbol t) as read off a clock. But when should we start the clock? That is, which frame should be labeled $t = 0$? This choice is much like that of choosing the origin $x = 0$ of a coordinate system: You can pick any arbitrary point in the motion and label it "$t = 0$ seconds." This is simply the instant you decide to start your clock or stopwatch, so it is the origin of your time coordinate. A video frame labeled "$t = 4$ seconds" means it was taken 4 seconds after you started your clock. We typically choose $t = 0$ to represent the "beginning" of a problem, but the object may have been moving before then.

To illustrate, Figure 1.11 shows the motion diagram for a car moving at a constant speed, and then braking to a halt. Two possible choices for the frame labeled $t = 0$ seconds are shown; our choice depends on what part of the motion we're interested in. Each successive position of the car is then labeled with the clock reading in seconds (abbreviated by the symbol "s").

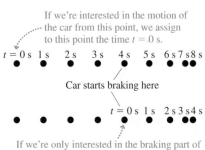

If we're interested in the motion of the car from this point, we assign to this point the time $t = 0$ s.

$t = 0$ s 1 s 2 s 3 s 4 s 5 s 6 s 7 s 8 s

Car starts braking here

$t = 0$ s 1 s 2 s 3 s 4 s

If we're only interested in the braking part of the motion, we would assign $t = 0$ s here.

FIGURE 1.11 The motion diagram of a car that travels at constant speed and then brakes to a halt.

Changes in Position and Displacement

Now that we've seen how to measure position and time, let's return to the problem of motion. To describe motion we'll need to measure the *changes* in position that occur with time. Consider the following:

> Sam is standing 50 feet (ft) east of the corner of 12th Street and Vine. He then walks to a second point 150 ft east of Vine. What is Sam's change of position?

Figure 1.12 shows Sam's motion on a map. We've placed a coordinate system on the map, using the coordinate x. We are free to place the origin of our coordinate system wherever we wish, so we have placed it at the intersection. Sam's initial position is then at $x_i = 50$ ft. The positive value for x_i tells us that Sam is east of the origin.

> NOTE ▶ We will label special values of x or y with subscripts. The value at the start of a problem is usually labeled with a subscript "i," for *initial*, and that at the end is labeled with a subscript "f," for *final*. For cases having several special values, we will usually use subscripts "1," "2," etc. ◀

Sam's final position is $x_f = 150$ ft, indicating that he is 150 feet east of the origin. You can see that Sam has changed position, and a *change* of position is called a **displacement.** His displacement is the distance labeled Δx in Figure 1.12. The Greek letter delta (Δ) is used in math and science to indicate the *change* in a quantity. Thus Δx indicates a change in the position x.

> NOTE ▶ Δx is a *single* symbol. You cannot cancel out or remove the Δ in algebraic operations. ◀

To get from the 50 ft mark to the 150 ft mark, Sam clearly had to walk 100 ft, so the change in his position—his displacement—is 100 ft. We can think about displacement in a more general way, however. **Displacement is the *difference* between a final position x_f and an initial position x_i.** Thus we can write

$$\Delta x = x_f - x_i = 150 \text{ ft} - 50 \text{ ft} = 100 \text{ ft}$$

> NOTE ▶ A general principle, used throughout this book, is that the change in any quantity is the final value of the quantity minus its initial value. ◀

Displacement is a *signed quantity*. That is, it can be either positive or negative. If, as shown in Figure 1.13, Sam's final position x_f had been at the origin instead of the 150 ft mark, his displacement would have been

$$\Delta x = x_f - x_i = 0 \text{ ft} - 50 \text{ ft} = -50 \text{ ft}$$

The negative sign tells us that he moved to the *left* along the x-axis, or 50 ft *west*.

Change in Time

A displacement is a change in position. In order to quantify motion, we'll need to also consider changes in *time*, which we call **time intervals.** We've seen how we can label each frame of a motion diagram with a specific time, as determined by our stopwatch. Figure 1.14 on the next page shows the motion diagram of a bicycle moving at a constant speed, with the times of measured points indicated.

The displacement between the initial position x_i and the final position x_f is

$$\Delta x = x_f - x_i = 120 \text{ ft} - 0 \text{ ft} = 120 \text{ ft}$$

Similarly, we define the time interval between these two points to be

$$\Delta t = t_f - t_i = 6 \text{ s} - 0 \text{ s} = 6 \text{ s}$$

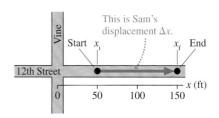

FIGURE 1.12 Sam undergoes a displacement Δx from position x_i to position x_f.

The size and the direction of the displacement both matter. Roy Riegels (pursued above by teammate Benny Lom) found this out in dramatic fashion in the 1928 Rose Bowl when he recovered a fumble and ran 69 yards—toward his own team's end zone. An impressive distance, but in the wrong direction!

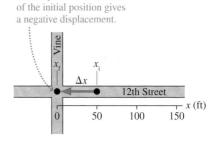

FIGURE 1.13 A displacement is a signed quantity. Here Δx is a negative number.

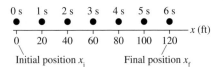

Initial position x_i Final position x_f

FIGURE 1.14 The motion diagram of a bicycle moving to the right at a constant speed.

A time interval Δt measures the elapsed time as an object moves from an initial position x_i at time t_i to a final position x_f at time t_f. Note that unlike Δx, Δt is always positive because t_f is always greater than t_i.

> **STOP TO THINK 1.3**   Sarah starts at a positive position along the x-axis. She then undergoes a negative displacement. Her final position
>
> A. Is positive.
> B. Is negative.
> C. Could be either positive or negative.

During each second, the car moves twice as far as the bicycle. Hence the car is moving at a greater speed.

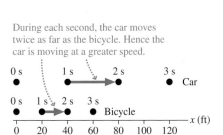

FIGURE 1.15 Motion diagrams for a car and a bicycle.

1.3 Velocity

We all have an intuitive sense of whether something is moving very fast or just cruising slowly along. To make this intuitive idea more precise, let's start by examining the motion diagrams of some objects moving along a straight line at a *constant* speed, objects that are neither speeding up nor slowing down. This motion at a constant speed is called **uniform motion.** As we saw for the skateboarder in Section 1.1, for an object in uniform motion successive frames of the motion diagram are *equally spaced*. We know now that this means that the object's displacement Δx is the same between successive frames.

To see how an object's displacement between successive frames is related to its speed, consider the motion diagrams of a bicycle and a car, traveling along the same street as shown in Figure 1.15. Clearly the car is moving faster than the bicycle: In any one-second time interval, the car undergoes a displacement $\Delta x = 40$ ft, while the bicycle's displacement is only 20 ft.

The distances traveled in one second by the bicycle and the car are a measure of their speeds. The greater the distance traveled by an object in a given time interval, the greater its speed. This idea leads us to define the speed of an object as

$$\text{speed} = \frac{\text{distance traveled in a given time interval}}{\text{time interval}} \qquad (1.1)$$

Speed of a moving object

For the bicycle, this gives

$$\text{speed} = \frac{20 \text{ ft}}{1 \text{ s}} = 20 \, \frac{\text{ft}}{\text{s}}$$

while for the car we have

$$\text{speed} = \frac{40 \text{ ft}}{1 \text{ s}} = 40 \, \frac{\text{ft}}{\text{s}}$$

The speed of the car is twice that of the bicycle, which seems reasonable.

NOTE ▶ The division gives units that are a fraction: ft/s. This is read as "feet per second," just like the more familiar "miles per hour." ◀

To fully characterize the motion of an object, it is important to specify not only the object's speed but also the *direction* in which it is moving. For example,

Figure 1.16 shows the motion diagrams of two bicycles traveling at the same speed of 20 ft/s. The two bicycles have the same speed. but something about their motion is different—the *direction* of their motion.

The problem is that the "distance traveled" in Equation 1.1 doesn't capture any information about the direction of travel. But we've seen that the *displacement* of an object does contain this information. We can then introduce a new quantity, the **velocity,** as

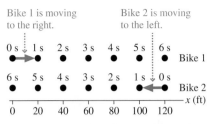

Bike 1 is moving to the right.   Bike 2 is moving to the left.

FIGURE 1.16 Two bicycles traveling at the same speed, but with different velocities.

$$\text{velocity} = \frac{\text{displacement}}{\text{time interval}} = \frac{\Delta x}{\Delta t} \qquad (1.2)$$

Velocity of a moving object

The velocity of bicycle 1 in Figure 1.16, computed using the one-second time interval between the $t = 2$ s and $t = 3$ s positions, is

$$v = \frac{\Delta x}{\Delta t} = \frac{x_3 - x_2}{3\,\text{s} - 2\,\text{s}} = \frac{60\,\text{ft} - 40\,\text{ft}}{1\,\text{s}} = +20\,\frac{\text{ft}}{\text{s}}$$

while the velocity for bicycle 2, during the same time interval, is

$$v = \frac{\Delta x}{\Delta t} = \frac{x_3 - x_2}{3\,\text{s} - 2\,\text{s}} = \frac{60\,\text{ft} - 80\,\text{ft}}{1\,\text{s}} = -20\,\frac{\text{ft}}{\text{s}}$$

NOTE ▶ We have used x_2 for the position at time $t = 2$ seconds, and x_3 for the position at time $t = 3$ seconds. The subscripts 2 and 3 serve the same role as before—identifying particular positions—but in this case the positions are identified by the time at which each position is reached. ◀

The two velocities have opposite signs because the bicycles are traveling in opposite directions. **Speed measures only how fast an object moves, but velocity tells us both an object's speed *and its direction.*** A positive velocity indicates motion to the right or, for vertical motion, upward. Similarly, an object moving to the left, or down, has a negative velocity.

NOTE ▶ Learning to distinguish between speed, which is always a positive number, and velocity, which can be either positive or negative, is one of the most important tasks in the analysis of motion. ◀

The velocity as defined by Equation 1.2 is actually what is called the *average* velocity. On average, over each 1 s interval bicycle 1 moves 20 ft, but we don't know if it sped up or slowed down a little during that 1 s. In Chapter 2, we'll develop the idea of *instantaneous* velocity, the velocity of an object at a particular instant in time. Since our goal in this chapter is to *visualize* motion with motion diagrams, we'll somewhat blur the distinction between average and instantaneous quantities, refining these definitions in Chapter 2, where our goal will be to develop the mathematics of motion.

The "Per" in Meters Per Second

The units for speed and velocity are those of a distance (feet, meters, miles) divided by a unit of time (seconds, hours). Thus we could measure velocity in units of m/s or mph, pronounced "meters *per* second" and "miles *per* hour." The word "per" will often arise in physics when we consider the ratio of two quantities. What do we mean, exactly, by "per"?

If a car moves with a speed of 23 m/s, we mean that it travels 23 meters *for each* 1 second of elapsed time. The word "per" thus associates the number of

300 million light years
= 2.8 × 10²⁴ m

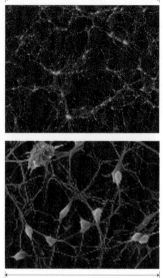

120 μm = 1.2 × 10⁻⁴ m

From galaxies to cells . . .   BIO   In science, we need to express numbers both very large and very small. The top image is of a computer simulation of the structure of the universe. Bright areas represent regions of clustered galaxies. The bottom image is of cortical nerve cells. Nerve cells relay signals to each other through a complex web of dendrites. These images, though similar in appearance, differ in scale by a factor of about 2 × 10²⁸!

These calipers have a precision of 0.001 in.

A tape measure has a precision of about 1 mm.

FIGURE 1.17 The precision of a measurement depends on how the measurement is made.

units in the numerator (23 m) with *one* unit of the denominator (1 s). We'll see many other examples of this idea as the book progresses. You may already know a bit about *density;* you can look up the density of gold and you'll find that it is 19.3 g/cm³ ("grams *per* cubic centimeter"). This means that there are 19.3 grams of gold *for each* 1 cubic centimeter of the metal. Thinking about the word "per" in this way will help you better understand physical quantities whose units are the ratio of two other units.

1.4 A Sense of Scale: Significant Figures, Scientific Notation, and Units

Physics attempts to explain the natural world, from the very small to the exceedingly large. And in order to understand our world, we need to be able to *measure* quantities both minuscule and enormous. A properly reported measurement has three elements. First, we can only measure our quantity with a certain precision. To make this precision clear, we need to make sure that we report our measurement with the correct number of *significant figures.*

Second, writing down the really big and small numbers that often come up in physics can be awkward. To avoid writing all those zeros, scientists use *scientific notation* to express numbers both big and small.

Finally, we need to choose an agreed-upon set of *units* for the quantity. For speed, common units include meters per second and miles per hour. For mass, the kilogram is the most commonly used unit. Later, we'll study more esoteric quantities such as magnetic fields, which have the units of "tesla." Every physical quantity that we can measure has an associated set of units.

Measurements and Significant Figures

When we measure any quantity, such as the length of a bone or the weight of a specimen, we can do so only with a certain *precision.* The digital calipers in Figure 1.17 can make a measurement to within ±0.001 in, so they have a precision of 0.001 in. If you used the tape shown to make a measurement, you probably couldn't do so to better than about ±1 mm, so the precision of the tape measure is about 1 mm. The precision of a measurement can also be affected by the skill or judgment of the person performing the measurement. A stopwatch might have a precision of 0.001 s, but, due to your reaction time, your measurement of the time of a sprinter would be much less precise.

It is important that your measurement be reported in a way that reflects its actual precision. Suppose, for example, that you use a ruler to measure the length of a particular specimen of a newly discovered species of frog. You judge that you can make this measurement with a precision of about 1 mm, or 0.1 cm. In this case, the frog's length should be reported as, say, 6.2 cm. We interpret this to mean that the actual value falls between 6.15 cm and 6.25 and thus rounds to 6.2 cm. Reporting the frog's length as simply 6 cm is saying less than you know; you are withholding information. On the other hand, to report the number as 6.213 cm is wrong. Any person reviewing your work would interpret the number 6.213 cm as meaning that the actual length falls between 6.2125 cm and 6.2135 cm, thus rounding to 6.213 cm. In this case, you are claiming to have knowledge and information that you do not really possess.

This example shows that one way to state your knowledge precisely is through the proper use of **significant figures.** You can think of a significant figure as being a digit that is reliably known. A measurement such as 6.2 cm has *two* significant figures, the 6 and the 2. The next decimal place—the one-hundredths—is not reliably known, and is thus not a significant figure. Similarly, a time measurement of 34.62 s has four significant figures, implying that the 2 in the hundredths place is reliably known.

When we perform a calculation such as adding or multiplying two or more measured numbers, we can't claim more accuracy for the result than was present in the initial measurements. Calculations with measured numbers follow the "weakest link" rule. The saying, which you probably know, is that "a chain is only as strong as its weakest link." If nine out of ten links in a chain can support a 1000 pound weight, that strength is meaningless if the tenth link can support only 200 pounds. Similarly, nine out of the ten numbers used in a calculation might be known with a precision of 0.01%; but if the tenth number is poorly known, with a precision of only 10%, then the result of the calculation cannot possibly be more precise than 10%. The weak link rules!

Determining the proper number of significant figures is straightforward, but there are a few definite rules to follow. We will often spell out such technical details in what we call a "Tactics Box." A Tactics Box is designed to teach you particular skills and techniques. Each Tactics Box will use the icon to designate exercises in the *Student Workbook* that you can use to practice these skills.

Tatyana Lebedeva won the 2004 Olympic gold medal with a long jump reported as 7.07 m. This number implies that the long jump is measured to an accuracy of about 0.01 m, or 1 cm.

(MP) TACTICS BOX 1.1 Using significant figures ✎ Exercise 16

❶ When multiplying or dividing several numbers, or when taking roots, the number of significant figures in the answer should match the number of significant figures of the *least* precisely known number used in the calculation:

Three significant figures

$$3.73 \times 5.7 = 21$$

Two significant figures

Answer should have the *lower* of the two, or two significant figures.

❷ When adding or subtracting several numbers, the number of decimal places in the answer should match the *smallest* number of decimal places of any number used in the calculation.

18.54 — Two decimal places
+106.6 — One decimal place
=125.1 ⬅ Answer should have the *lower* of the two, or one decimal place.

❸ **Exact numbers** have no uncertainty and, when used in calculations, do not change the number of significant figures of measured numbers. Examples of exact numbers are π and the number 2 in the relation $d = 2r$ between a circle's diameter and radius.

There is one notable exception to these rules:

■ It is acceptable to keep one or two extra digits during *intermediate* steps of a calculation. The goal here is to minimize round-off errors in the calculation. But the *final* answer must be reported with the proper number of significant figures.

TRY IT YOURSELF

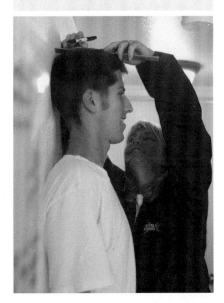

How tall are you really? If you measure your height in the morning, just after you wake up, and then in the evening, after a full day of activity, you'll find that your evening height is *less* by as much as 3/4 inches. Your height decreases over the course of the day as gravity compresses and reshapes your spine. If you give your height as 66 3/16 in, you are claiming more significant figures than are truly warranted; the 3/16 in isn't really reliably known, as your height can vary by more than this. Expressing your height to the nearest inch is plenty!

EXAMPLE 1.1 **Measuring the velocity of a car**

To measure the velocity of a car, clocks A and B are set up at two points along the road, as shown in Figure 1.18. Clock A is precise to 0.01 s, while B is precise only to 0.1 s. The distance between these two clocks is carefully measured to be 124.5 m. The two clocks are automatically started when the car passes a trigger in the road; each clock stops automatically when the car passes that clock. After the car has passed both clocks, clock A is found to read $t_A = 1.22$ s, and clock B to read $t_B = 4.5$ s. The time from the less-precise clock B is correctly reported with fewer significant figures than that from A. What is the velocity of the car, and how should it be reported with the correct number of significant figures?

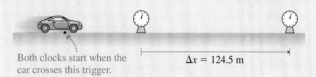

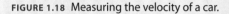
Both clocks start when the car crosses this trigger.

$\Delta x = 124.5$ m

FIGURE 1.18 Measuring the velocity of a car.

SOLVE We've already determined the car's displacement $\Delta x = 124.5$ m as it moves between the two clocks. To calculate its velocity, we need to determine the time interval Δt.

This is

This number has one decimal place. | This number has two decimal places.

$$\Delta t = t_B - t_A = (4.5 \text{ s}) - (1.22 \text{ s}) = 3.3 \text{ s}$$

By rule 2 of Tactics Box 1.1, the result should have *one* decimal place.

We can now calculate the velocity with the displacement and time interval from above:

The displacement has four significant figures.

$$v = \frac{\Delta x}{\Delta t} = \frac{124.5 \text{ m}}{3.3 \text{ s}} = 38 \text{ m/s}$$

The time interval has two significant figures. ⋯ By rule 1 of Tactics Box 1.1, the result should have *two* significant figures.

ASSESS Our final value has two significant figures. Suppose you had been hired to measure the speed of a car this way, and you reported 37.72 m/s. It would be reasonable for someone looking at your result to assume that the measurements you used to arrive at this value were correct to four significant figures and thus that you had measured time to the nearest 0.01 second. Our correct result of 38 m/s has all of the accuracy that you can claim, but no more!

Scientific Notation

It's easy to write down measurements of ordinary-sized objects: your height might be 1.72 meters, the weight of an apple 0.34 pounds. But the radius of a hydrogen atom is 0.000 000 000 053 m and the distance to the moon is 384 000 000 m. Writing and keeping track of all those zeros is quite cumbersome.

> **NOTE** ▶ Scientists usually write numbers with many digits by arranging the digits in groups of three, with the groups separated by spaces instead of commas. This makes it easier to read long numbers. ◀

Beyond requiring you to deal with all the zeros, writing quantities this way makes it unclear how many significant figures are involved. In the distance to the moon given above, how many of those digits are significant? Three? Four? All nine?

Writing numbers using scientific notation avoids both these problems. A value in scientific notation is a number with one digit to the left of the decimal point and zero or more to the right of it, multiplied by a power of ten. This solves the problem of all the zeros and makes the number of significant digits immediately apparent. In scientific notation, writing the distance to the sun as 1.50×10^{11} m implies that three digits are significant; writing it as 1.5×10^{11} m implies that only two digits are.

Even for smaller values, scientific notation can clarify the number of significant figures. Suppose a distance is measured as 1200 m. If this distance is known to within 1 m, we could write it as 1.200×10^3 m, showing that all four digits are significant; if it were accurate to only 100 m or so, we would report it as 1.2×10^3 m, indicating two significant figures.

Tactics Box 1.2 shows how to convert a number to scientific notation, and how to correctly indicate the number of significant figures.

(MP) TACTICS BOX 1.2 Using scientific notation   ✐ Exercises 17, 18

To convert a number into scientific notation:

❶ For a number greater than 10, move the decimal point to the left until only one digit remains to the left of the decimal point. The remaining number is then multiplied by 10 to a power; this power is given by the number of spaces the decimal point was moved. Here we convert the diameter of the earth to scientific notation:

We move the decimal point until there is only one digit to its left, counting the number of steps.

Since we moved the decimal point 6 steps, the power of ten is 6.

$$6\,370\,000 \text{ m} = 6.37 \times 10^{6} \text{ m}$$

The number of digits here equals the number of significant figures.

❷ For a number less than 1, move the decimal point to the right until it passes the first digit that isn't a zero. The remaining number is then multiplied by 10 to a negative power; the power is given by the number of spaces the decimal point was moved. For the diameter of a red blood cell we have

We move the decimal point until it passes the first digit that is not a zero, counting the number of steps.

Since we moved the decimal point 6 steps, the power of ten is −6.

$$0.000\,007\,5 \text{ m} = 7.5 \times 10^{-6} \text{ m}$$

The number of digits here equals the number of significant figures.

Proper use of significant figures is part of the "culture" of science. We will frequently emphasize these "cultural issues" because you must learn to speak the same language as the natives if you wish to communicate effectively! Most students "know" the rules of significant figures, having learned them in high school, but many fail to apply them. It is important that you understand the reasons for significant figures and that you get in the habit of using them properly.

Units

As we have seen, in order to measure a quantity we need to give it a numerical value. But a measurement is more than just a number—it requires a *unit* to be given. You can't go to the grocery and ask for "three-and-a-half of flour." You need to use a unit—here, one of weight, such as pounds—in addition to the number.

In your daily life, you generally tend to use the English system of units, in which distances are measured in inches, feet, and miles. These units are well adapted for daily life, but they are rarely used in scientific work. Given that science is an international discipline, it is also important to have a system of units that is recognized around the world. For these reasons, scientists use a system of units called *le Système Internationale d'Unités,* commonly referred to as **SI units.** In casual speaking we often refer to these as *metric units,* because the meter is the basic standard of length.

The importance of units In 1999, the $125 million Mars Climate Orbiter burned up in the Martian atmosphere instead of entering a safe orbit from which it could perform observations. The problem was faulty units! An engineering team had provided critical data on spacecraft performance in English units, but the navigation team assumed these data were in metric units. As a consequence, the navigation team had the spacecraft fly too close to the planet, and it burned up in the atmosphere.

TABLE 1.1 Common SI units

Quantity	Unit	Abbreviation
time	second	s
length	meter	m
mass	kilogram	kg

The three basic SI quantities, shown in Table 1.1, are time, length (or distance), and mass. Other quantities needed to understand motion can be expressed as combinations of these basic units. For example, speed or velocity are expressed in meters per second or m/s. This combination is a ratio of the length unit (the meter) to the time unit (the second).

The SI units have a long and interesting history. SI units were originally developed by the French in the late 1700s as a way of standardizing and regularizing numbers for commerce and science. Some of their other innovations of the time did not survive (such as the 10-day week), but their units did.

Using Prefixes

TABLE 1.2 Common prefixes

Prefix	Abbreviation	Power of 10
mega-	M	10^6
kilo-	k	10^3
centi-	c	10^{-2}
milli-	m	10^{-3}
micro-	μ	10^{-6}
nano-	n	10^{-9}

We will have many occasions to use lengths, times, and masses that are either much less or much greater than the standards of 1 meter, 1 second, and 1 kilogram. We will do so by using *prefixes* to denote various powers of ten. For instance, the prefix "kilo" (abbreviation k) denotes 10^3, or a factor of 1000. Thus 1 km equals 1000 m, 1 MW equals 10^6 watts, and 1 μV equals 10^{-6} V. Table 1.2 lists the common prefixes that will be used frequently throughout this book. Memorize it! Few things in physics are learned by rote memory, but this list is one of them. A more extensive list of prefixes is shown inside the cover of the book.

Although prefixes make it easier to talk about quantities, the proper SI units are meters, seconds, and kilograms. Quantities given with prefixed units must be converted to base SI units before any calculations are done. Thus 23.0 cm must be converted to 0.230 m before starting calculations. The exception is the kilogram, which is already the base SI unit.

Unit Conversions

TABLE 1.3 Useful unit conversions

1 inch (in) = 2.54 cm
1 foot (ft) = 0.305 m
1 mile (mi) = 1.609 km
1 mile per hour (mph) = 0.447 m/s
1 m = 39.37 in
1 km = 0.621 mi
1 m/s = 2.24 mph

Although SI units are our standard, we cannot entirely forget that the United States still uses English units. Even after repeated exposure to metric units in classes, most of us "think" in the English units we grew up with. Thus it remains important to be able to convert back and forth between SI units and English units. Table 1.3 shows a few frequently used conversions that will come in handy.

One effective method of performing unit conversions begins by noticing that since, for example, 1 mi = 1.609 km, the ratio of these two distances—*including their units*—is equal to one, so that

$$\frac{1 \text{ mi}}{1.609 \text{ km}} = \frac{1.609 \text{ km}}{1 \text{ mi}} = 1$$

A ratio of values equal to one is called a **conversion factor.** The following Tactics Box shows how to make a unit conversion. It uses the example of converting 60 mi into the equivalent distance in km.

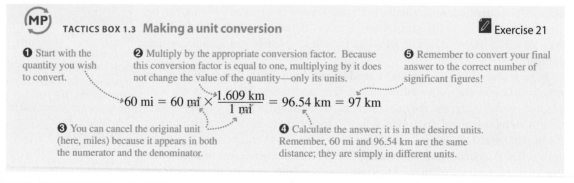

(MP) **TACTICS BOX 1.3** Making a unit conversion ✎ Exercise 21

❶ Start with the quantity you wish to convert.

❷ Multiply by the appropriate conversion factor. Because this conversion factor is equal to one, multiplying by it does not change the value of the quantity—only its units.

❺ Remember to convert your final answer to the correct number of significant figures!

$$60 \text{ mi} = 60 \text{ mi} \times \frac{1.609 \text{ km}}{1 \text{ mi}} = 96.54 \text{ km} = 97 \text{ km}$$

❸ You can cancel the original unit (here, miles) because it appears in both the numerator and the denominator.

❹ Calculate the answer; it is in the desired units. Remember, 60 mi and 96.54 km are the same distance; they are simply in different units.

Note that we've rounded the answer to 97 kilometers because the distance we're converting, 60 miles, has only two significant figures.

More complicated conversions can be accomplished with several successive multiplications of conversion factors, as we see in the next example.

EXAMPLE 1.2 **Can a bicycle go that fast?**

In Section 1.3, we calculated the speed of a bicycle to be 20 ft/s. Is this a reasonable speed for a bicycle?

SOLVE In order to determine whether or not this speed is reasonable, we will convert it to more familiar units. For speed, the unit you are most familiar with is likely miles per hour.

We first collect the necessary unit conversions:

$$1 \text{ mi} = 5280 \text{ ft} \qquad 1 \text{ hour (1 h)} = 60 \text{ min} \qquad 1 \text{ min} = 60 \text{ s}$$

We then multiply our original value by successive factors of 1 in order to convert the units:

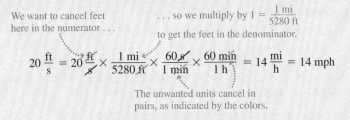

We want to cancel feet here in the numerator . . .

. . . so we multiply by $1 = \dfrac{1 \text{ mi}}{5280 \text{ ft}}$

to get the feet in the denominator.

$$20 \, \frac{\text{ft}}{\text{s}} = 20 \, \frac{\cancel{\text{ft}}}{\cancel{\text{s}}} \times \frac{1 \text{ mi}}{5280 \, \cancel{\text{ft}}} \times \frac{60 \, \cancel{\text{s}}}{1 \, \cancel{\text{min}}} \times \frac{60 \, \cancel{\text{min}}}{1 \text{ h}} = 14 \, \frac{\text{mi}}{\text{h}} = 14 \text{ mph}$$

The unwanted units cancel in pairs, as indicated by the colors.

Our final result of 14 miles per hour (14 mph) is a very reasonable speed for a bicycle, which gives us confidence in our answer. If we had calculated a speed of 140 miles per hour, we would have suspected that we had made an error, as this is quite a bit faster than the average bicyclist can travel!

Estimation

When scientists and engineers first approach a problem, they may do a quick measurement or calculation to establish the rough physical scale involved. This will help establish the procedures that should be used to make a more accurate measurement—or the estimate may well be all that is needed.

Suppose you see a rock fall off a cliff and would like to know how fast it was going when it hit the ground. By doing a mental comparison with the speeds of familiar objects, such as cars and bicycles, you might judge that the rock was traveling at "about" 20 mph. This is a one-significant-figure estimate. With some luck, you can probably distinguish 20 mph from either 10 mph or 30 mph, but you certainly cannot distinguish 20 mph from 21 mph just from a visual appearance. A one-significant-figure estimate or calculation, such as this estimate of speed, is called an **order-of-magnitude estimate.** An order-of-magnitude estimate is indicated by the symbol $\sim$ which indicates even less precision than the "approximately equal" symbol $\approx$. You would report your estimate of the speed of the falling rock as $v \sim 20$ mph.

A useful skill is to make reliable order-of-magnitude estimates on the basis of known information, simple reasoning, and common sense. This is a skill that is acquired by practice. Several chapters in this book will have homework problems that ask you to make order-of-magnitude estimates. Tables 1.4 and 1.5 have information that will be useful for doing estimates.

Later in the book, we will do some analysis of locomotion and look at the walking and running speeds of different animals. To help put things in perspective, it might be useful to have an estimate of how fast a person walks.

How many jellybeans are in the jar? Some reasoning about the size of one bean and the size of the jar can give you a one-significant-figure estimate.

TABLE 1.4 Some approximate lengths

	Length (m)
Circumference of the earth	4×10^7
New York to Los Angeles	5×10^6
Distance you can drive in 1 hour	1×10^5
Altitude of jet planes	1×10^4
Distance across a college campus	1000
Length of a football field	100
Length of a classroom	10
Length of your arm	1
Width of a textbook	0.1
Length of your little fingernail	0.01
Diameter of a pencil lead	1×10^{-3}
Thickness of a sheet of paper	1×10^{-4}
Diameter of a dust particle	1×10^{-5}

TABLE 1.5 Some approximate masses

	Mass (kg)
Large airliner	1×10^5
Small car	1000
Large human	100
Medium-size dog	10
Science textbook	1
Apple	0.1
Pencil	0.01
Raisin	1×10^{-3}
Fly	1×10^{-4}

Vectors and scalars

Scalars

Time, temperature, and weight are all *scalar* quantities. To specify your weight, only one number—150 pounds—need be given. The temperature is reported by a single number, such as 70° F, and the time of day is really just the number of seconds after midnight, although we break it into hours and minutes for convenience.

Vectors

The velocity of the race car is a *vector*. To fully specify a velocity, we need to give its magnitude (e.g., 120 mph) *and* its direction (e.g., west).

The force with which the boy pushes on his friend is another example of a vector. To completely specify this force, we must know not only how hard he pushes (the magnitude) but also in which direction.

EXAMPLE 1.3   How fast do you walk?
Estimate how fast you walk, in meters per second.

SOLVE In order to compute speed, we will need a distance and a time. If you walked a mile to campus, how long would this take? You'd probably say 30 minutes or so—a half an hour. Let's use this rough number in our estimate.

We have

$$\text{speed} = \frac{\text{distance}}{\text{time}} \sim \frac{1 \text{ mile}}{1/2 \text{ hour}} = 2 \frac{\text{mi}}{\text{h}}$$

But we want this in meters per second. Since our calculation is only an estimate, we use an approximate form of the conversion factor from Table 1.3:

$$1 \frac{\text{mi}}{\text{h}} \approx 0.5 \frac{\text{m}}{\text{s}}$$

This gives an approximate walking speed of about 1 m/s.

ASSESS Is this a reasonable value? Let's do another estimate. Your stride is probably about one yard long—about one meter. And you take about one step per second; next time you are walking, you can count and see. So a walking speed of 1 meter per second sounds pretty reasonable.

This sort of estimation is very valuable. We will see many cases in which we need to know an approximate value for a quantity before we start a problem or after we finish a problem, in order to assess our results.

STOP TO THINK 1.4   Rank in order, from the most to the fewest, the number of significant figures in the following numbers. For example, if B has more than C, C has the same number as A, and A has more than D, you would give your answer as B > C = A > D.

A. 0.43   B. 0.0052   C. 0.430   D. 4.321×10^{-10}

1.5 Vectors and Motion: A First Look

Many physical quantities, such as time, mass, and temperature, can be described completely by a number with a unit. For example, the mass of an object might be 6 kg and its temperature 30° C. When a physical quantity is described by a single number (with a unit), we call it a **scalar quantity.** A scalar can be positive, negative, or zero.

Many other quantities, however, have a directional quality and cannot be described by a single number. To describe the motion of a car, for example, you must specify not only how fast it is moving, but also the *direction* in which it is moving. A **vector quantity** is a quantity that has both a *size* (the "How far?" or "How fast?") and a *direction* (the "Which way?"). The size or length of a vector is called its **magnitude.** The magnitude of a vector can be positive or zero, but it cannot be negative.

Some examples of vector and scalar quantities are given at right.

We graphically represent a vector as an *arrow,* as illustrated for the velocity and force vectors in the table at right. The arrow is drawn to point in the direction of the vector quantity, and the *length* of the arrow is proportional to the magnitude of the vector quantity. If we choose to draw an arrow 2 cm long to represent a velocity with magnitude 23 m/s, we will draw an arrow 4 cm long to represent a velocity with magnitude 46 m/s. This graphical notation for representing vectors is so useful that we often think of the arrow as being the vector itself. Thus we might say, "draw a vector pointing to the right," and you would draw an arrow pointing to the right.

When we want to represent a vector quantity with a *symbol*, we need somehow to indicate that the symbol is for a vector rather than for a scalar. We do this by drawing an arrow over the letter that represents the quantity. Thus $\vec{r}$ and $\vec{A}$ are symbols for vectors, whereas r and A, without the arrows, are symbols for scalars. In handwritten work you *must* draw arrows over all symbols that represent vectors. This may seem strange until you get used to it, but it is very important because we will often use both r and $\vec{r}$, or both A and $\vec{A}$, in the same problem, and they mean different things! Without the arrow, you will be using the same symbol with two different meanings and will likely end up making a mistake. Note that the arrow over the symbol always points to the right, regardless of which direction the actual vector points. Thus we write $\vec{r}$ or $\vec{A}$, never $\overleftarrow{r}$ or $\overleftarrow{A}$.

Displacement Vectors

For motion along a line, we found in Section 1.2 that the displacement is a quantity that specifies not only how *far* an object moves, but also the *direction*—to the left or to the right—that the object moves. Since displacement is a quantity that has both a magnitude ("How far") and a direction, it can be represented by a vector, the **displacement vector.** Figure 1.19 shows the displacement vector for Sam's trip that we discussed earlier. We've simply drawn an arrow—the vector— from his initial to his final positions and assigned it the symbol $\vec{d}_S$. Because $\vec{d}_S$ has both a magnitude and a direction, it is convenient to write Sam's displacement as $\vec{d}_S = (100 \text{ ft, east})$. The first value in the parentheses is the magnitude of the vector (i.e., the size of the displacement) and the second value specifies its direction.

Also shown in Figure 1.19 is the displacement vector $\vec{d}_J$ for Jane, who started on 12th Street and ended up on Vine. As with Sam, we draw her displacement vector as an arrow from her initial to her final position. In this case, $\vec{d}_J = (100 \text{ ft, } 30° \text{ east of north})$.

Jane's trip illustrates an important point about displacement vectors. Jane started her trip on 12th Street and ended up on Vine, leading to the displacement vector shown. But to get from her initial to her final position, she needn't have walked along the straight-line path denoted by $\vec{d}_J$. If she walked east along 12th Street to the intersection, then headed north on Vine, her displacement would still be the vector shown. **An object's displacement vector is drawn from the object's initial position to its final position, regardless of the actual path followed between these two points.**

Vector Addition

Let's consider one more trip for the peripatetic Sam. In Figure 1.20, he starts at the intersection and walks east 50 ft; then he walks 100 ft to the northeast through a vacant lot. His displacement vectors for the two legs of his trip are labeled $\vec{d}_1$ and $\vec{d}_2$ in the figure.

Sam's trip consists of two legs that can be represented by the two vectors $\vec{d}_1$ and $\vec{d}_2$, but we can represent his trip as a whole, from his initial starting position to his overall final position, with the *net* displacement vector labeled $\vec{d}_{net}$. Sam's net displacement is in a sense the *sum* of the two displacements that made it up, so we can write

$$\vec{d}_{net} = \vec{d}_1 + \vec{d}_2$$

Sam's net displacement thus requires the *addition* of two vectors, but vector addition obeys different rules from the addition of two scalar quantities. The directions of the two vectors, as well as their magnitudes, must be taken into account. Sam's trip suggests that we can add vectors together by putting the "tail" of one

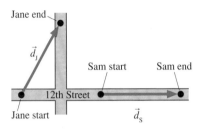

FIGURE 1.19 Two displacement vectors.

The boat's displacement is the straight-line connection from its initial to its final position.

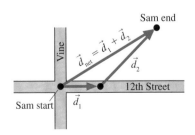

FIGURE 1.20 Sam undergoes two displacements.

vector at the tip of the other. This idea, which is reasonable for displacement vectors, in fact is how *any* two vectors are added. Tactics Box 1.4 shows how to add two vectors $\vec{A}$ and $\vec{B}$.

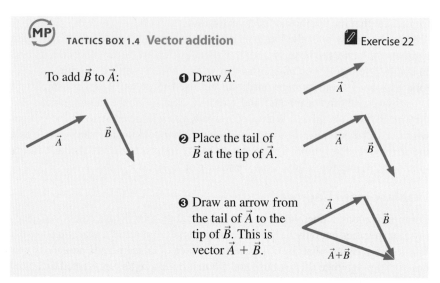

TACTICS BOX 1.4 Vector addition ✎ Exercise 22

To add $\vec{B}$ to $\vec{A}$:

❶ Draw $\vec{A}$.

❷ Place the tail of $\vec{B}$ at the tip of $\vec{A}$.

❸ Draw an arrow from the tail of $\vec{A}$ to the tip of $\vec{B}$. This is vector $\vec{A} + \vec{B}$.

EXAMPLE 1.4 Finding Sam's net displacement

Find Sam's net displacement in Figure 1.20, writing it in the form $\vec{d}_{net} =$ (magnitude of displacement, direction).

SOLVE We'll solve this graphically, using a ruler and a protractor. As shown in Figure 1.21, we first draw vector $\vec{d}_1$ pointing to the east, or to the right on our paper. We'll choose a scale where 1 cm on our paper represents 25 ft of Sam's neighborhood. Thus the length of $\vec{d}_1$ on the paper is 2 cm, representing the 50 ft magnitude of Sam's first displacement.

We then draw the second vector $\vec{d}_2$ with its tail at the tip of $\vec{d}_1$. Sam walked to the northeast during this leg, so we draw the direction of the vector at 45° to the horizontal; since he walked a distance of 100 ft, we draw the vector with a length of 4 cm.

The net displacement is the vector sum of the two displacements $\vec{d}_1$ and $\vec{d}_2$. It extends from the tail of $\vec{d}_1$ to the tip of $\vec{d}_2$. Using a ruler, we measure its length to be about 5.6 cm, corresponding to 5.6 × 25 ft = 140 ft. We can use a protractor to

find that the angle θ (the Greek letter *theta*) is about 30°. We thus have

$$\vec{d}_{net} = (140 \text{ ft, } 30° \text{ north of east})$$

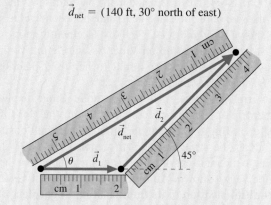

FIGURE 1.21 Graphical addition of two vectors.

Vectors and Trigonometry

Adding two vectors together using a ruler and protractor isn't very precise or practical. We need a more accurate and efficient method that can be used for adding any two vectors. Trigonometry provides us with just such a method.

Before seeing how trigonometry can be used for vector addition, let's review some of the basic ideas. Suppose we have a right triangle with hypotenuse H, angle θ, side opposite the angle O, and side adjacent to the angle A, as shown in Figure 1.22.

The sine, cosine, and tangent (which we write as "sin," "cos," and "tan") of angle θ are defined as ratios of the sides of the triangle:

$$\sin\theta = \frac{O}{H} \qquad \cos\theta = \frac{A}{H} \qquad \tan\theta = \frac{O}{A} \qquad (1.3)$$

If we know two of the sides of the triangle, we can find the angle θ.

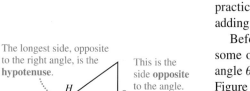

The longest side, opposite to the right angle, is the **hypotenuse**.

This is the side **opposite** to the angle.

This is the side **adjacent** to the angle.

FIGURE 1.22 A right triangle.

Conversely, if we know the angle θ and the length of one side, we can use the sine, cosine, or tangent to find the lengths of the other sides. For example, if you know θ and the length A of the adjacent side, and you need to find the hypotenuse H, you can rearrange the middle Equation 1.3 to give $H = A/\cos\theta$.

We will make regular use of these relationships in the following chapters.

EXAMPLE 1.5   Determining the sides of a triangle

A right triangle has an angle of 30° and a hypotenuse of length 10.0 m, as shown in Figure 1.23. What are the lengths of the other two sides of the triangle?

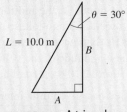

FIGURE 1.23 A triangle with two unknown sides.

SOLVE This is a problem that uses the trigonometric relationships of Equations (1.3). In Figure 1.23, the hypotenuse is labeled L, the adjacent side B, and the opposite side A. For each problem, the hypotenuse and adjacent and opposite sides will need to be determined; they will not in general be labeled H, O, and A as in Equations (1.3).

Because we know the hypotenuse and an angle, we can compute

$$A = L\sin\theta = (10.0 \text{ m})\sin(30°) = 5.00 \text{ m}$$

$$B = L\cos\theta = (10.0 \text{ m})\cos(30°) = 8.66 \text{ m}$$

ASSESS Since we have found all three sides of a right triangle, we can check our math by seeing if the Pythagorean theorem $L^2 = A^2 + B^2$ holds for our values. We have

$$L^2 = (10.0 \text{ m})^2 = 100 \text{ m}^2$$

and

$$A^2 + B^2 = (5.00 \text{ m})^2 + (8.66 \text{ m})^2 = 100 \text{ m}^2$$

The values agree, giving us confidence that our answer is correct.

As the next example shows, we can use the rules of trigonometry to add vectors together by considering each vector to be the hypotenuse of a right triangle. If A and B are two vertices (corners) of a triangle, then we denote the length of the side between A and B as $\overline{AB}$.

EXAMPLE 1.6   Finding Sam's displacement using trigonometry

Find Sam's net displacement in Figure 1.20, this time using methods of trigonometry.

SOLVE The situation is shown once more in Figure 1.24. We will first find sides $\overline{AB}$ and $\overline{BC}$ of triangle ABC, then use these lengths to find the hypotenuse and angle of triangle DBC. (Here, $\overline{AB}$ means the side between points A and B.)

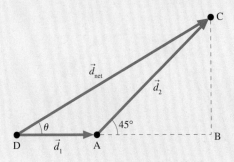

FIGURE 1.24 Using trigonometry to find Sam's displacement.

The hypotenuse AC has length 100 ft. From Equation 1.3 we have

$$\overline{AB} = \overline{AC}\cos 45° = (100 \text{ ft})\cos 45° = 71 \text{ ft}$$

$$\overline{BC} = \overline{AC}\sin 45° = (100 \text{ ft})\sin 45° = 71 \text{ ft}$$

Now consider triangle DBC. Side $\overline{BC}$, with length 71 ft, is opposite angle θ. The side adjacent to θ is $\overline{DB} = \overline{DA} + \overline{AB} = 50 \text{ ft} + 71 \text{ ft} = 121 \text{ ft}$. Then, using Equation 1.3 once again, we find

$$\tan\theta = \frac{\overline{BC}}{\overline{DB}} = \frac{71 \text{ ft}}{121 \text{ ft}} = 0.59$$

from which $\theta = \tan^{-1}(0.59) = 30°$, where $\tan^{-1}$ is the *arctangent* or *inverse tangent*. Finally, we can find the magnitude of the net displacement from the Pythagorean theorem on triangle DCB:

$$\overline{DC} = \sqrt{(\overline{DB})^2 + (\overline{BC})^2} = \sqrt{(121 \text{ ft})^2 + (71 \text{ ft})^2} = 140 \text{ ft}$$

Thus Sam's net displacement is $\vec{d}_{net} = (140 \text{ ft}, 30° \text{ north of east})$. This length, and the angle θ, agree with the values obtained using graphical methods in Example 1.4.

Velocity Vectors

We've seen that a basic quantity that describes the motion of an object is its velocity. Velocity is a vector quantity, since its specification involves not only how fast an object is moving (its speed), but also the direction in which the object is moving. We thus represent the velocity of an object by a **velocity vector** $\vec{v}$ that points in the direction of the object's motion, and whose magnitude is the object's speed. In this section, we'll learn how to draw velocity vectors on a motion diagram.

Figure 1.25a shows (using the particle model) the motion diagram of a car accelerating from rest. We've drawn vectors showing the car's displacement between successive positions of the motion diagram. To draw the car's velocity vectors, we note first that the direction of the displacement vector indicates the direction of motion between successive points in the motion diagram. But the velocity of an object also points in the direction of motion, so **an object's velocity vector points in the same direction as its displacement vector.**

Second, we've already noted that the magnitude of the velocity vector—"how fast"—is the object's speed. From Equation 1.1, the speed of an object is given by

$$\text{speed} = \frac{\text{distance traveled in a given time interval}}{\text{time interval}}$$

Now between any two successive points of the motion diagram, the distance traveled is equal to the magnitude of the displacement, that is, to the length of the displacement vector. Further, in a motion diagram the time interval between successive points is always the same. This means that the speed of an object, and thus the length of the velocity vector, is proportional to the length of the displacement vector between successive points on a motion diagram. Consequently, the vectors connecting each dot of a motion diagram to the next, which we previously labeled as displacement vectors, could equally well be identified as velocity vectors. This is shown for our car in Figure 1.25b. From now on, we'll show and label velocity vectors on motion diagrams rather than displacement vectors.

NOTE ▶ Again, the velocity vectors shown in Figure 1.25 are actually *average* velocity vectors. Because the velocity is increasing, it's actually a bit less than this average at the start of each time interval, and a bit more at the end. In Chapter 2 we'll refine these ideas and develop the idea of instantaneous velocity. ◀

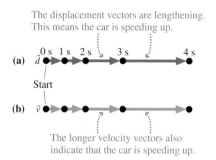

The displacement vectors are lengthening. This means the car is speeding up.

(a) $\vec{d}$ 0 s   1 s   2 s   3 s   4 s

Start

(b) $\vec{v}$

The longer velocity vectors also indicate that the car is speeding up.

FIGURE 1.25 The motion diagram for a car starting from rest.

EXAMPLE 1.7 Drawing a ball's motion diagram

Jake hits a ball at a 60° angle from the horizontal. It is caught by Jim. Draw a motion diagram of the ball that shows velocity vectors rather than displacement vectors.

SOLVE This example is typical of how many problems in science and engineering are worded. The problem does not give a clear statement of where the motion begins or ends. Are we interested in the motion of the ball just during the time it is in the air between Jake and Jim? What about the motion *as* Jake hits it (ball rapidly speeding up) or *as* Jim catches it (ball rapidly slowing down)? Should we include Jim dropping the ball after he catches it? The point is that *you* will often be called on to make a *reasonable interpretation* of a problem statement. In this problem, the details of hitting and catching the ball are complex. The motion of the ball through the air is easier to describe, and it's a motion you might expect to learn about in a physics class. So our *interpretation* is that the motion diagram should start as the ball leaves Jake's bat (ball already moving) and should end the instant it touches Jim's hand (ball still moving). We will model the ball as a particle.

With this interpretation in mind, Figure 1.26 shows the motion diagram of the ball. Notice how, in contrast to the car of Figure 1.25, the ball is already moving as the motion diagram movie begins. As before, the velocity vectors are found by connecting the dots with arrows. You can see that the velocity vectors get shorter (ball slowing down), get longer (ball speeding up), and change direction. Each $\vec{v}$ is different, so this is *not* constant velocity motion.

Jake $\vec{v}$ Jim

FIGURE 1.26 The motion diagram of a ball traveling from Jake to Jim.

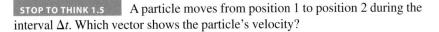

STOP TO THINK 1.5   A particle moves from position 1 to position 2 during the interval Δt. Which vector shows the particle's velocity?

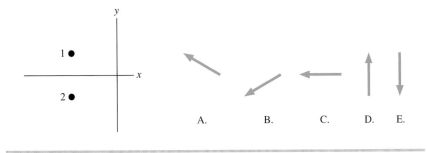

1.6 Making Models: The Power of Physics

You've now seen that we often make drastic simplifications when we analyze a situation in physics. For example, we may represent a speeding car as simply a moving dot. When we analyze a situation or solve a problem, we are making a *model* of a physical situation, an idealized version of the problem that allows us to focus on its most important features.

We will introduce many different models that allow us to focus in this way. Earlier in the chapter we introduced the *particle model,* which allowed us to visualize the motion of an object as a single particle. By ignoring the details of the object, we could concentrate on the object's overall motion. This is a very useful model in many cases, as we have seen.

Another model that we will use regularly is the **atomic model.** Matter is made of atoms, and it is useful to take this into account. Later, we will model solids as being composed of particle-like atoms connected by springs. A rubber band modeled in this way is shown in Figure 1.27. This is a simplification, but a simplification grounded in reality: For the purpose of analyzing the elastic behavior of solids, what really matters is that the atoms are connected by bonds—and that these bonds behave quite a bit like little springs.

Applying the concepts that you learn in this course to real problems is also a form of modeling: You are choosing a simplified way of looking at the problem that avoids extraneous detail. It is a skill you will acquire with practice.

Mathematical Forms

In this course, we will also make frequent use of *mathematical relationships* between physical quantities. In fact, we have already introduced some in this chapter. An important part of physics—but not the only part!—is analyzing nature using such mathematical relationships. As we do so, we find that certain ones show up in many different contexts.

As an example, consider the fairly simple mathematical equation

$$y = 4x^2 \tag{1.4}$$

This relationship between y and x is plotted in Figure 1.28a. As x increases, y increases more rapidly, so that the curve gets ever steeper.

In Figure 1.28b, we plot the important physical quantity known as the *kinetic energy K*, which we'll learn about in Chapter 5. The kinetic energy depends on the speed v of an object according to the equation

$$K = \frac{1}{2}mv^2 \tag{1.5}$$

Note how similar the shape of this curve is to that of Figure 1.28a.

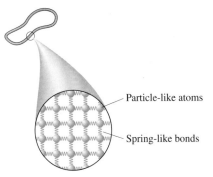

FIGURE 1.27 An atomic model of a rubber band.

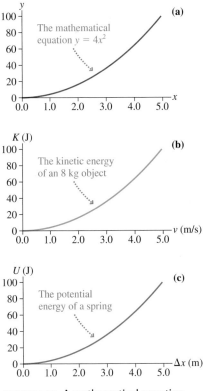

FIGURE 1.28 A mathematical equation models a physical quantity.

Finally, in Figure 1.28c we plot the *potential energy U* of a spring. In Chapter 5 we'll find that this energy depends on the displacement *x* of the end of the spring according to the equation

$$U = \frac{1}{2}kx^2 \tag{1.6}$$

The shape of this curve is the same as the previous two.

In looking at Figure 1.28, then, it is evident that graphs of all three of these expressions have the same overall appearance. They differ in their variables; kinetic energy depends on *v* and potential energy on *x*. They also differ in some of the constants in the equations—the $\frac{1}{2}m$ for kinetic energy, the $\frac{1}{2}k$ for potential energy. But they are all versions of the same mathematical relationship. We say that all three equations have the same mathematical *form*.

The mathematical form that all three of the plots in Figure 1.28 share is that they depend on the *square* of their variable. The variable *y* in Equation 1.4 depends on the square of *x*. The kinetic energy depends on the square of *v*. And the potential energy depends on the square of *x*. We express this dependence of each equation on the square of its variable using the symbol ∝. This symbol is often read as "varies as" or "depends on." We can then write

$$y \propto x^2 \qquad K \propto v^2 \qquad U \propto x^2$$

Writing expressions in this way emphasizes how the quantity depends on its variable. In many problems the form of this variation is more important than other details in the equations, such as *m* or factors of 1/2.

Table 1.6 shows four common mathematical forms that we'll encounter in this book, with some examples of each. There will be others as well. Because certain physical principles share the same mathematical form, we can use these similarities to help us learn new concepts. Thus, much of what you learn about gravity can later be applied to electricity, because the force of gravity and the electric force share the same mathematical form, $y \propto 1/x^2$.

As we meet each mathematical model for the first time, we will insert a section in the text that gives an overview of the form. When we see the form again, we will refer back to that overview section.

TABLE 1.6 Common mathematical forms

Mathematical form	Physical example
Proportional $y \propto x$	Dependence of acceleration on force
	Force due to a spring
Square $y \propto x^2$	Potential energy of a spring
	Kinetic energy
Inverse $y \propto \dfrac{1}{x}$	Potential energy of two charges
	Magnetic field due to a current
Inverse square $y \propto \dfrac{1}{x^2}$	Gravitational force between two masses
	Electric force between two charges

1.7 Where Do We Go from Here?

This first chapter has been an introduction to some of the fundamental ideas about motion and some of the basic techniques that you will use in the rest of the course. You have seen some examples of how to make *models* of a physical situation, thereby focusing in on the essential elements of the situation. You have learned some practical ideas, such as how to convert quantities from one kind of units to another. The rest of this book—and the rest of your course—will extend these themes. You will learn how to model many kinds of physical systems, and learn the technical skills needed to set up and solve problems using these models.

As we go along, you will learn a set of very practical and useful models that will allow you to discuss and analyze a very wide range of problems. For example,

- We will study the forces in joints, the flow of blood in arteries, how you make the sounds of speech, and how your eyes analyze light from the world around you.
- We will look at steel beams, bones, and spiders' silk and find which is strongest. The answer may surprise you!

Radio signals travel from tower to receiver in the form of invisible *electromagnetic waves*.

- We will learn how radio signals are generated, how they travel, how an antenna picks them up, how the speaker in the radio turns the signals into sound, and how this sound is analyzed by your ears.
- We will look at how electricity is generated and transmitted, whether it's the electricity that comes to your house or the electrical signal that propagates through your nerve cells.

This is all very practical, and will be quite useful in your current field of study. But in the midst of solving such practical problems, you will also learn what physics teaches us about the world, and how truly amazing some of it is. Did you know that:

- All of the energy that you use on a daily basis comes from nuclear energy?
- Certain animals, such as mice, can survive falls from any height?
- There are creatures that use the earth's magnetic field to navigate?
- It is possible for something to be in two places at once, or for two things to be in the same place at the same time?
- It is possible to go on a long trip—and return years younger than your twin?

As you work through this course and learn to solve problems, don't lose sight of this big picture! The universe is a remarkable place, and physics is a wonderful tool for showing both its depth and its underlying simplicity.

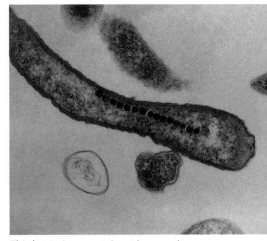

This bacterium contains microscopic magnetic particles that allow it to navigate using the earth's magnetic field.

SUMMARY

The goal of Chapter 1 has been to introduce the fundamental concepts of motion and to review the related basic mathematical principles.

IMPORTANT CONCEPTS

Motion Diagrams

The particle model represents a moving object as if all its mass were concentrated at a single point. Using this model, we can represent motion with a **motion diagram** where dots indicate the object's position at successive times. In a motion diagram, the time interval between successive dots is always the same.

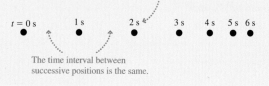

Each dot represents the position of the object. Each position is labeled with the time at which the dot was there.

$t = 0$ s   1 s   2 s   3 s   4 s   5 s   6 s

The time interval between successive positions is the same.

Describing Motion

Position locates an object with respect to a chosen coordinate system. It is described by a **coordinate**.

The *coordinate* is the variable used to describe the position.

$-6 \ -5 \ -4 \ -3 \ -2 \ -1 \ \ 0 \ \ 1 \ \ 2 \ \ 3 \ \ 4 \ \ 5$ x (mi)

This cow is at $x = -5$ miles.   This car is at $x = +4$ miles.

A change in position is called a **displacement**. For motion along a line, a displacement is a signed quantity. The displacement from x_i to x_f is $\Delta x = x_f - x_i$.

Time is measured from a particular instant to which we assign $t = 0$. A **time interval** is the elapsed time between two specific instants t_i and t_f. It is given by $\Delta t = t_f - t_i$.

Velocity is the ratio of the displacement of an object to the time interval during which this displacement occurs:

$$v = \frac{\Delta x}{\Delta t}$$

Scalars and Vectors

Scalar quantities have only a magnitude, and can be represented by a single number. Temperature, time, and mass are scalars.

A vector is a quantity described by both a magnitude and a direction. Velocity and displacement are vectors.

Velocity vectors can be drawn on a motion diagram by connecting successive points with a vector.

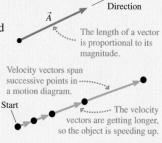

Direction

$\vec{A}$

The length of a vector is proportional to its magnitude.

Velocity vectors span successive points in a motion diagram.

Start

The velocity vectors are getting longer, so the object is speeding up.

Units

Every measurement of a quantity must include a unit.

The standard system of units used in science is the SI system. Common SI units include:

- Length: meters (m)
- Time: seconds (s)
- Mass: kilograms (kg)

APPLICATIONS

Working with Numbers

In scientific notation, a number is expressed as a decimal number between 1 and 10 multiplied by a power of ten. In scientific notation, the diameter of the earth is 1.27×10^7 m.

A prefix can be used before a unit to indicate a multiple of 10 or 1/10. Thus we can write the diameter of the earth as 12,700 km, where the k in km denotes 1000.

We can perform a unit conversion to convert the diameter of the earth to a different unit, such as miles. We do so by multiplying by a conversion factor equal to one, such as 1 = 1 mi/1.61 km.

Significant figures are reliably known digits. The number of significant figures for:

- **Multiplication, division, and powers** is set by the value with the fewest significant figures.
- **Addition and subtraction** is set by the value with the smallest number of decimal places.

An order-of-magnitude-estimate is an estimate that has an accuracy of about one significant figure. Such estimates are usually made using rough numbers from everyday experience.

For instructor-assigned homework, go to www.masteringphysics.com

Problems labeled BIO are of biological or medical interest.

Problem difficulty is labeled as | (straightforward) to ||||| (challenging).

QUESTIONS

Conceptual Questions

1. a. Write a paragraph describing the *particle model*. What is it, and why is it important?
   b. Give two examples of situations, different from those described in the text, for which the particle model is appropriate.
   c. Give an example of a situation, different from those described in the text, for which it would be inappropriate.

2. A softball player slides into second base. Use the particle model to draw a motion diagram of the player from the time he begins to slide until he reaches the base. Number the dots in order, starting with zero.

3. A car travels to the left at a steady speed for a few seconds, then brakes for a stop sign. Use the particle model to draw a motion diagram of the car for the entire motion described here. Number the dots in order, starting with zero.

4. A ball is dropped from the roof of a tall building and students in a physics class are asked to sketch a motion diagram for this situation. A student submits the diagram shown in Figure Q1.4. Is the diagram correct? Explain.

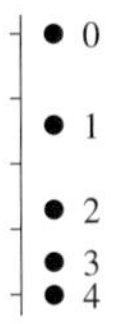

   FIGURE Q1.4

   • 0
   • 1
   • 2
   • 3
   • 4

5. Write a sentence or two describing the difference between position and displacement. Give one example of each.

6. Doug starts at position $x = 10$ m. He then undergoes a displacement $\Delta x = +15$ m. During his motion, is it possible that he passed through the origin, at $x = 0$ m?

7. Write a sentence or two describing the difference between speed and velocity. Give one example of each.

8. The motion of a skateboard along a horizontal axis is observed for 5 s. The initial position of the skateboard is negative with respect to a chosen origin, and its velocity throughout the 5 s is also negative. At the end of the observation time, is the skateboard closer to or further from the origin than initially? Explain.

9. Can the velocity of an object be positive during a time interval in which its position is always negative? Can its velocity be positive during a time interval in which its displacement is negative?

10. Two friends watch a jogger complete a 400 m lap around the track in 100 s. One of the friends states, "The jogger's velocity was 4 m/s during this lap." The second friend objects, saying, "No, the jogger's speed was 4 m/s." Who is correct? Justify your answer.

11. A softball player hits the ball and starts running toward first base. Draw a motion diagram, using the particle model, showing her position and her velocity vectors during the first few seconds of her run.

12. A child is sledding on a smooth, level patch of snow. She encounters a rocky patch and slows to a stop. Draw a motion diagram, using the particle model, showing her position and her velocity vectors.

13. A roof tile falls straight down from a two-story building. It lands in a swimming pool and settles gently to the bottom. Draw a motion diagram, using the particle model, showing the tile's position and its velocity vectors.

14. Your roommate drops a tennis ball from a third story balcony. It hits the sidewalk and bounces as high as the second story. Draw a motion diagram, using the particle model, showing the ball's velocity vectors from the time it is released until it reaches the maximum height on its bounce.

15. A car is driving north at a steady speed. It makes a gradual 90° left turn without losing speed, then continues driving to the west. Draw a motion diagram, using the particle model, showing the car's velocity vectors as seen from a helicopter hovering over the highway.

16. A toy car rolls down a ramp, then across a smooth, horizontal floor. Draw a motion diagram, using the particle model, showing the car's velocity vectors.

17. Estimate the average speed with which you go from home to campus (or another trip you commonly make) via whatever mode of transportation you use most commonly. Give your answer in both mph and m/s. Describe how you arrived at this estimate.

18. Estimate the number of times you sneezed during the past year. Describe how you arrived at this estimate.

19. Density is the ratio of an object's mass to its volume. Would you expect density to be a vector or a scalar quantity? Explain.

Multiple-Choice Questions

20. | A student walks 1.0 mi west and then 1.0 mi north. Afterward, how far is she from her starting point?
    A. 1.0 mi   B. 1.4 mi   C. 1.6 mi   D. 2.0 mi

21. | Which of the following motions is described by the motion diagram of Figure Q1.21?
    A. An ice skater gliding across the ice.
    B. An airplane braking to a stop after landing.
    C. A car pulling away from a stop sign.
    D. A pool ball bouncing off a cushion and reversing direction.

    FIGURE Q1.21

    0 1 2   3   4   5
    •• •   •   •   •

22. | A bird flies 3.0 km due west and then 2.0 km due north. What is the magnitude of the bird's displacement?
    A. 2.0 km   B. 3.0 km   C. 3.6 km   D. 5.0 km

23. ⫶ A bird flies 3.0 km due west and then 2.0 km due north. Another bird flies 2.0 km due west and 3.0 km due north. What is the angle between the net displacement vectors for the two birds?
    A. 23°   B. 34°   C. 56°   D. 90°

24. ⫼ A woman walks briskly at 2.00 m/s. How much time will it take her to walk one mile?
    A. 8.30 min B. 13.4 min C. 21.7 min D. 30.0 min

25. ⎮ Compute 3.24 m + 0.532 m to the correct number of significant figures.
    A. 3.7 m   B. 3.77 m   C. 3.772 m   D. 3.7720 m

26. ⎮ A rectangle has length 3.24 m and height 0.532 m. To the correct number of significant figures, what is its area?
    A. 1.72 m²   B. 1.723 m²
    C. 1.7236 m²   D. 1.72368 m²

27. ⎮ The earth formed 4.57×10^9 years ago. What is this time in seconds?
    A. 1.67×10^{12} s   B. 4.01×10^{13} s
    C. 2.40×10^{15} s   D. 1.44×10^{17} s

28. ⎮ An object's density ρ is defined as the ratio of its mass to its volume: $\rho = M/V$. The earth's mass is 5.94×10^{24} kg, and its volume is 1.08×10^{12} km³. What is the earth's density?
    A. 5.50×10^3 kg/m³   B. 5.50×10^6 kg/m³
    C. 5.50×10^9 kg/m³   D. 5.50×10^{12} kg/m³

PROBLEMS

Section 1.1 Motion: A First Look

1. ⎮ You've made a video of a car as it skids to a halt to avoid hitting an object in the road. Use the images from the video to draw a motion diagram of the car from the time the skid begins until the car is stopped.

2. ⎮ A man rides a bike along a straight road for 5 min, then has a flat tire. He stops for 5 min to repair the flat, but then realizes he cannot fix it. He continues his journey by walking the rest of the way, which takes him another 10 min. Use the particle model to draw a motion diagram of the man for the entire motion described here. Number the dots in order, starting with zero.

3. ⎮ A jogger running east at a steady pace suddenly develops a cramp. He is lucky: A westbound bus is sitting at a bus stop just ahead. He gets on the bus and enjoys a quick ride home. Use the particle model to draw a motion diagram of the jogger for the entire motion described here. Number the dots in order, starting with zero.

Section 1.2 Position and Time: Putting Numbers on Nature

4. ⎮ Figure P1.4 shows Sue between her home and the cinema. What is Sue's position x if
    a. her home is the origin?   b. the cinema is the origin?

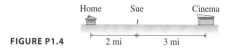

FIGURE P1.4   2 mi   3 mi

5. ⎮ Keira starts at position $x = 23$ m along a coordinate axis. She then undergoes a displacement of -45 m. What is her final position?

6. ⎮ A car travels along a straight east-west road. A coordinate system is established on the road, with x increasing to the east. The car ends up 14 mi west of the intersection with Mulberry Road. If its displacement was -23 mi, how far from and on which side of Mulberry Road did it start?

7. ⎮ Lisa is enjoying a bicycle ride on the country road shown earlier in Figure 1.7. Suppose that increasing x means moving east. At noon, she is 2 mi west of the post office. A half hour later, she is 3 mi east of the post office. What is her displacement Δx during that half hour?

Section 1.3 Velocity

8. ⎮ A security guard walks 110 m in one trip around the perimeter of the building. It takes him 240 s to make this trip. What is his speed?

9. ⎮ List the following items in order of decreasing speed, from greatest to least: (i) A wind-up toy car that moves 0.15 m in 2.5 s. (ii) A soccer ball that rolls 2.3 m in 0.55 s. (iii) A bicycle that travels 0.60 m in 0.075 s. (iv) A cat that runs 8.0 m in 2.0 s.

10. ⫼ Figure P1.10 shows the motion diagram for a horse galloping in one direction along a straight path. Not every dot is labeled, but the dots are at equally spaced instants of time. What is the horse's velocity
    a. during the first ten seconds of its gallop?
    b. during the interval from 30 s to 40 s?
    c. during the interval from 50 s to 70 s?

```
70 s      50 s 30 s   10 s
 ●    ●  ● ● ● ●   ●   ●
                              x (m)
 50  150 250 350 450 550 650
```
FIGURE P1.10

11. ⫼ It takes Harry 35 s to walk from $x = -12$ m to $x = -47$ m. What is his velocity?

12. ⫼ A dog trots from $x = -12$ m to $x = 3$ m in 10 s. What is its velocity?

13. ⎮ A ball rolling along a straight line with velocity 0.35 m/s goes from $x = 2.1$ m to $x = 7.3$ m. How much time does this take?

Section 1.4 A Sense of Scale: Significant Figures, Scientific Notation, and Units

14. ⫼ Convert the following to SI units:
    a. 9.12 μs   b. 3.42 km
    c. 44 cm/ms   d. 80 km/hour

15. ‖ Convert the following to SI units:
    a. 8.0 in   b. 66 ft/s   c. 60 mph
16. | Convert the following to SI units:
    a. 1.0 hour   b. 1.0 day   c. 1.0 year
17. ‖ List the following three speeds in order, from smallest to largest: 1 mm per μs, 1 km per ks, 1 cm per ms.
18. | How many significant figures does each of the following numbers have?
    a. 6.21   b. 62.1   c. 0.620   d. 0.062
19. | How many significant figures does each of the following numbers have?
    a. 0.621   b. 0.006200
    c. 1.0621   d. 6.21×10^3
20. | Compute the following numbers to 3 significant figures.
    a. 33.3×25.4 b. $33.3 - 25.4$
    c. $\sqrt{33.3}$ d. $333.3 \div 25.4$
21. | The Empire State Building has a height of 1250 ft. Express this height in meters, giving your result in scientific notation with three significant figures.
22. ‖ We interpret a measurement of $x_1 = 77$ m to mean a distance somewhere between 76.5 m and 77.5 m, thus rounding to 77 m. Similarly, $x_2 = 813.8$ m implies a distance between 813.75 m and 813.85 m. Use these values to justify the rule for determining significant figures in addition by finding the smallest and largest possible values of $x_1 + x_2$.
23. ‖ We can interpret a distance traveled of 7.43 m to mean a distance between 7.425 m and 7.435 m, thus rounding to 7.43 m. Similarly, a time interval of 0.83 s implies a time interval between 0.825 s and 0.835 s. Use these values to justify the rule for determining significant figures in division by finding the smallest and largest possible values of the speed.
24. ‖ Estimate (don't measure!) the length of a typical car. Give your answer in both feet and meters. Briefly describe how you arrived at this estimate.
25. | Estimate the height of a telephone pole. Give your answer in both feet and meters. Briefly describe how you arrived at this estimate.
26. | Estimate the average speed with which the hair on your
BIO head grows. Give your answer in both m/s and μm/hr. Briefly describe how you arrived at this estimate.
27. ‖ Estimate the average speed at which your fingernails grow,
BIO in both m/s and μm/hr. Briefly describe how you arrived at this estimate.

Section 1.5 Vectors and Motion: A First Look

28. | Carol and Robin share a house. To get to work, Carol walks north 2.0 km while Robin drives west 7.5 km. How far apart are their workplaces?
29. | Joe and Max shake hands and say goodbye. Joe walks east 0.55 km to a coffee shop, and Max flags a cab and rides north 3.25 km to a bookstore. How far apart are their destinations?
30. ‖‖ A city has streets laid out in a square grid, with each block 135 m long. If you drive north for three blocks, then west for two blocks, how far are you from your starting point?
31. ‖ A butterfly flies from the top of a tree in the center of a garden to rest on top of a red flower at the garden's edge. The tree is 8.0 m taller than the flower, and the garden is 12 m wide. Determine the magnitude of the butterfly's displacement.

32. ‖ A garden has a circular path of radius 50 m. John starts at the easternmost point on this path, then walks counterclockwise around the path until he is at its southernmost point. What is John's displacement? Use the (magnitude, direction) notation for your answer.
33. ‖ Anna walks 130 m due north, 50 m due east, and then 40 m due south. What is her net displacement? Use the (magnitude, direction) notation for your answer.
34. ‖‖‖ A ball on a porch rolls 60 cm to the porch's edge, drops 40 cm, continues rolling on the grass, and eventually stops 80 cm from the porch's edge. What is the magnitude of the ball's net displacement, in centimeters?

Section 1.6 Making Models: The Power of Physics

35. ‖ Sketch a graph of each function over a range of x values from 0.1 to 10. You may need to use different scales on the y axis.
    a. $y = x$ (proportional)
    b. $y = x^2$ (square)
    c. $y = \dfrac{1}{x}$ (inverse)
    d. $y = \dfrac{1}{x^2}$ (inverse square)

General Problems

Problems 36 through 42 are motion problems similar to those you will learn to solve in Chapter 2. For now, simply *interpret* the problem by drawing a motion diagram showing the object's position and its velocity vectors. **Do *not* solve these problems** or do any mathematics.

36. ‖ A Porsche accelerates from a stoplight at 5.0 m/s² for five seconds, then coasts for three more seconds. How far has it traveled?
37. ‖ Billy drops a watermelon from the top of a three-story building, 10 m above the sidewalk. How fast is the watermelon going when it hits?
38. ‖ Sam is recklessly driving 60 mph in a 30 mph speed zone when he suddenly sees the police. He steps on the brakes and slows to 30 mph in three seconds, looking nonchalant as he passes the officer. How far does he travel while braking?
39. ‖ A speed skater moving across frictionless ice at 8.0 m/s hits a 5.0-m-wide patch of rough ice. She slows steadily, then continues on at 6.0 m/s. What is her acceleration on the rough ice?
40. ‖ You would like to stick a wet spit wad on the ceiling, so you toss it straight up with a speed of 10 m/s. How long does it take to reach the ceiling, 3.0 m above?
41. ‖‖ A ball rolls along a smooth horizontal floor at 10 m/s, then starts up a 20° ramp. How high does it go before rolling back down?
42. ‖ A motorist is traveling at 20 m/s. He is 60 m from a stop light when he sees it turn yellow. His reaction time, before stepping on the brake, is 0.50 s. What steady deceleration while braking will bring him to a stop right at the light?

Problems 43 through 50 show a motion diagram. For each of these problems, write a one or two sentence "story" about a *real object* that has this motion diagram. Your stories should talk about people or objects by name and say what they are doing. Problems 36–42 are examples of motion short stories.

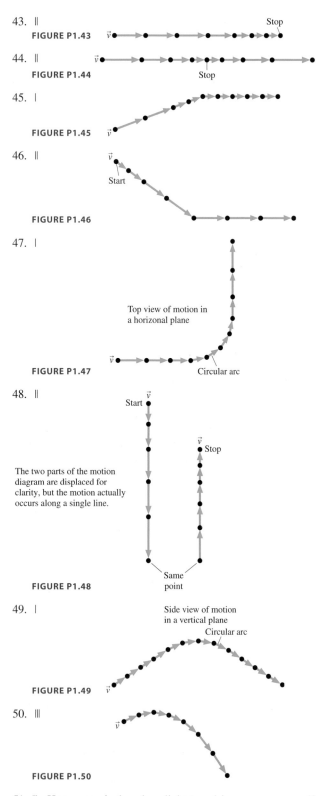

43. ‖
FIGURE P1.43

44. ‖
FIGURE P1.44

45. |
FIGURE P1.45

46. ‖
Start
FIGURE P1.46

47. |
Top view of motion in a horizontal plane
FIGURE P1.47
Circular arc

48. ‖
Start
Stop
The two parts of the motion diagram are displaced for clarity, but the motion actually occurs along a single line.
FIGURE P1.48
Same point

49. |
Side view of motion in a vertical plane
Circular arc
FIGURE P1.49

50. ‖‖
FIGURE P1.50

51. ‖‖ How many inches does light travel in one nanosecond? The speed of light is 3.0×10^8 m/s.

52. ‖ Joseph watches the roadside mile markers during a long car trip on an interstate highway. He notices that at 10:45 A.M. they are passing a marker labeled 101, and at 11:00 A.M. the car reaches marker 119. What is the car's speed, in mph?

53. ‖ Alberta is going to have dinner at her grandmother's house, but she is running a bit behind schedule. As she gets onto the highway, she knows that she must exit the highway within 45 min if she is not going to arrive late. Her exit is 32 mi away. What is the slowest speed at which she could drive and still arrive in time? Express your answer in miles per hour.

54. | Dave hits a hockey puck at 10 m/s toward the goal. If the puck travels 15 m to the goal, how long does it take to get there?

55. | In many living systems, information propagates through
BIO the body in the form of electrical signals called *nerve impulses*. Nerve impulses travel along nerve fibers consisting of many *axons* (fiber-like extensions of nerve cells) aligned in series. For example, when your foot accidentally kicks a rock the feeling of pain is transmitted from the foot to your brain along hundreds of axons that span the distance between your foot and head. Axons come in two varieties: one with a sheath called myelin around it, the other without. Myelinated (sheathed) axons conduct nerve impulses roughly 100 times faster than unmyelinated (unsheathed) axons. Nerve impulses travel at a speed of about 1.0 m/s or 2.2 mph (a walking pace) along unmyelinated axons and about 100 m/s or 220 mph (like a race car) along myelinated axons. Figure P1.55 shows three equal-length nerve fibers consisting of eight axons in a row. Nerve impulses enter at the left side simultaneously and travel to the right.
a. Draw motion diagrams for the nerve impulses traveling along fibers A, B, and C.
b. Which nerve impulse arrives at the right side first?
c. Which will be last?

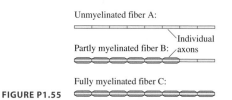

Unmyelinated fiber A:
Individual axons
Partly myelinated fiber B:
Fully myelinated fiber C:
FIGURE P1.55

56. ‖‖ The bacterium *Escherichia coli* (or *E. coli*) is a single-celled
BIO organism that lives in the gut of healthy humans and animals. Its body shape can be modeled as a 2-μm-long cylinder with a 1 μm diameter, and it has a mass of 1×10^{-12} g. Its chromosome consists of a single double-stranded chain of DNA 700 times longer than its body length. The bacterium moves at a constant speed of 20 μm/s, though not always in the same direction. Answer the following questions about *E. coli* using SI units (unless specifically requested otherwise) and correct significant figures.
a. What is its length?
b. Diameter?
c. Mass?
d. What is the length of its DNA, in millimeters?
e. If the organism were to move along a straight path, how many meters would it travel in one day?

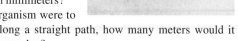

57. ⫼ The bacterium *Escher-*
BIO *ichia coli* (or *E. coli*) is a
single-celled organism that
lives in the gut of healthy
humans and animals. When
grown in a uniform medium
rich in salts and amino acids,
it swims along zig-zag paths
at a constant speed. Fig-
ure P1.57 shows the posi-
tions of an *E. coli* as it moves

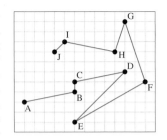

FIGURE P1.57

from point A to point J. Each segment of the motion can be
identified by two letters, such as segment BC. During which
segments, if any, does the bacterium have the same
a. Displacement?   b. Speed?   c. Velocity?

58. ⫼ In 2003, the population of the United States was 291 million people. The per-capita income was $31,459. What was
the total income of everyone in the United States? Express
your answer in scientific notation, with the correct number of
significant figures.

59. ⫼ The sun is 30° above the horizon. It makes a 52-m-long
shadow of a tall tree. How high is the tree?

60. ⫼ An airplane accelerates down the runway for 500 m, then
lifts into the air at an angle of 20.0 degrees above the ground.
When the plane has traveled 300 m in the air, what is its distance from where it started on the runway?

61. ⫼ Starting from its nest, an eagle flies at constant speed for
3.0 min due east, then 4.0 min due north. From there the eagle
flies directly to its nest at the same speed. How long is the
eagle in the air?

62. ⫼ John walks 1.00 km north, then turns right and walks
1.00 km east. His speed is 1.50 m/s during the entire stroll.
a. What is the magnitude of his displacement, from beginning to end?
b. If Jane starts at the same time and place as John, but walks
in a straight line to the endpoint of John's stroll, at what
speed should she walk to arrive at the endpoint just when
John does?

Passage Problems

Growth Speed

The images of trees in Figure P1.63 come from a catalog advertis-
ing fast-growing trees. If we mark the position of the top of the tree
in the successive years, as shown in the graph in the figure, we
obtain a motion diagram much like ones we have seen for other
kinds of motion. The motion isn't steady, of course. In some
months the tree grows rapidly; in other months, quite slowly. We
can see, though, that the average speed of growth is fairly constant
for the first few years.

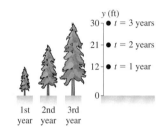

FIGURE P1.63

63. ⫼ What is the tree's speed of growth, in feet per year, from
$t = 1$ yr to $t = 3$ yr?
A. 12 ft/yr   B. 9 ft/yr   C. 6 ft/yr   D. 3 ft/yr
64. ⫼ What is this speed in m/s?
A. 9×10^{-8} m/s   B. 3×10^{-9} m/s
C. 5×10^{-6} m/s   D. 2×10^{-6} m/s
65. ⫼ At the end of year 3, a rope is tied to the very top of the tree
to steady it. This rope is staked into the ground 15 feet away
from the tree. What angle does the rope make with the
ground?
A. 63°   B. 60°   C. 30°   D. 27°

Stop to Think 1.1: B. The images of B are further apart, so it travels a larger distance than does A during the same intervals of time.

Stop to Think 1.2: A. Dropped ball. **B.** Dust particle. **C.** Descending rocket.

Stop to Think 1.3: C. Depending on her initial positive position,
and how far she moves in the negative direction, she could end up
on either side of the origin.

Stop to Think 1.4: D > C > B = A.

Stop to Think 1.5: E. The velocity vector is found by connecting
one dot on the motion diagram to the next.

2 MOTION IN ONE DIMENSION

A horse can run at 35 mph, much faster than a human. And yet, surprisingly, a man can win a race against a horse if the length of the course is right. When, and why, can a man outrun a horse?

Looking Ahead ▶▶

The goal of Chapter 2 is to describe and analyze linear motion. In this chapter you will learn to:

▶ Represent one-dimensional (straight-line) motion in different ways: using numbers, graphs, pictures, words, and equations.

▶ Use general physics problem-solving strategies and techniques.

▶ Solve problems of motion in one dimension.

Looking Back ◀◀

The material in this chapter builds on what you learned in Chapter 1 about motion and measurement. Please review:

◀ Sections 1.2–1.3 Definitions of displacement and velocity.

◀ Section 1.4 Units and significant figures.

◀ Section 1.5 Velocity vectors and motion diagrams.

A race, whether between runners, bicyclists, or drag racers, exemplifies the idea of motion. Today, we use electronic stopwatches, video recorders, and other sophisticated instruments to analyze motion, but it hasn't always been this way. Galileo, who in the early 1600s was the first scientist to study motion experimentally, used his pulse to measure time! Galileo made a useful distinction between the *cause* of motion and the *description* of motion. The modern name for the mathematical description of motion, without regard to causes, is **kinematics.** The term comes from the Greek word *kinema,* meaning "movement." You know this word through its English variation *cinema*—motion pictures!

This chapter will focus on the kinematics of motion in one dimension—that is, motion along a straight line. The motion of runners, drag racers, and skiers can be considered as motion in one dimension. But even in one dimension, there are many interesting issues to consider. For example, which is faster, a man or a horse? The answer depends on what you mean by "faster." Making such commonplace notions more precise will be one of our goals in this chapter. The other half of Galileo's distinction—the cause of motion—is a topic we will take up in Chapter 3 after first learning to describe motion.

2.1 Describing Motion

In Chapter 1 you learned about quantities that you could use to describe an object's motion. Position and velocity are measured with respect to a coordinate system, a grid or axis that *you* impose on a system. We will use an *x*-axis to analyze both horizontal motion and motion on a ramp; a *y*-axis will be used for vertical motion.

We will adopt the convention that the positive end of an *x*-axis is to the right and the positive end of a *y*-axis is up. This convention is illustrated in Figure 2.1.

Velocity is a vector; it has both a magnitude and a direction. When we draw a velocity vector on a diagram, we will use an arrow labeled with the symbol $\vec{v}$ to represent the magnitude and the direction. For motion in one dimension, vectors are restricted to point only "forward" or "backward" for horizontal motion (or "up" or "down" for vertical motion). This restriction lets us simplify our notation for vectors in one dimension. When we solve problems for motion along an *x*-axis we will represent velocity with the symbol v_x. v_x will be positive or negative, corresponding to motion to the right or the left, as shown in Figure 2.2. For motion along a *y*-axis, we will use the symbol v_y to represent the velocity; the sign conventions are also illustrated in Figure 2.2. We will use the symbol v, with no subscript, to represent the speed of an object. **Speed is the *magnitude* of the velocity vector** and is always positive.

Motion Diagrams and Graphs

We saw in Chapter 1 that a motion diagram is a useful tool for analyzing the one-dimensional motion of an object. Let's continue our discussion of motion by using a motion diagram to study a straightforward situation.

Figure 2.3 is a motion diagram, made at 1 frame per minute, of a student walking to school. We have included velocity vectors connecting successive positions on the motion diagram, as we saw we could do in Chapter 1. The motion diagram shows that she leaves home at a time we choose to call $t = 0$ min, and then makes steady progress for a while. Beginning at $t = 3$ min there is a period in which the distance traveled during each time interval becomes less—perhaps she slowed down to speak with a friend. Then, at $t = 6$ min she begins walking more quickly and the distances traveled within each interval are longer.

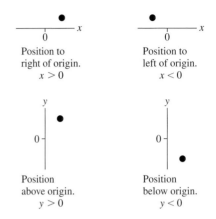

FIGURE 2.1 Sign conventions for position.

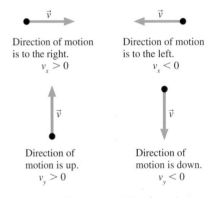

FIGURE 2.2 Sign conventions for velocity.

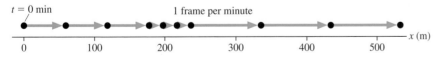

FIGURE 2.3 The motion diagram of a student walking to school and a coordinate axis for making measurements.

Figure 2.3 includes a coordinate axis, and we can see that every dot in a motion diagram occurs at a specific position. Table 2.1 shows the student's positions at different times as measured along this axis. For example, she is at position $x = 120$ m at $t = 2$ min.

The motion diagram of Figure 2.3 is one way to represent the student's motion. Presenting the data as in Table 2.1 is a second way to represent this motion; you can easily see where the student was at any particular time. A third way to represent

TABLE 2.1 Measured positions of a student walking to school

Time t (min)	Position x (m)	t	x
0	0	5	220
1	60	6	240
2	120	7	340
3	180	8	440
4	200	9	540

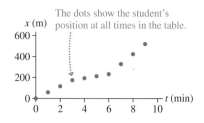

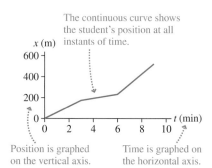

FIGURE 2.4 A graph of the student's motion.

FIGURE 2.5 Extending the graph of Figure 2.4 to a position-versus-time graph.

the motion is to make a graph of these measurements. Figure 2.4 is a graph of the position of the student at different times; we say it is a graph of x versus t for the student. We have merely taken the data from the table and plotted these particular points on the graph.

NOTE ▶ A graph of "a versus b" means that a is graphed on the vertical axis and b on the horizontal axis. ◄

We can flesh out the graph of Figure 2.4, though. Common sense tells us a few things. First, the student was *somewhere specific* at all times. That is, there was never a time when she failed to have a well-defined position, nor could she occupy two positions at one time. (As reasonable as this belief appears to be, it will be found to be not entirely accurate when we get to quantum physics!) Second, from the start to the end of her motion, the student moved *continuously* through all intervening points of space. She could not go from $x = 100$ m to $x = 200$ m without passing through every point in between. It is thus quite reasonable to believe that her motion can be shown as a continuous curve that passes through the measured points, as shown in Figure 2.5. A continuous curve that shows an object's position as a function of time is called a **position-versus-time graph** or, sometimes, just a *position graph*.

NOTE ▶ In making the graph continuous, we made some assumptions about her motion. For example, we assumed that the curve is smooth from point to point. This may not be quite true, but in most cases it is a reasonable assumption. ◄

NOTE ▶ A graph is *not* a "picture" of the motion. The student is walking along a straight line, but the graph itself is not a straight line. Further, we've graphed her position on the vertical axis even though her motion is horizontal. A graph is an *abstract representation* of motion. We will place significant emphasis on the process of interpreting graphs, and many of the exercises and problems will give you a chance to practice these skills. ◄

CONCEPTUAL EXAMPLE 2.1 Interpreting a car's position-versus-time graph

The graph in Figure 2.6 represents the motion of a car along a straight road. Describe (in words) the motion of the car.

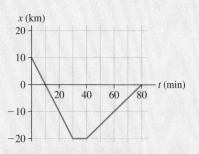

FIGURE 2.6 Position-versus-time graph for the car.

REASON The vertical axis in Figure 2.6 is labeled as "x (km)"; position is measured in kilometers. Our convention for motion along the x-axis given in Figure 2.1 tells us that x increases as the car moves to the right and x decreases as the car moves to the left. The graph thus represents the motion of a car that travels to the left for 30 minutes, stops for 10 minutes, then travels to the right for 40 minutes. It ends up 10 km to the left of where it began. Figure 2.7 gives a full explanation of the reasoning.

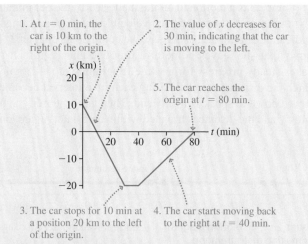

1. At $t = 0$ min, the car is 10 km to the right of the origin.

2. The value of x decreases for 30 min, indicating that the car is moving to the left.

5. The car reaches the origin at $t = 80$ min.

3. The car stops for 10 min at a position 20 km to the left of the origin.

4. The car starts moving back to the right at $t = 40$ min.

FIGURE 2.7 Looking at the position-versus-time graph in detail.

ASSESS The car travels to the left for 30 minutes and to the right for 40 minutes. Nonetheless, it ends up to the left of where it started. This means that the car was moving faster when it was moving to the left than when it was moving to the right. We can deduce this fact from the graph as well, as we will see in the next section.

Velocity Is the Slope of the Position-Versus-Time Graph

Let's look more closely at the graph of Figure 2.6 showing the motion of a car. Suppose we want to compute the velocity of the car during the 40 minutes when it moves to the right. For motion along a line, the definition of velocity from Chapter 1 can be written as

$$v_x = \frac{\Delta x}{\Delta t} \tag{2.1}$$

We can give a graphical interpretation to Equation 2.1: It is the *slope* of the section of the graph representing this motion. Recall that the slope of a straight-line graph is defined as "rise over run." Because position is graphed on the vertical axis, the "rise" of a position-versus-time graph is the object's displacement Δx. The "run" is the time interval Δt. Consequently, the slope of a straight-line segment is $\Delta x/\Delta t$. This idea is graphically illustrated in Figure 2.8. We can associate the slope of the position-versus-time graph, a *geometrical* quantity, with the *physical* quantity velocity. This will be an important aspect of interpreting position-versus-time graphs, as outlined in Tactics Box 2.1.

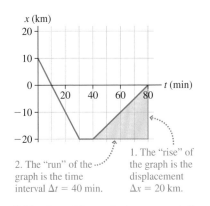

FIGURE 2.8 Calculating velocity from a position-versus-time graph.

1. The "rise" of the graph is the displacement $\Delta x = 20$ km.
2. The "run" of the graph is the time interval $\Delta t = 40$ min.
3. The slope of the graph, rise over run, is the car's velocity during this phase of motion:

v_x = slope of position-versus-time graph
$= \frac{\Delta x}{\Delta t} = \frac{20 \text{ km}}{40 \text{ min}} = 0.50$ km/min

(MP)   TACTICS BOX 2.1 Interpreting position-versus-time graphs   ✐ Exercises 2–4

Information about motion can be obtained from position-versus-time graphs as follows:

❶ Determine the *position* at time t by reading the graph at that instant of time.
❷ Determine the *speed* at time t by finding the magnitude of the slope at that point. Steeper slopes correspond to greater speeds.
❸ Determine the *direction of motion* by noting the sign of the slope. Positive slopes correspond to positive velocities and, hence, to motion to the right (or up). Negative slopes correspond to negative velocities and, hence, to motion to the left (or down).

NOTE ▶ The slope is a ratio of intervals, $\Delta x/\Delta t$, not a ratio of coordinates. That is, the slope is *not* simply x/t. ◀

NOTE ▶ We are distinguishing between the actual slope and the *physically meaningful* slope. If you were to use a ruler to measure the rise and the run of the graph, you could compute the actual slope of the line as drawn on the page. That is not the slope we are referring to when we equate the velocity with the slope of the line. Instead, we find the *physically meaningful* slope by measuring the rise and run using the scales along the axes. The "rise" Δx is some number of meters; the "run" Δt is some number of seconds. The physically meaningful rise and run include units, and the ratio of these units gives the units of the slope. ◀

Time lines BIO This section of the trunk of a pine tree shows the light bands of spring growth and the dark bands of summer and fall growth in successive years. If you focus on the spacing of successive dark bands, you can think of this picture as a motion diagram for the tree, representing its growth in diameter. The years of rapid growth (large distance between dark bands) during wet years and slow growth (small distance between dark bands) during years of drought are readily apparent.

EXAMPLE 2.1 Calculating a car's velocity
Looking again at Figure 2.6, what is the velocity of the car during the period from 0 to 30 min? What is the speed?

SOLVE We find the velocity by computing the slope of the graph:

$$v_x = \frac{\Delta x}{\Delta t} = \frac{-30 \text{ km}}{30 \text{ min}} = -1.0 \text{ km/min}$$

The speed is the magnitude of the velocity:

$$v = |v_x| = 1.0 \text{ km/min}$$

ASSESS The slope of the graph is negative; the value of the distance is decreasing with time, leading to a negative displacement and a negative velocity. The "−" sign in the velocity tells us that the motion is to the left. The speed for this phase of the motion is greater than that of the final phase, as we noted it should be.

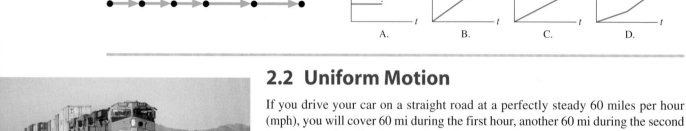

Which position-versus-time graph below best describes the motion diagram at left?

A.   B.   C.   D.

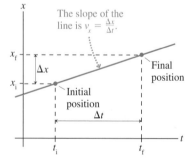

A freight train moving steadily on a straight run of track is a practical example of uniform motion.

Uniform motion

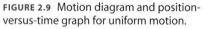

The displacements between successive frames are the same. Dots are equally spaced. v_x is constant.

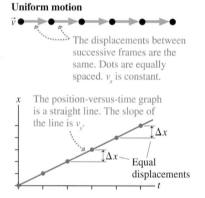

The position-versus-time graph is a straight line. The slope of the line is v_x.

Δx

Δx Equal displacements

FIGURE 2.9 Motion diagram and position-versus-time graph for uniform motion.

The slope of the line is $v_x = \frac{\Delta x}{\Delta t}$.

x_f

Δx Final position

x_i Initial position

Δt

t_i t_f

FIGURE 2.10 Position-versus-time graph for an object in uniform motion.

2.2 Uniform Motion

If you drive your car on a straight road at a perfectly steady 60 miles per hour (mph), you will cover 60 mi during the first hour, another 60 mi during the second hour, yet another 60 mi during the third hour, and so on. This is an example of what we call *uniform motion*. In this case, 60 mi is not your position, but rather the *change* in your position during each hour; that is, your displacement Δx. Similarly, 1 hour is a time interval Δt rather than a specific instant of time. This suggests the following definition: **Straight-line motion in which equal displacements occur during any successive equal-time intervals is called uniform motion or constant-velocity motion.**

The qualifier "any" is important. If during each hour you drive 120 mph for 30 min and stop for 30 min, you will cover 60 mi during each successive 1-hour interval. But you would *not* have equal displacements during successive 30-min intervals, so this motion is not uniform. Your constant 60 mph driving is uniform motion because you will find equal displacements no matter how you choose your successive time intervals.

Figure 2.9 shows a motion diagram and a graph for an object in uniform motion. Notice that the position-versus-time graph for uniform motion is a straight line. This follows from the requirement that all values of Δx corresponding to the same value of Δt be equal. In fact, an alternative definition of uniform motion is: **An object's motion is uniform if and only if its position-versus-time graph is a straight line.**

Equations of Uniform Motion

We have seen how to represent motion in four ways:

- Using words
- Using a motion diagram
- Using a table of data of positions at certain times
- Using a graph of position versus time

Now we will add a fifth representation: equations.

Consider an object in uniform motion along the x-axis with the linear position-versus-time graph shown in Figure 2.10. Recall from the previous chapter that we denote the object's initial position as x_i at time t_i. The term "initial" refers to the starting point of our analysis or the starting point in a problem. The object may or may not have been in motion prior to t_i. We use the term "final" for the ending point of our analysis or the ending point of a problem, and denote the object's final position x_f at the time t_f. The object's velocity v_x along the x-axis can be determined by finding the slope of the graph:

$$v_x = \frac{\text{rise}}{\text{run}} = \frac{\Delta x}{\Delta t} = \frac{x_f - x_i}{t_f - t_i} \tag{2.2}$$

Equation 2.2 can be rearranged to give

$$x_f = x_i + v_x \, \Delta t \tag{2.3}$$

Position equation for an object in uniform motion
(v_x is constant)

where $\Delta t = t_f - t_i$ is the interval of time in which the object moves from position x_i to position x_f. Equation 2.3 applies to any time interval Δt during which the velocity is constant. We can also write this in terms of the object's displacement, $\Delta x = x_f - x_i$:

$$\Delta x = v_x \Delta t \qquad (2.4)$$

The velocity of an object in uniform motion tells us the amount by which its position changes during each second. An object with a velocity of 20 m/s *changes* its position by 20 m during every second of motion: by 20 m during the first second of its motion, by another 20 m during the next second, and so on. We say that position is changing at the *rate* of 20 m/s. If the object starts at $x_i = 10$ m, it will be at $x = 30$ m after 1 s of motion and at $x = 50$ m after 2 s of motion. Thinking of velocity like this will help you develop an intuitive understanding of the connection between velocity and position—something we will explore further in the next section.

Physics may seem densely populated with equations, but most equations follow a few basic forms, as we saw in Chapter 1. The mathematical form of Equation 2.3 is a type that we will see again—a *linear relationship*.

NOTE ▶ The important features of a linear relationship are described below. In this text, the first time we use a particular mathematical form we will provide such an overview. In future chapters, when we see other examples of this type of relationship, we will refer back to this overview. ◀

Linear relationships
Exercises 5, 6 (MP)

Two quantities are said to have a **linear relationship** if the graph of y versus x is a straight line. We write the mathematical relationship as

$$y = Ax + B$$

y is a linear function of x

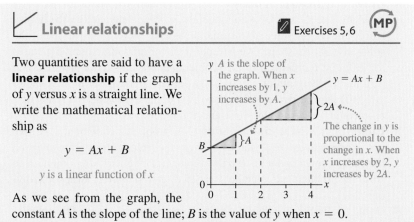

y A is the slope of the graph. When x increases by 1, y increases by A.

$y = Ax + B$

$2A$

The change in y is proportional to the change in x. When x increases by 2, y increases by $2A$.

As we see from the graph, the constant A is the slope of the line; B is the value of y when $x = 0$.

A change in x leads to a **proportional** change in y. If we have initial and final values:

$$y_f = Ax_f + B$$

$$y_i = Ax_i + B$$

We can subtract these equations to find that

$$y_f - y_i = A(x_f - x_i)$$

$$\Delta y = A \, \Delta x$$

Therefore, we can write

$$\Delta y \propto \Delta x$$

SCALING Linear scaling means, for example:

- If you double Δx, you double Δy, as you can see in the graph.
- If you decrease Δx by a factor of 3, you decrease Δy by a factor of 3.

EXAMPLE 2.2 How far does the car travel?

A car takes 2.0 min to travel 1.0 mi. How far does it travel in 10 min?

SOLVE The statement of the problem assumes that the car is in uniform motion—traveling at a constant velocity. The distance will be related to the time by the *linear relationship* of Equation 2.3; this means that the change in the distance is proportional to the change in time. 10 min is a time interval that is 5 times the original 2.0 min time interval, so the car will travel 5 times as far, 5.0 mi.

A Problem-Solving Strategy

Before we introduce any more physics concepts, we'll take a break to look at a strategy for using these concepts to solve practical problems. The first step in solving a seemingly complicated problem is to break it down into a series of smaller steps. In worked examples in the text, we will use a problem-solving strategy that consists of three steps: *prepare, solve* and *assess*. Each of these steps has important elements that you should follow when you solve problems on your own.

Building a complex structure requires careful planning. The architect's visualization and drawings have to be complete before the detailed procedures of construction get underway. The same is true for solving problems in physics.

(MP) Problem-Solving Strategy

PREPARE The "Prepare" step of a solution is where you identify important elements of the problem and collect information you will need to solve it. It's tempting to jump right to the "solve" step, but a skilled problem solver will spend the most time on this step, the preparation. Preparation includes:

- **Drawing a picture.** In many cases, this is the most important part of a problem. The picture lets you model the problem and identify the important elements. As you add information to your picture, the outline of the solution will take shape. We will give tips for drawing effective pictures for different problems. For the problems in this chapter, a picture could be a motion diagram or a graph—or perhaps both. Later in the chapter you will learn a strategy for drawing a complete *visual overview* of a problem that incorporates these and other elements.
- **Collecting necessary information.** The problem's statement may give you some values of variables. Other important information may be implied, or must be looked up in a table. Gather everything you need to solve the problem, and include it as part of your picture or an accompanying table.
- **Doing preliminary calculations.** In some cases, there are a few calculations, such as unit conversions, that are best done in advance of the main part of the solution.

SOLVE The "Solve" step of a solution is where you actually do the mathematics or reasoning necessary to arrive at the answer needed. This is the part of the problem-solving strategy that you likely think of when you think of "solving problems." But don't make the mistake of starting here! If you just choose an equation and plug in numbers, you will likely go wrong and will waste time trying to figure out why. The "Prepare" step will help you be certain you understand the problem before you start putting numbers in equations.

ASSESS The "Assess" step of your solution is very important. When you have an answer, you should check to see if it makes sense. Ask yourself:

- **Does my solution answer the question that was asked?** Make sure you have addressed all parts of the question and clearly written down your solutions.

Continued

- **Does my answer have the correct units and number of significant figures?**
- **Does the value I computed make physical sense?** In this book all calculations use physically reasonable numbers. You will not be given a problem to solve in which the final velocity of a bicycle is 100 miles per hour! If your final answer seems unreasonable, you should go back and check your work.
- **Can I estimate what the answer should be to check my solution?**
- **Does my final solution make sense in the context of the material I am learning?**

EXAMPLE 2.3 Using the problem-solving strategy to analyze the motion of a baseball

In a game of baseball, a batter hits the ball straight toward the pitcher, who stands 60 ft from the batter. The ball comes off the bat at a speed of 100 ft/s. How far is the ball from the batter 1.0 s after it passes the pitcher?

PREPARE Start by drawing a picture. In this case, we will draw a position-versus-time graph of the motion, shown in Figure 2.11. We've chosen the origin of our coordinate system to be at the

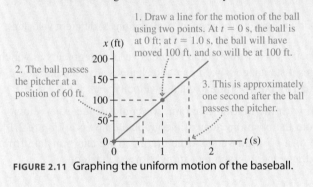

1. Draw a line for the motion of the ball using two points. At $t = 0$ s, the ball is at 0 ft; at $t = 1.0$ s, the ball will have moved 100 ft. and so will be at 100 ft.

2. The ball passes the pitcher at a position of 60 ft.

3. This is approximately one second after the ball passes the pitcher.

FIGURE 2.11 Graphing the uniform motion of the baseball.

position where the batter hits the ball. As the ball leaves the bat, its position increases at the rate of 100 ft/s. This is uniform motion, so the graph will be a straight line. We now add important information to our picture. One important distance to note on the graph is the position of the pitcher. When the ball is at this position, we can see that the time is a bit over 0.5 s.

We are interested in the position of the ball 1.0 s after this point. A quick look at the graph shows us that this position will be a bit over 150 ft.

SOLVE As the ball is in uniform motion, we will use Equation 2.3 for our solution. We take x_i to be 60 ft, when the ball passes the pitcher. We are interested in the position x_f 1.0 s later, so Δt is 1.0 s. Thus

$$x_f = x_i + v_x \Delta t = 60 \text{ ft} + (100 \text{ ft/s})(1.0 \text{ s}) = 160 \text{ ft}$$

ASSESS The final value is close to our estimate from the graph in the Prepare step. It also seems physically reasonable; if you have ever watched a baseball game, you know that 1.0 s after a struck ball passes the pitcher it is well on its way to the outfield.

This was a straightforward problem, but you can see that making such a complete picture in the "Prepare" step let us visualize the important points in the motion, aiding our solution. It also allowed us to estimate what the final solution should be. For more involved problems, the picture is much more important.

From Position to Velocity

We've focused thus far on graphs of position versus time. Now let's see what we can learn by graphing velocity versus time. In section 2.1, we considered the motion of a student walking to school; the motion diagram is repeated in Figure 2.12. Rather than looking at her position, let's now focus on her velocity, as represented by the green arrows. A long arrow corresponds to a large velocity, a short arrow a small velocity.

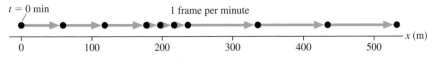

FIGURE 2.12 The motion diagram for the student walking to school, revisited.

The green arrow between $t = 0$ min and $t = 1$ min represents her velocity during this period of time. Looking at the data in Table 2.1, we see that her velocity during this interval is

$$v_x = \frac{\Delta x}{\Delta t} = \frac{60 \text{ m}}{1 \text{ min}} \times \frac{1 \text{ min}}{60 \text{ s}} = 1.0 \text{ m/s}$$

We see from the motion diagram that she moved at this constant velocity until $t = 3$ min, then she suddenly slowed down. We can use the data in Table 2.1 to find that her velocity from $t = 3$ min to $t = 6$ min is 0.33 m/s. She then increased her velocity to 1.7 m/s. Using all this information gives us the **velocity-versus-time graph** shown in Figure 2.13.

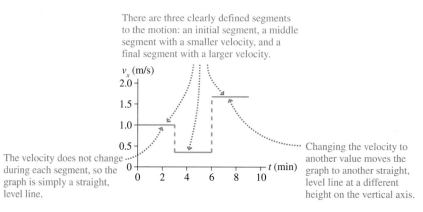

There are three clearly defined segments to the motion: an initial segment, a middle segment with a smaller velocity, and a final segment with a larger velocity.

The velocity does not change during each segment, so the graph is simply a straight, level line.

Changing the velocity to another value moves the graph to another straight, level line at a different height on the vertical axis.

FIGURE 2.13 The student's motion is a series of uniform motions at different velocities.

NOTE ▶ This velocity-versus-time graph includes vertical segments in which the velocity changes instantaneously. Such rapid changes are an idealization; it actually takes a small amount of time to change velocity. ◀

Rather than begin with the motion diagram, we could deduce the velocity-versus-time graph from the position-versus-time graph as shown in Figure 2.14. Velocity is the slope of a position-versus-time graph, so we can translate from the position graph to the velocity graph in a straightforward fashion.

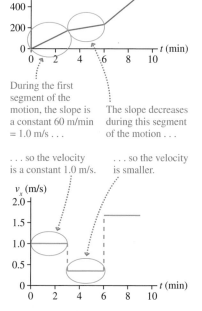

During the first segment of the motion, the slope is a constant 60 m/min = 1.0 m/s . . .

The slope decreases during this segment of the motion . . .

. . . so the velocity is a constant 1.0 m/s.

. . . so the velocity is smaller.

FIGURE 2.14 Deducing the velocity-versus-time graph from the position-versus-time graph.

EXAMPLE 2.4 **Analyzing a car's position graph**

Figure 2.15 gives the position-versus-time graph of a car.

a. Draw the car's velocity-versus-time graph.
b. Describe the car's motion in words.

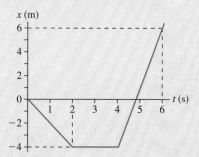

FIGURE 2.15 The position-versus-time graph of a car.

PREPARE Figure 2.15 is a graphical representation of the motion. The car's position-versus-time graph is a sequence of

three straight lines. Each of these straight lines represents uniform motion at a constant velocity. We can determine the car's velocity during each interval of time by measuring the slope of the line.

SOLVE

a. From $t = 0$ s to $t = 2$ s ($\Delta t = 2$ s) the car's displacement is $\Delta x = -4$ m $- 0$ m $= -4$ m. The velocity during this interval is

$$v_x = \frac{\Delta x}{\Delta t} = \frac{-4 \text{ m}}{2 \text{ s}} = -2 \text{ m/s}$$

The car's position does not change from $t = 2$ s to $t = 4$ s ($\Delta x = 0$ m), so $v_x = 0$ m/s. Finally, the displacement between $t = 4$ s and $t = 6$ s ($\Delta t = 2$ s) is $\Delta x = 10$ m. Thus the velocity during this interval is

$$v_x = \frac{10 \text{ m}}{2 \text{ s}} = 5 \text{ m/s}$$

Continued

These velocities are represented graphically in Figure 2.16.

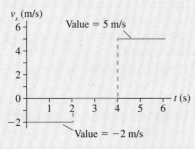

FIGURE 2.16 The velocity-versus-time graph for the car.

b. The velocity-versus-time graph of Figure 2.16 shows the motion in a way that we can describe in a straightforward manner: The car backs up for 2 s at 2 m/s, sits at rest for 2 s, then drives forward at 5 m/s for 2 s.

ASSESS Notice that the velocity graph and the position graph look completely different. The value of the velocity graph at any instant of time equals the *slope* of the position graph. Since the position graph is made up of segments of constant slope, the velocity graph will be made up of segments of constant *value*.

From Velocity to Position

We have seen how to convert from position-versus-time information to velocity-versus-time information. It is possible to go the other way as well: Given information about an object's velocity, we can determine its position.

Suppose a car moves at a constant velocity of 12 m/s for 4.0 s. How far does it travel—that is, what is its displacement during this time interval?

Equation 2.4, $\Delta x = v_x \Delta t$, describes the displacement mathematically; for a graphical interpretation, we consider the graph of velocity versus time in Figure 2.17. In the figure, we've shaded a rectangle whose height is the velocity v_x (12 m/s) and whose base is the time interval Δt (4.0 s). The area of this rectangle is $v_x \Delta t$. Looking at Equation 2.4, we see that this quantity is also equal to the displacement of the car. The area of this rectangle is the area between the axis and the line representing the velocity; we call it the "area under the graph." We see that the **displacement Δx is equal to the area under the velocity graph during interval Δt.**

Whether we use Equation 2.4 or the area under the graph to compute the displacement, we get the same result:

$$\Delta x = v_x \Delta t = (12 \text{ m/s})(4.0 \text{ s}) = 48 \text{ m}$$

Although we've shown that the displacement is the area under the graph only for uniform motion, where the velocity is constant, we'll soon see that this result applies to any one-dimensional motion.

> **NOTE** ▶ Wait a minute! The displacement $\Delta x = x_f - x_i$ is a length. How can a length equal an area? Recall earlier, when we found that the velocity is the slope of the position graph, we made a distinction between the *actual* slope and the *physically meaningful* slope? The same distinction applies here. The velocity graph does indeed bound a certain area on the page. That is the actual area, but it is *not* the area to which we are referring. Once again, we need to measure the quantities we are using, v_x and Δt, by referring to the scales on the axes. Δt is some number of seconds while v_x is some number of meters per second. When these are multiplied together, the *physically meaningful* area has units of meters, appropriate for a displacement. ◀

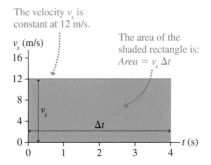

FIGURE 2.17 Displacement is the area under a velocity-versus-time graph.

STOP TO THINK 2.2 An object moves with the velocity-versus-time graph shown at left below. Which of the position-versus-time graphs matches this motion?

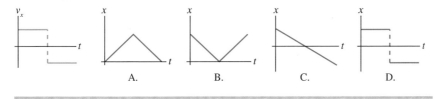

A.   B.   C.   D.

A drag racer moves with rapidly changing velocity.

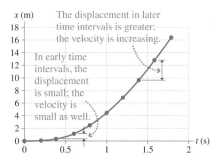

FIGURE 2.18 Position-versus-time graph for a drag racer.

2.3 Motion with Changing Velocity

The objects we've studied so far have moved with a constant, unchanging velocity or, like the car in Example 2.4, changed abruptly from one constant velocity to another. This is not very realistic. Real moving objects speed up and slow down, *changing* their velocity. As an extreme example, think about a drag racer. In a typical race, the car begins at rest but, one second later, is moving at over 25 miles per hour!

For one-dimensional motion, an object changing its velocity is either speeding up or slowing down. When you drive your car, as you speed up or slow down—changing your velocity—a glance at your speedometer tells you how fast you're going *at that instant*. An object's velocity—a speed *and* a direction—at a specific *instant* of time *t* is called the object's **instantaneous velocity.**

But what does it mean to have a velocity "at an instant"? An instantaneous velocity of magnitude 60 mph means that the rate at which your car's position is changing—at that exact instant—is such that it would travel a distance of 60 miles in 1 hour *if* it continued at that rate without change. Said another way, if *just for an instant* your car matches the velocity of another car driving at a steady 60 mph, then your instantaneous velocity is 60 mph. Whether or not your car actually does travel at that velocity for another hour is not relevant. **From now on, the word "velocity" will always mean instantaneous velocity.**

For uniform motion, we found that an object's position-versus-time graph is a straight line and the object's velocity is the slope of that line. In contrast, Figure 2.18 shows that the position-versus-time graph for a drag racer is a *curved* line. The displacement Δ*x* during equal intervals of time gets larger as the car speeds up. Even so, we can still use the slope of the line to measure the car's velocity.

Finding the instantaneous velocity

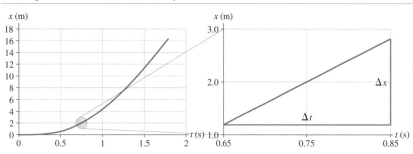

If the velocity changes, the position graph is no longer a straight line: It is clearly curved. How are we to compute the slope to find the velocity? The key is to focus in on a small segment of the motion. Let's look at the motion in a very small time interval right around *t* = 0.75 s. This is highlighted with a circle, and we show a "close-up" in the next graph, at right.

Now that we have magnified a small part of the position graph, we see that the graph in this small part appears to have a constant slope. It is always possible to make the graph appear as a straight line by choosing a small enough time interval. Now we can find the slope of the line by calculating the rise over run, just as we did before:

$$v_x = \frac{1.6 \text{ m}}{0.20 \text{ s}} = 8.0 \text{ m/s}$$

This is the slope of the graph at *t* = 0.75 s, and thus the velocity at this instant of time.

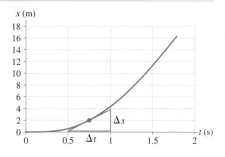

Graphically, the slope of the curve at a particular point is the same as the slope of a straight line drawn *tangent* to the curve at that point. **The slope of the tangent line is the instantaneous velocity at that instant of time.**

Calculating rise over run for the tangent line, we get

$$v_x = \frac{4.0 \text{ m}}{0.50 \text{ s}} = 8.0 \text{ m/s}$$

This is the same value we obtained from considering the close-up view.

CONCEPTUAL EXAMPLE 2.2 **Analyzing an elevator's position graph**

Figure 2.19 shows the position-versus-time graph of an elevator.

a. Sketch an approximate velocity-versus-time graph.
b. At which point or points is the elevator moving the fastest?
c. Is the elevator ever at rest? If so, at which point or points?

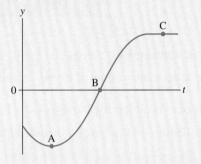

FIGURE 2.19 The position-versus-time graph for an elevator.

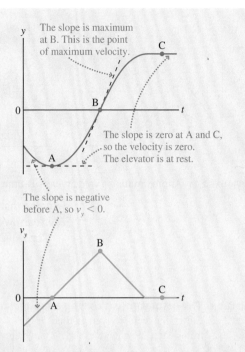

FIGURE 2.20 Finding a velocity graph from a position graph.

REASON a. Notice that the position graph shows y versus t, rather than x versus t, indicating that the motion is vertical rather than horizontal. Our analysis of one-dimensional motion has made no assumptions about the direction of motion, so it applies equally well to both horizontal and vertical motion. Let's start by sketching an approximate velocity-versus-time graph. As we just found, the velocity at a particular instant of time is the slope of a tangent line to the position-versus-time graph at that time. We can move point-by-point along the position-versus-time graph, noting the slope of the tangent at each point. This will give us the velocity at that point.

Initially, to the left of point A, the slope is negative and thus the velocity is negative (i.e., the elevator is moving downward). But the slope decreases as the curve flattens out, and by the time the graph gets to point A, the slope is zero. The slope then increases to a maximum value at point B, decreases back to zero a little before point C, and remains at zero thereafter. This reasoning process is outlined in Figure 2.20a, and Figure 2.20b shows the approximate velocity-versus-time graph that results.

The other questions were really answered during the construction of the graph:

b. The elevator moves the fastest at point B where the slope of the position graph is the steepest.
c. A particle at rest has $v_y = 0$. Graphically, this occurs at points where the tangent line to the position-versus-time graph is horizontal and thus has zero slope. Figure 2.20 shows that the slope is zero at points A and C. At point A, the velocity is only instantaneously zero as the particle reverses direction from downward motion (negative velocity) to upward motion (positive velocity). At point C, the elevator has actually stopped and remains at rest.

ASSESS Once again, the shape of the velocity graph bears no resemblance to the shape of the position graph. You must translate between slope information on the position graph and value information on the velocity graph.

For uniform motion we showed that the displacement Δx is the area under the velocity-versus-time graph during time interval Δt. We can generalize this idea to the case of an object whose velocity varies. Figure 2.21a on the next page is the velocity-versus-time graph for an object whose velocity changes with time. Suppose we know the object's position to be x_i at an initial time t_i. Our goal is to find its position x_f at a later time t_f.

Because we know how to handle constant velocities, let's *approximate* the velocity function of Figure 2.21a as a series of constant-velocity steps of width Δt. The velocity during each step is constant (uniform motion), so we can calculate the displacement during each step as the area of the rectangle under the curve. The total displacement of the object between t_i and t_f can be found as the sum of all the individual displacements during each of the constant-velocity steps. We can see in Figure 2.21c that the total displacement is approximately equal to the area under the graph, even in the case where the velocity varies. Although the approximation shown in the figure is rather rough, with only nine steps, we can

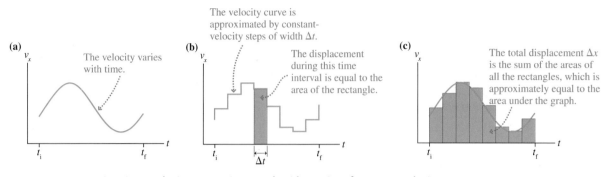

FIGURE 2.21 Approximating a velocity-versus-time graph with a series of constant-velocity steps.

imagine that it could be made as accurate as desired by having more and more ever-narrower steps.

Consequently, an object's displacement is related to its velocity by

$$x_f - x_i = \Delta x = \text{area under the velocity graph } v_x \text{ between } t_i \text{ and } t_f \quad (2.5)$$

EXAMPLE 2.5 The displacement during a rapid start

Figure 2.22 shows the velocity-versus-time graph of a car pulling away from a stop. How far does the car move during the first 3.0 s?

PREPARE Figure 2.22 is a graphical representation of the motion. The question "how far" indicates that we need to find a displacement Δx rather than a position x. According to Equation 2.5, the

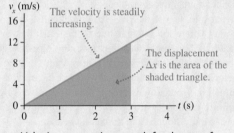

FIGURE 2.22 Velocity-versus-time graph for the car of Example 2.5.

car's displacement $\Delta x = x_f - x_i$ between $t = 0$ s and $t = 3$ s is the area under the curve from $t = 0$ s to $t = 3$ s.

SOLVE The curve in this case is an angled line, so the area is that of a triangle:

$$\Delta x = \text{area of triangle between } t = 0 \text{ s and } t = 3 \text{ s}$$

$$= \tfrac{1}{2} \times \text{base} \times \text{height} = \tfrac{1}{2} \times 3 \text{ s} \times 12 \text{ m/s} = 18 \text{ m}$$

The car moves 18 m during the first 3 seconds as its velocity changes from 0 to 12 m/s.

ASSESS The "area" is a product of s with m/s, so Δx has the proper units of m. Let's check the numbers. The final velocity, 12 m/s, is about 25 mph. Pulling away from a stop, you might expect to reach this speed in about 3 s—at least if you have a reasonably sporty vehicle! If the car had moved at a constant 12 m/s (the final velocity) during these 3 s, the distance would be 36 m. The actual distance traveled during the 3 s is 18 m— half of 36 m. This makes sense, as the velocity was 0 m/s at the start of the problem and increased steadily to 12 m/s.

STOP TO THINK 2.3 Which velocity-versus-time graph goes with the position-versus-time graph on the left?

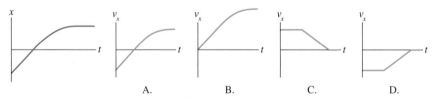

TABLE 2.2 Performance data for vehicles

Vehicle	Time to go from 0 to 60 mph
1997 Porsche 911 Turbo S	3.6 s
1973 Volkswagen Super Beetle Convertible	24 s

2.4 Acceleration

One of the goals of this chapter is to describe motion. Position, time, and velocity are important concepts, but we need one more motion concept, one that will describe a *change* in the velocity.

As an example, a frequently quoted measurement of car performance is the time it takes the car to change its velocity from 0 to 60 mph. Table 2.2 shows this time for two rather different cars.

Let's look at motion diagrams for the Porsche and the Volkswagen in Figure 2.23. We can see two important facts about the motion. First, the lengths of the velocity vectors are increasing, showing that the speeds are increasing. Second, the velocity vectors for the Porsche are increasing in length more rapidly than those of the VW. The quantity we seek is one that measures how rapidly an object's velocity vectors change in length.

FIGURE 2.23 Motion diagrams for the Porsche and Volkswagen.

When we wanted to measure changes in position, the ratio $\Delta x/\Delta t$ was useful. This ratio, which we defined as the velocity, is the *rate of change of position.* Similarly, we can measure how rapidly an object's velocity changes with the ratio $\Delta v_x/\Delta t$. Given our experience with velocity, we can say a couple of things about this new ratio:

- The ratio $\Delta v_x/\Delta t$ is the *rate of change of velocity.*
- The ratio $\Delta v_x/\Delta t$ is the *slope of a velocity-versus-time graph.*

We will define this ratio as the **acceleration,** for which we use the symbol a_x:

$$a_x = \frac{\Delta v_x}{\Delta t} \tag{2.6}$$

Definition of the acceleration as rate of change of velocity

Similarly, $a_y = \Delta v_y/\Delta t$ for vertical motion.

As an example, let's calculate the acceleration for the Porsche and the Volkswagen. For both, the initial velocity $(v_x)_i$ is zero and the final velocity $(v_x)_f$ is 60 mph. Thus the *change* in velocity is $\Delta v_x = 60$ mph. In m/s, our SI unit of velocity, $\Delta v_x = 27$ m/s.

Now we can use Equation 2.6 to compute acceleration. Let's start with the Porsche, which speeds up to 27 m/s in $\Delta t = 3.6$ s:

$$a_{\text{Porsche }x} = \frac{\Delta v_x}{\Delta t} = \frac{27 \text{ m/s}}{3.6 \text{ s}} = 7.5 \frac{\text{m/s}}{\text{s}}$$

Notice the units; they are velocity over time. In the first second of motion, the Porsche's velocity increases by 7.5 m/s; in the next second, it increases by another 7.5 m/s, and so on. After 1 second, the velocity is 7.5 m/s; after 2 seconds, it is 15 m/s. This increase continues as long as the Porsche has an acceleration of 7.5 (m/s)/s.

The Volkswagen's acceleration is

$$a_{\text{VW }x} = \frac{\Delta v_x}{\Delta t} = \frac{27 \text{ m/s}}{24 \text{ s}} = 1.1 \frac{\text{m/s}}{\text{s}}$$

In each second, the Volkswagen changes its speed by 1.1 m/s. This is about 1/7 the acceleration of the Porsche! The reasons why the Porsche is capable of greater acceleration have to do with what *causes* the motion. We will explore the reasons for acceleration in Chapter 3. For now, we will simply note that the Porsche is capable of much larger acceleration, something you would have suspected.

NOTE ► It is customary to abbreviate the acceleration units (m/s)/s as m/s². For example, the Volkswagen has an acceleration of 1.1 m/s². We will use this notation, but keep in mind the *meaning* of the notation as "(meters per second) per second." ◄

Cushion kinematics When a car hits an obstacle head-on, the damage to the car and its occupants can be reduced by making the acceleration as small as possible. As we can see from Equation 2.6, acceleration can be reduced by making the *time* for a change in velocity as long as possible. This is the purpose of the yellow crash cushion barrels you may have seen in work zones on highways.

Acceleration is a fairly abstract concept. Position and time are our real hands-on measurements of an object, and they are easy to understand. You can "see" where the object is located and the time on the clock. Velocity is a bit more abstract, being a relationship between the change of position and the change of time. Motion diagrams help us visualize velocity as the vector arrows connecting one position of the object to the next. Acceleration is an even more abstract idea about changes in the velocity, but we can use graphs to help us better understand it.

Acceleration Is the Slope of the Velocity-Versus-Time Graph

Let's use the values we have computed for acceleration to make a table of velocities for the Porsche and the Volkswagen. Table 2.3 uses the idea that the VW's velocity increases by 1.1 m/s every second while the Porsche's velocity increases by 7.5 m/s every second. The data in Table 2.3 are the basis for the velocity-versus-time graphs in Figure 2.24.

Look at the graph for the Porsche; it's a straight line. The slope is computed using the rise over the run:

$$\text{slope of velocity-versus-time graph} = \frac{\Delta v_x}{\Delta t}$$

Compare this with Equation 2.6; the equation for the slope is the same as that for the acceleration. **Acceleration is the slope of a velocity-versus-time graph.** The VW has a smaller acceleration, so its graph has a smaller slope. The slope could be negative; this would mean that velocity is *decreasing,* as we will see in the next example.

TABLE 2.3 Velocity data for the Volkswagen and the Porsche

Time (s)	Velocity of VW (m/s)	Velocity of Porsche (m/s)
0	0	0
1	1.1	7.5
2	2.2	15.0
3	3.3	22.5
4	4.4	30.0

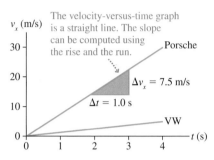

FIGURE 2.24 Velocity-versus-time graphs for the two cars.

CONCEPTUAL EXAMPLE 2.3 Analyzing a car's velocity graph

Figure 2.25a is a graph of velocity versus time for a car. Sketch a graph of the car's acceleration versus time.

REASON The graph can be divided into three sections:

- An initial segment, in which the velocity increases at a steady rate.
- A middle segment, in which the velocity is constant.
- A final segment, in which the velocity decreases at a steady rate.

In each section, the acceleration is the slope of the velocity-versus-time graph. Thus the initial segment has constant, posi-tive acceleration, the middle segment has zero acceleration, and the final segment has a constant, *negative* acceleration. The acceleration graph appears in Figure 2.25b.

ASSESS This process is analogous to finding a velocity graph from the slope of a position graph. In the middle segment, notice that zero acceleration does *not* mean that the velocity is zero. The velocity is constant, which means it is *not changing* and thus the car is not accelerating. The car does accelerate during the initial and final segments. The magnitude of the acceleration is a measure of how quickly the velocity is chang-ing. How about the sign? This is an issue we will address in the next section.

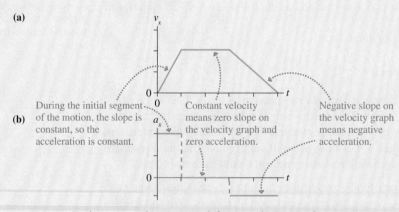

FIGURE 2.25 Finding an acceleration graph from a velocity graph.

The Sign of the Acceleration

A natural tendency is to think that a positive value of a_x or a_y describes an object that is speeding up while a negative value describes an object that is slowing down (decelerating). Unfortunately, this simple interpretation *does not work*.

Because an object can move right or left (or, equivalently, up and down) while either speeding up or slowing down, there are four situations to consider. Figure 2.26 shows a motion diagram and a velocity graph for each of these situations. As we've seen, an object's acceleration is the slope of its velocity graph, so a positive slope implies a positive acceleration and a negative slope implies a negative acceleration.

Acceleration, like velocity, is really a vector quantity. Figure 2.26 shows the acceleration vector for the four situations. The acceleration vector points in the same direction as the velocity vector $\vec{v}$ for an object that is speeding up and opposite to $\vec{v}$ for an object that is slowing down.

An object that speeds up as it moves to the right (positive v_x) has a positive acceleration, but an object that speeds up as it moves to the left (negative v_x) has a negative acceleration. Whether or not an object that is slowing down has a negative acceleration depends on whether the object is moving to the right or to the left. This is admittedly a bit more complex than thinking that negative acceleration always means slowing down, but our definition of acceleration as the slope of the velocity graph forces us to pay careful attention to the sign of the acceleration.

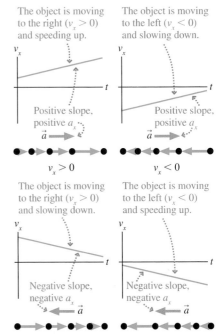

FIGURE 2.26 Determining the sign of the acceleration.

STOP TO THINK 2.4 A particle moves with the following velocity-versus-time graph. At which labeled point is the magnitude of the acceleration the greatest?

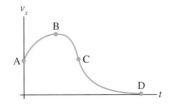

2.5 Motion with Constant Acceleration

For uniform motion—motion with constant velocity—we found in Equation 2.3 a simple relationship between position and time. It's no surprise that there are also simple relationships that connect the various kinematic variables in constant-acceleration motion. We will start with a concrete example, the launch of a Saturn V rocket like the one that carried the Apollo astronauts to the moon in the 1960s and 1970s. Figure 2.27 shows one frame from a video of a rocket lifting off the launch pad. The red dots show the position of the top of the rocket at equally spaced intervals of time. This is a motion diagram for the rocket, and we can see that the velocity is increasing. The graph of velocity versus time in Figure 2.28 shows that the velocity is increasing at a fairly constant rate. We can approximate the rocket's motion as constant acceleration.

We can use the slope of the graph in Figure 2.28 to determine the acceleration of the rocket:

$$a_y = \frac{\Delta v_y}{\Delta t} = \frac{27 \text{ m/s}}{1.5 \text{ s}} = 18 \text{ m/s}^2$$

This acceleration is more than double the acceleration of the Porsche, and it goes on for quite a long time—the first phase of the launch lasts 2 minutes! How fast is the rocket moving at the end of this acceleration, and how far has it traveled? To answer these questions, we first need to work out some basic kinematic formulas for motion with constant acceleration.

FIGURE 2.27 The red dots show the position of the top of the Saturn V rocket at equally spaced intervals during liftoff.

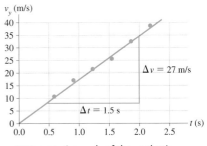

FIGURE 2.28 A graph of the rocket's velocity versus time.

(a) Acceleration

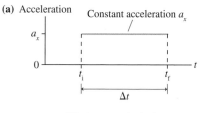

(b) Velocity

Displacement Δx is the area under the curve. The area can be divided into a rectangle of height $(v_x)_i$ and a triangle of height $a_x \Delta t$.

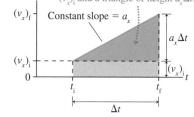

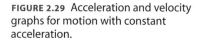

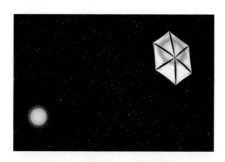

FIGURE 2.29 Acceleration and velocity graphs for motion with constant acceleration.

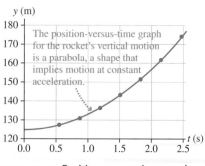

Solar sailing A rocket achieves a high speed by having a very high acceleration. A different approach is represented by a solar sail. A spacecraft with a solar sail accelerates due to the pressure of sunlight from the sun on a large, mirrored surface. The acceleration is minuscule, but it can continue for a long, long time. After an acceleration period of a few *years,* the spacecraft will reach a respectable speed!

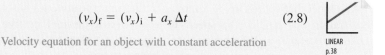

FIGURE 2.30 Position-versus-time graph for the Saturn V rocket launch.

Constant Acceleration Equations

Consider an object whose acceleration a_x remains constant during the time interval $\Delta t = t_f - t_i$. At the beginning of this interval, the object has initial velocity $(v_x)_i$ and initial position x_i. Note that t_i is often zero, but it need not be. Figure 2.29a shows the acceleration-versus-time graph. It is a horizontal line between t_i and t_f, indicating a *constant* acceleration.

The object's velocity is changing because the object is accelerating. We can use the acceleration to find $(v_x)_f$ at a later time t_f. We defined acceleration as

$$a_x = \frac{\Delta v_x}{\Delta t} = \frac{(v_x)_f - (v_x)_i}{\Delta t} \qquad (2.7)$$

which is rearranged to give

$$(v_x)_f = (v_x)_i + a_x \Delta t \qquad (2.8)$$

Velocity equation for an object with constant acceleration

LINEAR
p. 38

NOTE ▶ We have expressed this equation for motion along the *x*-axis, but it is a general result that will apply to any axis. ◀

The velocity-versus-time graph for this constant-acceleration motion, shown in Figure 2.29b, is a straight line that starts at $(v_x)_i$ and has slope a_x. This is another example of a linear relationship.

We would also like to know the object's position x_f at time t_f. As you learned in the last section, the displacement Δx during the time interval Δt is the area under the velocity-versus-time graph. The shaded area in Figure 2.29b can be subdivided into a rectangle of area $(v_x)_i \Delta t$ and a triangle of area $\frac{1}{2}(a_x \Delta t)(\Delta t) = \frac{1}{2}a_x(\Delta t)^2$. Adding these gives

$$x_f = x_i + (v_x)_i \Delta t + \tfrac{1}{2}a_x(\Delta t)^2 \qquad (2.9)$$

Position equation for an object with constant acceleration

where $\Delta t = t_f - t_i$ is the elapsed time. The fact that the time interval Δt appears in the equation as $(\Delta t)^2$ causes the position-versus-time graph for constant-acceleration motion to have a parabolic shape. For the rocket launch of Figure 2.27, a graph of position of the top of the rocket versus time appears as in Figure 2.30.

Equations 2.8 and 2.9 are two of the basic kinematic equations for motion with constant acceleration. They allow us to predict an object's position and velocity at a future instant of time. We need one more equation to complete our set, a direct relationship between displacement and velocity. To derive this relationship, we first use Equation 2.8 to write $\Delta t = ((v_x)_f - (v_x)_i)/a_x$. We can substitute this into Equation 2.9 to obtain

$$(v_x)_f^2 = (v_x)_i^2 + 2a_x \Delta x \qquad (2.10)$$

Relating velocity and displacement for constant-acceleration motion

In Equation 2.10 $\Delta x = x_f - x_i$ is the *displacement* (not the distance!). Notice that Equation 2.10 does not require knowing the time interval Δt. This is an important equation in problems where you're not given information about times.

Equations 2.8, 2.9, and 2.10 are the key equations for motion with constant acceleration. These results are summarized in Table 2.4.

Figure 2.31 is a graphical comparison of motion with constant velocity (uniform motion) and motion with constant acceleration. Notice that uniform motion is really a special case of constant-acceleration motion in which the acceleration happens to be zero.

TABLE 2.4 Kinematic equations for motion with constant acceleration

$$(v_x)_f = (v_x)_i + a_x \Delta t$$
$$x_f = x_i + (v_x)_i \Delta t + \tfrac{1}{2}a_x(\Delta t)^2$$
$$(v_x)_f^2 = (v_x)_i^2 + 2a_x \Delta x$$

1.1–1.3

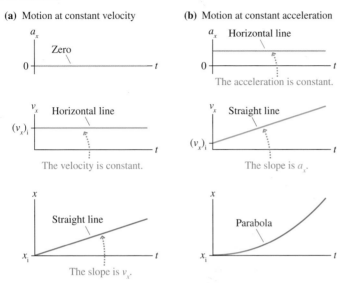

(a) Motion at constant velocity

(b) Motion at constant acceleration

FIGURE 2.31 Motion with constant velocity and constant acceleration. These graphs assume $x_i = 0$, $(v_x)_i > 0$, and (for constant acceleration) $a_x > 0$.

For motion at constant acceleration, a graph of position versus time is a *parabola*. This is a new mathematical form, one that we will see again. If $(v_x)_i = 0$, the second equation in Table 2.4 is simply

$$\Delta x = \tfrac{1}{2}a_x(\Delta t)^2 \qquad (2.11)$$

Δx depends on the *square* of Δt; we call this a *quadratic relationship*.

Getting up to speed BIO A bird must have a minimum speed to fly. Generally, the larger the bird, the larger the takeoff speed. Small birds can get moving fast enough to fly with a vigorous jump, but larger birds may need a running start. This swan must accelerate for a long distance in order to achieve the high speed it needs to fly, so it makes a frenzied dash across the frozen surface of a pond. Swans require a long, clear stretch of water or land to become airborne. Airplanes require an even higher takeoff speed and thus an even longer runway, as we will see.

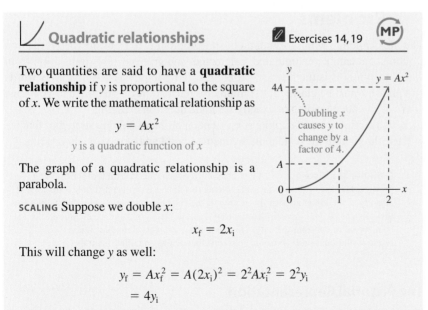

Quadratic relationships   Exercises 14, 19   (MP)

Two quantities are said to have a **quadratic relationship** if y is proportional to the square of x. We write the mathematical relationship as

$$y = Ax^2$$

y is a quadratic function of x

The graph of a quadratic relationship is a parabola.

Doubling x causes y to change by a factor of 4.

SCALING Suppose we double x:

$$x_f = 2x_i$$

This will change y as well:

$$y_f = Ax_f^2 = A(2x_i)^2 = 2^2 Ax_i^2 = 2^2 y_i$$
$$= 4y_i$$

Increasing x by a factor of 2 causes y to increase by a factor of 2^2, or 4.

Generally, we can say that

Changing x by a factor C changes y by a factor C^2.

EXAMPLE 2.6 Displacement of a drag racer

A drag racer, starting from rest, travels 6.0 m in 1.0 s. Suppose the car continues this acceleration for an additional 4.0 s. How far from the starting line will the car be?

SOLVE We assume that the acceleration is constant, so the displacement will follow Equation 2.11. This is a *quadratic relationship,* so the displacement will scale as the square of the time. After 1.0 s, the car has traveled 6.0 m; after another 4.0 s, a total of 5.0 s will have elapsed. The time has increased by a factor of 5, so the displacement will increase by a factor of 5^2, or 25. The total displacement is

$$\Delta x = 25(6.0 \text{ m}) = 150 \text{ m}$$

STOP TO THINK 2.5   A car is moving toward the right. The driver puts on the brakes, reducing the speed. The car then continues to the right at a reduced speed. Which of the following velocity-versus-time graphs matches this motion?

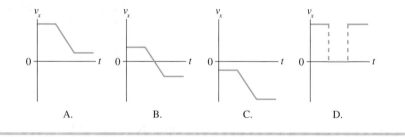

A.   B.   C.   D.

2.6 Solving One-Dimensional Motion Problems

The big challenge when solving a physics problem is to translate the words into symbols that can be manipulated, calculated, and graphed. This translation from words to symbols is the heart of problem solving in physics. Ambiguous words and phrases must be clarified, the imprecise must be made precise, and you must arrive at an understanding of exactly what the question is asking.

In this section we will explore some general problem-solving strategies that we will use throughout the text, applying them to problems of motion along a line.

▶ **Dinner at a distance** BIO A chameleon's tongue is a powerful tool for catching prey. Certain species can extend the tongue to a distance of over 1 ft in less than 0.1 s! A study of the kinematics of the motion of the chameleon tongue, using techniques like those in this chapter, reveals that the tongue has a period of rapid acceleration followed by a period of constant velocity. This knowledge is a very valuable clue in the analysis of the evolutionary relationships between chameleons and other animals.

The Pictorial Representation

You'll find that motion problems and other physics problems often have several variables and other pieces of information to keep track of. The best way to tackle such problems is to draw a picture, as we noted when we introduced a general problem-solving strategy. But what kind of picture should we draw?

In this section, we will begin to draw **pictorial representations** as an aid to solving problems. A pictorial representation shows all of the important details that we need to keep track of in a problem. Pictorial representations will be very important in solving motion problems.

MP TACTICS BOX 2.2 **Drawing a pictorial representation**   Exercise 21

❶ **Sketch the situation.** Not just any sketch: Show the object at the *beginning* of the motion, at the *end*, and at any point where the character of the motion changes. Very simple drawings are adequate.

❷ **Establish a coordinate system.** Select your axes and origin to match the motion.

❸ **Define symbols.** Use the sketch to define symbols representing quantities such as position, velocity, acceleration, and time. *Every* variable used later in the mathematical solution should be defined on the sketch.

We will generally combine the pictorial representation with a **list of values,** which will include

- *Known information.* Make a table of the quantities whose values you can determine from the problem statement or that can be found quickly with simple geometry or unit conversions.
- *Desired unknowns.* What quantity or quantities will allow you to answer the question?

EXAMPLE 2.7 Drawing a pictorial representation

Complete a pictorial representation and a list of values for the following problem: A rocket sled accelerates at 50 m/s² for 5 s. What are the total distance traveled and the final velocity?

PREPARE Figure 2.32a shows a pictorial representation as drawn by an artist in the style of the figures in this book. This is cer-

tainly neater and more artistic than the sketches you will make when solving problems yourself! Figure 2.32b shows a sketch like one you might actually do. It's less formal, but it contains all of the important information you need to solve the problem.

NOTE ▶ Throughout this book we will illustrate select examples with actual hand-drawn figures so that you have them to refer to as you work on your own pictures for homework and practice. ◀

Let's look at how these pictures were constructed. The motion has a clear beginning and end; these are the points sketched. A coordinate system has been chosen with the origin at the starting point. The quantities x, v_x, and t are needed at both points, so these have been defined on the sketch and distinguished by subscripts. The acceleration is associated with an interval between these points. Values for two of these quantities are given in the problem statement. Others, such as $x_i = 0$ m and $t_i = 0$ s, are inferred from our choice of coordinate system. The value $(v_x)_i = 0$ m/s is part of our *interpretation* of the problem. Finally, we identify x_f and $(v_x)_f$ as the quantities that will answer the question. We now understand quite a bit about the problem and would be ready to start a quantitative analysis.

ASSESS We didn't *solve* the problem; that was not our purpose. Constructing a pictorial representation and a list of values is part of a systematic approach to interpreting a problem and getting ready for a mathematical solution.

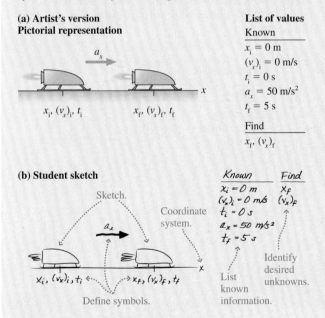

(a) Artist's version
Pictorial representation

List of values
Known
$x_i = 0$ m
$(v_x)_i = 0$ m/s
$t_i = 0$ s
$a_x = 50$ m/s²
$t_f = 5$ s

Find
x_f, $(v_x)_f$

(b) Student sketch

FIGURE 2.32 Constructing a pictorial representation and a list of values.

The Visual Overview

The pictorial representation and the list of values are a very good complement to the motion diagram and other ways of looking at a problem that we have seen. As we translate a problem into a form we can solve, we will combine all of these elements into what we will term a **visual overview.** The visual overview will consist of some or all of the following elements:

- A *motion diagram.* A good strategy for solving a motion problem is to start by drawing a motion diagram.
- A *pictorial representation,* as defined above.
- A *graphical representation.* For motion problems, it is often quite useful to include a graph of position and/or velocity.
- A *list of values.* This list should sum up all of the important values in the problem.

Future chapters will add other elements (such as forces) to this visual overview of the physics.

EXAMPLE 2.8 Kinematics of a rocket launch

A Saturn V rocket is launched straight up with a constant acceleration of 18 m/s². After 150 s, how fast is the rocket moving and how far has it traveled?

PREPARE Figure 2.33 shows a visual overview of the rocket launch that includes a motion diagram, a pictorial representation and a list of values. The visual overview shows the whole problem in a nutshell. The motion diagram illustrates the motion of the rocket, the pictorial representation (produced according to Tactics Box 2.2) shows axes, identifies the important points of the motion and defines variables. Finally, we have included a list of values that gives the known and unknown quantities. In the visual overview we have taken the statement of the problem in words and made it much more precise; it contains everything you need to know about the problem.

SOLVE Our first task is to find the final velocity. We can use the first kinematic equation of Table 2.4:

$$(v_y)_f = (v_y)_i + a_y \, \Delta t = 0 \text{ m/s} + (18 \text{ m/s}^2)(150 \text{ s})$$

$$= 2700 \text{ m/s}$$

The distance traveled is found using the second equation in Table 2.4:

$$y_f = y_i + (v_y)_i \, \Delta t + \tfrac{1}{2} a_y (\Delta t)^2$$

$$= 0 \text{ m} + (0 \text{ m/s})(150 \text{ s}) + \tfrac{1}{2}(18 \text{ m/s}^2)(150 \text{ s})^2$$

$$= 2.0 \times 10^5 \text{ m} = 200 \text{ km}$$

ASSESS The acceleration is very large, and it goes on for a long time, so the large final velocity and large distance traveled seem reasonable.

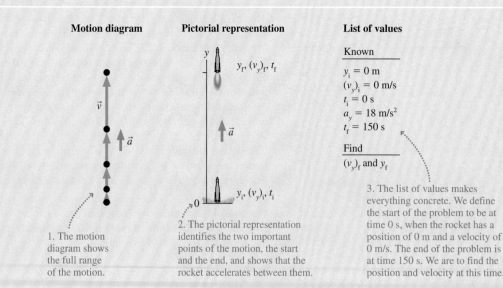

Motion diagram	Pictorial representation	List of values

Known

$y_i = 0$ m
$(v_y)_i = 0$ m/s
$t_i = 0$ s
$a_y = 18$ m/s²
$t_f = 150$ s

Find

$(v_y)_f$ and y_f

1. The motion diagram shows the full range of the motion.

2. The pictorial representation identifies the two important points of the motion, the start and the end, and shows that the rocket accelerates between them.

3. The list of values makes everything concrete. We define the start of the problem to be at time 0 s, when the rocket has a position of 0 m and a velocity of 0 m/s. The end of the problem is at time 150 s. We are to find the position and velocity at this time.

FIGURE 2.33 Visual overview of the rocket launch.

Problem-Solving Strategy for Motion with Constant Acceleration

Earlier in the chapter, we introduced a general problem-solving strategy. In this section, we will adapt this general strategy to solving problems of motion with constant acceleration. We will introduce such specific problem-solving strategies in future chapters as well.

Activ
Physics
ONLINE

1.4–1.6, 1.8, 1.9,
1.11–1.14

(MP) PROBLEM-SOLVING
STRATEGY 2.1 **Motion with constant acceleration**

PREPARE Draw a visual overview of the problem. This should include a motion diagram, a pictorial representation and a list of values; a graphical representation may be useful for certain problems.

SOLVE The mathematical solution is based on the three equations in Table 2.4.

- Though the equations are phrased in terms of the variable x, it's customary to use y for motion in the vertical direction.
- Use the equation that best matches what you know and what you need to find. For example, if you know acceleration and time and are looking for a change in velocity, the first equation is the best one to use.
- Uniform motion with constant velocity has $a = 0$.

ASSESS Is your result believable? Does it have proper units? Does it make sense?

EXAMPLE 2.9 Calculating the minimum length of a runway

A fully-loaded 747 with all engines at full thrust accelerates at 2.6 m/s^2. Its minimum takeoff speed is 70 m/s. How much time will the plane take to reach its takeoff speed? What minimum length of runway does the plane require for takeoff?

PREPARE The visual overview of Figure 2.34 summarizes the important details of the problem. We set x_i and t_i equal to zero at the starting point of the motion, when the plane is at rest and the acceleration begins. The final point of the motion is when the plane achieves the necessary takeoff speed of 70 m/s. The plane is accelerating to the right, so we will compute the time for the plane to reach a velocity of 70 m/s and the position of the plane at this time, giving us the minimum length of the runway.

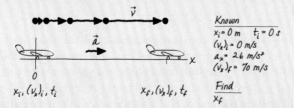

Known	
$x_i = 0 \text{ m}$	$t_i = 0 \text{ s}$
$(v_x)_i = 0 \text{ m/s}$	
$a_x = 2.6 \text{ m/s}^2$	
$(v_x)_f = 70 \text{ m/s}$	

Find
x_f

FIGURE 2.34 Visual overview for an accelerating plane.

SOLVE First we solve for the time required for the plane to reach takeoff speed. We can use the first equation in Table 2.4 to compute this time:

$$(v_x)_f = (v_x)_i + a_x \, \Delta t$$

$$70 \text{ m/s} = 0 \text{ m/s} + (2.6 \text{ m/s}^2) \, \Delta t$$

$$\Delta t = \frac{70 \text{ m/s}}{2.6 \text{ m/s}^2} = 26.9 \text{ s}$$

We keep an extra significant figure here as we will use this result in the next step of the calculation.

Given the time that the plane takes to reach takeoff speed, we can compute the position of the plane when it reaches this speed using the second equation in Table 2.4:

$$x_f = x_i + (v_x)_i \, \Delta t + \tfrac{1}{2} a_x (\Delta t)^2$$

$$= 0 \text{ m} + (0 \text{ m/s})(26.9 \text{ s}) + \tfrac{1}{2}(2.6 \text{ m/s}^2)(26.9 \text{ s})^2$$

$$= 940 \text{ m}$$

Our final answers are thus that the plane will take 27 s to reach takeoff speed, with a minimum runway length of 940 m.

ASSESS Think about the last time you flew; 27 s seems like a reasonable time for a plane to accelerate on takeoff. Actual runway lengths at major airports are 3000 m or more, a few times greater than the minimum length, because they have to allow for emergency stops during an aborted takeoff. (If we had calculated a distance far greater than 3000 m, we would know we had done something wrong!)

EXAMPLE 2.10 Finding the braking distance

A car is traveling at a speed of 30 m/s, a typical highway speed, on wet pavement. The driver sees an obstacle ahead and decides to stop. From this instant, it takes him 0.75 s to begin applying the brakes. Once the brakes are applied, the car experiences an acceleration of -6.0 m/s^2. How far does the car travel from the instant the driver notices the obstacle until stopping?

PREPARE This problem is more involved than previous problems we have solved, so we will take more care with the visual overview in Figure 2.35. In addition to a motion diagram and a pictorial representation, we include a graphical representation. Notice that there are two different phases of the motion, a constant-velocity phase before braking begins, and a steady slowing down once the brakes are applied. We will need to do two different calculations, one for each phase. Consequently, we've used numerical subscripts rather than a simple i and f.

SOLVE From t_1 to t_2 the velocity stays constant at 30 m/s. This is uniform motion, so the position at time t_2 is computed using Equation 2.3:

$$x_2 = x_1 + (v_x)_1(t_2 - t_1) = 0 \text{ m} + (30 \text{ m/s})(0.75 \text{ s})$$
$$= 22.5 \text{ m}$$

At t_2, the velocity begins to decrease at a steady -6.0 m/s^2 until the car comes to rest at t_3. This time interval can be computed using the first equation in Table 2.4, $(v_x)_3 = (v_x)_2 + a_x \Delta t$:

$$\Delta t = t_3 - t_2 = \frac{(v_x)_3 - (v_x)_2}{a_x} = \frac{0 \text{ m/s} - 30 \text{ m/s}}{-6.0 \text{ m/s}^2} = 5.0 \text{ s}$$

The position at time t_3 is computed using the second equation in Table 2.4; we take point 2 as the initial point and point 3 as the final point for this phase of the motion and use $\Delta t = t_3 - t_2$:

$$x_3 = x_2 + (v_x)_2 \Delta t + \tfrac{1}{2}a_x(\Delta t)^2$$
$$= 22.5 \text{ m} + (30 \text{ m/s})(5.0 \text{ s}) + \tfrac{1}{2}(-6.0 \text{ m/s}^2)(5.0 \text{ s})^2$$
$$= 98 \text{ m}$$

x_3 is the position of the car at the end of the problem—and so the car travels 98 m before coming to rest!

ASSESS The numbers for the reaction time and the acceleration on wet pavement are reasonable ones for an alert driver in a car with good tires. The final distance is quite large—it is more than the length of a football field.

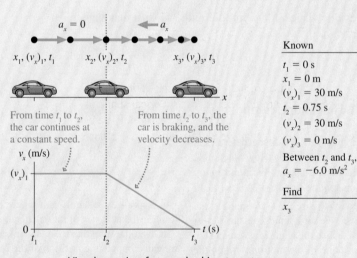

$a_x = 0$ a_x

$x_1, (v_x)_1, t_1$ $x_2, (v_x)_2, t_2$ $x_3, (v_x)_3, t_3$

From time t_1 to t_2, the car continues at a constant speed.

From time t_2 to t_3, the car is braking, and the velocity decreases.

v_x (m/s)

$(v_x)_1$

0

t_1 t_2 t_3 t (s)

Known

$t_1 = 0$ s
$x_1 = 0$ m
$(v_x)_1 = 30$ m/s
$t_2 = 0.75$ s
$(v_x)_2 = 30$ m/s
$(v_x)_3 = 0$ m/s

Between t_2 and t_3,
$a_x = -6.0$ m/s^2

Find

x_3

FIGURE 2.35 Visual overview for a car braking to a stop.

2.7 Free Fall

1.7, 1.10   Activ Physics ONLINE

A particularly important example of constant acceleration is the motion of an object moving under the influence of gravity only, and no other forces. This motion is called **free fall.** Strictly speaking, free fall occurs only in a vacuum, where there is no air resistance. But if you drop a hammer, air resistance is negligible, so we'll make only a very slight error in treating it *as if* it were in free fall. If you drop a feather, air resistance is *not* negligible, and we can't make this approximation. Motion with air resistance is a problem we will study in Chapter 4. Until then, we will restrict our attention to situations in which air resistance can be ignored, and will make the reasonable assumption that falling objects are in free fall.

As part of his early studies of motion, Galileo did the first careful experiments on free fall and made the somewhat surprising observation that two objects of different weight dropped from the same height will, if air resistance can be neglected, hit the ground at the same time and with the same speed. In fact—as Galileo surmised, and as a famous demonstration on the moon showed—in a vacuum, where there is no air resistance, this holds true for *any* two objects!

Galileo's discovery about free fall means that **any two objects in free fall, regardless of their mass, have the same acceleration.** This is an especially important conclusion. Figure 2.36a shows the motion diagram of an object that was released from rest and falls freely. The motion diagram and graph would be identical for a falling baseball or a falling boulder! Figure 2.36b shows the object's velocity graph. As we can see, the velocity changes at a steady rate. The slope of the velocity-versus-time graph is the free-fall acceleration $a_{\text{free fall}}$.

"Looks like Mr. Galileo was correct . . ." was the comment made by Apollo 15 astronaut David Scott, who dropped a hammer and a feather on the moon. The objects were dropped from the same height at the same time and hit the ground simultaneously—something that would not happen in the atmosphere of the earth!

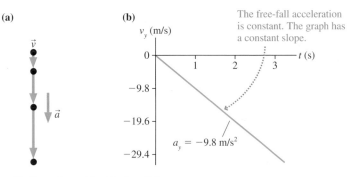

FIGURE 2.36 Motion of an object in free fall.

Careful measurements show that the value of the free-fall acceleration varies slightly at different places on the earth, due to the slightly nonspherical shape of the earth, the fact that different positions on the surface of the earth may be at different heights above sea level, and the fact that the earth is rotating. A global average, at sea level, is

$$\vec{a}_{\text{free fall}} = (9.80 \text{ m/s}^2, \text{ vertically downward}) \qquad (2.12)$$

Standard value for the acceleration of an object in free fall

The magnitude of the **free-fall acceleration** has the special symbol g:

$$g = 9.80 \text{ m/s}^2$$

We will generally work with 2 significant figures, and so will use $g = 9.8 \text{ m/s}^2$. Several points about free fall are worthy of note:

- g, by definition, is *always* positive. **There will never be a problem that uses a negative value for g.**
- The velocity graph in Figure 2.36b has a negative slope. Even though a falling object speeds up, it has *negative* acceleration. Alternatively, notice that the acceleration vector $\vec{a}_{\text{free fall}}$ points down. Thus g is *not* the object's acceleration, simply the magnitude of the acceleration. The one-dimensional acceleration is

$$a_y = a_{\text{free fall}} = -g$$

It is a_y that is negative, not g.

Some of the children are moving up and some are moving down, but all are in free fall—and so are accelerating downward at 9.8 m/s^2.

TRY IT YOURSELF

A reaction time challenge Hold a $1 (or larger!) bill by an upper corner. Have a friend prepare to grasp a lower corner, putting her fingers *near but not touching* the bill. Tell her to try to catch the bill when you drop it by simply closing her fingers without moving her hand downward—and that if she can catch it, she can keep it. Don't worry; the bill's free fall will keep your money safe. In the few tenths of a second that it takes your friend to react, the bill will move beyond her grasp.

■ Because free fall is motion with constant acceleration, we can use the kinematic equations of Table 2.4 with the acceleration being due to gravity, $a_y = -g$.

■ g is not called "gravity." Gravity is a force, not an acceleration. g is the *free-fall acceleration*.

■ $g = 9.80 \text{ m/s}^2$ only on earth. Other planets have different values of g.

■ We will sometimes compute acceleration in units of g. An acceleration of 9.8 m/s^2 is an acceleration of 1 g; an acceleration of 19.6 m/s^2 is 2 g. Generally, we can compute

$$\text{acceleration (in units of } g) = \frac{\text{acceleration (in units of m/s}^2)}{9.8 \text{ m/s}^2} \quad (2.13)$$

This allows us to express accelerations in units that have a definite physical reference.

NOTE ▶ Despite the name, free fall is not restricted to objects that are literally falling. Any object moving under the influence of gravity only, and no other forces, is in free fall. This includes objects falling straight down, objects that have been tossed or shot straight up, objects in projectile motion (such as a passed football) and, as we will see, satellites in orbit. In this chapter we consider only objects that move up and down along a vertical line. ◀

EXAMPLE 2.11 Analyzing a rock's fall
A heavy rock is dropped from rest at the top of a cliff and falls 100 m before hitting the ground. How long does the rock take to fall to the ground, and what is its velocity when it hits?

PREPARE Figure 2.37 shows a visual overview with all necessary data. We have placed the origin at the ground, which makes $y_i = 100$ m.

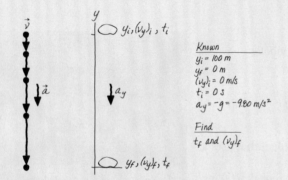

FIGURE 2.37 Visual overview of a falling rock.

SOLVE Free fall is motion with the specific constant acceleration $a_y = -g$. The first question involves a relation between time and distance, a relation expressed by the second equation in Table 2.4 Using $(v_y)_i = 0$ m/s and $t_i = 0$ s, we find

$$y_f = y_i + (v_y)_i \Delta t + \tfrac{1}{2} a_y \Delta t^2 = y_i - \tfrac{1}{2} g \Delta t^2 = y_i - \tfrac{1}{2} g t_f^2$$

We can now solve for t_f, finding:

$$t_f = \sqrt{\frac{2(y_i - y_f)}{g}} = \sqrt{\frac{2(100 \text{ m} - 0 \text{ m})}{9.80 \text{ m/s}^2}} = 4.52 \text{ s}$$

Now that we know the fall time, we can use the first kinematic equation to find $(v_y)_f$:

$$(v_y)_f = (v_y)_i - g \Delta t = -g t_f = -(9.80 \text{ m/s}^2)(4.52 \text{ s})$$

$$= -44.3 \text{ m/s}.$$

ASSESS Are the answers reasonable? Well, 100 m is about 300 feet, which is about the height of a 30-floor building. How long does it take something to fall 30 floors? Four or five seconds seems pretty reasonable. How fast would it be going at the bottom? Using an approximate version of our conversion factor 1 m/s ≈ 2 mph, we find that 44.3 m/s ≈ 90 mph. That also seems like a pretty reasonable speed for something that has fallen 30 floors. Suppose we had made a mistake. If we misplaced a decimal point we could have calculated a speed of 443 m/s, or about 900 mph! This is clearly *not* reasonable. If we had misplaced the decimal point in the other direction, we would have calculated a speed of 4.3 m/s ≈ 9 mph. This is another unreasonable result, as this is slower than a typical bicycling speed.

CONCEPTUAL EXAMPLE 2.4 **Analyzing the motion of a ball tossed upward**

Draw a motion diagram and a velocity-versus-time graph for a ball tossed straight up in the air from the point that it leaves the hand until just before it is caught.

REASON You know what the motion of the ball looks like: The ball goes up, and then it comes back down again. This compli- cates the drawing of a motion diagram a bit, as the ball retraces its route as it falls. A literal motion diagram would show the upward motion and downward motion on top of each other, leading to confusion. We can avoid this difficulty by horizon- tally separating the upward motion and downward motion dia- grams. This will not affect our conclusions because it does not change any of the vectors. The motion diagram and velocity- versus-time graph appear as in Figure 2.38.

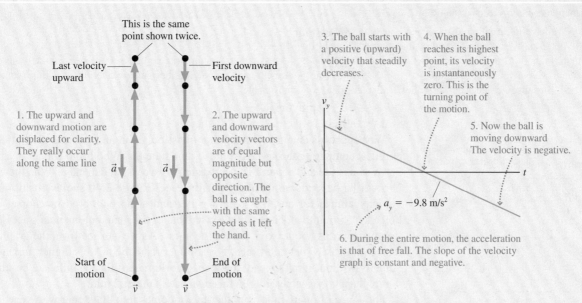

FIGURE 2.38 Motion diagram and velocity graph of a ball tossed straight up in the air.

ASSESS The highest point in the ball's motion, where it reverses direction, is called a *turning point*. What are the velocity and the acceleration at this point? We can see from the motion diagram that the velocity vectors are pointing upward but getting shorter as the ball approaches the top. As it starts to fall, the velocity vectors are pointing downward and getting longer. There must be a moment—just an instant as $\vec{v}$ switches from pointing up to pointing down—when the velocity is zero. Indeed, the ball's velocity *is* zero for an instant at the precise top of the motion! We can also see on the velocity graph that there is one instant of time when $v_y = 0$. This is the turning point.

But what about the acceleration at the top? Many people expect the acceleration to be zero at the highest point. But recall that the velocity at the top point is changing—from up to down. If the velocity is changing, there *must* be an acceleration. The slope of the velocity graph at the instant when $v_y = 0$—that is, at the highest point—is no different than at any other point in the motion. The ball is still in free fall with acceleration $a_y = -g$!

Another way to think about this is to note that zero accelera- tion would mean no change of velocity. When the ball reached zero velocity at the top, it would hang there and not fall if the acceleration were also zero!

EXAMPLE 2.12 **Finding the height of a leap**

A springbok is an antelope found in southern Africa that gets its name from its remarkable jump- ing ability. When a springbok is startled, it will leap straight up into the air—a maneuver called a "pronk." If a springbok leaves the ground at 7.0 m/s, a typical value, how high will it go?

PREPARE We will begin with the visual overview shown in Figure 2.39. Even though the springbok is moving upward, this is a free-fall problem because the springbok (after leaving the ground) is moving under the influence of gravity *only*.

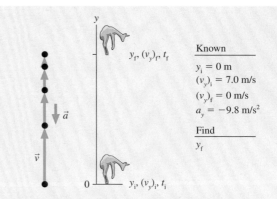

FIGURE 2.39 Visual overview of the springbok's leap.

A critical aspect of solving this sort of problem is knowing what to take as the end point of the motion. The clue is this: The very top point of the trajectory is a *turning point,* and the instantaneous velocity at this point is zero. Thus we can characterize the "top" of the trajectory—the highest point of the leap—as the point where $(v_y)_f = 0$ m/s. If we solve for y at this point, we will know the height of the leap. None of this was explicitly stated in the problem. Part of our job in solving a problem is to supply a reasonable *interpretation* of events and thus to gain the information needed to reach a solution.

SOLVE We have information about displacement and velocity, but we don't know anything about the time interval. The third kinematic equation in Table 2.4, a relationship among displacement, velocity, and acceleration, is perfect for situations like this. Because $y_i = 0$, the springbok's displacement is

$\Delta y = y_f - y_i = y_f$. Its final velocity is $(v_y)_f = 0$ m/s, so we can compute

$$(v_y)_f^2 = 0 = (v_y)_i^2 - 2g\,\Delta y = (v_y)_i^2 - 2gy_f$$

which gives

$$(v_y)_i^2 = 2gy_f$$

By solving for y_f, we find that the springbok reaches a height of

$$y_f = \frac{(v_y)_i^2}{2g} = \frac{(7.0\ \text{m/s})^2}{2(9.8\ \text{m/s}^2)} = 2.5\ \text{m}$$

ASSESS 2.5 m is a remarkable leap—a bit over 8 ft—but these animals are known for their jumping ability, so this seems reasonable.

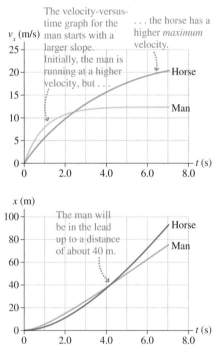

FIGURE 2.40 Velocity-versus-time and position-versus-time graphs for a sprint between a man and a horse.

We began this chapter with another question about animals and their athletic abilities: comparing the speeds of horses and humans. Who is the winner in a race between a horse and a man? The surprising answer is "It depends." Who the winner will be depends on the length of the race! Figure 2.40 shows position and velocity graphs for an elite male sprinter and a thoroughbred racehorse. The horse's maximum velocity is about twice that of the man, but the man's acceleration from rest is about twice that of the horse. As we can see from the graphs, a man could win a *very* short race. For a longer race, the horse's higher maximum velocity will put it in the lead; the men's world record for the mile is a bit under 4 min, but a horse can easily run this distance in under 2 min.

For a race of many miles, another factor comes into play: energy. A very long race is less about velocity and acceleration than about endurance—the ability to continue expending energy for a long time. In such endurance trials, humans often win. We will explore such energy issues in Chapter 6.

In this chapter, we have explored motion along a line—that is, motion in one dimension. In the next chapter, we will explore motion in two dimensions. We will begin with a more thorough treatment of vectors, and then pick up where we left off, exploring objects moving under the influence of gravity.

STOP TO THINK 2.6   A volcano ejects a chunk of rock straight up at a velocity of $v_y = 30$ m/s. Ignoring air resistance, what will be the velocity v_y of the rock when it falls back into the volcano's crater?

A. >30 m/s   B. 30 m/s   C. 0 m/s   D. −30 m/s   E. <−30 m/s

SUMMARY

The goal of Chapter 2 has been to describe and analyze linear motion.

GENERAL STRATEGIES

Problem-Solving Strategy

Our general problem-solving strategy has three parts:

PREPARE Set up the problem:

- Draw a picture
- Collect necessary information
- Do preliminary calculations

SOLVE Do the necessary mathematics or reasoning.

ASSESS Check your answer to see if it is complete in all details and makes physical sense.

Visual Overview

A visual overview consists of several pieces that completely specify a problem. This may include any or all of the elements below:

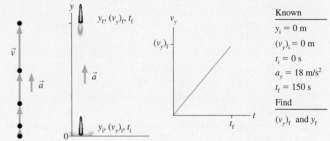

IMPORTANT CONCEPTS

Velocity is the rate of change of position

$$v_x = \frac{\Delta x}{\Delta t}$$

Acceleration is the rate of change of velocity.

$$a_x = \frac{\Delta v_x}{\Delta t}$$

The units of acceleration are m/s^2.

An object is speeding up if v_x and a_x have the same sign, slowing down if they have opposite signs.

A position-versus-time graph plots position on the vertical axis against time on the horizontal axis.

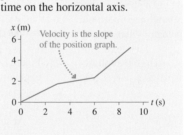

A velocity-versus-time graph plots velocity on the vertical axis against time on the horizontal axis.

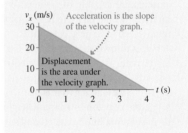

APPLICATIONS

Uniform motion

An object in uniform motion has a constant velocity. Its velocity graph is a horizontal line; its position graph is linear.

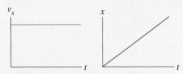

Kinematic equation for uniform motion:

$$x_f = x_i + v_x \, \Delta t$$

Uniform motion is a special case of constant-acceleration motion, with $a_x = 0$.

Motion with constant acceleration

An object with constant acceleration has a constantly changing velocity. Its velocity graph is linear; its position graph is a parabola.

Kinematic equations for motion with constant acceleration:

$$(v_x)_f = (v_x)_i + a_x \, \Delta t$$

$$x_f = x_i + (v_x)_i \, \Delta t + \tfrac{1}{2} a_x (\Delta t)^2$$

$$(v_x)_f^2 = (v_x)_i^2 + 2a_x \, \Delta x$$

Free fall

Free fall is a special case of constant-acceleration motion; the acceleration has magnitude $g = 9.80 \ m/s^2$ and is always directed vertically downward whether an object is moving up or down.

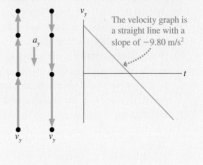

QUESTIONS

Conceptual Questions

1. A person gets in an elevator on the ground floor and rides it to the top floor of a building. Sketch a velocity-versus-time graph for this motion.

2. a. Give an example of a vertical motion with a positive velocity and a negative acceleration.
   b. Give an example of a vertical motion with a negative velocity and a negative acceleration.

3. Sketch a velocity-versus-time graph for a rock that is thrown straight upward, from the instant it leaves the hand until the instant it hits the ground.

4. You're driving along the highway at a steady speed of 60 mph when another driver decides to pass you. At the moment when the front of his car is exactly even with the front of your car, and you turn your head to smile at him, do the two cars have equal velocities? Explain.

5. A car is traveling north. Can its acceleration vector ever point south? Explain.

6. Certain animals are capable of running at great speeds; other BIO animals are capable of tremendous accelerations. Speculate on which would be more beneficial to a predator—large maximum speed or large acceleration.

7. A ball is thrown straight up into the air. At each of the following instants, is the ball's acceleration a_y equal to g, $-g$, 0, $<g$, or $>g$?
   a. Just after leaving your hand?
   b. At the very top (maximum height)?
   c. Just before hitting the ground?

8. A rock is *thrown* (not dropped) straight down from a bridge into the river below.
   a. Immediately after being released, is the magnitude of the rock's acceleration greater than g, less than g, or equal to g? Explain.
   b. Immediately before hitting the water, is the magnitude of the rock's acceleration greater than g, less than g, or equal to g? Explain.

9. Figure Q2.9 at right shows an object's position-versus-time graph. The letters A to E correspond to various segments of the motion in which the graph has constant slope.
   a. Write a realistic motion short story for an object that would have this position graph.
   b. In which segment(s) is the object at rest?
   c. In which segment(s) is the object moving to the right?
   d. Is the speed of the object during segment C greater than, equal to, or less than its speed during segment E? Explain.

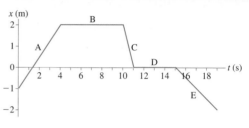

FIGURE Q2.9

10. Figure Q2.10 shows the position graph for an object moving along the horizontal axis.
    a. Write a realistic motion short story for an object that would have this position graph.
    b. Draw the corresponding velocity graph.

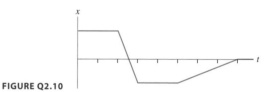

FIGURE Q2.10

11. Figure Q2.11 shows the position-versus-time graphs for two objects, A and B, that are moving along the same axis.
    a. At the instant $t = 1$ s, is the speed of A greater than, less than, or equal to the speed of B? Explain.
    b. Do objects A and B ever have the *same* speed? If so, at what time or times? Explain.

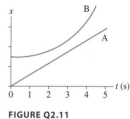

FIGURE Q2.11

12. Do the two position graphs in Figure Q2.12 represent possible motions of an object? If so, describe that motion in words. If not, why not?

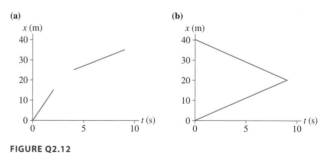

FIGURE Q2.12

---

13. Figure Q2.13 shows a position-versus-time graph for a moving object. At which lettered point or points
    a. Is the object moving the fastest?
    b. Is the object moving to the left?
    c. Is the object speeding up?
    d. Is the object slowing down?
    e. Is the object turning around?

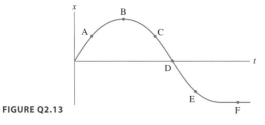

FIGURE Q2.13

14. Figure Q2.14 is the velocity-versus-time graph for an object moving along the *x*-axis. The graph is divided into six labeled segments.
    a. During which segment(s) is the velocity constant?
    b. During which segment(s) is the object speeding up?
    c. During which segment(s) is the object slowing down?
    d. During which segment(s) is the object standing still?
    e. During which segment(s) is the object moving to the right?

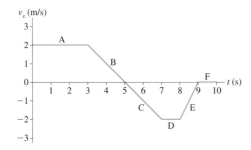

FIGURE Q2.14

15. A car traveling at velocity v takes distance d to stop after the brakes are applied. What is the stopping distance if the car is initially traveling at velocity $2v$? Assume that the acceleration due to the braking is the same in both cases.

Multiple-Choice Questions

16. | Figure Q2.16 shows the position graph of a car traveling on a straight road. At which labeled instant is the speed of the car greatest?

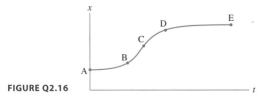

FIGURE Q2.16

17. ‖ Figure Q2.17 shows the position graph of a car traveling on a straight road. The velocity at instant 1 is _____ and the velocity at instant 2 is _____.
    A. positive, negative
    B. positive, positive
    C. negative, negative
    D. negative, zero
    E. positive, zero

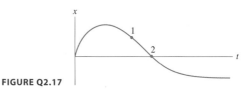

FIGURE Q2.17

18. ‖ Figure Q2.18 shows an object's position-versus-time graph. What is the velocity of the object at $t = 6$ s?
    A. 0.67 m/s   B. 0.83 m/s   C. 3.3 m/s
    D. 4.2 m/s   E. 25 m/s

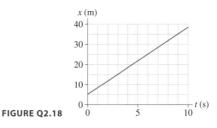

FIGURE Q2.18

19. | The following options describe the motion of four cars A–D. Which car has the largest acceleration?
    A goes from 0 m/s to 10 m/s in 5.0 s
    B goes from 0 m/s to 5.0 m/s in 2.0 s
    C goes from 0 m/s to 20 m/s in 7.0 s
    D goes from 0 m/s to 3.0 m/s in 1.0 s

20. | A car is traveling at $v_x = 20$ m/s. The driver applies the brakes, and the car slows with $a_x = -4.0$ m/s². What is the stopping distance?
    A. 5.0 m   B. 25 m   C. 40 m   D. 50 m

21. ‖ Velocity-versus-time graphs for three drag racers are shown in Figure Q2.21. At $t = 5.0$ s, which car has traveled the furthest?
    A. Andy   B. Betty   C. Carl
    D. All have traveled the same distance

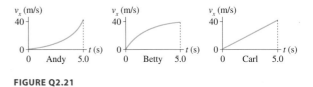

FIGURE Q2.21

22. | Which of the three drag racers in Question 21 had the greatest acceleration at $t = 0$ s?
    A. Andy   B. Betty   C. Carl
    D. All had the same acceleration

23. ‖ Ball 1 is thrown straight up in the air and, at the same instant, ball 2 is released from rest and allowed to fall. Which velocity graph in Figure Q2.23 best represents the motion of the two balls?

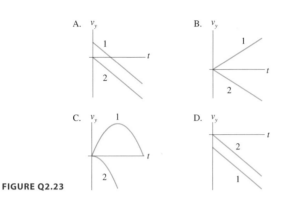

FIGURE Q2.23

Questions 24 and 25 refer to the graph in Figure Q2.24, which is the acceleration graph for an object moving along the *x*-axis.

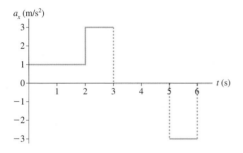

FIGURE Q2.24

24. ‖ If the object's velocity at $t = 0$ s is -1 m/s, what is its velocity at $t = 2$ s?
    A. 0 m/s   B. 0.5 m/s   C. -1 m/s
    D. 1 m/s   E. 2 m/s

25. ‖ Which graph in Figure Q2.25 could represent the velocity of the object?

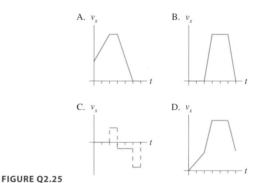

FIGURE Q2.25

26. | Figure Q2.26 shows a motion diagram with the clock reading (in seconds) shown at each position. From $t = 9$ s to $t = 15$ s the object is at the same position. After that, it returns along the same track. The positions of the dots for $t \geq 16$ s are offset for clarity. Which graph best represents the object's *velocity?*

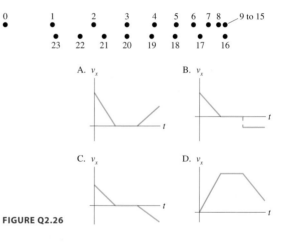

FIGURE Q2.26

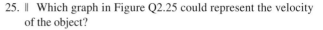

PROBLEMS

Section 2.1 Describing Motion

1. | Figure P2.1 shows a motion diagram of a car traveling down a street. The camera took one frame every second. A distance scale is provided.
    a. Measure the *x*-value of the car at each dot. Place your data in a table, similar to Table 2.1, showing each position and the instant of time at which it occurred.
    b. Make a graph of *x* versus *t*, using the data in your table. Because you have data only at certain instants of time, your graph should consist of dots that are not connected together.

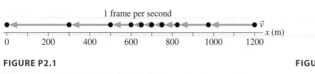

FIGURE P2.1

2. | For each motion diagram in Figure P2.2, determine the sign (positive or negative) of the position and the velocity.

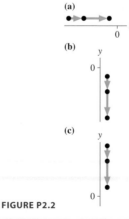

FIGURE P2.2

3. | Write a short description of the motion of a real object for which Figure P2.3 would be a realistic position-versus-time graph.

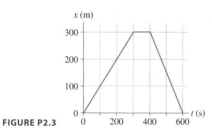

FIGURE P2.3

4. | Write a short description of the motion of a real object for which Figure P2.4 would be a realistic position-versus-time graph.

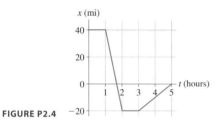

FIGURE P2.4

Section 2.2 Uniform Motion

5. ‖ Suppose a car is moving with constant velocity along a straight road. Its position was $x_1 = 15$ m at $t_1 = 0.0$ s and is $x_2 = 30$ m at $t_2 = 3.0$ s.
   a. What was its position at $t = 1.5$ s?
   b. What will its position be at $t = 5.0$ s?
6. | A car starts at the origin and moves with velocity $\vec{v} = (10$ m/s, northeast). How far from the origin will the car be after traveling for 45 s?
7. | Larry leaves home at 9:05 A.M. and runs at constant speed to the lamppost, shown in Figure P2.7. He reaches the lamppost at 9:07 A.M., immediately turns, and runs to the tree, again at constant speed. Larry arrives at the tree at 9:10 A.M. What is Larry's velocity during each of these two intervals?

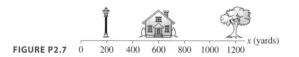

FIGURE P2.7

8. ‖ Alan leaves Los Angeles at 8:00 A.M. to drive to San Francisco, 400 mi away. He travels at a steady 50 mph. Beth leaves Los Angeles at 9:00 A.M. and drives a steady 60 mph.
   a. Who gets to San Francisco first?
   b. How long does the first to arrive have to wait for the second?
9. ‖| Richard is driving home to visit his parents. 125 mi of the trip are on the interstate highway where the speed limit is 65 mph. Normally Richard drives at the speed limit, but today he is running late and decides to take his chances by driving at 70 mph. How many minutes does he save?
10. ‖| In a 5.00 km race, one runner runs at a steady 12.0 km/h and another runs at 14.5 km/h. How long does the faster runner have to wait at the finish line to see the slower runner cross?

11. ‖‖‖ In an 8.00 km race, one runner runs at a steady 11.0 km/h and another runs at 14.0 km/h. How far from the finish line is the slower runner when the faster runner finishes the race?
12. ‖ A bicyclist has the position-versus-time graph shown in Figure P2.12. What is the bicyclist's velocity at $t = 10$ s, at $t = 25$ s, and at $t = 35$ s?

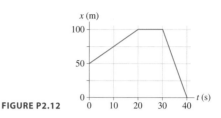

FIGURE P2.12

Section 2.3 Motion with Changing Velocity

13. ‖ Figure P2.13 shows the position graph of a particle.
   a. Draw the particle's velocity graph for the interval $0 \text{ s} \leq t \leq 4 \text{ s}$.
   b. Does this particle have a turning point or points? If so, at what time or times?

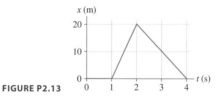

FIGURE P2.13

14. ‖‖| A car starts from $x_i = 10$ m at $t_i = 0$ s and moves with the velocity graph shown in Figure P2.14.
   a. What is the object's position at $t = 2$ s, 3 s, and 4 s?
   b. Does this car ever change direction? If so, at what time?

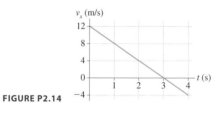

FIGURE P2.14

Section 2.4 Acceleration

15. ‖ Figure P2.15 shows the velocity graph of a bicycle. Draw the bicycle's acceleration graph for the interval $0 \text{ s} \leq t \leq 4 \text{ s}$. Give both axes an appropriate numerical scale.

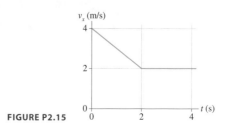

FIGURE P2.15

16. | Figure P2.16 shows the velocity graph of a train that starts from the origin at $t = 0$ s.
    a. Draw position and acceleration graphs for the train.
    b. Find the acceleration of the train at $t = 3.0$ s.

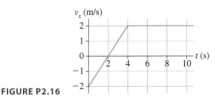

FIGURE P2.16

17. | Figure P2.17 shows the velocity graph of a bicycle moving along the x-axis. Its initial position is $x_i = 2.0$ m at $t_i = 0.0$ s. At $t = 2.0$ s, what are the bicycle's (a) position, (b) velocity, and (c) acceleration?

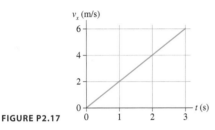

FIGURE P2.17

18. || For each motion diagram shown earlier in Figure P2.2, determine the sign (positive or negative) of the acceleration.
19. || Figure P2.19 is a somewhat simplified velocity graph for Olympic sprinter Carl Lewis starting a 100 m dash. Estimate his acceleration during each of the intervals A, B, and C.

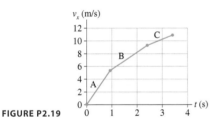

FIGURE P2.19

Section 2.5 Motion with Constant Acceleration

20. | A Thompson's gazelle can reach a speed of 13 m/s in 3.0 s.
BIO A lion can reach a speed of 9.5 m/s in 1.0 s. A trout can reach a speed of 2.8 m/s in 0.12 s. Which animal has the greatest acceleration?

21. || When striking, the pike, a
BIO predatory fish, can accelerate from rest to a speed of 4.0 m/s in 0.11 s.
    a. What is the acceleration of the pike during this strike?
    b. How far does the pike move during this strike?

22. ||| a. What constant acceleration, in SI units, must a car have to go from zero to 60 mph in 10 s?
    b. What fraction of g is this?
    c. How far has the car traveled when it reaches 60 mph? Give your answer both in SI units and in feet.

23. ||| A car travels with constant acceleration along a straight road. It was at the origin and at rest at $t_1 = 0$ s; its position is $x_2 = 144$ m at $t_2 = 6.00$ s.
    a. What was the car's position at $t = 3.00$ s?
    b. What will its position be at $t = 9.00$ s?

24. |||| A jet plane is cruising at 250 m/s when suddenly the pilot turns the engines up to full throttle. After traveling an additional 2.0 km, the jet is moving with a speed of 300 m/s.
    a. What is the jet's acceleration, assuming it to be a constant acceleration?
    b. Is your answer reasonable? Explain.

25. ||| A speed skater moving across frictionless ice at 8.0 m/s hits a 5.0-m-wide patch of rough ice. She slows steadily, then continues on at 6.0 m/s. What is her acceleration on the rough ice?

Section 2.6 Solving One-Dimensional Motion Problems

26. ||| A driver has a reaction time of 0.50 s, and the maximum deceleration of her car is 6.0 m/s². She is driving at 20 m/s when suddenly she sees an obstacle in the road 50 m in front of her. Can she stop the car in time to avoid a collision?

27. |||| You're driving down the highway late one night at 20 m/s when a deer steps onto the road 35 m in front of you. Your reaction time before stepping on the brakes is 0.50 s, and the maximum deceleration of your car is 10 m/s².
    a. How much distance is between you and the deer when you come to a stop?
    b. What is the maximum speed you could have and still not hit the deer?

28. | A light-rail train going from one station to the next on a straight section of track accelerates from rest at 1.4 m/s² for 15 s. It then proceeds at constant speed for 1100 m before slowing down at 2.2 m/s² until it stops at the station.
    a. What is the distance between the stations?
    b. How much time does it take the train to go between the stations?

29. || A simple model for a person running the 100 m dash is to assume the sprinter runs with constant acceleration until reaching top speed, then maintains that speed through the finish line. If a sprinter reaches his top speed of 11.2 m/s in 2.14 s, what will be his total time?

Section 2.7 Free Fall

30. ||| Ball bearings can be made by letting spherical drops of molten metal fall inside a tall tower—called a *shot tower*—and solidify as they fall.
    a. If a bearing needs 4.0 s to solidify enough for impact, how high must the tower be?
    b. What is the bearing's impact velocity?

31. | In the chapter, we saw that a person's reaction time is gen-
BIO erally not quick enough to allow the person to catch a dollar bill dropped between the fingers. If a typical reaction time in this case is 0.25 s, how long would a bill need to be for a person to have a good chance of catching it?

32. || A ball is thrown vertically upward with a speed of 19.6 m/s.
    a. What are the ball's velocity and height after 1.00, 2.00, 3.00, and 4.00 s?
    b. Draw the ball's velocity-versus-time graph. Give both axes an appropriate numerical scale.

33. ‖ A student at the top of a building of height h throws ball A straight upward with speed v_0 and throws ball B straight downward with the same initial speed.

　a. Compare the balls' accelerations, both direction and magnitude, immediately after they leave her hand. Is one acceleration larger than the other? Or are the magnitudes equal?

　b. Compare the final speeds of the balls as they reach the ground. Is one speed larger than the other? Or are they equal?

34. ‖‖‖ In an action movie, the villain is rescued from the ocean by grabbing onto the ladder hanging from a helicopter. He is so intent on gripping the ladder that he lets go of his briefcase of counterfeit money when he is 130 m above the water. If the briefcase hits the water 6.0 s later, what was the speed at which the helicopter was ascending?

35. ‖‖‖ A rock climber stands on top of a 50-m-high cliff overhanging a pool of water. He throws two stones vertically downward 1.0 s apart and observes that they cause a single splash. The initial speed of the first stone was 2.0 m/s.

　a. How long after the release of the first stone does the second stone hit the water?

　b. What was the initial speed of the second stone?

　c. What is the speed of each stone as they hit the water?

General Problems

36. ‖ Macrophages are cells referred to as "big eaters" or "killing
BIO machines" that destroy any foreign agents (pathogens) or antibodies found in the body. When a pathogen is detected, the macrophage moves toward it and literally devours it almost instantly. Suppose a large number of pathogen molecules are lined up 1.0 μm apart on a straight fiber of tissue. A macrophage initially 0.50 μm from the nearest one moves toward it at a constant speed of 30 nm/s.

　a. How long does it take until the first pathogen molecule is devoured?

　b. How about 100 molecules?

　c. What is the total distance traveled by the macrophage by the time 100 molecules have been eaten?

　d. How many pathogen molecules will one microphage destroy in 10 minutes?

Questions 37 and 38 concern *nerve impulses,* signals that propagate along *nerve fibers* consisting of many *axons* (fiber-like extensions of nerve cells) connected end-to-end. The speed of the signal depends on whether the axon has a sheath called myelin around it or not. Nerve impulses move along axons with myelin at 100 m/s, one hundred times as quickly as on axons without it. Figure P2.37 shows small portions of three nerve fibers consisting of axons of equal size. Two-thirds of the axons in fiber B are myelinated.

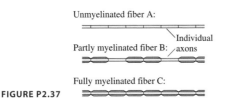

Unmyelinated fiber A:

Individual axons

Partly myelinated fiber B:

Fully myelinated fiber C:

FIGURE P2.37

37. ‖ Suppose nerve impulses simultaneously enter the left side
BIO of the nerve fibers sketched in Figure P2.37, then propagate to the right. Draw qualitatively accurate position and velocity graphs for the nerve impulses in all three cases. A nerve fiber is made up of many axons, but show the propagation of the impulses only over the six axons shown here.

38. ‖ Suppose that the nerve fibers in Figure P2.37 connect a
BIO finger to your brain, a distance of 1.2 m.

　a. What are the travel times of a nerve impulse from finger to brain along fibers A and C?

　b. For fiber B, 2/3 of the length is composed of myelinated axons, 1/3 unmyelinated axons. Compute the travel time for a nerve impulse on this fiber.

　c. When you touch a hot stove with the finger, the sensation of pain must reach your brain as a nerve signal along a nerve fiber before your muscles can react. Which of the three fibers gives you the best protection against a burn? Are any of these fibers unsuitable for transmitting urgent sensory information?

39. ‖ A driver travels along a straight east-west road. Starting from rest, he drives east for a while at highway speeds. Spotting some cows in the road, he brakes and comes to a halt. After waiting a few minutes, he backs slowly down the road until reaching the nearest crossroad.

　Draw graphs of the driver's position, velocity, and acceleration as functions of time. There are no numbers in this problem, but your graphs should have the correct shapes. Draw the three graphs one above the other so that the time axes line up.

40. ‖ A truck driver has a shipment of apples to deliver to a destination 440 miles away. The trip usually takes him 8 hours. Today he finds himself daydreaming and realizes 120 miles into his trip that he is running 15 minutes later than his usual pace at this point. At what speed must he drive for the remainder of the trip to complete the trip in the usual amount of time?

41. ‖ When you sneeze, the air in your lungs accelerates from
BIO rest to approximately 150 km/hr in about 0.50 seconds.

　a. What is the acceleration of the air in m/s^2?

　b. What is this acceleration, in units of g?

42. ‖‖‖ Two stones are released from the edge of a cliff, one a short time after the other.

　a. As they fall, the first is always going faster than the second. Does the *difference* between their speeds get larger, get smaller, or stay the same? Explain.

　b. Does their separation increase, decrease, or stay the same? Explain.

　c. Will the time interval between the instants at which they hit the ground be smaller than, equal to, or larger than the time interval between the instants of their release? Explain.

43. ‖ Figure P2.43 shows the motion diagram, made at two frames of film per second, of a ball rolling along a track. The track has a 3.0-m-long sticky section.

　a. Use the meter stick to determine the positions of the center of the ball. Place your data in a table, similar to Table 2.1, showing each position and the instant of time at which it occurred.

　b. Make a graph of x versus t for the ball. Because you have data only at certain instants of time, your graph should consist of dots that are not connected together.

c. What is the *change* in the ball's position from $t = 0$ s to $t = 1.0$ s?

d. What is the *change* in the ball's position from $t = 2.0$ s to $t = 4.0$ s?

e. What is the ball's velocity before reaching the sticky section?

f. What is the ball's velocity after passing the sticky section?

g. Determine the ball's acceleration on the sticky section of the track.

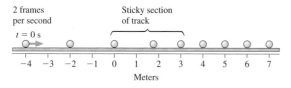

FIGURE P2.43

44. ‖ Figure P2.44 shows a velocity-versus-time graph for a particle moving along the *x*-axis. Its initial position is $x_i = 2.0$ m at $t_i = 0$ s.

a. What are the particle's position, velocity, and acceleration at $t = 1.0$ s?

b. What are the particle's position, velocity, and acceleration at $t = 3.0$ s?

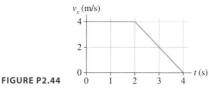

FIGURE P2.44

45. | Figure P2.45 shows a velocity graph for a particle having initial position $x_i = 0$ m at $t_i = 0$ s.

a. At what time or times is the particle found at $x = 35$ m? Work with the geometry of the graph, not with kinematic equations.

b. Draw a motion diagram for the particle.

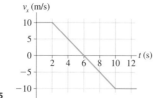

FIGURE P2.45

46. ‖‖ Julie drives 100 mi to Grandmother's house. On the way to Grandmother's, Julie drives half the *distance* at 40 mph and half the distance at 60 mph. On her return trip, she drives half the *time* at 40 mph and half the time at 60 mph.

a. How long does it take Julie to complete the trip to Grandmother's house?

b. How long does the return trip take?

47. ‖ The takeoff speed for an Airbus A320 jetliner is 80 m/s. Velocity data measured during takeoff are as follows:

t (s)	v_x (m/s)
0	0
10	23
20	46
30	69

a. What is the takeoff speed in miles per hour?

b. What is the jetliner's acceleration during takeoff?

c. At what time do the wheels leave the ground?

d. For safety reasons, in case of an aborted takeoff, the runway must be three times the takeoff distance. Can an A320 take off safely on a 2.5-mi-long runway?

48. ‖‖‖ Does a real automobile have constant acceleration? Measured data for a Porsche 944 Turbo at maximum acceleration are as follows:

t (s)	v_x (mph)
0	0
2	28
4	46
6	60
8	70
10	78

a. Convert the velocities to m/s, then make a graph of velocity versus time. Based on your graph, is the acceleration constant? Explain.

b. Draw a smooth curve through the points on your graph, then use your graph to *estimate* the car's acceleration at 2.0 s and 8.0 s. Give your answer in SI units. **Hint:** Remember that acceleration is the slope of the velocity graph.

49. ‖ a. How many days will it take a spaceship to accelerate to the speed of light (3.0×10^8 m/s) with the acceleration *g*?

b. How far will it travel during this interval?

c. What fraction of a light year is your answer to part b? A *light year* is the distance light travels in one year.

NOTE ▶ We know, from Einstein's theory of relativity, that no object can travel at the speed of light. So this problem, while interesting and instructive, is not realistic. ◀

50. ‖‖‖ You are driving to the grocery store at 20 m/s. You are 110 m from an intersection when the traffic light turns red. Assume that your reaction time is 0.70 s and that your car brakes with constant acceleration.

a. How far are you from the intersection when you begin to apply the brakes?

b. What acceleration will bring you to rest right at the intersection?

c. How long does it take you to stop?

51. ‖ When you blink your eye, the upper lid goes from rest with
BIO your eye open to completely covering your eye in a time of 0.024 s.

a. Estimate the distance that the top lid of your eye moves during a blink.

b. What is the acceleration of your eyelid? Assume it to be constant.

c. What is your upper eyelid's final speed as it hits the bottom eyelid?

52. |||| A bush baby, an African
BIO primate, is capable of leaping vertically to the remarkable height of 2.26 m. To jump this high, the bush baby accelerates over a distance of 0.16 m while rapidly extending its legs. The acceleration during the jump is approximately constant. What is the acceleration in m/s² and in g's?

53. |||| When jumping, a flea reaches a takeoff speed of 1.0 m/s
BIO over a distance of 0.50 mm.
   a. What is the flea's acceleration during the jump phase?
   b. How long does the acceleration phase last?
   c. If the flea jumps straight up, how high will it go? (Ignore air resistance for this problem; in reality, air resistance plays a large role, and the flea will not reach this height.)

54. |||| Divers compete by diving into a 3.0-m-deep pool from a platform 10 m above the water. What is the magnitude of the minimum acceleration in the water needed to keep a diver from hitting the bottom of the pool? Assume the acceleration is constant.

55. |||| With a man on first base, Hank hits a ball to the corner of the outfield. The outfielder has trouble retrieving the ball, so Hank decides to try for an inside-the-park home run. As he rounds third base at a speed of 18 ft/s, Hank sees that the player in front of him is two-thirds of the way from third base to home and is limping at 6.0 ft/s. It is 90 ft between bases. If Hank wants to arrive at home plate just behind the slower runner, what should be the magnitude of his acceleration as he slows?

56. ||| A student standing on the ground throws a ball straight up. The ball leaves the student's hand with a speed of 15 m/s when the hand is 2.0 m above the ground. How long is the ball in the air before it hits the ground? (The student moves her hand out of the way.)

57. || A rock is tossed straight up with a speed of 20 m/s. When it returns, it falls into a hole 10 m deep.
   a. What is the rock's velocity as it hits the bottom of the hole?
   b. How long is the rock in the air, from the instant it is released until it hits the bottom of the hole?

58. |||| A 200 kg weather rocket is loaded with 100 kg of fuel and fired straight up. It accelerates upward at 30.0 m/s² for 30.0 s, then runs out of fuel. Ignore any air resistance effects.
   a. What is the rocket's maximum altitude?
   b. How long is the rocket in the air?
   c. Draw a velocity-versus-time graph for the rocket from liftoff until it hits the ground.

59. |||| A juggler throws a ball straight up into the air with a speed of 10 m/s. With what speed would she need to throw a second ball half a second later, starting from the same position as the first, in order to hit the first ball at the top of its trajectory?

60. |||| A lead ball is dropped into a lake from a diving board 5.0 m above the water. After entering the water, it sinks to the bottom with a constant velocity equal to the velocity with which it hit the water. The ball reaches the bottom 3.0 s after it is released. How deep is the lake?

61. ||| A hotel elevator ascends 200 m with a maximum speed of 5.0 m/s. Its acceleration and deceleration both have a magnitude of 1.0 m/s².
   a. How far does the elevator move while accelerating to full speed from rest?
   b. How long does it take to make the complete trip from bottom to top?

62. ||| A car starts from rest at a stop sign. It accelerates at 2.0 m/s² for 6.0 seconds, coasts for 2.0 s, and then slows down at a rate of 1.5 m/s² for the next stop sign. How far apart are the stop signs?

63. || A toy train is pushed forward and released at $x_i = 2.0$ m with a speed of 2.0 m/s. It rolls at a steady speed for 2.0 s, then one wheel begins to stick. The train comes to a stop 6.0 m from the point at which it was released. What is the train's acceleration after its wheel begins to stick?

64. ||| Bob is driving the getaway car after the big bank robbery. He's going 50 m/s when his headlights suddenly reveal a nail strip that the cops have placed across the road 150 m in front of him. If Bob can stop in time, he can throw the car into reverse and escape. But if he crosses the nail strip, all his tires will go flat and he will be caught. Bob's reaction time before he can hit the brakes is 0.60 s, and his car's maximum deceleration is 10 m/s². Is Bob in jail?

65. || Heather and Jerry are standing on a bridge 50 m above a river. Heather throws a rock straight down with a speed of 20 m/s. Jerry, at exactly the same instant of time, throws a rock straight up with the same speed. Ignore air resistance.
   a. How much time elapses between the first splash and the second splash?
   b. Which rock has the faster speed as it hits the water?

66. ||| A motorist is driving at 20 m/s when she sees that a traffic light 200 m ahead has just turned red. She knows that this light stays red for 15 s, and she wants to reach the light just as it turns green again. It takes her 1.0 s to step on the brakes and begin slowing at a constant deceleration. What is her speed as she reaches the light at the instant it turns green?

67. ||||| A "rocket car" is launched along a long straight track at $t = 0$ s. It moves with constant acceleration $a_1 = 2.0$ m/s². At $t = 2.0$ s, a second car is launched with constant acceleration $a_2 = 8.0$ m/s².
   a. At what time does the second car catch up with the first one?
   b. How far down the track do they meet?

68. | A Porsche challenges a Honda to a 400 m race. Because the Porsche's acceleration of 3.5 m/s² is larger than the Honda's 3.0 m/s², the Honda gets a 50-m head start. Assume, somewhat unrealistically, that both cars can maintain these accelerations the entire distance. Who wins, and by how much time?

69. |||| The minimum stopping distance for a car traveling at a speed of 30 m/s is 60 m, including the distance traveled during the driver's reaction time of 0.50 s.
   a. What is the minimum stopping distance for the same car traveling at a speed of 40 m/s?
   b. Draw a position-versus-time graph for the motion of the car in part a. Assume the car is at $x_i = 0$ m when the driver first sees the emergency situation ahead that calls for a rapid halt.

70. |||| A rocket is launched straight up with constant acceleration. Four seconds after liftoff, a bolt falls off the side of the rocket. The bolt hits the ground 6.0 s later. What was the rocket's acceleration?

In Problems 71 through 73 you are given the kinematic equation that is used to solve a problem. For each of these, you are to

a. Write a *realistic* problem for which this is the correct equation. Be sure that the answer your problem requests is consistent with the equation given.

b. Draw the motion diagram and the pictorial representation for your problem.

c. Finish the solution of the problem.

71. ‖ $64 \text{ m} = 0.0 \text{ m} + (32 \text{ m/s})(4.0 \text{ s} - 0.0 \text{ s})$
$\qquad + \frac{1}{2}a_x(4.0 \text{ s} - 0.0 \text{ s})^2$

72. ‖ $0.0 \text{ m/s} = 36 \text{ m/s} - (3.0 \text{ m/s}^2)t$

73. ‖ $(10 \text{ m/s})^2 = (v_y)_i^2 - 2(9.8 \text{ m/s}^2)(10 \text{ m} - 0 \text{ m})$

Passage Problems

Free Fall on Different Worlds

Objects in free fall on the earth have acceleration $a_y = -9.8 \text{ m/s}^2$. On the moon, free-fall acceleration is approximately 1/6 of the acceleration on earth. This changes the scale of problems involving free fall. For instance, suppose you jump straight upward, leaving the ground with velocity v_i and then steadily slowing until reaching zero velocity at your highest point. Because your initial velocity is determined mostly by the strength of your leg muscles, we can assume your initial velocity would be the same on the moon. But considering the final equation in Table 2.4 we can see that, with a smaller free-fall acceleration, your maximum height would be greater. The following questions ask you to think about how certain athletic feats might be performed in this reduced-gravity environment.

74. ‖ If an astronaut can jump straight up to a height of 0.50 m on earth, how high could he jump on the moon?
A. 1.2 m   B. 3.0 m   C. 3.6 m   D. 18 m

75. ‖ On the earth, an astronaut can safely jump to the ground from a height of 1.0 m; her velocity when reaching the ground is low enough to not cause injury. From what height could the astronaut safely jump to the ground on the moon?
A. 2.4 m   B. 6.0 m   C. 7.2 m   D. 36 m

76. ‖ On the earth, an astronaut throws a ball straight upward; it stays in the air for a total time of 3.0 s before reaching the ground again. If a ball were to be thrown upward with the same initial speed on the moon, how much time would pass before it hit the ground?
A. 7.3 s   B. 18 s   C. 44 s   D. 108 s

STOP TO THINK ANSWERS

Stop to Think 2.1: D. The motion consists of two constant-velocity phases; the second one has a larger velocity. The correct graph has two straight-line segments, with the second one having a larger slope.

Stop to Think 2.2: A. The motion consists of two constant-velocity phases; the first one is positive velocity, the second is negative. The correct graph has two straight-line segments, the first with a positive slope and the second with a negative slope.

Stop to Think 2.3: C. Consider the slope of the position-versus-time graph; it starts out positive and constant, then decreases to zero. Thus the velocity graph must start with a constant positive value, then decrease to zero.

Stop to Think 2.4: C. Acceleration is the slope of the velocity-versus-time graph. The largest magnitude of the slope is at point C.

Stop to Think 2.5: A. The car is always moving to the right, so the velocity is positive at all times. There should be two constant-velocity segments, with the second having a smaller velocity.

Stop to Think 2.6: D. The final velocity will have the same *magnitude* as the initial velocity, but the velocity is negative because the rock will be moving downward.

3 FORCES AND NEWTON'S LAWS OF MOTION

These ice boats sail across the ice at great speeds. What gets the boats moving in the first place? What keeps them from going even faster?

Looking Ahead ▶▶

The goal of Chapter 3 is to establish a connection between force and motion. In this chapter you will learn to:

▶ Recognize what a force is and is not.

▶ Identify the specific forces acting on an object.

▶ Draw free-body diagrams.

▶ Understand the connection between force and motion.

Looking Back ◀◀

To master the material introduced in this chapter, you must understand how acceleration is determined and how vectors are used. Please review:

◀ Section 1.5 Vectors and motion.

◀ Section 2.4 Acceleration.

These ice sailers fly across the frozen lake at some 60 mph. Pretty amazing! We could use kinematics to describe a boat's motion with pictures, graphs, and equations. By defining position, velocity, and acceleration and dressing them in mathematical clothing, kinematics provides a language to describe *how* something moves. But kinematics would tell us nothing about *why* the boat accelerates briskly before reaching a top speed. For the more fundamental task of understanding the *cause* of motion, we turn our attention to **dynamics.** Dynamics joins with kinematics to form **mechanics,** the general science of motion. We study dynamics qualitatively in this chapter, then develop it quantitatively in the next four chapters.

The theory of mechanics originated in the mid-1600s when Sir Isaac Newton formulated his laws of motion. These fundamental principles of mechanics explain how motion occurs as a consequence of forces. Newton's laws are more than 300 years old, but they still form the basis for our contemporary understanding of motion.

A challenge in learning physics is that a textbook is not an experiment. The book can assert that an experiment will have a certain outcome, but you may not be convinced unless you see or do the experiment yourself. Newton's laws are frequently contrary to our intuition, and a lack of familiarity with the evidence for Newton's laws is a source of difficulty for many people. You should have an opportunity through lecture demonstrations and in the laboratory to see for yourself the evidence supporting Newton's laws. Physics is not an arbitrary collection of definitions and formulas, but a consistent theory as to how the universe really works. It is only with experience and evidence that we learn to separate physical fact from fantasy.

3.1 What Causes Motion?

The rocks in this rockslide quickly came to rest. Is this the "natural state" of objects?

Interstellar coasting A nearly perfect example of Newton's first law is the pair of Voyager space probes launched in 1977. Both spacecraft long ago ran out of fuel and are now coasting through the frictionless vacuum of space. Although not entirely free of influence from the sun's gravity, they are now so far from the sun and other stars that gravitational influences are very nearly zero. Thus, according to the first law, they will continue at their current speed of about 40,000 miles per hour essentially forever. Billions of years from now, long after our solar system is dead, the Voyagers will still be drifting through the stars.

As we remarked in Chapter 1, Aristotle (384–322 BC) and his contemporaries in the world of ancient Greece were very interested in motion. One question they asked was: What is the "natural state" of an object if left to itself? It does not take an expensive research program to see that every moving object on earth, if left to itself, eventually comes to rest. You have certainly seen countless examples of this: You must push a shopping cart to keep it rolling, but when you stop pushing, the cart soon comes to rest; a boulder bounds downhill and then tumbles to a halt. Having observed many such examples himself, Aristotle concluded that the natural state of an earthly object is to be *at rest*. An object at rest requires no explanation; it is doing precisely what comes naturally to it. We'll soon see, however, that this simple viewpoint is *incomplete*.

Aristotle further pondered moving objects. A moving object is *not* in its natural state and thus requires an explanation: Why is this object moving? What keeps it going and prevents it from being in its natural state? When a puck is sliding across the ice, what keeps it going? Why does an arrow fly through the air once it is no longer being pushed by the bowstring? Although these questions seem like reasonable ones to pose, it was Galileo who first showed that the questions being asked were, in fact, the wrong ones.

Galileo reopened the question of the "natural state" of objects. He suggested focusing on the *idealized case* in which resistance to the motion (e.g., friction or air resistance) is zero. He performed many experiments to study motion. Let's imagine a modern experiment of this kind, as shown in Figure 3.1.

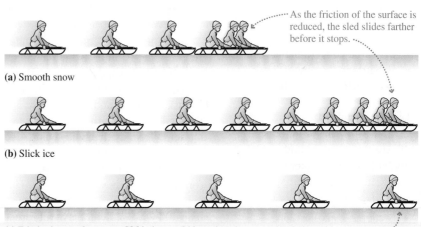

As the friction of the surface is reduced, the sled slides farther before it stops.

(a) Smooth snow

(b) Slick ice

(c) Frictionless surface   If friction could be reduced to zero, the sled would *never* stop.

FIGURE 3.1 Sleds sliding on increasingly smooth surfaces.

Tyler slides down a hill on his sled, then out onto a horizontal patch of smooth snow, which is shown in Figure 3.1a. Even if the snow is quite smooth, the friction between the sled and the snow will soon cause the sled to come to rest. What if Tyler slides down the hill onto some very slick ice, as in Figure 3.1b? This gives very low friction, and the sled could slide for quite a distance before stopping. Galileo's genius was to imagine the case where *all* sources of friction, air resistance, and other retarding influences were removed, as for the sled in Figure 3.1c sliding on imaginary *frictionless* ice. We can imagine in that case that the sled, once started in its motion, would continue in its motion *forever*, moving in a straight line with no loss of speed. In other words, **the natural state of an object—its behavior if free of external influences—is *uniform motion* with constant velocity!** Further, "at rest" has no special significance in Galileo's view of motion; it is simply uniform motion that happens to have a velocity of zero. This implies that an object at rest, in the absence of external influences, will remain at rest forever.

Galileo's ideas were completely counter to those of the ancient Greeks. We no longer need to explain why a sled continues to slide across the ice; that motion is its "natural" state. What needs explanation, in this new viewpoint, is why objects *don't* continue in uniform motion. Why does a sliding puck eventually slow to a stop? Why does a stone, thrown upward, slow and eventually fall back down? Galileo's new viewpoint was that the stone and the puck are *not* free of "influences": the stone is somehow pulled toward the earth, and some sort of retarding influence acted to slow the sled down. Today, we call such influences that lead to deviations from uniform motion **forces.**

Galileo's experiments were limited to motion along horizontal surfaces. It was left to Newton to generalize Galileo's conclusions, and today we call it Newton's first law of motion.

> **Newton's first law** Consider an object with no force acting on it. If it is at rest, it will remain at rest; if it is moving, it will continue to move in a straight line at a constant speed.

As an important application of Newton's first law, consider the crash test of Figure 3.2. The car contacts the wall and begins to slow. The wall is an external influence—a force—that alters the car's uniform motion. But the wall is a force on the *car*, not on the dummy. In accordance with Newton's first law, the unbelted dummy continues to move straight ahead at his original speed. Only when he collides violently with the dashboard of the stopped car is there a force acting to halt the dummy's uniform motion. If he had been wearing a seatbelt, the influence (i.e., the force) of the seatbelt would have slowed the dummy at the much lower rate with which the car slows down. We'll study the forces of collisions in detail in Chapter 5.

3.2 Force

Newton's first law tells us that an object in motion subject to no forces will continue to move in a straight line forever. But this law does not explain in any detail exactly what a force *is*. Unfortunately, there is no simple one-sentence definition of force. The concept of force is best introduced by looking at examples of some common forces and considering the basic properties shared by all forces. This will be our task in the next two sections. Let's begin by examining the properties that all forces have in common, as outlined in the table on the next page.

Getting the ketchup out The ketchup stuck at the bottom of the bottle is initially at rest. If you hit the bottom of the bottle, the bottle suddenly moves down, taking the ketchup on the bottom of the bottle with it, so that the ketchup just stays stuck to the bottom. But if instead you hit *up* on the bottle, as shown, you force the bottle rapidly upward. By the first law, the ketchup that was stuck to the bottom stays at rest, so it separates from the upward-moving bottle: the ketchup has moved forward with respect to the bottle!

At the instant of impact, the car and driver are moving at the same speed;

The car slows as it hits, but the driver continues at the same speed . . .

. . . until he hits the now-stationary dashboard. Ouch!

FIGURE 3.2 Newton's first law tells us: "Wear your seatbelts!"

What is a force?

A force is a push or a pull.

Our commonsense idea of a **force** is that it is a *push* or a *pull.* We will refine this idea as we go along, but it is an adequate starting point. Notice our careful choice of words: We refer to "*a* force," rather than simply "force." We want to think of a force as a very specific *action,* so that we can talk about a single force or perhaps about two or three individual forces that we can clearly distinguish. Hence the concrete idea of "a force" acting on an object.

A force acts on an object.

Implicit in our concept of force is that **a force acts on an object.** In other words, pushes and pulls are applied *to* something—an object. From the object's perspective, it has a force *exerted* on it. Forces do not exist in isolation from the object that experiences them.

A force requires an agent.

Every force has an **agent,** something that acts or pushes or pulls. That is, a force has a specific, identifiable *cause.* As you throw a ball, it is your hand, while in contact with the ball, that is the agent or the cause of the force exerted on the ball. *If* a force is being exerted on an object, you must be able to identify a specific cause (i.e., the agent) of that force. Conversely, a force is not exerted on an object *unless* you can identify a specific cause or agent. Note that an agent can be an inert object such as a tabletop or a wall. Such agents are the cause of many common forces.

A force is a vector.

If you push an object, you can push either gently or very hard. Similarly, you can push either left or right, up or down. To quantify a push, we need to specify both a magnitude *and* a direction. It should thus come as no surprise that a force is a vector quantity. The symbol for a force is a vector symbol such as $\vec{F}$, $\vec{w}$, or $\vec{T}$. The size or strength of such a force is its magnitude F (or w or T).

A force can be either a contact force . . .

There are two basic classes of forces, depending on whether the agent touches the object or not. **Contact forces** are forces that act on an object by touching it at a point of contact. The bat must touch the ball to hit it. A string must be tied to an object to pull it. The majority of forces that we will examine are contact forces.

. . . or a long-range force.

Long-range forces are forces that act on an object without physical contact. Magnetism is an example of a long-range force. You have undoubtedly held a magnet over a paper clip and seen the paper clip leap up to the magnet. A coffee cup released from your hand is pulled to the earth by the long-range force of gravity.

Let's summarize these ideas as our definition of force:

- A force is a push or a pull on an object.
- A force is a vector. It has both a magnitude and a direction.
- A force requires an agent. Something does the pushing or pulling. The agent can be an inert object such as a tabletop or a wall.
- A force is either a contact force or a long-range force. Gravity is the only long-range force we will deal with until much later in the book.

There's one more important aspect of forces. If you push against a door (the object) to close it, the door pushes back against your hand (the agent). If a tow rope pulls on a car (the object), the car pulls back on the rope (the agent). In general, if an agent exerts a force on an object, the object exerts a force on the agent. We really need to think of a force as an *interaction* between two objects. Although the interaction perspective is a more exact way to view forces, it adds complications that we would like to avoid for now. Our approach will be to start by focusing on how a single object responds to forces exerted on it. Later in this chapter, we'll return to the larger issue of how two or more objects interact with each other.

Force Vectors

We can use a simple diagram to visualize how forces are exerted on objects. Because we are using the particle model, in which objects are treated as points, the process of drawing a force vector is straightforward. Here is how it goes:

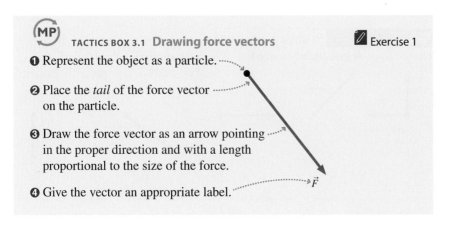

TACTICS BOX 3.1 Drawing force vectors   Exercise 1

❶ Represent the object as a particle.

❷ Place the *tail* of the force vector on the particle.

❸ Draw the force vector as an arrow pointing in the proper direction and with a length proportional to the size of the force.

❹ Give the vector an appropriate label.

Step 2 may seem contrary to what a "push" should do (it may look as if the force arrow is *pulling* the object rather than *pushing* it), but recall that moving a vector does not change it as long as the length and angle do not change. The vector $\vec{F}$ is the same regardless of whether the tail or the tip is placed on the particle. Our reason for using the tail will become clear when we consider how to combine several forces.

Figure 3.3 shows three examples of force vectors. One is a pull, one a push, and one a long-range force, but in all three the *tail* of the force vector is placed on the particle representing the object.

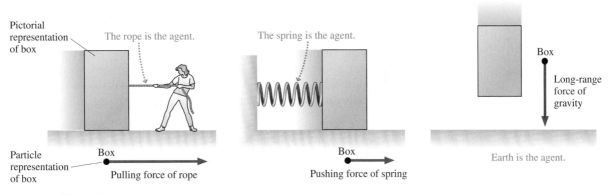

FIGURE 3.3 Three force vectors.

(a)

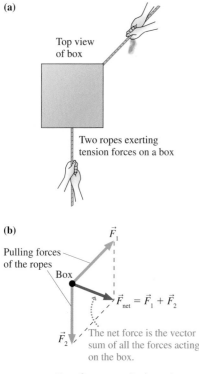

Top view of box

Two ropes exerting tension forces on a box

(b)

Pulling forces of the ropes

Box

$\vec{F}_1$

$\vec{F}_{net} = \vec{F}_1 + \vec{F}_2$

$\vec{F}_2$

The net force is the vector sum of all the forces acting on the box.

FIGURE 3.4 Two forces applied to a box.

Combining Forces

Figure 3.4a shows a top view of a box being pulled by two ropes, each exerting a force on the box. How will the box respond? Experimentally, we find that when several forces $\vec{F}_1$, $\vec{F}_2$, $\vec{F}_3$, . . . are exerted on an object, they combine to form a **net force** that is the *vector* sum of all the forces:

$$\vec{F}_{net} = \vec{F}_1 + \vec{F}_2 + \vec{F}_3 \cdots \qquad (3.1)$$

Mathematically, this summation is called a *superposition* of forces. The net force is sometimes called the *resultant force*. Figure 3.4b shows the net force on the box.

NOTE ► It is important to realize that the net force $\vec{F}_{net}$ is not a new force acting *in addition* to the original forces $\vec{F}_1$, $\vec{F}_2$, $\vec{F}_3$ . . . Instead, we should think of the original forces being *replaced* by $\vec{F}_{net}$. ◄

STOP TO THINK 3.1 Two of the three forces exerted on an object are shown. The net force points directly to the left. Which is the missing third force?

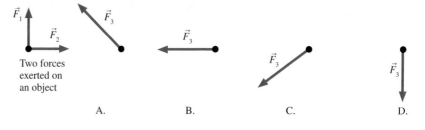

Two forces exerted on an object

A.   B.   C.   D.

3.3 A Short Catalog of Forces

There are many forces we will deal with over and over. This section will introduce you to some of them. Many of these forces have special symbols. As you learn the major forces, be sure to learn the symbol for each.

Weight

A falling rock is pulled toward the earth by the long-range force of gravity. Gravity is what keeps you in your chair, keeps the planets in their orbits around the sun, and shapes the large-scale structure of the universe. For now we'll concentrate on objects on or near the surface of the earth (or other planet).

The gravitational pull of the earth on an object on or near the surface of the earth is called **weight.** The symbol for weight is $\vec{w}$. Weight is the only long-range force we will encounter in the next few chapters. The agent for the weight force is the *entire earth* pulling on an object. The weight force is in some ways the simplest force we'll study. As Figure 3.5 shows, **an object's weight vector always points vertically downward,** no matter how the object is moving.

NOTE ► We often refer to "the weight" of an object. This is an informal expression for w, the magnitude of the weight force exerted on the object. Note that **weight is not the same thing as mass.** We will briefly examine mass later in the chapter and explore the connection between weight and mass in Chapter 4. ◄

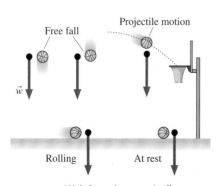

Free fall

Projectile motion

$\vec{w}$

Rolling

At rest

FIGURE 3.5 Weight points vertically downward.

Spring Force

Springs exert one of the most basic contact forces. A spring can either push (when compressed) or pull (when stretched). Figure 3.6 shows the spring force. In both cases, pushing and pulling, the tail of the force vector is placed on the particle in the force diagram. There is no special symbol for a spring force, so we simply use a subscript label: $\vec{F}_{sp}$.

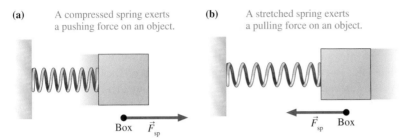

(a) A compressed spring exerts a pushing force on an object.

(b) A stretched spring exerts a pulling force on an object.

Box $\vec{F}_{sp}$

$\vec{F}_{sp}$ Box

FIGURE 3.6 The spring force is parallel to the spring.

Although you may think of a spring as a metal coil that can be stretched or compressed, this is only one type of spring. Hold a ruler, or any other thin piece of wood or metal, by the ends and bend it slightly. It flexes. When you let go, it "springs" back to its original shape. This is just as much a spring as is a metal coil.

Springs come in many forms. When deflected, they push or pull with a spring force.

Tension Force

When a string or rope or wire pulls on an object, it exerts a contact force that we call the **tension force,** represented by a capital $\vec{T}$. **The direction of the tension force is always in the direction of the string or rope,** as you can see in Figure 3.7. When we speak of "the tension" in a string, this is an informal expression for T, the size or magnitude of the tension force. Note that the tension force can only *pull* in the direction of the string; if you try to *push* with a string, it will go slack and be unable to exert a force.

The rope exerts a tension force on the sled.

Sled $\vec{T}$

FIGURE 3.7 Tension is parallel to the rope.

We can think about the tension force using a microscopic picture. If you were to use a very powerful microscope to look inside a rope, you would "see" that it is made of *atoms* joined together by *molecular bonds*. Molecular bonds are not rigid connections between the atoms. They are more accurately thought of as tiny *springs* holding the atoms together, as in Figure 3.8. Pulling on the ends of a string or rope stretches the molecular springs ever so slightly. The tension within a rope and the tension experienced by an object at the end of the rope are really the net spring force being exerted by billions and billions of microscopic springs.

This atomic-level view of tension introduces a new idea: a microscopic **atomic model** for understanding the behavior and properties of **macroscopic** (i.e., containing many atoms) objects. We will frequently use atomic models to obtain a deeper understanding of our observations.

The atomic model of tension also helps to explain one of the basic properties of ropes and strings. When you pull on a rope tied to a heavy box, the rope in turn exerts a tension force on the box. If you pull harder, the tension force on the box becomes greater. How does the box "know" that you are pulling harder on the other end of the rope? According to our atomic model, when you pull harder on the rope its microscopic springs stretch a bit more, increasing the spring force they exert on each other—and on the box they're attached to.

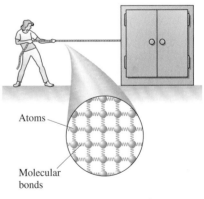

Atoms

Molecular bonds

FIGURE 3.8 An atomic model of tension.

Normal Force

If you sit on a bed, the springs in the mattress compress and, as a consequence of the compression, exert an upward force on you. Stiffer springs would show less

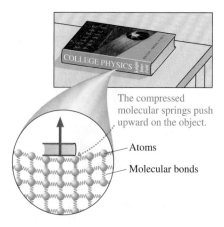

The compressed molecular springs push upward on the object.

Atoms

Molecular bonds

FIGURE 3.9 An atomic model of the force exerted by a table.

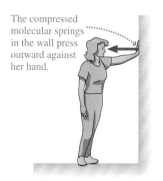

The compressed molecular springs in the wall press outward against her hand.

FIGURE 3.10 The wall pushes outward against your hand.

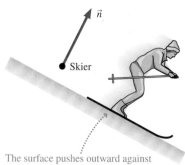

$\vec{n}$

Skier

The surface pushes outward against the bottom of the skis. The force is perpendicular to the surface.

FIGURE 3.11 The normal force is perpendicular to the surface.

compression but would still exert an upward force. The compression of extremely stiff springs might be measurable only by sensitive instruments. Nonetheless, the springs would compress ever so slightly and exert an upward spring force on you.

Figure 3.9 shows a book resting on top of a sturdy table. The table may not visibly flex or sag, but—just as you do to the bed—the book compresses the molecular springs in the table. The size of the compression is very small, but it is not zero. As a consequence, the compressed molecular springs *push upward* on the book. We say that "the table" exerts the upward force, but it is important to understand that the pushing is *really* done by molecular springs. Similarly, an object resting on the ground compresses the molecular springs holding the ground together and, as a consequence, the ground pushes up on the object.

We can extend this idea. Suppose you place your hand on a wall and lean against it, as shown in Figure 3.10. Does the wall exert a force on your hand? As you lean, you compress the molecular springs in the wall and, as a consequence, they push outward *against* your hand. So the answer is "yes," the wall does exert a force on you. It's not hard to see this if you examine your hand as you lean: you can see that your hand is slightly deformed, and becomes more so the harder you lean. This deformation is direct evidence of the force that the wall exerts on your hand. Consider also what would happen if the wall suddenly vanished. Without the wall there to push against you, you would topple forward.

The force the table surface exerts is vertical, while the force the wall exerts is horizontal. In all cases, the force exerted on an object that is pressing against a surface is in a direction *perpendicular* to the surface. Mathematicians refer to a line that is perpendicular to a surface as being *normal* to the surface. In keeping with this terminology, we define the **normal force** as the force exerted by a surface (the agent) against an object that is pressing against the surface. The symbol for the normal force is $\vec{n}$.

We're not using the word *normal* to imply that the force is an "ordinary" force or to distinguish it from an "abnormal force." A surface exerts a force *perpendicular* (i.e., normal) to itself as the molecular springs press *outward*. Figure 3.11 shows an object on an inclined surface, a common situation. Notice how the normal force $\vec{n}$ is perpendicular to the surface.

We have spent a lot of time describing the normal force because many people have a difficult time understanding it. The normal force is a very real force arising from the very real compression of molecular bonds. It is in essence just a spring force, but one exerted by a vast number of microscopic springs acting at once. The normal force is responsible for the "solidness" of solids. It is what prevents you from passing right through the chair you are sitting in and what causes the pain and the lump if you bang your head into a door. Your head can then tell you that the force exerted on it by the door was very real!

Friction

You've certainly observed that a rolling or sliding object, if not pushed or propelled, slows down and eventually stops. You've probably discovered that you can slide better across a sheet of ice than across asphalt. And you also know that most objects stay in place on a table without sliding off even if the table is tilted a bit. The force responsible for these sorts of behavior is **friction.** The symbol for friction is a lower case $\vec{f}$.

Friction, like the normal force, is exerted by a surface. Unlike the normal force, however, **the frictional force is always *parallel* to the surface,** not perpendicular to it. (In many cases, a surface will exert *both* a normal and a frictional force.) On a microscopic level, friction arises as atoms from the object and atoms on the surface run into each other. The rougher the surface is, the more these atoms are forced into close proximity and, as a result, the larger the friction force. We will develop a simple model of friction in the next chapter that will be sufficient for our needs. For now, it is useful to distinguish between two kinds of friction:

- *Kinetic friction,* denoted $\vec{f}_k$, appears as an object slides across a surface. Kinetic friction is a force that always "opposes the motion," meaning that the friction force $\vec{f}_k$ on a sliding object points in a direction opposite to the direction of the object's motion.
- *Static friction,* denoted $\vec{f}_s$, is the force that keeps an object "stuck" on a surface and prevents its motion. Finding the direction of $\vec{f}_s$ is a little trickier than finding it for $\vec{f}_k$. Static friction points opposite the direction in which the object *would* move if there were no friction. That is, it points in the direction necessary to *prevent* motion.

Figure 3.12 shows examples of kinetic and static friction.

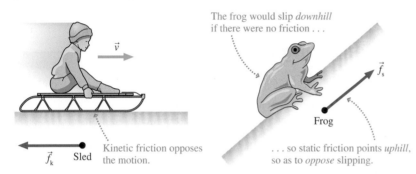

FIGURE 3.12 Kinetic and static friction are parallel to the surface.

It's a drag At the high speeds attained by racing cyclists, air drag can become very significant. The world record for the longest distance traveled in one hour on an ordinary bicycle is 56.38 km, set by Chris Boardman in 1996. But a bicycle with an aerodynamic shell has a much lower drag force, allowing it to attain significantly higher speeds. The bike shown here was pedaled 84.22 km in one hour by Sam Whittingham in 2004, for an amazing average speed of 52.3 mph!

Drag

Friction at a surface is one example of a *resistive force,* a force that opposes or resists motion. Resistive forces are also experienced by objects moving through *fluids*—gases (like air) and liquids (like water). This kind of resistive force—the force of a fluid on a moving object—is called **drag** and is symbolized as $\vec{D}$. Like kinetic friction, **drag points opposite to the direction of motion.** Figure 3.13 shows an example of drag.

Drag can be a large force for objects moving at high speeds or in dense fluids. Hold your arm out the window as you ride in a car and feel how hard the air pushes against your arm; note also how the air resistance against your arm increases rapidly as the car's speed increases. Drop a lightweight bead into a beaker of water and watch how slowly it settles to the bottom. The drag force of the water on the bead is very significant.

On the other hand, for objects that are heavy and compact, that move in air, and whose speed is not too great, the drag force of air resistance is fairly small. To keep things as simple as possible, **you can neglect air resistance in all problems unless a problem explicitly asks you to include it.** The error introduced into calculations by this approximation is generally pretty small. Later, when we consider objects moving in liquids, we'll find that drag will be a very significant force that we'll *have* to include.

Thrust

A jet airplane obviously has a force that propels it forward during takeoff. Likewise for the rocket being launched in Figure 3.14. This force, called **thrust,** occurs when a jet or rocket engine expels gas molecules at high speed. Thrust is a contact force, with the exhaust gas being the agent that pushes on the engine. The process by which thrust is generated is rather subtle, and requires an appreciation of Newton's third law, introduced later in this chapter. For now, we need only

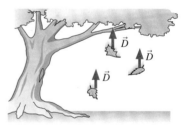

Air resistance is a significant force on falling leaves. It points opposite the direction of motion.

FIGURE 3.13 Air resistance is an example of drag.

Thrust force is exerted on a rocket by exhaust gases.

FIGURE 3.14 The thrust force on a rocket is opposite to the direction of the expelled gases.

consider that **thrust is a force opposite to the direction in which the exhaust gas is expelled.** There's no special symbol for thrust, so we will call it $\vec{F}_{\text{thrust}}$.

Electric and Magnetic Forces

Electricity and magnetism, like gravity, exert long-range forces. The forces of electricity and magnetism act on charged particles. It is worth noting that the forces holding molecules together—the molecular bonds—are not actually tiny springs. Atoms and molecules are made of charged particles—electrons and protons—and what we call a molecular bond is really an electric force between these particles. So when we say that the normal force and the tension force are due to "molecular springs," or that friction is due to atoms running into each other, what we're really saying is that these forces, at the most fundamental level, are actually electric forces between the charged particles in the atoms.

3.4 Identifying Forces

TABLE 3.1 Common forces and their notation

Force	Notation
General force	$\vec{F}$
Weight	$\vec{w}$
Spring force	$\vec{F}_{\text{sp}}$
Tension	$\vec{T}$
Normal force	$\vec{n}$
Static friction	$\vec{f}_{\text{s}}$
Kinetic friction	$\vec{f}_{\text{k}}$
Drag	$\vec{D}$
Thrust	$\vec{F}_{\text{thrust}}$

Force and motion problems generally have two basic steps:

1. Identify all of the forces acting on an object.
2. Use Newton's laws and kinematics to determine the motion.

Understanding the first step is the primary goal of this chapter. We'll turn our attention to step 2 in the next chapter.

A typical physics problem describes an object that is being pushed and pulled in various directions. Some forces are given explicitly, while others are only implied. In order to proceed, it is necessary to determine all the forces that act on the object. It is also necessary to avoid including forces that do not really exist. Now that you have learned the properties of forces and seen a catalog of typical forces, we can develop a step-by-step method for identifying each force in a problem. A summary of the most common forces we'll come across in the next few chapters is given in Table 3.1.

TACTICS BOX 3.2 Identifying forces   Exercises 4–8

❶ **Identify "the system" and "the environment."** The system is the object whose motion you wish to study; the environment is everything else.

❷ **Draw a picture of the situation.** Show the object—the system—and everything in the environment that touches the system. Ropes, springs, and surfaces are all parts of the environment.

❸ **Draw a closed curve around the system.** Only the object is inside the curve; everything else is outside.

❹ **Locate every point on the boundary of this curve where the environment touches the system.** These are the points where the environment exerts *contact forces* on the object.

❺ **Name and label each contact force acting on the object.** There is at least one force at each point of contact; there may be more than one. When necessary, use subscripts to distinguish forces of the same type.

❻ **Name and label each long-range force acting on the object.** For now, the only long-range force is weight.

CONCEPTUAL EXAMPLE 3.1 **Identifying forces on a bungee jumper**

A bungee jumper has leapt off a bridge and is nearing the bottom of her fall. What forces are being exerted on the bungee jumper?

REASON

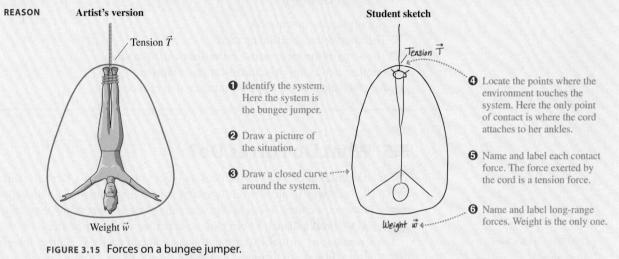

Artist's version

Tension $\vec{T}$

Weight $\vec{w}$

Student sketch

Tension $\vec{T}$

Weight $\vec{w}$

❶ Identify the system. Here the system is the bungee jumper.

❷ Draw a picture of the situation.

❸ Draw a closed curve around the system.

❹ Locate the points where the environment touches the system. Here the only point of contact is where the cord attaches to her ankles.

❺ Name and label each contact force. The force exerted by the cord is a tension force.

❻ Name and label long-range forces. Weight is the only one.

FIGURE 3.15 Forces on a bungee jumper.

CONCEPTUAL EXAMPLE 3.2 **Identifying forces on a skier**

A skier is being towed up a snow-covered hill by a tow rope. What forces are being exerted on the skier?

REASON

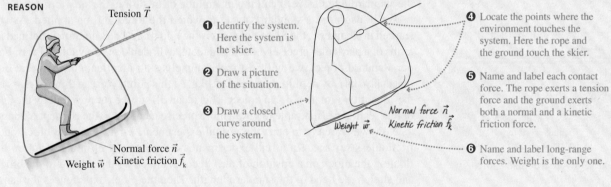

Tension $\vec{T}$

Normal force $\vec{n}$
Weight $\vec{w}$ Kinetic friction $\vec{f}_k$

❶ Identify the system. Here the system is the skier.

❷ Draw a picture of the situation.

❸ Draw a closed curve around the system.

Weight $\vec{w}$ Normal force $\vec{n}$
Kinetic friction $\vec{f}_k$

❹ Locate the points where the environment touches the system. Here the rope and the ground touch the skier.

❺ Name and label each contact force. The rope exerts a tension force and the ground exerts both a normal and a kinetic friction force.

❻ Name and label long-range forces. Weight is the only one.

FIGURE 3.16 Forces on a skier.

NOTE ▶ You might have expected two friction forces and two normal forces in Example 3.2, one on each ski. Keep in mind, however, that we're working within the particle model, which represents the skier by a single point. A particle has only one contact with the ground, so there is a single normal force and a single friction force. The particle model is valid if we want to analyze the motion of the skier as a whole, but we would have to go beyond the particle model to find out what happens to each ski. ◀

CONCEPTUAL EXAMPLE 3.3 **Identifying forces on a rocket**

A rocket is being launched to place a new satellite in orbit. Air resistance is not negligible. What forces are being exerted on the rocket?

REASON

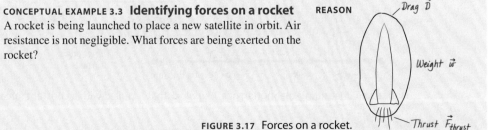

Drag $\vec{D}$

Weight $\vec{w}$

Thrust $\vec{F}_{thrust}$

FIGURE 3.17 Forces on a rocket.

STOP TO THINK 3.2   You've just kicked a rock, and it is now sliding across the ground about 2 meters in front of you. Which of these are forces acting on the rock? List all that apply.

A. Gravity, acting downward.
B. The normal force, acting upward.
C. The force of the kick, acting in the direction of motion.
D. Friction, acting opposite the direction of motion.
E. Air resistance, acting opposite the direction of motion.

3.5 What Do Forces Do?

The fundamental question is: How does an object move when a force is exerted on it? The only way to answer this question is to do experiments. To do experiments, however, we need a way to reproduce the same amount of force again and again, and we need a standard object so our experiments are repeatable.

Let's conduct a "virtual experiment," one you can easily visualize. Imagine using your fingers to stretch a rubber band to a certain length—say 10 centimeters—that you can measure with a ruler. We'll call this the *standard length*. Figure 3.18 shows the idea. You know that a stretched rubber band exerts a force because your fingers *feel* the pull. Furthermore, this is a reproducible force. The rubber band exerts the same force every time you stretch it to the standard length. We'll call the magnitude of this force the *standard force F*.

We'll also need a standard object to which the force will be applied. As we learned in Chapter 1, the SI unit of mass is the kilogram. The kilogram is defined in terms of a particular precisely machined metal cylinder kept in a vault in Paris. For our standard object, we will just make ourselves an identical copy, so that our object also has, by definition, a mass of 1 kg. At this point, you can think of mass as the "quantity of matter" in an object. This idea will suffice for now, but by the end of this section we'll be able to give a more precise meaning to the concept of mass.

Now we're ready to start the virtual experiment. First, place the block on a frictionless surface. (In a real experiment, we can nearly eliminate friction by floating the block on a cushion of air.) Second, attach a rubber band to the block and stretch the band to the standard length. Then the block experiences the same force *F* as did your finger. As the block starts to move, in order to keep the pulling force constant you must *move your hand* in just the right way to keep the length of the rubber band—and thus the force—*constant*. Figure 3.19 shows the

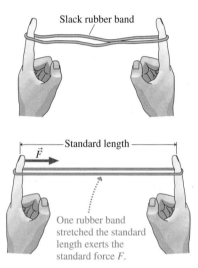

FIGURE 3.18 A reproducible force.

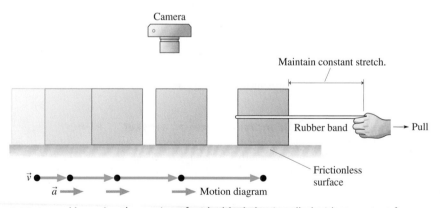

FIGURE 3.19 Measuring the motion of a 1 kg block that is pulled with a constant force.

experiment being carried out. Once the motion is complete, you can use motion diagrams (made from movie frames from the camera) and kinematics to analyze the block's motion.

The motion diagram in Figure 3.19 shows that the velocity vectors are getting longer, so the velocity is increasing: the block is *accelerating.* In order to study the acceleration more carefully, we make a velocity-versus-time graph, as shown in Figure 3.20. We know that the *slope* of such a graph is the acceleration. We see that the slope of the graph—and thus the acceleration—is the same at all times: it is *constant.* This is the first important finding of this experiment: **an object pulled with a constant force moves with a constant acceleration.** This finding could not have been anticipated in advance. It's conceivable that the object would speed up for a while, then move with a steady speed. Or that it would continue to speed up, but that the *rate* of increase, the acceleration, would steadily decline. These are conceivable motions, but they're not what happens. Instead, the object accelerates *with a constant acceleration* for as long as you pull it with a constant force. Let's use the symbol a_1 for this acceleration of our standard 1 kg block when it's pulled by the standard force.

The next experiment is to see what happens if a different force is used. To get a larger force, we can use more rubber bands. If two rubber bands are each pulling equally hard, like those in Figure 3.21, the net pull is twice that of one rubber band, and the force is 2*F*. Three side-by-side rubber bands, each pulled to the standard length, will exert three times the standard force, and so on. So we now have a way of applying forces of different strengths to our block. Figure 3.22 shows what happens in our experiment when we apply larger forces using more bands. When two rubber bands act instead of just one, the slope of the *v*-versus-*t* graph is twice as large, hence the acceleration is twice as large. When three bands act, the acceleration is three times greater than with just one. This is our second important finding: **The acceleration is directly proportional to the size of the force.**

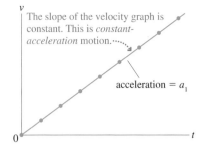

FIGURE 3.20 Velocity-versus-time graph for a 1 kg block pulled with a constant force.

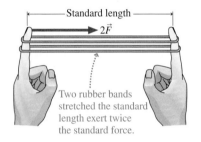

FIGURE 3.21 Doubling the standard force.

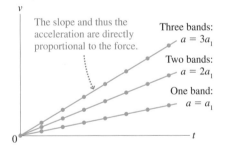

FIGURE 3.22 Velocity-versus-time graphs for a block pulled by one, two, and three rubber bands.

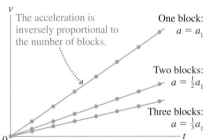

FIGURE 3.23 Velocity-versus-time graphs for one, two, and three blocks pulled with the same force.

The final question for our virtual experiment is: How does the acceleration of an object depend on the "quantity of matter" it contains? To find out, glue two identical 1 kg blocks together, so we have twice the quantity of matter. Now apply the same force—a single rubber band—as you applied to the original block. Figure 3.23 shows that the acceleration is *one-half* as great as that of the original 1 kg block. If we glue three blocks together and pull with one rubber band, we find that the acceleration is only *one-third* of the original acceleration. In general, we find that the acceleration is proportional to the *inverse* of the number of blocks. So our third important result is that **the acceleration is inversely proportional to the number of blocks.**

Inverse proportion

Exercise 12

Two quantities are said to be **inversely proportional** to each other if one quantity is the *inverse* of the other. Mathematically, this means that

$$y = \frac{A}{x}$$

y is inversely proportional to *x*

Here, *A* is a constant.

If *y* is inversely proportional to *x*, *x* is also inversely proportional to *y*.

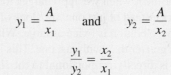

SCALING

- If you double *x*, you halve *y*.
- If you triple *x*, *y* is reduced by a factor of 3.
- If you halve *x*, *y* doubles.
- If you reduce *x* by a factor of 3, *y* becomes 3 times as large.

RATIOS
For any two values of *x*, say x_1 and x_2, we have

$$y_1 = \frac{A}{x_1} \quad \text{and} \quad y_2 = \frac{A}{x_2}$$

so that

$$\frac{y_1}{y_2} = \frac{x_2}{x_1}$$

That is, the ratio of *y* values is the inverse of the ratio of corresponding values of *x*.

LIMITS

- As *x* gets very large, *y* approaches zero.
- As *x* approaches zero, *y* gets very large.

Mass

So far, our idea of mass is that it is a measure of the "quantity of matter" an object contains. But this definition is a little vague. Exactly what do we mean by the "quantity" of matter in an object? The object's volume? The number of atoms it contains? Or some other measure? Our experiments indicate that an unambiguous way to define the mass of an object is in terms of its *acceleration*. We've just found that the more matter an object has, the more it *resists* accelerating in response to a force. You're familiar with this idea: your car is much harder to get moving than your bicycle. The tendency of an object to resist a *change* in its velocity (i.e., to resist acceleration) is called *inertia*.

To make these ideas more quantitative, we can start with the observation made above that the acceleration is inversely proportional to the number of blocks. But the number of blocks is directly related to the mass: One block has (by definition) a mass of 1 kg, so it seems reasonable that two such blocks, with twice the "quantity of matter," should have a mass of 2 kg, and so on. So we can state more generally that, when acted upon by the standard force, **the acceleration is inversely**

proportional to the mass on which the force acts. We can write this mathematically as $a = A/m$, where A is a constant and m is the mass.

For one block we know that $m = 1$ kg and $a = a_1$. Suppose now we take an unknown object, one not made of a simple combination of 1 kg blocks. We measure its acceleration a. What is its mass m? Because $a = A/m$, we can use the discussion in the math relationship box on inverse proportion to write

$$\frac{a_1}{a} = \frac{m}{1 \text{ kg}}$$

or

$$m = 1 \text{ kg} \times \frac{a_1}{a} \tag{3.2}$$

This result tells us how to think about mass: The greater an object's mass, the greater its resistance to being accelerated. If an object is more difficult to accelerate than a 1 kg object (i.e., a is smaller than a_1), then its mass is greater than 1 kg. If the object is easier to accelerate, then its mass is less than 1 kg. Any object that undergoes the *same* acceleration as the standard 1 kg object, using the same force, must have a mass of exactly 1 kg. **Mass, then, is the property of an object that determines how it accelerates in response to an applied force.**

Feel the difference Because of its high sugar content, a can of regular soda has a mass about 4% greater than that of a can of diet soda. If you try to judge which can is more massive by simply holding one in each hand, this small difference is almost impossible to detect. If you *move* the cans up and down, however, the difference becomes subtly but noticeably apparent: People evidently are more sensitive to how the mass of each can resists acceleration.

EXAMPLE 3.1 Finding the mass of an unknown block

When a rubber band is stretched to pull on a 1.0 kg block with a constant force, the acceleration of the block is measured to be 3.0 m/s^2. When a block with an unknown mass is pulled with the same rubber band, using the same force, its acceleration is 5.0 m/s^2. What is the mass of the unknown block?

PREPARE The acceleration a_1 of the 1 kg block is 3.0 m/s^2, and the acceleration a of the unknown block is 5.0 m/s^2.

SOLVE From the definition of mass in terms of acceleration, we find that

$$m = 1.0 \text{ kg} \times \frac{a_1}{a} = 1.0 \text{ kg} \times \frac{3.0 \text{ m/s}^2}{5.0 \text{ m/s}^2} = 0.60 \text{ kg}$$

ASSESS With the same force applied, the unknown block had a *larger* acceleration than the 1.0 kg block. It makes sense, then, that its mass—its resistance to acceleration—is *less* than 1.0 kg.

STOP TO THINK 3.3   Two rubber bands stretched to the standard length cause an object to accelerate at 2 m/s^2. Suppose another object with twice the mass is pulled by four rubber bands stretched to the standard length. The acceleration of this second object is

A. 1 m/s^2.　　B. 2 m/s^2.　　C. 4 m/s^2.　　D. 8 m/s^2.　　E. 16 m/s^2.

3.6 Newton's Second Law

We can now summarize the results of our experiments. We've seen that **a force causes an object to accelerate. The acceleration a is directly proportional to the force F and inversely proportional to the mass m.** We can express both these relationships in equation form as

$$a = \frac{F}{m} \tag{3.3}$$

Note that if we double the size of the force F, the acceleration a will double, as we found experimentally. And if we triple the mass m, the acceleration will be only one-third as great, again in accord with experiment.

Equation 3.3 tells us the magnitude of an object's acceleration in terms of its mass and the force applied. But our experiments also had another important finding: The *direction* of the acceleration was the same as the direction of the force. We can express this fact by writing Equation 3.3 in *vector* form as

$$\vec{a} = \frac{\vec{F}}{m} \tag{3.4}$$

Recall that any vector (such as $\vec{F}$), when multiplied by an ordinary number (such as $1/m$), gives a vector (such as $\vec{a}$) that points in the *same* direction as the original vector $\vec{F}$. So the relationship between force and acceleration expressed by Equation 3.4 indicates that $\vec{a}$ and $\vec{F}$ point in the same direction.

Finally, our experiment was limited to looking at an object's response to a *single* applied force. Realistically, an object is likely to be subjected to several distinct forces $\vec{F}_1$, $\vec{F}_2$, $\vec{F}_3$, . . . that may point in different directions. What happens then? Experiments show that the acceleration of the object is determined by the *net force* acting on it. Recall from Figure 3.4 and Equation 3.1 that the net force is the *vector sum* of all forces acting on the object. So if several forces are acting, we use the *net* force in Equation 3.4.

Newton was the first to recognize these connections between force and motion. This relationship is known today as Newton's second law.

> **Newton's second law** An object of mass m subjected to forces $\vec{F}_1$, $\vec{F}_2$, $\vec{F}_3$, . . . will undergo an acceleration $\vec{a}$ given by
>
> $$\vec{a} = \frac{\vec{F}_{\text{net}}}{m} \tag{3.5}$$
>
> INVERSE
> p. 118
>
> where the net force $\vec{F}_{\text{net}} = \vec{F}_1 + \vec{F}_2 + \vec{F}_3 + \cdots$ is the vector sum of all forces acting on the object. **The acceleration vector $\vec{a}$ points in the same direction as the net force vector $\vec{F}_{\text{net}}$.**

We'll use Newton's second law in Chapter 4 to solve many kinds of motion problems; for the moment, however, the critical idea is that an object accelerates in the direction of the net force acting on it.

The significance of Newton's second law cannot be overstated. There was no reason to suspect that there should be any simple relationship between force and acceleration. Yet a simple but exceedingly powerful equation relates the two. Newton's work, preceded to some extent by Galileo's, marks the beginning of a highly successful period in the history of science during which it was learned that the behavior of physical objects can often be described and predicted by mathematical relationships. While some relationships are found to apply only in special circumstances, others seem to have universal applicability. Those equations that appear to apply at all times and under all conditions have come to be called "laws of nature." Newton's second law is a law of nature; you will meet others as we go through this book.

We can rewrite Newton's second law in the form

$$\vec{F}_{\text{net}} = m\vec{a} \tag{3.6}$$

which is how you'll see it presented in many textbooks and how, in practice, we'll often use the second law. Equations 3.5 and 3.6 are mathematically equivalent,

An unfair advantage? Race car driver Danica Patrick was the subject of controversial comments by other drivers who thought her small mass of 45 kg gave her an advantage over heavier drivers; the next-lightest driver's mass was 61 kg. Because every driver's car must have the same mass, Patrick's overall racing mass was lower than any other driver's. Because a car's acceleration is inversely proportional to its mass, her car could be expected to have a slightly greater acceleration.

but Equation 3.5 better describes the central idea of Newtonian mechanics: A force applied to an object causes the object to accelerate.

NOTE ▶ When several forces act on an object, be careful not to think that the strongest force "overcomes" the others to determine the motion on its own. Forces are not in competition with each other! It is $\vec{F}_{net}$, the sum of *all* the forces, that determines the acceleration $\vec{a}$. ◀

CONCEPTUAL EXAMPLE 3.4 Acceleration of a wind-blown basketball

A basketball is released from rest in a stiff breeze directed to the right. In what direction does the ball accelerate?

REASON As shown in Figure 3.24a, two forces are acting on the ball: its weight $\vec{w}$ directed downward, and a wind force $\vec{F}_{wind}$ pushing the ball to the right. Newton's second law tells us that the direction of the acceleration is the same as the direction of the net force $\vec{F}_{net}$. In Figure 3.24b we find $\vec{F}_{net}$ by graphical vector addition of $\vec{w}$ and $\vec{F}_{wind}$. We see that $\vec{F}_{net}$ and therefore $\vec{a}$ point down and to the right.

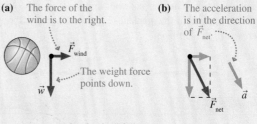

(a) The force of the wind is to the right.

The weight force points down.

(b) The acceleration is in the direction of $\vec{F}_{net}$.

FIGURE 3.24 A basketball falling in a strong breeze.

Units of Force

Because $\vec{F}_{net} = m\vec{a}$, the unit of force must be mass units multiplied by acceleration units. We've previously specified the SI unit of mass as the kilogram. We can now define the basic unit of force as "the force that causes a 1 kg mass to accelerate at 1 m/s²." From Newton's second law, this force is

$$1 \text{ basic unit of force} = (1 \text{ kg}) \times (1 \text{ m/s}^2) = 1\frac{\text{kg} \cdot \text{m}}{\text{s}^2}$$

This basic unit of force is called a *newton:* One **newton** is the force that causes a 1 kg mass to accelerate at 1 m/s². The abbreviation for newton is N. Mathematically, $1 \text{ N} = 1 \text{ kg} \cdot \text{m/s}^2$.

The newton is a *secondary unit,* meaning that it is defined in terms of the *primary units* of kilograms, meters, and seconds. We will introduce other secondary units as needed.

It is important to develop a feeling for what the size of forces should be. Table 3.2 shows some typical forces. As you can see, "typical" forces on "typical" objects are likely to be in the range 0.01–10,000 N. Forces less than 0.01 N are too small to consider unless you are dealing with very small objects. Forces greater than 10,000 N would make sense only if applied to very massive objects.

The unit of force in the English system is the *pound* (abbreviated lb). Although the definition of the pound has varied throughout history, it is now defined in terms of the newton:

$$1 \text{ pound} = 1 \text{ lb} = 4.45 \text{ N}$$

You very likely associate pounds with kilograms rather than with newtons. Everyday language often confuses the ideas of mass and weight, but we're going to need to make a clear distinction between them. We'll have more to say about this in the next chapter.

TABLE 3.2 Approximate magnitude of some typical forces

Force	Approximate magnitude (newtons)
Weight of a U.S. nickel	0.05
Weight of a 1-pound object	5
Weight of a 110-pound person	500
Propulsion force of a car	5,000
Thrust force of a rocket motor	5,000,000

EXAMPLE 3.2 Pulling an airplane

In 2000, a team of 60 British police officers set a world record by pulling a Boeing 747, with a mass of 205,000 kg, a distance of 100 m in 53.3 s. Estimate the force with which each officer pulled on the plane.

PREPARE If we assume that the plane undergoes a constant acceleration, we can use kinematics to find the magnitude of that acceleration. Then we can use Newton's second law to find the force applied to the airplane. Figure 3.25 shows the visual overview of the airplane.

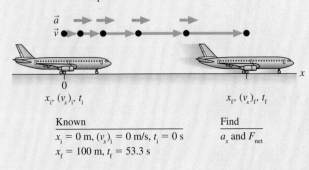

FIGURE 3.25 Visual overview of the airplane accelerating.

SOLVE Because we know the net displacement of the plane, and the time it took to move, we can use the kinematic equation

$$x_f = x_i + (v_x)_i \, \Delta t + \tfrac{1}{2} a_x \, (\Delta t)^2$$

to find the airplane's acceleration a_x. Using the known values $x_i = 0$ m and $(v_x)_i = 0$ m/s, we can solve for the acceleration to get

$$a_x = \frac{2x_f}{(\Delta t)^2} = \frac{2(100 \text{ m})}{(53.3 \text{ s})^2} = 0.0704 \text{ m/s}^2$$

Now we apply Newton's second law. The net force is

$$F_{net} = ma_x = (205,000 \text{ kg})(0.0704 \text{ m/s}^2) = 1.44 \times 10^4 \text{ N}$$

This is the force applied by all 60 men. Each man thus applies about 1/60th of this force, or around 240 N.

ASSESS Converting this force to pounds, we have

$$F = 240 \text{ N} \times \frac{1 \text{ lb}}{4.45 \text{ N}} = 54 \text{ lb}$$

Burly policemen can certainly apply a greater force than this. We have neglected the rolling friction of the plane's tires, which apply a force opposite to the plane's motion. Friction lowers the plane's acceleration, leading to an underestimate of the force applied by the men.

STOP TO THINK 3.4 Three forces act on an object. In which direction does the object accelerate?

$\vec{F}_1$

$\vec{F}_2$ In which direction does the object accelerate?

$\vec{F}_3$

$\vec{a}$ A. $\vec{a}$ B. $\vec{a}$ C. $\vec{a}$ D. $\vec{a}$ E.

3.7 Free-Body Diagrams

Having discussed at length what is and is not a force, and what forces do to an object, we are ready to assemble our knowledge about force and motion into a single diagram called a **free-body diagram.** A free-body diagram represents the object as a particle and shows *all* of the forces acting on the object. Now that we have forces to consider, we expand our visual overview to include force identification and a free-body diagram. Learning how to draw a correct free-body diagram is a very important skill, one that in the next chapter will become a critical part of our strategy for solving motion problems. For now, let's concentrate on the basic skill of constructing a correct free-body diagram.

(MP) **TACTICS BOX 3.3 Drawing a free-body diagram** ✐ Exercises 17–22

❶ **Identify all forces acting on the object.** This step was described in Tactics Box 3.2.
❷ **Draw a coordinate system.** Use the axes defined in your pictorial representation (Tactics Box 2.2). If those axes are tilted, for motion along an incline, then the axes of the free-body diagram should be similarly tilted.
❸ **Represent the object as a dot at the origin of the coordinate axes.** This is the particle model.
❹ **Draw vectors representing each of the identified forces.** This was described in Tactics Box 3.1. Be sure to label each force vector.
❺ **Draw and label the *net force* vector $\vec{F}_{net}$.** Draw this vector beside the diagram, not on the particle. Or, if appropriate, write $\vec{F}_{net} = \vec{0}$. Then check that $\vec{F}_{net}$ points in the same direction as the acceleration vector $\vec{a}$ on your motion diagram.

EXAMPLE 3.3 Forces on an upward-accelerating elevator

An elevator, suspended by a cable, speeds up as it moves upward from the ground floor. Draw a free-body diagram of the elevator.

PREPARE Figure 3.26 illustrates the steps outlined in Tactics Box 3.3.

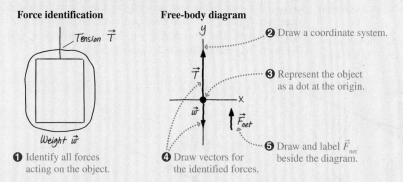

Force identification

Free-body diagram

❶ Identify all forces acting on the object.
❷ Draw a coordinate system.
❸ Represent the object as a dot at the origin.
❹ Draw vectors for the identified forces.
❺ Draw and label $\vec{F}_{net}$ beside the diagram.

FIGURE 3.26 Free-body diagram of an elevator accelerating upward.

ASSESS The coordinate axes, with a vertical *y*-axis, are the ones we would use in a pictorial representation of the motion. The elevator is accelerating upward, so $\vec{F}_{net}$ must point upward. For this to be true, the magnitude of $\vec{T}$ must be larger than the magnitude of $\vec{w}$. The diagram has been drawn accordingly.

EXAMPLE 3.4 Forces on a rocket-propelled ice block

Bobby straps a small model rocket to a block of ice and shoots it across the smooth surface of a frozen lake. Friction is negligible. Draw a visual overview—a motion diagram, force identification diagram, and free-body diagram—of the block of ice.

PREPARE Treat the block of ice as a particle. The visual overview consists of a motion diagram to determine $\vec{a}$, a force

identification picture, and a free-body diagram. The statement of the situation tells us that friction is negligible. We can draw these three pictures using Problem Solving Strategy 1.1 for the motion diagram, Tactics Box 3.2 to identify the forces, and Tactics Box 3.3 to draw the free-body diagrams. These pictures are shown in Figure 3.27 on the next page.

Continued

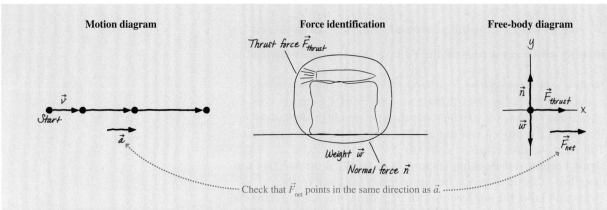

FIGURE 3.27 Visual overview for a block of ice shooting across a frictionless frozen lake.

ASSESS The motion diagram tells us that the acceleration is in the positive x-direction. According to the rules of vector addition, this can be true only if the upward-pointing $\vec{n}$ and the downward-pointing $\vec{w}$ are equal in magnitude and thus cancel each other. The vectors have been drawn accordingly, and this leaves the net force vector pointing toward the right, in agreement with $\vec{a}$ from the motion diagram.

EXAMPLE 3.5 Forces on a towed skier

A tow rope pulls a skier up a snow-covered hill at a constant speed. Draw a full visual overview of the skier.

PREPARE This is Example 3.2 again with the additional information that the skier is moving at constant speed. If we were doing a kinematics problem, the pictorial representation would use a tilted coordinate system with the x-axis parallel to the slope, so we use these same tilted coordinate axes for the free-body diagram. The motion diagram, force identification, and free-body diagram are shown in Figure 3.28.

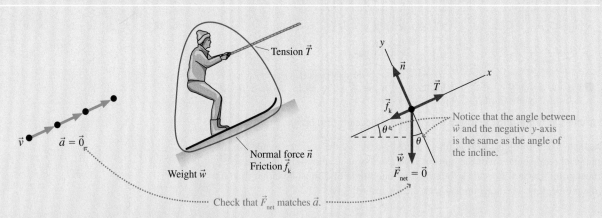

FIGURE 3.28 Visual overview for a skier being towed at a constant speed.

ASSESS We have shown $\vec{T}$ pulling parallel to the slope and $\vec{f}_k$, which opposes the direction of motion, pointing down the slope. The normal force $\vec{n}$ is perpendicular to the surface and thus along the y-axis. Finally, and this is important, the weight $\vec{w}$ is *vertically* downward, *not* along the negative y-axis.

The skier moves in a straight line with constant speed, so $\vec{a} = \vec{0}$. Newton's second law then tells us that $\vec{F}_{net} = m\vec{a} = \vec{0}$. Thus we have drawn the vectors such that the forces add to zero. We'll learn more about how to do this in Chapter 4.

Free-body diagrams will be our major tool for the next several chapters. Careful practice with the workbook exercises and homework in this chapter will pay immediate benefits in the next chapter. Indeed, it is not too much to assert that a problem is half solved, or even more, when you complete the free-body diagram.

STOP TO THINK 3.5   An elevator suspended by a cable is moving upward and slowing to a stop. Which free-body diagram is correct?

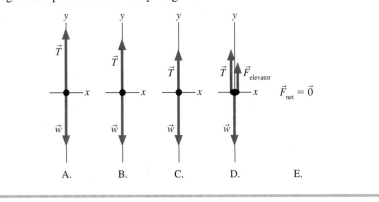

A.   B.   C.   D.   E.

3.8 Newton's Third Law

Thus far, we've focused on the motion of a single particle—which we called the *system*—responding to well-defined forces applied by objects outside the system—that is, from the *environment*. A skier sliding downhill, for instance, is subject to frictional and normal forces from the slope, and the pull of gravity on his body. Once we know these forces, we can use Newton's second law to calculate the acceleration, and hence the overall motion, of the skier.

But motion in the real world often involves two or more objects *interacting* with each other. Consider the two sumo wrestlers in Figure 3.29. The harder one wrestler pushes, the harder the other pushes back. A hammer and a nail, your foot and a soccer ball, and the earth-moon system are other examples of interacting objects.

Newton's second law is not sufficient to explain what happens when two or more objects interact. It does not explain how the force of the hammer on the nail is related to that of the nail on the hammer. In this section we will introduce a new law of physics, Newton's *third* law, that describes how two objects interact with each other.

FIGURE 3.29 The two sumo wrestlers are a system of interacting objects.

Interacting Objects

Think about the hammer and nail in Figure 3.30. The hammer certainly exerts a force on the nail as it drives the nail forward. At the same time, the nail exerts a force on the hammer. If you are not sure that it does, imagine hitting the nail with a glass hammer. It's the force of the nail on the hammer that would cause the glass to shatter.

Indeed, if you stop to think about it, any time that object A pushes or pulls on object B, object B pushes or pulls back on object A. As sumo wrestler A pushes on sumo wrestler B, B pushes back on A. (If A pushed forward without B pushing back, A would fall over in the same way you do if someone suddenly opens a door you're leaning against.) Your chair pushes upward on you (a normal force) while, at the same time, you push down on the chair. These are examples of what we call an *interaction*. An **interaction** is the mutual influence of two objects on each other.

These examples illustrate a key aspect of interactions: The forces involved in an interaction between two objects always occur as a *pair*. To be more specific, if object A exerts a force $\vec{F}_{A\,on\,B}$ on object B, then object B exerts a force $\vec{F}_{B\,on\,A}$ on

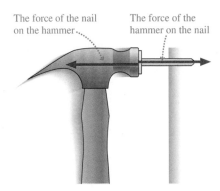

The force of the nail on the hammer...   The force of the hammer on the nail

FIGURE 3.30 The hammer and nail are interacting with each other.

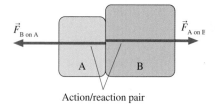

FIGURE 3.31 An action/reaction pair of forces.

object A. This pair of forces, shown in Figure 3.31, is called an **action/reaction pair.** Two objects interact by exerting an action/reaction pair of forces on each other. Notice the very explicit subscripts on the force vectors. The first letter is the *agent*—the source of the force—and the second letter is the *object* on which the force acts. $\vec{F}_{\text{A on B}}$ is thus the force exerted *by* A *on* B. The distinction is important, and this way of labeling forces will be of great help when we discuss how to identify the members of an action/reaction pair.

NOTE ▶ The name "action/reaction pair" is somewhat misleading. The forces occur simultaneously, and we cannot say which is the "action" and which the "reaction." Neither is there any implication about cause and effect; the action does not cause the reaction. **An action/reaction pair of forces exists as a pair, or not at all.** In identifying action/reaction pairs, the labels are the key. Force $\vec{F}_{\text{A on B}}$ is paired with force $\vec{F}_{\text{B on A}}$. ◀

Reasoning with Newton's Third Law

We've discovered that two objects always interact via an action/reaction pair of forces. Newton was the first to recognize how the two members of an action/reaction pair of forces are related to each other. Today we know this as Newton's third law:

> **Newton's third law** Every force occurs as one member of an action/reaction pair of forces.
>
> - The two members of an action/reaction pair act on two *different* objects.
> - The two members of an action/reaction pair point in *opposite* directions, and are *equal in magnitude*.

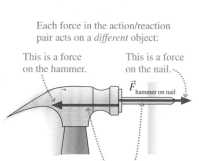

Each force in the action/reaction pair acts on a *different* object:

This is a force on the hammer.

This is a force on the nail.

$\vec{F}_{\text{hammer on nail}}$

The members of the pair point in *opposite directions*, but are of *equal magnitude*.

FIGURE 3.32 Newton's third law.

Newton's third law is often stated as "For every action there is an equal but opposite reaction." While this is a catchy phrase, it lacks the preciseness of our preferred version. In particular, it fails to capture an essential feature of action/reaction pairs—that they each act on a *different* object. This is shown in Figure 3.32, where a hammer hitting a nail exerts a force $\vec{F}_{\text{hammer on nail}}$ on the nail; by the third law, the nail must exert a force $\vec{F}_{\text{nail on hammer}}$ to complete the action/ reaction pair.

Figure 3.32 also illustrates that these two forces point in *opposite directions*. This feature of the third law is also in accord with our experience. If the hammer hits the nail with a force directed to the right, the force of the nail on the hammer is directed to the left; if the force of my chair on me pushes up, the force of me on the chair pushes down.

Finally, Figure 3.32 shows that, according to Newton's third law, the two members of an action/reaction pair have *equal* magnitudes, so that $F_{\text{hammer on nail}} = F_{\text{nail on hammer}}$. This is something new, and it is by no means obvious. Indeed, this statement causes students the most trouble when applying the third law because it seems so counter to our intuition. Consider, for instance, the collision between a bug and the windshield of a truck. The third law tells us that the magnitude of the force of the windshield on the bug is *equal* to that of the bug on the windshield! How can this be, when the bug is so small compared to the truck? The source of puzzlement in problems like this is that Newton's third law equates the size of the *forces* acting on the two objects, not their *accelerations*. The acceleration of each object depends not only on the force applied to it, but also, according to Newton's second law, its mass. The bug and the truck do in fact feel forces of equal strength from the other, but the bug, with its very small mass, undergoes an extreme acceleration from this force while the acceleration of the heavy truck is negligible. It is important to separate the *effects* of the forces (the accelerations) from the causes (the forces themselves). Because two interacting objects can have very different masses, their accelerations can be very different even though the interaction forces are of the same strength.

Identifying Forces for Interacting Objects

In order to understand the motion of a single object subject to external forces, we took the object to be the *system* and everything else to be the *environment*. Now we're interested in the motion of two or more objects that interact with each other, so we'll expand our system to include all these interacting objects. For example, for a truck pushing a car, we would take the car and truck together as the system, while the road and the earth would make up the environment, as shown in Figure 3.33.

With the system chosen in this way, we can make a distinction between two classes of forces, again shown in Figure 3.33. **External forces** are forces on objects in the system that originate from outside the system; that is, they are forces of the environment on the system. For example, the weight forces of the car and truck are external forces because they are the forces of the earth (part of the environment) on the vehicles. **Internal forces,** on the other hand, are forces *between* objects in the system. The force that the truck exerts on the car is an internal force between the two objects in this system.

Newton's third law tells us that *every* force is a member of an action/reaction pair. For an external force—a force of the environment on the system—the other member of the pair is a force of the *system* on the *environment*. But forces on the *environment* have no effect on the motion of objects in the *system*. Thus, for finding the motion of an object in the system, we don't need to identify action/reaction pairs involving external forces.

Finding both members of an action/reaction pair made up of *internal* forces is crucial, however, because both of these forces act on objects *within* the system and thus affect their motion. Only after identifying such pairs can we use Newton's third law, which relates their directions and magnitudes. The following Tactics Box 3.4 shows you how to correctly identify external forces, and the action/reaction pairs of internal forces.

Revenge of the target We normally think of the damage that the force of a bullet inflicts on its target. But according to Newton's third law, the target exerts an equal force on the bullet. The photo shows the damage sustained by bullets fired at 1600, 1800, and 2000 ft/s, after impacting a test target. The appearance of the bullet before firing is shown at the left.

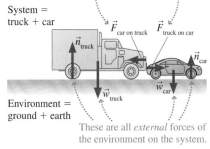

These are *internal* forces between objects in the system. They form an action/reaction pair.

System = truck + car

Environment = ground + earth

These are all *external* forces of the environment on the system.

FIGURE 3.33 External forces and action/reaction pairs.

(MP) **TACTICS BOX 3.4** Identifying forces for interacting objects   🖉 Exercises 23–27

❶ **Identify those objects whose motion you wish to study.** These objects make up the system; the environment is everything else.

❷ **Draw each object separately.** Place them in the correct position relative to each other.

❸ **Identify all forces on the system.** For each object in the system, use the techniques of Tactics Box 3.2 to find the forces acting on that object.

❹ ■ **Identify the action/reaction pairs.** For each force acting on an object, decide if it is of the form $\vec{F}_{A\,on\,B}$, where A and B are *both* objects in the system. If so, it is an internal force and forms an action/reaction pair with $\vec{F}_{B\,on\,A}$. Label the forces in a pair using notation like $\vec{F}_{car\,on\,truck}$ and $\vec{F}_{truck\,on\,car}$.

■ **Identify the external forces.** External forces are forces of the environment on an object in the system. Name each external force with its appropriate symbols such as $\vec{n}$ or $\vec{w}$. When needed, use subscripted labels such as $\vec{w}_1$ and $\vec{w}_2$ to distinguish between similar forces acting on different objects.

❺ **Draw separate free-body diagrams for each object.** For each object, include the forces acting on it found in Step 3. Connect the force vectors of action/reaction pairs with dotted lines.

CONCEPTUAL EXAMPLE 3.5 **Action/reaction pairs in a balancing act**

An acrobat balances a vase on his head. Define the system, then identify external forces acting on the system and action/reaction pairs of internal forces. Draw free-body diagrams for all objects in the system.

REASON We proceed by following the steps in Tactics Box 3.4, as shown in Figure 3.34a. We're interested in the motions of the acrobat and the vase, so they form the system. In accordance with step 2, we've drawn the objects separately with the vase above the acrobat.

Next we identify all the forces acting on both objects, using the methods of Tactics Box 3.2: We draw a closed curve around each object and decide where that object touches objects outside the curve. The vase makes contact only with the acrobat's head. Because the acrobat is part of the system, this is an internal force that we'll label $\vec{F}_{A \, on \, V}$. The only other force acting on the vase is its weight $\vec{w}_V$.

Now let's look at the forces on the acrobat. He is contacted in only two places, the floor and the top of his head where the vase touches. The floor pushes up on his feet with a normal force $\vec{n}$, an external force. The force on his head is more subtle. You might be tempted to say that this force is "the weight of the vase." But recall that *weight* is a force on an object due to the gravitational pull of the earth. Thus the "weight of the vase" is a force *on the vase* due to gravity; that is, it is the force $\vec{w}_V$ that we've already identified. So the force *on the acrobat* cannot be this weight. In fact, the force on his head is simply that due to the vase itself pushing down on him. It is thus an internal force, and we give it the label $\vec{F}_{V \, on \, A}$. Finally, we must include the long-range force of the acrobat's weight $\vec{w}_A$.

We have identified two internal forces, $\vec{F}_{V \, on \, A}$ and $\vec{F}_{A \, on \, V}$. Because every internal force must be one member of an action/reaction pair, these two must form such a pair. We can check this by noting that the subscripts are reverses of each other: A on V is just V on A flipped.

In Figure 3.34b we show the free-body diagram for the acrobat and vase. Because neither acrobat nor vase is accelerating, we know that the net force on each must be zero by Newton's second law. Thus we draw the vector $\vec{F}_{A \, on \, V}$ to have the same length as the vase's weight $\vec{w}_V$, so that these two vectors cancel. Similarly, the three forces acting on the acrobat must sum to zero. Finally, because $\vec{F}_{V \, on \, A}$ and $\vec{F}_{A \, on \, V}$ form an action/reaction pair, their *magnitudes must be the same,* as we've drawn.

Figure 3.34c shows the drawing as you should draw it. Although much simpler than the artist's version, it still contains all the steps of Tactics Box 3.4.

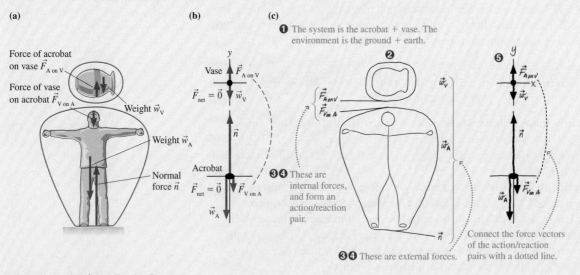

FIGURE 3.34 Applying Tactics Box 3.4.

ASSESS Using Newton's third law is the key to solving problems of interacting objects. The two forces of the action/reaction pair in Figure 3.34 really connect the two free-body diagrams together. If we know the magnitude of one of these forces in one free-body diagram, we automatically know the magnitude of its paired member in the other free-body diagram.

Propulsion

A sprinter accelerates out of the blocks. Because he's accelerating, there must be a force on him in the forward direction. For a system with an internal source of energy, a force that drives the system is a force of **propulsion.** Propulsion is an important feature not only of walking or running but also of the forward motion of cars, jets, and rockets. Propulsion is somewhat counterintuitive, so it is worth a closer look.

If you tried to walk across a frictionless floor, your foot would slip and slide *backward.* In order for you to walk, the floor needs to have friction so that your foot *sticks* to the floor as you straighten your leg, moving your body forward. The friction that prevents slipping is *static* friction. Static friction, you will recall, acts in the direction that prevents slipping, so the static friction force $\vec{f}_{\text{S on P}}$ (for *Surface* on *Person*) has to point in the *forward* direction to prevent your foot from slipping backward. As shown in Figure 3.35a, it is this forward-directed static friction force that propels you forward! The force of your foot on the floor, $\vec{f}_{\text{P on S}}$, is the other half of the action/reaction pair, and it points in the opposite direction as you push backward against the floor.

Similarly, the car in Figure 3.35b uses static friction to propel itself. The car uses its motor to turn the tires, causing the tires to push backward against the road ($\vec{f}_{\text{tire on road}}$). The road surface responds by pushing the car forward ($\vec{f}_{\text{road on tire}}$). This force of the road on the tire can be seen in photos of drag racers, where the forces are very great (Figure 3.36). Again, the forces involved are *static* friction forces. The tire is rolling, but the bottom of the tire, where it contacts the road, is instantaneously at rest. If it weren't, you would leave one giant skid mark as you drove and would burn off the tread within a few miles.

Rocket motors are somewhat different because they are not pushing *against* anything external. That's why rocket propulsion works in the vacuum of space. Instead, the rocket engine pushes hot, expanding gases out of the back of the rocket, as shown in Figure 3.37. In response, the exhaust gases push the rocket forward with the force we've called *thrust.*

STOP TO THINK 3.6 A small car is pushing a larger truck that has a dead battery. The mass of the truck is larger than the mass of the car. Which of the following statements is true?

A. The car exerts a force on the truck, but the truck doesn't exert a force on the car.
B. The car exerts a larger force on the truck than the truck exerts on the car.
C. The car exerts the same amount of force on the truck as the truck exerts on the car.
D. The truck exerts a larger force on the car than the car exerts on the truck.
E. The truck exerts a force on the car, but the car doesn't exert a force on the truck.

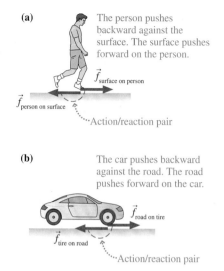

(a) The person pushes backward against the surface. The surface pushes forward on the person.

$\vec{f}_{\text{surface on person}}$

$\vec{f}_{\text{person on surface}}$

Action/reaction pair

(b) The car pushes backward against the road. The road pushes forward on the car.

$\vec{f}_{\text{road on tire}}$

$\vec{f}_{\text{tire on road}}$

Action/reaction pair

FIGURE 3.35 Examples of propulsion.

$\vec{F}_{\text{road on tire}}$

You can *see* that the force of the road on the tire points forward by the way it twists the rubber of the tire.

FIGURE 3.36 When the driver hits the gas, the force of the track on the tire is so great that the tire deforms.

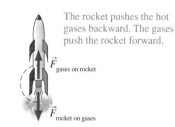

The rocket pushes the hot gases backward. The gases push the rocket forward.

$\vec{F}_{\text{gases on rocket}}$

$\vec{F}_{\text{rocket on gases}}$

FIGURE 3.37 Rocket propulsion.

Now we've assembled all the pieces we need in order to start solving problems in dynamics. We have seen what forces are and how to identify them, and we've learned how forces cause objects to accelerate according to Newton's second law. We've also found how Newton's third law governs the interaction forces between two objects. Our goal in the next chapter is to apply Newton's laws to a variety of problems involving straight-line and circular motion.

SUMMARY

The goal of Chapter 3 has been to establish a connection between force and motion.

GENERAL PRINCIPLES

Newton's First Law

Consider an object with no net force acting on it. If it is at rest, it will remain at rest. If it is in motion, then it will continue to move in a straight line at a constant speed.

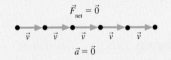

The first law tells us that no "cause" is needed for motion. Uniform motion is the "natural state" of an object.

Newton's Second Law

An object with mass m will undergo acceleration

$$\vec{a} = \frac{1}{m}\vec{F}_{\text{net}}$$

where $\vec{F}_{\text{net}} = \vec{F}_1 + \vec{F}_2 + \vec{F}_3 + \cdots$ is the vector sum of all the individual forces acting on the object.

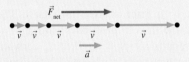

The second law tells us that a net force causes an object to accelerate. This is the connection between force and motion. The acceleration points in the direction of $\vec{F}_{\text{net}}$.

Newton's Third Law

Every force occurs as one member of an **action/reaction** pair of forces. The two members of an action/reaction pair:

- act on two *different* objects.
- point in opposite directions and are equal in magnitude:

$$\vec{F}_{\text{A on B}} = -\vec{F}_{\text{B on A}}$$

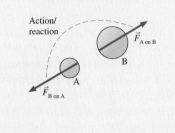

IMPORTANT CONCEPTS

Force is a push or pull on an object.

- Force is a vector, with a magnitude and a direction.
- A force requires an agent.
- A force is either a contact force or a long-range force.

The SI unit of force is the **newton** (N). A 1 N force will cause a 1 kg mass to accelerate at 1 m/s².

Net force is the vector sum of all the forces acting on an object.

The net force determines the acceleration according to Newton's second law.

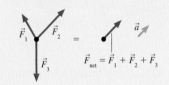

Mass is the property of an object that determines its resistance to acceleration.

If the same force is applied to different objects, their masses in kg are found from

$$m = \frac{a_1}{a} \times 1 \text{ kg}$$

where a is an object's acceleration, and a_1 that of a 1 kg object.

APPLICATIONS

Identifying Forces

Forces are identified by locating the points where the environment touches the system. These are points where contact forces are exerted. In addition, objects with mass feel a long-range weight force.

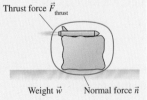

Free-Body Diagrams

A free-body diagram represents the object as a particle at the origin of a coordinate system. Force vectors are drawn with their tails on the particle. The net force vector is drawn beside the diagram.

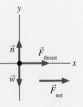

For instructor-assigned homework, go to www.masteringphysics.com

Problem difficulty is labeled as | (straightforward) to ||||| (challenging).

Problems labeled INT integrate significant material from earlier chapters; BIO are of biological or medical interest.

QUESTIONS

Conceptual Questions

1. A hockey puck slides along the surface of the ice. If friction and air resistance are negligible, what force is required to keep the puck moving?
2. If an object is not moving, does that mean that there are no forces acting on it? Explain.
3. An object moves in a straight line at a constant speed. Is it true that there must be no forces of any kind acting on this object? Explain.
4. Write several sentences explaining why you agree or disagree with the statement "Forces cause an object to move."
5. If you know all of the forces acting on a moving object, can you tell in which direction the object is moving? If the answer is Yes, explain how. If the answer is No, give an example.
6. Three arrows are shot horizontally. They have left the bow and are traveling parallel to the ground as shown in Figure Q3.6. Air resistance is negligible. Rank in order, from largest to smallest, the magnitudes of the *horizontal* forces F_1, F_2, and F_3 acting on the arrows. Some may be equal. State your reasoning.

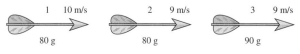

1
10 m/s
80 g
2
9 m/s
80 g
3
9 m/s
90 g

FIGURE Q3.6

7. A carpenter wishes to tighten the heavy head of his hammer onto its light handle. Which method shown in Figure Q3.7 will better tighten the head? Explain.

FIGURE Q3.7

8. BIO Internal injuries in vehicular accidents may be due to what is called the "third collision." The first collision is the vehicle hitting the external object. The second collision is the person hitting something on the inside of the car, such as the dashboard or windshield. This may cause external lacerations. The third collision, possibly the most damaging to the body, is when organs, such as the heart or brain, hit the ribcage, skull, or other confines of the body, bruising the tissues on the leading edge and tearing the organ from its supporting structures on the trailing edge.
   a. Why is there a third collision? In other words, why are the organs still moving after the second collision?
   b. If the vehicle was traveling at 60 mph before the first collision, would the organs be traveling more than, equal to, or less than 60 mph just before the third collision?
9. a. Give an example of the motion of an object in which the frictional force on the object is directed opposite to the motion.
   b. Give an example of the motion of an object in which the frictional force on the object is in the same direction as the motion.
10. Suppose you are an astronaut in deep space, far from any source of gravity. You have two objects that look identical, but one has a large mass and the other a small mass. How can you tell the difference between the two?
11. Newton's second law says that $\vec{F}_{net} = m\vec{a}$. Is $m\vec{a}$ thus a force? If so, what is its origin?
12. Superman can hover in midair if he wishes. Does this mean that he must exert a force on some other object? Explain.
13. A ball weighs 2.0 N when placed on a scale. It is then thrown straight up. What is its weight at the very top of its motion? Explain.
14. A book sits on a table. List all the forces acting on the book.
15. A person sits on a sloped hillside. Is it ever possible to have the static friction force on this person point down the hill? Explain.
16. BIO Walking without slipping requires a static friction force between your feet (or footwear) and the floor. As described in this chapter, the force on your foot as you push off the floor is forward while the force exerted by your foot on the floor is backward. But what about your *other* foot, the one moved during a stride? What is the direction of the force on that foot as it comes in contact with the floor? Explain.
17. Figure 3.35 shows a case in which the force of the road on the car's tire points forward. In other cases, the force points backward. Give an example of such a case.
18. a. A tightrope walker at the circus steps onto the high wire, causing it to sag slightly. Is the tension in the wire less than, greater than, or equal to the performer's weight? Explain. Include a free-body diagram as part of your explanation.
    b. The leading circus magazine advertises a new wire made of a material called DreamRope. The ad says that a DreamRope wire will remain perfectly straight and horizontal, with absolutely no sag, as the performer walks across. Should you order some? Explain.
19. A very smart three-year-old child is given a wagon for her birthday. She refuses to use it. "After all," she says, "Newton's third law says that no matter how hard I pull, the wagon will exert an equal but opposite force on me. So I will never be able to get it to move forward." What would you say to her in reply?
20. Will hanging a magnet in front of an iron cart, as shown in Figure Q3.20, make it go? Explain why or why not.

N
S

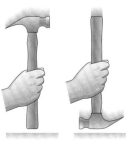

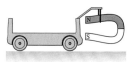

FIGURE Q3.20

Multiple-Choice Questions

21. ‖   Figure Q3.21 shows the view looking down onto a frictionless sheet of ice. A puck, tied with a string to point P, slides on the surface of the ice in the circular path shown. If the string suddenly snaps when the puck is in the position shown, which path best represents the puck's subsequent motion?

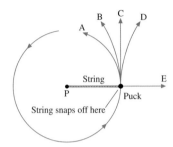

FIGURE Q3.21

22. ‖   A block has acceleration *a* when pulled by a string. If two identical blocks are glued together and pulled with twice the original force, their acceleration will be
    A. $(1/4)a$ B. $(1/2)a$ C. a D. $2a$ E. $4a$

23. ‖   A person gives a box a shove so that it slides up a ramp, then reverses its motion and slides down. The direction of the force of friction is
    A. Always down the ramp.
    B. Up the ramp and then down the ramp.
    C. Always down the ramp.
    D. Down the ramp and then up the ramp.

24. ‖   Tennis balls experience a large drag force. A tennis ball is hit so that it goes straight up and then comes back down. The direction of the drag force is
    A. Always up.   B. Up and then down.
    C. Always down.   D. Down and then up.

25. ‖   Rachel is pushing a box across the floor while Jon, at the same time, is hoping to stop the box by pushing in the opposite direction. There is friction between the box and floor. If the box is moving at constant speed, then the magnitude of Rachel's pushing force is
    A. Greater than the magnitude of Jon's force.
    B. Equal to the magnitude of Jon's force.
    C. Less than the magnitude of Jon's force.
    D. The problem can't be answered without knowing how large the friction force is.

26. ‖   A person is pushing horizontally on a box with a constant force, causing it to slide across the floor with a constant speed. If the person suddenly stops pushing on the box, the box will
    A. Immediately come to a stop.
    B. Continue moving at a constant speed for a while, then gradually slow down to a stop.
    C. Immediately change to a slower but constant speed.
    D. Immediately begin slowing down and eventually stop.

27. ‖‖   Figure Q3.27 shows block A sitting on top of block B. A constant force $\vec{F}$ is exerted on block B, causing block B to accelerate to the right. Block A rides on block B without slipping. Which statement is true?
    A. Block B exerts a friction force on block A, directed to the left.
    B. Block B exerts a friction force on block A, directed to the right.
    C. Block B does not exert a friction force on block A.

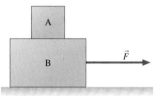

FIGURE Q3.27

28. ‖   Dave pushes his four-year-old son Thomas across the snow on a sled. As Dave pushes, Thomas speeds up. Which statement is true?
    A. The force of Dave on Thomas is larger than the force of Thomas on Dave.
    B. The force of Thomas on Dave is larger than the force of Dave on Thomas.
    C. Both forces have the same magnitude.
    D. It depends on how hard Dave pushes on Thomas.

29. ‖   A truck hits a small car. During this collision,
    A. The truck exerts a larger force on the car than the car on the truck.
    B. The car exerts a larger force on the truck than the truck on the car.
    C. The force of the truck on the car and of the car on the truck have the same magnitude.
    D. The net force is zero.

PROBLEMS

Section 3.1 What Causes Motion?

1. ‖   Whiplash injuries during an automobile accident are
BIO   caused by the inertia of the head. If someone is wearing a seatbelt, her body will tend to move with the car seat. However, her head is free to move until the neck restrains it, causing damage to the neck. Brain damage can also occur.
    Figure P3.1 shows two sequences of head and neck motion for a passenger in an auto accident. One corresponds to a head-on collision, the other to a rear-end collision. Which is which? Explain.

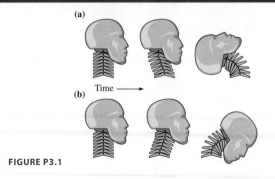

FIGURE P3.1

2. | An automobile has a head-on collision. A passenger in the
BIO car experiences a compression injury to the brain. Is this
injury most likely to be in the front or rear portion of the
brain? Explain.

3. | Passengers in the back seat of an automobile should wear
seatbelts, not only for their own protection, but also for the
protection of the people in the front seats of the car. Explain.

Section 3.2 Force

Problems 4 through 6 show two forces acting on an object at rest.
Redraw the diagram, then add a third force that will allow the
object to remain at rest. Label the new force $\vec{F}_3$.

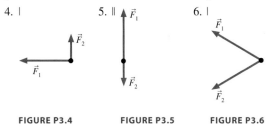

4.		5. ‖	6.	
FIGURE P3.4	**FIGURE P3.5**	**FIGURE P3.6**

Section 3.3 A Short Catalog of Forces

Section 3.4 Identifying Forces

7. ‖ A mountain climber is hanging from a rope in the middle
of a crevasse. The rope is vertical. Identify the forces on the
mountain climber.

8. | A circus clown hangs from one end of a large spring. The
other end is anchored to the ceiling. Identify the forces on the
clown.

9. | A baseball player is sliding into second base. Identify the
forces on the baseball player.

10. ‖ A jet plane is speeding down the runway during takeoff.
Air resistance is not negligible. Identify the forces on the jet.

11. | A skier is sliding down a 15° slope. Friction is not negligi-
ble. Identify the forces on the skier.

12. | A tennis ball is flying horizontally across the net. Air resis-
tance is not negligible. Identify the forces on the ball.

Section 3.5 What Do Forces Do?

13. ‖‖ Figure P3.13 shows an acceleration-versus-force graph for
three objects pulled by rubber bands. The mass of object 2 is
0.20 kg. What are the masses of objects 1 and 3? Explain your
reasoning.

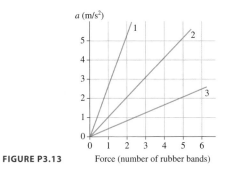

FIGURE P3.13   Force (number of rubber bands)

14. | A constant force applied to object A causes it to accelerate
at 5 m/s². The same force applied to object B causes an accel-

eration of 3 m/s². Applied to object C, it causes an acceleration of 8 m/s².
a. Which object has the largest mass?
b. Which object has the smallest mass?
c. What is the ratio of mass A to mass B (m_A/m_B)?

15. | Two rubber bands pulling on an object cause it to acceler-
ate at 1.2 m/s².
a. What will be the object's acceleration if it is pulled by four
rubber bands?
b. What will be the acceleration of two of these objects glued
together if they are pulled by two rubber bands?

16. | A constant force is applied to an object, causing the object
to accelerate at 10 m/s². What will the acceleration be if
a. The force is halved?
b. The object's mass is halved?
c. The force and the object's mass are both halved?
d. The force is halved and the object's mass is doubled?

17. | A constant force is applied to an object, causing the object
to accelerate at 8.0 m/s². What will the acceleration be if
a. The force is doubled?
b. The object's mass is doubled?
c. The force and the object's mass are both doubled?
d. The force is doubled and the object's mass is halved?

18. ‖‖ A man pulling an empty wagon causes it to accelerate at
1.4 m/s². What will the acceleration be if he pulls with the
same force when the wagon contains a child whose mass is
three times that of the wagon?

19. | A car has a maximum acceleration of 5.0 m/s². What will
the maximum acceleration be if the car is towing another car
of the same mass?

Section 3.6 Newton's Second Law

20. | Figure P3.20 shows an acceleration-versus-force graph for
a 500 g object. Redraw this graph and add appropriate acceleration values on the vertical scale.

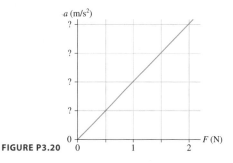

FIGURE P3.20

21. | Figure P3.21 shows an object's acceleration-versus-force
graph. What is the object's mass?

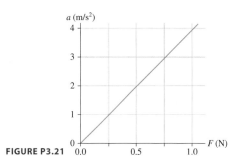

FIGURE P3.21

22. | Two children fight over a 200 g stuffed bear. The 25 kg boy pulls to the right with a 15 N force and the 20 kg girl pulls to the left with a 17 N force. Ignore all other forces on the bear (such as its weight).
   a. At this instant, can you say what the velocity of the bear is? If so, what are the magnitude and direction of the velocity?
   b. At this instant, can you say what the acceleration of the bear is? If so, what are the magnitude and direction of the acceleration?

23. | Based on the information in Table 3.2, estimate in newtons
   a. The weight of a laptop computer.
   b. The propulsion force of a bicycle.
   c. The propulsion force of a sprinter.

24. || Very small forces can have tremendous effects on the motion of very small objects. Consider a single electron, with a mass of 9.1×10^{-31} kg, subject to a single force equal to the weight of a penny, 2.5×10^{-2} N. What is the acceleration of the electron?

25. || The motion of a very massive object is hardly affected by what would seem to be a substantial force. Consider a supertanker, with a mass of 3.0×10^8 kg. If it is pushed by a rocket motor (see Table 3.2) and is subject to no other forces, what will be the magnitude of its acceleration?

Section 3.7 Free-Body Diagrams

Problems 26 through 28 show a free-body diagram. For each, (a) Redraw the free-body diagram and (b) Write a short description of a real object for which this is the correct free-body diagram. Use Examples 3.3, 3.4, and 3.5 as models of what a description should be like.

26. |

FIGURE P3.26

27. |

FIGURE P3.27

28. |

FIGURE P3.28

Problems 29 through 35 describe a situation. For each, identify all forces acting on the object and draw a free-body diagram of the object.

29. | Your car is sitting in the parking lot.
30. | Your car is accelerating from a stop.
31. || Your car is slowing to a stop from a high speed.
32. | An ice hockey puck glides across frictionless ice.
33. | An elevator, hanging from a cable, descends at steady speed.
34. | Your physics textbook is sliding across the table.
35. || You hold a picture motionless against a wall by pressing on it, as shown in Figure P3.35.

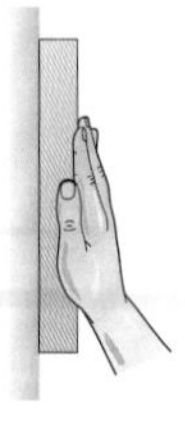

FIGURE P3.35

Section 3.8 Newton's Third Law

36. || A weight lifter stands up from a squatting position while holding a heavy barbell across his shoulders. Identify all the third-law pairs of forces, then draw free-body diagrams for the weight lifter and the barbell. Use dotted lines to connect the members of all action/reaction pairs.

37. || A softball player is throwing the ball. Her arm has come forward to where it is beside her head, but she hasn't yet released the ball. Identify all the third-law pairs of forces, then draw free-body diagrams for the ballplayer and the ball. Use dotted lines to connect the members of all action/reaction pairs.

38. | A soccer ball and a bowling ball roll across a hard floor and collide head on. Identify all the third-law pairs of forces at the moment of the collision, then draw free-body diagrams for each ball. Use dotted lines to connect the members of all action/reaction pairs. Friction is negligible.

General Problems

39. | Redraw the motion dia-
   INT gram shown in Figure P3.39, then draw a vector beside it to show the direction of the net force acting on the object. Explain your reasoning.

40. | Redraw the motion dia-
   INT gram shown in Figure P3.40, then draw a vector beside it to show the direction of the net force acting on the object. Explain your reasoning.

41. | Redraw the motion dia-
   INT gram shown in Figure P3.41, then draw a vector beside it to show the direction of the net force acting on the object. Explain your reasoning.

FIGURE P3.39   **FIGURE P3.40**

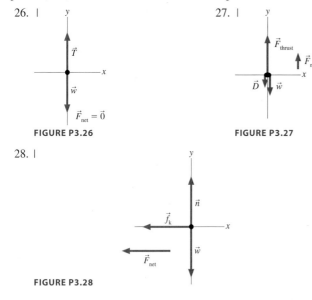

FIGURE P3.41   **FIGURE P3.42**

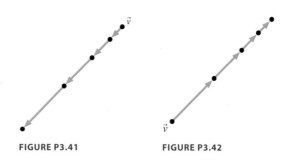

42. || Redraw the motion diagram shown in Figure P3.42, then
   INT draw a vector beside it to show the direction of the net force acting on the object. Explain your reasoning.

Problems 43 through 49 show a free-body diagram. For each:
a. Redraw the diagram.
b. Identify the direction of the acceleration vector $\vec{a}$ and show it as a vector next to your diagram. Or, if appropriate, write $\vec{a} = \vec{0}$.
c. If possible, identify the direction of the velocity vector $\vec{v}$ and show it as a labeled vector.
d. Write a short description of a real object for which this is the correct free-body diagram. Use Examples 3.3, 3.4, and 3.5 as models of what a description should be like.

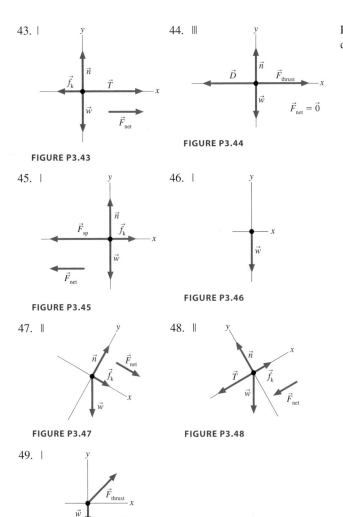

43. |

FIGURE P3.43

44. |||

FIGURE P3.44

45. |

FIGURE P3.45

46. |

FIGURE P3.46

47. ||

FIGURE P3.47

48. ||

FIGURE P3.48

49. |

FIGURE P3.49

50. ‖ A student draws the flawed free-body diagram shown in Figure P3.50 to represent the forces acting on a car traveling at constant speed on a level road. Identify the errors in the diagram, then draw a correct free-body diagram for this situation.

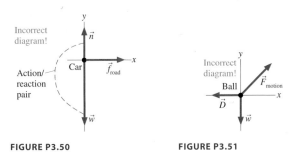

FIGURE P3.50   **FIGURE P3.51**

51. ‖ A student draws the flawed free-body diagram shown in Figure P3.51 to represent the forces acting on a golf ball that is traveling upward and to the right a very short time after being hit off the tee. Air resistance is assumed to be relevant. Identify the errors in the diagram, then draw a correct free-body diagram for this situation.

Problems 52 through 63 describe a situation. For each, draw a motion diagram, a force identification diagram, and a free-body diagram.

52. ‖ An elevator, suspended by a single cable, has just left the tenth floor and is speeding up as it descends toward the ground floor.

53. | A rocket is being launched straight up. Air resistance is not negligible.

54. | A jet plane is speeding down the runway during takeoff. Air resistance is not negligible.

55. | You've slammed on the brakes and your car is skidding to a stop while going down a 20° hill.

56. ‖‖ A skier is going down a 20° slope. A *horizontal* headwind is blowing in the skier's face. Friction is small, but not zero.

57. | You've just kicked a rock and it is now sliding down the sidewalk.

58. | A Styrofoam ball has just been shot straight up. Air resistance is not negligible.

59. ‖ A spring-loaded gun shoots a plastic ball. The trigger has just been pulled and the ball is starting to move down the barrel. The barrel is horizontal.

60. ‖ A person on a bridge throws a rock straight down toward the water. The rock has just been released.

61. ‖ A gymnast has just landed on a trampoline. She's still moving downward as the trampoline stretches.

62. ‖ A heavy box is in the back of a truck. The truck is accelerating to the right. Apply your analysis to the box.

63. ‖ A bag of groceries is on the back seat of your car as you stop for a stop light. The bag does not slide. Apply your analysis to the bag.

64. ‖ A rubber ball bounces. We'd like to understand *how* the ball bounces.

   a. A rubber ball has been dropped and is bouncing off the floor. Draw a motion diagram of the ball during the brief time interval that it is in contact with the floor. Show 4 or 5 frames as the ball compresses, then another 4 or 5 frames as it expands. What is the direction of $\vec{a}$ during each of these parts of the motion?

   b. Draw a picture of the ball in contact with the floor and identify all forces acting on the ball.

   c. Draw a free-body diagram of the ball during its contact with the ground. Is there a net force acting on the ball? If so, in which direction?

   d. During contact, is the force of the ground on the ball larger, smaller, or equal to the weight of the ball? Use your answers to parts a–c to explain your reasoning.

65. ‖ If a car stops suddenly, you feel "thrown forward." We'd like to understand what happens to the passengers as a car stops. Imagine yourself sitting on a *very* slippery bench inside a car. This bench has no friction, no seat back, and there's nothing for you to hold on to.

   a. Draw a picture and identify all of the forces acting on you as the car travels in a straight line at a perfectly steady speed on level ground.

   b. Draw your free-body diagram. Is there a net force on you? If so, in which direction?

   c. Repeat parts a and b with the car slowing down.

   d. Describe what happens to you as the car slows down.

   e. Use Newton's laws to explain why you seem to be "thrown forward" as the car stops. Is there really a force pushing you forward?

66. ▥ The fastest pitched baseball was clocked at 46 m/s. If the
BIO pitcher exerted his force (assumed to be horizontal and constant)
over a distance of 1.0 m, and a baseball has a mass of 145 g,
a. Draw a free-body diagram of the ball during the pitch.
b. What force did the pitcher exert on the ball during this
record-setting pitch?
c. Estimate the force in (b) as a fraction of the pitcher's
weight.

67. ▎ The froghopper, champion leaper of the insect world, can
BIO jump straight up at 4.0 m/s. The jump itself lasts a mere
1.0 ms before the insect is clear of the ground.
a. Draw a free-body diagram of this mighty leaper while the
jump is taking place.
b. While the jump is taking place, is the force that the ground
exerts on the froghopper greater than, less than, or equal to
the insect's weight? Explain.

68. ▥ A beach ball is thrown straight up, and some time later it
lands on the sand. Is the magnitude of the net force on the ball
greatest when it is going up or when it is on the way down? Or
is it the same in both cases? Explain. Air resistance should not
be neglected for a large, light object.

Passage Problems

A Simple Solution for a Stuck Car

If your car is stuck in the mud and you don't have a winch to pull
it out, you can use a piece of rope and a tree to do the trick. First,
you tie one end of the rope to your car and the other to a tree, then
pull as hard as you can on the middle of the rope, as shown in
Figure P3.69a. This technique applies a force to the car much larger
than the force that you can apply directly. To see why the car experiences such a large force, look at the forces acting on the center
point of the rope, as shown in Figure 3.69b. The sum of the forces
is zero, thus the tension is much greater than the force you apply. It
is this tension force that acts on the car and, with luck, pulls it free.

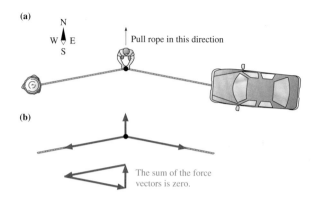

FIGURE P3.69

69. ▎ The sum of the three forces acting on the center point of
the rope is assumed to be zero because
A. This point has a very small mass.
B. Tension forces in a rope always cancel.
C. This point is not accelerating.
D. The angle of deflection is very small.

70. ▎ When you are pulling on the rope as shown, what is the
approximate direction of the tension force on the tree?
A. North   B. South   C. East   D. West

71. ▎ Assume that you are pulling on the rope but the car is not
moving. What is the approximate direction of the force of the
mud on the car?
A. North   B. South   C. East   D. West

72. ▎ Suppose your efforts work, and the car begins to move for-
ward out of the mud. As it does so, the force of the car on the
rope is
A. Zero.
B. Less than the force of the rope on the car.
C. Equal to the force of the rope on the car.
D. Greater than the force of the rope on the car.

STOP TO THINK ANSWERS

Stop to Think 3.1: C.

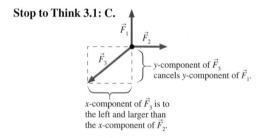

Stop to Think 3.2: A, B, and D. Friction and the normal force are
the only contact forces. Nothing is touching the rock to provide a
"force of the kick." We've agreed to ignore air resistance unless a
problem specifically calls for it.

Stop to Think 3.3: B. Acceleration is proportional to force, so doubling the number of rubber bands doubles the acceleration of the
original object from 2 m/s^2 to 4 m/s^2. But acceleration is also
inversely proportional to mass. Doubling the mass cuts the acceleration in half, back to 2 m/s^2.

Stop to Think 3.4: D.

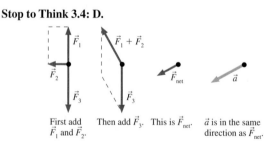

Stop to Think 3.5: C. The acceleration vector points downward as
the elevator slows. $\vec{F}_{net}$ points in the same direction as $\vec{a}$, so $\vec{F}_{net}$
also points down. This will be true if the tension is less than the
weight: $T < w$.

Stop to Think 3.6: C. Newton's third law says that the force of A
on B is *equal* and opposite to the force of B on A. This is always
true. The mass of the objects isn't relevant.

4 APPLYING NEWTON'S LAWS

Before his parachute opens, why does this skydiver fall at a constant speed? And why does he suddenly slow down when his parachute opens?

Looking Ahead ▶▶

The goal of Chapter 4 is to learn how to solve problems about motion in a straight line. In this chapter you will learn to:

▶ Use Newton's first law to solve problems of static and dynamic equilibrium.
▶ Use Newton's second law to solve dynamics problems.
▶ Understand how mass, weight, and apparent weight differ.
▶ Use simple models of friction and drag.
▶ Use Newton's third law to solve problems involving interacting objects.

Looking Back ◀◀

This chapter pulls together many strands of thought from Chapters 1–4. Please review:

◀ Sections 2.4–2.5 Constant acceleration kinematics, including free fall.
◀ Sections 3.4, 3.7, and 3.8 Identifying forces, drawing free-body diagrams, and identifying action/reaction pairs.

After jumping from the plane, a skydiver accelerates until reaching a *terminal speed* of about 140 mph. But when his parachute is opened, he then slows down to only some 10–20 mph. To understand the skydiver's motion, we need to look closely at the forces exerted on him. We also need to understand how those forces determine his motion.

Chapter 4 introduced Newton's three laws of motion. Now, in Chapter 4, we want to use these laws to solve force and motion problems. As will be the case throughout this textbook, our strategy will be to learn a set of *procedures* that can be applied to a wide variety of problems, not to memorize a set of equations.

This chapter focuses on objects that are at rest or that move in a straight line, such as runners, bicycles, cars, planes, and rockets. Weight, tension, thrust, friction, and drag forces will be essential to our understanding of this motion.

4.1 Equilibrium

The simplest applications of Newton's laws are those for which the net force $\vec{F}_{net}$ on an object is *zero*. According to Newton's first law, an object on which there is no net force moves with constant velocity $(\vec{a} = \vec{0})$. One way an object can have

99

This human tower is in equilibrium because the net force on each man is zero.

$\vec{a} = \vec{0}$ is to be at rest. An object that remains at rest is said to be in **static equilibrium.** A second way for an object to have $\vec{a} = \vec{0}$ is to move in a straight line at a constant speed. Such an object is in **dynamic equilibrium.** The defining property of both these cases of **equilibrium** is that the net force acting on the object is $\vec{F}_{net} = \vec{0}$.

To use Newton's laws, we have to identify all the forces acting on an object and then evaluate $\vec{F}_{net}$. Recall that $\vec{F}_{net}$ is the vector sum

$$\vec{F}_{net} = \vec{F}_1 + \vec{F}_2 + \vec{F}_3 + \cdots$$

where $\vec{F}_1$, $\vec{F}_2$, and so on are the individual forces, such as tension or friction, acting on the object. Vector sums can be evaluated in terms of the x- and y-components of the vectors. That is, the x-component of the net force is $(F_{net})_x = F_{1x} + F_{2x} + F_{3x} + \cdots$ If we restrict ourselves to problems where all the forces are in the xy-plane, then the equilibrium requirement $\vec{F}_{net} = \vec{0}$ is a shorthand way of writing two simultaneous equations:

$$(F_{net})_x = F_{1x} + F_{2x} + F_{3x} + \cdots = 0$$
$$(F_{net})_y = F_{1y} + F_{2y} + F_{3y} + \cdots = 0$$

Recall from your math classes that the Greek letter Σ (sigma) stands for "the sum of." It will be convenient to abbreviate the sum of the x-components of all forces as

$$F_{1x} + F_{2x} + F_{3x} + \cdots = \sum F_x$$

With this notation, the requirement that an object be in equilibrium—Newton's first law—can be written as the two equations

$$\sum F_x = 0 \qquad \text{and} \qquad \sum F_y = 0 \tag{4.1}$$

In equilibrium, the sums of the x- and y-components of the force are zero

Although this may look a bit forbidding, we'll soon see how to use a free-body diagram of the forces to evaluate these sums.

When an object is in equilibrium, we are usually interested in finding the forces that keep it in equilibrium. Newton's first law is the basis for a strategy for solving equilibrium problems.

(MP) PROBLEM-SOLVING
STRATEGY 4.1 **Equilibrium problems**

PREPARE First check that the object is in equilibrium: Does $\vec{a} = \vec{0}$?

■ An object at rest is in static equilibrium.
■ An object moving at a constant velocity is in dynamic equilibrium.

Then identify all forces acting on the object and show them on a free-body diagram. Determine which forces you know and which you need to solve for.

SOLVE An object in equilibrium must satisfy Newton's first law. In component form, the requirement is

$$\sum F_x = 0 \qquad \text{and} \qquad \sum F_y = 0$$

You can find the force components that go into these sums directly from your free-body diagram. From these two equations, solve for the unknown forces in the problem.

ASSESS Check that your result has the correct units, is reasonable, and answers the question.

Static Equilibrium

EXAMPLE 4.1 Forces supporting an orangutan

An orangutan weighing 500 N hangs from a vertical vine. What is the tension in the vine?

PREPARE The orangutan is in static equilibrium, so all the forces acting on it must cancel to give zero net force. Figure 4.1 first identifies the forces acting on the orangutan: the upward force of the tension in the vine and the downward, long-range force of gravity. These forces are then shown on a free-body diagram, where it's noted that equilibrium requires $\vec{F}_{net} = \vec{0}$.

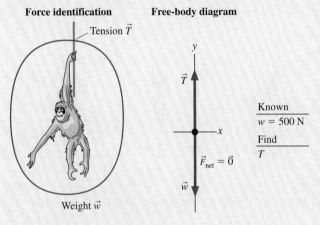

FIGURE 4.1 The forces on an orangutan.

SOLVE Neither force has an x-component, so we need to examine only the y-components of the forces. In this case, the y-component of Newton's first law is

$$\sum F_y = T_y + w_y = 0$$

You might have been tempted to write $T_y - w_y$ because the weight force points down. But remember that T_y and w_y are *components* of vectors, and can thus be positive (for a vector such as $\vec{T}$ that points up) or negative (for a vector such as $\vec{w}$ that points down). The fact that $\vec{w}$ points down is taken into account when we *evaluate* the components; that is, when we write them in terms of the *magnitudes* T and w of the vectors $\vec{T}$ and $\vec{w}$.

Because the tension vector $\vec{T}$ points straight up, in the positive y-direction, its y-component is $T_y = T$. Because the weight vector $\vec{w}$ points straight down, in the negative y-direction, its y-component is $w_y = -w$. This is where the signs enter. With these components, Newton's second law becomes

$$T - w = 0$$

This equation is easily solved for the tension in the vine:

$$T = w = 500 \text{ N}$$

ASSESS It's not surprising that the tension in the vine equals the weight of the orangutan. However, we'll soon see that this is *not* the case if the object is accelerating.

EXAMPLE 4.2 Readying a wrecking ball

A wrecking ball weighing 2500 N hangs from a cable. Prior to swinging, it is pulled back to a 20° angle by a second, horizontal cable. What is the tension in the horizontal cable?

PREPARE The ball hangs in static equilibrium until it is released. In Figure 4.2, we start by identifying all of the forces acting on the ball: a tension force from each cable and the ball's weight. We've used different symbols $\vec{T}_1$ and $\vec{T}_2$ for the two different tension forces. We then construct a free-body diagram for these three forces, noting that $\vec{F}_{net} = \vec{0}$. We're looking for the magnitude T_1 of the tension force $\vec{T}_1$ in the horizontal cable.

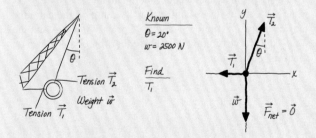

FIGURE 4.2 Visual overview of a wrecking ball just before release.

SOLVE The requirement of equilibrium is $\vec{F}_{net} = \vec{0}$. In component form, we have the two equations

$$\sum F_x = T_{1x} + T_{2x} + w_x = 0$$
$$\sum F_y = T_{1y} + T_{2y} + w_y = 0$$

As always, we *add* the force components together. Now we're ready to write the components of each force vector in terms of the magnitudes and directions of those vectors. With practice you'll learn to read the components directly off the free-body diagram, but to begin it's worthwhile to organize the components into a table.

Force	Name of x-component	Value of x-component	Name of y-component	Value of y-component
$\vec{T}_1$	T_{1x}	$-T_1$	T_{1y}	0
$\vec{T}_2$	T_{2x}	$T_2 \sin\theta$	T_{2y}	$T_2 \cos\theta$
$\vec{w}$	w_x	0	w_y	$-w$

We see from the free-body diagram that $\vec{T}_1$ points along the negative x-axis, so $T_{1x} = -T_1$ and $T_{1y} = 0$. We need to be careful with our trigonometry as we find the components of $\vec{T}_2$.

Continued

Remembering that the side adjacent to the angle is related to the cosine, we see that the vertical (y) component of $\vec{T}_2$ is $T_2\cos\theta$. Similarly, the horizontal (x) component is $T_2\sin\theta$. The weight vector points straight down, so its y-component is $-w$. Notice that negative signs enter as we evaluate the components of the vectors, *not* when we write Newton's first law. This is a critical aspect of solving force and motion problems. With these components, Newton's first law now becomes

$$-T_1 + T_2\sin\theta + 0 = 0 \quad \text{and} \quad 0 + T_2\cos\theta - w = 0$$

We can rewrite these as

$$T_2\sin\theta = T_1 \quad \text{and} \quad T_2\cos\theta = w$$

These are two simultaneous equations with two unknowns: T_1 and T_2. To eliminate T_2 from the two equations, solve the second equation for T_2, giving $T_2 = w/\cos\theta$. Insert this expression for T_2 into the first equation to get

$$T_1 = \frac{w}{\cos\theta}\sin\theta = \frac{\sin\theta}{\cos\theta}w = w\tan\theta = (2500\ \text{N})\tan 20° = 910\ \text{N}$$

where we made use of the fact that $\tan\theta = \sin\theta/\cos\theta$.

ASSESS It seems reasonable that to pull the ball back to this modest angle, a force substantially less than the ball's weight will be required.

CONCEPTUAL EXAMPLE 4.1 Forces in static equilibrium
A rod is free to slide on a frictionless sheet of ice. One end of the rod is lifted by a string. Once the rod comes to rest, which diagram in Figure 4.3 shows the correct angle of the string?

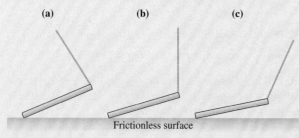

(a)   **(b)**   **(c)**

Frictionless surface

FIGURE 4.3 Which is the correct angle of the string?

REASON If the rod is to hang motionless, it must be in static equilibrium with $\sum F_x = 0$ and $\sum F_y = 0$. Figure 4.4 shows free-body diagrams for the three string orientations. Remember that tension always acts along the direction of the string and that the weight force always points straight down. The ice pushes up

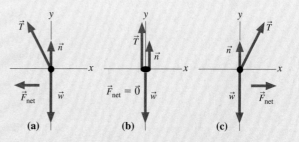

(a)   **(b)**   **(c)**

FIGURE 4.4 Free-body diagrams for three angles of the string.

with a normal force perpendicular to the surface, but frictionless ice cannot exert any horizontal force. If the string is angled, we see that its horizontal component exerts a net force on the rod. Only in case b, where the tension—and the string—are vertical, can the net force be zero.

ASSESS Frictionless surfaces are an idealization, but one that we will often use when friction is very small compared to other forces. This example illustrates that a frictionless surface has no component of force parallel to the surface.

Dynamic Equilibrium

EXAMPLE 4.3 Tension in towing a car
A car with a mass of 1500 kg is being towed at a steady speed by a rope held at a 20° angle. A friction force of 320 N opposes the car's motion. What is the tension in the rope?

PREPARE The car is moving in a straight line at a constant speed, so it is in dynamic equilibrium and must have $\vec{F}_{net} = \vec{0}$. Figure 4.5 shows three contact forces acting on the car—the tension force $\vec{T}$, friction $\vec{f}$, and the normal force $\vec{n}$—and the long-range force of gravity $\vec{w}$. These four forces are shown on the free-body diagram.

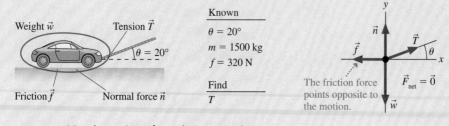

FIGURE 4.5 Visual overview of a car being towed.

SOLVE This is still an equilibrium problem, even though the car is moving, so our problem-solving procedure is unchanged. With four forces, the requirement of equilibrium is

$$\sum F_x = n_x + T_x + f_x + w_x = 0$$

$$\sum F_y = n_y + T_y + f_y + w_y = 0$$

We can again determine the horizontal and vertical components of the forces by "reading" the free-body diagram. The results are shown in the following table.

Force	Name of x-component	Value of x-component	Name of y-component	Value of y-component
$\vec{n}$	n_x	0	n_y	n
$\vec{T}$	T_x	$T\cos\theta$	T_y	$T\sin\theta$
$\vec{f}$	f_x	$-f$	f_y	0
$\vec{w}$	w_x	0	w_y	$-w$

With these components, Newton's first law reads

$$T\cos\theta - f = 0$$

$$T\sin\theta + n - w = 0$$

The first equation can be used to solve for the tension in the rope:

$$T = \frac{f}{\cos\theta} = \frac{320 \text{ N}}{\cos 20°} = 340 \text{ N}$$

to two significant figures. It turned out that we did not need the y-component equation in this problem. We would need it if we wanted to find the normal force $\vec{n}$.

ASSESS Had we pulled the car with a horizontal rope, the tension would need to exactly balance the friction force of 320 N. Because we are pulling at an angle, however, part of the tension in the rope pulls *up* on the car instead of in the forward direction. Thus we need a little more tension in the rope when it's at an angle.

4.2 Dynamics and Newton's Second Law

Newton's second law is the essential link between force and motion. The essence of Newtonian mechanics can be expressed in two steps:

Activ
Physics ONLINE   2.1–2.4

- The forces acting on an object determine its acceleration $\vec{a} = \vec{F}_{net}/m$.
- The object's motion can be found by using $\vec{a}$ in the equations of kinematics.

We want to develop a strategy to solve a variety of problems in mechanics, but first we need to write the second law in terms of its components. To do so, let's first rewrite Newton's second law in the form

$$\vec{F}_{net} = \vec{F}_1 + \vec{F}_2 + \vec{F}_3 + \cdots = m\vec{a}$$

where $\vec{F}_1, \vec{F}_2, \vec{F}_3$, and so on are the forces acting on an object. To write the second law in component form merely requires that we use the x- and y-components of the acceleration. Thus Newton's second law, $\vec{F}_{net} = m\vec{a}$, is

$$\sum F_x = ma_x \quad \text{and} \quad \sum F_y = ma_y \qquad (4.2)$$

Newton's second law in component form

The first equation says that **the component of the acceleration in the x-direction is determined by the sum of the x-components of the forces acting on the object.** A similar statement applies to the y-direction.

There are two basic types of problems in mechanics. In the first, you use information about forces to find an object's acceleration, then use kinematics to determine the object's motion. In the second, you use information about the object's motion to determine its acceleration, then solve for unknown forces. Either way, the two equations of Equation 4.2 are the link between force and motion, and they form the basis of a problem-solving strategy. The primary goal of this chapter is to illustrate the use of this strategy. We'll then follow the strategy with some examples.

(MP)   **PROBLEM-SOLVING**
STRATEGY 4.2 Dynamics problems

PREPARE Sketch a visual overview consisting of

- A list of values that identifies known quantities and what the problem is trying to find.
- A force-identification diagram to help you identify all forces acting on the object.
- A free-body diagram that shows all the forces acting on the object.

If you'll need to use kinematics to find velocities or positions, you'll also need to sketch

- A motion diagram to determine the direction of the acceleration.
- A pictorial representation that establishes a coordinate system, shows important points in the motion, and defines symbols.

It's OK to go back and forth between these steps as you visualize the situation.

SOLVE Write Newton's second law in component form as

$$\sum F_x = ma_x \quad \text{and} \quad \sum F_y = ma_y$$

You can find the components of the forces directly from your free-body diagram. Depending on the problem, either

- Solve for the acceleration, then use kinematics to find velocities and positions, or
- Use kinematics to determine the acceleration, then solve for unknown forces.

ASSESS Check that your result has the correct units, is reasonable, and answers the question.

EXAMPLE 4.4 Putting a golf ball

A golfer putts a 46 g ball with a speed of 3.0 m/s. Friction exerts a 0.020 N retarding force on the ball, slowing it down. Will her putt reach the hole, 10 m away?

PREPARE Figure 4.6 is a visual overview of the problem. We've collected the known information, drawn a sketch, and identified what we want to find. The motion diagram shows that the ball is slowing down as it rolls to the right, so the acceleration vector points to the left. Next, we identify the forces acting on the ball and show them on a free-body diagram. Note that the net force points to the left, as it must because the acceleration points to the left.

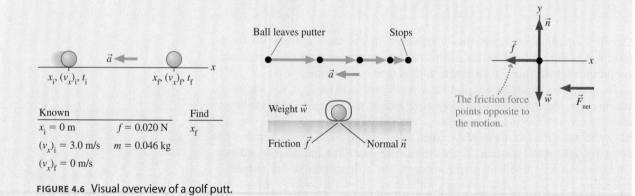

Known
$x_i = 0$ m $f = 0.020$ N
$(v_x)_i = 3.0$ m/s $m = 0.046$ kg
$(v_x)_f = 0$ m/s

Find
x_f

Weight $\vec{w}$

Friction $\vec{f}$ Normal $\vec{n}$

The friction force points opposite to the motion.

FIGURE 4.6 Visual overview of a golf putt.

SOLVE Newton's second law in component form is

$$\sum F_x = n_x + f_x + w_x = 0 - f + 0 = ma_x$$

$$\sum F_y = n_y + f_y + w_y = n + 0 - w = ma_y = 0$$

We've written the equations as sums, as we did with equilibrium problems, then "read" the values of the force components from the free-body diagram. The components are simple enough in this problem that we don't really need to show them in a table. It is particularly important to notice that we set $a_y = 0$ in the second equation. This is because the ball does not move in the y-direction, so it can't have any acceleration in the y-direction. This will be an important step in many problems.

The first equation is $-f = ma_x$, from which we find

$$a_x = -f/m = -(0.020 \text{ N})/(0.046 \text{ kg}) = -0.43 \text{ m/s}^2$$

(Recall from Chapter 3 that $1 \text{ N} = 1 \text{ kg} \cdot \text{m/s}^2$, so the units above work out correctly.) The negative sign shows that the acceleration is directed to the left, as expected.

Now that we know the acceleration, we can use kinematics to find how far the ball will roll before stopping. We don't have any information about the time it takes for the ball to stop, so we'll use the kinematic equation $(v_x)_f^2 = (v_x)_i^2 + 2a_x(x_f - x_i)$. This gives

$$x_f = x_i + \frac{(v_x)_f^2 - (v_x)_i^2}{2a_x} = 0 \text{ m} + \frac{(0 \text{ m/s})^2 - (3.0 \text{ m/s})^2}{2(-0.43 \text{ m/s}^2)} = 10.5 \text{ m}$$

If her aim is true, the ball will just make it into the hole.

ASSESS The key steps in any dynamics problem are to draw a correct free-body diagram and to use the free-body diagram to write Newton's second law in component form. Once you've mastered these two steps, you're well on your way to solving any dynamics problem!

EXAMPLE 4.5 Finding a rocket cruiser's acceleration

A rocket cruiser with a mass of 2200 kg and weighing 5000 N is flying horizontally over the surface of a distant planet. At its present speed, a 3000 N drag force acts on the cruiser. The cruiser's engines can be tilted so as to provide a thrust angled up or down. The pilot turns the thrust up to 14,000 N while pivoting the engines to continue flying horizontally. What is the cruiser's acceleration?

PREPARE Figure 4.7 is a visual overview in which we've listed known information, identified the forces on the cruiser, and drawn a free-body diagram. (Because kinematics is not needed to find the acceleration, we don't need a pictorial diagram.) As discussed in Chapter 3, the thrust force points *opposite* to the direction of the rocket exhaust, which we've shown at angle θ. The thrust must be directed upward to balance the weight force; otherwise the cruiser would fall. To continue flying horizontally requires the net force to be directed forward.

SOLVE Newton's second law in component form is

$$\sum F_x = (F_{\text{thrust}})_x + D_x + w_x = ma_x$$

$$\sum F_y = (F_{\text{thrust}})_y + D_y + w_y = ma_y$$

From the free-body diagram, we see that $(F_{\text{thrust}})_x = F_{\text{thrust}}\cos\theta$, $(F_{\text{thrust}})_y = F_{\text{thrust}}\sin\theta$, $D_x = -D$, $D_y = 0$, $w_x = 0$, and $w_y = -w$. We know that a_y must be zero because the cruiser is to accelerate *horizontally*. Thus the second law becomes

$$F_{\text{thrust}}\cos\theta - D = ma_x$$

$$F_{\text{thrust}}\sin\theta - w = 0$$

The first of these equations contains a_x, the quantity we want to find, but we can't solve for a_x without knowing what θ is. Fortunately, we can use the second equation to find θ, then use this value of θ in the first equation to find a_x.

The second equation gives

$$\sin\theta = w/F_{\text{thrust}} = (5000 \text{ N})/(14,000 \text{ N}) = 0.357$$

$$\theta = \sin^{-1}(0.357) = 20.9°$$

Now we can use this value in the first equation to get

$$a_x = \frac{1}{m}(F_{\text{thrust}}\cos\theta - D)$$

$$= \frac{1}{2200 \text{ kg}}\left[(14,000 \text{ N})\cos(20.9°) - 3000 \text{ N}\right] = 4.6 \text{ m/s}^2$$

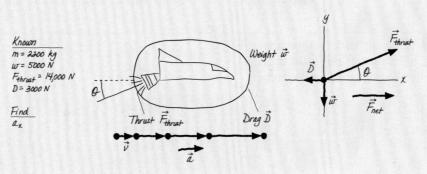

FIGURE 4.7 Visual overview of a rocket cruiser.

Continued

ASSESS An important key to solving this problem was to use the information that the cruiser accelerates only in the horizontal direction. Mathematically, this means that $a_y = 0$. Because the thrust is much greater than the weight, we need only a mod-

est downward component of the thrust to cancel the weight and let the cruiser accelerate horizontally. So our engine tilt seems reasonable.

EXAMPLE 4.6 Towing a car with acceleration

A car with a mass of 1500 kg is being towed by a rope held at a 20° angle. A friction force of 320 N opposes the car's motion. What is the tension in the rope if the car goes from rest to 12 m/s in 10 s?

PREPARE You should recognize that this problem is almost identical to Example 4.3. The difference is that the car is now accelerating, so it is no longer in equilibrium. This means, as shown in Figure 4.8, that the net force is not zero. We've already identified all the forces in Example 4.3.

SOLVE Newton's second law in component form is

$$\sum F_x = n_x + T_x + f_x + w_x = ma_x$$
$$\sum F_y = n_y + T_y + f_y + w_y = ma_y = 0$$

We've again used the fact that $a_y = 0$ for motion that is purely along the x-axis. The components of the forces were worked out

in Example 4.3. Using that information, Newton's second law in component form is

$$T\cos\theta - f = ma_x$$
$$T\sin\theta + n - w = 0$$

Because the car speeds up from rest to 12 m/s in 10 s, we can use kinematics to find the acceleration:

$$a_x = \frac{\Delta v_x}{\Delta t} = \frac{(v_x)_f - (v_x)_i}{t_f - t_i} = \frac{(12 \text{ m/s}) - (0 \text{ m/s})}{(10 \text{ s}) - (0 \text{ s})} = 1.2 \text{ m/s}^2$$

We can now use the first Newton's-law equation above to solve for the tension. We have

$$T = \frac{ma_x + f}{\cos\theta} = \frac{(1500 \text{ kg})(1.2 \text{ m/s}^2) + 320 \text{ N}}{\cos 20°} = 2300 \text{ N}$$

ASSESS The tension is substantially more than the 341 N found in Example 4.3. It takes much more force to accelerate the car than to keep it rolling at constant speed.

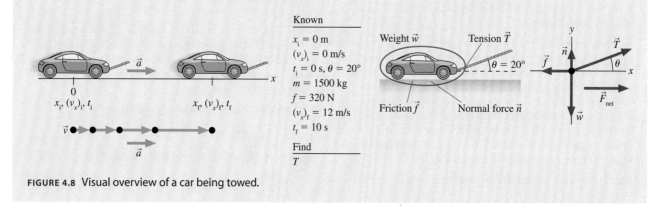

Known

$x_i = 0 \text{ m}$
$(v_x)_i = 0 \text{ m/s}$
$t_i = 0 \text{ s}, \theta = 20°$
$m = 1500 \text{ kg}$
$f = 320 \text{ N}$
$(v_x)_f = 12 \text{ m/s}$
$t_f = 10 \text{ s}$

Find
T

FIGURE 4.8 Visual overview of a car being towed.

These first examples have shown all the details of our problem-solving strategy. Our purpose has been to demonstrate how the strategy is put into practice. Future examples will be briefer, but the basic *procedure* will remain the same.

STOP TO THINK 4.1   A Martian lander is approaching the surface. It is slowing its descent by firing its rocket motor. Which is the correct free-body diagram for the lander?

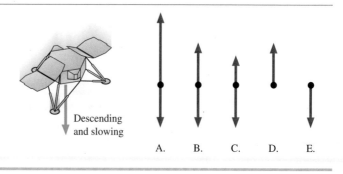

4.3 Mass and Weight

When the doctor asks what you weigh, what does she really mean? We do not make much distinction in our ordinary use of language between the terms *weight* and *mass,* but in physics their distinction is of critical importance.

Mass, you'll recall from Chapter 3, is a quantity that describes an object's inertia, its tendency to resist being accelerated. Loosely speaking, it also describes the amount of matter in an object. Mass, measured in kilograms, is an intrinsic property of an object; it has the same value wherever the object may be and whatever forces might be acting on it.

Weight, on the other hand, is a *force.* Specifically, it is the gravitational force exerted on an object by a planet. Weight is a vector, not a scalar, and the vector's direction is always straight down. Weight is measured in newtons.

Mass and weight are not the same thing, but they are related. We can use Galileo's discovery about free fall to make the connection. Figure 4.9 shows the free-body diagram of an object in free fall. The *only* force acting on this object is its weight $\vec{w}$, the downward pull of gravity. Newton's second law for this object is

$$\vec{F}_{net} = \vec{w} = m\vec{a} \tag{4.3}$$

Recall Galileo's discovery that *any* object in free fall, regardless of its mass, has the same acceleration:

$$\vec{a}_{free\,fall} = (g, \text{downward}) \tag{4.4}$$

where $g = 9.80$ m/s² is the free-fall acceleration at the earth's surface. So a_y in Equation 4.3 is equal to $-g$, and we have $-w = -mg$, or

$$w = mg \tag{4.5}$$

The magnitude of the weight force, which we call simply "the weight," is directly proportional to the mass, with g as the constant of proportionality. Thus, for example, the weight of a 3.6 kg book is $w = (3.6\ \text{kg})(9.8\ \text{m/s}^2) = 35$ N.

> NOTE ▶ Although we derived the relationship between mass and weight for an object in free fall, the weight of an object is *independent* of its state of motion. Equation 4.5 holds for an object at rest on a table, sliding horizontally, or moving in any other way. ◀

Because an object's weight depends on g, and the value of g varies from planet to planet, weight is not a fixed, constant property of an object. The value of g at the surface of the moon is about one-sixth its earthly value, so an object on the moon would have only one-sixth its weight on earth. The object's weight on Jupiter would be larger than its weight on earth. Its mass, however, would be the same. The amount of matter has not changed, only the gravitational force exerted on that matter.

So when the doctor asks what you weigh, she really wants to know your *mass.* That's the amount of matter in your body. You can't really "lose weight" by going to the moon, even though you would weigh less there!

Measuring Mass and Weight

A *pan balance,* shown in Figure 4.10, is a device for measuring *mass.* You may have used a pan balance to "weigh" chemicals in a chemistry lab. An unknown mass is placed in one pan, then known masses are added to the other until the pans balance. Gravity pulls down on both sides, effectively *comparing* the masses, and the unknown mass equals the sum of the known masses that balance it. Although a pan balance requires gravity in order to function, it does not depend on the value of g. Consequently, the pan balance would give the same result on another planet.

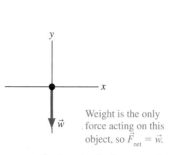

Weight is the only force acting on this object, so $\vec{F}_{net} = \vec{w}$.

FIGURE 4.9 The free-body diagram of an object in free fall.

On the moon, astronaut John Young jumps 2 feet straight up, despite his spacesuit that weighs 370 pounds on earth. On the moon, where $g = 1.6$ m/s², he and his suit together weighed only 90 pounds.

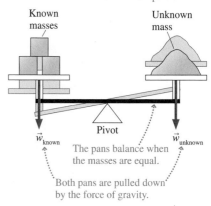

If the unknown mass differs from the known masses, the beam will rotate about the pivot.

Known masses

Unknown mass

Pivot

$\vec{w}_{known}$

$\vec{w}_{unknown}$

The pans balance when the masses are equal.

Both pans are pulled down by the force of gravity.

FIGURE 4.10 A pan balance measures mass.

(a)

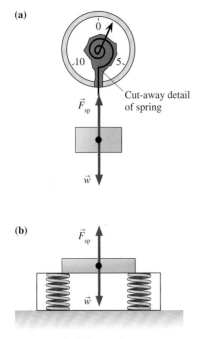

Cut-away detail of spring

$\vec{F}_{sp}$

$\vec{w}$

(b)

$\vec{F}_{sp}$

$\vec{w}$

FIGURE 4.11 A spring scale measures weight.

Spring scales, such as the two shown in Figure 4.11, measure weight, not mass. Hanging an item on the scale in Figure 4.11a, which might be used to weigh items in the grocery store, stretches the spring. The spring in the "bathroom scale" in Figure 4.11b is compressed when you stand on it.

A spring scale can be understood on the basis of Newton's first law. The object being weighed is at rest, in static equilibrium, so the net force on it must be zero. The stretched spring in Figure 4.11a *pulls* up on the object with force $\vec{F}_{sp}$; the compressed spring in Figure 4.11b *pushes* up with force $\vec{F}_{sp}$. But in both cases, in order to have $\vec{F}_{net} = \vec{0}$, the upward spring force must exactly balance the downward weight force:

$$F_{sp} = w = mg \tag{4.6}$$

The *reading* of a spring scale is F_{sp}, the magnitude of the force that the spring is exerting. If the object is in equilibrium, then F_{sp} is exactly equal to the object's weight w. The scale does not "know" the weight of the object. All it can do is to measure how much its spring is stretched or compressed. On a different planet, with a different value for g, the expansion or compression of the spring would be different and the scale's reading would be different.

The unit of force in the English system is the *pound.* We noted in Chapter 3 that the pound is defined as 1 lb = 4.45 N. An object whose weight $w = mg$ is 4.45 N has a mass

$$m = \frac{w}{g} = \frac{4.45 \text{ N}}{9.80 \text{ m/s}^2} = 0.454 \text{ kg} = 454 \text{ g}$$

You may have learned in previous science classes that "1 pound = 454 grams" or, equivalently, that "1 kg = 2.2 lb." Strictly speaking, these well-known "conversion factors" are not true. They are comparing a weight (pounds) to a mass (kilograms). The correct statement would be, "A mass of 1 kg has a weight on *earth* of 2.2 pounds." On another planet, the weight of a 1 kg mass would be something other than 2.2 pounds.

EXAMPLE 4.7 Masses of people

What is the mass, in kilograms, of a 90 pound gymnast, a 160 pound professor, and a 240 pound football player?

SOLVE We must convert their weights into newtons; then we can find their masses from $m = w/g$. We have

$$w_{gymnast} = 90 \text{ lb} \times \frac{4.45 \text{ N}}{1 \text{ lb}} = 400 \text{ N} \qquad m_{gymnast} = \frac{w_{gymnast}}{g} = \frac{400 \text{ N}}{9.80 \text{ m/s}^2} = 41 \text{ kg}$$

$$w_{prof} = 160 \text{ lb} \times \frac{4.45 \text{ N}}{1 \text{ lb}} = 710 \text{ N} \qquad m_{prof} = \frac{w_{prof}}{g} = \frac{710 \text{ N}}{9.80 \text{ m/s}^2} = 72 \text{ kg}$$

$$w_{football} = 240 \text{ lb} \times \frac{4.45 \text{ N}}{1 \text{ lb}} = 1070 \text{ N} \qquad m_{football} = \frac{w_{football}}{g} = \frac{1070 \text{ N}}{9.80 \text{ m/s}^2} = 110 \text{ kg}$$

ASSESS It's worth remembering that a *typical* adult has a mass in the range of 60 to 80 kg.

Apparent Weight

The weight of an object is the force of gravity on that object. You may never have thought about it, but gravity is not a force that you can feel or sense directly. Your *sensation* of weight—how heavy you feel—is due to *contact forces* pressing against you. Surfaces touch you and activate nerve endings in your skin. As you read this, your sensation of weight is due to the normal force exerted on you by

This popular amusement park ride shoots you straight up with an acceleration of $4g$. Your apparent weight is then five times your true weight.

the chair in which you are sitting. When you stand, you feel the contact force of the floor pushing against your feet. If you hang from a rope, your sensation of weight is due to the tension force pulling up on you.

Figure 4.12a shows how a standing man *feels* the normal force of the ground on his feet. The free-body diagram of Figure 4.12b shows that if he is at rest, with $\vec{a} = \vec{0}$, then the normal force pressing against his feet is exactly equal in magnitude to his weight. So the relationship between your weight and the forces you feel would be simple if objects were always at rest, but what happens if $\vec{a} \neq \vec{0}$?

Recall the sensations you feel while being accelerated. You feel "heavy" when an elevator suddenly accelerates upward or when an airplane accelerates for take-off. This sensation vanishes as soon as the elevator or airplane reaches a steady cruising speed. Your stomach seems to rise a little and you feel lighter than normal as the upward-moving elevator brakes to a halt or a roller coaster goes over the top. Your true weight $w = mg$ has not changed during these events, but your *apparent weight* has.

To investigate this, imagine a man weighing himself by standing on a spring scale in an elevator as it accelerates upward. What does the scale read? How does the scale reading correspond to the man's *sensation* of weight?

As Figure 4.13 shows, the only forces acting on the man are the upward spring force of the scale and the downward weight force. This seems to be the same situation as Figure 4.12, but there's one big difference. The man is accelerating; he's not in equilibrium. Thus, according to Newton's second law, there must be a net force acting on the man in the direction of $\vec{a}$.

For the net force $\vec{F}_{net}$ to point upward, the magnitude of the spring force must be *greater* than the magnitude of the weight force. That is, $F_{sp} > w$. This conclusion has major implications. Looking at the free-body diagram in Figure 4.13, we see that the y-component of Newton's second law is

$$\sum F_y = (F_{sp})_y + w_y = F_{sp} - w = ma_y \qquad (4.7)$$

where m is the man's mass.

The scale reading is the value of F_{sp}, the magnitude of the force that the scale exerts on the man. Solving Equation 4.7 for F_{sp} gives

$$F_{sp} = w + ma_y \qquad (4.8)$$

If the elevator is either at rest or moving with constant velocity, then $a_y = 0$ and the man is in equilibrium. In that case, $F_{sp} = w$ and the scale correctly reads his weight. But if $a_y \neq 0$, the scale's reading is *not* the man's true weight.

Let's define an object's **apparent weight** w_{app} as the magnitude of the contact force that supports the object. From Equation 4.8, this is

$$w_{app} = w + ma_y = mg + ma_y = m(g + a_y) \qquad (4.9)$$

If the elevator is accelerating upward, then $a_y = +a$, and Equation 4.9 reads $w_{app} = w + ma$. Thus $w_{app} > w$ and the man *feels* heavier than normal. If the elevator is accelerating downward, the acceleration vector $\vec{a}$ points downward and $a_y = -a$. Thus $w_{app} < w$ and the man feels lighter. Indeed, the scale reads less than his true weight.

An object doesn't have to be on a scale for its apparent weight to differ from its true weight. An object's apparent weight is the magnitude of the contact force supporting it. It makes no difference whether this is the spring force of the scale or simply the normal force of the floor.

The idea of apparent weight has important applications. Astronauts are nearly crushed by their apparent weight during a rocket launch when a is much greater than g. Much of the thrill of amusement park rides, such as roller coasters, comes from rapid changes in your apparent weight.

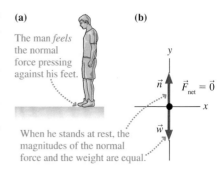

FIGURE 4.12 The sensation of weight for a man at rest.

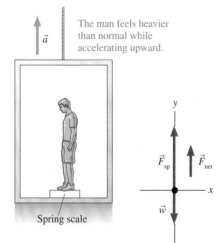

FIGURE 4.13 A man weighing himself in an accelerating elevator.

TRY IT YOURSELF

Physics students can't jump The next time you ride up in an elevator, try jumping in the air just as the elevator starts to rise. You'll feel like you can hardly get off the ground. This is because with $a_y > 0$ your apparent weight is *greater* than your actual weight; for an elevator with a large acceleration it's like trying to jump while carrying an extra 20 pounds. What will happen if you jump as the elevator slows at the top?

EXAMPLE 4.8 Apparent weight in an elevator

Anjay's mass is 70 kg. He's standing on a scale in an elevator. As the elevator stops, the scale reads 750 N. Had the elevator been moving up or down? If the elevator had been moving at 5.0 m/s, how long does it take to stop?

PREPARE The scale reading as he stops is his apparent weight, so w_{app} = 750 N. Because we know his mass m, we can then use Equation 4.9 to find the elevator's acceleration a_y. Then we can use kinematics to find the time it takes to stop the elevator.

SOLVE From Equation 4.9 we have $w_{app} = m(g + a_y)$, so that

$$a_y = \frac{w_{app}}{m} - g = \frac{750 \text{ N}}{70 \text{ kg}} - 9.80 \text{ m/s}^2 = 0.91 \text{ m/s}^2$$

This is a *positive* acceleration. If the elevator is stopping with a positive acceleration it must have been moving *down*, with a negative velocity.

To find the stopping time, we can use the kinematic equation

$$(v_y)_f = (v_y)_i + a_y \, \Delta t$$

to get

$$\Delta t = \frac{(v_y)_f - (v_y)_i}{a_y} = \frac{(0 \text{ m/s}) - (-5.0 \text{ m/s})}{0.91 \text{ m/s}^2} = 5.5 \text{ s}$$

Notice that we used -5.0 m/s as the initial velocity because the elevator was moving down before it stopped.

ASSESS Anjay's true weight is $mg = (70 \text{ kg})(9.8 \text{ m/s}^2) =$ 670 N. Thus his apparent weight is *greater* than his true weight. You have no doubt experienced this sensation in an elevator that is stopping as it reaches the ground floor. If it had stopped while going up, you'd feel *lighter* than your true weight.

Weightlessness

One last issue before leaving this topic: Suppose the elevator cable breaks and the elevator, along with the man and his scale, plunges straight down in free fall! What will the scale read? The acceleration in free fall is $a_y = -g$. When this acceleration is used in Equation 4.9, we find that $w_{app} = 0$! In other words, the man has *no sensation* of weight.

Think about this carefully. Suppose, as the elevator falls, the man inside releases a ball from his hand. In the absence of air resistance, as Galileo discovered, both the man and the ball would fall at the same rate. From the man's perspective, the ball would appear to "float" beside him. Similarly, the scale would float beneath him and not press against his feet. He is what we call *weightless*.

Surprisingly, "weightless" does *not* mean "no weight." An object that is **weightless** has no *apparent* weight. The distinction is significant. The man's weight is still mg, because gravity is still pulling down on him, but he has no *sensation* of weight as he free falls. The term "weightless" is a very poor one, likely to cause confusion because it implies that objects have no weight. As we see, that is not the case.

But isn't this exactly what happens to astronauts orbiting the earth? You've seen films of astronauts and various objects floating inside the Space Shuttle. If an astronaut tries to stand on a scale, it does not exert any force against her feet and reads zero. She is said to be weightless. But if the criterion to be weightless is to be in free fall, and if astronauts orbiting the earth are weightless, does this mean that they are in free fall?

A weightless experience You probably wouldn't want to experience weightlessness in a falling elevator. But objects undergoing projectile motion are in free fall as well. The special plane shown flies in the same parabolic trajectory as would a projectile with no air resistance. Objects inside, such as these passengers, are then moving along a perfect free fall trajectory. Just as for the man in the elevator, they then float with respect to the plane's interior. Such flights can last up to 30 seconds.

STOP TO THINK 4.2 An elevator that has descended from the 50th floor is coming to a halt at the 1st floor. As it does, your apparent weight is

A. More than your true weight.   B. Less than your true weight.
C. Equal to your true weight.   D. Zero.

4.4 Normal Forces

In Chapter 3 we saw that an object at rest on a table is subject to an upward force due to the table. This force is called the *normal force* because it is always directed normal, or perpendicular, to the surface of contact. As we saw, the normal force has its origin in the atomic "springs" that make up the surface. The harder the object bears down on the surface, the more these springs are compressed and the harder they push back. Thus the normal force *adjusts* itself so that the object stays on the surface without penetrating it. This fact is key in solving for the normal force.

EXAMPLE 4.9 Normal force on a pressed book

A 1.2 kg book lies on a table. The book is pressed down from above with a force of 15 N. What is the normal force acting on the book from the table below?

PREPARE The book is not moving and is thus in static equilibrium. We need to identify the forces acting on the book, and prepare a free-body diagram showing these forces. These steps are illustrated in Figure 4.14.

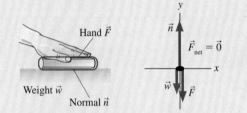

FIGURE 4.14 Finding the normal force of a book pressed from above.

SOLVE Because the book is in static equilibrium, the net force on it must be zero. The only forces acting are in the y-direction, so Newton's first law is

$$\sum F_y = n_y + w_y + F_y = n - w - F = 0$$

We learned in the last section that the weight force is $w = mg$. The weight of the book is thus

$$w = mg = (1.2 \text{ kg})(9.8 \text{ m/s}^2) = 12 \text{ N}$$

With this information, we see that the normal force exerted by the table is

$$n = F + w = 15 \text{ N} + 12 \text{ N} = 27 \text{ N}$$

ASSESS The magnitude of the normal force is *larger* than the weight of the book. From the table's perspective, the extra force from the hand pushes the book further into the atomic springs of the table. These springs then push back harder, giving a larger normal force.

A common situation is that of an object on a ramp or incline. If friction is neglected, there are only two forces acting on the object: gravity and the normal force. However, we need to carefully work out the components of these two forces. Figure 4.15a shows how. Be sure you avoid the two common errors shown in Figure 4.15b.

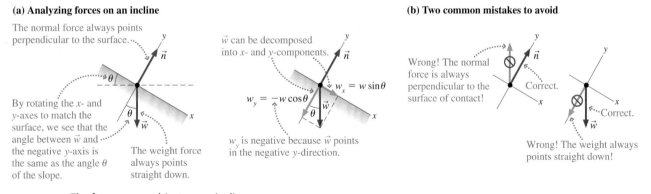

FIGURE 4.15 The forces on an object on an incline.

EXAMPLE 4.10 Acceleration of a downhill skier

A skier slides down a steep slope of 27° on ideal, frictionless snow. What is his acceleration?

PREPARE Figure 4.16 on the next page is a visual overview. We choose a coordinate system tilted so that the x-axis points down

the slope. This greatly simplifies the analysis, because with this choice $a_y = 0$ (the skier does not move in the y-direction at all). The free-body diagram is based on the information in Figure 4.15.

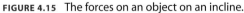

Continued

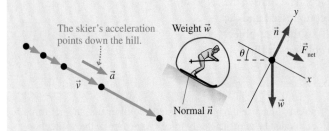

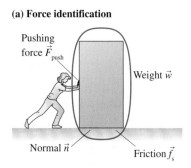

FIGURE 4.16 Visual overview of a downhill skier.

SOLVE We can now use Newton's second law in component form to find the skier's acceleration. We have

$$\sum F_x = w_x + n_x = ma_x$$
$$\sum F_y = w_y + n_y = ma_y$$

Because $\vec{n}$ points directly in the positive y-direction, $n_y = n$ and $n_x = 0$. Figure 4.15a showed the important fact that the angle between $\vec{w}$ and the negative y-axis is the *same* as the slope angle θ. With this information, the components of $\vec{w}$ are $w_x = w\sin\theta = mg\sin\theta$ and $w_y = -w\cos\theta = -mg\cos\theta$, where

we used the fact that $w = mg$. With these components in hand, Newton's second law becomes

$$\sum F_x = w_x + n_x = mg\sin\theta = ma_x$$
$$\sum F_y = w_y + n_y = -mg\cos\theta + n = ma_y = 0$$

In the second equation we used the fact that $a_y = 0$. The m cancels in the first Newton's-law equation, leaving us with

$$a_x = g\sin\theta$$

This is the expression for acceleration on a surface that we presented, without proof, in Chapter 3. Now we've justified our earlier assertion. We can use this to calculate the skier's acceleration:

$$a_x = g\sin\theta = (9.8 \text{ m/s}^2)\sin(27°) = 4.4 \text{ m/s}^2$$

ASSESS The skier's acceleration falls between $a_x = 0$, which it would be on a horizontal surface, and $a_x = 9.80 \text{ m/s}^2$, its value for a vertical drop. This seems reasonable. Notice that the mass cancelled out, so we didn't need to know the skier's mass.

4.5 Friction

In everyday life, friction is everywhere. Friction is absolutely essential for many things we do. Without friction you could not walk, drive, or even sit down (you would slide right off the chair!). It is sometimes useful to think about idealized frictionless situations, but it is equally necessary to understand a real world where friction is present. Although friction is a complicated force, many aspects of friction can be described with a simple model.

Static Friction

(a) Force identification

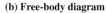

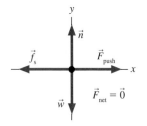

(b) Free-body diagram

FIGURE 4.17 Static friction keeps an object from slipping.

Chapter 3 defined *static friction* $\vec{f}_s$ as the force on an object that keeps it from slipping. Figure 4.17a shows a woman pushing on a box with horizontal force $\vec{F}_{push}$. If the box remains at rest, "stuck" to the floor, it must be because of a static friction force pushing back to the left. The box is in static equilibrium, so, as shown in 4.17b, the static friction must exactly balance the pushing force:

$$f_s = F_{push}$$

To determine the *direction* of $\vec{f}_s$, decide which way the object would move if there were no friction. The static friction force $\vec{f}_s$ then points in the opposite direction, to prevent the motion. Determining the *magnitude* of $\vec{f}_s$ is a bit trickier. Unlike weight, which has the precise and unambiguous magnitude $w = mg$, the magnitude f_s of the static friction force depends on how hard you push. As shown in Figures 4.18a and 4.18b on the next page, the harder the woman pushes, the harder the friction force from the floor pushes back. If she reduces her pushing force, the friction force will automatically be reduced to match. Static friction acts in *response* to an applied force.

But there's clearly a limit to how big f_s can get. If you push hard enough, the object will slip and start to move. In other words, the static friction force has a *maximum* possible magnitude $f_{s\,max}$, as illustrated in Figure 4.18c. Experiments with friction (first done by Leonardo da Vinci) show that $f_{s\,max}$ is proportional to the magnitude of the normal force between the surface and the object. That is,

$$f_{s\,max} = \mu_s n \qquad (4.10)$$

where μ_s is called the **coefficient of static friction.** The coefficient is a number that depends on the materials of which the object and the surface are made. The higher the coefficient of static friction, the greater the "stickiness" between the object and the surface, and the harder it is to make the object slip. Table 4.1 shows some typical values of coefficients of friction. It is to be emphasized that these are only approximate. The exact value of the coefficient depends on the roughness, cleanliness, and dryness of the surfaces.

> NOTE ▶ Equation 4.10 does *not* say $f_s = \mu_s n$. The value of f_s depends on the force or forces that static friction has to balance to keep the object from moving. It can have any value from zero up to, but not exceeding, $\mu_s n$. ◀

It is interesting to note that $f_{s\,max}$ does *not* depend on the contact area between the object and the surface on which it rests.

So our rules for static friction are

- The direction of static friction is such as to oppose motion.
- The magnitude f_s of static friction adjusts itself so that the net force is zero and the object doesn't move.
- The magnitude of static friction cannot exceed the maximum value $f_{s\,max}$ given by Equation 4.10. If the friction force needed to keep the object stationary is larger than $f_{s\,max}$, the object slips and starts to move.

Kinetic Friction

Once the box starts to slide, as in Figure 4.19, the static friction force is replaced by a kinetic (or sliding) friction force $\vec{f}_k$. Kinetic friction is in some ways simpler than static friction: The direction of $\vec{f}_k$ is always opposite to the direction in which an object slides across the surface, and experiments show that kinetic friction, unlike static friction, has a nearly *constant* magnitude, given by

$$f_k = \mu_k n \qquad (4.11)$$

where μ_k is called the **coefficient of kinetic friction.** Equation 4.11 also shows that kinetic friction, like static friction, is proportional to the magnitude of the

(a) Pushing gently: friction pushes back gently.

$\vec{f}_s$ balances $\vec{F}_{push}$ and the box does not move.

(b) Pushing harder: friction pushes back harder.

$\vec{f}_s$ grows as $\vec{F}_{push}$ increases, but they still cancel and the box remains at rest.

(c) Pushing harder still: $\vec{f}_s$ is now pushing back as hard as it can.

Now the magnitude of f_s has reached its maximum value $f_{s\,max}$. If $\vec{F}_{push}$ gets any bigger, the forces will *not* cancel and the box will start to move.

FIGURE 4.18 Static friction acts in *response* to an applied force.

TABLE 4.1 Coefficients of friction

Materials	Static μ_s	Kinetic μ_k	Rolling μ_r
Rubber on concrete	1.00	0.80	0.02
Steel on steel (dry)	0.80	0.60	0.002
Steel on steel (lubricated)	0.10	0.05	
Wood on wood	0.50	0.20	
Wood on snow	0.12	0.06	
Ice on ice	0.10	0.03	

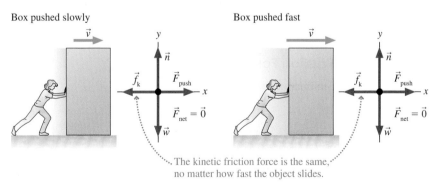

The kinetic friction force is the same, no matter how fast the object slides.

FIGURE 4.19 The kinetic friction force is *opposite* to the direction of motion.

FIGURE 4.20 The bottom of the wheel is stationary.

The wheel flattens where it touches the road.

Soon, this part of the tire will be flattened. To flatten it the road must push *back* on the tire.

FIGURE 4.21 Rolling friction is due to deformation of a wheel.

normal force n. Notice that **the magnitude of the kinetic friction force does not depend on how fast the object is sliding.**

Table 4.1 includes typical values of μ_k. You can see that $\mu_k < \mu_s$, which explains why it is easier to keep a box moving than it was to start it moving.

Rolling Friction

If you slam on the brakes hard enough, your car tires slide against the road surface and leave skid marks. This is kinetic friction, because the tire and the road are *sliding* against each other. A wheel *rolling* on a surface also experiences friction, but not kinetic friction: The portion of the wheel that contacts the surface is stationary with respect to the surface, not sliding. The photo in Figure 4.20 was taken with a stationary camera. Note how the part of the wheel touching the ground is not blurred, indicating that this part of the wheel is not moving with respect to the ground.

Textbooks draw wheels as circles, but no wheel is perfectly round. The weight of the wheel, and of any object supported by the wheel, causes the bottom of the wheel to flatten where it touches the surface, as Figure 4.21 shows. As a wheel rolls forward, the leading part of the tire must become deformed. This requires that the road push *backward* on the tire. In this way the road causes a backward force, even without slipping between the tire and the road.

The force of this *rolling friction* can be calculated in terms of a **coefficient of rolling friction** μ_r:

$$f_r = \mu_r n \tag{4.12}$$

with the *direction* of the force opposing the direction of motion. Thus rolling friction acts very much like kinetic friction, but values of μ_r (see Table 4.1) are much less than values of μ_k. This is why it is easier to roll an object on wheels than to slide it.

STOP TO THINK 4.3 Rank in order, from largest to smallest, the size of the friction forces $\vec{f}_A$ to $\vec{f}_E$ in the 5 different situations (one or more friction forces could be zero). The box and the floor are made of the same materials in all situations.

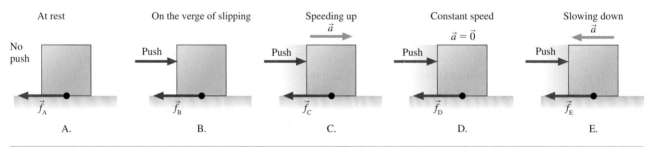

At rest — No push — $\vec{f}_A$ — A.
On the verge of slipping — Push — $\vec{f}_B$ — B.
Speeding up — $\vec{a}$ — Push — $\vec{f}_C$ — C.
Constant speed — $\vec{a} = \vec{0}$ — Push — $\vec{f}_D$ — D.
Slowing down — $\vec{a}$ — Push — $\vec{f}_E$ — E.

Working with Friction Forces

2.5, 2.6 Activ Physics

These ideas can be summarized in a *model* of friction:

> Static: $\vec{f}_s = $ (magnitude $\leq f_{s\,max} = \mu_s n$, direction as necessary to prevent motion)
> Kinetic: $\vec{f}_k = (\mu_k n$, direction opposite the motion)
> Rolling: $\vec{f}_r = (\mu_r n$, direction opposite the motion) (4.13)

LINEAR p. 38

Here "motion" means "motion relative to the surface." The maximum value of static friction $f_{s\,max} = \mu_s n$ occurs at the point where the object slips and begins to move. Note that only one kind of friction force at a time can act on an object.

NOTE ► Equations 4.13 are a "model" of friction, not a "law" of friction. These equations provide a reasonably accurate, but not perfect, description of how friction forces act. For example, we've ignored the surface area of the object because surface area has little effect. Likewise, our model assumes that the kinetic friction force is independent of the object's speed. This is a fairly good, but not perfect, approximation. Equations 4.13 are a simplification of reality that works reasonably well, which is what we mean by a "model." They are not a "law of nature" on a level with Newton's laws. ◄

(MP) TACTICS BOX 4.1 Working with friction forces   🖉 Exercises 20, 21

❶ If the object is *not moving* relative to the surface it's in contact with, the friction force is **static friction.** Draw a free-body diagram of the object. The *direction* of the friction force is such as to oppose sliding of the object. Then use Problem-Solving Strategy 4.1 or 4.2 to solve for f_s. If f_s is greater than $f_{s\,max} = \mu_s n$, then static friction cannot hold the object in place. The assumption that the object is at rest is not valid, and you need to redo the problem using kinetic friction.

❷ If the object is *sliding* relative to the surface, then **kinetic friction** is acting. From Newton's second law, find the normal force n. Equation 4.13 then gives the magnitude and direction of the friction force.

❸ If the object is *rolling* along the surface, then **rolling friction** is acting. From Newton's second law, find the normal force n. Equation 4.13 then gives the magnitude and direction of the friction force.

Optimized braking If you slam on your brakes, your wheels will lock up and you'll go into a skid. Then it is the *kinetic* friction force between the road and your tires that slows your car to a halt. If, however, you apply the brakes such that you don't quite skid and your tires continue to roll, the force stopping you is the *static* friction force between the road and your tires. This is a better way to brake, because the maximum static friction force is always larger than the kinetic friction force. *Antilock braking systems* (ABS) automatically do this for you when you slam on the brakes, stopping you in the shortest possible distance.

EXAMPLE 4.11 Finding the force to push a box

Carol pushes a 10.0 kg wood box across a wood floor at a steady speed of 2.0 m/s. How much force does Carol exert on the box?

PREPARE Let's assume the box slides to the right. In this case, a kinetic friction force $\vec{f}_k$ opposes the motion by pointing to the left. In Figure 4.22 we identify the forces acting on the box and construct a free-body diagram.

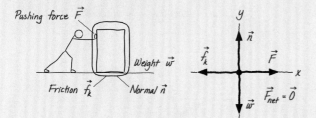

FIGURE 4.22 Forces on a box being pushed across a floor.

SOLVE The box is moving at a constant speed, so it is in dynamic equilibrium with $\vec{F}_{net} = \vec{0}$. This means that the x- and y-components of the net force must each be zero:

$$\sum F_x = n_x + w_x + F_x + (f_k)_x = 0 + 0 + F - f_k = 0$$

$$\sum F_y = n_y + w_y + F_y + (f_k)_y = n - w + 0 + 0 = 0$$

In the first equation, the x-component of $\vec{f}_k$ is equal to $-f_k$ because $\vec{f}_k$ is directed to the left. Similarly, $w_y = -w$ because the weight force points down.

From the first equation, we see that Carol's pushing force is $F = f_k$. To evaluate this, we need f_k. Here we can use our model for kinetic friction:

$$f_k = \mu_k n$$

Because the friction is wood sliding on wood, we can use Table 4.1 to find $\mu_k = 0.20$. Further, we can use the second Newton's-law equation to find that the normal force is $n = w = mg$. Thus

$$F = f_k = \mu_k n = \mu_k mg$$
$$= (0.20)(10.0 \text{ kg})(9.80 \text{ m/s}^2) = 20 \text{ N}$$

This is the force that Carol needs to apply to the box to keep it moving at a steady speed.

ASSESS The speed of 2.0 m/s with which Carol pushes the box does not enter into the answer. This is because our model of kinetic friction does not depend on the speed of the sliding object.

CONCEPTUAL EXAMPLE 4.2 To push or pull a lawn roller?

A lawn roller is a heavy cylinder used to flatten a bumpy lawn, as shown in Figure 4.23. Is it easier to push or pull such a roller? Which is more effective for flattening the lawn, pushing or pulling?

FIGURE 4.23 Pushing and pulling a lawn roller.

REASON Figure 4.24 shows free-body diagrams for the two cases. We assume that the roller is pushed at a constant speed so that it is in dynamic equilibrium with $\vec{F}_{net} = \vec{0}$. Because the roller does not move in the y-direction, the y-component of the net force must be zero. According to our model, the magnitude f_r of rolling friction is proportional to the magnitude n of the normal force. If we *push* on the roller, our pushing force $\vec{F}$ will have a downward y-component. To compensate for this, the normal force must increase and, because $f_r = \mu_r n$, the rolling friction will increase as well. This makes the roller harder to move. If we *pull* on the roller, the now upward y-component of

$\vec{F}$ will lead to a *reduced* value of n and hence of f_r. Thus the roller is easier to pull than to push.

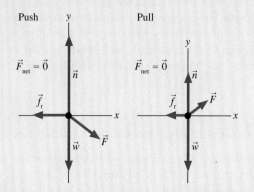

FIGURE 4.24 Free-body diagrams for the lawn roller.

However, the purpose of the roller is to flatten the soil. If the normal force $\vec{n}$ of the ground on the roller is larger, by Newton's third law the force of the roller on the ground will be larger as well. So for smoothing your lawn, it's better to push.

ASSESS You've probably experienced this effect while using an upright vacuum cleaner. The vacuum is harder to push on the forward stroke than when drawing it back.

EXAMPLE 4.12 How to dump a file cabinet

A 50.0 kg steel file cabinet is in the back of a dump truck. The truck's bed, also made of steel, is slowly tilted. What is the size of the static friction force on the cabinet when the bed is tilted 20°? At what angle will the file cabinet begin to slide?

PREPARE We'll use our model of static friction. The file cabinet will slip when the static friction force reaches its maximum possible value $f_{s max}$. Figure 4.25 shows the visual overview when the truck bed is tilted at angle θ. We can make the analysis easier if we tilt the coordinate system to match the bed of the truck. To prevent the file cabinet from slipping, the static friction force must point *up* the slope.

SOLVE Before it slips, the file cabinet is in static equilibrium. Newton's first law reads

$$\sum F_x = n_x + w_x + (f_s)_x = 0$$
$$\sum F_y = n_y + w_y + (f_s)_y = 0$$

From the free-body diagram we see that f_s has only a negative x-component and that n has only a positive y-component. We also have $w_x = w \sin\theta$ and $w_y = -w \cos\theta$. Thus the first law becomes

$$\sum F_x = w \sin\theta - f_s = mg \sin\theta - f_s = 0$$
$$\sum F_y = n - w \cos\theta = n - mg \cos\theta = 0$$

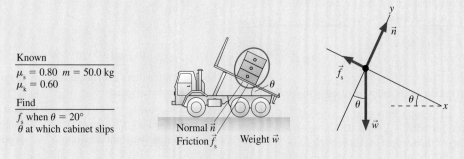

Known

$\mu_s = 0.80$ $m = 50.0$ kg
$\mu_k = 0.60$

Find

f_s when $\theta = 20°$
θ at which cabinet slips

Normal $\vec{n}$
Friction $\vec{f}_s$ Weight $\vec{w}$

FIGURE 4.25 Visual overview of a file cabinet in a tilted dump truck.

where we've used $w = mg$. The x-component equation allows us to determine the size of the static friction force when $\theta = 20°$:

$$f_s = mg\sin\theta = (50.0\text{ kg})(9.80\text{ m/s}^2)\sin 20° = 168\text{ N}$$

This value does not require knowing μ_s. The coefficient of static friction only enters when we want to find the angle at which the file cabinet slips. Slipping occurs when the static friction reaches its maximum value

$$f_s = f_{s\,max} = \mu_s n$$

From the y-component of Newton's second law we see that $n = mg\cos\theta$. Consequently,

$$f_{s\,max} = \mu_s mg\cos\theta$$

The x-component of the second law gave

$$f_s = mg\sin\theta$$

Setting $f_s = f_{s\,max}$ then gives

$$mg\sin\theta = \mu_s mg\cos\theta$$

The mg in both terms cancels, and we find

$$\frac{\sin\theta}{\cos\theta} = \tan\theta = \mu_s$$

$$\theta = \tan^{-1}\mu_s = \tan^{-1}(0.80) = 39°$$

ASSESS Steel doesn't slide all that well on unlubricated steel, so a fairly large angle is not surprising. The answer seems reasonable. It is worth noting that $n = mg\cos\theta$ in this example. A common error is to use simply $n = mg$. Be sure to evaluate the normal force within the context of each specific problem.

Causes of Friction

It is worth a brief pause to look at the *causes* of friction. All surfaces, even those quite smooth to the touch, are very rough on a microscopic scale. When two objects are placed in contact, they do not make a smooth fit. Instead, as Figure 4.26 shows, the high points on one surface become jammed against the high points on the other surface while the low points are not in contact at all. Only a very small fraction (typically 10^{-4}) of the surface area is in actual contact. The amount of contact depends on how hard the surfaces are pushed together, which is why friction forces are proportional to n.

For an object to slip, you must push it hard enough to force these contact points over each other. Once the two surfaces are sliding against each other, their high points undergo constant collisions, deformations, and even brief bonding that leads to the resistive force of kinetic friction.

4.6 Drag

Fluids—liquids and gases—exert a drag force on objects as they move through the fluid. You experience drag forces every day as you jog, bicycle, ski, or drive your car. The drag force is especially important for the skydiver at the beginning of the chapter and for unicellular animals swimming through water.

The drag force $\vec{D}$

- Is opposite in direction to the velocity $\vec{v}$.
- Increases in magnitude as the object's speed increases.

Experimental studies have found that the drag force depends on an object's speed in a complicated way. We'll look separately at drag forces in air and in liquids because different models apply.

Drag in Air

At relatively low speeds, the drag force in air is small and can usually be neglected, but drag plays an important role as speeds increase. Fortunately, we can use a fairly simple *model* of drag if the following three conditions are met:

- The object's size (diameter) is between a few millimeters and a few meters.
- The object's speed is less than a few hundred meters per second.
- The object is moving through the air near the earth's surface.

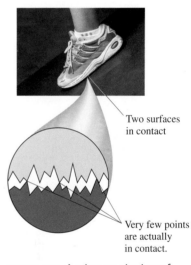

Two surfaces in contact

Very few points are actually in contact.

FIGURE 4.26 A microscopic view of friction.

These conditions are usually satisfied for balls, people, cars, and many other objects of the everyday world. Under these conditions, the drag force can be written

$$\vec{D} = \left(\tfrac{1}{2}C_{D}\rho A v^{2}, \text{ direction opposite to the motion}\right) \qquad (4.14)$$

Drag force on an object of cross-section area A moving at speed v

QUADRATIC
p.50

Here, ρ is the density of air ($\rho = 1.29$ kg/m³ at sea level), A is the cross-section area of the object (in m²), and the **drag coefficient** C_{D} depends on the details of the object's shape. However, the value of C_{D} for everyday moving objects is roughly 1/2, so a good approximation to the drag force is

$$D \approx \tfrac{1}{4}\rho A v^{2} \qquad (4.15)$$

This is the expression for the magnitude of the drag force that we'll use in this chapter.

The size of the drag force in air is proportional to the *square* of the object's speed: If the speed doubles, the drag increases by a factor of *four.* This model of drag fails for objects that are very small (such as dust particles) or very fast (such as jet planes) or that move in other media (such as water).

Figure 4.27 shows that the area A in Equation 4.14 is the cross section of the object as it "faces into the wind." It's interesting to note that the magnitude of the drag force depends on the object's *size and shape* but not on its *mass.* This has important consequences for the motion of falling objects.

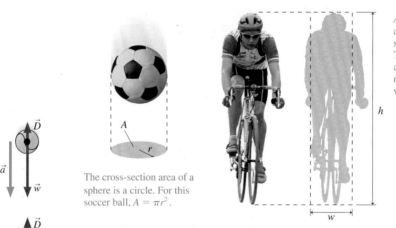

A is the cross-section area of the cyclist as seen from the front. This area is approximated by the rectangle shown, with area $A = h \times w$.

The cross-section area of a sphere is a circle. For this soccer ball, $A = \pi r^{2}$.

FIGURE 4.27 How to calculate the cross-section area A.

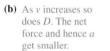

(a) At low speeds D is small and the ball falls with $a \approx g$.

(b) As v increases so does D. The net force and hence a get smaller.

(c) Eventually, v reaches a value such that $D = w$. Then the net force is zero and the ball falls at a constant speed.

FIGURE 4.28 A falling object eventually reaches terminal speed.

Terminal Speed

Just after an object is released from rest, its speed is low and the drag force is small (as shown in Figure 4.28a). Because the net force is nearly equal to the weight, the object will fall with an acceleration only a little less than g. As it falls further, its speed and hence the drag force increase. Now the net force is smaller, so the acceleration is smaller (as shown in Figure 4.28b). It's still speeding up, but at a lower *rate.* Eventually the speed will increase to a point such that the magnitude of the drag force *equals* the weight (as shown in Figure 4.28c). The net force—and hence the acceleration—at this speed are then *zero,* and the object falls with a *constant* speed. The speed at which the exact balance between the upward drag force and the downward weight force causes an object to fall without acceleration is called the **terminal speed** v_{term}. Once an **object has reached terminal speed, it will continue falling at that speed until it hits the ground.**

It's straightforward to compute the terminal speed. It is the speed, by definition, at which $D = w$ or, equivalently, $\frac{1}{4}\rho A v^2 = mg$. This speed is then

$$v_{\text{term}} \approx \sqrt{\frac{4mg}{\rho A}} \qquad (4.16)$$

This equation shows that a more massive object has a larger terminal speed than a less massive object of equal size. A 10-cm-diameter lead ball, with a mass of 6 kg, has a terminal speed of 150 m/s while a 10-cm-diameter Styrofoam ball, with a mass of 50 g, has a terminal speed of only 14 m/s.

EXAMPLE 4.13 Terminal speeds of a skydiver and a mouse

A skydiver and his pet mouse jump from a plane. Estimate their terminal speeds.

PREPARE To use Equation 4.16 we need to estimate the mass m and cross-section area A of both man and mouse. Figure 4.29 shows how. A typical skydiver might be 1.8 m long and 0.40 m wide ($A = 0.72 \text{ m}^2$) with a mass of 75 kg, while a mouse has a mass of perhaps 20 g (0.020 kg) and is 7 cm long and 3 cm wide ($A = 0.07 \text{ m} \times 0.03 \text{ m} = 0.0021 \text{ m}^2$).

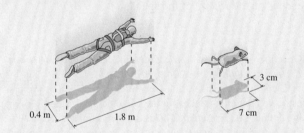

0.4 m   1.8 m   3 cm   7 cm

FIGURE 4.29 The cross-section areas of a skydiver and a mouse.

SOLVE We can use Equation 4.16 to find that for the skydiver

$$v_{\text{term}} \approx \sqrt{\frac{4mg}{\rho A}} = \sqrt{\frac{4(75 \text{ kg})(9.8 \text{ m/s}^2)}{(1.29 \text{ kg/m}^3)(0.72 \text{ m}^2)}} = 56 \text{ m/s}$$

This is roughly 130 mph. A higher speed can be reached by falling feet first or head first, which reduces the area A. Fortunately the skydiver can open his parachute, greatly increasing A. This brings his terminal speed down to a safe value.

For the mouse we have

$$v_{\text{term}} \approx \sqrt{\frac{4mg}{\rho A}} = \sqrt{\frac{4(0.020 \text{ kg})(9.8 \text{ m/s}^2)}{(1.29 \text{ kg/m}^2)(0.0021 \text{ m}^2)}} = 17 \text{ m/s}$$

The mouse has no parachute—nor does he need one! A mouse's terminal speed is low enough that he can fall from any height, even out of an airplane, and survive. Cats, too, have relatively low terminal speeds. In a study of cats that fell from high rises, over 90% survived—including one that fell 45 stories!

ASSESS The mouse survives the fall not only because of its lower terminal speed. The smaller an animal's body, the proportionally more robust it is. Further, a small animal's low mass and terminal speed mean that it has a very small *kinetic energy*, an idea we'll study in Chapter 5.

Although we've focused our analysis on falling objects, the same ideas apply to objects moving horizontally. If an object is thrown or shot horizontally, D causes the object to slow down. An airplane reaches its maximum speed, which is analogous to the terminal speed, when the drag is equal and opposite to the thrust: $D = F_{\text{thrust}}$. The net force is then zero and the plane cannot go any faster. The maximum speed of a passenger jet is about 550 mph.

We will continue to neglect drag unless a problem specifically calls for drag to be considered.

STOP TO THINK 4.4   The terminal speed of a Styrofoam ball is 15 m/s. Suppose a Styrofoam ball is shot straight down with an initial speed of 30 m/s. Which velocity graph is correct?

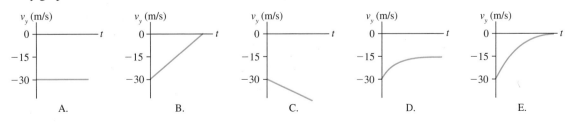

Drag in Liquids

The drag force in a liquid is quite different from that in air. Drag forces in air are largely the result of the object having to push the air out of its way as it moves. For an object moving slowly through a liquid, however, the drag force is mostly due to the *viscosity* of the liquid. For the moment, you can think of the viscosity of a fluid as a measure of how much resistance to flow the fluid has: Honey, which drizzles slowly out of its container, has a much higher viscosity than water, which flows fairly freely. Drag forces have particularly important effects on the motion of single-celled organisms in water, blood cells in the body, and many aquatic creatures.

The drag force in a liquid depends on the shape of the object, but there is a simple result called **Stokes's law** for the drag on a *sphere*. This law is useful because many biological objects, such as cells, can at least roughly be approximated as spheres. The drag on a sphere moving with speed v is

$$\vec{D} = (6\pi\eta rv, \text{ direction opposite to motion}) \qquad (4.17)$$

Stokes's law for the drag on a sphere of radius r moving at speed v

LINEAR
p. 38

Here, η is the viscosity of the liquid. (Water has a viscosity $\eta = 0.0010 \text{ N} \cdot \text{s/m}^2$ at 20° C.) Notice that the drag force in a liquid depends *linearly* on the speed, whereas drag in air depends on the *square* of the speed.

EXAMPLE 4.14 Drag force on a paramecium

A paramecium is a single-celled animal able to propel itself quite rapidly through water by using its *cilia,* rapidly beating hair-like fibers that ring its body. A typical paramecium has a diameter of 50 μm. What is the drag force on a paramecium swimming at a speed of 0.25 mm/s? If its mass is 1.0×10^{-11} kg, estimate how long it takes for the paramecium to come to a stop once it stops swimming.

PREPARE Although a real paramecium has an elongated shape, we'll model the paramecium as a sphere of radius 25 μm and use Stokes's law to find the drag force on it. Once the paramecium stops swimming, the drag force will be the only force acting, and we can use Newton's second law to find its acceleration and time to come to a stop.

SOLVE The drag force is

$$D = 6\pi\eta rv = (6\pi)(0.0010 \text{ N} \cdot \text{s/m}^2)(25 \times 10^{-6} \text{ m})$$
$$\times (0.25 \times 10^{-3} \text{ m/s}) = 1.2 \times 10^{-10} \text{ N}$$

Once the paramecium stops swimming, its acceleration is $a = F_{net}/m = -D/m = -(1.2 \times 10^{-10} \text{ N})/(1.0 \times 10^{-11} \text{ kg}) = -12 \text{ m/s}^2$. This acceleration is a little greater than g. We can estimate how long it takes for the paramecium to stop by using the definition $a = \Delta v/\Delta t$. (This is only an estimate, because the drag force and hence the acceleration decrease as the paramecium slows down.) This estimated stopping time is

$$\Delta t = \Delta v/a = \frac{-0.25 \times 10^{-3} \text{ m/s}}{-12 \text{ m/s}^2} = 2 \times 10^{-5} \text{ s} = 20 \text{ } \mu\text{s}$$

This is a *very* short time!

ASSESS In estimating the stopping time, we used the initial speed of the paramecium. Suppose its initial speed v were doubled. Then the drag force, which is proportional to the speed, would also double, and its acceleration a would double as well. But if both v and a double, $\Delta t = \Delta v/a$ would remain the same. Thus the stopping time of an object moving in a liquid is *independent of its initial speed.*

A paramecium, along with bacteria and other small organisms that live in water, lives in a very strange world where inertia—the tendency of a moving body to continue in motion—is negligible. To keep a shopping cart rolling you need to push it, but if you stop pushing it will continue to roll for some distance. A frictionless cart would roll forever at constant speed. In contrast, a paramecium comes to a halt essentially instantaneously, as soon as it stops actively swimming.

The reverse is also true: When it starts swimming again, it almost instantly reaches a constant speed, analogous to a terminal speed, at which the drag force $\vec{D}$ is equal and opposite to the paramecium's propulsion force $\vec{F}_{\text{propulsion}}$. Using Stokes's law for $\vec{D}$, we see that speed of swimming is directly proportional to the propulsion force:

$$v = \frac{F_{\text{propulsion}}}{6\pi\eta r}$$

If a small organism in water wants to go twice as fast, it has to double its propulsion force. (For objects without drag, doubling the force causes the *acceleration,* not the speed, to double.) Life in a world dominated by drag is very different from the world of accelerating objects in which we humans live.

4.7 Interacting Objects

Up to this point we have studied the dynamics of a single object subject to forces from the environment. In Example 4.11, for instance, a sliding box was acted upon by friction, normal, weight, and pushing forces that came from outside the box—from the floor, the earth, and the person pushing. As we've seen, such problems can be solved by an application of Newton's second law after all the forces have been identified.

Actjv
Physjcs 2.7–2.9

But in Chapter 3 we found that real-world motion often involves two or more objects interacting with each other. We further found that forces always come in action/reaction *pairs* that are related by Newton's third law. To remind you, Newton's third law states:

- Every force occurs as one member of an action/reaction pair of forces. The two members of the pair always act on *different* objects.
- The two members of an action/reaction pair point in *opposite* directions and are *equal* in magnitude.

Our goal in this section is to learn how to apply the second *and* third laws to systems of interacting objects.

Acceleration Constraints

Newton's third law is one relationship needed to solve problems of interacting objects. In addition, we frequently have other information about the motion in a problem. For example, consider the two boxes in Figure 4.30. As long as they're touching, box A *has* to have exactly the same acceleration as box B. If they were to accelerate differently, either box B would take off on its own, or it would suddenly slow down and box A would run over it! Our problem implicitly assumes that neither of these is happening. Thus the two accelerations are *constrained* to be equal: $\vec{a}_{A} = \vec{a}_{B}$. A well-defined relationship between the accelerations of two or more systems is called an **acceleration constraint.** It is an independent piece of information that can help solve a problem.

In practice, we'll express acceleration constraints in terms of the x- and y-components of $\vec{a}$. Consider the car being towed in Figure 4.31. As long as the cable is under tension, the accelerations are constrained to be equal: $\vec{a}_{C} = \vec{a}_{T}$. This is one-dimensional motion, so for problem solving we would use just the x-components a_{Cx} and a_{Tx}. In terms of these components, the acceleration constraint is

$$a_{Cx} = a_{Tx} = a_{x}$$

Because the accelerations of both systems are equal, we can drop the subscripts C and T and call both of them a_{x}.

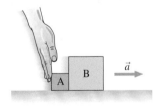

FIGURE 4.30 Two boxes moving together have the same acceleration.

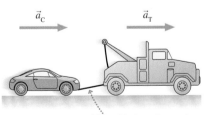

The cable is under tension.

FIGURE 4.31 The car and the truck have the same acceleration.

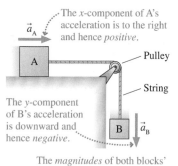

The *x*-component of A's acceleration is to the right and hence *positive.*

Pulley

String

The *y*-component of B's acceleration is downward and hence *negative.*

The *magnitudes* of both blocks' accelerations are equal.

FIGURE 4.32 The string constrains the two systems to accelerate together.

Don't assume the accelerations of A and B will always have the same sign. Consider blocks A and B in Figure 4.32. The blocks are connected by a string, so they are constrained to move together and their accelerations have equal magnitudes. But A has a positive acceleration (to the right) in the *x*-direction while B has a negative acceleration (downward) in the *y*-direction. Thus the acceleration constraint on the components of the acceleration is

$$a_{Ax} = -a_{By}$$

This relationship does *not* say that a_{Ax} is a negative number. It is simply a relational statement, saying that a_{Ax} is (-1) times whatever a_{By} happens to be. In fact, the acceleration a_{By} in Figure 4.32 is a negative number, so a_{Ax} is actually positive. In many problems, the signs of a_{Ax} and a_{By} may not be known until the problem is solved, but the *relationship* is known from the beginning.

A Revised Strategy for Interacting-Object Problems

Problems of interacting objects can be solved with a few modifications to the basic Problem-Solving Strategy 4.2 we developed earlier in this chapter. A revised problem-solving strategy is shown below.

(MP) PROBLEM-SOLVING STRATEGY 4.3 Interacting-object problems

PREPARE Identify the interacting objects that make up the system. Everything else is part of the environment. Make simplifying assumptions.

Prepare a visual overview: Make a sketch of the situation. Define symbols and identify what the problem is trying to find. Identify all forces acting on each object and all action/reaction pairs. Draw a *separate* free-body diagram for each object and connect the force vectors of action/reaction pairs with dotted lines. Use subscript labels to distinguish forces, such as $\vec{n}$ and $\vec{w}$, that act independently on more than one object. Identify any acceleration constraints and add these to your list of values.

SOLVE Use Newton's second and third laws:

- Write Newton's second law in component form for each object. Find the force components from the free-body diagrams.
- Equate the magnitudes of action/reaction pairs.
- If relevant, include the acceleration constraints and the friction model.
- Solve for the unknown forces or acceleration.

ASSESS Check that your result has the correct units, is reasonable, and answers the question.

NOTE ▶ Two steps are especially important when drawing the free-body diagrams. First, draw a *separate* diagram for each object. They need not have the same coordinate system. Second, show only the forces acting *on* that object. The force $\vec{F}_{A\,on\,B}$ goes on the free-body diagram of Object B, but $\vec{F}_{B\,on\,A}$ goes on the diagram of Object A. The two members of an action/reaction pair *always* appear on two different free-body diagrams—*never* on the same diagram. ◀

You might be puzzled that the Solve step calls for the use of the third law to equate just the *magnitudes* of action/reaction forces. What about the "opposite in direction" part of the third law? You have already used it! Your free-body diagrams should show the two members of an action/reaction pair to be opposite in direction, and that information will have been utilized in writing the second-law equations. Because the directional information has already been used, all that is left is the magnitude information.

EXAMPLE 4.15 Pushing two blocks

Figure 4.33 shows a 5.0 kg block A being pushed with a 3.0 N force. In front of this block is a 10 kg block B; the two blocks move together. What force does block A exert on block B?

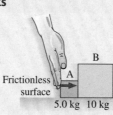

FIGURE 4.33 Two blocks are pushed by a hand.

PREPARE The visual overview of Figure 4.34 lists known information, what we want to find, and—new to problems of interacting objects—the acceleration constraint. Because the blocks move together in the positive x-direction, they both must have the same x-component of acceleration:

$$a_{Ax} = a_{Bx} = a_x$$

We've identified all the forces acting on blocks A and B, then drawn *separate* free-body diagrams. Because both blocks have a weight force and a normal force, we used subscripts A and B to distinguish between them. A key step is to include the forces of interaction between the two blocks, $\vec{F}_{AonB}$ and $\vec{F}_{BonA}$. Notice that $\vec{F}_{AonB}$ is drawn as acting on box B; it is the force *of* A *on* B. Because action/reaction pairs act in opposite directions, force $\vec{F}_{BonA}$ pushes *backward* on block A. Force vectors are always drawn on the free-body diagram of the object that *experiences* the force, not the object exerting the force.

SOLVE We begin by writing Newton's second law in component form for each block. Because the motion is only in the x-direction, we need only the x-component of the second law. For block A,

$$\sum F_x = (F_H)_x + (F_{BonA})_x = m_A a_{Ax}$$

The force components can be "read" from the free-body diagram, where we see $\vec{F}_H$ pointing to the right and $\vec{F}_{BonA}$ pointing to the left. Thus

$$F_H - F_{BonA} = m_A a_x$$

We used the acceleration constraint to write $a_{Ax} = a_x$. For B, we have

$$\sum F_x = (F_{AonB})_x = m_B a_{Bx}$$

or, again using the acceleration constraint,

$$F_{AonB} = m_B a_x$$

We have an additional piece of information: Newton's third law tells us that $F_{BonA} = F_{AonB}$. With this information, the two x-component equations become

$$F_{AonB} = m_B a_x$$
$$F_H - F_{AonB} = m_A a_x$$

Our goal is to find F_{AonB}, so we need to eliminate the unknown acceleration a_x. From the first equation, $a_x = F_{AonB}/m_B$. Substituting this into the second equation gives

$$F_H - F_{AonB} = \frac{m_A}{m_B} F_{AonB}$$

This can be solved for the force of block A on block B, giving

$$F_{AonB} = \frac{F_H}{1 + m_A/m_B} = \frac{3.0 \text{ N}}{1 + (5.0 \text{ kg})/(10 \text{ kg})} = \frac{3.0 \text{ N}}{1.5} = 2.0 \text{ N}$$

ASSESS The critical step in solving this problem was correctly identifying the forces and drawing the two free-body diagrams. The rest of the problem consists of writing the second-law equations directly from the free-body diagram and then using the new information of the acceleration constraint to solve for the desired quantity.

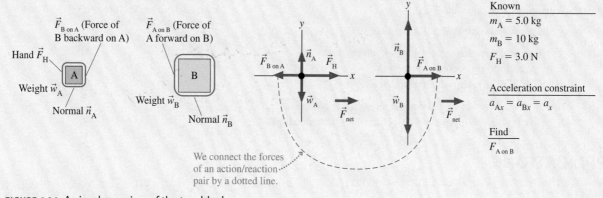

We connect the forces of an action/reaction pair by a dotted line.

FIGURE 4.34 A visual overview of the two blocks.

STOP TO THINK 4.5 Boxes P and Q are sliding to the right across a frictionless table. The hand H is slowing them down. The mass of P is larger than the mass of Q. Rank in order, from largest to smallest, the *horizontal* forces on P, Q, and H.

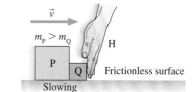

A. $F_{QonH} = F_{HonQ} = F_{PonQ} = F_{QonP}$
B. $F_{QonH} = F_{HonQ} > F_{PonQ} = F_{QonP}$
C. $F_{QonH} = F_{HonQ} < F_{PonQ} = F_{QonP}$
D. $F_{HonQ} = F_{HonP} > F_{PonQ}$

SUMMARY

The goal of Chapter 4 has been to learn how to solve problems about motion in a straight line.

GENERAL STRATEGY

All examples in this chapter follow a three-part strategy. You'll become a better problem solver if you adhere to it as you do the homework problems. The *Dynamics Worksheets* in the *Student Workbook* will help you structure your work in this way.

Equilibrium Problems

Object at rest or moving at constant velocity.

PREPARE Make simplifying assumptions.

- Check that the object is either at rest or moving with constant velocity.
- Identify forces and show them on a free-body diagram.

SOLVE Use Newton's first law in component form:

$$\sum F_x = 0$$
$$\sum F_y = 0$$

"Read" the components from the free-body diagram

ASSESS Is your result reasonable?

Dynamics Problems

Object accelerating.

PREPARE Make simplifying assumptions.
Make a **visual overview:**

- Sketch a pictorial representation
- Identify known quantities and what the problem is trying to find.
- Identify all forces and show them on a free-body diagram.

SOLVE Use Newton's second law in component form:

$$\sum F_x = ma_x \text{ and } \sum F_y = ma_y$$

"Read" the components of the vectors from the free-body diagram. If needed, use kinematics to find positions and velocities.

ASSESS Is your result reasonable?

Interacting Objects

Two or more objects interacting.

PREPARE Identify the system and the environment.
Make a **visual overview:**

- Sketch a pictorial representation.
- Identify any acceleration constraints.
- Identify all forces acting on *each* object.
- Identify action/reaction pairs between objects in the system.
- Draw separate free-body diagrams for each object. Connect action/reaction pairs with dotted lines and show them on the free-body diagram.

SOLVE Write Newton's second law for each object. Use Newton's third law to equate the magnitudes of action/reaction pairs. Include acceleration constraints.

ASSESS Is your result reasonable?

IMPORTANT CONCEPTS

Specific information about three important forces:

Weight $\vec{w} = (mg, \text{downwards})$

Friction $\vec{f_s} = (0 \text{ to } \mu_s n, \text{ direction as necessary to prevent motion})$
$\vec{f_k} = (\mu_k n, \text{ direction opposite the motion})$
$\vec{f_r} = (\mu_r n, \text{ direction opposite the motion})$

Drag $\vec{D} \approx \left(\frac{1}{4}\rho A v^2, \text{ direction opposite to the motion}\right)$ for motion in air
$\vec{D} = (6\pi\eta r v, \text{ direction opposite the motion})$ for motion in liquid

Newton's laws are vector expressions. You must write them out by components:

$$(F_{net})_x = a \quad F_x = ma_x \text{ or } 0$$
$$(F_{net})_y = a \quad F_y = ma_y \text{ or } 0$$

APPLICATIONS

Apparent weight is the magnitude of the contact force supporting an object. It is what a scale would read, and it is your sensation of weight.

$$w_{app} = m(g + a_y)$$

Apparent weight equals your true weight $w = mg$ only when $a_y = 0$.

Acceleration constraints
Objects that are constrained to move together must have accelerations of equal magnitude: $a_A = a_B$.

This must be expressed in terms of components, such as $a_{Ax} = -a_{By}$.

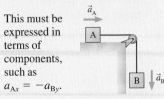

Strings and pulleys

- A string or rope pulls what it's connected to with a force equal to its tension. $F_{\text{rope on wall}} = \text{tension}$
- The tension in a rope is equal to the force pulling on the rope. $F_{\text{hand on rope}} = \text{tension}$
- The tension in a massless rope is the same at all points in the rope.
- Tension does not change when a rope passes over a massless, frictionless pulley.

For instructor-assigned homework, go to www.masteringphysics.com

Problem difficulty is labeled as I (straightforward) to IIIII (challenging).

Problems labeled ✐ can be done on a Workbook Dynamics Worksheet; INT integrate significant material from earlier chapters; BIO are of biological or medical interest.

QUESTIONS

Conceptual Questions

1. An object is subject to two forces that do not point in opposite directions. Is it possible to choose their magnitudes so that the object is in equilibrium? Explain.

2. Are the objects described here in static equilibrium, dynamic equilibrium, or not in equilibrium at all?
   a. A girder is lifted at constant speed by a crane.
   b. A girder is lowered by a crane. It is slowing down.
   c. You're straining to hold a 200 lb barbell over your head.
   d. A jet plane has reached its cruising speed and altitude.
   e. A rock is falling into the Grand Canyon.
   f. A box in the back of a truck doesn't slide as the truck stops.

3. What forces are acting on you right now? What net force is acting on you right now?

4. Decide whether each of the following is true or false. Give a reason!
   a. The mass of an object depends on its location.
   b. The weight of an object depends on its location.
   c. Mass and weight describe the same thing in different units.

5. An astronaut takes his bathroom scale to the moon and then stands on it. Is the reading of the scale his true weight? Explain.

6. A light block of mass m and a heavy block of mass M are attached to the ends of a rope. A student holds the heavier block and lets the lighter block hang below it, as shown in Figure Q4.6. Then she lets go. Air resistance can be neglected.
   a. What is the tension in the rope while the blocks are falling, before either hits the ground?
   b. Would your answer be different if she had been holding the lighter block initially?

FIGURE Q4.6

7. Four balls are thrown straight up. Figure Q4.7 is a "snapshot" showing their velocities. They have the same size but different mass. Air resistance is negligible. Rank in order, from largest to smallest, the magnitudes of the net forces, $F_{net 1}$, $F_{net 2}$, $F_{net 3}$, $F_{net 4}$, acting on the balls. Some may be equal. Give your answer in the form A > B = C > D, and state your reasoning.

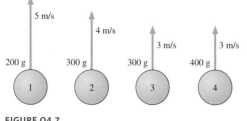
FIGURE Q4.7

8. Suppose you attempt to pour out 100 g of salt, using a pan balance for measurements, while in an elevator that is accelerating upward. Will the quantity of salt be too much, too little, or the correct amount? Explain.

9. a. Can the normal force on an object be directed horizontally? If not, why not? If so, provide an example.
   b. Can the normal force on an object be directed downward? If not, why not? If so, provide an example.

10. A ball is thrown straight up. Taking the drag force of air into account, does it take longer for the ball to travel to the top of its motion or for it to fall back down again?

11. Three objects move through the air as shown in Figure Q4.11. Rank in order, from largest to smallest, the three drag forces D_1, D_2, and D_3. Some may be equal. Give your answer in the form A > B = C and state your reasoning.

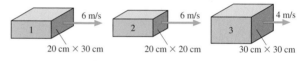
FIGURE Q4.11

12. A skydiver is falling at her terminal speed. Right after she opens her parachute, which has a very large area, what is the direction of the net force on her?

13. Raindrops can fall at different speeds; some fall quite quickly, others quite slowly. Why might this be true?

14. An airplane moves through the air at a constant speed. The jet engine's thrust applies a force in the direction of motion. Reducing thrust will cause the plane to fly at a slower—but still constant—speed. Explain why this is so.

15. Is it possible for an object to travel in air faster than its terminal speed? If not, why not? If so, explain how this might happen.

Multiple-Choice Questions

16. I A 2.0 kg ball is suspended by two light strings as shown in Figure Q4.16. What is the tension T in the angled string?
    A. 9.5 N   B. 15 N
    C. 20 N   D. 26 N
    E. 30 N

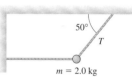
FIGURE Q4.16

17. I While standing in a low tunnel, you raise your arms and push against the ceiling with a force of 100 N. Your mass is 70 kg.
    a. What force does the ceiling exert on you?
       A. 10 N   B. 100 N   C. 690 N
       D. 790 N   E. 980 N
    b. What force does the floor exert on you?
       A. 10 N   B. 100 N   C. 690 N
       D. 790 N   E. 980 N

18. | A 5.0 kg dog sits on the floor of an elevator that is accelerating *downward* at 1.20 m/s².
    a. What is the magnitude of the normal force of the elevator floor on the dog?
       A. 34.2 N   B. 43.0 N   C. 49.0 N
       D. 55.0 N   E. 74.0 N
    b. What is the magnitude of the force of the dog on the elevator floor?
       A. 4.2 N   B. 49.0 N   C. 55.0 N
       D. 43.0 N   E. 74.0 N

19. ‖ A 3.0 kg puck slides due east on a horizontal frictionless surface at a constant speed of 4.5 m/s. Then a force of magnitude 6.0 N, directed due north, is applied for 1.5 s. Afterward,
    a. What is the northward component of the puck's velocity?
       A. 0.50 m/s   B. 2.0 m/s   C. 3.0 m/s
       D. 4.0 m/s   E. 4.5 m/s
    b. What is the speed of the puck?
       A. 4.9 m/s   B. 5.4 m/s   C. 6.2 m/s
       D. 7.5 m/s   E. 11 m/s

20. ‖ A rocket in space, initially at rest, fires its main engines at a constant thrust. As it burns fuel, the mass of the rocket decreases. Which of the graphs in Figure Q4.20 best represents the velocity of the rocket as a function of time?

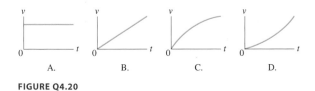

FIGURE Q4.20

21. | Eric has a mass of 60 kg. He is standing on a scale in an elevator that is accelerating downward at 1.7 m/s². What is the approximate reading on the scale?
    A. 0 N   B. 400 N   C. 500 N   D. 600 N

22. | The two blocks in Figure Q4.22 are at rest on frictionless surfaces. What must be the mass of the right block in order that the two blocks remain stationary?
    A. 4.9 kg   B. 6.1 kg   C. 7.9 kg
    D. 9.8 kg   E. 12 kg

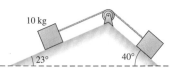

FIGURE Q4.22

23. | A football player at practice pushes a 60 kg blocking sled across the field at a constant speed. The coefficient of kinetic friction between the grass and the sled is 0.30. How much force must he apply to the sled?
    A. 18 N   B. 60 N   C. 180 N   D. 600 N

24. | Two football players are pushing a 60 kg blocking sled across the field at a constant speed of 2.0 m/s. The coefficient of kinetic friction between the grass and the sled is 0.30. Once they stop pushing, how far will the sled slide before coming to rest?
    A. 0.20 m   B. 0.68 m   C. 1.0 m   D. 6.6 m

25. ‖ Land Rover ads used to claim that their vehicles could climb a slope of 45°. For this to be possible, what must be the minimum coefficient of static friction between the vehicle's tires and the road?
    A. 0.5   B. 0.7   C. 0.9   D. 1.0

26. ‖ A truck is traveling at 30 m/s on a slippery road. The driver slams on the brakes and the truck starts to skid. If the coefficient of kinetic friction between the tires and the road is 0.20, how far will the truck skid before stopping?
    A. 230 m   B. 300 m   C. 450 m   D. 680 m

PROBLEMS

Section 4.1 Equilibrium

1. | The three ropes in Figure P4.1 are tied to a small, very light ring. Two of the ropes are anchored to walls at right angles, and the third rope pulls as shown. What are T_1 and T_2, the magnitudes of the tension forces in the first two ropes?

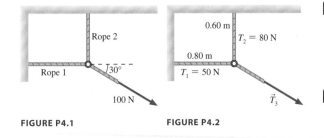

FIGURE P4.1   **FIGURE P4.2**

2. ‖ The three ropes in Figure P4.2 are tied to a small, very light ring. Two of these ropes are anchored to walls at right angles with the tensions shown in the figure. What are the magnitude and direction of the tension $\vec{T}_3$ in the third rope?

3. ‖ A 20 kg loudspeaker is suspended 2.0 m below the ceiling by two cables that are each 30° from vertical. What is the tension in the cables?

4. | A 1000 kg steel beam is supported by the two ropes shown in Figure P4.4. Each rope can support a maximum sustained tension of 5600 N. Do the ropes break?

5. ‖‖ A football coach sits on a sled while two of his players build their strength by dragging the sled across the field with ropes. The friction force on the sled is 1.0 kN and the angle between the two horizontal ropes is 20°. How hard must each player pull to drag the coach at a steady 2.0 m/s?

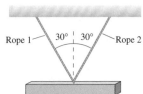

FIGURE P4.4

6. ‖ When you bend your knee,
BIO the quadriceps muscle is stretched. This increases the tension in
the quadriceps tendon attached
to your kneecap (patella), which,
in turn, increases the tension in
the patella tendon that attaches
your kneecap to your lower leg
bone (tibia). Simultaneously, the
end of your upper leg bone
(femur) pushes outward on the
patella. Figure P4.6 shows how
these parts of a knee joint are
arranged. What size force does
the femur exert on the kneecap

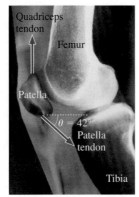

FIGURE P4.6

if the tendons are oriented as in the figure and the tension in
each tendon is 60 N?

Section 4.2 Dynamics and Newton's Second Law

7. | A force with x-component F_x acts on a 2.0 kg object as it
moves along the x-axis. The object's acceleration graph (a_x
versus t) is shown in Figure P4.7. Draw a graph of F_x versus t.

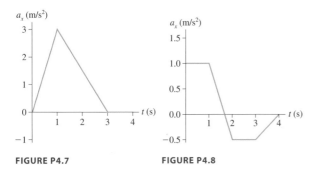

FIGURE P4.7   **FIGURE P4.8**

8. | A force with x-component F_x acts on a 500 g object as it
moves along the x-axis. The object's acceleration graph (a_x
versus t) is shown in Figure P4.8. Draw a graph of F_x versus t.

9. | A force with x-component F_x acts on a 2.0 kg object as it
moves along the x-axis. A graph of F_x versus t is shown in
Figure P4.9. Draw an acceleration graph (a_x versus t) for this
object.

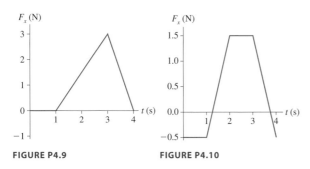

FIGURE P4.9   **FIGURE P4.10**

10. | A force with x-component F_x acts on a 500 g object as it
moves along the x-axis. A graph of F_x versus t is shown in
Figure P4.10. Draw an acceleration graph (a_x versus t) for this
object.

11. ‖ The forces in Figure P4.11 are acting on a 2.0 kg object.
Find the values of a_x and a_y, the x- and y-components of the
object's acceleration.

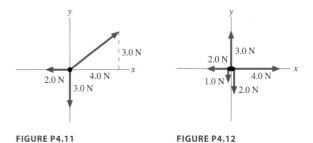

FIGURE P4.11   **FIGURE P4.12**

12. | The forces in Figure P4.12 are acting on a 2.0 kg object.
Find the values of a_x and a_y, the x- and y-components of the
object's acceleration.

13. | A horizontal rope is tied to a 50 kg box on frictionless ice.
What is the tension in the rope if
   a. The box is at rest?
   b. The box moves at a steady 5.0 m/s?
   c. The box has $v_x = 5.0$ m/s and $a_x = 5.0$ m/s²?

14. ‖ A crate pushed along the floor with velocity $\vec{v}_i$ slides a distance d after the pushing force is removed.
   a. If the mass of the crate is doubled but the initial velocity is
      not changed, what distance does the crate slide before
      stopping? Explain.
   b. If the initial velocity of the crate is doubled to $2\vec{v}_i$ but the
      mass is not changed, what distance does the crate slide
      before stopping? Explain.

15. | In a head-on collision, a car stops in 0.10 s from a speed of
14 m/s. The driver has a mass of 70 kg, and is, fortunately,
tightly strapped into his seat. What force is applied to the driver by his seat belt during that fraction of a second?

Section 4.3 Mass and Weight

16. | An astronaut's weight on earth is 800 N. What is his weight
on Mars, where $g = 3.76$ m/s²?

17. | A woman has a mass of 55.0 kg.
   a. What is her weight on earth?
   b. What are her mass and her weight on the moon, where
      $g = 1.62$ m/s²?

18. | A box with a 75 kg passenger inside is launched straight up
into the air by a giant rubber band. After the box has left the
rubber band but is still moving *upward,*
   a. What is the passenger's true weight?
   b. What is the passenger's apparent weight?

19. | a. How much force does an 80 kg astronaut exert on his
         chair while sitting at rest on the launch pad?
   b. How much force does the astronaut exert on his chair
      while accelerating straight up at 10 m/s²?

20. | It takes the elevator in a skyscraper 4.0 s to reach its cruis-
ing speed of 10 m/s. A 60 kg passenger gets aboard on the
ground floor. What is the passenger's apparent weight
   a. Before the elevator starts moving?
   b. While the elevator is speeding up?
   c. After the elevator reaches its cruising speed?

21. | Zach, whose mass is 80 kg, is in an elevator descending at 10 m/s. The elevator takes 3.0 s to brake to a stop at the first floor.
    a. What is Zach's apparent weight before the elevator starts braking?
    b. What is Zach's apparent weight while the elevator is braking?

22. | Figure P4.22 shows the velocity graph of a 75 kg passenger in an elevator. What is the passenger's apparent weight at $t = 1.0$ s? At 5.0 s? At 9.0 s?

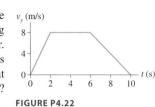

FIGURE P4.22

Section 4.4 Normal Forces

23. | a. A 0.60 kg bullfrog is sitting at rest on a level log. How large is the normal force of the log on the bullfrog?
    b. A second 0.60 kg bullfrog is on a log tilted 30° above horizontal. How large is the normal force of the log on this bullfrog?

24. ‖‖ A 23 kg child goes down a straight slide inclined 38° above horizontal. The child is acted on by his weight, the normal force from the slide, and kinetic friction.
    a. Draw a free-body diagram of the child.
    b. How large is the normal force of the slide on the child?

Section 4.5 Friction

25. ‖ Bonnie and Clyde are sliding a 300 kg bank safe across the floor to their getaway car. The safe slides with a constant speed if Clyde pushes from behind with 385 N of force while Bonnie pulls forward on a rope with 350 N of force. What is the safe's coefficient of kinetic friction on the bank floor?

26. ‖ A 4000 kg truck is parked on a 15° slope. How big is the friction force on the truck?

27. ‖ A 1000 kg car traveling at a speed of 40 m/s skids to a halt on wet concrete where $\mu_k = 0.60$. How long are the skid marks?

28. | A stubborn 120 kg mule sits down and refuses to move. To drag the mule to the barn, the exasperated farmer ties a rope around the mule and pulls with his maximum force of 800 N. The coefficients of friction between the mule and the ground are $\mu_s = 0.80$ and $\mu_k = 0.50$. Is the farmer able to move the mule?

29. ‖ A 10 kg crate is placed on a horizontal conveyor belt. The materials are such that $\mu_s = 0.50$ and $\mu_k = 0.30$.
    a. Draw a free-body diagram showing all the forces on the crate if the conveyer belt runs at constant speed.
    b. Draw a free-body diagram showing all the forces on the crate if the conveyer belt is speeding up.
    c. What is the maximum acceleration the belt can have without the crate slipping?
    d. If acceleration of the belt exceeds the value determined in part c, what is the acceleration of the crate?

Section 4.6 Drag

30. | What is the drag force on a 1.6 m wide, 1.4 m high car traveling at
    a. 10 m/s (≈22 mph)?　　b. 30 m/s (≈65 mph)?

31. ‖ A 75 kg skydiver can be modeled as a rectangular "box" with dimensions 20 cm × 40 cm × 1.8 m. What is his terminal speed if he falls feet first?

32. | A 22-cm-diameter bowling ball has a terminal speed of 85 m/s. What is the ball's mass?

33. ‖ In Example 4.14, the stopping of a paramecium due to the Stokes's law drag force was treated in an approximate fashion, taking the drag force to be independent of time.
    a. Use the same approximation to determine how *far* the paramecium drifts after it stops actively swimming at 0.25 mm/s.
    b. Is your answer to part a much less than, comparable to, or much greater than the size of the paramecium?

Section 4.7 Interacting Objects

34. ‖ A 1000 kg car pushes a 2000 kg truck that has a dead battery. When the driver steps on the accelerator, the drive wheels of the car push against the ground with a force of 4500 N.
    a. What is the magnitude of the force of the car on the truck?
    b. What is the magnitude of the force of the truck on the car?

35. ‖‖‖ Blocks with masses of 1.0 kg, 2.0 kg, and 3.0 kg are lined up in a row on a frictionless table. All three are pushed forward by a 12 N force applied to the 1.0 kg block. How much force does the 2.0 kg block exert on (a) the 3.0 kg block and (b) the 1.0 kg block?

General Problems

36. ‖‖ A 500 kg piano is being lowered into position by a crane while two people steady it with ropes pulling to the sides. Bob's rope pulls to the left, 15° below horizontal, with 500 N of tension. Ellen's rope pulls toward the right, 25° below horizontal.
    a. What tension must Ellen maintain in her rope to keep the piano descending vertically?
    b. What is the tension in the vertical main cable supporting the piano?

37. ‖‖ In an electricity experiment, a 1.00 g plastic ball is suspended on a 60.0-cm-long string and given an electric charge. A charged rod brought near the ball exerts a horizontal electrical force $\vec{F}_{elec}$ on it, causing the ball to swing out to a 20.0° angle and remain there.
    a. What is the magnitude of $\vec{F}_{elec}$?
    b. What is the tension in the string?

38. ‖ Figure P4.38 shows the velocity graph of a 2.0 kg object as it moves along the x-axis. What is the net force acting on this object at $t = 1$ s? At 4 s? At 7 s?

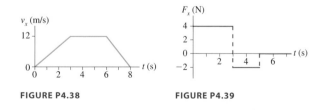

FIGURE P4.38　　　　　　　**FIGURE P4.39**

39. ‖ Figure P4.39 shows the force acting on a 2.0 kg object as it moves along the x-axis. The object is at rest at the origin at $t = 0$ s. What are its acceleration and velocity at $t = 6.0$ s?

40. ‖ A 50 kg box hangs from a rope. What is the tension in the rope if
    a. The box is at rest?
    b. The box has $v_y = 5.0$ m/s and is speeding up at 5.0 m/s²?

41. ‖ A 50 kg box hangs from a rope. What is the tension in the rope if
    a. The box moves up at a steady 5.0 m/s?
    b. The box has $v_y = 5.0$ m/s and is slowing down at 5.0 m/s²?

42. | Your forehead can withstand a force of about 6.0 kN force BIO before fracturing, while your cheekbone can only withstand about 1.3 kN.
    a. If a 140 g baseball strikes your head at 30 m/s and stops in 0.0015 s, what is the magnitude of the ball's acceleration?
    b. What is the magnitude of the force that stops the baseball?
    c. What force does the baseball apply to your head? Explain.
    d. Are you in danger of a fracture if the ball hits you in the forehead? In the cheek?

43. ‖ Seat belts and air bags save lives by reducing the forces exerted on the driver and passengers in an automobile colli-BIO sion. Cars are designed with a "crumple zone" in the front of the car. In the event of an impact, the passenger compartment decelerates over a distance of about 1 m as the front of the car crumples. An occupant restrained by seat belts and air bags decelerates with the car. By contrast, an unrestrained occupant keeps moving forward with no loss of speed (Newton's first law!) until hitting the dashboard or windshield, as we saw in Figure 4.2. These are unyielding surfaces, and the unfortunate occupant then decelerates over a distance of only about 5 mm.
    a. A 60 kg person is in a head-on collision. The car's speed at impact is 15 m/s. Estimate the net force on the person if he or she is wearing a seat belt and if the air bag deploys.
    b. Estimate the net force that ultimately stops the person if he or she is not restrained by a seat belt or air bag.
    c. How do these two forces compare to the person's weight?

44. ‖ Bob, who has a mass of 75 kg, can throw a 500 g rock with a speed of 30 m/s. The distance through which his hand INT moves as he accelerates the rock forward from rest until he releases it is 1.0 m.
    a. What constant force must Bob exert on the rock to throw it with this speed?
    b. If Bob is standing on frictionless ice, what is his recoil speed after releasing the rock?

45. ‖ An 80 kg spacewalking astronaut pushes off a 640 kg satel-lite, exerting a 100 N force for the 0.50 s it takes him to INT straighten his arms. How far apart are the astronaut and the satellite after 1.0 min?

46. ‖ What thrust does a 200 g model rocket need in order to have a vertical acceleration of 10.0 m/s²
    a. On earth?
    b. On the moon, where $g = 1.62$ m/s²?

47. ‖ A 20,000 kg rocket has a rocket motor that generates 3.0×10^5 N of thrust.
    a. What is the rocket's initial upward acceleration?
    b. At an altitude of 5.0 km the rocket's acceleration has increased to 6.0 m/s². What mass of fuel has it burned?

48. ‖ You've always wondered about the acceleration of the ele-vators in the 101-story-tall Empire State Building. One day, while visiting New York, you take your bathroom scales into

the elevator and stand on them. The scales read 150 lb as the door closes. The reading varies between 120 lb and 170 lb as the elevator travels 101 floors.
    a. What is the magnitude of the acceleration as the elevator starts upward?
    b. What is the magnitude of the acceleration as the elevator brakes to a stop?

49. ‖‖‖ A 23 kg child goes down a straight slide inclined 38° above horizontal. The child is acted on by his weight, the normal force from the slide, kinetic friction, and a horizontal rope exerting a 30 N force as shown in Fig-ure P4.49. How large is the nor-mal force of the slide on the child?

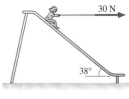

FIGURE P4.49

50. ‖‖‖ Researchers often use *force plates* to measure the forces that BIO people exert against the floor during movement. A force plate INT works like a bathroom scale, but it keeps a record of how the reading changes with time. Figure P4.50 shows the data from a force plate as a woman jumps straight up and then lands.
    a. What was the vertical component of her acceleration dur-ing push-off?
    b. What was the vertical component of her acceleration while in the air?
    c. What was the vertical component of her acceleration dur-ing the landing?
    d. What was her speed as her feet left the force plate?
    e. How high did she jump?

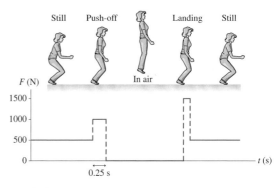

FIGURE P4.50

51. ‖‖‖ A 77 kg sprinter is running the 100 m dash. At one instant, BIO early in the race, his acceleration is 4.7 m/s².
    a. What *total* force does the track surface exert on the sprinter? Assume his acceleration is parallel to the ground. Give your answer as a magnitude and an angle with respect to the horizontal.
    b. This force is applied to one foot (the other foot is in the air), which for a fraction of a second is stationary with respect to the track surface. Because the foot is stationary, the net force on it must be zero. Thus the force of the lower leg bone on the foot is equal but opposite to the force of the track on the foot. If the lower leg bone is 60° from horizon-tal, what are the components of the leg's force on the foot in the directions parallel and perpendicular to the leg? (Force components perpendicular to the leg can cause dis-location of the ankle joint.)

52. ||| Sam, whose mass is 75 kg, takes off across level snow on his jet-powered skis. The skis have a thrust of 200 N and a coefficient of kinetic friction on snow of 0.10. Unfortunately, the skis run out of fuel after only 10 s.
    a. What is Sam's top speed?
    b. How far has Sam traveled when he finally coasts to a stop?

53. ||| A person with compromised pinch strength in his fingers can only exert a normal force of 6.0 N to either side of a pinch-held object, such as the book shown in Figure P4.53. What is the heaviest book he can hold onto vertically before it slips out of his fingers? The coefficient of static friction of the surface between the fingers and the book cover is 0.80.

BIO

FIGURE P4.53

54. | A 1.0 kg wood block is pressed against a vertical wood wall by a 12 N force as shown in Figure P4.55. If the block is initially at rest, will it move upward, move downward, or stay at rest?

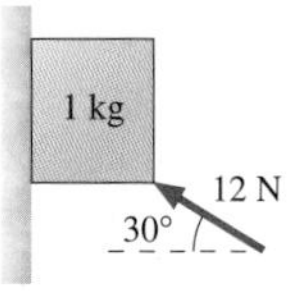

55. || A 50,000 kg locomotive, with steel wheels, is traveling at 10 m/s on steel rails when its engine and brakes both fail. How far will the locomotive roll before it comes to a stop?

FIGURE P4.55

56. ||| An Airbus A320 jetliner has a takeoff mass of 75,000 kg. It reaches its takeoff speed of 82 m/s (180 mph) in 35 s. What is the thrust of the engines? You can neglect air resistance but not rolling friction.

57. |||| A 2.0 kg wood block is launched up a wooden ramp that is inclined at a 35° angle. The block's initial speed is 10 m/s.
    a. What vertical height does the block reach above its starting point?
    b. What speed does it have when it slides back down to its starting point?

58. |||| A 2.7 g Ping-Pong ball has a diameter of 4.0 cm.
    a. The ball is shot straight up at twice its terminal speed. What is its initial acceleration?
    b. The ball is shot straight down at twice its terminal speed. What is its initial acceleration?

59. || The fastest recorded skydive was by an Air Force officer who jumped from a helium balloon at an elevation of 103,000 ft, three times higher than airliners fly. Because the density of air is so low at these altitudes, he reached a speed of 614 mph at an elevation of 90,000 ft, then gradually slowed as the air became more dense. Assume that he fell in the spread-eagle position and that his low-altitude terminal speed is 125 mph. Use this information to determine the density of air at 90,000 ft.

Passage Problems

Sliding on the Ice

In the winter sport of curling, players give a 20 kg stone a push across a sheet of ice. The stone moves approximately 40 m before coming to rest. The final position of the stone, in principle, only depends on the initial speed at which it is launched and the force of friction between the ice and the stone, but team members can use brooms to sweep the ice in front of the stone to adjust its speed and trajectory a bit; they must do this without touching the stone. Judicious sweeping can lengthen the travel of the stone by 3 m.

60. | A curler pushes a stone to a speed of 3.0 m/s over a time of 2.0 s. Ignoring the force of friction, how much force must the curler apply to the stone to bring it up to speed?
  A. 3.0 N   B. 15 N   C. 30 N   D. 150 N

61. | The sweepers in a curling competition adjust the trajectory of the stone by
  A. Decreasing the coefficient of friction between the stone and the ice.
  B. Increasing the coefficient of friction between the stone and the ice.
  C. Changing friction from kinetic to static.
  D. Changing friction from static to kinetic.

62. | Suppose the stone is launched with a speed of 3 m/s and travels 40 m before coming to rest. What is the *approximate* magnitude of the friction force on the stone?
  A. 0 N   B. 2 N   C. 20 N   D. 200 N

63. | Suppose the stone's mass is increased to 40 kg, but it is launched at the same 3 m/s. Which one of the following is true?
  A. The stone would now travel a longer distance before coming to rest.
  B. The stone would now travel a shorter distance before coming to rest.
  C. The coefficient of friction would now be greater.
  D. The force of friction would now be greater.

STOP TO THINK ANSWERS

Stop to Think 4.1: A. The lander is descending and slowing. The acceleration vector points upward, and so $\vec{F}_{net}$ points upward. This can be true only if the thrust has a larger magnitude than the weight.

Stop to Think 4.2: A. You are descending and slowing, so your acceleration vector points upward and there is a net upward force on you. The floor pushes up against your feet harder than gravity pulls down.

Stop to Think 4.3: $f_B > f_C = f_D = f_E > f_A$**.** Situations C, D, and E are all kinetic friction, which does not depend on either velocity or acceleration. Kinetic friction is smaller than the maximum static friction that is exerted in B. $f_A = 0$ because no friction is needed to keep the object at rest.

Stop to Think 4.4: D. The ball is shot *down* at 30 m/s, so $v_{0y} = -30$ m/s. This exceeds the terminal speed, so the upward drag force is *larger* than the downward weight force. Thus the ball *slows down* even though it is "falling." It will slow until $v_y = -15$ m/s, the terminal velocity, then maintain that velocity.

Stop to Think 4.5: B. $F_{QonH} = F_{HonQ}$ and $F_{PonQ} = F_{QonP}$ because these are action/reaction pairs. Box Q is slowing down and therefore must have a net force to the left. So from Newton's second law we also know that $F_{HonQ} > F_{PonQ}$.

Stop to Think 4.6: Equal to. Each block is hanging in equilibrium, with no net force, so the upward tension force is mg.

5

ENERGY AND WORK

Using just a fast run-up and flexible pole, how can a pole vaulter reach an astonishing 6 m (20 ft) off the ground?

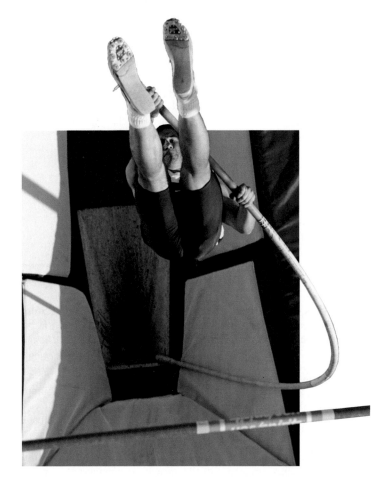

Looking Ahead ▶▶

The goal of Chapter 5 is to introduce the concept of energy and learn a new problem-solving strategy based on conservation of energy. In this chapter you will learn to:

▶ Understand some of the important forms of energy, and how energy can be transformed and transferred.

▶ Understand what work is, and how to calculate it.

▶ Understand and use the concepts of kinetic, potential, and thermal energy.

▶ Solve problems using the law of conservation of energy.

▶ Apply these ideas to elastic collisions.

Looking Back ◀◀

Part of our introduction to energy will be based on the kinematics of constant acceleration. In addition, we will need ideas from rotational motion. We will also use the before-and-after pictorial representation developed for impulse and momentum problems. Please review

◀ Section 2.4 Constant-acceleration kinematics.

nergy. It's a word you hear all the time. We use chemical energy to heat our homes and bodies, electrical energy to run our lights and computers, and solar energy to grow our crops and forests. We're told to use energy wisely and not to waste it. Athletes and weary students consume "energy bars" and "energy drinks."

But just what is energy? The concept of energy has grown and changed with time, and it is not easy to define in a general way just what energy is. Rather than starting with a formal definition, we'll let the concept of energy expand slowly over the course of several chapters. In this chapter we introduce several fundamental forms of energy, including kinetic energy, potential energy, and thermal energy. Our goal is to understand the characteristics of energy, how energy is used, and, especially important, how energy is transformed from one form to another. For example, this pole vaulter, after years of training, has become extraordinarily proficient at transforming his energy of motion into energy associated with height from the ground.

We'll also discover a very powerful conservation law for energy. Some scientists consider the law of conservation of energy to be the most important of all the laws of nature. But all that in due time. First we have to start with the basic ideas.

5.1 A "Natural Money" Called Energy

We will start by discussing what seems to be a completely unrelated topic: money. As you will discover, monetary systems have much in common with energy. Let's begin with a short story.

The Parable of the Lost Penny

John was a hard worker. His only source of income was the paycheck he received each month. Even though most of each paycheck had to be spent on basic necessities, John managed to keep a respectable balance in his checking account. He even saved enough to occasionally buy a few savings bonds, his investment in the future.

John never cared much for pennies, so he kept a jar by the door and dropped all his pennies into it at the end of each day. Eventually, he reasoned, his saved pennies would be worth taking to the bank and converting into crisp new dollar bills.

John found it fascinating to keep track of these various forms of money. He noticed, to his dismay, that the amount of money in his checking account did not spontaneously increase overnight. Furthermore, there seemed to be a definite correlation between the size of his paycheck and the amount of money he had in the bank. So John decided to embark on a systematic study of money.

He began, as would any good scientist, by using his initial observations to formulate a hypothesis, which he called a *model* of the monetary system. He found that he could represent his monetary model with the flowchart in Figure 5.1.

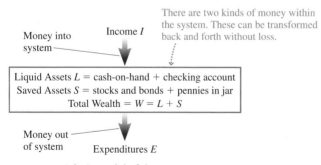

FIGURE 5.1 John's model of the monetary system.

As the chart shows, John divided his money into two basic types, liquid assets and saved assets. The *liquid assets* L, which included his checking account and the cash in his pockets, were moneys available for immediate use. His *saved assets* S, which included his savings bonds as well as the jar of pennies, had the potential to be converted into liquid assets, but they were not available for immediate use.

John decided to call the sum total of assets his *wealth:* $W = L + S$.

John's assets were, more or less, simply definitions. The more interesting question, he thought, was how his wealth depended on his *income I* and *expenditures E*. These represented money transferred *to* him by his employer and money transferred *by* him to stores and bill collectors. After painstakingly collecting and analyzing his data, John finally determined that the relationship between monetary transfers and wealth is

$$\Delta W = I - E$$

John interpreted this equation to mean that the *change* in his wealth, ΔW, was numerically equal to the *net* monetary transfer $I - E$.

During a week-long period when John stayed home sick, isolated from the rest of the world, he had neither income nor expenses. In grand confirmation of his hypothesis, he found that his wealth W_f at the end of the week was identical to his wealth W_i at the week's beginning. That is, $W_f = W_i$. This occurred despite the fact that he had moved pennies from his pocket to the jar and also, by telephone, had sold some bonds and transferred the money to his checking account. In other words, John found that he could make all of the *internal* conversions of assets from one form to another that he wanted, but his total wealth remained constant ($W =$ constant) as long as he was isolated from the world. This seemed such a remarkable rule that John named it the *law of conservation of wealth.*

One day, however, John added up his income and expenditures for the week, and the changes in his various assets, and he was 1¢ off! Inexplicably, some money seemed to have vanished. He was devastated. All those years of careful research, and now it seemed that his monetary hypothesis might not be true. Under some circumstances, yet to be discovered, it looked like $\Delta W \neq I - E$. Off by a measly penny. A wasted scientific life. . . .

But wait! In a flash of inspiration, John realized that perhaps there were other types of assets, yet to be discovered, and that his monetary hypothesis would still be valid if *all* assets were included. Weeks went by as John, in frantic activity, searched fruitlessly for previously *hidden* assets. Then one day, as John lifted the cushion off the sofa to vacuum out the potato chip crumbs—lo and behold, there it was!—the missing penny!

John raced to complete his theory, now including money in the sofa, the washing machine, and behind the radiator as previously unknown forms of assets that were easy to convert from other forms, but often rather difficult to recover. Other researchers soon discovered other types of assets, such as the remarkable find of the "cash in the mattress." To this day, when *all* known assets are included, monetary scientists have never found a violation of John's simple hypothesis that $\Delta W = I - E$. John was last seen sailing for Stockholm to collect the Nobel Prize for his Theory of Wealth.

5.2 The Basic Energy Model

John, despite his diligent efforts, did not discover a law of nature. The monetary system is a human construction that, by design, obeys John's "laws." Monetary system laws, such as that you cannot print money in your basement, are enforced by society, not by nature. But suppose that physical objects possessed a "natural money" that was governed by a theory, or model, similar to John's. An object might have several forms of natural money that could be converted back and forth, but the total amount of an object's natural money would *change* only if natural money were *transferred* to or from the object. Two key words here, as in John's model, are *transfer* and *change*.

One of the greatest and most significant discoveries of science is that there is such a "natural money" called **energy.** You have heard of some of the many forms of energy, such as solar energy or nuclear energy, but others may be new to you. These forms of energy can differ as much as a checking account differs from loose change in the sofa. Much of our study is going to be focused on the *transformation* of energy from one form to another. Much of modern technology is concerned with transforming energy, such as changing the chemical energy of oil molecules to electrical energy or to the kinetic energy of your car.

As we use energy concepts, we will be "accounting" for energy that is transferred in or out of a system or that is transformed from one form to another within a system. Figure 5.2 shows a simple model of energy that is based on John's model of the monetary system. Many details must be added to this model, but it's a good starting point. The fact that nature "balances the books" for energy is one of the most profound discoveries of science.

A major goal of ours is to discover the conditions under which energy is conserved. Surprisingly, the *law of conservation of energy* was not recognized until the mid-nineteenth century, long after Newton. The reason, similar to John's lost penny, was that it took scientists a long time to realize how many types of energy there are and the various ways that energy can be converted from one form to another. As you'll soon learn, energy ideas go well beyond Newtonian mechanics to include new concepts about heat, about chemical energy, and about the energy of the individual atoms and molecules that comprise an object. All of these forms of energy will ultimately have to be included in our accounting scheme for energy.

Systems and Energy

Earlier, we introduced the idea of a *system* of interacting objects. A system can be quite simple, such as a saltshaker sliding across the table, or much more complex, such as a city or a human body. But whether simple or complex, every system in nature has associated with it a quantity we call its **total energy** E. Like John's total wealth, which was made up of assets of many kinds, the total energy of a system is made up of many kinds of energies. In the table below, we give a brief overview of some of the more important forms of energy; in the rest of the chapter we'll look at several of these forms of energy in much greater detail.

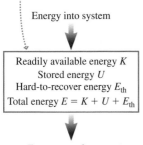

There are several kinds of energy within the system. These can be transformed back and forth without loss.

Energy into system

Readily available energy K
Stored energy U
Hard-to-recover energy E_{th}
Total energy $E = K + U + E_{th}$

Energy out of system

FIGURE 5.2 An initial model of energy.

Some important forms of energy

Kinetic energy K	Gravitational potential energy U_g	Elastic or spring potential energy U_s

Kinetic energy is the energy of *motion.* All moving objects have kinetic energy. The heavier an object, and the faster it moves, the more kinetic energy it has. The wrecking ball in this picture is effective in part because of its large kinetic energy.

Gravitational potential energy is *stored* energy associated with an object's *height above the ground.* As this roller coaster ascends the track, energy is stored as increased gravitational potential energy. As it descends, this stored energy is converted into kinetic energy.

Elastic potential energy is energy stored when a spring or other elastic object, such as this archer's bow, is *stretched.* This energy can later be transformed into the kinetic energy of the arrow. We'll sometimes use the symbol U to represent potential energy when it is not important to distinguish between U_g and U_s.

Thermal energy E_{th}	Chemical energy E_{chem}	Nuclear energy $E_{nuclear}$

Hot objects have more *thermal energy* than cold ones because the molecules in a hot object jiggle around more than those in a cold object. Thermal energy is really just the sum of the microscopic kinetic and potential energies of all the molecules in an object. In boiling water, some molecules have enough energy to escape the water as steam.

Electric forces cause atoms to bind together to make molecules. Energy can be stored in these bonds, energy that can later be released as the bonds are rearranged during chemical reactions. When we burn fuel to run our car, or eat food to power our bodies, we are using *chemical energy.*

An enormous amount of energy is stored in the *nucleus,* the tiny core of an atom. Certain nuclei can be made to break apart, releasing some of this *nuclear energy,* which is transformed into the kinetic energy of the fragments and then into thermal energy. This is the source of energy of nuclear power plants and nuclear weapons.

A system may have many of these kinds of energy present in it at once. For instance, a moving car has kinetic energy of motion, chemical energy stored in its gasoline, thermal energy in its hot engine, and other forms of energy in its many other parts. The total energy of the system, E, is just the *sum* of the different energies present in the system, so that we have

$$E = K + U_g + U_s + E_{th} + E_{chem} + \cdots \qquad (5.1)$$

The energies shown in this sum are the forms of energy in which we'll be most interested in this and the next chapter. The ellipses (. . .) represent other forms of energy, such as nuclear or electric, that also might be present. We'll treat these and others in later chapters.

Energy Transformations

We've seen that all systems contain energy in many different forms. But if the amounts of each form of energy never changed, the world would be a very dull place. What makes the world interesting is that **energy of one kind can** *transform*

into energy of another kind. The gravitational potential energy of the roller coaster at the top of the track is rapidly converted into kinetic energy as the coaster descends; the chemical energy of gasoline is converted into the kinetic energy of your moving car. The following table illustrates a few common energy transformations. In this table, we'll use an arrow → as a shorthand way of representing an energy transformation.

Some energy transformations

A weightlifter lifts a barbell over her head
The barbell has much more gravitational potential energy when high above her head than when on the floor. To lift the barbell, she is transforming chemical energy in her body into gravitational potential energy of the barbell.

$$E_{chem} \rightarrow U_g$$

A base runner slides into the base
When running, he has lots of kinetic energy. After sliding, he has none. His kinetic energy is transformed mainly into thermal energy: the ground and his legs are slightly warmer.

$$K \rightarrow E_{th}$$

A burning campfire
The wood contains considerable chemical energy. When the carbon in the wood combines chemically with oxygen in the air, this chemical energy is transformed largely into thermal energy of the hot gases and embers.

$$E_{chem} \rightarrow E_{th}$$

A springboard diver
Here's a two-step energy transformation. The picture shows the diver after his first jump onto the board itself. At the instant shown, the board is flexed to its maximum extent. There is a large amount of elastic potential energy stored in the board. Soon this energy will begin to be transformed into kinetic energy; as he rises into the air and slows, this kinetic energy will be transformed into gravitational potential energy.

$$U_s \rightarrow K \rightarrow U_g$$

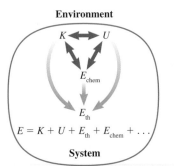

FIGURE 5.3 Energy transformations occur within the system.

Figure 5.3 reinforces the idea that **energy transformations are changes of energy *within* the system from one form to another.** Note that it is easy to convert kinetic, potential, or chemical energies into thermal energy. But converting thermal energy back into these other forms is not so easy. How it can be done, and what possible limitations there might be in doing so, will form a large part of the next chapter.

Energy Transfers: Work and Heat

We've just seen that energy *transformations* occur between forms of energy *within* a system. In our monetary model, these transformations are like John's shifting of money between his own various assets, such as from his savings account to stocks. But John also interacted with the greater world around him, receiving money as income and outlaying it as expenditures. Every physical system also interacts with the world around it, that is, with its *environment*. In the course of these interactions, the system can exchange energy with the environment. **An exchange of energy between system and environment is called an energy** *transfer.* There are two primary energy transfer processes: **work,** the *mechanical* transfer of energy to or from a system by pushing or pulling on it, and **heat,** the *nonmechanical* transfer of energy from the environment to the system (or vice versa) *because of a temperature difference between the two.* Figure 5.4 shows how our energy model is modified to include energy transfers. In this chapter we'll focus mainly on work; the concept of heat will be developed much further in Chapters 6 and 7.

Work is a common word in the English language, with many meanings. When you first think of work, you probably think of the first two definitions in this list. After all, we talk about "working out," or we say, "I just got home from work." But that is *not* what work means in physics.

In physics we use *work* in the sense of definition 6: Work is the process of *transferring* energy from the environment to a system, or from a system to the environment, by the application of mechanical forces—pushes and pulls—to the system. Once the energy has been transferred to the system, it can appear in many forms. Exactly what form it takes depends on the details of the system and how the forces are applied. The table below gives a few examples of energy transfers due to work. We use W as the symbol for work.

FIGURE 5.4 Work and heat are energy transfers into and out of the system.

Energy is transferred from the environment to the system.

Work, heat

Energy is transferred from the system to the environment.

Environment

System

K ↔ U

E_{chem}

E_{th}

One dictionary defines *work* as:

1. Physical or mental effort; labor.
2. The activity by which one makes a living.
3. A task or duty.
4. Something produced as a result of effort, such as a *work of art.*
5. Plural *works:* The essential or operating parts of a mechanism.
6. The transfer of energy to a body by application of a force.

Energy transfers: work

Putting a shot

The system: The shot.

The environment: The athlete.

As the athlete pushes on the shot to get it moving, he is doing work on the system. That is, he is transferring energy from himself to the ball. The energy transferred to the system appears as kinetic energy.

The transfer: $W \rightarrow K$

Striking a match

The system: The match and matchbox.

The environment: The hand.

As the hand quickly pulls the match across the box, the hand does work on the system, increasing its thermal energy. The match-head becomes hot enough to ignite.

The transfer: $W \rightarrow E_{th}$

Firing a slingshot

The system: The slingshot.

The environment: The boy.

As the boy pulls back on the elastic bands, he does work on the system, increasing its elastic potential energy.

The transfer: $W \rightarrow U_s$

Notice that in each example above, the environment applies a force while the system undergoes a *displacement.* Energy is transferred as work only when the system *moves* while the force acts. A force applied to a stationary object, such as when you push against a wall, transfers no energy to the object and thus does no work.

NOTE ▶ In the table above, energy is being transferred *from* the athlete *to* the shot by the force of his hand. We say he "does work" on the shot, or "work is done" by the force of his hand. ◀

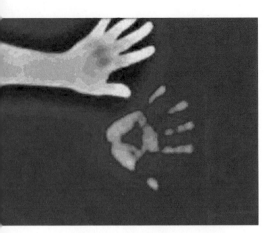

As the hand in the photo was held against the wall, heat was transferred from the warm hand to the cool wall, warming up the wall. The warm "handprint" can be imaged using a special camera sensitive to the temperature of objects.

It is also possible to convert work into gravitational potential, electric, or even chemical energy. We'll have much more to say about work in the next section. But the key points to remember are that **work is the transfer of energy to or from a system by the application of forces,** and that **the system must undergo a displacement for this energy to be transferred.**

There is a second, nonmechanical means of transferring energy between a system and its environment, which we discuss here only briefly. As mentioned before, we'll have much more to say about heat in the next two chapters. When a hot object is placed in contact with a cooler one, energy flows naturally from the hot object to the cool one. **The transfer of energy from a hot to a cold object is called *heat,*** and it is given the symbol Q. It is important to note that heat is not an energy *of* a system, as are kinetic energy and chemical energy. Rather, heat is energy *transferred* between two systems.

STOP TO THINK 5.1   A child slides down a playground slide at constant speed. The energy transformation is

A. $U_g \rightarrow K$ B. $K \rightarrow U_g$ C. $W \rightarrow K$ D. $U_g \rightarrow E_{th}$ E. $K \rightarrow E_{th}$

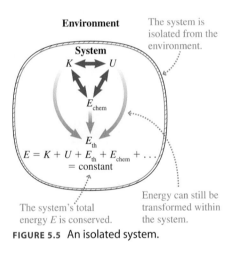

Environment

The system is isolated from the environment.

System

$K \longleftrightarrow U$

E_{chem}

E_{th}

$E = K + U + E_{th} + E_{chem} + \ldots$ = constant

The system's total energy E is conserved.

Energy can still be transformed within the system.

FIGURE 5.5 An isolated system.

5.3 The Law of Conservation of Energy

Remember that when John was *isolated* from the rest of the world—having neither income nor expenses—his internal wealth could be converted between its many forms, but his *total* wealth remained constant. A similar but much more fundamental law is found for the "natural money" of energy.

Let's start our study of this law by considering an **isolated system** that is separated from its surrounding environment in such a way that no energy can flow into or out of the system. This means that no work is done on the system, nor is any energy transferred as heat. We've already seen that the total energy of a system is made up of many forms of energy that are continually transforming from one kind to another. It is a deep and remarkable fact of nature that during these transformations, the total energy of an isolated system—the *sum* of all of the individual kinds of energy—remains *constant.* Any increase in, say, the system's kinetic energy must be accompanied by a decrease in its potential or thermal energies so that the total energy remains unchanged, as shown in Figure 5.5. We say that **the total energy of an isolated system is *conserved,*** giving us the following *law of conservation of energy.*

> **Law of conservation of energy for an isolated system** The total energy of an isolated system remains constant:
>
> The energies in the system are constantly transforming from one kind to another . . .   . . . but their *sum* is a constant: it doesn't change.
>
> $$K + U_g + U_s + E_{th} + E_{chem} + \ldots = E = \text{constant}$$ (5.2)

Another way to think of this conservation law is in terms of energy *changes.* Recall that we denote the change in a quantity by the symbol Δ, so we write the change in a system's kinetic energy, for instance, as ΔK. Now suppose that an isolated system has its kinetic energy change by ΔK, its gravitational potential energy by ΔU_g, and so on. Then the sum of these changes is the change in the total energy. But since the total energy is constant, its change is *zero.* We can thus write the law of conservation of energy in an alternate form as

> **Law of conservation of energy for an isolated system (alternate form)**
> The change in the total energy of an isolated system is zero:
>
> $$\Delta E = \Delta K + \Delta U_g + \Delta U_s + \Delta E_{th} + \Delta E_{chem} + {}^C = 0 \qquad (5.3)$$

Any increase in one form of energy must be accompanied by a decrease in other forms, so that the total change is zero.

The law of conservation of energy sets a fundamental constraint on those processes that can occur in nature. In any process that occurs within an isolated system, the changes in each form of energy must add up to zero, as required by Equation 5.3.

CONCEPTUAL EXAMPLE 5.1 **Energy changes in a bungee ride**

A popular fair attraction is the trampoline bungee ride. The rider bounces up and down on large bungee cords. During part of her motion she is found to be moving upward with the cords becoming more stretched. Is she speeding up or slowing down during this interval?

REASON We'll take our system to include the rider, the bungee cords, and the *earth*. We'll see later how gravitational potential energy is stored in the *system* consisting of the earth and an object such as the rider. With this choice of system, to a good approximation the system is isolated, with no energy being transferred into or out of the system. Thus the total energy of the system is constant: $\Delta E = 0$.

Because she's moving upward, her height is increasing—and thus so is her gravitational potential energy. Thus $\Delta U_g > 0$. We also know that the cords are getting more stretched, hence more elastic potential energy is being stored. Thus $\Delta U_s > 0$ as well. Now the law of conservation of energy, Equation 5.3, states that $\Delta E = \Delta K + \Delta U_g + \Delta U_s = 0$, so that $\Delta K = -(\Delta U_g + \Delta U_s)$. Both ΔU_g and ΔU_s are positive, so ΔK must be *negative*. This means that her kinetic energy is *decreasing*. Since kinetic energy is energy of motion, this means that she's slowing down.

ASSESS In that part of her motion where she's moving upward and the cords are stretching, she's approaching the highest point of her motion. It makes sense that she's slowing down here, since at the high point her speed is instantaneously zero.

Systems That Aren't Isolated

When John had income and expenses, his total wealth could change. Indeed, he found that his wealth increased by exactly the amount of his income, and decreased by exactly the amount of his expenditures. Similarly, if a system is *not* isolated, so that it can exchange energy with its environment, the system's energy can change. We have seen that the two primary means of energy exchange are work and heat. If an amount of work W is done on the system, this means that an amount of energy W is transferred from the environment to the system, increasing the system's energy by exactly W. Similarly, if a certain amount of energy is transferred from a hot environment to a cooler system as heat Q, the system's energy will increase by exactly the amount Q. As illustrated in Figure 5.6, **the change in the system's energy is simply the sum of the work done on the system and the heat transferred to the system:**

$$\Delta E = W + Q$$

This gives us a more general statement of conservation of energy:

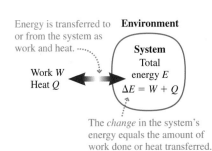

Energy is transferred to or from the system as work and heat.

Work W
Heat Q

Environment

System
Total energy E
$\Delta E = W + Q$

The *change* in the system's energy equals the amount of work done or heat transferred.

FIGURE 5.6 The law of conservation of energy.

> **Law of conservation of energy including energy transfers** The change in the total energy of a nonisolated system is equal to the energy transferred into or out of the system as work W or heat Q:
>
> $$\Delta K + \Delta U_g + \Delta U_s + \Delta E_{th} + \Delta E_{chem} + {}^C = W + Q \qquad (5.4)$$

Airplanes are assisted in takeoff from aircraft carriers by a steam-powered catapult under the flight deck. The force of this catapult does work W on the plane, leading to a large increase ΔK in the plane's kinetic energy.

Equation 5.4 is the fullest expression of the law of conservation of energy. It's usually called the **first law of thermodynamics,** but it's really just a restatement of the law of conservation of energy to include the possibility of energy transfers. In this chapter we'll refer to it simply as the law of conservation of energy.

NOTE ▶ It's important to realize that even when the system is not isolated, energy is conserved overall. The energy transferred to the system as, say, work increases the energy of the system. But this energy is *removed* from the environment, so that the total energy of system *plus* environment is still conserved. ◀

Systems and Conservation of Energy

To apply the law of conservation of energy, you need to carefully define which objects make up the system and which belong to the environment. This choice will affect how we analyze the various energy transfers and tranformations that occur. In doing so, we need to make a distinction between two classes of forces. **Internal forces** are forces between objects *within* the system. If a weightlifter and barbell are both part of the system, the forces $\vec{F}_{\text{weightlifter on barbell}}$ and $\vec{F}_{\text{barbell on weightlifter}}$ are both internal forces. Internal forces are responsible for energy transformations within the system. Because they are internal to the system, however, **internal forces cannot do work on the system** and thereby change its energy. **External forces** act on the system, but their agent is part of the *environment*. **External forces *can* do work on the system,** transferring energy in or out of it. Whether a given force is an internal or external force depends on the choice of what's included in the system. The following table shows some choices for a crane accelerating a heavy ball upward.

Different choices of the system

Both these forces are due to the environment: They are *external* forces that do work. → Tension $\vec{T}$ ⟍ System boundary $\vec{a}$ → Weight $\vec{w}$	$\vec{T}$ ↑ $\vec{a}$ ↑ $\vec{T}$ is still an external force, but now $\vec{w}$ is *internal*. → Weight $\vec{w}$ Earth	Many other internal forces of crane All forces are now internal. The system is *isolated*. $\vec{T}$ $\vec{w}$ $\vec{a}$ ↑
System: The ball only	Ball + earth	Ball + earth + crane
Internal forces: None	$\vec{w}$	$\vec{T}, \vec{w}$, many internal forces of crane
External forces: $\vec{T}, \vec{w}$	$\vec{T}$	None
System energies: K	K, U_g	K, U_g, E_{chem}
Energy analysis: Tension does positive work and the weight does negative work, but since $T > w$ the net work is positive. This work serves to increase the only energy of the system, its kinetic energy. Notice that since the earth is *not* part of the system, the system has no gravitational potential energy.	The weight force is now an *internal* force. That is, it is an interaction force between two objects—the ball and the earth—that are part of the system. The tension force is still an *external* force that does work on the system. This work increases the gravitational potential energy and the kinetic energy of the system.	Now all the forces are internal, and no work is done on the system: The system is *isolated*. With this choice of system, the increased potential and kinetic energy of the ball come from an energy *transformation* from the chemical energy of the crane's fuel.
Energy equation: $\Delta K = W$	$\Delta K + \Delta U_g = W$	$\Delta K + \Delta U_g + \Delta E_{\text{chem}} = 0$

There are evidently many possible choices of the system for a given situation. However, certain choices can make problem solving using the law of energy conservation easier. For the crane above, we'd probably choose the second system consisting of the ball and the earth, since it is a good balance between reducing the number of external forces and having only simple system energies such as K

and U_g. The third choice would be hard to work with, since the many complicated internal forces are difficult to calculate. Tactics Box 5.1 gives some suggestions on how to make a good choice for the system.

 TACTICS BOX 5.1 Choosing the system for conservation-of-energy problems   Exercise 6

The system should include all of the objects identified as follows:

❶ If the speed of an object or objects is changing, the system should include these moving objects because their kinetic energy is changing.

❷ If the height of an object or objects is changing, the system should include the raised object(s) *plus* the earth. This is because potential energy is stored via the gravitational interaction of the earth and object(s).

❸ If the compression or extension of a spring is changing, the system should include the spring because elastic potential energy is stored in the spring itself.

❹ If kinetic or rolling friction is present, the system should include the moving object and the surface on which it slides or rolls. This is because thermal energy is created in both the moving object and the surface, and we want this thermal energy to all be within the system.

Working with Energy Transformations

The law of conservation of energy applies to every form of energy, from kinetic to chemical to nuclear. For the rest of this chapter, however, we'll narrow our focus a bit and only concern ourselves with the forms of energy typically transformed during the motion of ordinary objects. These energies are the kinetic energy K, the potential energy U (which includes both U_g and U_s), and thermal energy E_{th}. The sum of the kinetic and potential energy, $K + U = K + U_g + U_s$, is called the **mechanical energy** of the system. We'll also limit our analysis to energy transfers in the form of work W. In Chapter 6 we'll expand our scope to include other forms of energy listed in the earlier table, as well as energy transfers as heat Q.

The fact that energy is conserved can be a powerful tool for analyzing the dynamics of moving objects. To see how we can apply the law of conservation of energy to dynamics problems, let's use the fact that the change in any quantity is its final value minus its initial value so that, for example, $\Delta K = K_f - K_i$. Then we can write the law of conservation of energy, Equation 5.4 (with $Q = 0$), as

$$(K_f - K_i) + (U_f - U_i) + \Delta E_{th} = W \qquad (5.5)$$

NOTE ▶ We don't rewrite ΔE_{th} as $(E_{th})_f - (E_{th})_i$ because the initial thermal energy of an object is typically unknown. Only the *change* in E_{th} can be measured. ◀

Rearranging, we have

$$\underbrace{K_i + U_i}_{} + W = \underbrace{K_f + U_f + \Delta E_{th}}_{} \qquad (5.6)$$

The initial energy of the system...   ...plus the energy transferred to the system as work...   ...equals the final system energy, now possibly including extra thermal energy.

If no external forces do work on the system, $W = 0$ in Equation 5.6 and the system is *isolated*. **If no kinetic friction is present, ΔE_{th} will be zero and mechanical energy will be conserved.** Equation 5.6 then becomes the **law of conservation of mechanical energy:**

$$K_i + U_i = K_f + U_f \tag{5.7}$$

Equations 5.6 and 5.7 summarize what we have learned about the conservation of energy, and they will be the basis of our strategy for solving problems using the law of conservation of energy. Much of the rest of this chapter will be concerned with finding quantitative expressions for the different forms of energy in the system and discussing the important question of what to include in the system. We'll use the following Problem-Solving Strategy as we further develop these ideas.

Spring into action BIO A locust can jump as far as one meter, an impressive distance for such a small animal. To make such a jump, its legs must extend much more rapidly than muscles can ordinarily contract. Thus, instead of using its muscles to make the jump directly, the locust uses them to more slowly stretch an internal "spring" near its knee joint. This stores elastic potential energy in the spring. When the muscles relax, the spring is suddenly released, and its energy is rapidly converted into kinetic energy of the insect.

(MP) PROBLEM-SOLVING
STRATEGY 5.1   **Conservation of energy problems**

PREPARE   Choose what to include in your system (see Tactics Box 5.1). Draw a before-and-after visual overview. Note known quantities, and determine what quantity you're trying to find. If the system is isolated and if there is no friction, your solution will be based on Equation 5.7, otherwise you should use Equation 5.6.

Identify which mechanical energies in the system are changing:

- If the *speed* of the object is changing, include K_i and K_f in your solution.
- If the *height* of the object is changing, include $(U_g)_i$ and $(U_g)_f$.
- If the *length* of a spring is changing, include $(U_s)_i$ and $(U_s)_f$.
- If kinetic friction is present, ΔE_{th} will be positive. Some kinetic or potential energy will be transformed into thermal energy.

If an external force acts on the system, you'll need to include the work W done by this force in Equation 5.6.

SOLVE   Depending on the problem, you'll need to calculate initial and/or final values of these energies and insert them into Equation 5.6 or 5.7. Then you can solve for the unknown energies, and from these any unknown speeds (from K), positions (from U), or displacements or forces (from W).

ASSESS   Check the signs of your energies. Kinetic energy, as we'll see, is always positive. In the systems we'll study in this chapter, thermal energy can only increase, so that its change is positive. In Chapters 6 and 7 we'll study systems for which the thermal energy can decrease.

5.4 Work

We've already discussed work as the transfer of energy between a system and its environment by the application of forces on the system. We also noted that in order for energy to be transferred in this way, the system must undergo a displacement—it must *move*—during the time that the force is applied. Let's further investigate the relationship between work, force, and displacement. We'll find that there is a simple expression for work, which we can then use to quantify other kinds of energy as well.

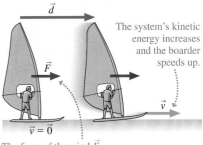

The system's kinetic energy increases and the boarder speeds up.

The force of the wind $\vec{F}$ does work on the system.

FIGURE 5.7 The force of the wind does work on the system, increasing its kinetic energy K.

Consider a system consisting of a windsurfer at rest, as shown on the left in Figure 5.7. Let's assume that there is no friction between his board and the water. Initially the system has no kinetic energy. But if a force from outside the system, such as the force due to the wind, begins to act on the system, the surfer will begin to speed up, and his kinetic energy will increase. In terms of energy transfers, we would say that the energy of the system has increased because of the work done on the system by the force of the wind.

What determines how much work is done by the force of the wind? First, we note that the greater the distance over which the wind pushes the surfer, the faster the surfer goes, and the more his kinetic energy increases. This implies a greater transfer of energy. So **the larger the displacement, the greater the work done.** Second, if the wind pushes with a stronger force, the surfer speeds up more rapidly, and the change in his kinetic energy is greater than with a weaker force. **The stronger the force, the greater the work done.**

This experiment suggests that the amount of energy transferred into a system by a force $\vec{F}$—that is, the amount of work done by $\vec{F}$—depends on both the magnitude F of the force *and* the displacement d of the system. Many experiments of this kind have established that the amount of work done by $\vec{F}$ is *proportional* to both F and d. For the simplest case described above, where the force $\vec{F}$ is constant and points in the direction of the object's displacement, the expression for the work done is found to be

$$W = Fd \tag{5.8}$$

Work done by a constant force $\vec{F}$
in the direction of a displacement $\vec{d}$

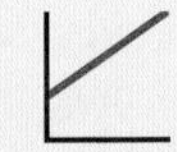

LINEAR
p. 38

The unit of work, that of force multiplied by distance, is N · m. This unit is so important that it has been given its own name, the **joule** (rhymes with *tool*). We define:

$$1 \text{ joule} = 1 \text{ J} = 1 \text{ N} \cdot \text{m}$$

Since work is simply energy being transferred, **the joule is the unit of *all* forms of energy.** Note that work is a *scalar* quantity.

EXAMPLE 5.1 Work done in pushing a crate

Sarah pushes a heavy crate 3.0 m along the floor at a constant speed. She pushes with a constant horizontal force of magnitude 70 N. How much work does Sarah do on the crate?

PREPARE We begin with the visual overview in Figure 5.8. Sarah pushes with a constant force in the direction of the crate's motion, so we can use Equation 5.8 to find the work done.

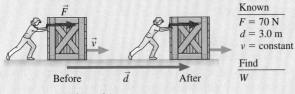

	Known
	$F = 70$ N
	$d = 3.0$ m
	$v =$ constant
	Find
	W

Before $\vec{d}$ After

FIGURE 5.8 Sarah pushing a crate.

SOLVE The work done by Sarah is given by

$$W = Fd = (70 \text{ N})(3.0 \text{ m}) = 210 \text{ J}$$

ASSESS Since the crate moves at a constant speed, it must be in dynamic equilibrium with $\vec{F}_{net} = \vec{0}$. This means that a friction force (not shown) must act opposite to Sarah's push. If friction is present, Tactics Box 5.1 suggests taking the crate *and* the floor as the system. The work Sarah does represents energy transferred *into* the system. In this case, the work increases the thermal energy in the crate and the part of the floor along which it slid. Contrast this with the windsurfer, where work increased the windsurfer's kinetic energy. Both situations are consistent with the energy model shown in Figure 5.4, which you should review at this point.

(b) The rider undergoes a displacement $\vec{d}$.

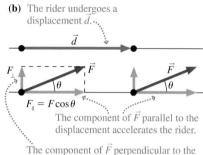

$F_{\parallel} = F\cos\theta$

The component of $\vec{F}$ parallel to the displacement accelerates the rider.

The component of $\vec{F}$ perpendicular to the displacement only pulls up on the rider. It doesn't accelerate him.

FIGURE 5.9 Finding the work done when the force is at an angle to the displacement.

Force at an Angle to the Displacement

Pushing a crate in the same direction as the crate's displacement is the most efficient way to transfer energy into the system, and so the largest possible amount of work is done. Less work is done if the force acts at an angle to the displacement. To see this, consider the kite buggy of Figure 5.9a, pulled along a horizontal path by the angled force of the kite string $\vec{F}$. As shown in Figure 5.9b, we can break $\vec{F}$ into a component $F_{\perp}$ perpendicular to the motion, and a component $F_{\parallel}$ parallel to the motion. Only the parallel component acts to accelerate the rider and increase his kinetic energy, so only the parallel component does work on the rider. From Figure 5.9b, we see that if the angle between $\vec{F}$ and the displacement is θ, then the parallel component is $F_{\parallel} = F\cos\theta$. So when the force acts at an angle θ to the direction of the displacement, we have

$$W = F_{\parallel}d = Fd\cos\theta \tag{5.9}$$

Work done by a constant force $\vec{F}$ at an angle θ to the displacement $\vec{d}$

Notice that this more general definition of work agrees with Equation 5.8 if $\theta = 0°$.

CONCEPTUAL EXAMPLE 5.2 Work done by a parachute

A drag racer is slowed by a parachute. What is the sign of the work done?

REASON The drag force on the drag racer is shown in Figure 5.10, along with the dragster's displacement as it slows. The force points in the opposite direction to the displacement, so that the angle θ in Equation 5.9 is 180°. Then $\cos\theta = \cos(180°) = -1$. Since F and d in Equation 5.9 are magnitudes, and hence positive, this means that the work $W = Fd\cos\theta = -Fd$ done by the drag force is *negative*.

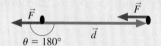

$\theta = 180°$

FIGURE 5.10 The force acting on a drag racer.

ASSESS Applying Equation 5.4, the law of conservation of energy, to this situation, we have

$$\Delta K = W$$

because the only system energy that changes is the racer's kinetic energy K. Since the kinetic energy is decreasing, its change ΔK is negative. This agrees with the sign of W. This example illustrates the general principle that **negative work represents a transfer of energy out of the system.**

Tactics Box 5.2 shows how to calculate the work done by a force at any angle to the direction of motion. The system illustrated is a block sliding on a frictionless horizontal surface, so that only the kinetic energy is changing. However, the same relationships hold for any object undergoing a displacement.

The quantities F and d are always positive, so **the sign of W is determined entirely by the angle θ between the force and the displacement.** Note that

Equation 5.9, $W = Fd\cos\theta$, is valid for any angle θ. In three special cases, $\theta = 0°$, $\theta = 90°$, and $\theta = 180°$, however, there are simple versions of Equation 5.9 that you can use. These are noted in Tactics Box 5.2.

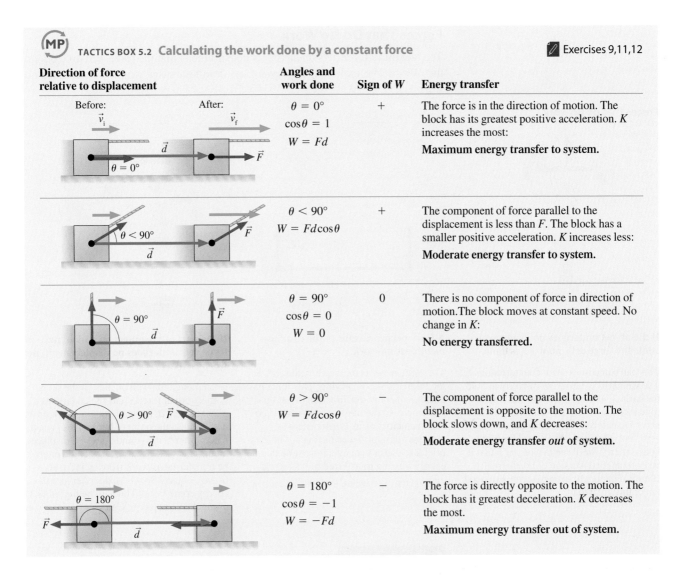

(MP) **TACTICS BOX 5.2** **Calculating the work done by a constant force**   📝 Exercises 9,11,12

Direction of force relative to displacement	Angles and work done	Sign of W	Energy transfer
Before: $\vec{v}_i$ **After:** $\vec{v}_f$ $\vec{d}$ $\theta = 0°$ $\vec{F}$	$\theta = 0°$ $\cos\theta = 1$ $W = Fd$	+	The force is in the direction of motion. The block has its greatest positive acceleration. K increases the most: **Maximum energy transfer to system.**
$\theta < 90°$ $\vec{F}$ $\vec{d}$	$\theta < 90°$ $W = Fd\cos\theta$	+	The component of force parallel to the displacement is less than F. The block has a smaller positive acceleration. K increases less: **Moderate energy transfer to system.**
$\theta = 90°$ $\vec{F}$ $\vec{d}$	$\theta = 90°$ $\cos\theta = 0$ $W = 0$	0	There is no component of force in direction of motion. The block moves at constant speed. No change in K: **No energy transferred.**
$\theta > 90°$ $\vec{F}$ $\vec{d}$	$\theta > 90°$ $W = Fd\cos\theta$	–	The component of force parallel to the displacement is opposite to the motion. The block slows down, and K decreases: **Moderate energy transfer *out* of system.**
$\theta = 180°$ $\vec{F}$ $\vec{d}$	$\theta = 180°$ $\cos\theta = -1$ $W = -Fd$	–	The force is directly opposite to the motion. The block has it greatest deceleration. K decreases the most. **Maximum energy transfer out of system.**

EXAMPLE 5.2 Work done in pulling a suitcase

A strap inclined upward at a 45° angle pulls a suitcase through the airport. The tension in the strap is 20 N. How much work does the tension do if the suitcase is pulled 100 m at a constant speed?

PREPARE Figure 5.11 shows a visual overview. Since the case moves at a constant speed, there must be a rolling friction force acting to the left. Tactics Box 5.1 suggests in this case that we take as our system the suitcase and the floor upon which it rolls.

SOLVE We can use Equation 5.9 to find that the tension does work

$$W = Td\cos\theta = (20\text{ N})(100\text{ m})\cos 45° = 1400\text{ J}$$

ASSESS Because a person is pulling on the other end of the strap, causing the tension, we would say informally that the person does 1400 J of work on the suitcase. This work represents

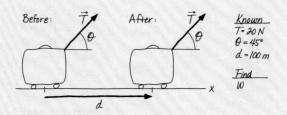

FIGURE 5.11 A suitcase pulled by a strap.

energy transferred into the suitcase/floor system. Since the suitcase moves at a constant speed, the system's kinetic energy doesn't change. Thus the work goes entirely into increasing the *thermal* energy E_{th} of the suitcase and the floor.

If several forces act on an object that undergoes a displacement, each does work on the object. The **total (or net) work** W_{total} is the sum of the work done by each force. The total work represents the total energy transfer *to* the system from the environment (if $W_{total} > 0$) or *from* the system to the environment (if $W_{total} < 0$).

Forces That Do No Work

The fact that a force acts on an object doesn't mean that the force will do work on the object. The table below shows three common cases where a force does no work.

Forces that do no work

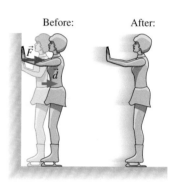

If the object undergoes no displacement while the force acts, no work is done.	**A force perpendicular to the displacement does no work.**	**If the part of the object on which the force acts undergoes no displacement, no work is done.**
This can sometimes seem counterintuitive. The weightlifter struggles mightily to hold the barbell over his head. But during the time the barbell remains stationary, he does no work on it because its displacement is zero. But why then is it so hard for him to hold it there? We'll see in Chapter 6 that it takes a rapid conversion of his internal chemical energy to keep his arms extended under this great load.	The woman exerts only a vertical force on the briefcase she's carrying. This force has no component in the direction of the displacement, so the briefcase moves at a constant velocity and its kinetic energy remains constant. Since the energy of the briefcase doesn't change, it must be that no energy is being transferred to it as work. (This is the case where $\theta = 90°$ in Tactics Box 5.2.)	Even though the wall pushes on the skater with a normal force $\vec{n}$ and she undergoes a displacement $\vec{d}$, the wall does no work on her, because the point of her body on which $\vec{n}$ acts—her hands—undergoes no displacement. This makes sense: How could energy be transferred as work from an inert, stationary object? So where does her kinetic energy come from? This will be the subject of much of Chapter 6. Can you guess?

STOP TO THINK 5.2   Which force does the most work?

A. The 10 N force.
B. The 8 N force.
C. The 6 N force.
D. They all do the same amount of work.

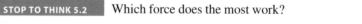

5.5 Kinetic Energy

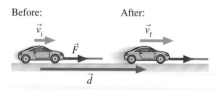

FIGURE 5.12 The work done by the tow rope increases the car's kinetic energy.

We've already qualitatively discussed kinetic energy, an object's energy of motion. Let's now use what we've learned about work, and some simple kinematics, to find a quantitative expression for kinetic energy. Consider the system consisting of a car being pulled by a tow rope as in Figure 5.12. The rope pulls with a constant force $\vec{F}$ while the car undergoes a displacement $\vec{d}$, so that the force does work $W = Fd$ on the car. If we ignore friction and drag, the work done by $\vec{F}$ will be transferred entirely into the car's energy of motion—its kinetic energy. In this case, the law of conservation of energy, Equation 5.6, reads

$$K_i + W = K_f$$

or

$$W = K_f - K_i \qquad (5.10)$$

Using kinematics, we can find another expression for the work done, in terms of the car's initial and final speeds. Recall from Chapter 2 the kinematic equation relating an object's displacement and its change in velocity:

$$v_f^2 = v_i^2 + 2a\Delta x$$

Applied to the motion of our car, $\Delta x = d$ is the car's displacement and, from Newton's second law, the acceleration is $a = F/m$. Thus we can write

$$v_f^2 = v_i^2 + \frac{2Fd}{m} = v_i^2 + \frac{2W}{m}$$

where we have replaced Fd with the work W. If we now solve for the work, we find

$$W = \frac{1}{2}m(v_f^2 - v_i^2) = \frac{1}{2}mv_f^2 - \frac{1}{2}mv_i^2$$

If we compare this result with Equation 5.10, we see that

$$K_f = \frac{1}{2}mv_f^2 \qquad \text{and} \qquad K_i = \frac{1}{2}mv_i^2$$

In general, then, an object moving at a speed v has kinetic energy

Act|v
Physics ONLINE 6.1

$$K = \frac{1}{2}mv^2 \qquad (5.11)$$

QUADRATIC
p. 50

Kinetic energy of an object of mass m moving with speed v

From Equation 5.11, the units of kinetic energy are mass times speed squared, or $kg \cdot (m/s)^2$. But

$$1\ kg \cdot (m/s)^2 = \underbrace{1\ kg \cdot (m/s^2)}_{1\,N} \cdot m = 1\,N \cdot m = 1\,J$$

We see that the units of kinetic energy are the same as those of work, as they must be. Table 5.1 gives some approximate kinetic energies. Everyday kinetic energies range from a tiny fraction of a fraction of a joule to nearly a million joules for a speeding car.

TABLE 5.1 Some approximate kinetic energies

Object	Kinetic energy
Walking ant	1×10^{-8} J
Penny dropped 1 m	2.5×10^{-3} J
Person walking	70 J
100 mph fastball	150 J
Bullet	5000 J
Car, 60 mph	5×10^5 J
Supertanker	2×10^{10} J

CONCEPTUAL EXAMPLE 5.3 Kinetic energy changes for a car

Compare the increase in a 1000 kg car's kinetic energy as it speeds up by 5.0 m/s starting from 5.0 m/s, to its increase in kinetic energy as it speeds up by 5.0 m/s starting from 10 m/s.

REASON The change in the car's kinetic energy in going from 5 m/s to 10 m/s is

$$\Delta K_{5 \to 10} = \frac{1}{2}mv_f^2 - \frac{1}{2}mv_i^2$$

This gives

$$\Delta K_{5 \to 10} = \frac{1}{2}(1000\ kg)(10\ m/s)^2 - \frac{1}{2}(1000\ kg)(5.0\ m/s)^2$$

$$= 3.8 \times 10^4\ J$$

while

$$\Delta K_{10 \to 15} = \frac{1}{2}(1000\ kg)(15\ m/s)^2 - \frac{1}{2}(1000\ kg)(10\ m/s)^2$$

$$= 6.3 \times 10^4\ J$$

Even though the increase in the car's *speed* was the same in both cases, the increase in kinetic energy is substantially larger in the second case.

ASSESS Kinetic energy depends on the *square* of the speed v. If we plot the kinetic energy of the car as in Figure 5.13, we see that the energy of the car increases rapidly with speed. We can also see graphically why the change in K for a fixed 5 m/s change in v is greater at high speeds than at low speeds. In part this is why it's harder to accelerate your car at high speeds than at low speeds.

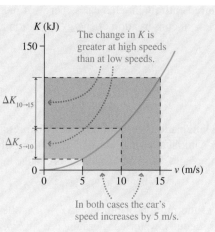

FIGURE 5.13 The kinetic energy increases as the *square* of the speed.

EXAMPLE 5.3 **Speed of a bobsled after pushing**

A two-man bobsled has a mass of 390 kg. Starting from rest, the two racers push the sled for the first 50 m with a net force of 270 N. Neglecting friction, what is the sled's speed at the end of the 50 m?

PREPARE This is the first example where we fully use Problem-Solving Strategy 5.1. We start by identifying the bobsled as the system; the two racers pushing the sled are part of the environment. The racers do work on the system by pushing it with force $\vec{F}$. Because the speed of the sled changes, we'll need to include kinetic energy. Neither U_g nor U_s changes, so we won't need to consider these energies. Figure 5.14 lists the known quantities and the quantity (v_f) that we want to find.

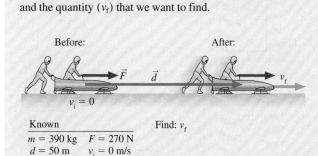

FIGURE 5.14 The work done by the pushers increases the sled's kinetic energy.

SOLVE With only kinetic energy changing, the conservation of energy equation, Equation 5.6, is

$$K_i + W = K_f$$

Using our expressions for kinetic energy and work, this becomes

$$\frac{1}{2}mv_i^2 + Fd = \frac{1}{2}mv_f^2$$

Because $v_i = 0$, the energy equation reduces to

$$Fd = \frac{1}{2}mv_f^2$$

We can solve for the final speed to get

$$v_f = \sqrt{\frac{2Fd}{m}} = \sqrt{\frac{2(270 \text{ N})(50 \text{ m})}{390 \text{ kg}}} = 8.3 \text{ m/s}$$

ASSESS We solved this problem using the concept of energy conservation. In this case, we could also have solved it using Newton's second law and kinematics. However, we'll soon see that energy conservation can solve problems that would be very difficult for us to solve using Newton's laws alone.

STOP TO THINK 5.3   Rank in order, from greatest to least, the kinetic energies of the sliding pucks.

1 kg 2.0 m/s	1 kg 3.0 m/s	–2.0 m/s 1 kg	2 kg 2.0 m/s
A.	B.	C.	D.

5.6 Potential Energy

When two or more objects in a system interact, it is sometimes possible to *store* energy in that system in a way that the energy can be easily recovered. For instance, the earth and a ball interact by the gravitational force between them. If the ball is lifted up into the air, energy is stored in the ball-earth system, energy that can later be recovered as kinetic energy when the ball is released and falls. Similarly, a spring is a system made up of countless atoms that interact via their atomic "springs." If we push a box against a spring, energy is stored that can be recovered when the spring later pushes the box across the table. This sort of stored energy is called **potential energy,** since it has the *potential* to be converted into other forms of energy such as kinetic or thermal energy.

The forces due to gravity and springs are special in that they allow for the storage of energy. Other interaction forces do not. When a crate is pushed across the floor, the crate and the floor interact via the force of friction, and the work done on the system is converted into thermal energy. But this energy is *not* stored up for later recovery—it slowly diffuses into the environment and cannot be recovered.

Interaction forces that can store useful energy are called **conservative forces.** The name comes from the important fact, which we'll soon look at in detail, that when only conservative forces act, the mechanical energy of a system is *conserved.* Gravity and elastic forces are conservative forces, and later we'll see that the electric force is a conservative force as well. Friction, on the other hand, is a **nonconservative force.** When two objects interact via a friction force, energy is not stored. It is usually transformed into thermal energy.

Let's look more closely at the potential energies associated with the two conservative forces—gravity and springs—that we'll study in this chapter.

Gravitational Potential Energy

To find an expression for gravitational potential energy, let's consider the system of the book and the earth shown in Figure 5.15a on the next page. The book is lifted at a constant speed from its initial position at y_i to a final height y_f.

We can analyze this situation using the approach of Problem-Solving Strategy 5.1. The lifting force of the hand is external to the system and so does work W on the system, increasing its energy. The book is lifted at a constant speed, so its kinetic energy doesn't change. Because there's no friction, the book's thermal energy doesn't change either. Thus the work done goes entirely into increasing the gravitational potential energy of the system. The law of conservation of energy, Equation 5.12, then reads

The initial gravitational potential energy. . . . . . . .plus the energy put into the system as work. . .

$$(U_g)_i + W = (U_g)_f \tag{5.12}$$

. . .equals the final gravitational potential energy.

The work done is $W = F\Delta y$, where $\Delta y = y_f - y_i$ is the vertical distance that the book is lifted. From the free-body diagram of Figure 5.15b, we see that $F = mg$. This gives $W = mg\Delta y$, so that

$$(U_g)_i + mg\Delta y = (U_g)_f$$

or

$$(U_g)_f = (U_g)_i + mg\Delta y \tag{5.13}$$

Since our final height was greater than our initial height, Δy is positive and $(U_g)_f > (U_g)_i$. **The higher the object is lifted, the greater the gravitational potential energy in the object/earth system.**

Equation 5.13 gives the final gravitational potential energy $(U_g)_f$ in terms of its initial value $(U_g)_i$. But what is the value of $(U_g)_i$? We can gain some insight by writing Equation 5.13 in terms of energy *changes*. We have

$$(U_g)_f - (U_g)_i = mg\Delta y$$

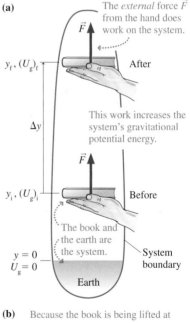

(a)

The *external* force $\vec{F}$ from the hand does work on the system.

$y_f, (U_g)_f$

After

Δy

This work increases the system's gravitational potential energy.

$\vec{F}$

$y_i, (U_g)_i$

Before

$y = 0$
$U_g = 0$

The book and the earth are the system.

System boundary

Earth

(b) Because the book is being lifted at a constant speed, it is in dynamic equilibrium with $\vec{F}_{net} = \vec{0}$. Thus $F = w = mg$.

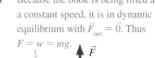

$\vec{F}$

$\vec{w}$

FIGURE 5.15 Lifting a book increases its gravitational potential energy.

or

$$\Delta U_g = mg\Delta y$$

For example, if we lift a 1.5 kg book up by 2.0 m, we increase its gravitational potential energy by $\Delta U_g = (1.5 \text{ kg})(9.8 \text{ m/s}^2)(2.0 \text{ m}) = 29.4$ J. This increase is *independent* of the book's starting height: We would get the *same* increase whether we lifted the book 2.0 m starting at sea level or starting at the top of Mount Everest. If we then dropped the book 2.0 m, we would recover the same 29.4 J as kinetic energy, whether in Miami or on Everest. This illustrates an important general fact about *every* form of potential energy: **Only *changes* in potential energy are significant.**

Because of this fact, we are free to choose a *reference level* where we define U_g to be zero. Our expression for U_g is particularly simple if we choose this reference level to be at $y = 0$. We then have

$$U_g = mgy \qquad (5.14)$$

Gravitational potential energy of an object of mass m at a height y
(assuming $U_g = 0$ when the object is at $y = 0$)

LINEAR
p.38

NOTE ▶ We've emphasized that gravitational potential energy is an energy of the earth-object *system*. In solving problems using the law of conservation of energy, you'll need to include the earth as part of your system. For simplicity, we'll usually speak of "the gravitational potential energy of the ball," but what we really mean is the potential energy of the earth-ball system. ◀

EXAMPLE 5.4 Hitting the bell

At the county fair, Katie tries her hand at the ring-the-bell attraction, as shown in Figure 5.16. She swings the mallet hard enough to give the ball an initial upward speed of 8.0 m/s. Will the ball ring the bell, 3.0 m from the bottom?

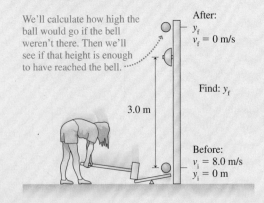

We'll calculate how high the ball would go if the bell weren't there. Then we'll see if that height is enough to have reached the bell.

After:
y_f
$v_f = 0$ m/s

Find: y_f

3.0 m

Before:
$v_i = 8.0$ m/s
$y_i = 0$ m

FIGURE 5.16 Before-and-after visual overview of the ring-the-bell attraction.

PREPARE As discussed above and in Tactics Box 5.1, we'll choose the ball *and* the earth as the system. Figure 5.16 shows the visual overview. If we assume that the track along which the ball moves is frictionless, then only the *mechanical* energy of the system changes. The only force on the ball after it leaves the bottom lever is gravity, but gravity is an *internal* force due to our choice of the ball *plus* the earth as the system. This means

that the gravitational interaction is included as gravitational potential energy rather than as external work. Since no *external* forces do work on the earth-ball system, the system is isolated. We can then use the law of conservation of mechanical energy, Equation 5.7.

SOLVE Equation 5.7 tells us that $K_i + (U_g)_i = K_f + (U_g)_f$. We can use our expressions for kinetic and potential energy to write this as

$$\frac{1}{2}mv_i^2 + mgy_i = \frac{1}{2}mv_f^2 + mgy_f$$

Let's ignore the bell for the moment and figure out how far the ball would rise if there were nothing in its way. We know that the ball starts at $y_i = 0$ m and that its speed v_f at the highest point is zero. Thus the energy equation simplifies to

$$mgy_f = \frac{1}{2}mv_i^2$$

This is easily solved for the height y_f:

$$y_f = \frac{v_i^2}{2g} = \frac{(8.0 \text{ m/s})^2}{2(9.8 \text{ m/s}^2)} = 3.3 \text{ m}$$

This is higher than the point where the bell sits, so the ball would actually hit it on the way up.

ASSESS Notice that the mass canceled and wasn't needed, a fact about free fall that you should remember from Chapter 2.

An important conclusion from Equation 5.14 is that **gravitational potential energy depends only on the height of the object above the reference level $y = 0$, not on the object's horizontal position.** Consider carrying a briefcase while walking on level ground at a constant speed. As shown in the table on page 15, the force of your hand on the briefcase is *vertical* and hence *perpendicular* to the displacement. No work is done on the briefcase and consequently its gravitational potential energy remains constant as long as its height above the ground doesn't change as you walk.

This idea can be applied to more complicated cases, such as the 51 kg hiker in Figure 5.17. His gravitational potential energy depends *only* on his height y above the reference level, so it's the same value $U_g = mgy = 50$ kJ at any point on path A where he is at a height $y = 100$ m above the reference level. If he had instead taken path B, his gravitational potential energy at 100 m would be the same 50 kJ. It doesn't matter *how* he gets to 100 m, his potential energy at that height will be the same. This demonstrates an important aspect of all potential energies: **The potential energy depends only on the *position* of the object and not on the path the object took to get to that position.** This fact will allow us to use the law of conservation of energy to easily solve a variety of problems that would be very difficult to solve using Newton's laws alone, because we won't need to know the details of the path of the object—just its starting and ending points.

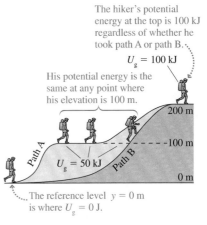

The hiker's potential energy at the top is 100 kJ regardless of whether he took path A or path B.

$U_g = 100$ kJ

His potential energy is the same at any point where his elevation is 100 m.

$U_g = 50$ kJ

Path A   Path B

200 m
100 m
0 m

The reference level $y = 0$ m is where $U_g = 0$ J.

FIGURE 5.17 The hiker's gravitational potential energy depends only on his height above the $y = 0$ reference level.

EXAMPLE 5.5 Speed at the bottom of a water slide

Still at the county fair, Katie tries the water slide, whose shape is shown in Figure 5.18. The starting point is 9.0 m above the ground. She pushes off with an initial speed of 2.0 m/s. If the slide is frictionless, how fast will Katie be traveling at the bottom?

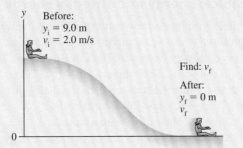

FIGURE 5.18 Before-and-after visual overview of Katie on the water slide.

Before:
$y_i = 9.0$ m
$v_i = 2.0$ m/s

Find: v_f

After:
$y_f = 0$ m
v_f

PREPARE Figure 5.18 on the next page shows a visual overview of the slide. Because there is no friction, Tactics Box 5.1 suggests that we take as our system Katie (the moving object) and the earth. With this choice of system, the only energies in the system are kinetic and gravitational potential energy. Note that the slope of the slide is not constant, so Katie's acceleration will not be constant either. Thus we can't use

constant-acceleration kinematics to find her speed. But we *can* use the law of conservation of energy to easily solve for her speed. Because there is no friction, the mechanical energy is conserved.

SOLVE Conservation of mechanical energy gives

$$K_i + (U_g)_i = K_f + (U_g)_f$$

or

$$\frac{1}{2}mv_i^2 + mgy_i = \frac{1}{2}mv_f^2 + mgy_f$$

Taking $y_f = 0$ m we have

$$\frac{1}{2}mv_i^2 + mgy_i = \frac{1}{2}mv_f^2$$

which we can solve to get

$$v_f = \sqrt{v_i^2 + 2gy_i}$$
$$= \sqrt{(2.0\ \text{m/s})^2 + 2(9.8\ \text{m/s}^2)(9.0\ \text{m})} = 13\ \text{m/s}$$

ASSESS It is important to realize that the *shape* of the slide does not matter because gravitational potential energy depends only on the *height* above a reference level. **In sliding down any (frictionless) slide of the same height, your speed at the bottom would be the same.**

STOP TO THINK 5.4 Rank in order, from largest to smallest, the gravitational potential energies of identical balls 1 to 4.

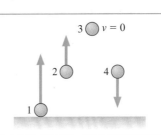

3   $v = 0$

2

4

1

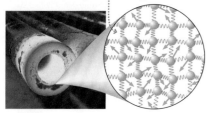

Hot object: Fast-moving molecules have lots of kinetic and elastic potential energy.

Cold object: Slow-moving molecules have little kinetic and elastic potential energy.

FIGURE 5.19 A molecular view of thermal energy.

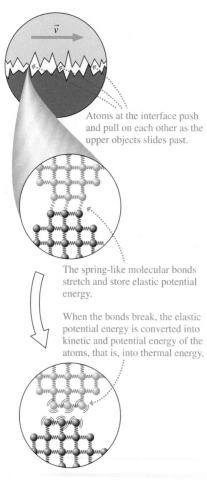

Atoms at the interface push and pull on each other as the upper objects slides past.

The spring-like molecular bonds stretch and store elastic potential energy.

When the bonds break, the elastic potential energy is converted into kinetic and potential energy of the atoms, that is, into thermal energy.

FIGURE 5.20 How friction causes an increase in thermal energy.

5.7 Thermal Energy

We noted earlier that thermal energy is related to the microscopic motion of the molecules of an object. As Figure 5.19 shows, the molecules in a hot object jiggle around their average positions more than the molecules in a cold object. This has two consequences. First, each atom is on average moving faster in the hot object. This means that each atom has a higher *kinetic energy*. Second, each atom in the hot object tends to stray further from its equilibrium position, leading to a greater stretching or compressing of the spring-like molecular bonds. This means that each atom has on average a higher *potential energy*. The potential energy stored in any one bond and the kinetic energy of any one atom are both exceedingly small, but there are incredibly many bonds and atoms. The sum of all these microscopic potential and kinetic energies is what we call **thermal energy.**

Is this microscopic energy worth worrying about? To see, consider a 500 g ($\approx$1 lb) iron ball moving at the respectable speed of $v_{ball} = 20$ m/s ($\approx$45 mph). Its kinetic energy is $K = \frac{1}{2}mv_{ball}^2 = 100$ J.

How fast do the atoms jiggle about their equilibrium positions? This speed depends on the temperature, but at room temperature it's very high—roughly 500 m/s. So each atom is on average traveling in a straight line at 20 m/s, but jiggling about this average motion at a speed of 500 m/s! This a factor of 25 times faster. And since kinetic energy is proportional to the *square* of the speed, the kinetic energy due to the microscopic motion is about 625 times greater than that due to the overall motion. And it turns out that the microscopic potential energy is just as large. Thus the ball that has an ordinary kinetic energy of 100 J has an internal thermal energy of 2 × 625 × 100 J = 125,000 J!

Transforming Mechanical Energy into Thermal Energy

Consider a snowboarder sliding on level snow. After a while, he will glide to a stop because of the friction force of the snow on his board. We can analyze this using the law of conservation of energy. Following Tactics Box 5.1 we'll take the system to be the boarder *plus* the snow. Then there are no forces external to the system that do work on it and, since he's moving horizontally, his potential energy doesn't change. Then the law of conservation of energy is $K_i = K_f + \Delta E_{th}$, or $\Delta E_{th} = K_i - K_f$. He's slowing to a stop, so $K_i > K_f$ and ΔE_{th} is positive. The system's thermal energy *increases* as kinetic energy is transformed into thermal energy.

This increase in thermal energy is a general feature of any system where friction between sliding objects is present: **When two objects slide against each other with friction present, mechanical energy is always transformed into thermal energy.** An atomic-level explanation is shown in Figure 5.20.

The presence of friction has two important consequences for our conservation of energy Problem-Solving Strategy 5.1:

1. As stated in Tactics Box 5.1, we must include in the system not only the moving object but also the surface against which it slides. This is because the thermal energy generated by friction resides in *both* object and surface (as in Figure 5.20), and it is usually impossible to tell what fraction resides in each. By choosing both object and surface to be in the system, we know that *all* the thermal energy ends up in the system.
2. In addition to the mechanical energy $K + U$ we now must include ΔE_{th} in the conservation of energy equation.

TRY IT YOURSELF

Agitating atoms Vigorously rub a some-what soft object such as a blackboard eraser on your desktop for about 10 seconds. If you then pass your fingers over the spot where you rubbed, you'll feel a distinct warm area. Congratulations: you've just set some 100,000,000,000,000,000,000,000 atoms into motion!

EXAMPLE 5.6 Thermal energy created sledding down a hill

George jumps onto his sled and starts from rest at the top of a 5.0-m-high hill. His speed at the bottom is 8.0 m/s. The mass of George and the sled is 55 kg. How much thermal energy was produced in this process?

PREPARE Figure 5.21 shows the before-and-after visual overview. The statement of the problem implies that thermal energy will be generated, so following Tactics Box 5.1, we'll take the system to include both George and the sled *and* the slope. Because his height is changing, his gravitational potential energy is changing and we'll need to include the earth in the system as well. No forces act from outside this system, so the work W is zero.

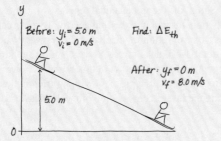

FIGURE 5.21 Visual overview of George sliding down the hill.

SOLVE Here the law of conservation of energy reads

$$K_i + (U_g)_i = K_f + (U_g)_f + \Delta E_{th}$$

In terms of positions and speeds,

$$\frac{1}{2}mv_i^2 + mgy_i = \frac{1}{2}mv_f^2 + mgy_f + \Delta E_{th}$$

Because $v_i = 0$ m/s and $y_f = 0$ m, this simplifies to

$$mgy_i = \frac{1}{2}mv_f^2 + \Delta E_{th}$$

from which we have

$$\Delta E_{th} = mgy_i - \frac{1}{2}mv_f^2$$

$$= (55 \text{ kg})(9.8 \text{ m/s}^2)(5.0 \text{ m}) - \frac{1}{2}(55 \text{ kg})(8.0 \text{ m/s})^2$$

$$= 940 \text{ J}$$

ASSESS The change in E_{th} is positive, as it must be. This extra thermal energy resides in the sled and all along the slope where George slid. You should be able to show that about 35% of George's original gravitational potential energy was transformed into thermal energy as he slid down the hill.

5.8 Further Examples of Conservation of Energy

In this section, we'll tie together what we've learned about using the law of conservation of energy to solve dynamics problems. In each, we use the key idea of setting the "before" energy equal to the "after" energy.

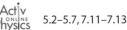 5.2–5.7, 7.11–7.13

EXAMPLE 5.7 Where will the sled stop?

A sledder, starting from rest, slides down a 10-m-high hill. At the bottom of the hill is a long horizontal patch of rough snow. The hill is nearly frictionless, but the coefficient of friction between the sled and the rough snow at the bottom is $\mu_k = 0.30$. How far will the sled slide along the rough patch?

PREPARE A picture of the sledder is shown in Figure 5.22. We'll break this problem into Part A, his motion down the hill; and Part B, his motion along the ice. We know how to use conservation of energy to find his speed at the bottom of the hill. Along the rough patch, however, we'll use kinematics and Newton's laws, to find how far he slides.

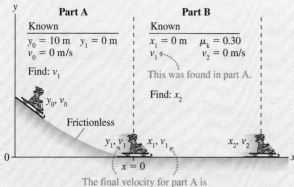
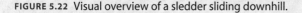
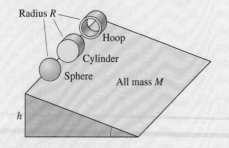

FIGURE 5.22 Visual overview of a sledder sliding downhill.

SOLVE We'll solve Part A first and find the sled's speed v_f at the bottom. The hill is frictionless, so mechanical energy is conserved and we have

$$mgy_i + \frac{1}{2}mv_i^2 = mgy_f + \frac{1}{2}mv_f^2$$

Since $v_i = 0$ m/s and $y_f = 0$ m, this reduces to

$$mgy_i = \frac{1}{2}mv_f^2$$

so that

$$v_f = \sqrt{2gy_i} = \sqrt{2(9.8 \text{ m/s}^2)(10 \text{ m})} = 14.0 \text{ m/s}$$

On the rough patch in Part B, where the only horizontal force is the kinetic friction force f_k pointing to the left, the sled's acceleration is

$$a = -\frac{f_k}{m} = -\frac{\mu_k n}{m} = -\frac{\mu_k mg}{m}$$

$$= -\mu_k g = -(0.30)(9.8 \text{ m/s}^2) = -2.94 \text{ m/s}^2$$

The negative acceleration indicates that the sled is slowing down, as expected.

We now use kinematics to find how far the sled slides. We know the acceleration a, as well as the initial and final velocities along the horizontal patch, and we want to know the final position x_2. This suggests using the kinematic equation

$$v_f^2 = v_i^2 + 2a(x_f - x_i)$$

to find the final position. For the motion of Part B, the final velocity $v_f = v_2 = 0$ m/s, the initial velocity is $v_1 = 14.0$ m/s, and the initial position is $x_i = x_1 = 0$ m. We can then solve for the final position in the kinematic equation to get

$$x_2 = -\frac{v_1^2}{2a} = -\frac{(14.0 \text{ m/s})^2}{-5.88 \text{ m/s}^2} = 33 \text{ m}$$

ASSESS When friction is present, mechanical energy is *not* conserved: Some of the mechanical energy of the system is inevitably transformed into thermal energy. Thus we cannot use the law of conservation of mechanical energy for such problems. Instead, we'll need to use Newton's laws and kinematics to find how far objects slide. As in this example, however, there will often be a part of the problem with no friction that we *can* solve using the law of conservation of mechanical energy.

EXAMPLE 5.8 Who wins the great downhill race?

Figure 5.23 shows a contest in which a sphere, a cylinder, and a circular hoop, each with mass M and radius R, are placed at height h on a slope of angle θ. All three are simultaneously released from rest and roll down the ramp without slipping. Which one will win the race to the bottom of the hill?

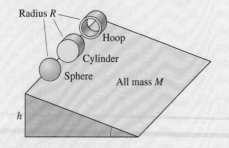

FIGURE 5.23 Which will win the downhill race?

PREPARE With no sliding friction, the total mechanical energy is conserved. However, the kinetic energy of each object must include a contribution from its rotational kinetic energy.

SOLVE Conservation of energy tells us that the gravitational potential energy $(U_g)_i = Mgh$ at the top will be transformed into an equal amount of kinetic energy K_f at the bottom.

$$(U_g)_i = Mgh = K_f = \frac{1}{2}\left(M + \frac{I}{R^2}\right)v^2$$

The speed at the bottom is then

$$v = \sqrt{\frac{2Mgh}{M + \dfrac{I}{R^2}}}$$

We have

Shape	Moment of Inertia I	$v = \sqrt{2Mgh/(M + I/R^2)}$
Sphere	$\dfrac{2}{5}MR^2$	$v = \sqrt{\dfrac{10}{7}gh} = 1.19\sqrt{gh}$
Cylinder	$\dfrac{1}{2}MR^2$	$v = \sqrt{\dfrac{4}{3}gh} = 1.15\sqrt{gh}$
Hoop	MR^2	$v = \sqrt{gh}$

The sphere has the largest speed at the bottom, a full 19% faster than the hoop. Because the sphere always travels faster than the hoop or the cylinder, it will win the race, followed by the cylinder and the hoop.

ASSESS All the objects have the same kinetic energy at the bottom, because they all started with the same energy, Mgh, at the top. But the object with the smallest I will have the smallest *rotational* kinetic energy at the bottom, and hence the largest *translational* kinetic energy and the largest v. An ordinary sliding object (no rotation) reaches the bottom with speed $v = \sqrt{2gh} = 1.41\sqrt{gh}$. This is significantly faster than any of the rolling objects. The sliding object is faster because *all* its kinetic energy is translational—and it's the translational motion that gets you down the hill.

5.9 Power

We've now studied how energy can be transformed from one kind to another and how it can be transferred between the environment and the system as work. In many situations we would like to know *how quickly* the energy is transformed or transferred. Is a transfer of energy very rapid, or does it take place over a long time? In passing a truck, your car needs to transform a certain amount of the chemical energy in its fuel into kinetic energy. It makes a *big* difference whether your engine can do this in 20 s or 60 s!

The question "How quickly?" implies that we are talking about a *rate*. For example, the velocity of an object—how fast it is going—is the *rate of change* of position. So when we raise the issue of how fast the energy is transformed, we are talking about the *rate of transformation* of energy. Suppose in a time interval Δt an amount of energy ΔE is transformed from one form to another. The rate at which this energy is transformed is called the **power** P, and it is defined as

$$P = \frac{\Delta E}{\Delta t} \tag{5.15}$$

Power when amount of energy ΔE is transformed in time interval Δt

The unit of power is the **watt,** which is defined as 1 watt = 1 W = 1 J/s.

Power also measures the rate at which energy is transferred into or out of a system as work W. If work W is done in time interval Δt, the rate of energy *transfer* is

$$P = \frac{W}{\Delta t} \tag{5.16}$$

Power when amount of work W is done in time interval Δt

A force that is doing work (i.e., transferring energy) at a rate of 3 J/s has an "output power" of 3 W. A system gaining energy at the rate of 3 J/s is said to "consume" 3 W of power. Common prefixes used with power are mW (milliwatts), kW (kilowatts), and MW (megawatts).

Both these cars take about the same energy to reach 60 mph, but the race car gets there in a much shorter time, so its *power* is much greater.

The English unit of power is the *horse-power*. The conversion factor to watts is

$$1 \text{ horsepower} = 1 \text{ hp} = 746 \text{ W}$$

Many common appliances, such as motors, are rated in hp.

We can express Equation 5.16 in a different form. If in the time interval Δt an object undergoes a displacement Δx, the work done by a force acting on the object is $W = F\Delta x$. Then Equation 5.16 can be written

$$P = \frac{W}{\Delta t} = \frac{F\Delta x}{\Delta t} = F\frac{\Delta x}{\Delta t} = Fv$$

The rate at which energy is transferred to an object as work—the power—is the product of the force that does the work, and the velocity of the object:

$$P = Fv \qquad (5.17)$$

Rate of energy transfer due to a force F
acting on an object moving at velocity v

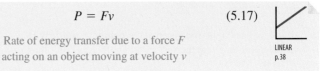

LINEAR
p.38

EXAMPLE 5.9 Power to pass a truck

You are behind a 1500 kg truck traveling at 60 mph (27 m/s). To pass it, you speed up to 75 mph (34 m/s) in 6.0 s. What power is required to do this?

PREPARE Your car is undergoing an energy transformation from the chemical energy of your fuel to the kinetic energy of the car. We can calculate the amount of energy transformed by finding the change ΔK in the kinetic energy.

SOLVE We have

$$K_i = \frac{1}{2}mv_i^2 = \frac{1}{2}(1500 \text{ kg})(27 \text{ m/s})^2 = 5.47 \times 10^5 \text{ J}$$

$$K_f = \frac{1}{2}mv_f^2 = \frac{1}{2}(1500 \text{ kg})(34 \text{ m/s})^2 = 8.67 \times 10^5 \text{ J}$$

so that

$$\Delta K = K_f - K_i$$
$$= 8.67 \times 10^5 \text{ J} - 5.47 \times 10^5 \text{ J} = 3.20 \times 10^5 \text{ J}$$

To transform this amount of energy in 6 s, the power required is

$$P = \frac{\Delta K}{\Delta t} = \frac{3.20 \times 10^5 \text{ J}}{6.0 \text{ s}} = 53,000 \text{ W} = 53 \text{ kW}$$

This is about 71 hp. This power is in addition to the power needed to overcome drag and friction and cruise at 60 mph, so the total power required from the engine will be even greater than this.

ASSESS You use a large amount of energy to perform a simple driving maneuver such as this. 3.20×10^5 J is enough energy to lift an 80 kg person 410 m in the air—the height of a tall skyscraper. And 53 kW would lift him there in only 6 s!

STOP TO THINK 5.5 Four students run up the stairs in the time shown. Rank in order, from largest to smallest, their power outputs P_A to P_D.

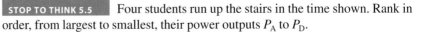
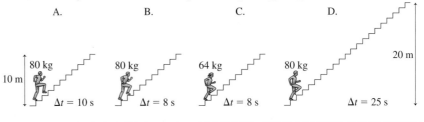

SUMMARY

The goal of Chapter 5 has been to learn about energy and how to solve problems using the law of conservation of energy.

GENERAL PRINCIPLES

General Energy Model

Within a system, energy can be **transformed** between various forms.

Energy can be **transferred** into or out of a system in two basic ways:

- **Work:** The transfer of energy by mechanical forces.

- **Heat:** The nonmechanical transfer of energy from a hotter to a colder object.

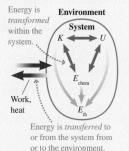

Energy is *transformed* within the system.

Environment

System

$K \longleftrightarrow U$

E_{chem}

E_{th}

Work, heat

Energy is *transferred* to or from the system from or to the environment.

Law of Conservation of Energy

Isolated system: No energy is transferred into or out of the system. Each form of energy within the system can change, but the total change in energy is zero. Energy of the system is *conserved*:

The change in the system's energy is zero.

$$\Delta K + \Delta U_g + \Delta U_s + \Delta E_{th} + \Delta E_{chem} + \ldots = 0$$

Nonisolated system: Energy can be exchanged with the environment as work or heat. The energy of the system changes by the amount of work done or heat transferred:

$$\Delta K + \Delta U_g + \Delta U_s + \Delta E_{th} + \Delta E_{chem} + \ldots = W + Q$$

The system's energy changes by the amount of work done and heat transferred.

Systems with mechanical and thermal energy only: The initial mechanical energy, plus the work done, equals the final mechanical energy plus additional thermal energy:

$$K_i + U_i + W = K_f + U_f + \Delta E_{th}$$

In terms of energy changes, this can be written

$$\Delta K + \Delta U_g + \Delta U_s + \Delta E_{th} = W$$

Solving Energy Conservation Problems

PREPARE Choose your system (Tactics Box 5.1). Decide what forms of energy are changing. If there is friction, then thermal energy will be created. Check for external forces that will do work on your system.

SOLVE Use Equation 5.6 to relate the initial energy of your system, plus the work done, to the final energy of the system:

$$K_i + U_i + W = K_f + U_f + \Delta E_{th}$$

ASSESS Kinetic energy is always positive. The *change* in thermal energy should be positive.

IMPORTANT CONCEPTS

Mechanical energy is the sum of a system's kinetic and potential energies:

Mechanical energy $= K + U = K + U_g + U_s$

Kinetic energy is an energy of motion

$$K = \frac{1}{2}mv^2 + \frac{1}{2}I\omega^2$$

Translational ··········· ˥   ˹ ··········· Rotational

Potential energy is energy stored in a system of interacting objects

- **Gravitational potential energy:** $U_g = mgy$

- **Elastic potential energy:** $U_s = \frac{1}{2}kx^2$

Thermal energy is the sum of the microscopic kinetic and potential energy of all the molecules in an object. The hotter an object, the more thermal energy it has. When kinetic (sliding) friction is present, mechanical energy will be transformed into thermal energy.

Work is the process by which energy is transferred to or from a system by the application of mechanical forces.

If a particle moves through a displacement $\vec{d}$ while acted upon by a constant force $\vec{F}$, the force does work

$$W = F_\parallel d = Fd\cos\theta$$

Only the component of the force parallel to the

APPLICATIONS

Power is the rate at which energy is transformed . . .

$$P = \frac{\Delta E}{\Delta t}$$ ◄·········· Amount of energy transformed
◄·········· Time required to transform it

. . . or at which work is done.

$$P = \frac{W}{\Delta t}$$ ◄·········· Amount of work done
◄·········· Time required to do work

QUESTIONS

Conceptual Questions

1. The brake shoes of your car are made of a material that can tolerate very high temperatures without being damaged. Why is this so?
2. When you pound a nail with a hammer, the nail gets quite warm. Describe the energy transformations that lead to the addition of thermal energy in the nail.

For Questions 3 through 8, give a specific example of a system with the energy transformation shown. In these questions, W is the work done on the system by the environment, and K and U are the kinetic and potential energies of the system, respectively.

3. $W \rightarrow K$ with $\Delta U = 0$.
4. $W \rightarrow U$ with $\Delta K = 0$.
5. $K \rightarrow U$ with $W = 0$.
6. $K \rightarrow W$ with $\Delta U = 0$.
7. $U \rightarrow K$ with $W = 0$.
8. $U \rightarrow W$ with $\Delta K = 0$.
9. A ball of putty is dropped from a height of 2 m onto a hard floor, where it sticks. What object or objects need to be included within the system if the system is to be isolated during this process?
10. A 0.5 kg mass on a 1-m-long string swings in a circle on a horizontal, frictionless table at a steady speed of 2 m/s. How much work does the tension in the string do on the mass during one revolution? Explain.
11. Particle A has less mass than particle B. Both are pushed forward across a frictionless surface by equal forces for 1 s. Both start from rest.
    a. Compare the amount of work done on each particle. That is, is the work done on A greater than, less than, or equal to the work done on B? Explain.
    b. Compare the impulses delivered to particles A and B. Explain.
    c. Compare the final speeds of particles A and B. Explain.
12. The meaning of the word "work" is quite different in physics from its everyday usage. Give an example of an action a person could do that "feels like work" but that does not involve any work as we've defined it in this chapter.
13. To change a tire, you need to use a jack to raise one corner of your car. While doing so, you happen to notice that pushing the jack handle down 20 cm raises the car only 0.2 cm. Use energy concepts to explain why the handle must be moved so far to raise the car by such a small amount.

Questions 14 through 17 refer to a weightlifter raising a barbell from the floor to above his head. Describe the energy transformations that occur if the system is chosen as specified in the question. Use the notation of Section 5.2 for the various forms of energy and energy transfer.

14. The system is the barbell alone.
15. The system is the weightlifter alone.
16. The system is the barbell plus the earth.
17. The system is the barbell plus the earth plus the weightlifter.

In Questions 18 through 20, imagine yourself doing a chin-up. You start from rest with your arms extended above your head, and end at rest with your elbows bent and your hands still gripping the bar. Describe the energy transformations that occur if the system is chosen as specified in the question. Use the notation of Section 5.2 for the various forms of energy and energy transfer.

18. The system is you alone.
19. The system is you plus the chin-up bar.
20. The system is you plus the chin-up bar plus the earth.
21. One kilogram of matter contains approximately 10^{17} J of nuclear energy. Why don't we need to include this energy when we study ordinary energy transformations?
22. A roller coaster car rolls down a frictionless track, reaching speed v_f at the bottom.
    a. If you want the car to go twice as fast at the bottom, by what factor must you increase the height of the track?
    b. Does your answer to part a depend on whether the track is straight or not? Explain.
23. A spring gun shoots out a plastic ball at speed v_i. The spring is then compressed twice the distance it was on the first shot.
    a. By what factor is the spring's potential energy increased?
    b. By what factor is the ball's speed increased? Explain.
24. Sandy and Chris stand on the edge of a cliff and throw identical mass rocks at the same speed. Sandy throws her rock horizontally while Chris throws his upward at an angle of 45° to the horizontal. Are the rocks moving at the same speed when they hit the ground, or is one moving faster than the other? If one is moving faster, which one? Explain.

Multiple-Choice Questions

25. || If you walk up a flight of stairs at constant speed, gaining vertical height h, the work done on you (the system, of mass m) is
    A. $+mgh$, by the normal force of the stairs.
    B. $-mgh$, by the normal force of the stairs.
    C. $+mgh$, by the gravitational force of the earth.
    D. $-mgh$, by the gravitational force of the earth.
26. | You and a friend each carry a 15 kg suitcase up two flights of stairs, walking at a constant speed. Take each suitcase to be the system. Suppose you carry your suitcase up the stairs in 30 s while your friend takes 60 s. Which of the following is true?
    A. You did more work, but both of you expended the same power.
    B. You did more work and expended more power.

C. Both of you did the same work, but you expended more power.

D. Both of you did the same work, but you expended less power.

27. | A woman uses a pulley and a rope to raise a 20 kg weight to a height of 2 m. If it takes 4 s to do this, about how much power is she supplying?

A. 100 W   B. 200 W   C. 300 W   D. 400 W

28. | A hockey puck sliding along frictionless ice with speed v to the right collides with a horizontal spring and compresses it by 2.0 cm before coming to a momentary stop. What will be the spring's maximum compression if the same puck hits it at a speed of $2v$?

A. 2.0 cm   B. 2.8 cm   C. 4.0 cm
D. 5.6 cm   E. 8.0 cm

29. ‖ A block slides down a smooth ramp, starting from rest at a height h. When it reaches the bottom it's moving at speed v_i. It then continues to slide up a second smooth ramp. At what height is its speed equal to $v_i/2$?

A. $h/4$ B. $h/2$ C. $3h/4$ D. $2h$

30. ‖ A wrecking ball is suspended from a 5.0-m-long cable that makes a 30° angle with the vertical. The ball is released and swings down. What is the ball's speed at the lowest point?

A. 7.7 m/s   B. 4.4 m/s   C. 3.6 m/s   D. 3.1 m/s

PROBLEMS

Section 5.4 Work

1. | During an etiquette class, you walk slowly and steadily at 0.20 m/s for 2.5 m with a 0.75 kg book balanced on top of your head. How much work does your head do on the book?

2. | A 2.0 kg book is lying on a 0.75-m-high table. You pick it up and place it on a bookshelf 2.3 m above the floor.
   a. How much work does gravity do on the book?
   b. How much work does your hand do on the book?

3. ‖ The two ropes seen in Figure P5.3 are used to lower a 255 kg piano exactly 5 m from a second-story window to the ground. How much work is done by each of the three forces?

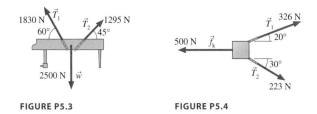

FIGURE P5.3   **FIGURE P5.4**

4. ‖ The two ropes shown in the bird's-eye view of Figure P5.4 are used to drag a crate exactly 3 m across the floor. How much work is done by each of the ropes on the crate?

5. ‖ a. At the airport, you ride a "moving sidewalk" that carries you horizontally for 25 m at 0.70 m/s. Assuming that you were moving at 0.70 m/s before stepping onto the moving sidewalk and continue at 0.70 m/s afterward, how much work does the moving sidewalk do on you? Your mass is 60 kg.
   b. An escalator carries you from one level to the next in the airport terminal. The upper level is 4.5 m above the lower level, and the length of the escalator is 7.0 m. How much work does the up escalator do on you when you ride it from the lower level to the upper level?
   c. How much work does the down escalator do on you when you ride it from the upper level to the lower level?

6. | A boy flies a kite with the string at a 30° angle to the horizontal. The tension in the string is 4.5 N. How much work does the string do on the boy if the boy
   a. stands still?
   b. walks a horizontal distance of 11 m away from the kite?
   c. walks a horizontal distance of 11 m toward the kite?

Section 5.5 Kinetic Energy

7. | Which has the larger kinetic energy, a 10 g bullet fired at 500 m/s or a 10 kg bowling ball sliding at 10 m/s?

8. | At what speed does a 1000 kg compact car have the same kinetic energy as a 20,000 kg truck going 25 km/hr?

9. ‖ An oxygen atom is four times as massive as a helium atom. In an experiment, a helium atom and an oxygen atom have the same kinetic energy. What is the ratio v_{He}/v_O of their speeds?

10. ‖ Sam's job at the amusement park is to slow down and bring to a stop the boats in the log ride. If a boat and its riders have a mass of 1200 kg and the boat drifts in at 1.2 m/s, how much work does Sam do to stop it?

11. ‖ A 20 g plastic ball is moving to the left at 30 m/s. How much work must be done on the ball to cause it to move to the right at 30 m/s?

Section 5.6 Potential Energy

12. | The lowest point in Death Valley is 85.0 m below sea level. The summit of nearby Mt. Whitney has an elevation of 4420 m. What is the change in gravitational potential energy of an energetic 65.0 kg hiker who makes it from the floor of Death Valley to the top of Mt. Whitney?

13. | a. What is the kinetic energy of a 1500 kg car traveling at a speed of 30 m/s ($\approx$65 mph)?
   b. From what height should the car be dropped to have this same amount of kinetic energy just before impact?
   c. Does your answer to part b depend on the car's mass?

14. ‖ A boy reaches out of a window and tosses a ball straight up with a speed of 10 m/s. The ball is 20 m above the ground as he releases it. Use conservation of energy to find
   a. The ball's maximum height above the ground.
   b. The ball's speed as it passes the window on its way down.
   c. The speed of impact on the ground.

15. ‖ a. With what minimum speed must you toss a 100 g ball straight up to just barely hit the 10-m-high ceiling of the gymnasium if you release the ball 1.5 m above the floor? Solve this problem using energy.
   b. With what speed does the ball hit the floor?

16. ‖ What minimum speed does a 100 g puck need to make it to the top of a frictionless ramp that is 3.0 m long and inclined at 20°?

17. ‖ A car is parked at the top of a 50-m-high hill. It slips out of gear and rolls down the hill. How fast will it be going at the bottom? (Ignore friction.)

18. ‖ A pendulum is made by tying a 500 g ball to a 75-cm-long string. The pendulum is pulled 30° to one side, then released.
    a. What is the ball's speed at the lowest point of its trajectory?
    b. To what angle does the pendulum swing on the other side?

19. ‖ A 1500 kg car is approaching the hill shown in Figure P5.19 at 10 m/s when it suddenly runs out of gas.
    a. Can the car make it to the top of the hill by coasting?
    b. If your answer to (a) is yes, what is the car's speed after coasting down the other side?

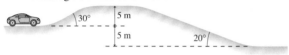

FIGURE P5.19

20. ‖ You're driving at 35 km/hr when the road suddenly descends 15 m into a valley. You take your foot off the accelerator and coast down the hill. Just as you reach the bottom you see the police officer hiding behind the speed limit sign that reads "70 km/hr." Are you going to get a speeding ticket?

21. ‖ Your friend's Frisbee has become stuck 16 m above the ground in a tree. You want to dislodge the Frisbee by throwing a rock at it. The Frisbee is stuck pretty tight, so you figure the rock needs to be traveling at least 5.0 m/s when it hits the Frisbee. If you release the rock 2.0 m above the ground, with what minimum speed must you throw it?

Section 5.7 Thermal Energy

22. | A 1500 kg car traveling at 20 m/s skids to a halt.
    a. What energy transfers and transformations occur during the skid?
    b. What is the change in the thermal energy of the car and the road surface?

23. ‖ A 20 kg child slides down a 3.0-m-high playground slide. She starts from rest, and her speed at the bottom is 2.0 m/s.
    a. What energy transfers and transformations occur during the slide?
    b. What is the change in the thermal energy of the slide and the seat of her pants?

24. ‖ A fireman of mass 80 kg slides down a pole. When he reaches the bottom, 4.2 m below his starting point, his speed is 2.2 m/s. By how much has thermal energy increased during his slide?

Section 5.9 Power

25. | a. How much work does an elevator motor do to lift a 1000 kg elevator a height of 100 m?
    b. How much power must the motor supply to do this in 50 s at constant speed?

26. ‖ a. How much work must you do to push a 10 kg block of steel across a steel table at a steady speed of 1.0 m/s for 3.0 s? The coefficient of kinetic friction for steel on steel is 0.60.
    b. What is your power output while doing so?

27. | Which consumes more energy, a 1.2 kW hair dryer used for 10 min or a 10 W night light left on for 24 hr?

28. ‖ A 1000 kg sports car accelerates from 0 to 30 m/s in 10 s. What is the average power of the engine?

29. ‖ In just 0.30 s, you compress a spring (spring constant 5000 N/m), which is initially at its equilibrium length, by 4.0 cm. What is your average power output?

30. ‖‖ In the winter sport of curling, players give a 20 kg stone a push across a sheet of ice. A curler accelerates a stone to a speed of 3.0 m/s over a time of 2.0 s.
    a. How much force does the curler exert on the stone?
    b. What average power does the curler use to bring the stone up to speed?

31. ‖‖ A 710 kg car drives at a constant speed of 23 m/s. It is subject to a drag force of 500 N. What power is required from the car's engine to drive the car
    a. on level ground?
    b. up a hill with a slope of 2.0°?

32. ‖ An elevator weighing 2500 N ascends at a constant speed of 8.0 m/s. How much power must the motor supply to do this?

General Problems

33. ‖ A 2.3 kg box, starting from rest, is pushed up a ramp by a 10 N force parallel to the ramp. The ramp is 2.0 m long and tilted at 17°. The speed of the box at the top of the ramp is 0.80 m/s. Consider the system to be the box + ramp + earth.
    a. How much work W does the force do on the system?
    b. What is the change ΔK in the kinetic energy of the system?
    c. What is the change ΔU_g in the gravitational potential energy of the system?
    d. What is the change ΔE_{th} in the thermal energy of the system?

34. ‖ A 55 kg skateboarder wants to just make it to the upper edge of a "half-pipe" with a radius of 3.0 m, as shown in Figure P5.34. What speed v_i does he need at the bottom if he is to coast all the way up?
    a. First do the calculation treating the skateboarder and board as a point particle, with the entire mass nearly in contact with the half-pipe.

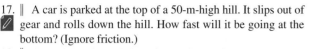

    FIGURE P5.34

    b. More realistically, the mass of the skateboarder in a deep crouch might be thought of as concentrated 0.75 m from the half-pipe. Assuming he remains in that position all the way up, what v_i is needed to reach the upper edge?

35. ‖ Fleas have remarkable jumping ability. If a 0.50 mg flea jumps straight up, it will reach a height of 40 cm if there is no air resistance. In reality, air resistance limits the height to 20 cm.
    a. What is the flea's kinetic energy as it leaves the ground?
    b. At its highest point, what fraction of the initial kinetic energy has been converted to potential energy?

36. ‖ A marble slides without friction in a *vertical* plane around the inside of a smooth, 20-cm-diameter horizontal pipe. The marble's speed at the bottom is 3.0 m/s; this is fast enough so that the marble makes a complete loop, never losing contact with the pipe. What is its speed at the top?

37. ||| A 20 kg child is on a swing that hangs from 3.0-m-long chains, as shown in Figure P5.37. What is her speed v_i at the bottom of the arc if she swings out to a 45° angle before reversing direction?

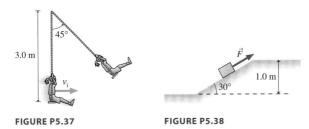

FIGURE P5.37   FIGURE P5.38

38. | Suppose you lift a 20 kg box by a height of 1.0 m.
   a. How much work do you do in lifting the box?
   Instead of lifting the box straight up, suppose you push it up a 1.0-m-high ramp that makes a 30° degree angle with the horizontal, as shown in Figure P5.38. Being clever, you choose a ramp with no friction.
   b. How much force F is required to push the box straight up the slope at a constant speed?
   c. How long is the ramp?
   d. Use your force and distance results to calculate the work you do in pushing the box up the ramp. How does this compare to your answer to part a?

39. || A cannon tilted up at a 30° angle fires a cannon ball at 80 m/s from atop a 10-m-high fortress wall. What is the ball's impact speed on the ground below? Ignore air resistance.

40. ||| The sledder shown in Figure P5.40 starts from the top of a frictionless hill and slides down into the valley. What initial speed v_i does the sledder need to just make it over the next hill?

FIGURE P5.40

41. ||| A 100 g granite cube slides down a frictionless 40° incline. At the bottom, just after it exits onto a horizontal table, the granite collides with a 200 g steel cube at rest. How high above the table should the granite cube be released to give the steel cube a speed of 150 cm/s?

42. || A 50 g ice cube can slide without friction up and down a 30° slope. The ice cube is pressed against a spring at the bottom of the slope, compressing the spring 10 cm. The spring constant is 25 N/m. When the ice cube is released, what distance will it travel up the slope before reversing direction?

43. |||| In a physics lab experiment, a spring clamped to the table shoots a 20 g ball horizontally. When the spring is compressed 20 cm, the ball travels horizontally 5.0 m and lands on the floor 1.5 m below the point at which it left the spring. What is the spring constant?

44. | The desperate contestants on a TV survival show are very hungry. The only food they can see is some fruit hanging on a branch high in a tree. Fortunately, they have a spring they can use to launch a rock. The spring constant is 1000 N/m, and they can compress the spring a maximum of 30 cm. All the rocks on the island seem to have a mass of 400 g.
   a. With what speed does the rock leave the spring?
   b. If the fruit hangs 15 m above the ground, will they feast or go hungry?

45. | The maximum energy a bone can absorb without breaking
BIO is surprisingly small. For a healthy human of mass 60 kg, experimental data show that the leg bones can absorb about 200 J.
   a. From what maximum height could a person jump and land rigidly upright on both feet without breaking his legs? Assume that all the energy is absorbed in the leg bones in a rigid landing.
   b. People jump from much greater heights than this; explain how this is possible.
   Hint: Think about how people land when they jump from greater heights.

46. || In an amusement park water slide, people slide down an essentially frictionless tube. They drop 3.0 m and exit the slide, moving horizontally, 1.2 m above a swimming pool. What horizontal distance do they travel from the exit point before hitting the water? Does the mass of the person make any difference?

47. || The 5.0-m-long rope in Figure P5.47 hangs vertically from a tree right at the edge of a ravine. A woman wants to use the rope to swing to the other side of the ravine. She runs as fast as she can, grabs the rope, and swings out over the ravine.
   a. As she swings, what energy conversion is taking place?
   b. When she's directly over the far edge of the ravine, how much higher is she than when she started?
   c. Given your answers to parts a and b, how fast must she be running when she grabs the rope in order to swing all the way across the ravine?

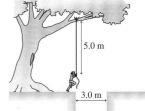

FIGURE P5.47

48. ||| You have been asked to design a "ballistic spring system" to measure the speed of bullets. A bullet of mass m is fired
INT into a block of mass M. The block, with the embedded bullet, then slides across a frictionless table and collides with a horizontal spring whose spring constant is k. The opposite end of the spring is anchored to a wall. The spring's maximum compression d is measured.
   a. Find an expression for the bullet's initial speed v_B in terms of m, M, k, and d.
   Hint: This is a two-part problem. The bullet's collision with the block is an inelastic collision. What quantity is conserved in an inelastic collision? Subsequently the block hits a spring on a frictionless surface. What quantity is conserved in this collision?
   b. What was the speed of a 5.0 g bullet if the block's mass is 2.0 kg and if the spring, with $k = 50$ N/m, was compressed by 10 cm?
   c. What fraction of the bullet's initial kinetic energy is "lost"? Where did it go?

49. || A new event, shown in Figure P5.49, has been proposed for the Winter Olympics. An athlete will sprint 100 m, starting
INT from rest, then leap onto a 20 kg bobsled. The person and

bobsled will then slide down a 50-m-long ice-covered ramp, sloped at 20°, and into a spring with a carefully calibrated spring constant of 2000 N/m. The athlete who compresses the spring the farthest wins the gold medal. Lisa, whose mass is 40 kg, has been training for this event. She can reach a maximum speed of 12 m/s in the 100 m dash.

FIGURE P5.49

a. How far will Lisa compress the spring?
b. The Olympic committee has very exact specifications about the shape and angle of the ramp. Is this necessary? If the committee asks your opinion, what factors about the ramp will you tell them are important?

50. ||| A 20 g ball is fired horizontally with initial speed v_i toward a 100 g ball that is hanging motionless from a 1.0-m-long string. The balls undergo a head-on, perfectly elastic collision, after which the 100 g ball swings out to a maximum angle $\theta_{max} = 50°$. What was v_i?

51. | A 70 kg human sprinter can accelerate from rest to 10 m/s in 3.0 s. During the same interval, a 30 kg greyhound can accelerate from rest to 20 m/s. Compute (a) the change in kinetic energy and (b) the average power output for each.

52. || A 50 g ball of clay traveling at speed v_i hits and sticks to a 1.0 kg block sitting at rest on a frictionless surface.
a. What is the speed of the block after the collision?
b. Show that the mechanical energy is *not* conserved in this collision. What percentage of the ball's initial kinetic energy is "lost"? Where did this kinetic energy go?

53. || A package of mass m is released from rest at a warehouse loading dock and slides down a 3.0-m-high frictionless chute to a waiting truck. Unfortunately, the truck driver went on a break without having removed the previous package, of mass $2m$, from the bottom of the chute as shown in Figure P5.53.
a. Suppose the packages stick together. What is their common speed after the collision?
b. Suppose the collision between the packages is perfectly elastic. To what height does the package of mass m rebound?

FIGURE P5.53

54. |||| A 50 kg sprinter, starting from rest, runs 50 m in 7.0 s at constant acceleration.
a. What is the magnitude of the horizontal force acting on the sprinter?
b. What is the sprinter's average power output during the first 2.0 s of his run?
c. What is the sprinter's average power output during the final 2.0 s?

55. ||| Bob can throw a 500 g rock with a speed of 30 m/s. He moves his hand forward 1.0 m while doing so.
a. How much force, assumed to be constant, does Bob apply to the rock?
b. How much work does Bob do on the rock?

56. |||| A 2.0 hp electric motor on a water well pumps water from 10 m below the surface. The density of water is 1.0 kg per L. How many liters of water can the motor pump in 1 hr?

57. | The human heart has to pump the average adult's 6.0 L of blood through the body every minute. The heart must do work to overcome frictional forces that resist the blood flow. The average blood pressure is 1.3×10^4 N/m².
a. Compute the work done moving the 6.0 L of blood completely through the body, assuming the blood pressure always takes its average value.
b. What power output must the heart have to do this task once a minute?
Hint: When the heart contracts, it applies force to the blood. Pressure is just force/area, so we can write work = (pressure)(area)(distance). But (area)(distance) is just the blood volume passing through the heart.

Passage Problems

Tennis Ball Testing

A tennis ball bouncing on a hard surface compresses and then rebounds. The details of the rebound are specified in tennis regulations. Tennis balls, to be acceptable for tournament play, must have a mass of 57.5 g. When dropped from a height of 2.5 m onto a concrete surface, a ball must rebound to a height of 1.4 m. During impact, the ball compresses by approximately 6 mm.

58. | How fast is the ball moving when it hits the concrete surface? (Ignore air resistance.)
A. 5 m/s   B. 7 m/s   C. 25 m/s   D. 50 m/s

59. | If the ball accelerates uniformly when it hits the floor, what is its approximate acceleration as it comes to rest before rebounding?
A. 1000 m/s² B. 2000 m/s² C. 3000 m/s² D. 4000 m/s²

60. | The ball's kinetic energy just after the bounce is less than just before the bounce. In what form does this lost energy end up?
A. Elastic potential energy
B. Gravitational potential energy
C. Thermal energy
D. Rotational kinetic energy

61. | By what percent does the kinetic energy decrease?
A. 35%   B. 45%   C. 55%   D. 65%

62. | When a tennis ball bounces from a racket, the ball loses approximately 30% of its kinetic energy to thermal energy. A ball that hits a racket at a speed of 10 m/s will rebound with approximately what speed?
A. 8.5 m/s   B. 7.0 m/s   C. 4.5 m/s   D. 3.0 m/s

Work and Power in Cycling

When you ride a bicycle at constant speed, almost all of the energy you expend goes into the work you do against the drag force of the air. In this problem, assume that *all* of the energy expended goes into working against drag. As we saw in Section 4.7, the drag force on an object is approximately proportional to the square of its speed with respect to the air. For this problem, assume that $F \propto v^2$ exactly and that the air is motionless with respect to the ground unless noted otherwise. Suppose a cyclist and her bicycle have a combined mass of 60 kg and she is cycling along at a speed of 5 m/s.

63. | If the drag force on the cyclist is 10 N, how much energy does she use in cycling 1 km?
    A. 6 kJ   B. 10 kJ   C. 50 kJ   D. 100 kJ

64. | Under these conditions, how much power does she expend as she cycles?
    A. 10 W   B. 50 W   C. 100 W   D. 200 W

65. | If she doubles her speed to 10 m/s, how much energy does she use in cycling 1 km?
    A. 20 kJ   B. 40 kJ   C. 400 kJ   D. 400 kJ

66. | How much power does she expend when cycling at that speed?
    A. 100 W   B. 200 W   C. 400 W   D. 1000 W

67. | Upon reducing her speed back down to 5 m/s, she hits a headwind of 5 m/s. How much power is she expending now?
    A. 100 W   B. 200 W   C. 500 W   D. 1000 W

STOP TO THINK ANSWERS

Stop to Think 5.1: D. Since the child slides at a constant speed, his kinetic energy doesn't change. But his gravitational potential energy at the top of the slide decreases as he descends, and is transformed into thermal energy in the slide and his bottom.

Stop to Think 5.2: C. $W = Fd\cos\theta$. The 10 N force at 90° does no work at all. $\cos 60° = \frac{1}{2}$, so the 8 N force does less work than the 6 N force.

Stop to Think 5.3: B > D > A = C. $K = (1/2)mv^2$. Using the given masses and velocities, we find $K_A = 2.0$ J, $K_B = 4.5$ J, $K_C = 2.0$ J, $K_D = 4.0$ J.

Stop to Think 5.4: $(U_g)_3 > (U_g)_2 = (U_g)_4 > (U_g)_1$. Gravitational potential energy depends only on height, not speed.

Stop to Think 5.5: $P_B > P_A = P_C > P_D$. The power here is the rate at which each runner's internal chemical energy is converted into gravitational potential energy. The change in gravitational potential energy is $mg\Delta y$, so the power is $mg\Delta y/\Delta t$. For runner A, the ratio $m\Delta y/\Delta t$ equal $(80 \text{ kg})(10 \text{ m})/(10 \text{ s}) = 80 \text{ kg} \cdot \text{m/s}$. For C, it's the same. For B, it's $100 \text{ kg} \cdot \text{m/s}$, while for D the ratio is $64 \text{ kg} \cdot \text{m/s}$.

6

USING ENERGY

The strange masks worn by the fighters have a very simple purpose: to measure how much oxygen their bodies are using. How can this tell us how efficiently their bodies are using energy?

Looking Ahead ▸▸

The goal of Chapter 6 is to learn more about energy transformations and transfers, the laws of thermodynamics, and theoretical and practical limitations on energy use. In this chapter, you will learn to:

▸ Use the concept of efficiency.
▸ Discuss how energy is used in the body.
▸ Understand the related concepts of heat, temperature, and thermal energy.
▸ Apply the first law of thermodynamics.

Looking Back ◂◂

This chapter is a companion chapter to Chapter 5. All of the concepts that you learned in that chapter will be used here. Please review especially:

Chapter 5 introduced the concept of energy, and in it you learned to solve problems in which energy is transformed from one form to another. For example, you now know how to calculate the energy required to lift a box a certain distance off the floor.

But how much energy would your body actually *use* to complete this task? We will find that the energy used by your body is more than the change in potential energy of the box. Why is this? As you lift the box, where does the energy come from? If you put the box back on the floor, where has the energy gone? Is it "lost"? In this chapter, we will consider just such questions of energy transformations and efficiency. Answering these questions will lead us to learn more about thermal energy, temperature, and heat.

6.1 Transforming Energy

As we saw in Chapter 5, energy can't be created or destroyed; it can only be converted from one form to another. When we say we are *using energy,* we mean that we are transforming it, such as transforming the chemical energy of food into the kinetic energy of your body. Let's revisit the idea of energy transformations, considering some realistic situations that have interesting theoretical and practical limitations.

Energy transformations

Light energy hitting a solar cell on top of these walkway lights is converted to electric energy and then stored as chemical energy in a battery. At night, the battery's chemical energy is converted to electric energy that is then converted to light energy in a light-emitting diode.

Light energy is absorbed by photosynthetic pigments in soybean plants, which use this energy to create concentrated chemical energy. The soybeans are harvested and their oil is used to make candles. When the candle burns, the stored chemical energy is transformed into light energy and thermal energy.

A wind turbine converts the translational kinetic energy of moving air into electric energy. Miles away, this energy can be used by a fan, which transforms the electric energy back into the kinetic energy of moving air.

In each of the processes in the table, energy is transformed from one form to another, ending up in the same form as it began. But some energy appears to have been "lost" along the way. The garden lights shine with a glow that is much less bright than the sun that shined on them! No energy is really lost, because energy is conserved; it is merely converted to other forms that are less useful to us.

Let's look at a practical example. Electric power companies sometimes use excess electric energy to pump water uphill. They can then reclaim this energy when demand is greater by letting the water generate electricity as it flows back down. Figure 6.1 shows the energy transformations in this process, assuming 100 J of electric energy at the start.

At the end of the process, only 50 J of electric energy is recovered. No energy is actually lost, but when other forms of energy are transformed to thermal energy, this change is *irreversible:* We cannot easily recover this thermal energy and convert it back to electric energy. **The energy isn't lost, but it is lost to our use.** In order to look at losses in energy transformations in more detail, we will define the notion of *efficiency.*

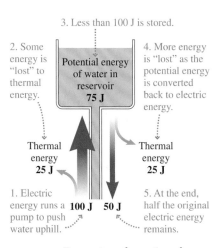

FIGURE 6.1 Energy transformations for a pumped storage system.

Efficiency

To get 50 J of energy out of your pumped storage plant, you would actually need to *pay* to put in 100 J of energy, as we saw in Figure 6.1. Because only 50% of the energy is returned as useful energy, we can say that this plant has an efficiency of 50%. Generally, we can define efficiency as

$$e = \frac{\text{what you get}}{\text{what you had to pay}} \qquad (6.1)$$

General definition of efficiency

The larger the energy losses in a system, the lower its efficiency.

The reductions in efficiency can arise from two different sources:

- **Process limitations.** In many cases that we will consider, the energy losses are due to practical details of an energy transformation process. You could, in principle, design a process that entailed smaller losses.
- **Fundamental limitations.** In other cases that we will consider, energy losses are due to physical laws that cannot be circumvented. The best process that could theoretically be designed will have less than 100% efficiency. As we will see, these limitations result from the difficulty of transforming thermal energy into other forms of energy.

As you walk up a flight of stairs, you increase your body's potential energy by about 1800 J. But a measurement of the energy used by your body to climb the stairs would show that your body uses 7200 J to complete this task. The 1800 J increase in potential energy is "what you get"; the 7200 J your body uses is "what you had to pay." We can use Equation 6.1 to compute the efficiency for this action to be

$$e = \frac{1800 \text{ J}}{7200 \text{ J}} = 0.25 = 25\%$$

This low efficiency is due to *process limitations*. The efficiency is limited by the biochemistry of how your food is digested and the biomechanics of how you move. This is not a fundamental limit; the process could be made more efficient. For instance, changing the angle of the stairs can allow a person to climb the same height with a smaller total energy expenditure.

The electric energy you use daily must be generated from other sources, in most cases the chemical energy in coal or other fossil fuels. The chemical energy is converted to thermal energy by burning, and the resulting thermal energy is converted to electric energy. A typical power plant cycle is shown in Figure 6.2. "What you get" is the energy output, the 35 J of electric energy. "What you had to pay" is the energy input, the 100 J of chemical energy, giving an efficiency of

$$e = \frac{35 \text{ J}}{100 \text{ J}} = 0.35 = 35\%$$

This low efficiency turns out to be largely due to a *fundamental limitation*. Thermal energy cannot be transformed to other forms of energy with 100% efficiency. A 35% efficiency is close to the theoretical maximum, and no power plant could be designed that would do better than this maximum. In later sections, we will explore the fundamental properties of thermal energy that make this so.

This idea of efficiency will form a thread that will run through this chapter. We will take some time to explore how to solve problems using this concept.

These cooling towers release thermal energy from a coal-fired power plant.

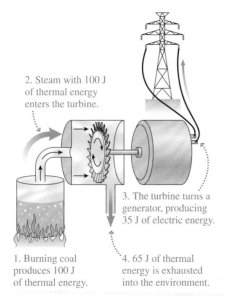

2. Steam with 100 J of thermal energy enters the turbine.

3. The turbine turns a generator, producing 35 J of electric energy.

1. Burning coal produces 100 J of thermal energy.

4. 65 J of thermal energy is exhausted into the environment.

FIGURE 6.2 Energy transformations in a coal-fired power plant.

(MP) PROBLEM-SOLVING
STRATEGY 6.1   **Energy efficiency problems**

PREPARE There are two key components to define as we prepare to compute efficiency:

❶ Choose what energy to count as "what you get." This could be the useful energy output of an engine or process or the work that is done in completing a process. For example, when you climb a flight of stairs, "what you get" is your change in potential energy.

❷ "What you had to pay" will generally be the total energy input needed for an engine, task, or process. For example, when you run your air conditioner, "what you had to pay" is the electric energy input.

SOLVE You may need to do additional calculations:

■ Compute values for "what you get" and "what you had to pay."
■ Be certain that all energy values are in the same units.

After this, compute the efficiency using $e = \dfrac{\text{what you get}}{\text{what you had to pay}}$.

ASSESS Check your answer to see if it is reasonable, given what you know about typical efficiencies for the process under consideration.

A Case Study in Energy Efficiency

We will now look at a practical example that involves energy transformations and energy transfers by work and heat: the energy transformations and transfers in moving a car along the road. How efficient is your car as you drive down the highway?

Why does your car use energy to move forward at all? In the absence of external forces, your car would continue at a constant speed once it was moving. But if you are driving at highway speed and take your foot off the gas, your car will slow down; this is almost entirely due to one external force, the drag force on the car. The car must apply a forward force to move through the air; it has to do work to move forward.

CONCEPTUAL EXAMPLE 6.1 **Energy transformations and transfers for a car**

A car is traveling along a level road at a steady 65 mph (approximately 30 m/s). What energy transformations and transfers are taking place?

REASON We will take the car as our system. Let's write the conservation of energy equation for a system that isn't isolated, Equation 5.4, including all types of energy which might apply to the car:

$$\Delta K + \Delta U_g + \Delta E_{th} + \Delta E_{chem} = W + Q$$

The car is moving at a constant speed, so the kinetic energy is not changing. The road is level, so there is no change in potential energy. If the car is running well, its temperature will be constant; its thermal energy isn't changing. Chemical energy does change, decreasing as fuel is burned. The equation thus reduces to

$$\Delta E_{chem} = W + Q$$

Chemical energy in the car's fuel is being used to do work because of the drag force and to transfer energy as heat to the environment. These are the only significant energy transfers taking place at constant speed.

ASSESS The car has kinetic energy, potential energy and thermal energy, but these forms of energy are all constant. Only the chemical energy changes.

We can now use what we know about the drag force to compute the minimum amount of energy necessary to move a car forward. We can take this as "what you get"; it is the minimum amount of energy that could be used to move the car forward. We can then use some real numbers to compute "what you had to pay"—the energy actually used to move the car forward. Once we have these two pieces of information, we can calculate an efficiency.

EXAMPLE 6.1 Minimum power for a car on a freeway

A Chevrolet Corvette has a drag coefficient of 0.30; the area of the front of the car is 1.8 m². What minimum power does this car need to move at a steady speed of 30 m/s on level ground?

PREPARE In Conceptual Example 6.1, we saw that the car was doing work because of drag. The car is pushing on the atmosphere with a force F equal in magnitude to the drag force D; this is the force that is doing work on the environment.

SOLVE In Chapter 4, we saw that the drag force on an object moving at a speed v is given by $D = \frac{1}{2}C\rho Av^2$, where C is the drag coefficient, ρ the density of air (approximately 1.2 kg/m²), A the area of the front of the car, and v the speed. Thus the drag force on the car moving at 30 m/s is

$$D = (\tfrac{1}{2})(0.30)(1.2 \text{ kg/m}^3)(1.8 \text{ m}^2)(30 \text{ m/s})^2 = 290 \text{ N}$$

Now that we know the magnitude of the force we can compute the necessary power by using Equation 5.22:

$$P = Fv = (290 \text{ N})(30 \text{ m/s}) = 8700 \text{ W}$$

ASSESS We can get a better idea of the size of this power by converting to horsepower:

$$P = 8700 \text{ W}\left(\frac{1 \text{ hp}}{746 \text{ W}}\right) = 12 \text{ hp}.$$

A Corvette will likely have a 350 hp engine. The power necessary to drive at highway speeds is just over 3% of the power available from the engine! The extra power is used to provide power for rapid acceleration (as we saw in Example 5.14) and for climbing hills. And, as we'll explore more later, quite a bit of the engine's power is "wasted" as heat energy transferred to the environment.

EXAMPLE 6.2 The efficiency of an automobile

The Corvette of the previous example is rated at 25 miles per gallon of gas at highway speeds. What is the efficiency of a Corvette driven 25 miles (40 km) at 30 m/s? (A gallon of gas contains 1.4×10^8 J of chemical energy.)

PREPARE We can use the steps outlined in Problem-Solving Strategy 6.1 for computing efficiency. "What you get" is the minimum energy to move the car forward as in the previous example; "what you had to pay" is the energy in one gallon of gas—the energy the car actually uses to drive this distance.

SOLVE As we saw in the previous example, the power necessary to overcome drag is 8700 W. The minimum energy needed to travel 40 km, which we will label ΔE_{min}, is

$$\Delta E_{min} = P\Delta t = P\left(\frac{\Delta x}{v}\right) = (8700 \text{ W})\left(\frac{40{,}000 \text{ m}}{30 \text{ m/s}}\right)$$
$$= 11.6 \times 10^6 \text{ J}$$

To drive 25 miles the car will use one gallon of gas, with energy 1.4×10^8 J. We can now use Equation 6.1 to find the efficiency:

$$e = \frac{\text{what you get}}{\text{what you had to pay}} = \frac{11.6 \times 10^6 \text{ J}}{1.4 \times 10^8 \text{ J}} = 0.083 = 8.3\%$$

ASSESS Only 8.3% of the chemical energy from the gasoline is used to overcome drag. The rest of the energy—about 92%—is "lost" as heat to the environment.

STOP TO THINK 6.1 Walking or running up a flight of stairs takes the same amount of energy. Which is more efficient?

A. Walking up the stairs.
B. Running up the stairs.
C. The efficiency is the same.

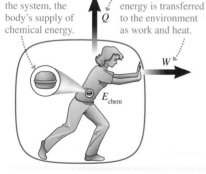

Once food is eaten, it becomes part of the system, the body's supply of chemical energy.

As chemical energy is used by the body, energy is transferred to the environment as work and heat.

Q

W

E_{chem}

FIGURE 6.3 Energy of the body, considered as the system.

6.2 Energy in the Body: Energy Inputs

In this section, we will look at energy in the body, which will give us the opportunity to explore a number of different energy transformations and transfers in another practical context. Figure 6.3 shows the body considered as the system for energy analysis. The chemical energy in food provides the necessary energy input for your body to function. It is this energy that is used for energy transfers with the environment.

Getting Energy from Food

Suppose you do a very simple exercise: lifting a mass and increasing its potential energy. Where did the energy come from to do this? At some point, the energy came from the food you ate, but what were the intermediate steps? The chemical energy in food is made available to the cells in the body by a two-step process. First, the digestive system breaks down food into simpler molecules such as glucose, a simple sugar, or long chains of glucose molecules called glycogen. These molecules are delivered via the bloodstream to cells in the body, where they are metabolized by combining with oxygen to produce simpler molecules, as in Equation 6.2.

Glucose from the digestion of food combines with oxygen that is breathed in to produce...   ...carbon dioxide, which is exhaled; water, which can be used by the body; and energy.

$$C_6H_{12}O_6 + 6O_2 \longrightarrow 6CO_2 + 6H_2O + \text{energy} \qquad (6.2)$$

Glucose   Oxygen   Carbon   Water
                      dioxide

This metabolism releases energy, some of which is stored in a molecule called ATP, or adenosine triphosphate. Cells in the body use this ATP to do all the work of life: Muscle cells use it to contract, nerve cells use it to produce electrical signals, and so on.

Oxidation reactions like those in Equation 6.2 "burn" the fuel that you obtain by eating. The oxidation of 1 g of glucose (or any other carbohydrate) will release approximately 17 kJ of energy. Table 6.1 compares the energy content of carbohydrates and other foods to other familiar sources of chemical energy.

It is possible to measure the chemical energy content of food by burning it. Burning food may seem quite different from metabolizing it, but if glucose is burned, the chemical formula for the reaction is exactly that of Equation 6.2; the two reactions are the same. Burning food transforms all of its chemical energy to thermal energy, which can be easily measured. Thermal energy is often measured in units of **calories (cal)** rather than in joules; 1.00 calorie is equivalent to 4.19 joules.

NOTE ▶ The energy content of food is usually quoted in Calories (Cal) (with a capital "c"); one Calorie (also called a "food calorie") is equal to 1000 calories or 1 kcal. If a candy bar contains 230 Cal, this means that, if burned, it would produce 230,000 cal (or 962 kJ) of thermal energy. ◀

TABLE 6.1 Energy in fuels

Fuel	Energy in 1 g of fuel (in kJ)
Hydrogen	121
Gasoline	44
Fat (in food)	38
Coal	27
Carbohydrates (in food)	17
Wood chips	15

Counting calories BIO Most foods burn quite well, as this photo of corn chips illustrates. You could set food on fire to measure its energy content, but this isn't really necessary. The chemical energies of the basic components of food (carbohydrates, proteins, fats) have been carefully measured—by burning—in a device called a *calorimeter*. Foods are analyzed to determine their composition, and their chemical energy can then be calculated.

EXAMPLE 6.3 Energy in food

A 12 oz can of soda contains approximately 40 g (or a bit less than 1/4 cup) of sugar, a simple carbohydrate. How much chemical energy in joules does this sugar contain? How many Calories is this?

SOLVE 1 g of sugar contains 17 kJ of energy; 40 g contains:

$$40 \text{ g} \times \frac{17 \times 10^3 \text{ J}}{1 \text{ g}} = 68 \times 10^4 \text{ J} = 680 \text{ kJ}$$

Converting to Calories, we get:

$$680 \text{ kJ} = 6.8 \times 10^5 \text{ J} = (6.8 \times 10^5 \text{ J})\frac{1.00 \text{ cal}}{4.19 \text{ J}}$$
$$= 1.6 \times 10^5 \text{ cal} = 160 \text{ Cal}$$

ASSESS 160 Calories is a typical value for the energy content of a 12 oz can of soda (check the nutrition label on one to see!), so this calculation seems reasonable.

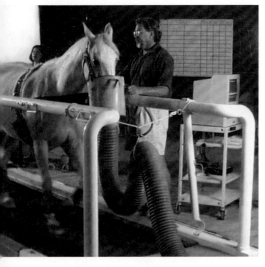

A respiratory apparatus can be used to measure metabolic energy use of animals as well as humans, in this case the energy used by a horse in walking.

TABLE 6.3 Energy usage at rest

Organ	Resting power (W) of 68 kg individual
Liver	26
Brain	19
Heart	7
Kidneys	11
Skeletal muscle	18
Remainder of body	19
Total	**100**

TABLE 6.4 Metabolic power use during activities by a 68 kg (150 lb) individual

Activity	Metabolic power (W) of 68 kg individual
Typing	125
Ballroom dancing	250
Walking at 5 km/hr	380
Cycling at 15 km/hr	480
Swimming at a fast crawl	800
Running at 15 km/hr	1150

TABLE 6.2 Energy content of foods

Food	Energy content in Cal	Energy content in kJ
Fried egg	100	420
Large apple	125	525
Slice of pizza	300	1260
Slice of apple pie	400	1680
Fast-food meal: Burger, fries, drink, large size	1350	5670

The first item on the nutrition label on packaged foods is Calories—a measure of the chemical energy in the food. (In Europe, where SI units are standard, you will also find the energy content listed in kJ.) The energy content of some common foods is given in Table 6.2.

6.3 Energy in the Body: Energy Outputs

Your body uses energy in many ways. Even at rest, your body uses energy for tasks such as building and repairing tissue, digesting food, and keeping warm. The number of joules used per second (that is, the power in watts) by different tissues in the resting body is given in Table 6.3.

Even at rest, your body uses energy at the rate of approximately 100 W. This energy comes from chemical energy in your body's stores, and is ultimately converted entirely to thermal energy, which is transferred as heat to the environment. If 100 people are in a lecture hall, they are adding thermal energy to the room at a rate of 10,000 W, and the air conditioning must be designed to take account of this!

Energy Use in Activities

Your body stores very little energy as ATP; as your body uses energy your cells must continually metabolize carbohydrates to produce it. This requires oxygen, as we saw in Equation 6.2. Physiologists can precisely measure the body's energy use by measuring how much oxygen the body is taking up with a respiratory apparatus, as seen in the photograph at the start of the chapter. The spirometer measures the body's *total metabolic energy use*—all of the energy used by the body while performing an activity. This total will include all of the body's basic processes such as breathing plus whatever additional energy is needed to perform the activity.

The metabolic energy used in an activity depends on an individual's size, level of fitness, and other variables. But we can make reasonable estimates for the power used in various activities for a typical individual. Some values are given in Table 6.4.

Your body uses energy above the resting rate to perform different activities. For instance, typing requires 125 W, as seen in Table 6.4. This corresponds to 100 W for basic functions plus 25 W for the work of typing.

Suppose you climb a set of stairs at a constant speed, as in Figure 6.4 on the next page. What is your body's efficiency for this process? To answer this question we will take the system to be your body together with the earth, so that we can consider gravitational potential energy.

Given how we have defined the system, there are no external forces that do work and there is no heat input—the system is isolated. Any energy transformations are internal to the system. We can use Equation 5.3 for the energy changes in the system, using the only forms of energy that change in this situation: gravitational potential, chemical (in your body), and thermal energy; kinetic energy does not change because your speed is constant:

$$\Delta U_g + \Delta E_{th} + \Delta E_{chem} = 0 \qquad (6.3)$$

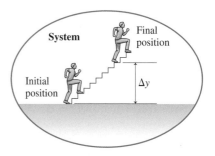

FIGURE 6.4 Pictorial representation of climbing a set of stairs.

Thermal energy and gravitational potential energy are increasing, so ΔE_{th} and ΔU_g are positive; chemical energy is being used, so ΔE_{chem} is a negative number. We can get a better feeling about what is happening by rewriting Equation 6.3 as

$$\left| \Delta E_{chem} \right| = \Delta U_g + \Delta E_{th}$$

The *magnitude* of the change in the chemical energy is equal to the sum of the changes in the gravitational potential and thermal energies. Chemical energy from your body is converted into potential energy and thermal energy; in the final position, you are at a greater height, and your body is slightly warmer!

Earlier in the chapter, we noted that the efficiency for stair climbing is about 25%. Let's see where that number comes from.

1. *What you get.* "What you get" is the change in potential energy: You have raised your body to the top of the stairs. If you climb a flight of stairs of vertical height Δy, we can easily compute the increase in potential energy $\Delta U_g = mg\Delta y$. Assuming a mass of 68 kg and a change in height of 2.7 m (about 9 ft, a reasonable value for a flight of stairs) we compute (to two significant figures)

$$\Delta U_g = (68 \text{ kg})(9.8 \text{ m/s}^2)(2.7 \text{ m}) = 1800 \text{ J}$$

2. *What you had to pay.* The cost is the metabolic energy the body used in completing the task. Physiologists can measure directly how much energy $\left| \Delta E_{chem} \right|$ your body uses to perform a task. A typical value for climbing a flight of stairs is

$$\left| E_{chem} \right| = 7200 \text{ J}$$

Given the definition of efficiency of Equation 6.2, we can compute an efficiency for climbing the stairs as

$$e = \frac{\Delta U_g}{\left| \Delta E_{chem} \right|} = \frac{1800 \text{ J}}{7200 \text{ J}} = 0.25 = 25\%$$

For the types of activities we will consider in this chapter, such as running, walking, and cycling, the body's efficiency is typically in the range of 20–30%.

In the above example, 25% of the energy used by your body ends up as increased potential energy; the other 75% ends up as thermal energy. Thermal energy losses arise from several sources, including the metabolism of glucose or glycogen to produce ATP, the use of ATP to make muscle cells contract, and from basic body processes that continue to be performed. Whenever you exercise, most

High heating costs? BIO The daily energy use of mammals is much higher than that of reptiles, largely because mammals use energy to maintain a constant body temperature. A 40 kg timber wolf uses approximately 19,000 kJ during the course of a day. A Komodo dragon, a reptilian predator of the same size, uses only 2100 kJ.

of the energy you use is converted to thermal energy; that's why you warm up when you work out!

EXAMPLE 6.4 How many flights?

If you have consumed a 12 oz can of soda, how many flights of stairs could you climb on the chemical energy it contains? Assume a mass of 68 kg and that a flight of stairs has a vertical height of 2.7 m.

PREPARE In Example 6.3, we calculated that the soda contains a chemical energy of 680 kJ. If the body uses this energy to climb stairs, we can assume that 25% of the energy is transformed to increased potential energy:

$$\Delta U_g = (0.25)(680 \times 10^3 \text{ J}) = 1.7 \times 10^5 \text{ J}$$

SOLVE Since $\Delta U_g = mg\Delta y$, the height gained is

$$\Delta y = \frac{\Delta U_g}{mg} = \frac{1.7 \times 10^5 \text{ J}}{(68 \text{ kg})(9.8 \text{ m/s}^2)} = 255 \text{ m}$$

If we assume that each flight has a height of 2.7 m, this gives

$$\text{Number of flights} = \frac{255 \text{ m}}{2.7 \text{ m}} \cong 94 \text{ flights}$$

ASSESS This is almost enough to get to the top of the Empire State Building—all fueled by one can of soda! This is a remarkable result.

FIGURE 6.5 Amazingly, a racing cyclist moving at 35 km/hr uses about the same power as an electric scooter moving at 5 km/hr.

The metabolic power values given in Table 6.4 represent the energy *used by the body* while these activities are being performed. Given that the body's efficiency is only 20–30%, the body's actual *useful power output* is quite a bit less than this. The table's value for cycling at 15 km/hr (a bit less than 10 mph) is 480 W. If we assume that the efficiency for cycling is approximately 25%, the actual power going to forward propulsion will only be 120 W. An elite racing cyclist going more than twice as fast as 15 km/hr might be using about 300 W for forward propulsion. This is a surprisingly low figure, as noted in Figure 6.5.

The energy you use per second running is proportional to your speed; running twice as fast takes approximately twice as much power. But running twice as fast takes you twice as far in the same time, so the energy you use to run a certain distance doesn't depend on how fast you run! Running a marathon takes approximately the same amount of energy whether you complete it in 2 hours, 3 hours or 4 hours; it is only the power that varies.

NOTE ▶ It is important to remember the distinction between the metabolic energy used to perform a task and the work done in a physics sense; these values can be quite different. Your muscles use power when applying a force, even when there is no motion. Holding a weight above your head involves no external work, but it clearly takes metabolic power to keep the weight in place! ◀

CONCEPTUAL EXAMPLE 6.2 Energy in weightlifting

A weightlifter lifts a 50 kg bar from the floor to a position over his head and back to the floor again 10 times in succession. At the end of this exercise, what energy transformations have taken place?

REASON We will take the system to be the weightlifter plus the bar. The environment does no work on the system, and we will assume that the time is short enough that no heat is transferred from the system to the environment. The bar has returned to its starting position and is not moving, so there has been no change in potential or kinetic energy. The equation for energy conservation is thus

$$\Delta E_{\text{chem}} + \Delta E_{\text{th}} = 0$$

Each time the bar is raised or lowered, the muscles use chemical energy. Ultimately, all of this energy is transformed to thermal energy.

ASSESS Most exercises in the gym—lifting weights, running on a treadmill—involve only the transformation of chemical energy to thermal energy.

EXAMPLE 6.5 Energy usage for a cyclist

A cyclist pedals for 20 min at a speed of 15 km/hr. How much metabolic energy is required?

PREPARE Table 6.4 gives a value of 480 W for the power used in cycling at a speed of 15 km/hr. This is the energy that is used per second.

SOLVE The cyclist uses energy at this rate for 20 min, or 1200 s. Power is the rate of using energy, $P = \Delta E / \Delta t$, so the energy required is

$$\Delta E = P\Delta t = (480 \text{ J/s})(1200 \text{ s}) = 580 \text{ kJ}$$

ASSESS How much energy is 580 kJ? A look at Table 6.2 shows that this is slightly more than the amount of energy available in a large apple, and only 10% of the energy available in a large fast-food meal. If you eat such a meal and plan to "work it off" by cycling, you should plan on cycling at a pretty good clip for a bit over 3 hr.

Energy Storage

The body gets energy from food; if this energy is not used, it will be stored. A small amount of energy needed for immediate use is stored as ATP. A larger amount of energy is stored as chemical energy of glycogen and glucose in muscle tissue and the liver. A healthy adult might store 400 g of these carbohydrates, which is a little more carbohydrate than is typically consumed in one day.

If the energy input from food continuously exceeds the energy outputs of the body, this energy will be stored in the form of fat under the skin and around the organs. From an energy point of view, gaining weight is simply explained!

EXAMPLE 6.6 Running out of fuel

The body stores about 400 g of carbohydrates. Approximately how far could a 68 kg runner travel on this stored energy?

PREPARE Table 6.1 gives a value of 17 kJ per g of carbohydrate. The 400 g of carbohydrates in the body contain an energy of

$$E_{\text{chem}} = (400 \text{ g})(17 \times 10^3 \text{ J/g}) = 6.8 \times 10^6 \text{ J}$$

SOLVE Table 6.4 gives the power used in running at 15 km/hr as 1150 W. The time that the stored chemical energy will last at this rate is

$$\Delta t = \frac{\Delta E_{\text{chem}}}{P} = \frac{6.8 \times 10^6 \text{ J}}{1150 \text{ W}} = 5.91 \times 10^3 \text{ s} = 1.64 \text{ hr}$$

And the distance that can be covered during this time at 15 km/hr is

$$\Delta x = v\Delta t = (15 \text{ km/hr})(1.64 \text{ hr}) = 25 \text{ km}$$

to two significant figures.

ASSESS A marathon is longer than this—just over 42 km. Even with "carbo loading" before the event (eating high-carbohydrate meals), many marathon runners "hit the wall" before the end of the race as they reach the point where they have exhausted their store of carbohydrates. The body has other energy stores (in fats, for instance), but the rate that they can be drawn on is much lower.

Energy and Locomotion

When you walk at a constant speed on level ground, your kinetic energy is constant. Your potential energy is also constant. So why does your body need energy to walk? Where does this energy go?

We use energy to walk because of mechanical inefficiencies in our gait. Figure 6.6 shows how the speed of your foot typically changes during each stride. The kinetic energy of your leg and foot increases, only to go to zero at the end of the stride. The kinetic energy is mostly transformed into thermal energy in your muscles and in your shoe. This thermal energy is lost; it can't be used for making further strides.

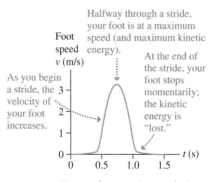

FIGURE 6.6 Human locomotion analysis.

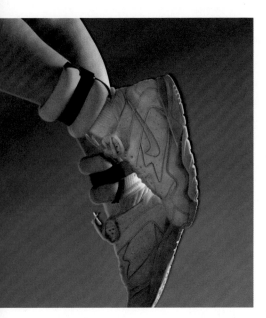

Where do you wear the weights? BIO
If you wear a backpack with a mass equal to 1% of your body mass, your energy expenditure for walking will increase by 1%. But if you wear ankle weights with a combined mass of 1% of your body mass, the increase in energy expenditure is 6%, because you must repeatedly accelerate this extra mass. If you want to "burn more fat," wear the weights on your ankles, not on your back!

Footwear can be designed to minimize the loss of kinetic energy to thermal energy. A spring in the sole of the shoe can store potential energy, which can be returned to kinetic energy during the next stride. Such a spring will make the collision with the ground more elastic. We saw in Chapter 5 that the tendons in the ankle do store a certain amount of energy during a stride; very stout tendons in the legs of kangaroos store energy even more efficiently. Their peculiar hopping gait is quite efficient at high speeds.

> **STOP TO THINK 6.2** A person is running at a constant speed on level ground. Chemical energy in the runner's body is being transformed to other forms of energy; most of the chemical energy is transformed to
>
> A. Kinetic energy.   B. Potential energy.   C. Thermal energy.

6.4 Thermal Energy and Temperature

We have frequently spoken of the energy that is transformed to thermal energy as being "lost." Regardless of whether "the system" is a car, a power plant, or your body, this thermal energy is exhausted into the environment as heat. But why is thermal energy in your body and other systems not converted to other forms of energy and used for practical purposes? To continue our study of how energy is used, we need to understand a bit more about one particular kind of energy— thermal energy.

What do you mean when you say something is "hot"? Do you mean that it has a high temperature? Or do you mean that it has a lot of thermal energy? Perhaps both of these definitions are the same? Let's give some thought to the definitions of temperature and thermal energy, and the relationship between them.

Measuring Temperature

We are all familiar with the idea of temperature. You hear the word used nearly every day. But just what is temperature a measure of? Velocity is a measure of how fast a system moves. What physical property of the system have you determined if you measure its temperature?

Let's start by looking at how you measure temperature. This is what a *thermometer* does. In a common glass-tube thermometer, for example, a small volume of mercury or alcohol expands or contracts when placed in contact with a "hot" or "cold" object. The object's temperature is determined by the height of the column of liquid.

A thermometer needs a *temperature scale* to be a useful measuring device. In 1742, the Swedish astronomer Anders Celsius sealed mercury into a small capillary tube and observed how it moved up and down the tube as the temperature changed. He selected two temperatures that anyone could reproduce, the freezing and boiling points of pure water, and labeled them 0 and 100. He then marked off the glass tube into one hundred equal intervals between these two reference points. By doing so, he invented the temperature scale that we today call the *Celsius scale*. The units of the Celsius temperature scale are "degrees Celsius," which we abbreviate as °C. The *Fahrenheit scale,* still widely used in the United States, is related to the Celsius scale by

$$T_C = \frac{5}{9}(T_F - 32°)$$ (6.4)

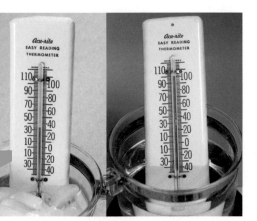

Thermal expansion of the liquid in the thermometer pushes it higher when immersed in hot water than in ice water.

An Atomic View of Thermal Energy and Temperature

When you add heat to an object, you increase its thermal energy; you also increase its temperature. In Chapter 5, we noted that the thermal energy of an object is the sum of the kinetic and potential energy of its atoms or molecules. Now we extend our discussion to include the concept of temperature. Let's start with the simplest possible system, a gas of atoms. In fact, we will make the system even simpler by defining the properties of what we will term an **ideal gas** in Figure 6.7. This is a rather simple model, but it gives a remarkably accurate description of the behavior of many real gases.

Because the ideal-gas atoms do not interact with each other (except for collisions), the system has no potential energy. The only internal energy in the ideal gas is the translational kinetic energy of the individual atoms. Thus, **the thermal energy of an ideal gas is equal to the total kinetic energy of the atoms that make up the gas.**

Adding heat to an ideal gas, as in Figure 6.8, will increase the thermal energy of the gas; the atoms will move faster. Adding heat to the gas will also increase its temperature. So temperature must be related to the kinetic energy of the individual atoms, but how? We can get one hint from the following fact: The temperature of a system doesn't depend on the size of the system. If you have two glasses of water, each at a temperature of 20°C, and you pour them together, you will have a larger volume of water at the same temperature of 20°C. There are more atoms, and therefore there is more *total* thermal energy, but the temperature has not changed. Even though there are more atoms, the *average* energy per atom is the same. It is this average kinetic energy of the atoms that is related to the temperature. **The temperature of an ideal gas is a measure of the average kinetic energy of the atoms that make up the gas.**

Let's consider the average kinetic energy of atoms in the gas. An atom of mass m and velocity v has kinetic energy $K = \frac{1}{2}mv^2$. The average kinetic energy of an atom is computed as the sum of the kinetic energies of all of the atoms divided by the number of atoms:

$$K_{avg} = \frac{\sum \frac{1}{2}mv^2}{N} = \frac{1}{2}m\frac{\sum v^2}{N} = \frac{1}{2}m(v^2)_{avg} \qquad (6.5)$$

The quantity $\sum v^2/N$ that appears in Equation 6.5 is the average of the speed squared, not the square of the average speed. If we want to know how fast a typical atom is moving, we should look at the square root of this average:

$$\text{Speed of a typical atom} = \sqrt{(v^2)_{avg}} = v_{rms} \qquad (6.6)$$

The quantity that we've defined as v_{rms} is called the **root mean square speed,** often referred to as the *rms speed*. Rewriting Equation 6.5 in terms of v_{rms} gives the average kinetic energy per atom:

$$K_{avg} = \frac{1}{2}mv_{rms}^2 \qquad (6.7)$$

If the gas consists of N atoms, the total kinetic energy of the atoms is just NK_{avg}. The total kinetic energy of the atoms in the gas is the thermal energy of the gas, so we find that

$$E_{th} = \frac{1}{2}Nmv_{rms}^2$$

If we can establish a connection between K_{avg} and the temperature T, which we will do in the next section, then we'll know how both the thermal energy E_{th} and the typical atomic speed are related to temperature.

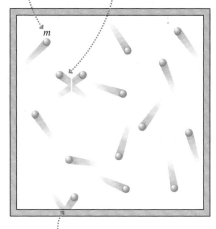

1. The gas is made of a large number N of atoms, each of mass m, all moving randomly.

2. The atoms in the gas are quite far from each other and interact only rarely when they collide.

3. The collisions of the atoms with each other (and with walls of the container) are elastic; no energy is lost in these collisions.

FIGURE 6.7 Motion of atoms in an ideal gas.

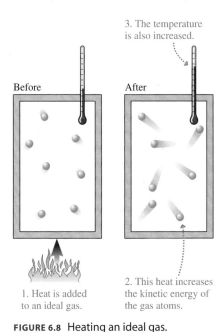

3. The temperature is also increased.

1. Heat is added to an ideal gas.

2. This heat increases the kinetic energy of the gas atoms.

FIGURE 6.8 Heating an ideal gas.

8.1–8.3

Optical molasses It isn't possible to reach absolute zero, where the atoms would be still, but it is possible to get quite close by slowing the atoms down directly. These crossed laser beams produce what is known as "optical molasses." Light is made of photons, which carry energy and momentum. Interactions of the atoms of a diffuse gas with the photons cause the atoms to slow down. Atoms can be slowed to very slow speeds that correspond to a temperature as cold as 5×10^{-10} K!

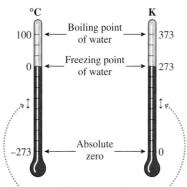

Temperature *differences* are the same on the Celsius and Kelvin scales. The temperature difference between the freezing point and boiling point of water is 100°C or 100 K.

FIGURE 6.9 Celsius and Kelvin temperature scales.

The Meaning of Temperature on the Kelvin Scale

When the Celsius temperature scale was defined, zero degrees was fixed to be the freezing point of water. The Fahrenheit scale has a zero point that was set as the temperature of an ice-salt mix. On both of these scales the choice of zero is arbitrary, and both scales allow temperatures that are negative or "below zero."

If we use the average kinetic energy of atoms as the basis for our definition of temperature, our temperature scale will have a very natural zero—the point at which kinetic energy is zero. Kinetic energy is always positive, so the zero on our temperature scale will be an **absolute zero;** no temperature below this is possible.

This is how zero is defined on the temperature scale called the *Kelvin scale:* **Zero degrees is the point at which the kinetic energy of atoms is zero.** All temperatures on the Kelvin scale are positive, so it is often called an *absolute temperature scale.* The units of the Kelvin temperature scale are "kelvin" (not degrees kelvin!), which is abbreviated K.

The spacing between divisions for the Kelvin scale is the same as that of the Celsius scale; the only difference is the position of the zero point. It is found experimentally that absolute zero—the temperature at which atoms would cease moving—is $-273°C$. Thus the Kelvin scale is obtained from the Celsius scale by shifting the zero point by 273 divisions. For this reason, the conversion between Celsius and Kelvin temperatures is quite straightforward:

$$T = T_C + 273 \tag{6.8}$$

Thus the freezing point of water at 0°C is $T = 0 + 273 = 273$ K. A 30°C warm summer day is $T = 303$ K on the Kelvin scale. A side-by-side comparison of these scales is given in Figure 6.9.

NOTE ▶ We will use the symbol T for temperature in kelvin. We will use subscripts to denote other scales. In the equations in this chapter and the rest of the text, **T must be interpreted as a temperature in kelvin.** ◀

EXAMPLE 6.7 Temperature scales

The coldest temperature ever measured on earth was $-129°F$, in Antarctica. What is this in °C and K?

SOLVE We use Equation 6.4 to convert the temperature to the Celsius scale:

$$T_C = \frac{5}{9}(-129° - 32°) = -89°C$$

We can then use Equation 6.8 to convert this to kelvin:

$$T = -89 + 273 = 184 \text{ K}$$

ASSESS This is quite cold, but quite a bit warmer than the coldest temperatures achieved in the laboratory.

We noted above that the temperature of an ideal gas is a measure of the average kinetic energy of the atoms. It can be shown that temperature on the Kelvin scale is related to the average kinetic energy per atom by

$$T = \frac{2}{3}\frac{K_{avg}}{k_B} \tag{6.9}$$

Temperature of an ideal gas in terms of the average kinetic energy per atom

LINEAR
p. 38

where k_B is a constant known as **Boltzmann's constant.** Its value is

$$k_B = 1.38 \times 10^{-23} \text{ J/K}$$

We can rewrite Equation 6.9 to express the average kinetic energy of the atoms in an ideal gas at a temperature T as

$$K_{avg} = \frac{3}{2}k_B T \qquad (6.10)$$

Interestingly, the average kinetic energy per atom depends *only* on the temperature, not on the atom's mass. For example, the average kinetic energy of an atom (of any gas) at room temperature (20°C, or 293 K) is

$$K_{avg} = \frac{3}{2}(1.38 \times 10^{-23} \text{ J/K})(293 \text{ K}) = 6.07 \times 10^{-21} \text{ J}$$

Combining Equation 6.10 with our definition of the root-mean-square speed of the atoms in a gas in Equation 6.7, we find that

$$v_{rms} = \sqrt{\frac{3k_B T}{m}} \qquad (6.11)$$

The rms speed is proportional to the *square root* of the temperature. This is a new mathematical form that we will see again, so we will take a look at its properties.

Martian airsicles The atmosphere of Mars is mostly carbon dioxide. At night, the temperature may drop so low that the molecules in the atmosphere will slow down enough to stick together—the atmosphere actually freezes. The frost on the surface in this image from the Viking 2 lander is composed partially of frozen carbon dioxide.

◣ Square-root relationships   ✐ Exercise 12 (MP)

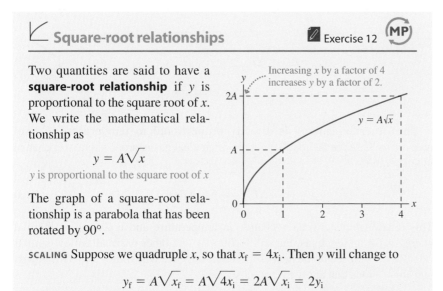

Two quantities are said to have a **square-root relationship** if y is proportional to the square root of x. We write the mathematical relationship as

$$y = A\sqrt{x}$$

y is proportional to the square root of x

The graph of a square-root relationship is a parabola that has been rotated by 90°.

Increasing x by a factor of 4 increases y by a factor of 2.

$y = A\sqrt{x}$

SCALING Suppose we quadruple x, so that $x_f = 4x_i$. Then y will change to

$$y_f = A\sqrt{x_f} = A\sqrt{4x_i} = 2A\sqrt{x_i} = 2y_i$$

Increasing x by a factor of 4 causes y to increase by a factor of $\sqrt{4}$, or 2. Similarly, if we *decrease* x by a factor of 4, y will decrease by a factor of 2. Generally, we can say that:

Changing x by a factor C changes y by a factor $\sqrt{C}$.

We have been treating ideal gases made of atoms, but our results are equally valid for real gases made of atoms or molecules. From Equation 6.11 we see that **a higher temperature corresponds to faster atomic or molecular speeds.** At a given temperature, the speed of atoms or molecules in a gas varies with the atomic or molecular mass. A gas with lighter atoms will have faster atoms, on average, than a gas with heavier atoms.

The masses of atoms and molecules in chemistry are measured in **atomic mass units,** denoted u; this is the atomic mass that you will find in a periodic table. The atomic mass of a hydrogen atom is 1 u, so that of an H_2 molecule is 2 u. However, the equations in this chapter require that the masses of atoms and molecules be in kg. The conversion factor is

$$1 \text{ u} = 1.66 \times 10^{-27} \text{ kg}$$

EXAMPLE 6.8 Speed of nitrogen molecules

Nitrogen gas consists of molecules, N_2. At 20°C, what is the root-mean-square speed of the molecules of nitrogen?

PREPARE In the periodic table, you can find that the mass of a nitrogen atom is 14 u. A N_2 molecule consists of two atoms, so its mass is 28 u. Thus the molecular mass in SI units (i.e., kg) is

$$m = 28 \text{ u} \times \frac{1.66 \times 10^{-27} \text{ kg}}{1 \text{ u}} = 4.65 \times 10^{-26} \text{ kg}$$

Convert the temperature to kelvin:

$$T = 20 + 273 = 293 \text{ K}$$

SOLVE We compute v_{rms} for the nitrogen atoms using Equation 6.11:

$$v_{rms} = \sqrt{\frac{3k_B T}{m}} = \sqrt{\frac{3(1.38 \times 10^{-23} \text{ J/K})(293 \text{ K})}{4.65 \times 10^{-26} \text{ kg}}} = 510 \text{ m/s}$$

ASSESS This is *very* fast, just a bit faster than the speed of sound in air. This result makes sense, however: Sound waves must be carried by moving air molecules, so we would expect the speed of sound to be close to the speed of the molecules.

Computing Thermal Energy

The speeds of gas atoms are quite high. The associated kinetic energy of the atoms in a gas will be quite high as well. The thermal energy of an ideal gas consisting of N atoms can be computed using the above result for the average kinetic energy:

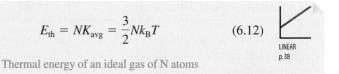

$$E_{th} = NK_{avg} = \frac{3}{2}Nk_B T \qquad (6.12)$$

Thermal energy of an ideal gas of N atoms

LINEAR
p. 38

Thus, **thermal energy is directly proportional to temperature.** Consequently, a change in the thermal energy of an ideal gas is proportional to a change in temperature:

$$\Delta E_{th} = \frac{3}{2}Nk_B \Delta T \qquad (6.13)$$

This relationship between a change in temperature and a change in thermal energy is for an ideal gas, but solids, liquids, and other gases all follow similar rules, as we will see in the next chapter. For now, we will simply note two important conclusions that apply to any substance:

1. The thermal energy of a substance is proportional to the number of atoms. A gas with more atoms has more thermal energy than a gas at the same temperature with fewer atoms.
2. A change in temperature causes a proportional change in the substance's thermal energy. A larger temperature change causes a larger change in thermal energy.

Is it cold in space? The space shuttle orbits in the upper thermosphere, about 300 km above the surface of the earth. There is still a trace of atmosphere left at this altitude, and it has quite a high temperature—over 1000°C. Although the average speed of the air molecules here is quite high, there are so few air molecules present that the thermal energy is extremely low.

EXAMPLE 6.9 Energy change in heating a gas

100 cm³ of gas at 1 atmosphere pressure and 20°C contains 2.5×10^{21} molecules. (You'll learn how to show this in the next chapter.) By how much does its thermal energy change if it is heated to 30°C?

SOLVE The temerature *change* is $\Delta T = 10$ K. Using Equation 6.13, we find

$$\Delta E_{th} = \frac{3}{2}Nk_B \Delta T = \frac{3}{2}(2.5 \times 10^{21})(1.38 \times 10^{-23} \text{ J/K})(10 \text{ K}) = 0.52 \text{ J}$$

ASSESS Although the number of molecules in a typical gas is vast, a typical change in thermal energy is quite comparable to the values we've been calculating for the kinetic and potential energies of macroscopic objects.

Consider gases of the following atoms or molecules, all at the same temperature. Which atoms or molecules have the fastest average speed?

A. H_2 B. He   C. N_2 D. O_2 E. All the same.

6.5 Heat and the First Law of Thermodynamics

In Chapter 5, we saw that a system could exchange energy with the environment through two different means: Work and heat. Work was treated in some detail in Chapter 5; now it is time to look at the transfer of energy by heat. This will begin our study of a topic called *thermodynamics,* the study of thermal energy and heat and their relationships to other forms of energy and energy transfer.

What Is Heat?

Heat is a more elusive concept than work. We use the word "heat" very loosely in the English language, often as synonymous with *hot.* We might say, on a very hot day, that "This heat is oppressive." If your apartment is cold you may say, "Turn up the heat." These expressions date to a time long ago when it was thought that heat was a *substance* with fluid-like properties.

If you place a hot object and a cold object together, they evolve toward a common final temperature. Common sense suggests that "something" flows from the hot object to the cold until equilibrium is achieved. This "heat fluid" was called *caloric.* The notion that objects somehow "contain" heat, and that heat can move around, lingers on in expressions like *heat flow, heat loss,* and *heat capacity*

One of the first to disagree with this notion, in the late 1700s, was Benjamin Thompson, known by his title Count Rumford. While watching the hot metal chips thrown off during the boring of cannons, he began to think about heat. If caloric is a substance, the cannon and borer should eventually run out of caloric and the heat generation ought to decrease with time. But it does not. Rumford noted that the heat generation appears to be "inexhaustible," which is not consistent with the idea of heat as a substance. He concluded that heat is not a substance—it is *motion!*

The British physicist James Joule carried out careful experiments in the 1840s to learn how it is that systems change their temperature. Using experiments like those shown in Figure 6.10, Joule found that you can raise the temperature of a beaker of water by two entirely different means:

1. Heating it with a flame, or
2. Doing work on it with a rapidly spinning paddle wheel.

Surprisingly, the final state of the water is *exactly* the same in both cases. This implies that heat and work are essentially equivalent to each other—**heat and work are simply two different ways of transferring energy to or from a system.**

Thermal energy is transferred between a system and the environment as a consequence of a temperature difference between them. When you place a pan of water on the stove, thermal energy is transferred *from* the hotter flame *to* the cooler water. If you place the water in a freezer, thermal energy is transferred from the warmer water to the colder air in the freezer.

Energy is transferred when the faster molecules in the hotter object collide with the slower molecules in the cooler object. On average, these collisions cause

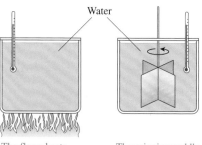

Water

The flame heats the water.

The spinning paddle does work on the water.

FIGURE 6.10 Joule's experiments to show the equivalence of heat and work.

TRY IT YOURSELF

Energetic cooking We can do a modern version of Joule's experiment in the kitchen. Next time you mix food in a blender, notice how it actually warms the food! As the blades rotate, friction increases the thermal energy of the food in the blender. A blender uses about as much power as a microwave, and most of this energy ends up as thermal energy in the food, so the temperature rises as the food is chopped and blended.

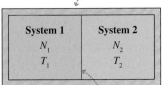

Insulation prevents heat from entering or leaving the container.

A thin barrier prevents atoms from moving from system 1 to 2 but still allows them to collide.

FIGURE 6.11 Two gases are separated by a thin barrier through which they can thermally interact.

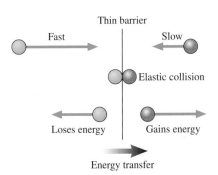

FIGURE 6.12 Collisions at a barrier transfer energy from faster molecules to slower molecules.

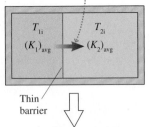

Collisions transfer energy from the warmer system to the cooler as more energetic atoms lose energy to less energetic atoms. This energy transfer is heat.

Thermal equilibrium occurs when the systems have the same average translational kinetic energy and thus the same temperature.

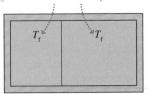

FIGURE 6.13 Two systems in thermal contact exchange thermal energy.

the faster molecules to lose energy and the slower molecules to gain energy. The net result is that energy is transferred from the hotter object to the colder object. The process itself, whereby energy is transferred between the system and the environment via atomic-level collisions, is called a *thermal interaction*. **Heat is the energy transfer during a thermal interaction.**

An Atomic Model of Heat

Let's look at a thermal interaction in some detail, considering what happens at an atomic level. Figure 6.11 shows a rigid, insulated container that is divided into two sections by a very thin membrane. Each side is filled with a gas of the same kind of atoms. The left side, which we'll call system 1, has N_1 atoms at an initial temperature T_{1i}. System 2 on the right has N_2 atoms at an initial temperature T_{2i}. We imagine the membrane to be so thin that atoms can collide at the boundary as if the membrane were not there, yet it is a barrier that prevents atoms from moving from one side to the other.

Suppose that system 1 is initially at a higher temperature: $T_{1i} > T_{2i}$. This means that the atoms in system 1 will have a higher average kinetic energy. Figure 6.12 shows a fast atom and a slow atom approaching the barrier from opposite sides. They undergo a perfectly elastic collision at the barrier. Although no net energy is lost in a perfectly elastic collision, the faster atom loses energy while the slower one gains energy. In other words, there is an energy *transfer* from the faster atom's side to the slower atom's side.

Because the atoms in system 1 are, on average, more energetic than the atoms in system 2, *on average* the collisions transfer energy from system 1 to system 2. This is not true for every collision. Sometimes a fast atom in system 2 collides with a slow atom in system 1, transferring energy from 2 to 1. But the net energy transfer, from all collisions, is from the warmer system 1 to the cooler system 2. This transfer of energy is heat; **thermal energy is transferred from the faster moving atoms on the warmer side to the slower moving atoms on the cooler side.**

This transfer will continue until a stable situation is reached. This is a situation we call **thermal equilibrium.** How do the systems "know" when they've reached thermal equilibrium? Energy transfer continues until the atoms on both sides of the barrier have the *same average kinetic energy.* Once the average kinetic energies are the same, individual collisions will still transfer energy from one side to the other. But since both sides have atoms with the same average kinetic energies, the amount of energy transferred from 1 to 2 will equal that transferred from 2 to 1. Once the average kinetic energies are the same, there will be no more net energy transfer.

An important result from the previous section is that the average kinetic energy of the atoms in a system is directly proportional to the system's temperature. If two systems exchange energy until their atoms have the same average kinetic energy, we can say that

$$T_{1f} = T_{2f} = T_f$$

That is, heat is transferred until the two systems reach a common final temperature; we call this final state **thermal equilibrium.** We considered a rather artificial system in this case, but the result is quite general: **Two systems placed in thermal contact will transfer thermal energy until their final temperatures are the same.** This process is illustrated in Figure 6.13.

Heat is a transfer of energy. The sign that we use for transfers is defined in Figure 6.14 on the next page. In the process of Figure 6.13, Q_1 is negative as system 1 loses energy; Q_2 is positive as system 2 gains energy. Because no energy escapes from the container, all of the energy that was lost by system 1 was gained by system 2

$$Q_2 = -Q_1$$

as required by energy conservation. That is, the heat energy lost by one system is gained by the other.

The above argument was made for gases, but it is completely general. We could make a similar analysis for different gases, solids, or liquids. In each case, the final result is the same: **Heat is transferred from hot to cold.**

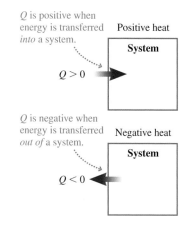

FIGURE 6.14 The sign of Q.

The First Law of Thermodynamics

In Chapter 5, we looked at several versions of the law of conservation of energy. The most general statement was the law of conservation of energy for systems that were not isolated, Equation 5.4:

$$\Delta K + \Delta U_g + \Delta U_s + \Delta E_{th} + \Delta E_{chem} + \cdots = W + Q$$

In Chapter 5, we focused on systems where the potential and kinetic energy could change, such as a sled moving down a hill. Earlier in this chapter, we looked at the body, where the chemical energy changes. Now let's consider systems in which only the thermal energy changes. That is, we will consider systems that aren't moving, that aren't changing chemically, but whose temperatures can change. Such systems are the province of what is called **thermodynamics.** The question of how to keep your house cool in the summer is a question of thermodynamics. If thermal energy is transferred into your house, the temperature will rise; if thermal energy is transferred out, the temperature will drop.

When the law of conservation of energy was introduced, we noted that it was sometimes called the first law of thermodynamics. This is true, but a more common statement of the first law of thermodynamics applies to systems in which only thermal energy changes take place.

First law of thermodynamics For systems in which only the thermal energy changes, the change in thermal energy is equal to the energy transferred into or out of the system as work W and/or heat Q:

$$\Delta E_{th} = W + Q \qquad (6.14)$$

Only work and heat, two ways of transferring energy between a system and the environment, cause the system's energy to change. In thermodynamic systems, the only energy change will be a change in thermal energy. Whether this energy increases or decreases depends on the signs of W and Q. In Chapter 5, we noted that when $W > 0$, work is done on the system, increasing its energy, and when $W < 0$ work is done by the system, decreasing its energy. A similar sign convention holds for heat, as we saw in Figure 6.14. The possible energy transfers between a system and the environment are illustrated in Figure 6.15.

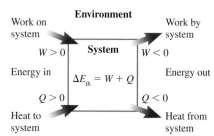

FIGURE 6.15 Energy transfers in a thermodynamic system.

CONCEPTUAL EXAMPLE 6.3 Compressing a gas
Suppose a gas is in an insulated container, so that no heat energy can escape. If a piston is used to compress the gas, what happens to the temperature of the gas?

REASON The piston applies a force to the gas, and there is a displacement. This means that work is done on the gas by the piston ($W > 0$). No thermal energy can be exchanged with the environment, meaning $Q = 0$. Since energy is transferred into the system, the thermal energy of the gas must increase. This means that the temperature must increase as well.

ASSESS When you use a bike pump to inflate a tire, you may have noticed that the pump and the tire get warm. This temperature increase is due to the warming of the air by the compression.

EXAMPLE 6.10 Work and heat in an ideal gas

Suppose a container holds 5.0×10^{22} molecules of an ideal gas. 50 J of work are done on the gas by a piston that compresses it. The temperature of the gas changes by 30°C during this process. How much heat is transferred to or from the environment?

SOLVE For an ideal gas, the change in thermal energy is proportional to the change in temperature, as we see in Equation 6.13. We compute the change in thermal energy to be

$$\Delta E_{\text{th}} = \frac{3}{2} N k_B \Delta T$$

$$= \left(\frac{3}{2}\right)(5.0 \times 10^{22})(1.38 \times 10^{-23} \text{ J/K})(30 \text{ K}) = 31 \text{ J}$$

The first law of thermodynamics, Equation 6.14, tells us that the change in thermal energy ΔE_{th} of the gas is equal to the sum of W and Q. W is known, and we have just calculated ΔE_{th}. Combining, we get

$$Q = \Delta E_{\text{th}} - W = 31 \text{ J} - 50 \text{ J} = -19 \text{ J}$$

ASSESS Q is negative, meaning that energy is transferred from the hot gas to the cooler environment in this process.

Energy-Transfer Diagrams

Suppose you drop a hot rock into the ocean. Heat is transferred from the rock to the ocean until the rock and ocean are at the same temperature. Although the ocean warms up ever so slightly, ΔT_{ocean} is so small as to be completely insignificant. For all practical purposes, the ocean is infinite and unchangeable.

An **energy reservoir** is an object or a part of the environment so large that its temperature does not noticeably change when heat is transferred between the system and the reservoir. A reservoir at a higher temperature than the system is called a *hot reservoir*. A vigorously burning flame is a hot reservoir for small objects placed in the flame. A reservoir at a lower temperature than the system is called a *cold reservoir*. The ocean is a cold reservoir for the hot rock. We will use T_H and T_C to designate the temperatures of the hot and cold reservoirs.

Heat energy is transferred between a system and a reservoir if they have different temperatures. We will define

$$Q_H = \text{amount of heat transferred to or from a hot reservoir}$$

$$Q_C = \text{amount of heat transferred to or from a cold reservoir}$$

By definition, Q_H and Q_C are *positive* quantities.

Figure 6.16a shows a heavy copper bar placed between a hot reservoir (at temperature T_H) and a cold reservoir (at temperature T_C). Heat Q_H is transferred from the hot reservoir into the copper and heat Q_C is transferred from the copper to the cold reservoir. Figure 6.16b is an **energy-transfer diagram** for this process. The hot reservoir is always drawn at the top, the cold reservoir at the bottom, and the system—the copper bar in this case—between them. The reservoirs and the system are connected by "pipes" that show the energy transfers. Figure 6.16b shows heat Q_H being transferred into the system and Q_C being transferred out.

Figure 6.17 illustrates an important fact about heat transfers that we have seen: Spontaneous transfers go in one direction only. The fact that heat is not transferred from a colder object to a hotter object is an important result that will have significant practical implications, as we will soon discover.

(a)

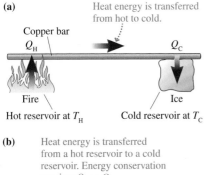

Heat energy is transferred from hot to cold.

Copper bar

Q_H Q_C

Fire   Ice

Hot reservoir at T_H Cold reservoir at T_C

(b)

Heat energy is transferred from a hot reservoir to a cold reservoir. Energy conservation requires $Q_C = Q_H$.

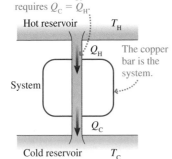

Hot reservoir T_H

Q_H The copper bar is the system.

System

Q_C

Cold reservoir T_C

FIGURE 6.16 Energy-transfer diagrams.

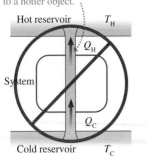

Heat is never spontaneously transferred from a colder object to a hotter object.

Hot reservoir T_H

Q_H

System

Q_C

Cold reservoir T_C

FIGURE 6.17 An impossible energy transfer.

CONCEPTUAL EXAMPLE 6.4 Energy transfers and the body

Why—in physics terms—is it more taxing on the body to exercise in very hot weather?

REASON Your body continuously converts chemical energy to thermal energy, as we have seen. In order to maintain a constant body temperature, your body must continuously transfer heat to the environment. This is a simple matter in cool weather when heat is spontaneously transferred to the environment, but when the air temperature is higher than your body temperature, your body cannot cool itself this way and must use other mechanisms to transfer this energy, such as perspiring. These mechanisms require additional energy expenditure.

ASSESS Strenuous exercise in hot weather can easily lead to a rise in body temperature if the body cannot exhaust heat quickly enough.

STOP TO THINK 6.4   The radiator in an automobile is at a higher temperature than the air around it. Considering the radiator as the system, we can say that

A. $Q > 0$ B. $Q = 0$ C. $Q < 0$

The goal of Chapter 6 has been to learn more about energy transformations and transfers, the laws of thermodynamics, and theoretical and practical limitations on energy use. [Please Note: Not all the topics covered on this summary page were included in this chapter.]

GENERAL PRINCIPLES

Energy and Efficiency

When energy is transformed from one form to another, some may be "lost," usually to thermal energy, due to practical or theoretical constraints. This limits the efficiency of processes. We define **efficiency** as:

$$e = \frac{\text{what you get}}{\text{what you had to pay}}$$

Entropy and Irreversibility

Systems move toward more probable states. These states have higher entropy—more disorder. This change is irreversible. Changing other forms of energy to thermal energy is irreversible.

Increasing probability
Increasing entropy

The Laws of Thermodynamics

The **first law of thermodynamics** is the law of conservation of energy for systems in which only thermal energy changes:

$$\Delta E_{th} = W + Q$$

The **second law of thermodynamics** can be stated in a few different ways:

- The entropy of an isolated system always increases.
- Heat energy spontaneously flows only from hot to cold.
- No heat engine can be 100% efficient.
- "The future" is the time direction of entropy increase.

Heat is the transfer of energy via a thermal interaction. Energy will be transferred until thermal equilibrium is reached.

| T_1 | $T_2 < T_1$ |
| $Q \rightarrow$ | |

IMPORTANT CONCEPTS

Thermal energy

- For a gas, the thermal energy is the **total kinetic energy** of motion of the atoms.

$$E_{th} = NK_{avg} = \frac{1}{2}Nmv_{rms}^2$$

- Thermal energy is random kinetic energy and thus has entropy.

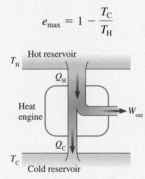

Temperature

- For a gas, temperature is proportional to the **average kinetic energy** of the motion of the atoms.

$$T = \frac{2}{3}\frac{K_{avg}}{k_B}$$

- Two systems are in **thermal equilibrium** if they are at the same temperature. No heat energy is transferred at thermal equilibrium.

A heat engine converts thermal energy from a hot reservoir into useful work. Some heat is exhausted into a cold reservoir.

$$e_{max} = 1 - \frac{T_C}{T_H}$$

A heat pump uses an energy input to transfer heat from a cold side to a hot side. When used for cooling:

$$COP_{max} = \frac{T_C}{T_H - T_C}$$

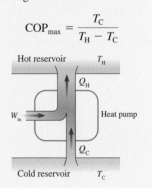

APPLICATIONS

Efficiencies

Energy in the body
Cells in the body metabolize chemical energy in food. Efficiency for most actions is about 25%.

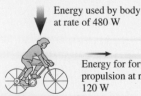

Energy used by body at rate of 480 W

Energy for forward propulsion at rate of 120 W

Power plants
A typical power plant converts about 1/3 of the energy input into useful work. The rest is exhausted as waste heat.

Chemical energy in

Waste heat

Useful work out

Temperature scales

Zero on the **Kelvin temperature scale** is the temperature at which the kinetic energy of atoms is zero. This is **absolute zero.** The conversion from °C to K is

$$T = T_C + 273$$

► All temperatures in equations must be in kelvin. ◄

Conceptual Questions

1. Rub your hands together vigorously. What happens? Discuss the energy transfers and transformations that take place.

2. Write a few sentences describing the energy transformations that occur from the time moving water enters a hydroelectric plant until you see some water being pumped out of a nozzle in a public fountain. Use the "Energy transformations" table on page 40 as an example.

3. BIO Describe the energy transfers and transformations that occur from the time you sit down to breakfast until you've completed a fast bicycle ride.

4. BIO According to Table 6.4, cycling at 15 km/hr requires less metabolic energy than running at 15 km/hr. Suggest reasons why this is the case.

5. For most automobiles, the number of miles per gallon decreases as highway speed increases. Fuel economy drops as speeds increase from 55 to 65 mph, then decreases further as speeds increase to 75 mph. Explain why this is the case.

6. When the space shuttle returns to earth, its surfaces get very hot as it passes through the atmosphere at high speed.
    a. Has the space shuttle been heated? If so, what was the source of the heat? If not, why is it hot?
    b. Energy must be conserved. What happens to the space shuttle's initial kinetic energy?

7. One end of a short aluminum rod is in a campfire and the other end is in a block of ice, as shown in Figure Q6.7. If 100 J of energy are transferred from the fire to the rod, and if the temperature at every point in the rod has reached a steady value, how much energy goes from the rod into the ice?

    FIGURE Q6.7

8. Two blocks of copper, 1 kg and 3 kg, are at the same temperature. Which block has more thermal energy? If the blocks are placed in thermal contact, will the thermal energy of the blocks change? If so, how?

9. If the temperature T of an ideal gas doubles, by what factor does the average kinetic energy of the atoms change?

10. A bottle of helium gas and a bottle of argon gas contain equal numbers of atoms at the same temperature. Which bottle, if either, has the greater total thermal energy?

For Questions 11 through 16, give a specific example of a process that has the energy changes and transfers described. (For example, if the question states "$\Delta E_{th} > 0$, $W = 0$," you are to describe a process that has an increase in thermal energy and no transfer of energy by work. You could write "Heating a pan of water on the stove.")

11. $\Delta E_{th} < 0$, $W = 0$
12. $\Delta E_{th} > 0$, $Q = 0$
13. $\Delta E_{th} < 0$, $Q = 0$
14. $\Delta E_{th} > 0$, $W \neq 0$, $Q \neq 0$
15. $\Delta E_{th} < 0$, $W \neq 0$, $Q \neq 0$
16. $\Delta E_{th} = 0$, $W \neq 0$, $Q \neq 0$

17. A drop of green ink falls into a beaker of clear water. First *describe* what happens. Then *explain* the outcome in terms of entropy.

18. If you hold a rubber band loosely between two fingers and let it rest against your lips, and then stretch the rubber band, the sensitive skin of your lips will detect a small temperature increase. The rubber band soon returns to its original temperature. What are the signs of W and Q for this process?

19. The exterior unit of a heat pump designed for heating is sometimes buried underground in order to use the earth as a thermal reservoir. Why is it worthwhile to bury the heat exchanger, even if the underground unit costs more to purchase and install than one above ground?

Multiple-Choice Questions

20. | A person is walking on level ground at constant speed. What energy transformation is taking place?
    A. Chemical energy is being transformed to thermal energy.
    B. Chemical energy is being transformed to kinetic energy.
    C. Chemical energy is being transformed to kinetic energy and thermal energy.
    D. Chemical energy and thermal energy are being transformed to kinetic energy.

21. ‖ A person walks 1 km, turns around, and runs back to where he started. Compare the energy used and the power during the two segments:
    A. The energy used and the power are the same for both segments.
    B. The energy used while walking is greater, the power while running is greater.
    C. The energy used while running is greater, the power while running is greater.
    D. The energy used is the same for both segments, the power while running is greater.

22. | The temperature of the air in a basketball increases as it is pumped up. This means that:
    A. The total kinetic energy of the air is increasing and the average kinetic energy of each atom is decreasing.
    B. The total kinetic energy of the air is increasing and the average kinetic energy of each atom is increasing.
    C. The total kinetic energy of the air is decreasing and the average kinetic energy of each atom is decreasing.
    D. The total kinetic energy of the air is decreasing and the average kinetic energy of each atom is increasing.

23. | The thermal energy of a container of helium gas is halved. What happens to the temperature, in kelvin?
    A. It decreases to one-fourth its initial value.
    B. It decreases to one-half its initial value.
    C. It stays the same.
    D. It increases to twice its initial value.

24. | An inventor approaches you with a device that he claims will take 100 J of thermal energy input and produce 200 J of electricity. You decide not to invest your money because this device would violate
    A. the first law of thermodynamics.
    B. the second law of thermodynamics.
    C. both the first and second laws of thermodynamics.

25. | While keeping your food cold, your refrigerator transfers energy from the inside to the surroundings. Thus thermal energy goes from a colder object to a warmer one. What can you say about this?
   A. It is a violation of the second law of thermodynamics.
   B. It is not a violation of the second law of thermodynamics because refrigerators can have efficiency of 100%.
   C. It is not a violation of the second law of thermodynamics because the second law doesn't apply to refrigerators.
   D. The second law of thermodynamics applies in this situation, but it is not violated because the energy did not spontaneously go from cold to hot.

PROBLEMS

Section 6.1 Transforming Energy

1. | A 20%-efficient engine accelerates a 1500 kg car from rest to 15 m/s. How much energy is transferred to the engine by burning gasoline?
2. | A 60% efficient device uses chemical energy to generate 600 J of electric energy.
   a. How much chemical energy is used?
   b. A second device uses twice as much chemical energy to generate half as much electric energy? What is its efficiency?
3. | A typical photovoltaic cell delivers 4.0×10^{-3} W of electric energy when illuminated with 1.2×10^{-1} W of light energy. What is the efficiency of the cell?
4. | A 15 W compact fluorescent bulb and a 75 W incandescent bulb each produce 3.0 W of visible light energy. What are the efficiencies of these two types of bulbs for converting electric energy into light?

FIGURE P6.4 Compact fluorescent and incandescent bulbs.

Section 6.2 Energy in the Body: Energy Inputs

5. || A fast-food hamburger (with cheese and bacon) contains 1000 Calories. (a) What is the burger's energy in joules? (b) If all this energy is used to lift a 10 kg mass, how high can it be lifted?
6. || In an average human, basic life processes require energy to be supplied at a steady rate of 100 W. What daily energy intake, in Calories, is required to maintain these basic processes? This is the minimum daily caloric intake needed to avoid starvation.
7. | An "energy bar" contains 6.0 g of fat. How much energy is this in joules? In calories? In Calories?
8. | An "energy bar" contains 22 g of carbohydrates. How much energy is this in joules? In calories? In Calories?

Section 6.3 Energy in the Body: Energy Outputs

9. || An "energy bar" contains 22 g of carbohydrates. If the energy bar was his only fuel, how far could a 68 kg person walk at 5.0 km/hr?
10. || Suppose your body was able to use the chemical energy in gasoline. How far could you pedal a bicycle at 15 km/hr on the energy in 1 gal of gas? (1 gal of gas has a mass of 3.2 kg.)

11. |||| The label on a candy bar says 400 Calories. Assuming a typical efficiency for energy use by the body, if a 60 kg person were to use the energy in this candy bar to climb stairs, how high could she go?
12. || A weightlifter curls a 30 kg bar, raising it each time a distance of 0.60 m. How many times must he repeat this exercise to burn off the energy in one slice of pizza?
13. |||| A weightlifter works out at the gym each day. Part of her routine is to lie on her back and lift a 40 kg barbell straight up from chest height to full arm extension, a distance of 0.50 m.
   a. How much work does the weightlifter do to lift the barbell one time?
   b. If the weightlifter does 20 repetitions a day, what total energy does she expend on lifting? Assume 25% efficiency.
   c. How many 400 Calorie donuts can she eat a day to supply that energy?

General Problems

14. || How many slices of pizza must you eat to walk for 1.0 hr at a speed of 5.0 km/hr? (Assume your mass is 68 kg.)
15. | A 60 kg person climbs to the top of a 500-m-high hill. If the energy necessary to do this were provided by burning coal, how much coal would be needed?
16. || For how long would a 68 kg person have to swim at a fast crawl to use all the energy available in a typical fast food meal of burger, fries, and a drink?
17. | a. How much metabolic energy is required for a 68 kg person to run at a speed of 15 km/hr for 20 min?
   b. How much metabolic energy is required for this person to walk at a speed of 5.0 km/hr for 60 min? Compare your result to your answer to part a.
   c. Compare your results of parts a and b to the result of Example 6.5. Of these three modes of human motion, which is the most efficient?
18. ||| To a good approximation, the only external force that does work on a cyclist moving on level ground is the force of air resistance. Suppose a cyclist is traveling at 15 km/hr on level ground. Assume he is using 480 W of metabolic power.
   a Estimate the amount of power he uses for forward motion.
   b. How much force must he exert to overcome the force of air resistance?
19. || The winning time for the 2005 annual race up 86 floors of the Empire State Building was 10 min and 49 s. The winner's mass was 60 kg.
   a. If each floor was 3.7 m high, what was the winner's change in gravitational potential energy?

b. If the efficiency in climbing stairs is 25%, what total energy did the winner expend during the race?

c. How many food Calories did the winner "burn" in the race?

d. Of those Calories, how many were converted to thermal energy?

e. What was the winner's metabolic power in watts during the race up the stairs?

20. ‖ Championship swimmers take about 22 s and about 30 arm
BIO strokes to move through the water in a 50 m freestyle race.
INT a. From Table 7.4, a swimmer's metabolic power is 800 W. If the efficiency for swimming is 25%, how much energy is expended moving through the water in a 50 m race?

b. If half the energy is used in arm motion and half in leg motion, what is the energy expenditure per arm stroke?

c. Model the swimmer's hand as a paddle. During one arm stroke, the paddle moves halfway around a 90-cm-radius circle. If all the swimmer's forward propulsion during an arm stroke comes from the hand pushing on the water and none from the arm (somewhat of an oversimplification), what is the average force of the hand on the water?

STOP TO THINK ANSWERS

Stop to Think 6.1: C. In each case, "what you get" is the same because the potential energy change is the same; "What you had to pay" is the same as well.

Stop to Think 6.2: C. As the body uses chemical energy from food, approximately 75% is transformed to thermal energy. Also, kinetic energy of motion of the legs and feet is transformed to thermal energy with each stride. Most of the chemical energy is transformed to thermal energy.

Stop to Think 6.3: A. The temperatures are the same, so all atoms have the same average kinetic energy. Hydrogen molecules, with the smallest mass, with thus have the highest typical speed.

Stop to Think 6.4: C. The radiator is at a higher temperature than the surrounding air. Thermal energy is transferred out of the system to the environment, so $Q < 0$.

7

HEAT TRANSFER

This image of an elephant shows its surface temperatures. Red represents warm patches (such as the trunk) and blue cool patches (such as the ears). The image shows energy that the elephant *radiates*. Why does an elephant (or any other warm object) radiate energy?

Looking Back ◀◀

This chapter will make extensive use of the concepts of energy and heat from Chapters 5 and 6. Please review:

◀ Section 5.7 The nature of thermal energy.

◀ Section 6.4 The connection between thermal energy and temperature, the nature of thermal energy and temperature for ideal gases.

◀ Section 6.5 Heat and the first law of thermodynamics.

Elephants, humans, and all other animals convert the chemical energy of food to thermal energy. This is the process of metabolism. But if an animal had no means of getting rid of excess thermal energy, its temperature would soon rise to dangerous levels.

Chapter 6 introduced the concepts of thermal energy, temperature, and heat, but many unanswered questions remain. For example:

■ How is heat transferred to or from a system? How can an elephant keep cool even in the hot African savanna?

■ What are the consequences of heating or cooling a system? Changing the temperature is one obvious possibility, but are there others? And what is the connection between the amount of heat transferred to a system and the amount by which its temperature changes?

■ How do the properties of matter depend on temperature? Whether a system is a solid or liquid depends on its temperature. So does the pressure of a gas.

7.1 Heat Transfer

You feel warmer when the sun is shining on you, colder when sitting on a cold concrete bench or when a stiff wind is blowing. This is due to the transfer of heat. Although we've talked about heat a lot in these last two chapters, we haven't said much about *how* heat is transferred from a hotter object to a colder object. There are four basic mechanisms, outlined in the table below, by which objects exchange heat with other objects or their surroundings. Evaporation was treated in an earlier section; in this section we will consider the other mechanisms.

Heat transfer mechanisms

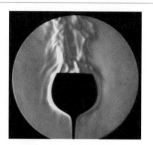

When two objects are in direct physical contact, such as the soldering iron and the circuit board, heat is transferred by *conduction.* **Energy is transferred by direct contact.**

This special photograph shows air currents near a warm glass of water. Air near the glass is warmed and rises, taking thermal energy with it in a process known as *convection.* **Energy is transferred by the motion of molecules with high thermal energy.**

The lamp shines on the lambs huddled below, warming them. The energy is transferred by infrared *radiation,* a form of electromagnetic waves. **Energy is transferred by electromagnetic waves.**

As we saw in a previous section, the *evaporation* of liquid can carry away significant quantities of thermal energy. When you blow on a cup of cocoa, this increases the rate of evaporation, rapidly cooling it. **Energy is transferred by the removal of molecules with high thermal energy.**

Conduction

If you hold a metal spoon in a cup of hot coffee, the handle of the spoon soon gets warm. Thermal energy is transferred along the spoon from the coffee to your hand. The difference in temperature between the two ends drives this heat transfer by a process known as **conduction.** Conduction is the transfer of thermal energy directly through a physical material.

Figure 7.1 shows a copper rod placed between a hot reservoir (a fire) and a cold reservoir (a block of ice). We can use our atomic model to see how thermal energy is transferred along the rod by the interaction between atoms in the rod; fast-moving atoms at the hot end transfer energy to slower-moving atoms at the cold end.

Suppose we set up a series of experiments to measure the heat Q transferred through various rods. We would find the following trends in our data:

- Q increases if the temperature difference ΔT between the hot end and the cold end is increased.
- Q increases if the cross-section area A of the rod is increased.
- Q decreases if the length L of the rod is increased.
- Some materials (such as metals) have a high value of Q; a lot of energy is transferred. Other materials (such as wood) have a low value of Q; very little energy is transferred.

The final observation is one that is familiar to you; if you are stirring a pot of hot soup on the stove, you use a wood or plastic spoon rather than a metal one.

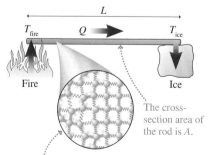

The particles on the left side of the rod are vibrating more vigorously than the particles on the right. The particles on the left transfer energy to the particles on the right via the bonds connecting them.

FIGURE 7.1 Conduction of heat in a solid rod.

These experimental observations about heat conduction can be summarized in a single formula. If heat Q is transferred in a time interval Δt, the *rate* of heat transfer (joules per second) is $Q/\Delta t$. For a material of cross-section area A and length L, spanning a temperature difference ΔT, the rate of heat transfer is

$$\frac{Q}{\Delta t} = \left(\frac{kA}{L}\right)\Delta T \tag{7.1}$$

Rate of conduction of heat across a temperature difference

The quantity k, which characterizes whether the material is a good conductor of heat or a poor conductor, is called the **thermal conductivity** of the material. Because the heat transfer rate J/s is a *power*, measured in watts, the units of k are W/m · K. Typical values of k for common materials are given in Table 7.1; a larger number for k means a material is a better conductor of heat.

Note that good conductors of electricity, such as silver and copper, are usually good heat conductors. One exception is diamond: Though diamond is a very poor electrical conductor, the strong bonds among atoms that make diamond such a hard material lead to a rapid transfer of thermal energy.

The weak bonds among molecules make most biological materials poor conductors of heat. Muscle is a better conductor than fat, so sea mammals have thick layers of fat for insulation. Land mammals insulate their bodies with fur, birds with feathers. Both fur and feathers trap a good deal of air, so their conductivity is similar to that of air. Air, like all gases, is a poor conductor of heat, as there are no bonds between adjacent atoms.

TABLE 7.1 Thermal conductivity values (measured at 20°C)

Material	k (W/m · K)
Diamond	1000
Silver	420
Copper	400
Iron	72
Stainless steel	14
Ice	1.7
Concrete	0.8
Plate glass	0.75
Skin	0.50
Muscle	0.46
Fat	0.21
Wood	0.2
Carpet	0.04
Fur, feathers	0.02–0.06
Air (27°C, 100 kPa)	0.026

Carpet or tile? If you walk around your house barefoot, you will notice that tile floors feel much colder than carpeted floors. The tile floor isn't really colder—the temperatures of all the floors in your house are nearly the same. But tile has a much higher thermal conductivity than carpet, so more heat will flow from your feet into the tile than into carpet. This causes the tile to feel colder. Standing or lying on carpet, with its low thermal conductivity, is much more comfortable than on tile!

EXAMPLE 7.1 Heat loss through a window
A 0.90 m by 1.2 m window (approximately 3 ft by 4 ft) in a house is made of a single pane of 3.0-mm-thick (approximately 1/8 in) glass. The temperature inside the house is 21°C; outside, it is a frosty −5°C. What power, in watts, must the furnace provide to compensate for heat loss through the window?

PREPARE The area through which heat is conducted is

$$A = (0.90\ \text{m})(1.2\ \text{m}) = 1.1\ \text{m}^2$$

The length of the conducting medium is the glass thickness, $L = 0.0030$ m. The temperature difference across the glass is

$$T = 21°C - (-5°C) = 26°C = 26\ \text{K}.$$

SOLVE Heat is transferred through the window to the outside. To keep the house at a constant temperature, the furnace must add heat energy at the same rate. The rate of conduction through the window is

$$\frac{Q}{\Delta t} = \left(\frac{(0.75\ \text{W/m} \cdot \text{K})(1.1\ \text{m}^2)}{0.0030\ \text{m}}\right)(26\ \text{K}) = 7100\ \text{W}$$

To compensate, the furnace must provide 7100 W of heating power.

ASSESS This is a great deal of power—three or four times the power of common electric space heaters. In modern construction, windows generally consist of two panes of glass with an air space in between. The low thermal conductivity of this air gap dramatically reduces the energy loss by conduction.

Convection

We noted that air is a poor conductor of heat. In fact, the data in Table 7.1 show that air has a thermal conductivity that is comparable to that of feathers. So why, on a cold day, will you be more comfortable if you are wearing a down jacket?

Thermal energy is easily transferred through air, water, and other fluids when the air and water can flow. A pan of water on the stove is heated at the bottom. This heated water expands and becomes less dense than the water above it, so it rises to the surface while cooler, denser water sinks to take its place. This transfer of thermal energy by the motion of a fluid is known as **convection.**

Convection is usually the main mechanism for heat transfer in fluid systems. On a small scale, convection mixes the pan of water that you heat on the stove; on a large scale, convection is responsible for making the wind blow and ocean currents circulate. Air is a very poor thermal conductor, but it is very effective at transferring energy by convection. To use air for thermal insulation, it is necessary to trap the air in small pockets to limit convection. And that's exactly what feathers, fur, double-paned windows, and fiberglass insulation do. Convection is much more rapid in water than in air, which is why people can die of hypothermia in 65°F water but can live quite happily in 65°F air.

Forced convection occurs when fluid is pushed by a pump or motor. In most buildings, forced hot-air heating transfers heat from the furnace to the rooms. Forced convection is also important for regulating body temperature. If your body is too hot, blood vessels near the cooler skin dilate to carry more blood. Blood flow transfers heat from the core of your body to the skin and then to your surroundings. Elephants use their ears for forced convection as well. The motion of air across the body from flapping ears is a very effective means of keeping cool.

Radiation

The sunlight that falls on the earth increases the thermal energy of the earth's surface each day. But the earth cools down at night; clearly, there must be some way for the earth to transfer energy back to space.

The earth and all other objects emit energy in the form of **radiation,** electromagnetic waves that are generated by oscillating electric charges in the atoms that form the object, an issue we'll explore further in later chapters on electricity and magnetism. These waves carry energy, transferring energy from the object that emits the radiation to the object that absorbs it. Electromagnetic waves carry energy from the sun; when this sunlight falls on your skin, the energy is absorbed, increasing your skin's thermal energy. Your skin also emits electromagnetic radiation, which reduces your skin's thermal energy. Radiation is a significant part of the energy balance that keeps your body at the proper temperature.

NOTE ▶ The word "radiation" comes from "radiate," which means "to beam." You have likely used the word to refer to x-rays and other forms of *ionizing radiation.* This is not the sense we will use in this chapter. Here, we will use radiation to mean light and other forms of electromagnetic waves that can "beam" from an object. ◀

Visible light, the red-to-violet colors of the rainbow, is an electromagnetic wave. Electromagnetic waves of somewhat lower frequency are called *infrared radiation;* we can't see these waves, but we can sometimes sense them as "heat" as they are absorbed on our skin. All objects radiate; objects at room temperature

Warm water (colored) moves by convection.

A feather coat BIO Penguins are birds and thus have feathers, even though they do not fly. The feathers are more obvious on this penguin chick than on the adults. A penguin's short, dense feathers serve a different role than the flight feathers of other birds: They trap air to provide thermal insulation. The feathers are equipped with muscles at the base of the shafts to flatten them and eliminate these air pockets, otherwise the penguins would be too buoyant to swim underwater.

Global heat transfer This satellite image shows radiation emitted by the waters of the ocean off the east coast of the United States. You can clearly see the warm waters of the Gulf Stream, a large-scale convection that transfers heat to northern latitudes. The satellite "sees" the radiation from the earth, so this radiation must readily pass through the atmosphere into space. In fact, the *only* means by which the earth as a whole can reduce its thermal energy is by radiation, as there is no conduction or convection in the vacuum of space. This has consequences for the energy balance of the earth.

and even somewhat higher temperatures emit virtually all of their radiation as infrared radiation. As the temperature increases, the charged particles oscillate more vigorously and an object becomes "red hot" and eventually "white hot"— some of the radiation is now in the form of visible light. The white light from an incandescent light bulb is radiation emitted by a thin wire filament that has been heated to a very high temperature by an electric current. The radiation that the earth emits, or that you emit, is no different, it is simply lower-frequency infrared radiation that you can't see.

Even though we can't see infrared radiation, some films and detectors are infrared sensitive and can record the infrared radiation from objects. The false-color thermal image of the elephant that opened this chapter shows the infrared emission as the elephant radiates energy into the cooler environment. Warmer patches, such as the trunk, emit more radiation and are easily distinguished from cooler patches that radiate less. Elephants do not sweat, so radiation from their trunk and ears is an important part of their temperature-regulation system.

If an object's temperature is increased, the increasingly vigorous oscillations radiate more energy. The energy radiated by any object thus shows a strong dependence on temperature. If heat energy Q is radiated in a time interval Δt by an object with surface area A and absolute temperature T, the *rate* of heat transfer $Q/\Delta t$ (joules per second) is found to be

$$\frac{Q}{\Delta t} = e\sigma A T^4 \qquad (7.2)$$

Rate of heat transfer by radiation at temperature T (Stefan's Law)

Quantities in this equation are defined as follows:

- e is the **emissivity** of a surface, a measure of the effectiveness of radiation. The value of e ranges from 0 to 1. Human skin is a very effective radiator at body temperature, with $e = 0.97$, regardless of skin color.
- T is the absolute temperature in kelvin.
- A is the surface area in m^2.
- σ is a constant known as the Stefan-Boltzmann constant, with the value $\sigma = 5.67 \times 10^{-8}$ W/m$^2 \cdot$ K^4.

Notice the very strong fourth-power dependence on temperature. Doubling the absolute temperature of an object increases the radiant heat transfer by a factor of 16!

The amount of energy radiated by an animal can be surprisingly large. An adult human with bare skin in a room at a comfortable temperature has a skin temperature of approximately 33°C, or 306 K. A typical value for the skin's surface area is 1.8 m^2. With these values and the emissivity of skin noted above, we can calculate the rate of heat transfer via radiation from the skin:

$$\frac{Q}{\Delta t} = e\sigma A T^4 = (0.97)\left(5.67 \times 10^{-8}\,\frac{\text{W}}{\text{m}^2 \cdot \text{K}^4}\right)(1.8\text{ m}^2)(306\text{ K})^4 = 870\text{ W}$$

As we learned in Chapter 6, the body at rest generates approximately 100 W of thermal energy. If the body radiated energy at 870 W, it would quickly cool. At this rate of emission, the body temperature would drop by 1°C every seven minutes! Clearly, there must be some mechanism to balance this emitted radiation: the radiation *absorbed* by the body.

When you sit in the sun, your skin warms due to the radiation you absorb. Even if you are not in the sun, you are absorbing the radiation emitted by the objects surrounding you. Suppose an object at temperature T is surrounded by an environment at temperature T_0. The *net* rate at which the object radiates heat energy—that is, radiation emitted minus radiation absorbed—is

$$\frac{Q_{net}}{\Delta t} = e\sigma A(T^4 - T_0^4) \tag{7.3}$$

This makes sense. An object should have no net energy transfer by radiation if it's in thermal equilibrium ($T = T_0$) with its surroundings. Note that the emissivity e appears for absorption as well; objects that are good emitters are good absorbers as well.

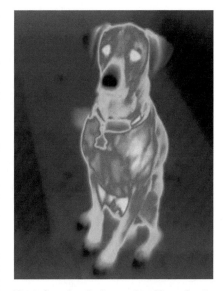

The infrared radiation emitted by a dog is captured in this image. His cool nose and paws radiate much less energy than the rest of his body.

EXAMPLE 7.2 Determining energy loss by radiation for the body

A person with skin temperature of 33°C is in a room at 24°C. What is the net rate of heat transfer by radiation?

SOLVE Body temperature is $T = 33 + 273 = 306$ K; the temperature of the room is $T_0 = 24 + 273 = 297$ K. The net radiation rate, given by Equation 7.30, is

$$\frac{Q_{net}}{\Delta t} = e\sigma A(T^4 - T_0^4)$$

$$= (0.97)\left(5.67 \times 10^{-8} \frac{W}{m^2 \cdot K^4}\right)(1.8 \text{ m}^2)[(306 \text{ K})^4 - (297 \text{ K})^4] = 98 \text{ W}$$

ASSESS This is a reasonable value, roughly matching your resting metabolic power. When you are dressed (little convection) and sitting on wood or plastic (little conduction), radiation is your body's primary mechanism for dissipating the excess thermal energy of metabolism.

STOP TO THINK 7.1   Suppose you are an astronaut in space, hard at work in your sealed spacesuit. The only way that you can transfer heat to the environment is by

A. Conduction.   B. Convection.   C. Radiation.   D. Evaporation.

7.2 The Electromagnetic Spectrum

Infrared, Visible Light, and Ultraviolet

Radio waves can be produced by oscillating charges in an antenna. At the higher frequencies of infrared, visible light, and ultraviolet, the "antennas" are individual atoms. This portion of the electromagnetic spectrum is *atomic radiation.*

Nearly all the atomic radiation in our environment is *thermal radiation* due to the thermal motion of the atoms in an object. Thermal radiation—a form of heat transfer—is described by Stefan's law: If heat energy Q is radiated in a time interval Δt by an object with surface area A and absolute temperature T, the *rate* of heat transfer $Q/\Delta t$ (joules per second) is

$$\frac{Q}{\Delta t} = e\sigma A T^4 \tag{7.4}$$

Increasing filament temperature

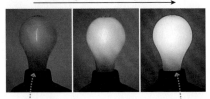

At lower filament temperatures, the bulb is dim, and the light is noticeably reddish.

When the filament is hotter, the bulb is brighter and the light is whiter.

FIGURE 7.2 The brightness of the bulb varies with the temperature of the filament.

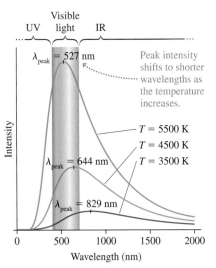

FIGURE 7.3 A thermal emission spectrum depends on the temperature.

The constant e in this equation is the object's emissivity, a measure of its effectiveness at emitting electromagnetic waves, and σ is the Stefan-Boltzmann constant, $\sigma = 5.67 \times 10^{-8} \text{ W/(m}^2 \cdot \text{K}^4)$.

Consider the amount of energy radiated and its dependence on temperature. The filament of an incandescent bulb glows simply because it is hot. If you increase the current through a lightbulb, the temperature increases and so does the total energy emitted by the bulb, in accordance with Stefan's law. The three pictures in Figure 7.2 show a glowing lightbulb with the filament at successively higher temperatures. We can clearly see an increase in brightness in the sequence of three photographs.

But it's not just the brightness that varies. The *color* of the emitted radiation changes as well. At low temperatures, the light from the bulb is quite red. (A dim bulb doesn't look this red to your eye because your brain, knowing that the light "should" be white, compensates. But the camera doesn't lie.) Looking at the change in color as the temperature of the bulb rises in Figure 7.2, we see that **the spectrum of thermal radiation changes with temperature.** It's this variation in the spectrum that we want to consider in this chapter.

If we measured the intensity of thermal radiation as a function of wavelength for an object at three temperatures, 3500 K, 4500 K, and 5500 K, the data would appear as in Figure 7.3. Notice two important features of the data:

- Increasing the temperature increases the intensity at all wavelengths. **Making the object hotter causes it to emit more radiation across the entire spectrum.**
- Increasing the temperature causes the peak intensity to shift to a shorter wavelength. **The higher the temperature, the shorter the wavelength of the peak of the spectrum.**

The wavelength corresponding to the peak of the intensity graph is given by

$$\lambda_{\text{peak}}(\text{in nm}) = \frac{2.9 \times 10^6 \text{ nm} \cdot \text{K}}{T} \qquad (7.3)$$

INVERSE
p. 118

Wien's law for the peak wavelength of a thermal emission spectrum

where the temperature *must* be in kelvin. The spectrum of a hotter object is a taller graph (more energy radiated) with its peak at a shorter wavelength.

EXAMPLE 7.3 Finding peak wavelengths

What are the wavelengths of peak intensity and the corresponding spectral regions for radiating objects at (a) normal human body temperature of 37°C, (b) the temperature of the filament in an incandescent lamp, 1500°C, and (c) the temperature of the surface of the sun, 5800 K?

PREPARE All of the objects emit thermal radiation.

SOLVE First, we convert temperatures to kelvin. The temperature of the human body is $T = 37 + 273 = 310$ K and the filament temperature is $T = 1500 + 273 = 1773$ K. Equation 25.22 then gives the wavelengths of peak intensity as

a. $\lambda_{\text{peak}}(\text{body}) = \dfrac{2.9 \times 10^6 \text{ nm} \cdot \text{K}}{310 \text{ K}} = 9.4 \times 10^3 \text{ nm} = 9.4 \text{ } \mu\text{m}$

b. $\lambda_{\text{peak}}(\text{filament}) = \dfrac{2.9 \times 10^6 \text{ nm} \cdot \text{K}}{1773 \text{ K}} = 1600 \text{ nm}$

c. $\lambda_{\text{peak}}(\text{sun}) = \dfrac{2.9 \times 10^6 \text{ nm} \cdot \text{K}}{5800 \text{ K}} = 500 \text{ nm}$

ASSESS The peak of the emission curve at body temperature is far into the infrared region of the spectrum, well below the range of sensitivity of human vision. The sun's emission peaks right in the middle of the visible spectrum, which seems reasonable. Interestingly, most of the energy radiated by an incandescent bulb is *not* visible light. The tail of the emission curve extends into the visible region, but the peak of the emission curve—and most of the emitted energy—is in the infrared region of the spectrum. A 100 W bulb emits only a few watts of visible light.

◄ **It's the pits . . .** BIO Rattlesnakes can hunt in total darkness. Prey animals are warm, and warm objects emit thermal radiation—which the snakes can sense. Rattlesnakes are in a group of snakes know as *pit vipers*. The name comes from a second set of vision organs that are simply pits with sensitive tissue at the bottom. In the photo, the pits appear as dark spots in front of the eyes. The pits are sensitive to infrared wavelengths of $\approx 10 \, \mu$m, near the wavelength of peak emission at mammalian body temperatures. Pit vipers sense the electromagnetic waves *emitted* by warm-blooded animals. They need no light to "see" you. You emit a "glow" they can detect.

Infrared radiation, with its relatively long wavelength and low photon energy, produces effects in tissue similar to those of microwaves—heating—but the penetration is much less than for microwaves. Infrared is absorbed mostly by the top layer of your skin and simply warms you up, as you know from sitting in the sun or under a heat lamp. The wave picture is generally most appropriate for infrared.

In contrast, ultraviolet photons have enough energy to interact with molecules in entirely different ways, ionizing molecules and breaking molecular bonds. The cells in skin are altered by ultraviolet radiation, causing sun tanning and sun burning. DNA molecules can be permanently damaged by ultraviolet radiation. There is a reasonably sharp threshold for such damage at 290 nm (corresponding to 4.3 eV photon energy). At longer wavelengths, damage to cells is slight; at shorter wavelengths, it is extensive. Ultraviolet lamps are very effective at sterilizing surfaces because they disrupt the genetic material of bacteria sufficiently to kill them. These interactions of ultraviolet radiation with matter are best understood from the photon perspective, with the absorption of each photon being associated with a particular molecular event.

STOP TO THINK 7.2 A group of four stars, all the same size, have the four different surface temperatures given below. Which of these stars emits the most red light?

A. 3000 K   B. 4000 K   C. 5000 K   D. 6000 K

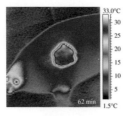

(MP) For instructor-assigned homework, go to
www.masteringphysics.com

Problem difficulty is labeled as | (straightforward) to |||| (challenging).

Problems labeled INT integrate significant material from earlier chapters; BIO are of biological or medical interest.

QUESTIONS

Conceptual Questions

1. People with body piercings are advised to remove their
BIO exposed body jewelry before engaging in cold-weather activities. The skin surrounding the metal in earrings, lip rings, nose rings, or eyebrow rings can get frostbite much more easily than other skin. Explain why.

2. If you live somewhere with cold, clear nights, you may have noticed some mornings when there was frost on open patches of ground but not under trees. This is because the ground under trees does not get as cold as open ground. Explain how tree cover keeps the ground under trees warmer.

3. Arc welding uses electric current to make an extremely hot electric arc that can melt metal. The arc emits ultraviolet light that can cause sunburn and eye damage if a welder is not wearing protective gear. Why does the arc give off ultraviolet light?

PROBLEMS

Section 7.1 Heat Transfer

1. | A 1.8-cm-thick wood floor covers a 4.0 m × 5.5 m room. The subfloor on which the flooring sits is at a temperature of 16.2°C, while the air in the room is at 19.6°C. What is the rate of heat conduction through the floor?

2. ||| A copper-bottomed kettle, its bottom 24 cm in diameter and 3.0 mm thick, sits on a burner. The kettle holds boiling water, and energy flows into the water from the kettle bottom at 800 W. What is the temperature of the bottom surface of the kettle?

3. ||| What is the rate of energy transfer by radiation from a metal cube 2.0 cm on a side that is at 700°C? Its emissivity is 0.20.

4. || What is the greatest possible rate of energy transfer by radiation for a 5.0-cm-diameter sphere that is at 100°C?

5. |||| Seals may cool themselves by
BIO using *thermal windows,* patches on their bodies with much higher than average surface temperature. Suppose a seal has a 0.030 m² thermal window at a temperature of 30°C. If the seal's surroundings are a frosty −10°C, what is the net rate of energy loss by radiation? Assume an emissivity equal to that of a human.

6. || The glowing filament in a lamp is radiating energy at a rate of 60 W. At the filament's temperature of 1500°C, the emissivity is 0.23. What is the surface area of the filament?

7. ||| The top layer of your goose down sleeping bag has a thickness of 5.0 cm and a surface area of 1.0 m². When the outside temperature is −20°C, you lose 25 Cal/hr by heat conduction through the bag (which remains at a cozy 35°C inside). Assume that you're sleeping on an insulated pad that eliminates heat conduction to the ground beneath you. What is the thermal conductivity of the goose down?

8. || Suppose you go outside in your fiber-filled jacket on a windless but very cold day. The thickness of the jacket is 2.5 cm, and it covers 1.1 m² of your body. The purpose of fiber- or down-filled jackets is to trap a layer of air, and it's really the air layer that provides the insulation. If your skin temperature is 34°C while the air temperature is −20°C, at what rate is heat being conducted through the jacket and away from your body?

9. ||| Two thin, square copper plates are radiating energy at the same rate. The edge length of plate 2 is four times that of plate 1. What is the ratio of absolute temperatures T_1/T_2 of the plates?

10. || The surface area of an adult human is about 1.8 m². Sup-
BIO pose a person with a skin temperature of 34°C is standing nude in a room where the air is 25°C but the walls are 17°C.
    a. There is a "dead-air" layer next to your skin that acts as insulation. If the dead-air layer is 5.0 mm thick, what is the person's rate of heat loss by conduction?
    b. What is the person's net radiation loss to the walls? The emissivity of skin is 0.97.
    c. Does conduction or radiation contribute more to the total rate of energy loss?
    d. If the person is metabolizing food at a rate of 155 W, does the person feel comfortable, chilly, or too warm?

Section 7.2 The Electromagnetic Spectrum

11. | The spectrum of a glowing filament has its peak at a wavelength of 1200 nm. What is the temperature of the filament, in °C?

12. || While using a dimmer switch to investigate a new type of incandescent light bulb, you notice that the light changes both its spectral characteristics and its brightness as the voltage is increased.

    a. If the wavelength of maximum intensity decreases from 1800 nm to 1600 nm as the bulb's voltage is increased, by how many °C does the filament temperature increase?

    b. By what factor does the total radiation from the filament increase due to this temperature change?

STOP TO THINK ANSWERS

Stop to Think 7.1 C. With a sealed suit and no matter around you, there is no way to transfer heat to the environment except by radiation.

Stop to Think 7.2: D. A hotter object emits more radiation across the *entire* spectrum than a cooler object. The 6000 K star has its maximum intensity in the blue region of the spectrum, but it still emits more red radiation than the somewhat cooler stars.

8

CURRENT AND RESISTANCE

This woman is measuring her percentage body fat by gripping a device that passes a small electric current through her body. How does a measurement of the current reveal such details of the body's structure?

Looking Ahead ▶▶

The goal of Chapter 8 is to learn how and why charge moves through a conductor as what we call a current. In this chapter you will learn to:

▶ Understand how charge moves through a conductor.

▶ Apply the law of conservation of current.

▶ Understand the emf of a battery.

▶ Use the concepts of resistance and resistivity to predict currents.

▶ Analyze the energy transfers as charges move through simple circuits.

We began our investigation of electric charges by looking at the forces between plastic rods rubbed with wool. We continued our investigation by building the concepts of electric field and potential. In this chapter, we will now look at practical applications of these concepts. When you press the power button on your laptop computer, cell phone, or digital camera, the device powers up because the electric potential of a battery causes charges to move through the circuits in what we call a *current*. We can explain the operation of these devices using the physics of charges, electric fields, and electric potentials—the same physics behind the force between the plastic rods.

Our goal in this chapter is to understand how to produce and manipulate electric currents, the controlled flow of charges. We will begin with a description of how charges flow through a wire. This model will help us understand how current depends on the properties of the conductor carrying the current. The measurement of an electric current can reveal something about the physical properties of an object, whether it's the temperature of a device or the percentage of fat in a person's body. The basic properties of current established in this chapter will be necessary groundwork for our further study of electric circuits in the next chapter.

8.1 A Model of Current

Let's start our exploration of current with a very simple experiment. Figure 8.1a shows a charged parallel-plate capacitor. If we connect the two capacitor plates to each other with a metal wire, as shown in Figure 8.1b, the plates quickly become neutral. We say that the capacitor has been *discharged.*

The wire is a conductor, a material through which charge easily moves. Earlier, we defined a *current* as the motion of charges through a material. Later in the chapter we will develop a quantitative expression for current, but for now this definition will suffice. Apparently the excess charge on one capacitor plate is able to move through the wire to the other plate, neutralizing both plates. **The capacitor is discharged by a current in the connecting wire.**

> NOTE ▶ Current is defined as the motion of charges, so we don't say that "current flows." It is *charges* that flow, not current. Current *is* the flow. ◀

If we observe the capacitor discharge, we see other effects. As Figure 8.2 shows, the connecting wire gets warmer. If the wire is very thin in places, such as the thin filament in a lightbulb, the wire gets hot enough to glow. The current-carrying wire also deflects a compass needle. For now, we will use "makes the wire warmer" and "deflects a compass needle" as *indicators* that a current is present in a wire.

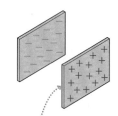

(a)

A charged parallel-plate capacitor

The net charge of each plate is decreasing.

(b)

A connecting wire discharges the capacitor.

FIGURE 8.1 A capacitor is discharged by a metal wire.

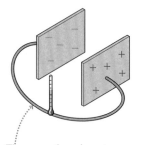

The connecting wire gets warm.

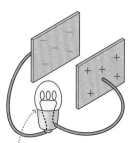

A lightbulb glows. The lightbulb filament is part of the connecting wire.

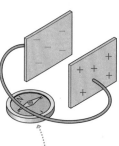

A compass needle is deflected.

FIGURE 8.2 Properties of a current.

Charge Carriers

Opposite charges attract, but the oppositely charged plates of a capacitor don't spontaneously discharge because the charges can't leap from one plate to the other. A connecting wire discharges the capacitor by providing a pathway for charge to move from one side of the capacitor to the other. However, merely observing that a wire discharges a capacitor doesn't answer an important question: Does positive charge move toward the negative plate, or does negative charge move toward the positive plate? *Either* motion would explain the observations we have made.

The charges that move in a current are called the *charge carriers.* The first experiments that could distinguish between positive and negative charge carriers didn't take place until the early 20th century, but the experimental evidence is now clear: **The charge carriers in metals are electrons.** As Figure 8.3 shows, it is the motion of the *conduction electrons,* which are free to move around, that forms a current—a flow of charge—in the metal. An *insulator* does not have such free charges and cannot carry a current. A *semiconductor* is an intermediate case, with relatively few charge carriers, which can be either positive or negative. It will carry a current, but not as easily as a conductor.

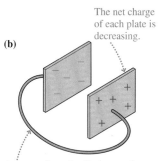

Ions (the metal atoms minus one electron) occupy fixed positions.

The conduction electrons (one per atom) are bound to the solid as a whole, not any particular atom. They are free to move around.

The metal as a whole is electrically neutral.

FIGURE 8.3 Conduction electrons in a metal.

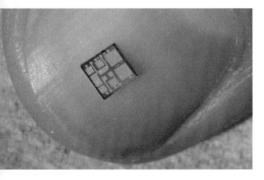

◄**Designer charge carriers** Silicon in its natural state is a semiconductor with few charge carriers. Adding other atoms to pure silicon can give it additional charge carriers that are positive or negative, changing the conducting properties of the silicon. An *integrated circuit* is built on a silicon wafer by creating small adjacent regions with different numbers and types of charge carriers, allowing a circuit with thousands or even millions of elements to be built on a single piece of silicon.

NOTE ▶ Electrons are the charge carriers in *metals*. Other materials, such as semiconductors, may have different charge carriers. In ionic solutions, such as seawater, blood, and intercellular fluids, the charge carriers are ions, both positive and negative. ◄

Creating a Current

Suppose you want to slide a book across the table to your friend. You give it a quick push to start it moving, but it begins slowing down because of friction as soon as you take your hand off of it. The book's kinetic energy is transformed into thermal energy, leaving the book and the table slightly warmer. The only way to keep the book moving at a *constant* speed is to continue pushing it.

Something similar happens in a conductor. As we saw earlier, we can use an electric field to push on the electrons in a conductor. Suppose we take a piece of metal and apply an electric field, as in Figure 8.4. The field exerts a force on the electrons, and they begin to move. But the electrons aren't moving in a vacuum. Collisions between the electrons and the atoms of the metal slow them down, transforming the electrons' kinetic energy into the thermal energy of the metal, making the metal warmer. (Recall that "makes the wire warmer" is one of our indicators of a current.) The motion of the electrons will cease *unless you continue pushing*. To keep the electrons moving, we must maintain an electric field. In a constant field, an electron's average motion will be opposite the field. We call this motion the electron's *drift velocity*. If the field goes to zero, so does the drift velocity.

One important conclusion is that $\vec{E} = \vec{0}$ inside a conductor in electrostatic equilibrium. But a conductor with electrons moving through it is *not* in electrostatic equilibrium—the charges are still in motion, so the field need not be zero. **A current is a motion of charges sustained by an internal electric field.** Thus the quick answer to "What creates a current?" is "An electric field."

But why is there an electric field in a current-carrying wire? Where does it come from? Let's recall a key piece of information: Wherever there's a potential difference, an electric field points from higher potential toward lower potential. Figure 8.5 shows how connecting a conducting wire between two points of different potential leads to a current.

Now we can understand how the capacitor in Figure 8.1 gets discharged. Initially, there's a potential difference between the two plates, due to the separation of charges. Connecting a wire between the plates establishes an electric field in the wire, and this electric field causes electrons to flow from the negative plate (which has an excess of electrons) toward the positive plate. In other words, **it is the *potential difference* that creates a current in the wire.** The potential difference across a capacitor depends on the capacitor's charge, so the potential difference—and hence the current—steadily falls as the discharging proceeds. The current ceases when the capacitor is fully discharged because there's no longer a potential difference to maintain the current.

One interesting observation is that the excess electrons on the negative plate need not move all the way to the positive plate. Don't forget that the wire is *already full* of electrons; recall the model of the *sea of electrons*. Let's use an analogy with water in a pipe. If a pipe is already full of water, adding a drop to one end quickly pushes a drop out the other end. Likewise with the wire. As soon

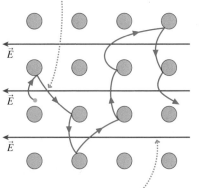

The collisions "reset" the motion of the electron. It then accelerates until the next collision.

$\vec{E}$

$\vec{E}$

$\vec{E}$

The electron has a net displacement opposite the electric field.

FIGURE 8.4 The motion of an electron in a conductor.

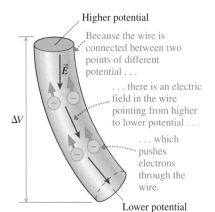

Higher potential

Because the wire is connected between two points of different potential . . .

$\vec{E}$

. . . there is an electric field in the wire pointing from higher to lower potential . . .

ΔV

. . . which pushes electrons through the wire.

Lower potential

FIGURE 8.5 Creating a current.

as some excess electrons move from the negative capacitor plate into the wire, an equal number of electrons are immediately (or very nearly so) pushed out the other end of the wire and onto the positive plate. We don't have to wait for electrons to move all the way through the wire from one plate to the other. Instead, we just need to slightly rearrange the charges on the plates *and* in the wire. No electron moves very far, and the time required is quite short.

CONCEPTUAL EXAMPLE 8.1 **Discharging a capacitor**

The two plates of a capacitor are charged to ± 10 nC, and are then connected with a wire. In the instant after the wire is connected, the electrons move through the wire with average speed v_i. At a slightly later time, when the discharge is 50% complete, the charge on the plates is ± 5 nC. How does the average speed of the electrons at this time compare to v_i?

REASON The electrons are pushed through the wire by an electric field. The source of the electric field is the potential differ- ence created by excess charges on the plates of the capacitor. As the capacitor charge decreases, so does the strength of the electric field. With a reduced "push," the electrons move at a speed less than v_i.

ASSESS To verify that this answer makes sense, let's take it to its logical conclusion: Suppose the current continues until the capacitor completely discharges. With no excess charges, there will be no field—and no motion of electrons. The current will cease, exactly as we expect.

Conservation of Current

In Figure 8.6 a lightbulb has been added to the wire connecting two capacitor plates. The bulb glows while the current is discharging the capacitor. How do you think the current at point A compares to the current at point B? Are the currents at these points the same? Or is one larger than the other? Think about this before going on.

You might have predicted that the current at B is less than the current at A because the bulb, in order to glow, must use up some of the current. It's easy to test this prediction; for instance, we could compare the currents at A and B by comparing how far two compass needles at these positions are deflected. All methods give the same result: The current at point B is *exactly equal* to the current at point A. **The current leaving a lightbulb is exactly the same as the current entering the lightbulb.**

This is an important observation, one that demands an explanation. After all, "something" makes the bulb glow, so why don't we observe a decrease in the current? Electrons are charged particles. The lightbulb can't destroy electrons without violating both the law of conservation of mass and the law of conservation of charge. Thus the *number* of electrons is not changed by the lightbulb. Further, the lightbulb can't store electrons. Were it to do so, the bulb would become increasingly negative until its repulsive force stopped the flow of new electrons and the bulb would go out. This doesn't happen. Every electron entering the lightbulb must be matched by an electron leaving the bulb, and thus the current at B is the same as at A.

Let's consider again our analogy with water flowing through a pipe. Suppose we put a turbine in the middle of the pipe so that the flow of the water turns the turbine, as in Figure 8.7. Water flows *through* the turbine. It is not consumed by the turbine, and the number of gallons of water per minute leaving the pipe is exactly the same as that entering. Nonetheless, the water must do work to turn the turbine, so the water *loses energy* as it passes through.

Similarly, the lightbulb doesn't "use up" current, but, like the turbine, it *does* use energy. The energy is dissipated by atomic-level friction as the electrons move through the wire, making the wire hotter until, in the case of the lightbulb filament, it glows.

There are many other issues we'll need to examine, but we can draw a first important conclusion:

Law of conservation of current The current is the same at all points in a current-carrying wire.

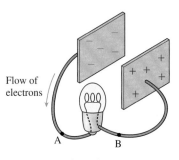

Flow of electrons

FIGURE 8.6 How does the current at A compare to the current at B?

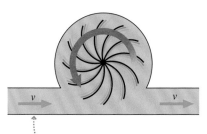

The amount of water that leaves the turbine is the same as that which entered, and the flow of electrons leaving the bulb is the same as that entering.

Flow of electrons

FIGURE 8.7 Water in a pipe turns a turbine.

The discharge of a capacitor lights two bulbs. Comparing the current in the two bulbs, we can say that

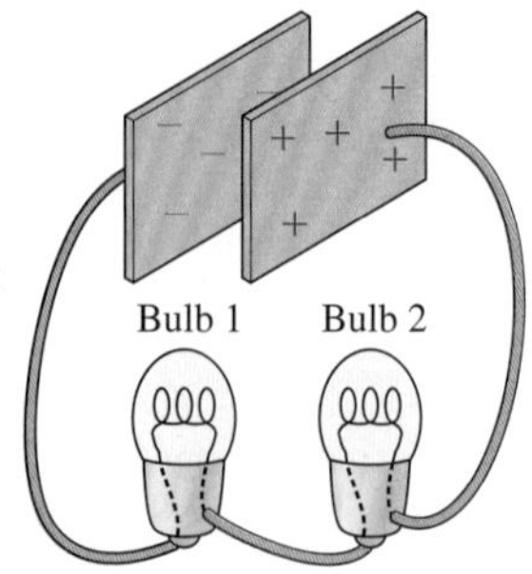

A. The current in bulb 1 is greater than the current in bulb 2.
B. The current in bulb 1 is less than the current in bulb 2.
C. The current in bulb 1 is equal to the current in bulb 2.

Bulb 1   Bulb 2

8.2 Defining and Describing Current

We have developed the idea of a current as the motion of electrons through metals. But currents were known and studied before it was known what the charge carriers are, and the direction of current was *defined* to be the direction in which positive charges *seem* to move, as illustrated in Figure 8.8. Because the charge carriers turned out to be negative, at least for a metal, the direction of the current in a metal is opposite the direction of motion of the electrons.

The fact that the definition of current is "wrong" in some sense isn't really a problem for the work we will do. A capacitor is discharged regardless of whether positive charges move toward the negative plate or negative charges move toward the positive plate. The primary application of the concept of current is to the analysis of circuits, and in a circuit—a macroscopic device—we simply can't tell the sign of the charges that are moving through the wires. **All of our calculations will be correct and all of our circuits will work perfectly well if we define current to be the flow of positive charge.** The distinction is important only at the microscopic level.

Definition of Current

Because the coulomb is the SI unit of charge, and because currents are charges in motion, we define current as the *rate,* in coulombs per second, at which charge moves through a wire. Figure 8.9 shows a wire in which the electric field is $\vec{E}$. This electric field causes charges to move through the wire. Because we are considering current as the motion of positive charges, the motion is in the direction of the field.

When traffic engineers measure the flow of traffic on a road, they place a wire across the road that detects the passage of cars. The flow of traffic is determined by the number of cars that pass this point in a certain time interval. We use a similar convention for current. As illustrated in Figure 8.9, we can measure the amount of charge ΔQ that passes through a cross section of the wire in a time interval Δt. We then define the current in the wire as

$$I = \frac{\Delta Q}{\Delta t} \qquad (8.1)$$

Definition of current

The current direction in a wire is from higher potential to lower potential or, equivalently, in the direction of the electric field $\vec{E}$. The SI unit for current is the coulomb per second, which is called the **ampere** A:

1 ampere = 1 A = 1 coulomb per second = 1 C/s

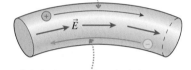

The *current* is defined to point in the direction of $\vec{E}$. It is the direction in which positive charge carriers *would* move . . .

. . . but electrons are the actual charge carriers. They move opposite to $\vec{E}$.

FIGURE 8.8 The current is opposite the direction of motion of the electrons in a metal.

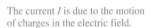
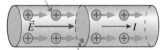

The current I is due to the motion of charges in the electric field.

We imagine an area across the wire through which the charges move. In a time Δt, charge ΔQ moves through this area.

FIGURE 8.9 The current I.

The current unit is named for the French scientist André Marie Ampère, who made major contributions to the study of electricity and magnetism in the early 19th century. The *amp* is an informal abbreviation of ampere. Household currents are typically ≈ 1 A. For example, the current through a 100 watt lightbulb is 0.83 A. Currents in electronic circuits, such as those in computers, are much less. They are typically measured in milliamps (1 mA = 10^{-3} A) or microamps (1 μA = 10^{-6} A).

For a *steady current,* which will be our primary focus, the total amount of charge delivered by current I during the time interval Δt is

$$Q = I\,\Delta t \qquad\qquad (8.2)$$

EXAMPLE 8.1   Charge flow in a lightbulb

A 100 W lightbulb carries a current of 0.83 A. How much charge flows through the bulb in one minute?

SOLVE According to Equation 8.2, the total charge passing through the bulb in 1 min = 60 s is

$$Q = I\,\Delta t = (0.83\text{ A})(60\text{ s}) = 50\text{ C}$$

ASSESS The charge that flows through devices such as lightbulbs or motors is enormous. This is a good check on the con-

cept of conservation of current. If even a minuscule fraction of the charge stayed in the bulb, the bulb would become highly charged. For comparison, a Van de Graaff generator develops a potential of several hundred thousand volts due to an excess charge of just a few μC, a ten-millionth of the charge that flows through the bulb in one minute. Lightbulbs do not develop a noticeable charge, so the current into and out of the bulb must be exactly the same.

Conservation of Current at a Junction

The law of conservation of current tells us that the current I is the same at all points in a current-carrying wire. But what happens when a wire splits, or when two wires come together?

Figure 8.10 shows two wires merging into one and one wire splitting into two. A point where a wire branches is called a **junction.** The presence of a junction doesn't change our basic reasoning. We cannot create or destroy charges in the wire, and neither can we store them in the junction. The rate at which electrons flow into one *or many* wires must, like water in a pipe, be exactly balanced by the rate at which they flow out of others. For a *junction,* the law of conservation of charge requires that

$$\Sigma I_{\text{in}} = \Sigma I_{\text{out}} \qquad\qquad (8.3)$$

where, as usual, the Σ symbol means "the sum of."

This basic conservation statement, that the sum of the currents into a junction equals the sum of the currents leaving, is called **Kirchhoff's junction law.** The junction law isn't a new law of physics; it is a consequence of the conservation of charge.

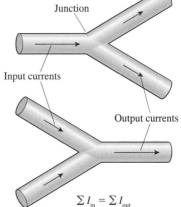

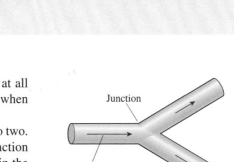

FIGURE 8.10 The sum of the currents into a junction must equal the sum of the currents leaving the junction.

EXAMPLE 8.2   Currents in a junction

Four wires have currents as noted in Figure 8.11. What are the direction and the magnitude of the current in the fifth wire?

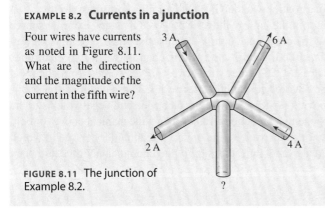

FIGURE 8.11 The junction of Example 8.2.

SOLVE Two of the wires have currents into the junction:

$$\Sigma I_{\text{in}} = 3\text{ A} + 4\text{ A} = 7\text{ A}$$

Two of the wires have currents out of the junction:

$$\Sigma I_{\text{out}} = 6\text{ A} + 2\text{ A} = 8\text{ A}$$

To conserve current, the fifth wire must carry a current of 1 A into the junction.

ASSESS This type of analysis will be very important when we begin to analyze circuits.

The discharge of a capacitor lights three bulbs. Comparing the current in bulbs 1 and 2, we can say that

A. The current in bulb 1 is greater than the current in bulb 2.
B. The current in bulb 1 is less than the current in bulb 2.
C. The current in bulb 1 is equal to the current in bulb 2.

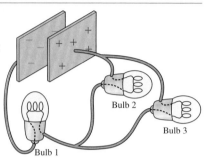

8.3 Batteries and EMF

There are practical devices, such as a camera flash, that use the charge on a capacitor to drive a current. But, as we have seen, a capacitor discharges and the current ceases. A camera flash gives a single, bright flash of light. If you want a light to illuminate your way along a dark path, you need a *continuous* source of light like a flashlight. Continuous light requires the current to be continuous as well.

Figure 8.12 shows a wire connecting the two terminals of a battery, much like the wire that connected the capacitor plates in Figure 8.1. Just like that wire, the wire connecting the battery terminals gets warm, deflects a compass needle, and makes a lightbulb inserted into it glow brightly. These indicators tell us that charges flow through the wire from one terminal to the other. The current in the wire is the same whether it is supplied by a capacitor or a battery. Everything you've learned so far about current applies equally well to the current supplied by a battery, with one important difference.

The difference is the duration of the current. The current that discharges a capacitor is transient; it quickly ceases. By contrast, the wire connecting the battery terminals *continues* to deflect the compass needle and *continues* to light the lightbulb. The capacitor quickly runs out of excess charge, but the battery can keep the charges in motion.

How does a battery produce this sustained motion of charge? A real battery involves a series of chemical reactions, but Figure 8.13 shows a simple model of a battery that illustrates the motion of charges. The inner workings of a battery act like a *charge escalator* between the two terminals. Charges are removed from the negative terminal and "lifted" to the positive terminal. It is the charge escalator that sustains the current in the wire by providing a continually renewed supply of charges at the positive terminal.

Once a charge reaches the positive terminal, it is able to flow through the wire as a current until reaching the negative terminal. The charge escalator then lifts the charge back to the positive terminal where it can start the loop all over again. This flow of charge in a continuous loop is what we call a **complete circuit.**

The charge escalator in the battery must be powered by some external source of energy. It is lifting the electrons "uphill" against the electric field. A battery consists of chemicals, called *electrolytes,* sandwiched between two electrodes made of different materials. The energy to move charges comes from chemical reactions between the electrolytes and the electrodes. These chemical reactions separate charge by moving positive ions to one electrode and negative ions to the other. In other words, chemical reactions, rather than a mechanical conveyor belt, transport charge from one electrode to the other. A dead battery is one in which the supply of chemicals, and thus the supply of chemical energy, has been exhausted.

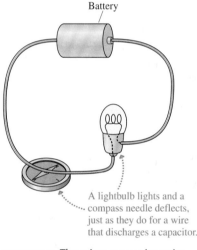

FIGURE 8.12 There is a current in a wire connecting the terminals of a battery.

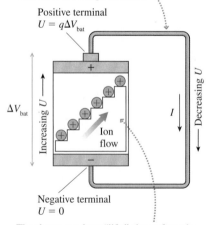

FIGURE 8.13 The charge escalator model of a battery.

By separating charge, the charge escalator establishes the potential difference ΔV_{bat} that is shown between the terminals of the battery in Figure 8.13. The process works like so: Suppose chemical reactions do work W_{chem} to move charge q from the negative to the positive terminal. In an ideal battery, in which there are no internal energy losses, the charge gains electric potential energy $\Delta U = W_{chem}$. This is analogous to a book gaining gravitational potential energy as you do work to lift it from the floor to a shelf.

The quantity W_{chem}/q, which is the work done *per charge* by the charge escalator, is called the **emf** of the battery. It is pronounced as the sequence of three letters "e-m-f." The symbol for emf is $\mathcal{E}$, a script E, and its units are those of the electric potential: joules per coulomb, or volts. The term emf was originally an abbreviation of "electromotive force." That is an outdated term, so today we just call it emf and it's not an abbreviation of anything.

The *rating* of a battery, such as 1.5 V, is the battery's emf. It is determined by the specific chemical reactions employed by the battery. An alkaline battery has an emf of 1.5 V; a rechargeable NiCd battery has an emf of 1.2 V. Larger emfs are created by using several smaller "cells" in a row, much like going to the fourth floor by taking four separate escalators.

By definition, the electric potential is related to the electric potential energy of charge q by $\Delta V = \Delta U/q$. But $\Delta U = W_{chem}$ for the charges in an ideal battery, hence the potential difference between the terminals of an ideal battery is

$$\Delta V_{bat} = \frac{W_{chem}}{q} = \mathcal{E} \tag{8.4}$$

In other words, the potential difference between the terminals of a battery, often called the **terminal voltage,** is the battery's emf. In practice, inevitable energy losses within the battery cause the terminal voltage of a real battery to be slightly less than the emf. We'll overlook this small difference and assume $\Delta V_{bat} = \mathcal{E}$.

Electric generators, photocells, and power supplies use different means to separate charge, but otherwise they function much like a battery. The common feature of all such devices is that **they use some source of energy to separate charge and, thus, to create a potential difference.** The emf of the device is the work done per charge to separate the charge. In contrast, a capacitor stores separated charges, but a capacitor has no means to *do* the separation. Hence a capacitor has a potential difference, but not an emf.

NOTE ▶ The term *emf,* often capitalized as EMF, is widely used in popular science articles in newspapers and magazines to mean "electromagnetic field." This is *not* how we will use the term *emf.* ◀

CONCEPTUAL EXAMPLE 8.2 Recharging a battery

As a battery creates a current in a circuit, the reactions that run the charge escalator deplete chemicals in the battery. However, you can "recharge" some types of batteries by forcing a current into the positive terminal. Clearly you are not literally *recharging* it, as you are not adding charge to the battery. What are you replenishing in the battery when you recharge it?

REASON When you recharge a battery, you reverse the direction of the current. This reverses the chemical reactions that produce the emf, replenishing the chemicals in the battery and storing energy as chemical energy.

ASSESS Because we are really adding energy to the battery, it would be more appropriate to say that we are "re-energizing" the battery. Note that only certain batteries can be recharged; the chemical reactions must be easily reversible.

TRY IT YOURSELF

Listen to your potential Put on a set of earphones from a portable music player and place the plug on the table. Moisten your fingertips and hold a penny in one hand and a paper clip in the other. This makes a very weak battery; the penny and the clip are the electrodes and your moist skin the electrolyte. Touch the paper clip to the innermost contact on the headphone plug and the penny to the outermost. You will hear a *very* soft click as the potential difference causes a small current in the headphones.

A shocking predator? BIO The torpedo ray captures and eats fish by paralyzing them with electricity. As we will see in Chapter 9, cells in the body use chemical energy to separate charge, just as in a battery. Special cells in the body of the ray called *electrocytes* produce an emf of a bit more than 0.10 V for a short time when stimulated. Such a small emf will not produce a large effect, but the torpedo ray has organs that contain clusters of hundreds of these electrocytes connected in a row. The total emf can be 50 V or more, enough to immobilize nearby prey.

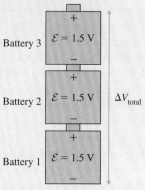

CONCEPTUAL EXAMPLE 8.3 Potential difference for batteries in series

Three batteries are connected one after the other as shown in Figure 8.14; we say they are connected in *series*. What's the total potential difference?

REASON We can think of this as three charge escalators, one after the other. Each one lifts charges to a higher potential. Because each battery raises the potential by 1.5 V, the total potential difference of the three batteries in series is 4.5 V.

ASSESS Common AA and AAA batteries are 1.5 V batteries. Many consumer electronics, such as digital cameras, use two or four of these batteries. Wires inside the device connect the batteries in series to produce a total 3.0 V or 6.0 V potential difference.

FIGURE 8.14 Three batter-ies in series.

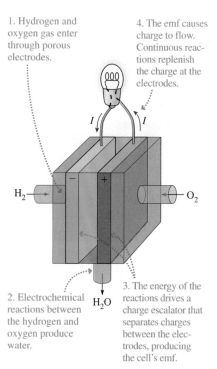

1. Hydrogen and oxygen gas enter through porous electrodes.

4. The emf causes charge to flow. Continuous reactions replenish the charge at the electrodes.

H_2 O_2

2. Electrochemical reactions between the hydrogen and oxygen produce water. H_2O

3. The energy of the reactions drives a charge escalator that separates charges between the electrodes, producing the cell's emf.

FIGURE 8.15 The electric energy to light a bulb comes from the reaction between hydrogen fuel and oxygen in a fuel cell.

Electricity generators, such as coal-burning power plants, burn fuel (a source of chemical energy), transform the resulting thermal energy to the mechanical energy of a spinning turbine, then use a generator, which we'll discuss in Chapter 24, to transform the mechanical energy to electricity. There are unavoidable thermodynamic inefficiencies associated with this process, as we learned in Chapter 6. In contrast, a battery converts chemical energy directly to electric energy. This is more efficient, but batteries have a limited store of chemicals.

A much more elegant solution to the generation of electricity is the *fuel cell*. A particular fuel cell, one that combines hydrogen fuel with oxygen, is illustrated in Figure 8.15. Rather than burning the fuel, as in a power plant, with the resulting thermal losses, the fuel cell's specially designed electrodes allow an electrochemical reaction that transforms the chemical energy of the hydrogen directly to electrical energy. A fuel cell thus works like a battery, but with the chemicals supplied externally. As long as fuel and oxygen are coming in, a fuel cell can produce electricity. A hydrogen-fueled car with a fuel cell and an electric motor under the hood would be very efficient, and it would generate no hazardous exhaust. The only "waste" product is water!

STOP TO THINK 8.3   A battery produces a current in a wire. As the current continues, which of the following quantities (perhaps more than one) decreases?

A. The positive charge in the battery.
B. The emf of the battery.
C. The chemical energy in the battery.

8.4 Connecting Potential and Current

An important conclusion of the charge escalator model is that **a battery is a source of potential difference.** When charges flow through a wire that connects the battery terminals, this current is a *consequence* of the battery's potential difference. You can think of the battery's emf as being the *cause*. Current, heat, light, sound, and so on are all *effects* that happen when the battery is used in certain ways.

Our goal in this section is to find the connection between potential and current. Let's start by connecting a wire between the two terminals of a battery, as shown in Figure 8.16. You learned earlier, the potential difference between any two points is independent of the path between them. Consequently, the potential difference between the two ends of the wire, along a path through the wire, is equal to the potential difference between the two terminals of the battery:

$$\Delta V_{wire} = \Delta V_{bat} \tag{8.5}$$

Figure 8.16 shows how the battery causes a current in the wire. Notice that **the current is in the direction of decreasing potential.** We can think of it this way: The charge escalator in the battery raises the charges "uphill," and then they flow "downhill" through the wire.

Resistance

If you connect a wire between the terminals of a battery, the battery's potential difference creates a current in the wire. Suppose we were to do a series of experiments to determine what factors affect this current, as in Figure 8.17. As you would expect, adding a second battery in series increases the current. Careful measurements show that the current in the wire is proportional to ΔV_{wire}. This is easily explained with our model of conduction: A larger potential difference creates a larger electric field that, in turn, pushes charges through the wire faster.

We would also find that increasing the length of the wire decreases the current, while increasing the thickness of the wire increases the current. This seems reasonable, because it should be harder to push charges through a long wire than a short one, and an electric field should be able to push more charges through a fat wire than a skinny one.

Finally, we would find that some materials carry more current than others. A material is a better conductor if the charges are able to move through the wire with fewer collisions. This allows the drift velocity to be higher and leads to a larger current.

For any particular wire, we can define a quantity called the **resistance** that is a measure of how hard it is to push charges through the wire. We use the symbol R for resistance. A large resistance implies that it is hard to move the charges through the wire; in a wire with low resistance, the charges move much more easily. The current in the wire depends on the potential difference ΔV_{wire} between the ends of the wire and the wire's resistance R as follows:

$$I = \frac{\Delta V_{wire}}{R} \tag{8.6}$$

Establishing a potential difference ΔV_{wire} between the ends of a wire of resistance R creates an electric field that, in turn, causes a current $I = \Delta V_{wire}/R$ in the wire. As we would expect, the smaller the resistance, the larger the current.

We can think of Equation 8.6 as the definition of resistance. If a potential difference V_{wire} causes current I in a wire, the wire's resistance is

$$R = \frac{\Delta V_{wire}}{I} \tag{8.7}$$

The SI unit of resistance is the **ohm,** defined as

$$1 \text{ ohm} = 1 \ \Omega = 1 \text{ V/A}$$

where Ω is an uppercase Greek omega. The unit takes its name from the German physicist Georg Ohm, whose work in the early 19th century helped clarify the relationship among potential difference, current, and resistance. The ohm is the basic unit of resistance, although kilohms ($1 \text{ k}\Omega = 10^3 \ \Omega$) and megohms ($1 \text{ M}\Omega = 10^6 \ \Omega$) are widely used.

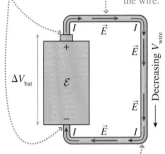

1. The potential difference between these two points is the same whether you go through the battery or the wire.

2. The potential difference between the ends of the wire establishes an electric field inside the wire.

3. The electric field drives a current through the wire, in the direction of decreasing potential.

FIGURE 8.16 The electric field and the current inside the wire.

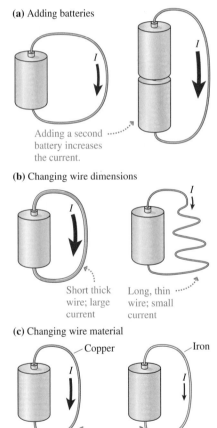

(a) Adding batteries

Adding a second battery increases the current.

(b) Changing wire dimensions

Short thick wire; large current

Long, thin wire; small current

(c) Changing wire material

Copper   Iron

A copper wire will carry a larger current than an iron wire of the same dimensions.

FIGURE 8.17 Factors affecting the current in a wire.

EXAMPLE 8.3 Resistance of a lightbulb

The glowing element in an incandescent lightbulb is the *filament,* a long, thin piece of tungsten wire that is heated by the electric current through it. When connected to the 120 V of an electric outlet, a 60 W bulb carries a current of 0.50 A. What is the resistance of the filament in the lamp?

SOLVE We can use Equation 8.7 to compute the resistance:

$$R = \frac{\Delta V_{\text{wire}}}{I} = \frac{120 \text{ V}}{0.50 \text{ A}} = 240 \ \Omega$$

ASSESS As we will see below, the resistance of the filament varies with temperature. This value holds for the lightbulb only when the bulb is glowing and the filament is hot.

Resistivity

TABLE 8.1 Resistivity of materials

Material	Resistivity ($\Omega \cdot$ m)
Copper	1.7×10^{-8}
Tungsten (20°C)	5.6×10^{-8}
Tungsten (1500°C)	5.0×10^{-7}
Iron	9.7×10^{-8}
Nichrome	1.5×10^{-6}
Seawater	0.22
Blood (average)	1.6
Muscle	13
Fat	25
Pure water	2.4×10^{5}
Cell membrane	3.6×10^{7}

Figure 8.17c noted that the resistance of a wire depends on what it is made of. We define a quantity called **resistivity,** for which we use the symbol ρ (a lowercase Greek rho), to characterize the electrical properties of materials. Materials that are good conductors have low resistivity; materials that are poor conductors (i.e., insulators) have high resistivity. The resistivity ρ has units of $\Omega \cdot$ m. The resistivity of some materials is given in Table 8.1.

The resistivity of materials varies quite a bit. Metals are generally good conductors (and so have very small resistivity), but metals such as copper are much better conductors than metals such as nichrome, an alloy of nickel and chromium that is used to make heating wires. Water is a poor conductor, but the dissolved salts in seawater produce ions that can carry charge, so seawater is a good conductor, with a resistivity one million times less than that of pure water. Glass is an excellent insulator with a resistivity in excess of $10^{14} \ \Omega \cdot$ m, 10^{22} times that of copper.

The resistivity of a material depends on the temperature, as you can see from the two values for tungsten listed in Table 8.1. As the temperature increases, so do the thermal vibrations of the atoms. This makes them "bigger targets" for the moving electrons, causing collisions to be more frequent. Thus the resistivity of a metal increases with increasing temperature.

The resistance of a wire depends both on the resistivity of its material and on the dimensions of the wire. A wire made of a material of resistivity ρ, with length L and cross-section area A, has resistance

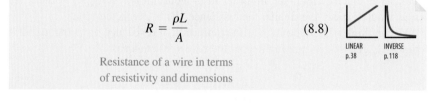

$$R = \frac{\rho L}{A} \qquad (8.8)$$

Resistance of a wire in terms of resistivity and dimensions

LINEAR p. 38   INVERSE p. 118

Resistivity is a property of a material. All copper wires (at the same temperature) have the same resistivity. But resistance is a property of a *specific* wire or conductor because it depends on the conductor's length and diameter as well as on the resistivity of the material from which it is made.

NOTE ▶ It is important to distinguish between resistivity and resistance. *Resistivity* describes just the *material,* not any particular piece of it. *Resistance* characterizes a specific piece of the conductor having a specific geometry. The relationship between resistivity and resistance is analogous to that between density and mass. ◀

▶ **Coils of coils** Most lightbulb filaments are made of tungsten, as it is one of a few materials that can withstand the necessary high temperatures. But a filament must have a large resistance. The resistivity of tungsten is quite low, so a tungsten filament must be very long and very thin. A close view of a typical bulb's filament shows that it is made of very thin wire that is coiled and then coiled again. The double-coil structure is necessary to fit the great length of the filament into the small space of the bulb's globe.

EXAMPLE 8.4 The length of a lightbulb filament

We calculated in Example 8.3 that a 60 W lightbulb has a resistance of 240 Ω. At the operating temperature of the tungsten filament, the resistivity is approximately $5.0 \times 10^{-7}\ \Omega \cdot m$. If the wire used to make the filament is 0.040 mm in diameter, how long must the filament be?

PREPARE The resistance of a wire depends on its length, its cross-section area, and the material of which it is made.

SOLVE The cross-section area of the wire is $A = \pi r^2 = \pi(2.0 \times 10^{-5}\ m)^2 = 1.26 \times 10^{-9}\ m^2$. Rearranging Equation 8.8 shows us that the filament must be of length

$$L = \frac{AR}{\rho} = \frac{(1.26 \times 10^{-9}\ m^2)(240\ \Omega)}{5.0 \times 10^{-7}\ \Omega \cdot m} = 0.60\ m$$

ASSESS The resistivity of tungsten is low, so the filament must be quite thin and quite long. This result is quite reasonable.

EXAMPLE 8.5 Making a heater

An amateur astronomer uses a heater to warm her telescope eyepiece so moisture does not collect on it. The heater is a 20-cm-long, 0.50-mm-diameter nichrome wire that wraps around the eyepiece. When the wire is connected to a 1.5 V battery, what is the current in the wire?

PREPARE The current in the wire depends on the emf of the battery and the resistance of the wire. The resistance of the wire depends on the resistivity of nichrome, given in Table 8.1, and the dimensions of the wire. Converted to meters, the relevant dimensions of the wire are $L = 0.20\ m$ and $r = 2.5 \times 10^{-4}\ m$.

SOLVE The wire's resistance is

$$R = \frac{\rho L}{A} = \frac{\rho L}{\pi r^2} = \frac{(1.5 \times 10^{-6}\ \Omega \cdot m)(0.20\ m)}{\pi(2.5 \times 10^{-4}\ m)^2} = 1.5\ \Omega$$

The wire is connected to the battery, so $\Delta V_{wire} = \Delta V_{bat} = 1.5\ V$. The current in the wire is

$$I = \frac{\Delta V_{wire}}{R} = \frac{1.5\ V}{1.5\ \Omega} = 1.0\ A$$

ASSESS The emf of the battery is small, but so is the resistance of the wire, so this is a reasonable current, enough to warm the wire and the eyepiece.

Electrical Measurements of Physical Properties

Measuring resistance is quite straightforward. Because resistance depends sensitively on the properties of materials, a measurement of resistance can be a simple but effective probe of other quantities of interest.

For example, the resistivity of water is strongly dependent on dissolved substances in the water, so it is easy to make a quick test of water purity by making a measurement of resistivity. In situations in which water must be absolutely pure, such as in the semiconductor industry, the resistivity of the water is continuously monitored. Even a small amount of contaminant can significantly reduce the resistivity, making resistivity a sensitive test of water purity.

CONCEPTUAL EXAMPLE 8.4 Testing drinking water

A house gets its drinking water from a well that has an intermittent problem with salinity. Before the water is pumped into the house, it passes between two electrodes in the circuit shown in Figure 8.18. The current passing through the water is measured with a meter. Which corresponds to increased salinity—an increased current or a decreased current?

REASON Increased salinity causes the water's resistivity to decrease. This decrease causes a decrease in resistance between the electrodes. Current is inversely proportional to resistance, so this leads to an increase in current.

ASSESS Increasing salinity means more ions in solution, and thus more charge carriers, so an increase in current is expected. Electrical systems similar to this can therefore provide a quick check of water purity.

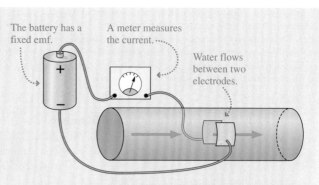

The battery has a fixed emf.

A meter measures the current.

Water flows between two electrodes.

FIGURE 8.18 A water-testing circuit for Conceptual Example 8.4

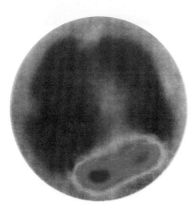

FIGURE 8.19 An electrical impedance map shows the cross section of a healthy patient's torso. You can clearly see the heart (blue) and lungs (red).

The discovery of superconductivity was quite unexpected. No less surprising was the discovery of the remarkable magnetic properties of superconductors, illustrated here by the stable levitation of a small, strong magnet above a wafer of high-temperature superconductor.

Different tissues in the body have quite different resistivities, as we see in Table 8.1. For example, fat has a higher resistivity than muscle. Consequently, a routine test to estimate the percentage of fat in a person's body is based on a measurement of the body's resistance, as illustrated in the photo at the start of the chapter. A higher resistance of the body means a higher proportion of fat.

More careful measurements of resistance can provide more detailed diagnostic information. Passing a small, safe current between two electrodes on opposite sides of a person's torso permits a measurement of the resistance of the intervening tissue. Figure 8.19 shows an image of a patient's torso generated from measurements of resistance between many pairs of opposing electrodes, created just as the heart contracted, sending blood to the lungs. Blood is a better conductor than the tissues of the heart and lungs, so this motion of blood decreased the resistance of the lungs (shown in red) and increased that of the heart (shown in blue). Such measurements are most useful for studying the heart, in the noninvasive diagnostic procedure called *impedance cardiography*.

Superconductivity

In 1911, the Dutch physicist Kamerlingh Onnes was studying the conductivity of metals at very low temperatures. As we noted above, metals become better conductors (i.e., they have lower resistivity) at lower temperatures. But the resistivity change with temperature is gradual. Onnes, however, found that mercury suddenly and dramatically loses *all* resistance to current when cooled below a temperature of 4.2 K. This complete loss of resistance at low temperatures is called **superconductivity.**

Later experiments established that the resistivity of a superconducting metal is not just small, *it is truly zero*. The electrons are moving in a frictionless environment, and charge will continue to move through a superconductor *without an electric field*. Superconductivity was not understood until the 1950s, when it was explained as being a specific quantum effect.

Superconducting wires can carry enormous currents, and superconducting electromagnets, such as those used in MRI machines, can generate very strong magnetic fields. But applications remained limited for many decades because all known superconductors required temperatures less than 20 K. This situation changed dramatically in 1986 with the discovery of *high-temperature superconductors*. These ceramic-like materials are superconductors at temperatures as "high" as 125 K. Although −150°C may not seem like a high temperature to you, the technology for producing such temperatures is simple and inexpensive. Thus many new superconductor applications are likely to appear in coming years.

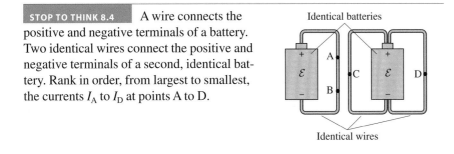

STOP TO THINK 8.4 A wire connects the positive and negative terminals of a battery. Two identical wires connect the positive and negative terminals of a second, identical battery. Rank in order, from largest to smallest, the currents I_A to I_D at points A to D.

8.5 Resistors and Ohm's Law

The relationship between the potential difference across a conductor and the current passing through it that we saw in the previous section was first deduced by Georg Ohm, and is known as **Ohm's law:**

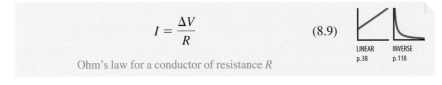

$$I = \frac{\Delta V}{R}$$ (8.9)

Ohm's law for a conductor of resistance R

If we know that a wire of resistance R carries a current I, we can compute the potential difference between the ends of the wire as $\Delta V = IR$.

NOTE ▶ We could write the equation for Ohm's law as $\Delta V = IR$, but $I = \Delta V/R$ is a better description of cause and effect because it is the potential difference that causes the current. ◀

Ohmic and Nonohmic Materials

Despite its name, Ohm's law is *not* a law of nature. It is limited to those materials whose resistance R remains constant—or very nearly so—during use. Materials to which Ohm's law applies are called **ohmic.** Figure 8.20a shows that the current through an ohmic material is directly proportional to the potential difference; doubling the potential difference results in a doubling of the current. This is a linear relationship, and the resistance R can be determined from the slope of the graph.

Many materials are ohmic over a reasonable range of operating conditions. The resistance of metals varies slightly with temperature, but a metal wire is ohmic as long as the temperature is reasonably constant, and we can give it a fixed resistance value.

Other materials and devices are **nonohmic,** meaning that the current through the device is *not* directly proportional to the potential difference. An example is a semiconductor device known as a *diode.* The graph in Figure 8.20b shows that a diode does not have a well-defined resistance. Three important examples of nonohmic devices are

1. Batteries, where $\Delta V = \mathcal{E}$ is determined by chemical reactions, independent of I.
2. Semiconductor devices, where the I-versus-ΔV curve is very nonlinear.
3. Capacitors, where, as you'll learn in Chapter 9, the relationship between I and ΔV is very different from that of a resistor.

The main point to remember is that Ohm's law does *not* apply to these nonohmic devices.

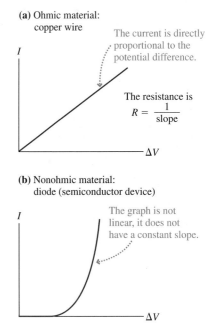

(a) Ohmic material: copper wire

The current is directly proportional to the potential difference.

The resistance is $R = \frac{1}{\text{slope}}$

(b) Nonohmic material: diode (semiconductor device)

The graph is not linear, it does not have a constant slope.

FIGURE 8.20 Current-versus-potential-difference graphs for ohmic and nonohmic materials.

Range of Resistance

In circuits, conductors that are designed to have a constant resistance are called **resistors.** A resistor has a specified value of resistance; typical values range from 1 Ω to 1 MΩ. By comparison, the resistance of metal wires is much lower; a 1 foot section of the copper wire in the wall of your house has a resistance of about 0.002 Ω. The resistance of insulators is much greater; a 1 foot section of a thin glass rod would have a resistance of about 1×10^{18} Ω.

We can identify three different classes of ohmic material, based on the size of their resistance:

- *Wires* are made of metals with very small resistivities ρ, thus wires have very small resistances ($R \ll 1$ Ω). In most cases, the resistance of wires is too small to make a practical difference, and we can make the approximation that $R = 0$ Ω.
- *Insulators* are materials such as glass, plastic, or air. All practical insulators have $R \gg 10^9$ Ω, much larger than the range of resistors we will consider. We can generally make the approximation that $R = \infty$ for an insulator.
- *Resistors,* as noted, have resistances in the range of about 1 Ω to 1 MΩ. These circuit elements will be the ones on which we focus our attention.

We will model many different circuit elements as resistors. For example, the filament in a lightbulb functions as a resistor, although its resistance when hot is larger than its room-temperature value. Other examples of resistors that you may work with are illustrated in the table below.

Light-sensitive resistor

◄ **The resistance goes up when the sun goes down** Many devices use circuit elements whose resistance varies. The sensor on the front of a night light is a *photoresistor*. In the dark, the resistance is large; when light shines on the photoresistor, its resistance decreases. During the day, the resistance is low; at night, the resistance rises. A circuit in the night light monitors the resistance, and switches on the light when the resistance is above a certain value.

Real resistors

Turning the dial changes the length of the wire between two contacts, changing the resistance.

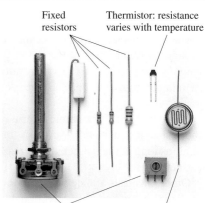

Fixed resistors

Thermistor: resistance varies with temperature

Variable resistors: resistance is varied by turning a knob or screw

Photoresistor: resistance varies with light intensity

The heating element in a toaster is a long nichrome wire that functions as a resistor. Current heats the wire until it glows. Other similar resistors include the heating element in a hair dryer, the heating coil on an electric stove, the rear window defroster in a car, and the filament in a lightbulb.

Volume control knobs are usually *variable* resistors. The resistor is a long wire wrapped as a coil. Turning the dial varies the effective length the wire and thus the resistance. This change in resistance affects the operation of a circuit, controlling the volume.

Practical circuits use a wide variety of resistors with different properties. Some are designed to have a constant resistance, others to have a resistance that varies as a dial is turned, still others to have a resistance that varies with light intensity, temperature, or some other physical parameter.

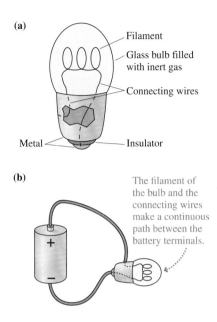

CONCEPTUAL EXAMPLE 8.5 **The changing current in a toaster**
When you press the lever on a toaster, a switch connects the heating wires to 120 V. The wires are initially cool, but the current in the wires raises the temperature until they are hot enough to glow. As the wire heats up, how does the current in the toaster change?

REASON As the wire heats up, its resistivity increases, as noted above, so the resistance of the wires increases. Because the potential difference stays the same, an increasing resistance causes the current to decrease. The current through a toaster is largest when the toaster is first turned on.

ASSESS This result makes sense. As the wire's temperature increases, the current decreases. This makes the temperature of the wire self-limiting. It will warm up to a certain temperature but no farther.

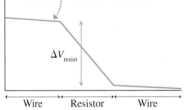

FIGURE 8.21 The basic circuit of a battery and a bulb.

The Ideal-Wire Model

Figure 8.21a shows the anatomy of a lightbulb. The important point is that a lightbulb, like a wire, has two "ends" and that current passes *through* the bulb. Connections to the filament in the bulb are made at the tip and along the side of the metal cylinder. It is often useful to think of a lightbulb as a resistor that happens to give off light when a current is present. Now, let's look at a circuit using a battery, a lightbulb, and wires to make the connection, as in Figure 8.21b. This is the basic circuit in a flashlight.

A typical flashlight bulb has a resistance of $\approx 3\ \Omega$, while a wire that one would use to connect such a bulb to a battery has a resistance of $\approx 0.01\ \Omega$. The resistance of the wires is so much less than that of the bulb that we can, with very little error, adopt the *ideal-wire model* and assume that any connecting wires in a circuit are ideal. An **ideal wire** has $R = 0\ \Omega$, hence the potential difference between the ends of an ideal wire is $\Delta V = 0$ V *even if there is a current in it.*

NOTE ▶ We know that, physically, the potential difference can't be zero. There must be an electric field in the wire for the charges to move, so it must have a potential difference. But in practice this potential difference is so small that we can assume it to be zero with little error. ◀

Figure 8.22 illustrates the ideal-wire model. Here we see wires connected to the two ends of a resistor and a current passing through. Current must be conserved, hence the current I in the resistor is the same as the current in each wire. However, the resistor's resistance is *much* larger than the resistance of the wires: $R_{resist} \gg R_{wire}$. Consequently, the potential difference across the resistor $\Delta V_{resist} = IR_{resist}$ is *much* larger than the potential difference $\Delta V_{wire} = IR_{wire}$ between the ends of each wire.

Figure 8.22b shows the potential along the wire-resistor-wire combination. We saw earlier that current moves in the direction of decreasing potential, so there is a large *voltage drop*—a decrease in potential—across the resistor as we go from left to right, the direction of the current. A very reasonable approximation is to assume that *all* the voltage drop occurs along the resistor, none along the wires. This is the approximation made by the ideal-wire model, which assumes that $R_{wire} = 0\ \Omega$ and $\Delta V_{wire} = 0$ V. With this approximation, shown in Figure 8.22c, the segments of the graph corresponding to the wires are horizontal.

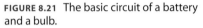

(a) The current is constant along the wire-resistor-wire combination.

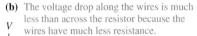

(b) The voltage drop along the wires is much less than across the resistor because the wires have much less resistance.

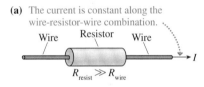

(c) In the ideal wire model, with $R_{wire} = 0\ \Omega$, there is no voltage drop along the wires. All the voltage drop is across the resistor.

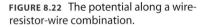

FIGURE 8.22 The potential along a wire-resistor-wire combination.

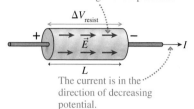

The electric field inside the resistor is uniform, and points from high to low potential.

The current is in the direction of decreasing potential.

FIGURE 8.23 Electric field inside a resistor.

The linear variation in the potential across the resistor is similar to the linear variation in potential between the plates of a parallel-plate capacitor. In a capacitor, this linear variation in potential corresponds to a uniform electric field; the same will be true here. As we see in Figure 8.23, the electric field in a resistor carrying a current in a circuit is uniform; the strength of the electric field is

$$E = \frac{\Delta V}{L}.$$

A larger potential difference corresponds to a larger field, as we would expect.

EXAMPLE 8.6 Analyzing a single-resistor circuit

A 15 Ω resistor is connected to the terminals of a 1.5 V battery.

a. Draw a graph showing the potential as a function of distance traveled through the circuit, starting from $V = 0$ V at the negative terminal of the battery.
b. What is the current in the circuit?

PREPARE To help us visualize the change in potential as charges move through the circuit, we begin with the sketch of the circuit in Figure 8.24. The zero point of potential is noted. We have drawn our sketch so that "up" corresponds to higher potential, which will help us make sense of the circuit. Charges are raised to higher potential in the battery, then travel "downhill" from the positive terminal through the resistor and back to the negative terminal. We assume ideal wires.

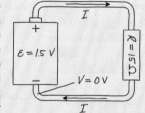

FIGURE 8.24 Single-resistor circuit for Example 8.6.

SOLVE a. Figure 8.25 is a graphical representation of the potential in the circuit. The distance s is measured from the battery's negative terminal, where $V = 0$ V. As we move around the circuit to the starting point, the potential must return to its original value. Because the wires are ideal, there is no change in potential along the wires. This means that the potential difference across the resistor must be equal to the potential difference across the battery: $\Delta V_R = \mathcal{E} = 1.5$ V.

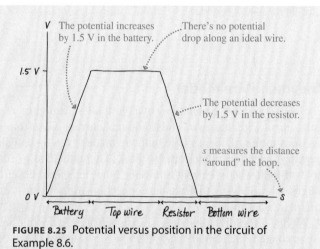

FIGURE 8.25 Potential versus position in the circuit of Example 8.6.

b. Now that we know the potential difference of the resistor, we can compute the current in the resistor by using Ohm's Law:

$$I = \frac{\Delta V_R}{R} = \frac{1.5 \text{ V}}{15 \text{ } \Omega} = 0.10 \text{ A}$$

Because current is conserved, this is the current at any point in the circuit. In other words, the battery's charge escalator lifts charge at the rate 0.10 C/s, and charge flows through the wires and the resistor at the rate 0.10 C/s.

ASSESS This is a reasonable value of the current in a battery-powered circuit.

As we noted, there are many devices whose resistance varies as a function of a physical variable that we might like to measure, such as light intensity, temperature, or sound intensity. As the following example shows, we can use resistance measurements to monitor a physical variable.

EXAMPLE 8.7 Using a thermistor

A thermistor is a device whose resistance varies in a well-defined way with temperature. A certain thermistor has a resistance of 2.8 kΩ at 20°C and 0.39 kΩ at 70°C. This thermistor is used in a water bath in a lab to monitor the temperature. The thermistor is connected in a circuit with a 1.5 V battery, and the current measured. What is the change in current in the circuit as the temperature rises from 20°C to 70°C?

SOLVE We can use Ohm's law to find the current in each case:

$$I(20°C) = \frac{\Delta V}{R} = \frac{1.5 \text{ V}}{2.8 \times 10^3 \text{ }\Omega} = 0.54 \text{ mA}$$

$$I(70°C) = \frac{\Delta V}{R} = \frac{1.5 \text{ V}}{0.39 \times 10^3 \text{ }\Omega} = 3.8 \text{ mA}$$

The change in current is thus 3.3 mA.

ASSESS A modest change in temperature leads to a large change in current, making this a very sensitive means of measuring temperature change.

STOP TO THINK 8.5 Two identical batteries are connected in series in a circuit with a single resistor. $V = 0$ V at the negative terminal of the lower battery. Rank in order, from highest to lowest, the potentials V_A to V_E at the labeled points, noting any ties. Assume the wires are ideal.

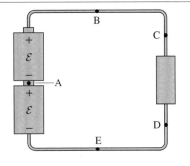

8.6 Energy and Power

When you flip the switch on a flashlight, a battery is connected to a lightbulb, which then begins to glow. The bulb is radiating energy. Where does this energy come from?

A battery not only supplies a potential difference, it also supplies energy, as shown in the battery and bulb circuit of Figure 8.26. The charge escalator is an energy-transfer process, transferring chemical energy E_{chem} stored in the battery to the electric potential energy U of the charges. That energy is then dissipated as the charges move through the lightbulb, keeping the filament warm and glowing.

Recall that charge q gains potential energy $\Delta U = q\,\Delta V$ as it moves through a potential difference ΔV. The potential difference of a battery is $\Delta V_{bat} = \mathcal{E}$, so the battery supplies energy $\Delta U = q\mathcal{E}$ to charge q as it lifts the charge up the charge escalator from the negative to the positive terminal.

It's more useful to know the *rate* at which the battery supplies energy. You learned in Chapter 5 that the rate at which energy is transformed is *power*, measured in joules per second or *watts*. Suppose an amount of charge Δq moves through the battery in a time Δt. The charge Δq will increase its potential energy by $\Delta U = (\Delta q)\mathcal{E}$. The *rate* at which energy is transferred from the battery to the moving charges is

$$P_{bat} = \text{rate of energy transfer} = \frac{\Delta U}{\Delta t} = \frac{\Delta q}{\Delta t}\mathcal{E} \qquad (8.10)$$

But $\Delta q/\Delta t$, the rate at which charge moves through the battery, is the current I. Hence the power supplied by a battery or any emf is

$$P_{emf} = I\mathcal{E} \qquad (8.11)$$

Power delivered by an emf

$I\mathcal{E}$ has units of J/s, or W.

Chemical energy in the battery is transferred to potential energy of the charges in the current.

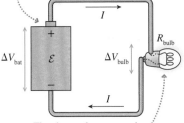

The charges lose energy in collisions as they pass through the filament of the bulb. This energy is transformed to the thermal energy of the glowing filament.

FIGURE 8.26 Energy transformations in a circuit with a battery and a lightbulb.

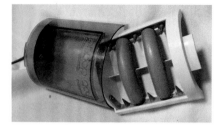

Cooking with electricity Before microwave ovens were common, there were devices that used a decidedly lower-tech approach to the rapid cooking of hot dogs. Prongs connected the hot dog to the 120 V of household electricity, making it the resistor in a circuit. The current through the hot dog dissipated energy as thermal energy, cooking the hot dog in about 2 minutes.

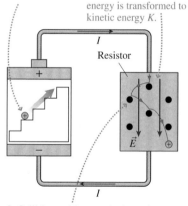

1. Charges gain potential energy U in the battery.

2. As charges accelerate in the electric field in the resistor, potential energy is transformed to kinetic energy K.

3. Collisions with atoms in the resistor transform the kinetic energy of the charges to thermal energy E_{th} of the resistor.

FIGURE 8.27 The power from the battery is dissipated in the resistor.

EXAMPLE 8.8 Power delivered by a car battery

A car battery has $\mathcal{E} = 12$ V. When the car's starter motor is running, the battery current is 320 A. What power does the battery supply?

SOLVE The power is the product of the emf of the battery and the current:

$$P_{bat} = I\mathcal{E} = (320 \text{ A})(12 \text{ V}) = 3.8 \text{ kW}$$

ASSESS This is a lot of power (about 5 hp), but this amount makes sense because turning over a car's engine is hard work. Car batteries are designed to reliably provide such intense bursts of power for starting the engine.

Suppose we consider a circuit consisting of a battery and a single resistor. $P_{bat} = I\mathcal{E}$ is the energy transferred per second from the battery's store of chemicals to the moving charges that make up the current. Figure 8.27 shows the entire sequence of energy transformations, which looks like

$$E_{chem} \rightarrow U \rightarrow K \rightarrow E_{th}$$

The net result is that **the battery's chemical energy is transferred to the thermal energy of the resistor,** raising its temperature.

In the resistor, the amount of charge Δq loses potential energy $\Delta U = (\Delta q)(\Delta V_R)$ as this energy is transformed into kinetic energy and then into the resistor's thermal energy. Thus the rate at which energy is transferred from the current to the resistor is

$$P_R = \frac{\Delta U}{\Delta t} = \frac{\Delta q}{\Delta t}\Delta V_R = I\,\Delta V_R \qquad (8.12)$$

We say that this power—so many joules per second—is *dissipated* by the resistor as charge flows through it.

Our analysis of the single-resistor circuit in Example 8.6 found that $\Delta V_R = \mathcal{E}$. That is, the potential difference across the resistor is exactly the emf supplied by the battery. Because the current is the same in the battery and the resistor, a comparison of Equations 8.11 and 8.12 shows that

$$P_R = P_{bat} \qquad (8.13)$$

The power dissipated in the resistor is exactly equal to the power supplied by the battery. The *rate* at which the battery supplies energy is exactly equal to the *rate* at which the resistor dissipates energy. This is, of course, exactly what we would have expected from energy conservation.

EXAMPLE 8.9 Finding the current in a lightbulb

How much current is "drawn" by a 100 W lightbulb connected to a 120 V outlet?

PREPARE We can model the lightbulb as a resistor.

SOLVE Because the lightbulb is operating as intended, it will dissipate 100 W of power. We can rearrange Equation 8.12 to find

$$I = \frac{P_R}{\Delta V_R} = \frac{100 \text{ W}}{120 \text{ V}} = 0.83 \text{ A}$$

ASSESS Most household appliances, such as a 100 W lightbulb or a 1500 W hair dryer, have a power rating. The rating does *not* mean that these appliances *always* dissipate that much power. These appliances are intended for use at a standard household voltage of 120 V, and their rating is the power they will dissipate *if* operated with a potential difference of 120 V. Their power consumption will differ from the rating if they are operated at any other potential difference.

A resistor obeys Ohm's law, $\Delta V_R = IR$. This gives us two alternative ways of writing the power dissipated by a resistor. We can either substitute IR for ΔV_R or substitute $\Delta V_R/R$ for I. Thus

$$P_R = I\,\Delta V_R = I^2 R = \frac{(\Delta V_R)^2}{R} \qquad (8.14)$$

QUADRATIC
p. 50

Power dissipated by resistance R with current I and potential difference ΔV_R

It is worth writing the different forms of this equation to illustrate that the power varies as the square of both the current and the potential difference.

EXAMPLE 8.10   Finding the power of a dim bulb

How much power is dissipated by a 60 W (120 V) lightbulb when operated, using a dimmer switch, at 100 V?

PREPARE The 60 W rating is for operation at 120 V. We can compute the resistance for this case, then compute the power with the dimmer switch.

SOLVE The lightbulb dissipates 60 W at $\Delta V_R = 120$ V. Thus the filament's resistance is

$$R = \frac{(\Delta V_R)^2}{P_R} = \frac{(120\ \text{V})^2}{60\ \text{W}} = 240\ \Omega$$

The power dissipation when operated at $\Delta V_R = 100$ V is

$$P_R = \frac{(\Delta V_R)^2}{R} = \frac{(100\ \text{V})^2}{240\ \Omega} = 42\ \text{W}$$

ASSESS Actually, this result is not quite correct. As noted previously, a filament is not a true ohmic material because the resistance changes somewhat with temperature. The filament's resistance at 100 V, where it glows less brightly, is not quite the same as its resistance at 120 V. The voltage in this example is still near 120 V, so the temperature of the filament will decrease only slightly, and our answer should be fairly accurate. However, this calculation would not give a good result for the power dissipation at 20 V, where the filament's temperature would be much less than at 120 V.

EXAMPLE 8.11   Determining the voltage of a stereo

Most stereo speakers are designed to have a resistance of 8.0 Ω. If an 8.0 Ω speaker is connected to a stereo amplifier with a rating of 100 W, what is the maximum possible potential difference the amplifier can apply to the speakers?

PREPARE The rating of an amplifier is the *maximum* power it can deliver. Most of the time it delivers far less, but the maximum might be needed for brief, intense sounds. The maximum potential difference will occur when the amplifier is providing the maximum power, so we will make our computation with this figure. We can model the speaker as a resistor.

SOLVE The maximum potential difference occurs when the power is a maximum. At the maximum power of 100 W,

$$P_R = 100\ \text{W} = \frac{(\Delta V_R)^2}{R} = \frac{(\Delta V_R)^2}{8.0\ \Omega}$$

$$\Delta V_R = \sqrt{(8.0\ \Omega)(100\ \text{W})} = 28\ \text{V}$$

This is the maximum potential difference the amplifier might provide.

ASSESS As a check on our result, we note that the resistance of the speaker is less than that of a lightbulb, so a smaller potential difference can provide 100 W of power. The amplifier works like a battery—it is an emf, providing energy to the speaker. Some of the amplifier's energy is transformed to sound energy, but most is simply dissipated as thermal energy because of the resistance of the wires in the speaker.

STOP TO THINK 8.6   Rank in order, from largest to smallest, the powers P_A to P_D dissipated in resistors A to D.

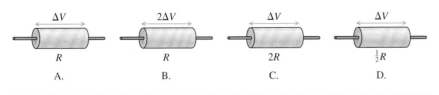

SUMMARY

The goal of Chapter 8 has been to learn how and why charge moves through a conductor as a current.

GENERAL PRINCIPLES

Current

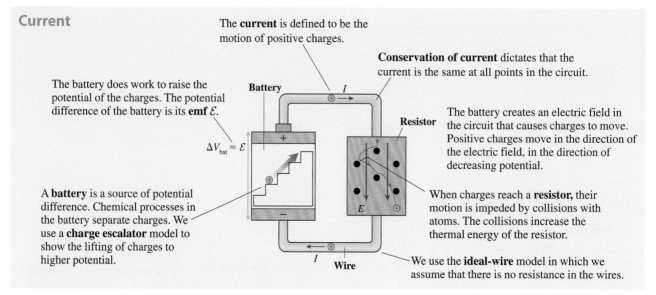

The **current** is defined to be the motion of positive charges.

The battery does work to raise the potential of the charges. The potential difference of the battery is its **emf** $\mathcal{E}$.

$$\Delta V_{bat} = \mathcal{E}$$

A **battery** is a source of potential difference. Chemical processes in the battery separate charges. We use a **charge escalator** model to show the lifting of charges to higher potential.

Conservation of current dictates that the current is the same at all points in the circuit.

The battery creates an electric field in the circuit that causes charges to move. Positive charges move in the direction of the electric field, in the direction of decreasing potential.

When charges reach a **resistor,** their motion is impeded by collisions with atoms. The collisions increase the thermal energy of the resistor.

We use the **ideal-wire** model in which we assume that there is no resistance in the wires.

IMPORTANT CONCEPTS

Resistance, resistivity, and Ohm's law

The **resistivity** ρ is a property of a material, a measure of how good a conductor the material is.

- Good conductors have low resistivity.
- Poor conductors have high resistivity.

The **resistance** is a property of a particular wire or conductor. The resistance of a wire depends on its resistivity and dimensions.

$$R = \frac{\rho L}{A}$$

Cross-section area A — Length L

Ohm's law describes the relationship between potential difference and current in a resistor.

$$I = \frac{\Delta V}{R}$$

Energy and power

The energy used by a circuit is supplied by the emf of the battery through a series of energy transformations:

$$E_{chem} \rightarrow U_{elec} \rightarrow K \rightarrow E_{th}$$

Chemical energy in the battery	Potential energy of separated charges	Kinetic energy of moving charges	Thermal energy of atoms in the resistor

The battery *supplies* power at the rate

$$P = I\mathcal{E}$$

The resistor *dissipates* power at the rate

$$P = I\,\Delta V_R = I^2 R = \frac{(\Delta V_R)^2}{R}$$

APPLICATIONS

Conducting materials

When a potential difference is applied to a wire, if the relationship between potential difference and current is linear, the material is **ohmic.**

The resistance is

$$R = \frac{1}{slope}$$

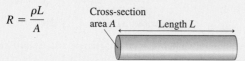

Resistors are made of ohmic materials and have a well-defined value of resistance.

$$R = \frac{\Delta V}{I}$$

If the variation is not linear, the material is **nonohmic.**

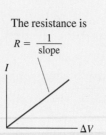

218

QUESTIONS

Conceptual Questions

1. Two wires connect a lightbulb to a battery, completing a circuit and causing the bulb to glow. Do the simple observations and measurements that you can make on this circuit prove that something is *flowing* through the wires? If so, state the observations and/or measurements that are relevant and the steps by which you can then infer that something must be flowing. If not, can you offer an alternative hypothesis about why the bulb glows that is at least plausible and that could be tested?

2. Two wires connect a lightbulb to a battery, completing a circuit and causing the bulb to glow. Are the simple observations and measurements you can make on this circuit able to distinguish a current composed of positive charge carriers from a current composed of negative charge carriers? If so, describe how you can tell which it is. If not, why not?

3. Are the charge carriers in a current always electrons? If so, why is this the case? If not, describe a situation in which a current is due to some other charge carrier.

4. What *causes* electrons to move through a wire as a current?

5. A lightbulb is connected to a battery by two copper wires of equal lengths but different thicknesses. A thick wire connects one side of the lightbulb to the positive terminal of the battery and a thin wire connects the other side of the bulb to the negative terminal.
   a. Which wire carries a greater current? Or is the current the same in both? Explain.
   b. If the two wires are switched, will the bulb get brighter, dimmer, or stay the same? Explain.

6. All wires in Figure Q8.6 are made of the same material and have the same diameter. Rank in order, from largest to smallest, the currents I_1 to I_4. Explain.

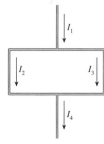

FIGURE Q8.6

7. A wire carries a 4 A current. What is the current in a second wire that delivers twice as much charge in half the time?

8. Metal 1 and metal 2 are each formed into 1-mm-diameter wires. The electric field needed to cause a 1 A current in metal 1 is larger than the electric field needed to cause a 1 A current in metal 2. Which metal has the larger resistivity? Explain.

9. A continuous metal wire connects the two ends of a 3 V battery with a rectangular loop, as shown in Figure Q8.9. The negative terminal of the battery has been chosen as the point where $V = 0$ V.
   a. Redraw this figure on your paper. Then locate and label the approximate points along the wire where $V = 3$ V, $V = 2$ V, and $V = 1$ V.
   b. Estimate the value of ΔV_{14}, the potential difference between points 1 and 4. Explain how you did so.
   c. In moving through the *wire* from point 2 to point 3, does the potential increase, decrease, or not change? If the potential changes, by how much?
   d. In moving through the *battery* from point 2 to point 3, does the potential increase, decrease, or not change? If the potential changes, by how much?
   e. In moving all the way around the loop in a clockwise direction, starting from point 2 and ending at point 2, is the net change in the potential positive, negative, or zero?

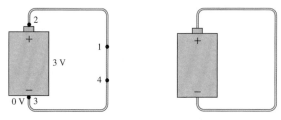

FIGURE Q8.9   **FIGURE Q8.10**

10. a. Which direction—clockwise or counterclockwise—does an electron travel through the wire in Figure Q8.10? Explain.
    b. Does an electron's electric potential energy increase, decrease, or stay the same as it moves through the wire? Explain.
    c. If you answered "decrease" in part b, where does the energy go? If you answered "increase" in part b, where does the energy come from?
    d. Which way—up or down—does an electron move through the *battery?* Explain.
    e. Does an electron's electric potential energy increase, decrease, or stay the same as it moves through the battery? Explain.
    f. If you answered "decrease" in part e, where does the energy go? If you answered "increase" in part e, where does the energy come from?

11. The wires in Figure Q8.11 are all made of the same material. Rank in order, from largest to smallest, the resistances R_1 to R_5 of these wires. Explain.

FIGURE Q8.11

12. The two circuits in Figure Q8.12 use identical batteries and wires of equal diameters. Rank in order, from largest to smallest, the currents I_1, I_2, I_3, and I_4 at points 1 to 4.

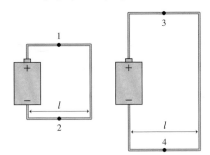

FIGURE Q8.12

13. The two circuits in Figure Q8.13 use identical batteries and wires of equal diameters. Rank in order, from largest to smallest, the currents I_1 to I_7 at points 1 to 7. Explain.

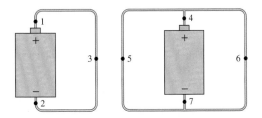

FIGURE Q8.13

14. Which, if any, of these statements are true? (More than one may be true.) Explain your choice or choices.
    a. A battery supplies the energy to a circuit.
    b. A battery is a source of potential difference. The potential difference between the terminals of the battery is always the same.
    c. A battery is a source of current. The current leaving the battery is always the same.

15. Rank in order, from largest to smallest, the currents I_1 to I_4 through the four resistors in Figure Q8.15. Explain.

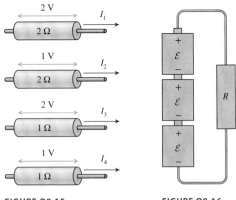

FIGURE Q8.15   **FIGURE Q8.16**

16. The circuit in Figure Q8.16 has three batteries of emf $\mathcal{E}$ in series. Assuming the wires are ideal, sketch a graph of the potential as a function of distance traveled around the circuit, starting from $V = 0$ V at the negative terminal of the bottom battery. Note all important points on your graph.

17. Is a superconducting wire an ideal wire? Explain.

18. When lightning strikes the ground, it generates a large electric field along the surface of the ground directed toward the point of the strike. People near a lightning strike are often injured not by the lightning itself but by a large current that flows up one leg and down the other due to this electric field. To minimize this possibility, you are advised to stand with your feet close together if you are trapped outside during a lightning storm. Explain why this is beneficial.
    Hint: The current path through your body, up one leg and down the other, has a certain resistance. The larger the current along this path, the greater the damage.

19. One way to find out if a wire has corroded is to measure its resistance. Explain why the resistance of a wire increases if it becomes corroded.

20. Rank in order, from largest to smallest, the powers P_1 to P_4 dissipated by the four resistors in Figure Q8.20.

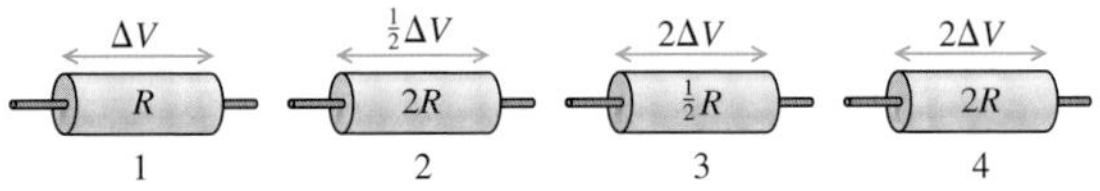

$$\xleftarrow{\Delta V} \boxed{R}_1 \quad \xleftarrow{\frac{1}{2}\Delta V} \boxed{2R}_2 \quad \xleftarrow{2\Delta V} \boxed{\frac{1}{2}R}_3 \quad \xleftarrow{2\Delta V} \boxed{2R}_4$$

FIGURE Q8.20

21. We can model the rear window defroster in a car as a resistor that is connected to the car's 12 V battery. The defroster is made of a material whose resistance increases rapidly as the temperature increases. When the defroster is cold, its resistance is low; when the defroster is warm, its resistance is high. Why is it better to make a defroster with a material like this than with a material whose resistance is independent of temperature? Think about how the resistance, the current, and the power will change as the window warms.

Multiple-Choice Questions

22. | Lightbulbs are typically rated by their power dissipation when operated at a given voltage. Which of the following lightbulbs has the largest current through it when operated at the voltage for which it's rated?
    A. 0.8 W, 1.5 V
    B. 6 W, 3 V
    C. 4 W, 4.5 V
    D. 8 W, 6 V

23. ||| Lightbulbs are typically rated by their power dissipation when operated at a given voltage. Which of the following lightbulbs has the largest resistance when operated at the voltage for which it's rated?
    A. 0.8 W, 1.5 V
    B. 6 W, 3 V
    C. 4 W, 4.5 V
    D. 8 W, 6 V

24. | A copper wire is stretched so that its length increases and its diameter decreases. As a result,
    A. The wire's resistance decreases, but its resistivity stays the same.
    B. The wire's resistivity decreases, but its resistance stays the same.
    C. The wire's resistance increases, but its resistivity stays the same.
    D. The wire's resistivity increases, but its resistance stays the same.

25. | The potential difference across a length of wire is increased. Which of the following does *not* increase as well?
    A. The electric field in the wire.
    B. The power dissipated in the wire.
    C. The resistance of the wire.
    D. The current in the wire.
26. ||| A stereo amplifier creates a 5.0 V potential difference across a speaker. To double the power dissipation of the speaker, the amplifier's potential difference must be increased to
    A. 7.1 V   B. 10 V   C. 14 V   D. 25 V

27. ||| If a 1.5 V battery stores 5.0 kJ of energy, for how many minutes could it sustain a current of 1.2 A?
    A. 2.7   B. 6.9   C. 9.0   D. 46
28. | Figure Q8.28 shows a side view of a wire of varying circular cross section. Rank in order the currents flowing in the three sections.

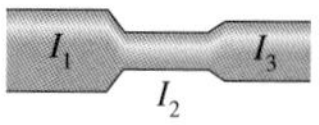

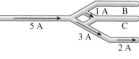

FIGURE Q8.28

    A. $I_1 > I_2 > I_3$ B. $I_2 > I_3 > I_1$
    C. $I_1 = I_2 = I_3$ D. $I_1 > I_3 > I_2$

PROBLEMS

Section 8.1 A Model of Current

Section 8.2 Defining and Describing Current

1. || The current in an electric hair dryer is 10 A. How much charge and how many electrons flow through the hair dryer in 5.0 min?
2. || 2.0×10^{13} electrons flow through a transistor in 1.0 ms. What is the current through the transistor?
3. | A wire carries a 1.0 A current for 30 s. How many electrons move past a point in the wire?
4. | A wire carries a 15 μA current. How many electrons pass a given point on the wire in 1.0 s?
5. | The moving belt on a Van de Graaff generator carries charges to the dome on the top at a constant rate. After 30 s, the dome has accumulated a charge of 5.0 μC. What is the current carried by the belt to the dome?
6. | In a typical lightning strike, 2.5 C flows from cloud to ground in 0.20 ms. What is the current during the strike?
7. || A capacitor is charged to 6.0×10^{-4} C, then discharged by connecting a wire between the two plates. 40 μs after the discharge begins, the capacitor still holds 13% of its original charge. What was the average current during the first 40 μs of the discharge?
8. | In an ionic solution, 5.0×10^{15} positive ions with charge $+2e$ pass to the right each second while 6.0×10^{15} negative ions with charge $-e$ pass to the left. What are the magnitude and direction of current in the solution?
9. | The starter motor of a car engine draws a current of 150 A from the battery. The copper wire to the motor is 5.0 mm in diameter and 1.2 m long. The starter motor runs for 0.80 s until the car engine starts. How much charge passes through the starter motor?
10. | A car battery is rated at 90 A · hr, meaning that it can supply a 90 A current for 1 hr before being completely discharged. If you leave your headlights on until the battery is completely dead, how much charge leaves the positive terminal of the battery?
11. || What are the values of currents I_B and I_C in Figure P8.11? The directions are as noted.

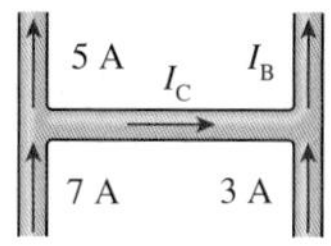

FIGURE P8.11

12. | The currents through several segments of a wire object are shown in Figure P8.12. What are the magnitudes and directions of the currents I_B and I_C in segments B and C?

FIGURE P8.12

Section 8.3 Batteries and EMF

13. | A battery supplies a steady 1.5 A current to a circuit. If the charges moving in the battery are positive ions with charge e, how many ions per second are transported from the negative terminal to the positive terminal?
14. | How much work is done to move 1.0 μC of charge from the negative terminal to the positive terminal of a 1.5 V battery?
15. | What is the emf of a battery that does 0.60 J of work to transfer 0.050 C of charge from the negative to the positive terminal?
16. || A 9.0 V battery supplies a 2.5 mA current to a circuit for 5.0 hr.
    a. How much charge has been transferred from the negative to the positive terminal?
    b. How much work has been done on the charges that passed through the battery?
17. | An individual hydrogen-oxygen fuel cell has an output of 0.75 V. How many cells must be connected to drive a 24.0 V motor?

Section 8.4 Connecting Potential and Current

18. | A wire with resistance R is connected to the terminals of a 6.0 V battery. What is the potential difference ΔV_{ends} between the ends of the wire and the current I through it if the wire has the following resistances? (a) 1.0 Ω (b) 2.0 Ω (c) 3.0 Ω.
19. | Wires 1 and 2 are made of the same metal. Wire 2 has twice the length and twice the diameter of wire 1. What are the ratios (a) ρ_2/ρ_1 of the resistivities and (b) R_2/R_1 of the resistances of the two wires?
20. ||| A wire has a resistance of 0.010 Ω. What will be the wire's resistance if it is stretched to twice its original length without changing the volume of the wire?
21. || What is the resistance of
    a. A 1.0-m-long copper wire that is 0.50 mm in diameter?
    b. A 10-cm-long piece of iron with a 1.0 mm $\times$ 1.0 mm square cross section?
22. | A 10-m-long wire with a diameter of 0.80 mm has a resistance of 1.1 Ω. Of what material is the wire likely made?

23. | The femoral artery is the large artery that carries blood to
BIO the leg. A person's femoral artery has an inner diameter of
1.0 cm. What is the resistance of a 20-cm-long column of
blood in this artery?

24. ||| A 3.0 V potential difference is applied between the ends of
a 0.80-mm-diameter, 50-cm-long nichrome wire. What is the
current in the wire?

25. || A 1.0-mm-diameter, 20-cm-long copper wire carries a
3.0 A current. What is the potential difference between the
ends of the wire?

26. | a. How long must a 0.60-mm-diameter copper wire be to
carry a 0.50 A current when connected to the terminals
of a 1.5 V flashlight battery?
b. What is the current if the wire is half this length?

27. || The terminals of a 0.70 V watch battery are connected by a
100-m-long copper wire with a diameter of 0.10 mm. What is
the current in the wire?

Section 8.5 Resistors and Ohm's Law

28. | Figure P8.28 is a current-versus-potential-difference graph
for a cylinder. What is the cylinder's resistance?

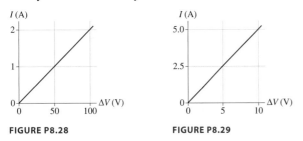

FIGURE P8.28   **FIGURE P8.29**

29. | Figure Q8.29 shows the current-versus-potential-dif-
ference graph for a resistor.
a. What is the resistance of this resistor?
b. Suppose the length of the resistor is doubled while keeping
its cross section the same. (This requires doubling the
amount of material the resistor is made of.) Copy the figure and add to it the current-versus-potential-difference
graph for the longer resistor.

30. | The electric field inside a 30-cm-long copper wire is
0.010 V/m. What is the potential difference between the ends
of the wire?

31. | In Example 8.4 the length of a 60 W, 240 Ω lightbulb fila-
ment was calculated to be 60 cm.
a. If the potential difference across the filament is 120 V,
what is the strength of the electric field inside the filament?
b. Suppose the length of the bulb's filament were doubled
without changing its diameter or the potential difference
across it. What would the electric field strength be in this
case?
c. Remembering that the current in the filament is proportional to the electric field, what is the current in the filament following the doubling of its length?
d. What is the resistance of the filament following the doubling of its length?

Section 8.6 Energy and Power

32. | a. What is the resistance of a 1500 W (120 V) hair dryer?
b. What is the current in the hair dryer when it is used?

33. || You've brought your 1000 W (120 V) hair dryer on vaca-
tion to Europe, where the standard outlet voltages are 220 V.
Assuming the hair dryer can operate safely at the higher voltage, can you actually use it if the outlet is rated at 15 A, or will
it draw more current than this?

34. | A 60-cm-long heating wire is connected to a 120 V outlet.
If the wire dissipates 45 W, what are (a) the current in and
(b) the resistance of the wire?

35. || The total charge a household battery can supply is given in
units of mA · hr. For example, a 9.0 V alkaline battery is rated
450 mA · hr, meaning that such a battery could supply a 1 mA
current for 450 hr, a 2 mA current for 225 hr, etc. How much
energy, in joules, is this battery capable of supplying?

General Problems

36. | A 3.0 V battery powers a flashlight bulb that has a resis-
tance of 6.0 Ω. How much charge moves through the battery
in 10 min?

37. || A sculptor has asked you to help electroplate gold onto a
brass statue. You know that the charge carriers in the ionic
solution are monovalent (charge e) gold ions, and you've calculated that you must deposit 0.50 g of gold to reach the necessary thickness. How much current do you need, in mA, to
plate the statue in 3.0 hr?

38. |||| For a science experiment you need to electroplate a
INT 100-nm-thick zinc coating onto both sides of a very thin,
2.0 cm × 2.0 cm copper sheet. You know that the charge carriers in the ionic solution are divalent (charge $2e$) zinc ions.
The density of zinc is 7140 kg/m^3. If the electroplating apparatus operates at 1.0 mA, how long will it take the zinc to
reach the desired thickness?

39. || The hot dog cooker described in the chapter heats hot dogs
INT by connecting them to 120 V household electricity. A typical
hot dog has a mass of 60 g and a resistance of 150 Ω. How
long will it take for the cooker to raise the temperature of the
hot dog from 20°C to 80°C? The specific heat of a hot dog is
approximately 2500 J/kg · K.

40. | The biochemistry that takes place inside cells depends on
BIO various elements, such as sodium, potassium, and calcium,
that are dissolved in water as ions. These ions enter cells
through narrow pores in the cell membrane known as *ion
channels*. Each ion channel, which is formed from a specialized protein molecule, is selective for one type of ion.
Measurements with microelectrodes have shown that a
0.30-nm-diameter potassium ion (K$^+$) channel carries a current of 1.8 pA. How many potassium ions pass through if
the ion channel opens for 1.0 ms?

41. | High-resolution measurements have shown that an ion
BIO channel (see Problem 40) is a 0.30-nm-diameter cylinder with
length of 5.0 nm. The intracellular fluid filling the ion channel
has resistivity 0.60 Ω · m. What is the resistance of the ion
channel?

42. | When an ion channel opens in a cell wall (see Problem 40),
BIO monovalent (charge e) ions flow through the channel at a rate
of 1.0×10^7 ions/s.
a. What is the current through the channel?
b. The potential difference across the ion channel is 70 mV.
What is the power dissipation in the channel?

43. ‖ The total charge a battery can supply is rated in mA · hr. For instance, a battery rated at 1000 mA · hr could supply a 1000 mA current for 1.0 hr, a 500 mA current for 2.0 hr, etc. A rechargeable 1.2 V battery stores 7800 J of energy when fully charged. What is the mA · hr rating of this battery?

44. | The heating element of a simple heater consists of a 2.0-m-long, 0.60-mm-diameter nichrome wire. When plugged into a 120 V outlet, the heater draws 8.0 A of current when hot.
    a. What is the wire's resistance when it is hot?
    b. Use your answer to part a to calculate the resistivity of nichrome. Why is it not the same as the value of ρ given for nichrome in Table 8.1?

45. | Variations in the resistivity of blood can give valuable clues
BIO to changes in the blood's viscosity and other properties. The resistivity is measured by applying a small potential difference and measuring the current. Suppose a medical device attaches electrodes into a 1.5-mm-diameter vein at two points 5.0 cm apart. What is the blood resistivity if a 9.0 V potential difference causes a 230 μA current through the blood in the vein?

46. | The resistance of a very fine tungsten wire with a 10 μm × 10 μm square cross section is 1000 Ω.
    a. How long is the wire?
    b. A 1000 Ω resistor is made by wrapping this wire in a spiral around a 3.0-mm-diameter glass core. How many turns of wire are needed?

47. ‖ Wires aren't really ideal. The voltage drop across a current-carrying wire can be significant unless the resistance of the wire is quite low. Suppose a 50 ft extension cord is being used to provide power to an electric lawn mower. The cord carries a 10 A current. The copper wire in a typical extension cord has a 1.3 mm diameter. What is the voltage drop across a 50 ft length of wire at this current?

48. ‖ When the starter motor on a car is engaged, there is a 300 A current in the wires between the battery and the motor. Suppose the wires are made of copper and have a total length of 1.0 m. What minimum diameter can the wires have if the voltage drop along the wires is to be less than 0.50 V?

49. | The electron beam inside a television picture tube is
INT 0.40 mm in diameter and carries a current of 50 μA. This electron beam impinges on the inside of the picture tube screen.
    a. How many electrons strike the screen each second?
    b. The electrons move with a velocity of 4.0×10^7 m/s. What electric field strength is needed to accelerate electrons from rest to this velocity in a distance of 5.0 mm?
    c. Each electron transfers its kinetic energy to the picture tube screen upon impact. What is the *power* delivered to the screen by the electron beam?
    Hint: What potential difference produced the field that accelerated electrons? This is an emf.

50. | The two segments of the wire in Figure P8.50 have equal diameters and equal lengths but different resistivities ρ_1 and ρ_2. Current I passes through this wire. If the resistivities have the ratio $\rho_2/\rho_1 = 2$, what is the ratio $\Delta V_1/\Delta V_2$ of the potential differences across the two segments of the wire?

FIGURE P8.50

51. ‖ A 15-cm-long nichrome wire is connected across the terminals of a 1.5 V battery. If the current in the wire is 2.0 A, what is the wire's diameter?

52. | A 1.0-m-long copper wire has a diameter of 0.23 mm. How long would a nichrome wire with 0.50 mm diameter need to be in order to have the same resistance as the copper wire?

53. | A wire is 2.3 m long and has a diameter of 0.38 mm. When connected to a 1.2 V battery, there is a current of 0.61 A. What material is the wire likely made of?

54. ‖ A 20-cm-long hollow nichrome tube of inner diameter 2.8 mm, outer diameter 3.0 mm is connected to a 3.0 V battery. What is the current in the tube?

55. ‖ The filament of a 100 W (120 V) lightbulb is a tungsten wire 0.035 mm in diameter. At the filament's operating temperature, the resistivity is 5.0×10^{-7} Ω · m. How long is the filament?

56. ‖ You've made the finals of the Science Olympics! As one of
INT your tasks, you're given 1.0 g of copper and asked to make a wire, using all the metal, with a resistance of 1.0 Ω. Copper has a density of 8900 kg/m^3. What length and diameter will you choose for your wire?

57. | Not too long ago houses were protected from excessive currents by fuses rather than circuit breakers. Sometimes a fuse blew out and a replacement wasn't at hand. Because a copper penny happens to have almost the same diameter as a fuse, some people replaced the fuse with a penny. Unfortunately, a penny never blows out, no matter how large the current, and the use of pennies in fuse boxes caused many house fires. Make the appropriate measurements on a penny, then calculate the resistance between the two faces of a solid-copper penny.

58. ‖ An immersion heater used to boil water for a single cup of
INT tea plugs into a 120 V outlet and is rated at 300 W.
    a. What is the resistance of the heater?
    b. Suppose your super-size, super-insulated tea mug contains 400 g of water at a temperature of 18°C. How long will this heater take to bring the water to a boil? You can ignore the energy needed to raise the temperature of the mug and the heater itself.

59. ‖ The graph in Figure P8.59 shows the current through a 1.0 Ω resistor as a function of time.
    a. How much charge flowed through the resistor during the 10 s interval shown?
    b. What was the total energy dissipated by the resistor during this time?

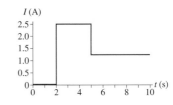

FIGURE P8.59

60. ‖‖‖ A toy car has a mass of 120 g, including two 1.5 V batteries
INT connected in series. Suppose the motor that drives the car is 80% efficient (i.e., 80% of the electric energy goes to the drive wheels, 20% is dissipated as heat) and that friction and air resistance are negligible. How much charge passes through the batteries during the time it takes the car to accelerate from rest to 1.5 m/s?

61. | If you touch the two terminals of a power supply with your
BIO two fingertips on opposite hands, the potential difference will
produce a current through your torso. The maximum safe current is approximately 5 mA.
    a. If your hands are completely dry, the resistance of your
    body from fingertip to fingertip is approximately 500 kΩ.
    If you accidentally touch both terminals of your 120 V
    household electricity supply with dry fingers, will you
    receive a dangerous shock?
    b. If your hands are moist, your resistance drops to approximately 1 kΩ. If you accidentally touch both terminals of
    your 120 V household supply with moist fingers, will you
    receive a dangerous shock?
    c. For the situation of part a, what electric power is dissipated
    in your body? Would you notice the heating?
62. | The average resistivity of the human body (apart from surface resistance of the skin) is about 5.0 Ω · m. The conducting
BIO face resistance of the skin) is about 5.0 Ω · m. The conducting
path between the hands can be approximated as a cylinder
1.6 m long and 0.10 m in diameter. The skin resistance can
be made negligible by soaking the hands in salt water.
    a. What is the resistance between the hands if the skin resistance is negligible?
    b. If skin resistance is negligible, what potential difference
    between the hands is needed for a lethal shock current of
    100 mA? Your result shows that even small potential differences can produce dangerous currents when skin is damp.
    c. What power is dissipated in the body by the current in b?

Passage Problems   Lightbulb Failure

You've probably observed that the most common time for an incandescent lightbulb to fail is the moment when it is turned on. Let's
look at the properties of the bulb's filament to see why this happens.

The current in the tungsten filament of a lightbulb heats the filament until it glows. The filament is so hot that some of the atoms
on its surface fly off and end up sticking on a cooler part of the
bulb. Thus the filament gets progressively thinner as the bulb ages.
There will certainly be one spot on the filament that is a bit thinner
than elsewhere. This thin segment will have a higher resistance
than the surrounding filament. More power will be dissipated at
this spot, so it won't only be a thin spot, it also will be a hot spot.

Now, let's look at the resistance of the filament. The graph in
Figure P8.63 shows data for the current in a lightbulb as a function
of the potential difference
across it. The graph is not linear, so the filament is not an
ohmic material with a constant
resistance. However, we can
define the resistance at any particular voltage ΔV to be $R =
\Delta V/I$. This ratio, and hence the
resistance, increases with ΔV
and thus with temperature.

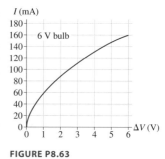

When the bulb is turned on,
the filament is cold and its resistance is much lower than during
normal, high-temperature operation. The low resistance causes a
surge of higher-than-normal current lasting a fraction of a second
until the filament heats up. Because power dissipation is I^2R, the
power dissipated during this first fraction of a second is much
larger than the bulb's rated power. This current surge concentrates
the power dissipation at the high-resistance thin spot, perhaps melting it and breaking the filament.

63. | For the bulb in Figure P8.63, what is the approximate resistance of the bulb at a potential difference of 6.0 V?
    A. 7.0 Ω   B. 17 Ω   C. 27 Ω   D. 37 Ω
64. | As the bulb ages, the resistance of the filament
    A. Increases.   B. Decreases.   C. Stays the same.
65. | Which of the curves in Figure P8.65 best represents the
    expected variation in current as a function of time in the short
    time interval immediately after the bulb is turned on?
66. | There are devices to put in a light socket that control the
    current through a lightbulb, thereby increasing its lifetime.

FIGURE P8.65

Which of the following strategies would increase the lifetime
of a bulb without making it dimmer?
    A. Reducing the average current through the bulb.
    B. Limiting the maximum current through the bulb.
    C. Increasing the average current through the bulb.
    D. Limiting the minimum current through the bulb.

STOP TO THINK ANSWERS

Stop to Think 8.1: C. Current is conserved. The connecting wires
and the wires in the lightbulbs form a single current path.

Stop to Think 8.2: A. From Kirchhoff's junction law the current
through bulb 1 is the sum of the currents through bulbs 2 and 3.

Stop to Think 8.3: C. Charge flows out one terminal of the battery
but back into the other; the amount of charge does not change. The
emf is determined by the chemical reactions in the battery and is
constant. But the chemical energy in the battery steadily decreases
as the battery converts it to the potential energy of charges.

Stop to Think 8.4: $I_A = I_B = I_C = I_D$. The current in each wire is
$I = \Delta V/R$. All the wires have the same resistance, because they are
identical, and they all have the same potential difference, because

the battery is a *source of potential*. Therefore all wires have the
same current. Conservation of current requires $I_A = I_B$.

Stop to Think 8.5: $V_B = V_C > V_A > V_D = V_E$. There's no potential difference along ideal wires, so $V_B = V_C$ and $V_D = V_E$. Potential increases in going from the − to the + terminal of a battery, so
$V_A > V_E$ and $V_B > V_A$. These imply $V_C > V_D$, which was expected
because potential decreases as current passes through a resistor.

Stop to Think 8.6: $P_B > P_D > P_A > P_C$. The power dissipated by
a resistor is $P_R = (\Delta V_R)^2/R$. Increasing R decreases P_R; increasing
ΔV_R increases P_R. But changing the potential has a larger effect
because P_R depends on the square of ΔV_R.

9

CIRCUITS

The electric eel isn't really an eel; it's a fish. But it is electric, producing pulses of up to 600 V that it uses to stun prey. How does the fish produce such a large potential difference?

Looking Ahead ▶▶

The goal of Chapter 9 is to understand the fundamental physical principles that govern electric circuits. In this chapter you will learn to:

▶ Draw and use basic circuit diagrams.

▶ Analyze circuits containing resistors in series and in parallel.

▶ Use Kirchhoff's laws to analyze circuits.

▶ Understand the growth and decay of current and voltage in *RC* circuits.

▶ Develop a model of signal propagation in the nervous system.

Looking Back ◀◀

This chapter will use much of the material of Chapter 8, in which we began looking at current and circuits. The final sections of the chapter will draw on many concepts from earlier chapters. Please review especially:

◀ Section 8.2 Current.

◀ Section 8.4–8.6 Resistors and circuits, energy and power.

Electricity is part of your life. You use a variety of electric devices each day, from lamps to telephones to computers, in which electrical signals process information and deliver energy. But you also use electricity in a more fundamental way. The signals in your body's nervous system are electrical signals, and the same physics that explains the timing of intermittent windshield wipers in your car also explains how signals get from your brain to your muscles. In some animals, such as the electric eel, the cells that produce electrical signals form circuits that create large voltages and currents.

The physics behind the operation of circuits is the physics of charges, forces, and fields—topics we have explored in detail in the previous chapters. This will be a very practical chapter, one in which we apply our knowledge to the analysis of circuits involving batteries, resistors and capacitors. We will look at many practical applications, culminating in a description of electrical conduction in the nervous system, a topic that will bring together many of the concepts we have explored in this part of the book.

9.1 Circuit Elements and Diagrams

In Chapter 8 we analyzed a very simple circuit, a resistor connected to a battery. In this chapter, we will explore more complex circuits involving more and different elements. As was the case with other topics in the book, we will learn a good deal about circuits by making appropriate drawings. We will begin our investigation by developing a system for representing circuits symbolically in a manner that highlights their essential features.

Figure 9.1 shows an electric circuit in which a resistor and a capacitor are connected by wires to a battery. To understand the functioning of this circuit, we do not need to know whether the wires are bent or straight, or whether the battery is to the right or to the left of the resistor. The literal picture of Figure 9.1 provides many irrelevant details. It is customary when describing or analyzing circuits to use a more abstract picture called a **circuit diagram.** A circuit diagram is a *logical* picture of what is connected to what. The actual circuit, once it is built, may *look* quite different from the circuit diagram, but it will have the same logic and connections.

In a circuit diagram we replace pictures of the circuit elements with symbols. Figure 9.2 shows the basic symbols that we will need. Notice that the *longer* line at one end of the battery symbol represents the positive terminal of the battery.

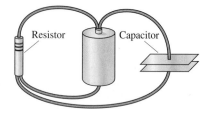

FIGURE 9.1 An electric circuit.

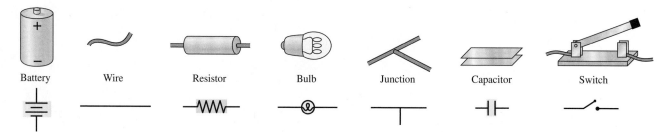

FIGURE 9.2 A library of basic symbols used for electric circuit drawings.

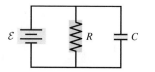

FIGURE 9.3 A circuit diagram for the circuit of Figure 9.1.

Figure 9.3 is a circuit diagram of the circuit shown in Figure 9.1. Notice how circuit elements are labeled. The battery's emf $\mathcal{E}$ is shown beside the battery, and the resistance R of the resistor and capacitance C of the capacitor are written beside them. We would use numerical values for $\mathcal{E}$, R and C if we knew them. The wires, which in practice may bend and curve, are shown as straight-line connections between the circuit elements. The positive potential of the battery is at the top of the diagram; in general, we try to put higher potentials toward the top. You should get into the habit of drawing your own circuit diagrams in a similar fashion.

STOP TO THINK 9.1   Which of these diagrams represent the same circuit?

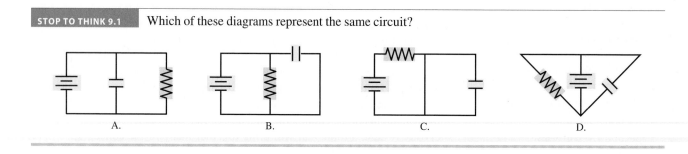

9.2 Kirchhoff's Laws

Once we have a diagram for a circuit, we can analyze it. In this chapter, a full analysis of a circuit means that we find:

1. The potential difference across each circuit component.
2. The current through each circuit component.

Our tools and techniques for analyzing circuits will be based on the physical principles of potential differences and currents.

You learned in Chapter 8 that, as a result of charge and current conservation, the total current into a junction must equal the total current leaving the junction, as in Figure 9.4a This result was called *Kirchhoff's junction law,* which we wrote as follows:

(a)

Junction law: $I_1 = I_2 + I_3$

$$\sum I_{\text{in}} = \sum I_{\text{out}} \tag{9.1}$$

Kirchhoff's junction law

Kirchhoff's junction law is one of the two basic tools of circuit analysis. The second tool deals with electric potential. When we learned about gravitational potential energy in Chapter 5, we saw that the gravitational potential energy of an object depends on its position, not on the path it took to get to that position. The same is true of electric potential energy. If a particle moves around a closed loop and returns to its starting point, there will be no net change in electric potential energy, $\Delta U_{\text{elec}} = 0$. Because $V = U_{\text{elec}}/q$, **the net change in the electric potential around any loop or closed path must be zero** as well.

We can apply this idea to circuits, as shown in Figure 9.4b. If we add all of the potential differences *around* the loop formed by the circuit, the sum of these potential differences must be zero. This result is known as **Kirchhoff's loop law:**

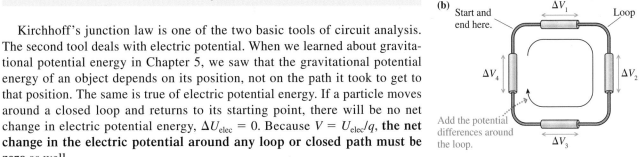

(b)

Loop law: $\Delta V_1 + \Delta V_2 + \Delta V_3 + \Delta V_4 = 0$

FIGURE 9.4 Kirchhoff's laws apply to junctions and loops in circuits.

$$\Delta V_{\text{loop}} = \sum_i \Delta V_i = 0 \tag{9.2}$$

Kirchhoff's loop law

In Equation 9.2, ΔV_i is the potential difference of the ith component in the loop.

Kirchhoff's loop law can be true only if at least one of the potential differences ΔV_i is negative. To apply the loop law, we need to explicitly identify which potential differences are positive and which are negative.

(MP)   TACTICS BOX 9.1 **Using Kirchhoff's loop law**   ✐ Exercises 5, 6

❶ **Draw a circuit diagram.** Label all known and unknown quantities.
❷ **Assign a direction to the current.** Draw and label a current arrow I to show your choice.
   ■ If you know the actual current direction, choose that direction.
   ■ If you don't know the actual current direction, make an educated guess. All that will happen if you choose wrong is that your value for I will end up negative.

Continued

❸ **"Travel" around the loop.** Start at any point in the circuit, then go all the way around the loop in the direction you assigned to the current in step 2. As you go through each circuit element, ΔV is interpreted to mean

$$\Delta V = V_{\text{downstream}} - V_{\text{upstream}}$$

■ For a battery with current in the negative-to-positive direction:

$$\Delta V_{\text{bat}} = +\mathcal{E}$$

■ For a battery in the positive-to-negative direction (i.e., the current is going into the positive terminal of the battery):

$$\Delta V_{\text{bat}} = -\mathcal{E}$$

■ For a resistor:

$$\Delta V_R = -IR$$

❹ **Apply the loop law:**

$$\sum \Delta V_i = 0$$

ΔV_{bat} can be positive or negative for a battery, but ΔV_R for a resistor is always negative because the potential in a resistor *decreases* along the direction of the current—charge flows "downhill," as we saw in Chapter 8. Because the potential across a resistor always decreases, we often speak of the *voltage drop* across the resistor.

NOTE ▶ The equation for ΔV_R in Tactics Box 9.1 seems to be the opposite of Ohm's law, but Ohm's law was only concerned with the *magnitude* of the potential difference. Kirchhoff's law requires us to recognize that the electric potential inside a resistor *decreases* in the direction of the current. ◀

The most basic electric circuit is that of a single resistor connected to the two terminals of a battery, as in Figure 9.5. We considered this circuit in Chapter 8, but let's now apply Kirchhoff's laws to its analysis.

This circuit of Figure 9.5 has no junctions, so the current is the same in all parts of the circuit. Kirchhoff's junction law is not needed. Kirchhoff's loop law is the tool we need to analyze this circuit, and Figure 9.6 shows the first three steps of Tactics Box 9.1. Notice that we're assuming the ideal-wire model in which there are no potential differences along the connecting wire. The fourth step is to apply Kirchhoff's loop law, $\sum \Delta V_i = 0$:

$$\Delta V_{\text{loop}} = \sum_i \Delta V_i = \Delta V_{\text{bat}} + \Delta V_R = 0 \tag{9.3}$$

Let's look at each of the two terms in Equation 9.3:

1. The potential *increases* as we travel through the battery on our clockwise journey around the loop, as we see in the conventions in Tactics Box 9.1. We enter the negative terminal and, farther downstream, exit the positive terminal after having gained potential $\mathcal{E}$. Thus

$$\Delta V_{\text{bat}} = +\mathcal{E}$$

2. The *magnitude* of the potential difference across the resistor is $\Delta V = IR$, but Ohm's law does not tell us whether this should be positive or negative—and the difference is crucial. The potential of a resistor *decreases*

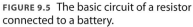
❶ Draw circuit diagram.

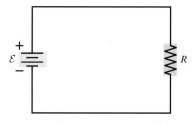
❷ The orientation of the battery indicates a clockwise current, so assign a clockwise direction to I.

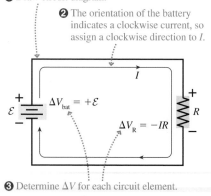

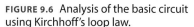
❸ Determine ΔV for each circuit element.

FIGURE 9.6 Analysis of the basic circuit using Kirchhoff's loop law.

FIGURE 9.5 The basic circuit of a resistor connected to a battery.

in the direction of the current, which we've indicated with the + and − signs in Figure 9.6. Thus

$$\Delta V_R = -IR$$

NOTE ▶ Determining which potential differences are positive and which negative is perhaps the most important step in circuit analysis. ◀

With this information about ΔV_{bat} and ΔV_R, the loop equation becomes

$$\mathcal{E} - IR = 0 \tag{9.4}$$

We can solve the loop equation to find that the current in the circuit is

$$I = \frac{\mathcal{E}}{R} \tag{9.5}$$

This is exactly the result we saw in the previous chapter. Notice again that the current in the circuit depends on the size of the resistance. The emf of a battery is a fixed quantity; the current that the battery delivers depends jointly on the emf and on the resistance.

EXAMPLE 9.1 Analyzing a circuit with two batteries

What is the current in the circuit of Figure 9.7? What is the potential difference across each resistor?

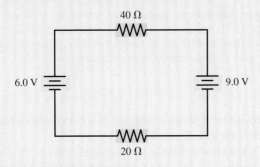

FIGURE 9.7 Circuit for Example 9.1.

PREPARE We will solve this circuit using Kirchhoff's loop law, as outlined in Tactics Box 9.1. But how do we deal with *two* batteries? What happens when charge flows "backward" through a battery, from positive to negative? Consider the charge-escalator analogy. Left to itself, a charge escalator lifts charge from lower to higher potential. But it *is* possible to run down an up escalator, as many of you have probably done. If two escalators are placed "head to head," whichever is "stronger" will, indeed, force the charge to run down the up

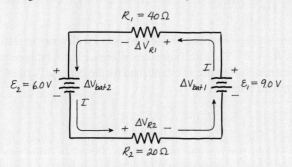

FIGURE 9.8 Analyzing the circuit of Example 9.1.

escalator of the other battery. The current in a battery *can* be from positive to negative if driven in that direction by a larger emf from a second battery. Indeed, this is how batteries are "recharged," as we saw in Chapter 8. The current goes in the direction that the larger emf—the 9.0 V battery—"wants" it to go. We have redrawn the circuit in Figure 9.8, showing the direction of the current and the direction of the potential difference for each circuit element.

SOLVE Kirchhoff's loop law requires us to add the potential differences as we travel around the circuit in the direction of the current. Let's do this starting at the negative terminal of the 9.0 V battery:

$$\sum_i \Delta V_i = +9.0 \text{ V} - I(40\ \Omega) - 6.0 \text{ V} - I(20\ \Omega) = 0$$

The 6.0 V battery has $\Delta V_{bat} = -\mathcal{E}$, in accord with Tactics Box 9.1, because the potential decreases as we travel through this battery in the positive-to-negative direction. We can solve this equation for the current:

$$I = \frac{3.0 \text{ V}}{60\ \Omega} = 0.050 \text{ A} = 50 \text{ mA}$$

Now that the current is known, we can use Ohm's $\Delta V = IR$ law to find the potential difference across each resistor. For the 40 Ω resistor

$$\Delta V_1 = (0.050 \text{ A})(40\ \Omega) = 2.0 \text{ V}$$

and for the 20 Ω resistor

$$\Delta V_2 = (0.050 \text{ A})(20\ \Omega) = 1.0 \text{ V}$$

ASSESS Let's look at the loop law again as a check on our result. As a charge travels around the circuit, the potential increases by 9.0 V in the first battery, then decreases by 2.0 V in the first resistor, decreases by 6.0 V in the second battery, and decreases by 1.0 V in the second resistor. The total decrease is 9.0 V, so the charge returns to its starting potential, as it must.

9.3 Series and Parallel Circuits

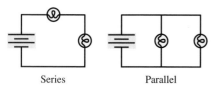

FIGURE 9.9 Series and parallel circuits.

Example 9.1 involved a circuit with multiple elements—two batteries and two resistors. As we introduce more circuit elements, we have possibilities for different types of connections. Suppose you use a single battery to light two lightbulbs. There are two possible ways that you can connect the circuit, as shown in Figure 9.9. These *series* and *parallel* circuits have very different properties. We will consider these two cases in turn.

We say two bulbs are connected in **series** if they are connected directly to each other with no junction in between. All series circuits share certain characteristics, as we will see.

CONCEPTUAL EXAMPLE 9.1 **Brightness of bulbs in series**

Figure 9.10 shows two identical lightbulbs connected in series. Which bulb is brighter, A or B? Or are they equally bright?

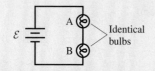

FIGURE 9.10 Two bulbs in series.

REASON Current is conserved, and there are no junctions in the circuit. Thus the current is the same at all points, as we see in Figure 9.11.

We learned in Chapter 8 that the power dissipated by a resistor is $P = I^2R$. If the two bulbs are identical (i.e., the same resistance) and have the same current through them, the power

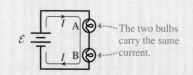

FIGURE 9.11 The current in the series circuit of Conceptual Example 9.1.

dissipated by each bulb is the same. This means that the brightness of the bulbs must be the same. The voltage across each of the bulbs will be the same as well, as $\Delta V = IR$.

ASSESS It's perhaps tempting to think that bulb A will be brighter than bulb B, thinking that something is "used up" before the current gets to bulb B. It is true that *energy* is being transformed in each bulb, but current must be conserved and so both bulbs dissipate energy at the same rate.

Series Resistors

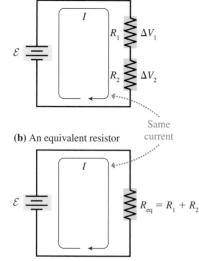

(a) Two resistors in series

(b) An equivalent resistor

Same current

FIGURE 9.12 Replacing two series resistors with an equivalent resistor.

Figure 9.12a shows two resistors in series connected to a battery. Because there are no junctions, the current I must be the same in both resistors.

We can use Kirchhoff's loop law to look at the potential differences. Starting at the battery's negative terminal and following the current clockwise around the circuit, we find:

$$\sum_i \Delta V_i = \mathcal{E} + \Delta V_1 + \Delta V_2 = 0 \tag{9.6}$$

The voltage drops across the two resistors, in the direction of the current, are $\Delta V_1 = -IR_1$ and $\Delta V_2 = -IR_2$, so we can use Equation 9.6 to find the current in the circuit:

$$\mathcal{E} = -\Delta V_1 - \Delta V_2 = IR_1 + IR_2$$
$$I = \frac{\mathcal{E}}{R_1 + R_2} \tag{9.7}$$

Suppose, as in Figure 9.12b, we replace the two resistors with a single resistor having the value $R_{eq} = R_1 + R_2$. The total potential difference across this resistor is still $\mathcal{E}$ because the potential difference is established by the battery. Further, the current in this single-resistor circuit is

$$I = \frac{\mathcal{E}}{R_{eq}} = \frac{\mathcal{E}}{R_1 + R_2}$$

which is the same as it had been in the two-resistor circuit. In other words, this single resistor is *equivalent* to the two series resistors in the sense that the circuit's current and potential difference are unchanged. Nothing anywhere else in the circuit would differ if we took out resistors R_1 and R_2 and replaced them with resistor R_{eq}.

We can extend this analysis to a case with more resistors. If we have N resistors in series, their **equivalent resistance** is the sum of the N individual resistances:

$$R_{eq} = R_1 + R_2 + \cdots + R_N \qquad (9.8)$$

Equivalent resistance of N series resistors

The behavior of the circuit will be unchanged if the N series resistors are replaced by the single resistor R_{eq}.

EXAMPLE 9.2 Analyzing a series resistor circuit

What is the current in the circuit of Figure 9.13?

PREPARE The three resistors are in series, so we can replace them with a single equivalent resistor as shown in Figure 9.14.

SOLVE The equivalent resistance is calculated using Equation 9.8:

$$R_{eq} = 25\ \Omega + 31\ \Omega + 19\ \Omega = 75\ \Omega$$

The current in the equivalent circuit of Figure 9.14 is:

$$I = \frac{\mathcal{E}}{R_{eq}} = \frac{9.0\ \text{V}}{75\ \Omega} = 0.12\ \text{A}$$

This is also the current in the original circuit.

ASSESS The current in the circuit is the same whether there are three resistors or a single equivalent resistor. The equivalent resistance is the sum of the individual resistance values, and so it is always greater than any of the individual values. This is a good check on your work.

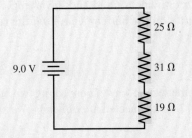

FIGURE 9.13 Circuit for Example 9.2.

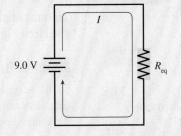

FIGURE 9.14 Analyzing a circuit with series resistors.

EXAMPLE 9.3 Potential difference of Christmas-tree minilights

A string of Christmas-tree minilights consists of 50 bulbs wired in series. What is the potential difference across each bulb when the string is plugged into a 120 V outlet?

PREPARE Figure 9.15 shows the minilight circuit, which has 50 bulbs in series. The current in each of the bulbs is the same because they are in series.

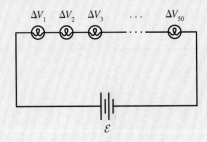

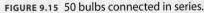

FIGURE 9.15 50 bulbs connected in series.

SOLVE Applying Kirchhoff's loop law around the circuit, we find:

$$\mathcal{E} = \Delta V_1 + \Delta V_2 + \cdots + \Delta V_{50}$$

The bulbs are all identical and, because the current in the bulbs is the same, all of the bulbs have the same potential difference. The potential difference across a single bulb is thus

$$\Delta V_1 = \frac{\mathcal{E}}{50} = \frac{120\ \text{V}}{50} = 2.4\ \text{V}$$

ASSESS Minilights are wired in series because the wiring is simpler and the bulbs can be inexpensive low-voltage bulbs. But there is a drawback that is true of all series circuits: If one bulb is removed, there is no longer a complete circuit, and there will be no current. Indeed, if you remove a bulb from a string of minilights, the entire string will go dark.

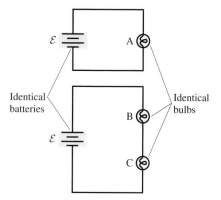

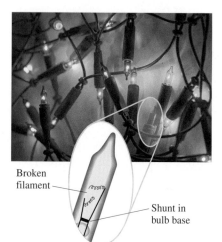

FIGURE 9.16 How does the brightness of bulb B compare to that of bulb A?

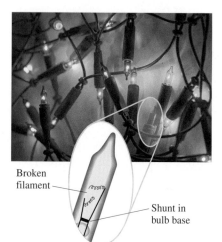

Broken filament

Shunt in bulb base

A seasonal series circuit puzzle
Christmas-tree minilights are connected in series. This is easy to verify: When you remove one bulb from a string of lights, the circuit is not complete, and the entire string of lights goes out. But when one bulb *burns* out, meaning its filament has broken, the string of lights stays lit. How is this possible? The secret is a *shunt* in the base of the bulb. Initially, the shunt is a good insulator. But if the filament breaks, the shunt is activated, and its resistance drops. The shunt can now carry the current, so the other bulbs will stay lit.

Let's use our knowledge of series circuits to look at another lightbulb puzzle. Figure 9.16 shows two different circuits, one with one battery and one lightbulb and a second with one battery and two lightbulbs. All of the batteries and bulbs are identical. You now know that B and C, which are connected in series, are equally bright, but how does the brightness of B compare to that of A?

Suppose the resistance of each identical lightbulb is R. In the first circuit, the battery drives current $I_A = \mathcal{E}/R$ through bulb A. In the second circuit, bulbs B and C are in series, with an equivalent resistance $R_{eq} = R_A + R_B = 2R$, but the battery has the same emf $\mathcal{E}$. Thus the current through bulbs B and C is $I_{B+C} = \mathcal{E}/R_{eq} = \mathcal{E}/2R = \frac{1}{2}I_A$. Bulb B has only half the current of bulb A, so B is dimmer.

Many people predict that A and B should be equally bright. It's the same battery, so shouldn't it provide the same current to both circuits? No! **A battery is a source of potential difference, *not* a source of current.** In other words, the battery's emf is the same no matter how the battery is used. When you buy a 1.5 V battery you're buying a device that provides a specified amount of potential difference, not a specified amount of current. The battery does provide the current to the circuit, but the *amount* of current depends on the resistance. Your 1.5 V battery causes 1 A to pass through a 1.5 Ω resistor but only 0.1 A to pass through a 15 Ω resistor.

As an analogy, think about a water faucet. The pressure in the water main underneath the street is a fixed quantity set by the water company. It's like the emf of a battery. But the amount of water coming out of a faucet depends on how far you open it. A faucet opened slightly has a "high resistance," so only a little water flows. A wide-open faucet has a "low resistance," and the water flow is large.

This is a critical idea for understanding circuits. A battery provides a fixed emf (potential difference). It does *not* provide a fixed and unvarying current. **The amount of current depends jointly on the battery's emf *and* the resistance of the circuit attached to the battery.**

Parallel Resistors

In the next example, we consider the second way of connecting two bulbs in a circuit. The two bulbs in Figure 9.17 are connected at *both* ends. We say that they are connected in **parallel.**

CONCEPTUAL EXAMPLE 9.2 Brightness of bulbs in parallel
Which lightbulb in the circuit of Figure 9.17 is brighter, A or B? Or are they equally bright?

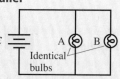

REASON Both ends of the two lightbulbs are connected together by wires. Because there's no potential difference along ideal wires, the potential at the top of bulb A must be the same as the potential at the top of bulb B. Similarly, the potential at the bottoms of the bulbs must be the same. This means that the potential *difference* ΔV across the two bulbs must be the same, as we see in Figure 9.18. Because the bulbs are identical (i.e., equal resistances), the currents $I = \Delta V/R$ through the two bulbs are equal and thus the bulbs are equally bright.

FIGURE 9.17 Two bulbs in parallel.

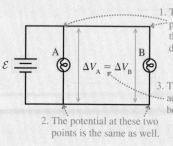

1. The potential at these two points is the same because there is no potential difference across the wire.

3. The potential differences across the two bulbs must be equal.

$\Delta V_A = \Delta V_B$

FIGURE 9.18 The potential differences of the bulbs.

2. The potential at these two points is the same as well.

ASSESS One might think that A would be brighter than B because current takes the "shortest route." But current is determined by potential difference, and two bulbs connected in parallel have the same potential difference.

Let's look at parallel circuits in more detail. The circuit of Figure 9.19a has a battery and two resistors connected in parallel. If we assume ideal wires, the potential differences across the two resistors are equal. In fact, the potential difference across each resistor is equal to the emf of the battery because both resistors are connected directly to the battery with ideal wires. That is, $\Delta V_1 = \Delta V_2 = \mathcal{E}$.

Now we apply Kirchhoff's junction law. The current I_{bat} from the battery splits into currents I_1 and I_2 at the top junction noted in Figure 9.19b. According to the junction law,

$$I_{bat} = I_1 + I_2 \tag{9.9}$$

We can apply Ohm's law to each resistor to find that the battery current is

$$I_{bat} = \frac{\Delta V_1}{R_1} + \frac{\Delta V_2}{R_2} = \frac{\mathcal{E}}{R_1} + \frac{\mathcal{E}}{R_2} = \mathcal{E}\left[\frac{1}{R_1} + \frac{1}{R_2}\right] \tag{9.10}$$

We found that we could replace a group of series resistors with a single equivalent resistor. Can we do the same for these parallel resistors? To be equivalent, the potential difference across the equivalent resistor must be $\Delta V = \mathcal{E}$, the same as for the two resistors it replaces. Further, so that the battery doesn't know there's been any change, the current through the equivalent resistor must be $I = I_{bat}$. According to Ohm's law, a resistor with this current and potential difference must have resistance

$$R_{eq} = \frac{\Delta V}{I} = \frac{\mathcal{E}}{I_{bat}} = \left[\frac{1}{R_1} + \frac{1}{R_2}\right]^{-1} \tag{9.11}$$

where we used Equation 9.10 for I_{bat}. This is the *equivalent resistance,* so a single resistor R_{eq} acts exactly the same as the two resistors R_1 and R_2.

We can extend this analysis to the case of N resistors in parallel. For this circuit, the equivalent resistance is the inverse of the sum of the inverses of the N individual resistances:

$$R_{eq} = \left(\frac{1}{R_1} + \frac{1}{R_2} + \cdots + \frac{1}{R_N}\right)^{-1} \tag{9.12}$$

Equivalent resistance of N parallel resistors

The behavior of the circuit will be unchanged if the N parallel resistors are replaced by the single resistor R_{eq}.

In Figure 9.19 each of the resistors "sees" the full potential difference of the battery. If one resistor were removed, the conditions of the second resistor would not change. This is an important property of parallel circuits.

Now, let's look at another lightbulb puzzle. Figure 9.20 shows two different circuits, one with one battery and one lightbulb and a second with one battery and two lightbulbs. As before, the batteries and the bulbs are identical. You know that B and C, which are connected in parallel, are equally bright, but how does the brightness of B compare to that of A?

▶ **Parallel circuits for safety** You have certainly seen cars with only one headlight lit. This tells us that automobile headlights are connected in parallel: The currents in the two bulbs are independent, so the loss of one bulb doesn't affect the other. The parallel wiring is very important, as the failure of one headlight will not leave the car without illumination.

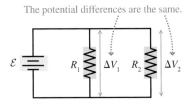
(a) Two resistors in parallel
The potential differences are the same.

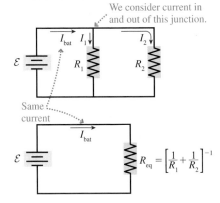
(b) Applying the junction law
We consider current in and out of this junction.

Same current

(c) An equivalent resistor

FIGURE 9.19 Replacing two parallel resistors with an equivalent resistor.

Actív Physics ONLINE 12.2, 12.5

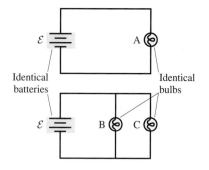

Identical batteries · Identical bulbs

Each of the bulbs A, B and C is connected to the same potential difference, that of the battery, so they each have the *same* brightness. Though all of the bulbs have the same brightness, there is a difference between the circuits. In the second circuit, the battery must power two lightbulbs, and so it must provide twice as much current. Recall that the battery is a source of fixed potential difference; the current depends upon the circuit that is connected to the battery. Adding a second lightbulb doesn't change the potential difference, but it does increase the current from the battery.

◀ **FIGURE 9.20** How does the brightness of bulb B compare to that of bulb A?

EXAMPLE 9.4 Current in a parallel resistor circuit

The three resistors of Figure 9.21 are connected to a 12 V battery. What current is provided by the battery?

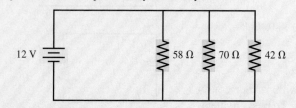

FIGURE 9.21 Circuit for Example 9.4.

PREPARE The three resistors are in parallel, so we can reduce them to a single equivalent resistor, as in Figure 9.22.

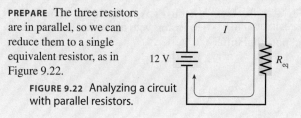

FIGURE 9.22 Analyzing a circuit with parallel resistors.

SOLVE We can use Equation 9.12 to calculate the equivalent resistance:

$$R_{eq} = \left(\frac{1}{58\ \Omega} + \frac{1}{70\ \Omega} + \frac{1}{42\ \Omega} \right)^{-1} = 18\ \Omega$$

Once we know the equivalent resistance, we can use Ohm's law to calculate the current leaving the battery:

$$I = \frac{\mathcal{E}}{R_{eq}} = \frac{12\ V}{18\ \Omega} = 0.67\ A$$

Because the battery can't tell the difference between the original three resistors and this single equivalent resistor, the battery in Figure 9.21 provides a current of 0.67 A to the circuit.

ASSESS Note that the resistance of the group of resistors is less than the resistance of any of the resistors in the group. This is always true for parallel resistors, and is a good check on your work.

The value of the total resistance in this example may seem surprising. The equivalent of a parallel combination of 58 Ω, 70 Ω, and 42 Ω is 18 Ω. Shouldn't more resistors imply more resistance? The answer is "yes" for resistors in series, but not for resistors in parallel. Even though a resistor is an obstacle to the flow of charge, parallel resistors provide more pathways for charge to get through. Consequently, **the equivalent of several resistors in parallel is always *less* than any single resistor in the group.** As an analogy, think about driving in heavy traffic. If there is an alternate route or an extra lane for cars to travel, more cars will be able to "flow."

STOP TO THINK 9.2 Rank in order, from brightest to dimmest, the identical bulbs A to D.

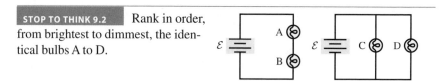

9.4 Measuring Voltage and Current

12.1, 12.4 · Activ Physics ONLINE

Suppose you want to use a meter to measure the voltage or the current in a circuit. How would you connect the meter? As we will see, the connection depends on the quantity you wish to measure.

A device that measures the current in a circuit element is called an **ammeter.** Because charge flows *through* circuit elements, an ammeter must be placed *in series* with the circuit element whose current is to be measured.

Figure 9.23a shows a simple one-resistor circuit with a fixed emf $\mathcal{E} = 1.5$ V and an unknown resistance R. Suppose we would like to determine the resistance. To do this, we must know the current in the circuit, which we measure using an ammeter. We insert the ammeter in the circuit as shown in Figure 9.23b. We have to *break the connection* between the battery and the resistor in order to insert the ammeter. The resistor and the ammeter now have the same current, because they are in series, so the reading of the ammeter is the current through the resistor.

Because the ammeter is in series with resistor R, the total resistance seen by the battery is $R_{eq} = R + R_{meter}$. In order to *measure* the current without *changing* the current, the ammeter's resistance must be much less than R. Thus **the resistance of an ideal ammeter is zero.** Real ammeters come quite close to this ideal.

The ammeter in Figure 9.23b reads 0.60 A, meaning that the current in the ammeter—and in the resistor—is $I = 0.60$ A. If the ammeter is ideal, which we will assume, then there is no potential difference across the ammeter ($\Delta V = IR = 0$ if $R = 0\,\Omega$) and thus the potential difference across the resistor is $\Delta V = \mathcal{E}$. The resistance can then be calculated as

$$R = \frac{\mathcal{E}}{I} = \frac{1.5 \text{ V}}{0.60 \text{ A}} = 2.5\ \Omega$$

A device that measures the potential difference across a circuit element is called a **voltmeter.** Because a potential difference is measured *across* a circuit element, from one side to the other, a voltmeter is placed in *parallel* with the circuit element whose potential difference is to be measured. We want to *measure* the voltage without *changing* the voltage—without affecting the circuit. Because the voltmeter is in parallel with the resistor, the voltmeter's resistance must be very large so that it draws very little current. **An ideal voltmeter has infinite resistance.** Real voltmeters come quite close to this ideal.

Figure 9.24a shows a simple circuit in which a 24 Ω resistor is connected in series with an unknown resistance, with the pair of resistors connected to a 9.0 V battery. To determine the unknown resistance we first characterize the circuit by measuring the potential difference across the known resistor with a voltmeter as shown in Figure 9.24b. The voltmeter is connected in parallel with the resistor; using a voltmeter does *not* require that we break the connections. The resistor and the voltmeter have the same potential difference, because they are in parallel, so the reading of the voltmeter is the voltage across the resistor.

The voltmeter in Figure 9.24b tells us that the potential difference across the 24 Ω resistor is 6.0 V, so the current through the resistor is

$$I = \frac{\Delta V}{R} = \frac{6.0 \text{ V}}{24\ \Omega} = 0.25 \text{ A} \qquad (9.13)$$

The two resistors are in series, so this is also the current in unknown resistor R. We can use Kirchhoff's loop law and the voltmeter reading to find the potential difference across the unknown resistor:

$$\sum_i \Delta V_i = 9.0 \text{ V} + \Delta V_R - 6.0 \text{ V} = 0 \qquad (9.14)$$

from which we find $\Delta V_R = -3.0$ V. We can now use $\Delta V_R = -IR$ to calculate

$$R = \frac{-\Delta V_R}{I} = -\frac{(-3.0 \text{ V})}{0.25 \text{ A}} = 12\ \Omega \qquad (9.15)$$

▶ In this text, we speak of ammeters and voltmeters, but in practice we generally make measurements with a *multimeter*. A dial on the front sets the meter to measure voltage, current, or other electrical quantities. When set to measure current, it works as an ammeter and must be connected in series. When set to measure voltage, it works as a voltmeter and must be connected in parallel. It can also work as an *ohmmeter*, directly measuring the resistance of a resistor not in a circuit.

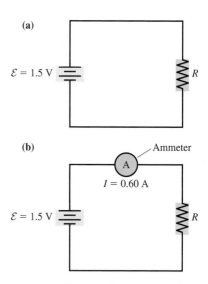

FIGURE 9.23 An ammeter measures the current in a circuit.

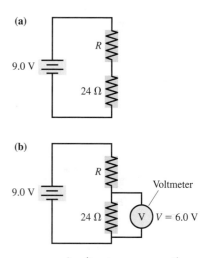

FIGURE 9.24 A voltmeter measures the potential difference across a circuit element.

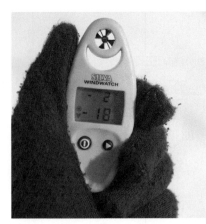

A circuit for all seasons This device displays wind speed and temperature, but these are computed from basic measurements of voltage and current. The wind turns a propeller attached to a generator; a rapid spin means a high voltage. A circuit in the device contains a *thermistor*, whose resistance varies with temperature; low temperatures mean high resistance and thus a small current.

Which is the right way to connect the meters to measure the potential difference across and the current through the resistor?

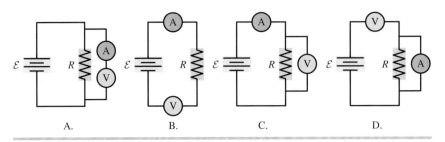

9.5 More Complex Circuits

In this section, we will consider circuits that involve both series and parallel resistors. The analysis of these circuits will take more steps, but the steps are ones with which we are now familiar. We can make the following general statements about series and parallel connections:

■ Circuit elements connected in series have the same current.
■ Circuit elements connected in parallel have the same potential difference.
■ Combinations of resistors can often be reduced to a single equivalent resistance through a step-by-step application of the series and parallel rules.

EXAMPLE 9.5 Combining resistors

What is the equivalent resistance of the group of resistors shown in Figure 9.25?

PREPARE We can analyze this circuit by reducing combinations of series and parallel resistors. We will do this in a series of steps, redrawing the circuit after each step.

FIGURE 9.25 Resistor circuit for Example 9.5.

SOLVE The process of simplifying the circuit is outlined in Figure 9.26. Note that the 10 Ω and 60 Ω resistors are *not* in parallel. They are connected at their top ends but not at their bottom ends. Resistors must be connected at *both* ends to be in parallel. Similarly, the 10 Ω and 45 Ω resistors are *not* in series because of the junction between them.

ASSESS If the original group of four resistors occurred within a larger circuit, they could be replaced with a single 24 Ω resistor without having any effect on the rest of the circuit. The first step in analyzing a complex circuit is often to reduce combinations of resistors in this manner.

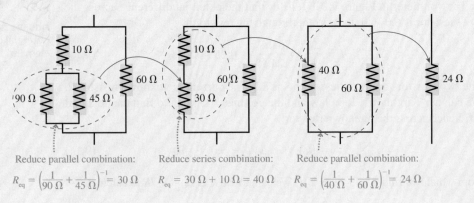

FIGURE 9.26 A combination of resistors is reduced to a single equivalent resistor.

Reduce parallel combination:
$$R_{eq} = \left(\frac{1}{90\ \Omega} + \frac{1}{45\ \Omega}\right)^{-1} = 30\ \Omega$$

Reduce series combination:
$$R_{eq} = 30\ \Omega + 10\ \Omega = 40\ \Omega$$

Reduce parallel combination:
$$R_{eq} = \left(\frac{1}{40\ \Omega} + \frac{1}{60\ \Omega}\right)^{-1} = 24\ \Omega$$

Two useful special cases (which will be helpful in the next example) are the equivalent resistances of two identical resistors $R_1 = R_2 = R$ in series and in parallel:

Two identical resistors in series: $R_{eq} = 2R$

Two identical resistors in parallel: $R_{eq} = \dfrac{R}{2}$

EXAMPLE 9.6 **How does the brightness change?**

Initially the switch in Figure 9.27 is open. Bulbs A and B are equally bright, and bulb C is not glowing. What happens to the brightness of A and B when the switch is closed? And how does the brightness of C then compare to that of A and B? Assume that all bulbs are identical.

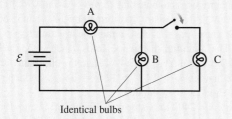

FIGURE 9.27 Lightbulb circuit for Example 9.6.

SOLVE Suppose the resistance of each bulb is R. Initially, before the switch is closed, bulbs A and B are in series; bulb C is not part of the circuit. A and B are identical resistors in series, so their equivalent resistance is $2R$ and the current from the battery is

$$I_{before} = \frac{\mathcal{E}}{R_{eq}} = \frac{\mathcal{E}}{2R} = \frac{1}{2}\frac{\mathcal{E}}{R}$$

This is the initial current in bulbs A and B, so they are equally bright.

Closing the switch places bulbs B and C in parallel with each other. The equivalent resistance of the two identical resistors in parallel is $R_{B+C} = R/2$. This equivalent resistance of B and C is in series with bulb A, hence the total resistance of the circuit is $R_{eq} = R + \frac{1}{2}R = \frac{3}{2}R$ and the current leaving the battery is

$$I_{after} = \frac{\mathcal{E}}{R_{eq}} = \frac{\mathcal{E}}{(3R/2)} = \frac{2}{3}\frac{\mathcal{E}}{R} > I_{before}$$

Closing the switch *decreases* the total circuit resistance and thus *increases* the current leaving the battery.

All the current from the battery passes through bulb A, so A *increases* in brightness when the switch is closed. The current I_{after} then splits at the junction. Bulbs B and C have equal resistance, so the current divides equally. The current in B is $\frac{1}{3}(\mathcal{E}/R)$, which is *less* than I_{before}. Thus B *decreases* in brightness when the switch is closed. With the switch closed, bulbs B and C are in parallel, so bulb C has the same brightness as bulb B.

ASSESS Even though bulb C is connected in parallel with bulb B, adding bulb C changes the brightness of bulb B because this isn't a simple parallel circuit. Bulbs B and C have the same potential difference and will have the same brightness—but this is less than the brightness of bulb B before the switch was closed.

Analyzing Complex Circuits

We can use the information in this chapter to analyze more complex but more realistic circuits. This will give us a chance to bring together the many ideas of this chapter and to see how they are used in practice. The techniques that we use for this analysis are general, so we present them as a Problem-Solving Strategy. You can use the steps outlined to analyze any resistor circuit, as we show in the example following.

(MP) PROBLEM-SOLVING STRATEGY 9.1 **Resistor circuits**

PREPARE Draw a circuit diagram. Label all known and unknown quantities.

SOLVE Base your mathematical analysis on Kirchhoff's laws and on the rules for series and parallel resistors:

■ Step by step, reduce the circuit to the smallest possible number of equivalent resistors.
■ Determine the current through and potential difference across the equivalent resistors.
■ Rebuild the circuit, using the facts that the current is the same through all resistors in series and the potential difference is the same across all parallel resistors.

ASSESS Use two important checks as you rebuild the circuit.

■ Verify that the sum of the potential differences across series resistors matches ΔV for the equivalent resistor.
■ Verify that the sum of the currents through parallel resistors matches I for the equivalent resistor.

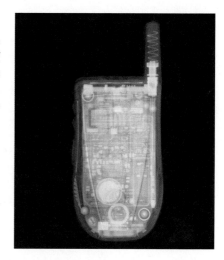

This x-ray image of a cell phone shows the complex circuitry inside. Though there are thousands of components, the analysis of such a circuit starts with the same basic rules we are studying in this chapter.

 12.3

EXAMPLE 9.7 **Analyzing a complex circuit**

Find the current through and the potential difference across each of the four resistors in the circuit shown in Figure 9.28.

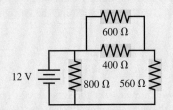

FIGURE 9.28 Multiple-resistor circuit of Example 9.7.

PREPARE Figure 9.29 shows the circuit diagram. We'll keep redrawing the diagram as we analyze the circuit.

SOLVE First, we break down the circuit, step-by-step, into one with a single resistor. Figure 9.29a does this in three steps, using the rules for series and parallel resistors. The final battery-and-resistor circuit is one we know well how to analyze. The current is

$$I = \frac{\mathcal{E}}{R} = \frac{12 \text{ V}}{400 \text{ }\Omega} = 0.030 \text{ A} = 30 \text{ mA}$$

The potential difference across the 400 Ω equivalent resistor is $\Delta V_{400} = \Delta V_{bat} = \mathcal{E} = 12$ V.

Second, we rebuild the circuit, step-by-step, finding the currents and potential differences at each step. Figure 9.29b repeats the steps of Figure 9.29a exactly, but in reverse order. The 400 Ω resistor came from two 800 Ω resistors in parallel. Because $\Delta V_{400} = 12$ V, it must be true that each $\Delta V_{800} = 12$ V. The current through each 800 Ω is then $I = \Delta V/R = 15$ mA. A check on our work is to note that 15 mA + 15 mA = 30 mA.

The right 800 Ω resistor was formed by 240 Ω and 560 Ω in series. Because $I_{800} = 15$ mA, it must be true that $I_{240} = I_{560} = 15$ mA. The potential difference across each is $\Delta V = IR$, so $\Delta V_{240} = 3.6$ V and $\Delta V_{560} = 8.4$ V. Here the check on our work is to note that 3.6 V + 8.4 V = 12 V = ΔV_{800}, so the potential differences add as they should.

Finally, the 240 Ω resistor came from 600 Ω and 400 Ω in parallel, so they each have the same 3.6 V potential difference as their 240 Ω equivalent. The currents are $I_{600} = 6.0$ mA and $I_{400} = 9.0$ mA. Note that 6.0 mA + 9.0 mA = 15 mA, which is our third check on our work. We now know all currents and potential differences.

ASSESS We *checked our work* at each step of the rebuilding process by verifying that currents summed properly at junctions and that potential differences summed properly along a series of resistances. This "check as you go" procedure is extremely important. It provides you, the problem solver, with a built-in error finder that will immediately inform you if a mistake has been made.

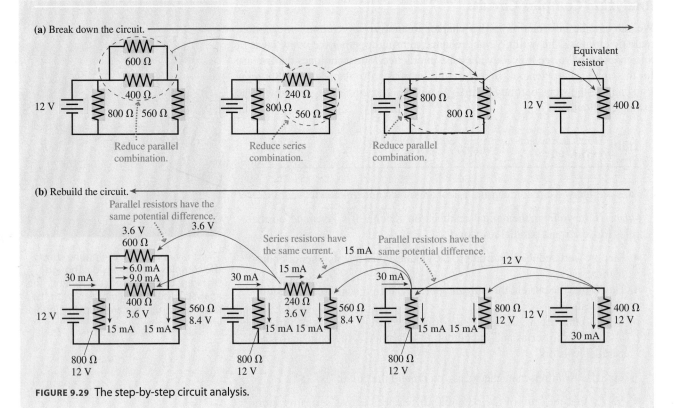

FIGURE 9.29 The step-by-step circuit analysis.

STOP TO THINK 9.4 Rank in order, from brightest to dimmest, the identical bulbs A to D.

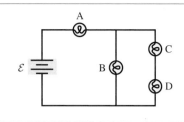

9.6 Household Electricity

Kirchhoff's laws and other principles that we have learned in this chapter apply to any circuit—including the circuits of devices that you plug into outlets in your house. We will use our knowledge of circuits to understand household electricity, focusing on elements of your household electrical supply that are present for your safety.

Getting Grounded

The circuit analysis procedures we have discussed so far deal only with potential *differences*. Although we are free to choose the zero point of potential anywhere that is convenient, our analysis of circuits has not revealed any need to establish a zero point. Potential differences are all we have needed.

Difficulties can begin to arise, however, if you want to connect two *different* circuits together. Perhaps you would like to connect your CD player to your amplifier or your computer monitor to the computer itself. Incompatibilities can arise unless all the circuits to be connected have a *common* reference point for the potential.

You learned previously that the earth itself is a conductor. Suppose we have two circuits. If we connect *one* point of each circuit to the earth by an ideal wire, and we also agree to call the potential of the earth $V_{earth} = 0$ V, then both circuits have a common reference point. A circuit connected to the earth in this way is said to be **grounded.** Figure 9.30 shows a circuit with a ground connection. Under normal circumstances, the ground connection does not carry any current, as it is not part of a complete circuit. In this case, it does not alter the behavior of the circuit.

Grounding serves two functions. First, it provides a common reference potential so that different circuits or instruments can be correctly interconnected. Second, it is an important safety feature. As we will see in the next section, a current to ground can quickly open a circuit breaker if an electric appliance malfunctions.

Electric Outlets Are Grounded Parallel Circuits

The electrical supply to your house is AC, meaning *alternating current.* The voltage isn't constant; it oscillates positive and negative in a sinusoidal manner. For most applications, though, we can model your household electrical supply as a constant 120 V source.

The electrical supply from the utility company is connected to electric outlets in your house via wires that run through the walls, as shown in Figure 9.31 on the next page. One terminal of the electrical supply is grounded with a metal bar sunk into the earth. The side that is grounded is called the **neutral** side; the other side at 120 V is the **hot** side. When you plug something in to an electric outlet, the device completes a circuit between the hot side and the neutral side. The potential difference across the device leads to a current, and the device turns on.

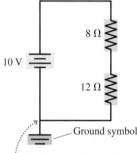

The circuit is grounded at this point. The potential at this point is $V = 0$ V.

FIGURE 9.30 A grounded circuit.

A two-prong "polarized" plug has one large prong and one small one. When plugged in to a standard outlet, the large prong is grounded. A three-prong plug has a round pin that makes a second ground connection.

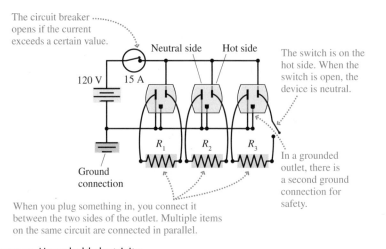

The circuit breaker opens if the current exceeds a certain value.

Neutral side   Hot side

120 V   15 A

The switch is on the hot side. When the switch is open, the device is neutral.

Ground connection

R_1 R_2 R_3

In a grounded outlet, there is a second ground connection for safety.

When you plug something in, you connect it between the two sides of the outlet. Multiple items on the same circuit are connected in parallel.

FIGURE 9.31 Household electricity.

With a few exceptions, each electric circuit in your house has multiple outlets connected in parallel. Everything that you plug in to an outlet is connected in parallel with other devices on the same circuit. We have seen that adding an additional resistor to a parallel circuit increases the current. The same is true here: When you plug in another device, the total current in the circuit increases. This can create a problem; although the wires in your walls are good conductors, they aren't ideal. The wires have a small resistance and heat up when carrying a current. If there is too much current, the wires could get hot enough to cause a fire.

To keep this from happening, the circuits in your house are protected with circuit breakers. A circuit breaker consists of a switch and an ammeter that measures the current in the circuit. If the ammeter measures too much current in the circuit, it sends a signal to open the switch to disconnect the circuit. You have probably had the experience of having a circuit breaker "trip" if you have too many things plugged in. The circuit breaker has prevented a potentially dangerous situation; the circuit was carrying too much current. To keep the problem from recurring, you must reduce the current in the circuit. Some things need to be turned off, unplugged, or moved to a different circuit.

Grounding of household circuits provides an important reference potential, as noted above, but the main reason for grounding is safety. The two slots in a standard outlet are different sizes; the neutral outlet is a bit larger. Most electrical devices are fitted with plugs that can only be inserted into an outlet in one orientation. A lamp, for instance, will almost certainly have this sort of plug. This is an important safety feature; when you turn the lamp off, the switch disconnects the hot wire, not the neutral wire. The lamp is then neutral, and thus safe, when it is off.

The round hole in a standard electrical outlet is a second ground connection that serves a second safety function. If a device has a metal case, whether it's a microwave oven or an electric drill, the case will likely be connected to this ground connection. Suppose a wire came loose inside the device and contacted the metal case. A person touching the case could get a shock or even be killed. But if the case is grounded, its potential is always 0 V, and it is always safe to touch. In addition, a hot wire touching the grounded case would be a *short circuit,* causing a sudden very large current that would trip the circuit breaker, disconnecting the hot wire and preventing any danger. If you plug something in and the circuit breaker trips, the device likely has an electrical fault and should be discarded or repaired.

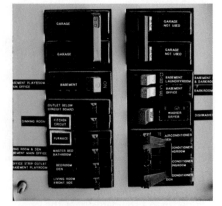

A typical circuit breaker panel. Each switch corresponds to a different circuit in the house.

EXAMPLE 9.8 Will the circuit breaker open?

A circuit in a student's room has a 15 A circuit breaker. One evening, the student plugs in a computer (240 W), a lamp (with two 60 W bulbs, for a total of 120 W), and a space heater (1200 W). Will this be enough to trip the circuit breaker?

PREPARE We start by sketching the circuit, as shown in Figure 9.32. Because the three devices are connected in the same circuit, they are in parallel. We can model them as resistors.

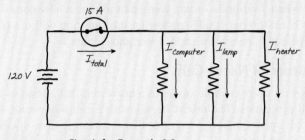

FIGURE 9.32 Circuit for Example 9.8.

SOLVE According to Kirchhoff's junction law, the current, which is provided by the 120 V supply and passes through the circuit breaker, is the sum of the currents in the individual devices:

$$I_{total} = I_{computer} + I_{lamp} + I_{heater}$$

The power dissipated by a resistor is $P_R = I\Delta V$, so we can calculate the current in the individual devices as $I = P_R/\Delta V$. All three devices are in parallel with the supply, so $\Delta V = 120$ V. The current is thus

$$I_{total} = \frac{240\ \text{W}}{120\ \text{V}} + \frac{120\ \text{W}}{120\ \text{V}} + \frac{1200\ \text{W}}{120\ \text{V}} = 13\ \text{A}$$

This is not enough to open the circuit breaker.

ASSESS Generally all of the outlets in one room (and perhaps the lights as well) are on the same circuit. You can see that it would be quite easy to plug in enough devices to trip the circuit breaker.

Kilowatt Hours

The energy dissipated (i.e., transformed into thermal energy) by a resistor during time Δt is $E_{th} = P_R\,\Delta t$. The product of watts and seconds is joules, the SI unit of energy. However, your local electric company prefers to use a different unit, called *kilowatt hours,* to measure the energy you use each month.

A device in your home that consumes P_R kW of electricity for Δt hours has used $P_R\,\Delta t$ **kilowatt hours** of energy, abbreviated kWh. For example, suppose you run a 1500 W electric water heater for 10 hours. The energy used in kWh is $(1.5\ \text{kW})(10\ \text{hr}) = 15$ kWh.

Despite the rather unusual name, a kilowatt hour is a unit of energy, as it is a power multiplied by a time. The conversion between kWh and J is

$$1.00\ \text{kWh} = (1.00 \times 10^3\ \text{W})(3600\ \text{s}) = 3.60 \times 10^6\ \text{J}$$

Your monthly electric bill specifies the number of kilowatt hours you used last month. This is the amount of energy that the electric company delivered to you, via an electric current, and that you transformed into light and thermal energy inside your home.

The electric meter on the side of your house or apartment records the kilowatt hours of electricity you use each month.

EXAMPLE 9.9 Computing the cost of electric energy

A hair dryer carries a current of 10 A. If electricity costs 10¢ per kWh (an approximate national average), what is the cost to run the dryer for 5.0 min?

SOLVE The power of the hair dryer, in kW, is $P_R = I\Delta V = (10\ \text{A})(120\ \text{V}) = 1200\ \text{W} = 1.2$ kW. The energy consumed is power multiplied by time. With the time in hours, $t = 5.0\ \text{min} = \frac{1}{12}$ hr, the energy is calculated to be

$$E = (1.2\ \text{kW})\left(\frac{1}{12}\ \text{hr}\right) = 0.10\ \text{kWh}$$

At 10¢ per kWh, the cost is 1.0¢.

9.7 Electricity in the Nervous System

In the late 1700s, the Italian scientist Galvani discovered that animal tissue has an electrical nature. He found that a frog's leg would twitch when stimulated with electricity, even when no longer attached to the frog. Further investigations by Galvani and others revealed that electrical signals can animate muscle cells, and that a small potential applied to the *axon* of a nerve cell can produce a signal that propagates down its length.

Our goal in this section will be to understand the nature of electrical signals in the nervous system. When your brain orders your hand to move, how does the signal get from your brain to your hand? Answering this question will use our knowledge of fields, potential, resistance, capacitance and circuits.

The Electrical Nature of Nerve Cells

We start our analysis with a very simple *model* of a nerve cell that allows us to describe its electrical properties. The model begins with a *cell membrane,* an insulating layer of lipids approximately 7 nm thick that separates regions of conducting fluid inside and outside the cell.

The cell membrane is not a passive structure. It has channels and pumps that transport ions between the inside and the outside of the cell. In our simple model we will consider the transport of only two positive ions, sodium (Na^+) and potassium (K^+), though other ions are also important to cell function. Ions, rather than electrons, are the charge carriers of the cell. These ions can slowly diffuse across the cell membrane. In addition, sodium and potassium ions are transported via the following structures:

- *Sodium-potassium exchange pumps.* These pump Na^+ ions out of the cell and K^+ ions in. In the cell's resting state, the concentration of sodium ions outside the cell is about ten times the concentration on the inside. Potassium ions are more concentrated on the inside.
- *Sodium and potassium channels.* These channels in the cell membrane are usually closed. When they are open, ions move in the direction of lower concentration. Thus Na^+ ions flow into the cell and K^+ ions flow out.

Our simple model, outlined in Figure 9.33, neglects many of the features of real cells, but it allows us to accurately describe the reaction of nerve cells to a stimulus and the conduction of electrical signals.

The ion exchange pumps act much like the charge escalator of a battery, using chemical energy to separate charge by transporting ions. The transport and subsequent diffusion of charged ions leads to a separation in charge across the cell membrane. Consequently, **a living cell generates an emf.** This emf takes energy to create and maintain. The ion pumps that produce the emf of neural cells account for 25–40% of the energy usage of the brain.

The charge separation produces an electric field inside the cell membrane, and results in a potential difference between the inside and the outside of the cell, as shown in Figure 9.34. The potential inside a nerve cell is typically 70 mV less than that outside the cell. This is called the cell's *resting potential.* Because this potential difference is produced by a charge separation across the membrane, we say that the membrane is *polarized.* As the potential difference is entirely across the membrane, we may call this potential difference the *membrane potential.*

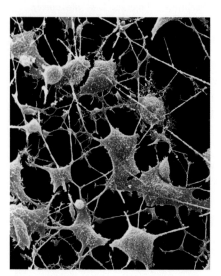

The long fibers connecting these nerve cells are *axons,* the transmission lines for electrical signals between cells.

The pump moves sodium out of the cell and potassium in, so the sodium concentration is higher outside the cell, the potassium concentration is higher inside.

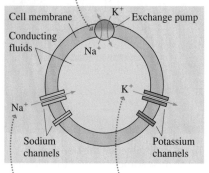

When a sodium channel is open, the higher sodium concentration outside the cell causes ions to flow into the cell.

When a potassium channel is open, the higher potassium concentration inside the cell causes ions to flow out of the cell.

FIGURE 9.33 A simple model of a nerve cell.

EXAMPLE 9.10 Electric field in a cell membrane

The thickness of a typical nerve cell membrane is 7.0 nm. What is the electric field inside the membrane of a resting nerve cell?

PREPARE The potential difference across the membrane of a resting nerve cell is −70 mV. The inner and outer surfaces of the membrane are equipotentials. We learned that the electric field is perpendicular to the equipotentials and is related to the potential difference by $E = \Delta V/d$.

SOLVE The magnitude of the potential difference between the inside and the outside of the cell is 70 mV. The field strength is thus

$$E = \frac{\Delta V}{d} = \frac{70 \times 10^{-3}\ \text{V}}{7.0 \times 10^{-9}\ \text{m}} = 1.0 \times 10^7\ \text{V/m}$$

The field points from positive to negative, so the electric field is

$$\vec{E} = (1.0 \times 10^7\ \text{V/m, inward})$$

ASSESS This is a very large electric field; in air it would be large enough to cause a spark! But we expect the fields to be large, to explain the cell's strong electrical character.

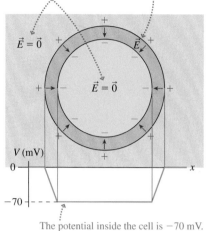

The conducting fluids inside and outside the cell have zero field.

Charges on the inside and outside surfaces of the insulating membrane create a field inside it.

The potential inside the cell is −70 mV.

FIGURE 9.34 The resting potential of a nerve cell.

EXAMPLE 9.11 Finding the resistance of a cell membrane

Ions can move across the cell membrane, so it is not a perfect insulator; the cell membrane will have a certain resistance. The resistivity of the cell membrane was given in Chapter 8 as $36 \times 10^6\ \Omega \cdot \text{m}$. What is the resistance of the 7.0-nm-thick membrane of a spherical cell with diameter 0.050 mm?

PREPARE Current—in this case, the motion of ions—travels *through* the membrane. As we learned in Chapter 8, an object's resistance depends on its resistivity, length, and cross-section area. What this means for a cell membrane is noted in Figure 9.35.

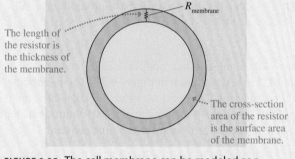

R_{membrane}

The length of the resistor is the thickness of the membrane.

The cross-section area of the resistor is the surface area of the membrane.

FIGURE 9.35 The cell membrane can be modeled as a resistor.

SOLVE The area of the membrane is the surface area of a sphere, $4\pi r^2$. We can calculate the resistance using the equation for the resistance of a conductor of length L and cross-section area A from Chapter 8:

$$R_{\text{membrane}} = \frac{\rho L}{A} = \frac{(3.6 \times 10^7\ \Omega \cdot \text{m})(7.0 \times 10^{-9}\ \text{m})}{4\pi(2.5 \times 10^{-5}\ \text{m})^2}$$

$$= 3.2 \times 10^7\ \Omega = 32\ \text{M}\Omega$$

ASSESS The resistance is quite high; the membrane is a good insulator, as we noted.

We can associate a resistance with the cell membrane, but we can associate other electrical quantities as well. The fluids inside and outside of the membrane are good conductors; they are separated by the membrane, which is not. Charges therefore accumulate on the inside and outside surfaces of the membrane. A cell thus looks like two charged conductors separated by an insulator—a capacitor.

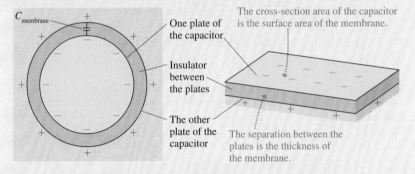

EXAMPLE 9.12 Finding the capacitance of a cell membrane

What is the capacitance of the membrane of the spherical cell specified in Example 9.11? The dielectric constant of a cell membrane is approximately 9.0.

PREPARE If we imagine opening up a cell membrane and flattening it out, we would get something that looks like a parallel-plate capacitor with the plates separated by a dielectric. The relevant dimensions are the same as those in Example 9.11.

$C_{membrane}$

One plate of the capacitor

Insulator between the plates

The other plate of the capacitor

The cross-section area of the capacitor is the surface area of the membrane.

The separation between the plates is the thickness of the membrane.

FIGURE 9.36 The cell membrane can also be modeled as a capacitor.

SOLVE The capacitance of the membrane is that of a parallel-plate capacitor filled with a dielectric. Inserting the dimensions from Example 9.11, we find

$$C_{membrane} = \frac{\kappa \epsilon_0 A}{d} = \frac{9.0(8.85 \times 10^{-12}\,\text{C}^2/\text{N} \cdot \text{m}^2)4\pi(2.5 \times 10^{-5}\,\text{m})^2}{7.0 \times 10^{-9}\,\text{m}}$$

$$= 8.9 \times 10^{-11}\,\text{F}$$

ASSESS Though the cell is small, the cell membrane has a reasonably large capacitance of ≈ 90 pF. This makes sense, because the membrane is quite thin.

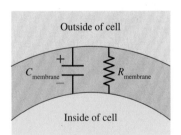

FIGURE 9.37 The cell membrane can be modeled as an *RC* circuit.

Because the cell membrane has both resistance and capacitance, it can be modeled as an *RC* circuit, as shown in Figure 9.37. The membrane, like any *RC* circuit, has a time constant. The previous examples calculated the resistance and capacitance of the 7.0-nm-thick membrane of a 0.050-mm-diameter cell. We can use these numbers to compute the membrane's time constant:

$$\tau = RC = (3.2 \times 10^7\,\Omega)(8.9 \times 10^{-11}\,\text{F}) = 2.8 \times 10^{-3}\,\text{s} \approx 3\,\text{ms}$$

Indeed, if we raise the membrane potential of a real nerve cell by 10 mV (large enough to easily measure but not enough to trigger a response in the cell) the potential will decay back to its resting value with a time constant of a few ms.

But the real action happens when some stimulus *is* large enough to trigger a response in the cell. In this case, ion channels open and the potential changes in much less time than the cell's time constant, as we will see in the next section.

The Action Potential

Suppose a nerve cell is sitting quietly at its resting potential. The membrane potential is approximately −70 mV. However, this potential can change drastically in response to a *stimulus*. Neurons—nerve cells—can be stimulated by neurotransmitter chemicals released at synapse junctions. A neuron can also be electrically stimulated by a changing potential, which is why Galvani saw the frog's leg jump.

Whatever the stimulus, the result is a rapid change called an *action potential;* this is the "firing" of a nerve cell. There are three phases in the action potential, as outlined below.

The action potential

| Depolarization | Repolarization | Reestablishing resting potential |

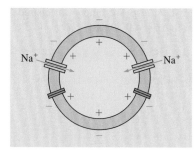

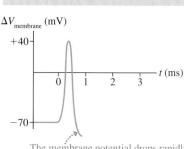

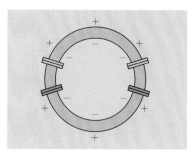

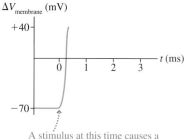

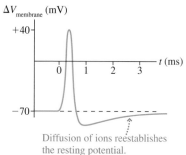

A stimulus at this time causes a quick rise in membrane potential.

The membrane potential drops rapidly, overshooting its initial value.

Diffusion of ions reestablishes the resting potential.

A stimulus causes the cell to "fire"; the first step is the opening of the sodium channels. The concentration of sodium ions is much higher outside the cell, so sodium ions flow rapidly into the cell. In less than 1 ms, this influx of positive ions raises the membrane potential from -70 mV to $+40$ mV, at which point the sodium channels close. This phase of the action potential is called *depolarization.*

The positive membrane potential that causes the sodium channels to close causes the potassium channels to open. The higher potassium concentration inside the cell drives these ions out of the cell, making the membrane potential negative. The negative potential closes the potassium channels, but a delayed response leads to a slight *overshoot* of the resting potential to about -80 mV. This phase of the action potential is called *repolarization.*

The reestablishment of the resting potential after the sodium and potassium channels close is a relatively slow process, because it is controlled by the motion of ions across the membrane. The time constant of the membrane determines how long this takes.

As soon as one action potential is complete, the cell is ready to be triggered again. The action potential is driven by ionic conduction through sodium and potassium channels, so the potential changes are quite rapid. The time for the potential to rise and then to fall is much less than the 3 ms time constant for diffusion of ions across the membrane.

The above discussion concerned nerve cells, but muscle cells undergo a similar cycle of depolarization and repolarization. The resulting potential changes are responsible for the dipole moment of the heart, and so provide the signal that is measured by an electrocardiogram. The potential differences in the human body are small, as the changes in potential are small. But some fish, such as the electric eel, have electric organs in which the action potentials of thousands of specially adapted cells are added in series, leading to very large potential differences—hundreds of volts in the case of the electric eel.

EXAMPLE 9.13 Counting ions through a channel

Investigators can measure the ion flow through a single ion channel with the *patch clamp* technique, as illustrated in Figure 9.38. A micropipette, a glass tube ≈1 μm in diameter, makes a seal on a patch of cell membrane that includes one sodium channel. This tube is filled with a conducting salt water solution, and a very sensitive ammeter measures the current as

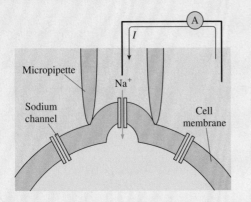

FIGURE 9.38 Measuring the current in a single sodium channel.

sodium ions flow into the cell. A sodium channel passes an average current of 4.0 pA during the 0.40 ms that the channel is open during an action potential. How many sodium ions pass through the channel?

PREPARE Current is the rate of flow of charge. Each ion has charge $q = e$.

SOLVE In Chapter 8, we saw that the charge delivered by a steady current in time Δt is $Q = I\Delta t$. The amount of charge flowing through the channel in $\Delta t = 4.0 \times 10^{-4}$ s is

$$Q = I\Delta t = (4.0 \times 10^{-12}\text{ A})(4.0 \times 10^{-4}\text{ s}) = 1.6 \times 10^{-15}\text{ C}$$

This charge is due to N ions, each with $q = e$, so the number of ions is

$$N = \frac{Q}{e} = \frac{1.6 \times 10^{-15}\text{ C}}{1.6 \times 10^{-19}\text{ C}} = 10{,}000$$

ASSESS The number of ions flowing through one channel is not large, but a cell has a great many channels. The patch clamp technique and other similar procedures have allowed investigators to elucidate the details of the response of the cell membrane to a stimulus.

TRY IT YOURSELF

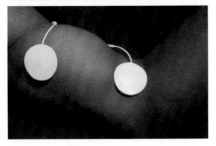

◀**Electrical exercising** Perhaps you have seen devices advertised on television that purport to allow you to "effortlessly" exercise the muscles of your body. These devices use electrodes that make good electrical contact with the skin. By applying small potential differences between the electrodes, it is possible to directly stimulate the nerve cells that signal muscles to contract. If you use one of these devices, the stimulation will cause your muscles to contract whether you want them to or not! The benefits of this "exercise" are questionable, and it carries significant risks.

The Propagation of Nerve Impulses

Let's return to the question posed at the start of the section: How is a signal transmitted from the brain to a muscle in the hand? The primary cells of the nervous system, responsible for signal transmission, are known as *neurons*. The transmission of a signal to a muscle is the function of a *motor neuron*, whose structure is sketched in Figure 9.39. The transmission of signals takes place along the *axon* of

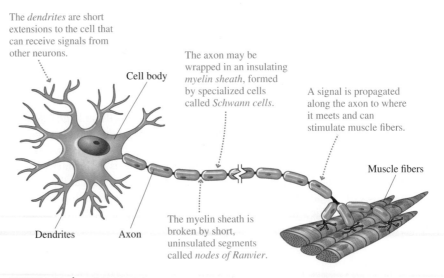

The *dendrites* are short extensions to the cell that can receive signals from other neurons.

Cell body

The axon may be wrapped in an insulating *myelin sheath*, formed by specialized cells called *Schwann cells*.

A signal is propagated along the axon to where it meets and can stimulate muscle fibers.

Muscle fibers

The myelin sheath is broken by short, uninsulated segments called *nodes of Ranvier*.

Dendrites   Axon

FIGURE 9.39 A motor neuron.

the neuron, a long fiber—up to 1 m in length—that connects the cell body to a muscle fiber. This particular neuron has a myelin sheath around the axon, though not all neurons do.

How is a signal transmitted along an axon? The axon is long enough that different points on its membrane may have different potentials. When one point on the axon's membrane is stimulated, the membrane will depolarize at this point. The resulting action potential may trigger depolarization in adjacent parts of the membrane. Stimulating the axon's membrane at one point can trigger a *wave* of action potential—a nerve impulse—that travels along the axon. When this signal reaches a muscle cell, the muscle cell depolarizes and produces a mechanical response.

Let's look at this process in more detail. We will start with a simple model of an axon with no myelin sheath in Figure 9.40a. The sodium channels are normally closed, but if the potential at some point is raised by ≈ 15 mV, from the resting potential of -70 mV to ≈ -55 mV, the sodium channels suddenly open, sodium ions rush into the cell, and an action potential is triggered. This is the key idea: **A small increase in the potential difference across the membrane causes the sodium channels to open, triggering a large action-potential response.**

This process begins at the cell body, in response to signals the neuron receives at its dendrites. If the cell body potential goes up by ≈ 15 mV, an action potential is initiated in the cell body. As the cell body potential quickly rises to a peak of $+40$ mV, it causes the potential on the nearest section of the axon—where the axon attaches to the cell body—to rise by 15 mV. This triggers an action potential in this first section of the axon. The action potential in the first section of the axon triggers an action potential in the next section of the axon, which triggers an action potential in the next section, and so on down the axon until reaching the end.

As Figure 9.40b shows, this causes a wave of action potential to propagate down the axon. The signal moves relatively slowly. At each point on the membrane, channels must open and ions must diffuse through, which takes time. On a typical axon with no myelin sheath, the action potential propagates at a speed of about 1 m/s. If all nerve signals traveled at this speed, a decision to move your hand would take about 1 s to travel from your brain to your hand. Clearly, at least some neurons in the nervous system must transmit signals at a greater speed than this!

One way to make the signals travel more quickly is to increase an axon's diameter. The giant axon in the squid triggers a rapid escape response when the squid is threatened. This axon may have a diameter of 1 mm, a thousand times that of a typical axon, providing for the necessary rapid signal transmission. But your nervous system consists of 300 billion neurons, and they can't all be 1 mm in diameter—there simply isn't enough space in your body. In your nervous system, higher neuron signal speed is achieved in a totally different manner.

Increasing Speed by Insulation

The axons of motor neurons and most other neurons in your body can transmit signals at very high speeds because they are insulated with a myelin sheath. Look back at the diagram of a motor neuron in Figure 9.39. Schwann cells wrap the axon with myelin, insulating it electrically and chemically, with breaks at the nodes of Ranvier. The ion channels are concentrated in these nodes because this is the only place where the extracellular fluid is in contact with the cell membrane. In an insulated axon, a signal propagates by jumping from one node to the next. This process is called *saltatory conduction,* from the Latin *saltare,* "to leap."

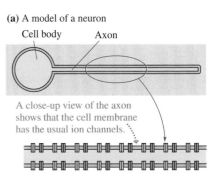

(a) A model of a neuron

A close-up view of the axon shows that the cell membrane has the usual ion channels.

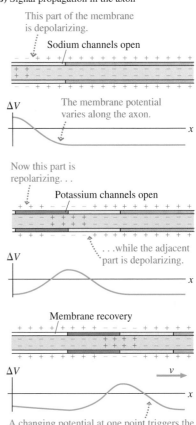

(b) Signal propagation in the axon

This part of the membrane is depolarizing.

Sodium channels open

The membrane potential varies along the axon.

Now this part is repolarizing. . .

Potassium channels open

. . .while the adjacent part is depolarizing.

Membrane recovery

A changing potential at one point triggers the membrane to the right, leading to a wave of action potential that moves along the axon.

FIGURE 9.40 Propagation of a nerve impulse.

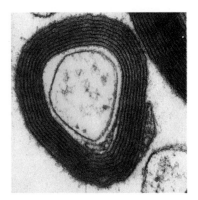

▶ This cross-section view of a myelinated axon shows that the axon (colored aqua) is wrapped several times by a Schwann cell (colored red). There is insulating myelin between each layer.

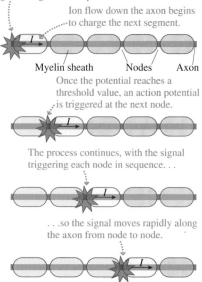

The ion channels at this node are triggered, generating an action potential.

Ion flow down the axon begins to charge the next segment.

Myelin sheath   Nodes   Axon

Once the potential reaches a threshold value, an action potential is triggered at the next node.

The process continues, with the signal triggering each node in sequence. . .

. . .so the signal moves rapidly along the axon from node to node.

FIGURE 9.41 Nerve propagation along a myelinated axon.

Figure 9.41 shows a model for saltatory conduction. The membrane is triggered to depolarize at the left node. An action potential is produced here, but it can't travel down the axon as before because the axon is insulated. Instead, the potential difference between this node and the next causes ions to flow in the body of the axon. As the charges flow down the axon, the potential at the next node rises. When the potential has risen by ≈ 15 mV, the next node is triggered and an action potential is produced at this node. This process continues, with the depolarization "jumping" from node to node down the axon. This dramatically increases the speed of propagation, as we can show.

How rapidly does a pulse move down a myelinated axon? Figure 9.42 provides a model of the process based on RC circuits. The critical time for propagation is the time constant $\tau = RC$ for charging the capacitance of the segments of the axon.

The resistance of an axon between one node and the next is ≈ 25 MΩ. The myelin insulation increases the separation between the inner conducting fluid and the outer conducting fluid. Because the capacitance of a capacitor depends inversely on the electrode spacing d, the myelin reduces the capacitance of the membrane from the ≈ 90 pF we calculated earlier to ≈ 1.6 pF per segment. With these values, the time constant for charging the capacitor in one segment is

$$\tau = R_{axon}C_{membrane} = (25 \times 10^6\ \Omega)(1.6 \times 10^{-12}\ F) = 40\ \mu s$$

We've modeled the axon as a series of such segments, and the time constant is a good estimate of how much time it takes for a signal to jump from one node to the next. Because the nodes of Ranvier are spaced about 1 mm apart, the speed at which the nerve impulse travels down the axon is approximately

$$v = \frac{L_{node}}{\tau} = \frac{1.0 \times 10^{-3}\ m}{40 \times 10^{-6}\ s} = 25\ m/s$$

Although our model of nerve-impulse propagation is very simple, this predicted speed is just about right for saltatory conduction of signals in myelinated axons. This speed is 25 times faster than that in unmyelinated axons; at this speed, your brain can send a signal to your hand in $\approx \frac{1}{25}$ s.

Your electric nature might not be as apparent as that of the electric eel, but the operation of your nervous system is inherently electrical. When you decide to move your hand, the signal from your brain travels to your hand in a process that is governed by the electrical nature of the cells in your body.

(a) A model of a myelinated axon

The fluid in the axon has a certain resistivity. The axon is thin, so the resistance is large.

The interior and exterior of the axon are conducting fluid separated by insulating membrane—a capacitor.

(b) Signal propagation in the myelinated axon

1. An action potential is triggered at this node; we close the switch.

2. Once the switch is closed, the action potential emf drives a current down the axon and charges the capacitance of the membrane.

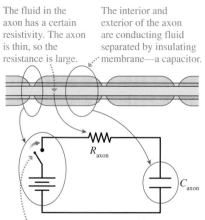

R_{axon}

C_{axon}

We model the triggering of an action potential as closing a switch connected to a battery.

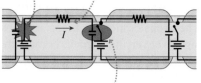

3. When the voltage on the capacitor exceeds a threshold, it triggers an action potential at this node—the next switch is closed.

FIGURE 9.42 A circuit model of nerve-impulse propagation along myelinated axons.

The goal of Chapter 9 has been to learn about the fundamental physical principles that govern electric circuits.

GENERAL PRINCIPLES

Kirchhoff's loop law

For a closed loop:

- Assign a direction to the current.
- Add potential differences around the loop.

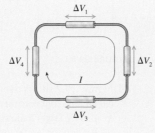

$$\sum_i \Delta V_i = 0$$

Kirchhoff's junction law

For a junction:

$$\sum I_{in} = \sum I_{out}$$

Analyzing circuits

PREPARE Draw a circuit diagram.

SOLVE *Break the circuit down:*

- Reduce the circuit to the smallest possible number of equivalent resistors.
- Find the current and potential difference.

Rebuild the circuit:

- Find current and potential difference for each resistor.

ASSESS Verify that

- The sum of potential differences across series resistors matches that for the equivalent resistor.
- The sum of the currents through parallel resistors matches that for the equivalent resistor.

IMPORTANT CONCEPTS

Series elements

A series connection has no junction.
The current in each element is the same.

Resistors in series can be reduced to an equivalent:

 $R_{eq} = R_1 + R_2 + R_3 + \cdots$

Parallel elements

Elements connected in parallel are connected by wires at both ends.
The potential difference across each element is the same.

Resistors in parallel can be reduced to an equivalent:

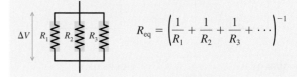 $R_{eq} = \left(\dfrac{1}{R_1} + \dfrac{1}{R_2} + \dfrac{1}{R_3} + \cdots \right)^{-1}$

(MP) For instructor-assigned homework, go to www.masteringphysics.com

Problem difficulty is labeled as | (straightforward) to ||||| (challenging).

Problems labeled INT integrate significant material from earlier chapters; BIO are of biological or medical interest.
Problems labeled: can be done on a Workbook

Conceptual Questions

1. The tip of a flashlight bulb is touching the top of a 3 V battery as shown in Figure Q9.1. Does the bulb light? Why or why not?

FIGURE Q9.1

2. A flashlight bulb is connected to a battery and is glowing; the circuit is shown in Figure Q9.2. Is current I_2 greater than, less than, or equal to current I_1? Explain.

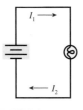

FIGURE Q9.2

3. Current I_{in} flows into three resistors connected together one after the other as shown in Figure Q9.3. The accompanying graph shows the value of the potential as a function of position.
   a. Is I_{out} greater than, less than, or equal to I_{in}? Explain.
   b. Rank in order, from largest to smallest, the three resistances R_1, R_2, and R_3. Explain.

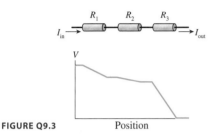

FIGURE Q9.3

4. a. What is the direction of the current through resistor R in Figure Q9.4?
   b. Which end of R is more positive, the right or left? Explain.
   c. If this circuit were analyzed in a clockwise direction, what numerical value would you assign to ΔV_R? Why?
   d. What value would ΔV_R have if the circuit were analyzed in a counterclockwise direction?

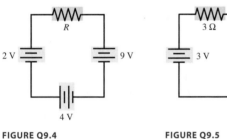

FIGURE Q9.4   **FIGURE Q9.5**

5. The wire is broken on the right side of the circuit in Figure Q9.5 at lower left. What is the potential difference ΔV_{12} between points 1 and 2? Explain.
6. The circuit in Figure Q9.6 has two resistors, with $R_1 > R_2$. Which resistor dissipates the larger amount of power? Explain.

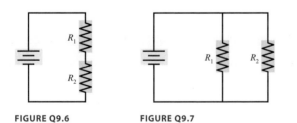

FIGURE Q9.6   **FIGURE Q9.7**

7. The circuit in Figure Q9.7 has a battery and two resistors, with $R_1 > R_2$. Which resistor dissipates the larger amount of power? Explain.
8. In the circuit shown in Figure Q9.8, bulbs A and B are glowing. Then the switch is closed. What happens to each bulb? Does it get brighter, stay the same, get dimmer, or go out? Explain.

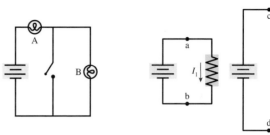

FIGURE Q9.8   **FIGURE Q9.9**

9. Figure Q9.7 shows two circuits. The two batteries are identical and the four resistors all have exactly the same resistance.
   a. Is ΔV_{ab} larger than, smaller than, or equal to ΔV_{cd}? Explain.
   b. Rank in order, from largest to smallest, the currents I_1, I_2, and I_3. Explain.
10. Figure Q9.10 shows two circuits. The two batteries are identical and the four resistors all have exactly the same resistance.
    a. Compare ΔV_{ab}, ΔV_{cd}, and ΔV_{ef}. Are they all the same? If not, rank them in order from largest to smallest. Explain.
    b. Rank in order, from largest to smallest, the five currents I_1 to I_5. Explain.

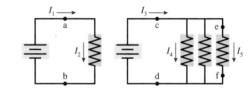

FIGURE Q9.10

11. a. In Figure Q9.11, what fraction of current I goes through the 3 Ω resistor?
    b. If the 9 Ω resistor is replaced with a larger resistor, will the fraction of current going through the 3 Ω resistor increase, decrease, or stay the same?

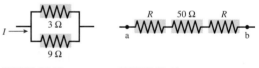

FIGURE Q9.11   **FIGURE Q9.12**

12. Two of the three resistors in Figure Q9.12 are unknown but equal. Is the total resistance between points a and b less than, greater than, or equal to 50 Ω? Explain.
13. Two of the three resistors in Figure Q9.13 are unknown but equal. Is the total resistance between points a and b less than, greater than, or equal to 200 Ω? Explain.

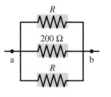

FIGURE Q9.13

14. Rank in order, from largest to smallest, the currents I_1, I_2, and I_3 in the circuit diagram in Figure Q9.14.

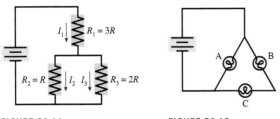

FIGURE Q9.14   **FIGURE Q9.15**

15. The three bulbs in Figure Q9.15 are identical. Rank the bulbs from brightest to dimmest. Explain.
16. The four bulbs in Figure Q9.16 are identical. Rank the bulbs from brightest to dimmest. Explain.

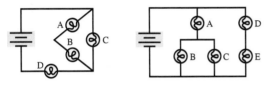

FIGURE Q9.16   **FIGURE Q9.17**

17. Figure Q9.17 shows five identical bulbs connected to a battery. All the bulbs are glowing. Rank the bulbs A to E, from brightest to dimmest. Explain.
18. a. The three bulbs in Figure Q9.18 are identical. Rank the bulbs from brightest to dimmest. Explain.
    b. Suppose a wire is connected between points 1 and 2. What happens to each bulb? Does it get brighter, stay the same, get dimmer, or go out? Explain.

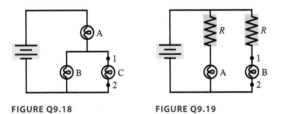

FIGURE Q9.18   **FIGURE Q9.19**

19. Initially, bulbs A and B in Figure Q9.19 are both glowing. Bulb B is then removed from its socket. Does removing bulb B cause the potential difference ΔV_{12} between points 1 and 2 to increase, decrease, or become zero? Explain.
20. a. Consider the points a and b in Figure Q9.20. Is the potential difference ΔV_{ab} between point a and b zero? If so, why? If not, which point is more positive?
    b. If a wire is connected between points a and b, does it carry a current? If so, in which direction—to the right or to the left? Explain.

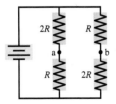

FIGURE Q9.20

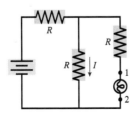

FIGURE Q9.21

21. Initially the lightbulb in Figure Q9.21 is glowing. It is then removed from its socket.
    a. What happens to the current I when the bulb is removed? Does it increase, stay the same, or decrease? Explain.
    b. What happens to the potential difference ΔV_{12} between points 1 and 2? Does it increase, stay the same, decrease, or become zero? Explain.

Multiple-Choice Questions

Questions 22 and 23 are about the circuit of Figure Q9.22.

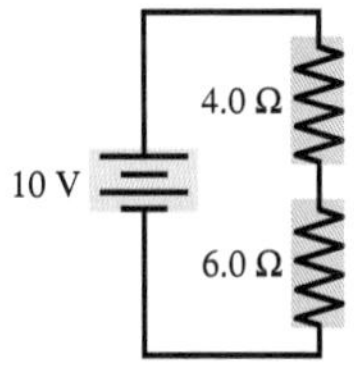

FIGURE Q9.22

22. | What is the current in the circuit?
    A. 1.0 A
    B. 1.7 A
    C. 2.5 A
    D. 4.2 A
23. | Which resistor dissipates the most power?
    A. The 4.0 Ω resistor.
    B. The 6.0 Ω resistor.
    C. Both dissipate the same power.
24. ||| Normally, household lightbulbs are connected in parallel to a power supply. Suppose a 40 W and a 60 W lightbulb are, instead, connected in series, as shown in Figure Q9.24. Which bulb is brighter?
    A. The 60 W bulb.
    B. The 40 W bulb.
    C. The bulbs are equally bright.

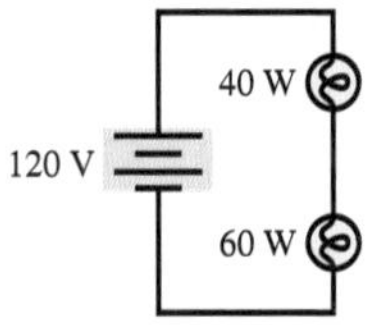

FIGURE Q9.24

25. || A metal wire of resistance R is cut into two pieces of equal length. The two pieces are connected together side by side. What is the resistance of the two connected wires?
    A. $R/4$
    B. $R/2$
    C. R
    D. $2R$
    E. $4R$
26. | What is the value of resistor R in Figure Q9.26?
    A. 4.0 Ω
    B. 12 Ω
    C. 36 Ω
    D. 72 Ω
    E. 96 Ω

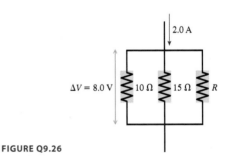

FIGURE Q9.26

PROBLEMS

Section 9.1 Circuit Elements and Diagrams

1. ‖ Draw a circuit diagram for the circuit of Figure P9.1.

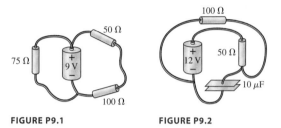

FIGURE P9.1　　　　**FIGURE P9.2**

2. ‖ Draw a circuit diagram for the circuit of Figure P9.2.
3. ‖ Draw a circuit diagram for the circuit of Figure P9.3.

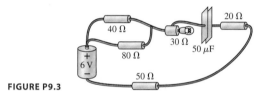

FIGURE P9.3

Section 9.2 Kirchhoff's Laws

4. ‖ In Figure P9.4, what is the current in the wire above the junction? Does charge flow toward or away from the junction?

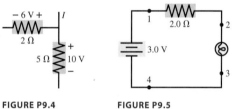

FIGURE P9.4　　　　**FIGURE P9.5**

5. ‖ The lightbulb in the circuit diagram of Figure P9.5 has a resistance of $1.0\ \Omega$. Let ΔV_{ab} represent the magnitude of the potential difference between points a and b.
   a. What are the values of ΔV_{12}, ΔV_{23}, and ΔV_{34}?
   b. What are the values if the bulb is removed?
6. ‖ a. What are the magnitude and direction of the current in the $30\ \Omega$ resistor in Figure P9.6?
   b. Draw a graph of the potential as a function of the distance traveled through the circuit, traveling clockwise from $V = 0$ V at the lower left corner.

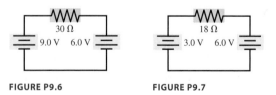

FIGURE P9.6　　　　**FIGURE P9.7**

7. ‖ a. What are the magnitude and direction of the current in the $18\ \Omega$ resistor in Figure P9.7?
   b. Draw a graph of the potential as a function of the distance traveled through the circuit, traveling clockwise from $V = 0$ V at the lower left corner. See Figure P9.7 for an example of such a graph.

8. ‖ a. What is the potential difference across each resistor in Figure P9.8?
   b. Draw a graph of the potential as a function of the distance traveled through the circuit, traveling clockwise from $V = 0$ V at the lower left corner. See Figure P9.7 for an example of such a graph.

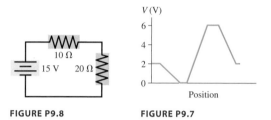

FIGURE P9.8　　　　**FIGURE P9.7**

9. ‖ The current in a circuit with only one battery is 2.0 A. Figure P9.7 shows how the potential changes when going around the circuit in the clockwise direction, starting from the lower left corner. Draw the circuit diagram.

Section 9.3 Series and Parallel Circuits

10. ‖ What is the equivalent resistance of each group of resistors shown in Figure P9.10?

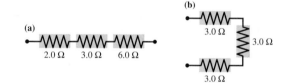

FIGURE P9.10

11. ‖ What is the equivalent resistance of each group of resistors shown in Figure P9.11?

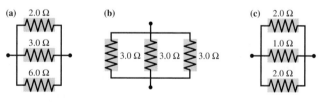

FIGURE P9.11

12. ‖ An 80-cm-long wire is made by welding a 1.0-mm-diameter, 20-cm-long copper wire to a 1.0-mm-diameter, 60-cm-long iron wire. What is the resistance of the composite wire?
13. ‖ You have a collection of $1.0\ k\Omega$ resistors. How can you connect four of them to produce an equivalent resistance of $0.25\ k\Omega$?
14. ‖ You have a collection of six $1.0\ k\Omega$ resistors. What is the smallest resistance you can make by combining them?
15. ‖ You have three $6.0\ \Omega$ resistors and one $3.0\ \Omega$ resistor. How can you connect them to produce an equivalent resistance of $5.0\ \Omega$?
16. ‖ You have four identical resistors. How can you connect them to produce an equivalent resistance which is the same as the resistance of each individual resistor?

Section 9.4 Measuring Voltage and Current

Section 9.5 More Complex Circuits

17. ‖‖ What is the equivalent resistance between points a and b in Figure P9.17?

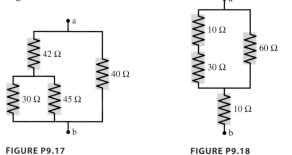

FIGURE P9.17   **FIGURE P9.18**

18. | What is the equivalent resistance between points a and b in Figure P9.18?

19. | Part of a circuit is shown in Figure P9.19.
   a. What is the current through the 3.0 Ω resistor?
   b. What is the value of the current I?

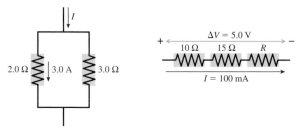

FIGURE P9.19   **FIGURE P9.20**

20. | What is the value of resistor R in Figure P9.20?

21. | What are the resistance R and the emf of the battery in Figure P9.21?

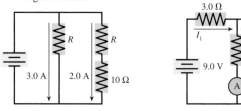

FIGURE P9.21   **FIGURE P9.22**

22. ‖‖ The ammeter in Figure P9.22 reads 3.0 A. Find I_1, I_2, and $\mathcal{E}$.

23. ‖‖ For the circuit shown in Figure P9.23, find the current through and the potential difference across each resistor. Place your results in a table for ease of reading.

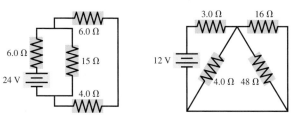

FIGURE P9.23   **FIGURE P9.24**

24. | For the circuit shown in Figure P9.24, find the current through and the potential difference across each resistor. Place your results in a table for ease of reading.

Section 9.6 Household Electricity

25. ‖ A typical American family uses 1000 kWh of electricity a month.
   a. What is the average current in the 120 V power line to the house?
   b. On average, what is the resistance of a household?

26. | The wiring in the wall of your house to and from an outlet
INT has a total resistance of typically 0.10 Ω. Suppose a device plugged into a 120 V outlet draws 10.0 A of current.
   a. What is the voltage drop along the wire?
   b. How much power is dissipated in the wire?
   c. What is the voltage drop across the device?
   d. At what rate does the device use electric energy?

27. | The following appliances are connected to a single 120 V,
INT 15 A circuit in a kitchen: a 330 W blender, a 1000 W coffeepot, a 150 W coffee grinder, and a 750 W microwave oven. If these are all turned on at the same time, will they trip the circuit breaker?

28. | A 60 W (120 V) night light is turned on for an average 12 hr a day year round. What is the annual cost of electricity at a billing rate of $0.10/kWh?

29. ‖ Suppose you leave a 110 W television and two 100 W lightbulbs on in your house to scare off burglars while you go out dancing. If the cost of electric energy in your town is $0.12/kWh and you stay out for 4.0 hr, how much does this robbery-prevention measure cost?

General Problems

30. | How much power is dissipated by each resistor in Fig-
INT ure P9.30?

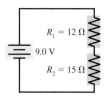

FIGURE P9.30

31. ‖‖ Two 75 W (120 V) lightbulbs are wired in series, then the
INT combination is connected to a 120 V supply. How much power is dissipated by each bulb?

32. ‖‖ The corroded contacts in a lightbulb socket have 5.0 Ω total
INT resistance. How much actual power is dissipated by a 100 W (120V) lightbulb screwed into this socket?

33. ‖ A real battery is not just an emf. We can
INT model a real 1.5 V battery as a 1.5 V emf in series with a resistor known as the "internal resistance," as shown in Figure P9.33. A typical battery has 1.0 Ω internal resistance due to imperfections that limit current through the battery. When there's no current through the battery, and thus no voltage drop across the internal resistance, the potential difference between its terminals is 1.5 V, the value of the emf. Suppose the terminals of this battery are connected to a 2.0 Ω resistor.

FIGURE P9.33

a. What is the potential difference between the terminals of the battery?

b. What fraction of the battery's power is dissipated by the internal resistance?

34. | For the real battery shown in Figure P9.33, calculate the power dissipated by a resistor R connected to the battery when (a) $R = 0.25\ \Omega$, (b) $R = 0.50\ \Omega$, (c) $R = 1.0\ \Omega$, (d) $R = 2.0\ \Omega$, and (e) $R = 4.0\ \Omega$. (Your results should suggest that maximum power dissipation is achieved when the external resistance R equals the internal resistance. This is true in general.)

35. ‖| When two resistors are connected in parallel across a battery of unknown voltage, one resistor carries a current of 3.2 A while the second carries a current of 1.8 A. What current will be supplied by the same battery if these two resistors are connected to it in series?

36. ‖ The 10 Ω resistor in Figure P9.36 is dissipating 40 W of power. How much power are the other two resistors dissipating?

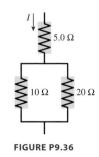

FIGURE P9.36

STOP TO THINK ANSWERS

Stop to Think 9.1: A, B, and **D.** These three are the same circuit because the logic of the connections is the same. In C, the functioning of the circuit is changed by the extra wire connecting the two sides of the capacitor.

Stop to Think 9.2: C = D > A = B. The two bulbs in series are of equal brightness, as are the two bulbs in parallel. But the two bulbs in series have a larger resistance than a single bulb, so there will be less current through the bulbs in series than the bulbs in parallel.

Stop to Think 9.3: C. The voltmeter must be connected in parallel with the resistor, and the ammeter in series.

Stop to Think 9.4: A > B > C = D. All the current from the battery goes through A, so it is brightest. The current divides at the junction, but not equally. Because B is in parallel with C + D, but has half the resistance, twice as much current travels through B as through C + D. So B is dimmer than A but brighter than C and D. C and D are equal because of conservation of current.

10 GLOBAL ENERGY BALANCE: THE GREENHOUSE EFFECT

Earth is heated by visible radiation from the Sun and cools by radiating infrared energy back to space. Earth's surface temperature depends on the amount of incident sunlight, the planet's reflectivity, and the greenhouse effect of its atmosphere. Certain gases in the atmosphere absorb outgoing infrared radiation and reradiate part of that energy back down to the surface. If this process did not occur, Earth's average surface temperature would be well below the freezing point of water, and life could not survive. Both the greenhouse effect and the amount of absorbed sunlight are strongly influenced by the presence of clouds. Clouds can either warm or cool the surface, depending on their altitude and thickness. Built-in feedback loops involving atmospheric water vapor and the extent of snow and ice cover are also fundamental aspects of the climate system. All these factors need to be considered in order to predict the response of Earth's climate to future increases in greenhouse gas concentrations.

10.1 Introduction

That Earth is suitable for life is largely a consequence of its temperate climate. A fundamental requirement for life as we know it is liquid water, and Earth is the only planet in our solar system that has liquid water at its surface. Venus, our nearest neighbor toward the Sun, has an average surface temperature of 460°C (860°F), hot enough to melt lead. Mars, the closest planet away from the Sun, has an average surface temperature of −55°C (−67°F), the coldest temperatures experienced at the South Pole. Earth's average surface temperature is 15°C (59°F), the same as the mean annual temperature of San Francisco. Earth is not only habitable, it is a relatively pleasant place to live.

FIGURE 10.1 Venus, Earth, and Mars, shown roughly to scale. (Left: From NASA/Marten, Photo Researchers, Inc. Center: From NASA/Science Source, Photo Researchers, Inc. Right: From Photo Disc, Inc.)

Why is Venus too hot, Mars too cold, and Earth just right? This question is sometimes called the "Goldilocks problem" of comparative planetology. Intuition suggests that the answer is that Earth happens to lie at the right distance from the Sun (and hence would receive exactly the right amount of sunlight), whereas Venus and Mars do not (Figure 10.1). A closer look, however, reveals that it is not just the amount of sunlight that a planet receives that determines its surface temperature. A planet's surface is also warmed by the greenhouse effect of its atmosphere. A planet's atmosphere allows sunlight to come in but slows down the rate at which heat is lost. Without this greenhouse effect, Earth's average surface temperature would be about 33°C (59°F) colder than the observed value. Earth would be an icy, desolate world.

In this chapter, we discuss how the greenhouse effect works. We begin by considering the nature of electromagnetic radiation and why the Sun emits primarily one form of radiation (visible light), whereas Earth emits another (infrared radiation). We show that the incoming solar energy and outgoing infrared energy must be approximately in balance, and we demonstrate how this balance allows us to calculate the magnitude of the atmospheric greenhouse effect. Next, we discuss how both forms of energy are affected by atmospheric gases and by clouds, and we explain why some gases are greenhouse gases but others are not. Finally, we use the systems notation to introduce real climate feedback mechanisms, and we show why it is necessary to understand these feedbacks in order to estimate the climate changes that are occurring now as well as those that may occur in the future.

10.2 Electromagnetic Radiation

What exactly does it mean to say that Earth is heated by radiation from the Sun? From our sense of sight, we know that the Sun emits about 50% of its energy in the form of *visible light*. Let us start by considering what makes up light and other forms of *electromagnetic radiation*.

Properties of Electromagnetic Radiation. A physicist would describe an electromagnetic wave as a propagating disturbance consisting of oscillating (regularly fluctuating) electric and magnetic fields that are perpendicular to each other. For our purposes, we can think of **electromagnetic radiation** as a self-propagating electric and magnetic wave that is similar to a wave that moves on the surface of a pond. A wave of any form of electromagnetic radiation—such as light, ultraviolet, or infrared radiation—moves at a fixed speed c (the "speed of light"). The numerical value of c for a light wave in a vacuum is 3.00×10^8 m/s. The wave consists of a series of crests and troughs (Figure 10.2). The distance between two adjacent

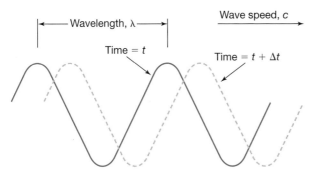

FIGURE 10.2 Simplified representation of an electromagnetic wave, illustrating the concept of wavelength. The solid curve shows the position of the wave at some time t. The dashed curve shows the wave at time $t + \Delta t$.

crests is called the **wavelength.** It is typically denoted by the Greek letter λ (lambda). An observer standing at a fixed point in the path of the wave would be passed by a given number of crests in one second. This number is called the **frequency** of the wave. It is represented by the Greek letter ν (nu).

If we neglect complexities like polarization, an electromagnetic wave can be described by these three characteristics: speed, wavelength, and frequency. Not all of these characteristics are independent. The speed of the wave must equal the product of the number of wave crests that pass a given point each second (the frequency) and the distance between the crests (the wavelength). We can express this relationship mathematically as

$$\lambda \nu = c,$$

or equivalently as

$$\nu = \frac{c}{\lambda}.$$

The longer the wavelength of an electromagnetic wave, the lower must be its frequency, and vice versa. Conversely, the shorter the wavelength, the higher the frequency.

Photons and Photon Energy

Although we can think of electromagnetic radiation as a wave, at times it behaves more like a stream of particles. A single "particle," or pulse, of electromagnetic radiation is referred to as a **photon.** A photon is the smallest discrete (independent) amount of energy that can be transported by an electromagnetic wave of a given frequency. The energy E of a photon is proportional to its frequency:

$$E = h\nu = \frac{hc}{\lambda},$$

where h is a constant called *Planck's constant*, after the famous German physicist Max Planck. Its numerical value is 6.63×10^{-34} J-s (joule-seconds). Thus, high-frequency (short-wavelength) photons have high energy, and low-frequency (long-wavelength) photons have low energy. This difference in photon energy becomes important when electromagnetic radiation interacts with matter, because high-energy and low-energy photons have very different effects. High-energy photons can break

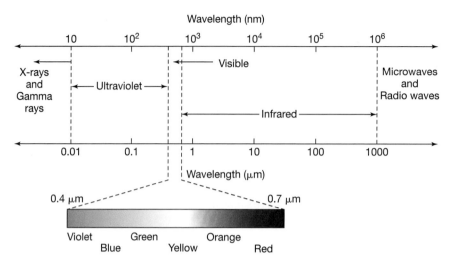

FIGURE 10.3 [See color section] The electromagnetic spectrum.

molecules apart and hence cause chemical reactions to occur, whereas low-energy photons merely cause molecules to rotate faster or vibrate more strongly.

The fact that electromagnetic radiation behaves both as a particle and as a wave was one of the great discoveries of physics of the early part of the 20th century. This *wave-particle duality* is not restricted to electromagnetic waves. Rather, it is a general characteristic of matter and energy.

The Electromagnetic Spectrum

The full range of forms of electromagnetic radiation, which differ by their wavelengths (or by their frequencies), makes up the **electromagnetic spectrum** (Figure 10.3). Wavelengths in the visible range are typically measured in nanometers (nm). One *nanometer* is one-billionth of 1 meter. **Visible radiation,** or visible light, consists of a relatively narrow range of wavelengths, from about 400 nm to 700 nm. Within this range, the color of the light depends on its wavelength. Anyone who has observed a rainbow has witnessed this phenomenon. The longest visible wavelengths appear to our eyes as the color red, whereas the shortest wavelengths register as blue to violet. The colors of the rainbow—in other words, the range of component wavelengths of visible light—are referred to as the **visible spectrum.** The term "spectrum" indicates that the light has been separated into its component wavelengths.

About 40% of the Sun's energy is emitted at wavelengths longer than the visible limit of 700 nm in a region referred to as the *infrared* region of the electromagnetic spectrum. Wavelengths of **infrared (IR) radiation** are significantly longer than those of visible light. Hence, it is convenient to keep track of them in units called *micrometers* (μm) rather than in nanometers. One micrometer (formerly called *micron*) equals one-millionth (10^{-6}) of 1 meter. So, 1 μm equals 1000 nm. Infrared wavelengths range from 0.7 μm to 1000 μm. At even longer wavelengths within the electromagnetic spectrum, radiation is transmitted in the form of *microwaves* and *radio waves.* Radio waves can have wavelengths of many meters.

About 10% of the Sun's energy is emitted at wavelengths shorter than those of visible light as **ultraviolet (UV) radiation.** Wavelengths of the ultraviolet region extend from 400 nm down to about 10 nm. At shorter wavelengths are *X-rays* and *gamma rays.* These high-energy forms of electromagnetic radiation have little effect on our story here, but they do affect the chemistry of the uppermost atmosphere. X-rays, of course, are also used in medicine because they can penetrate skin and muscle tissue and allow us to see the underlying bones.

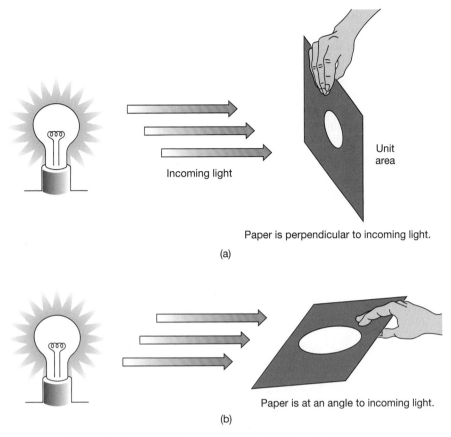

Paper is perpendicular to incoming light.

(a)

Paper is at an angle to incoming light.

(b)

FIGURE 10.4 Schematic diagram of the concept of flux. The flux of radiation into the paper is reduced when the paper is tilted at an angle to the incoming light.

The regions of the electromagnetic spectrum that are most important to climate are the visible and the infrared. The Sun emits energy in both of these spectral regions. Earth, as we shall see, emits primarily in the infrared. Solar ultraviolet radiation also affects the Earth system significantly by driving atmospheric chemistry. In addition, UV radiation would be lethal to most forms of life were it not almost totally blocked out by oxygen and ozone in Earth's atmosphere.

Flux

We will need one other basic concept from electromagnetic theory in order to proceed: the notion of flux. In general terms, *flux* (*F*) is the amount of energy or material that passes through a given area (perpendicular to that area) per unit time. In terms of fluid flow, for example, the flux is the volume of fluid that flows perpendicularly into or out of a unit area per unit time. Applied to electromagnetic radiation, **flux** is the amount of energy (or number of photons) in an electromagnetic wave that passes perpendicularly through a unit surface area per unit time.

To demonstrate the concept of flux, let us consider the light given off by an electric lightbulb. A typical, small lightbulb is labeled "60 Watts." A *Watt* (W) is a unit of *power*—formally, the rate at which work is done; informally, the intensity of the bulb in the SI system. One Watt equals one Joule per second. Suppose that a person is standing some distance from such a lightbulb and holds up a sheet of paper directly facing the light (Figure 10.4A). The paper is illuminated by radiant energy from the bulb. The radiation crosses the paper perpendicularly from the lightbulb at a certain flux, or intensity per unit area. That flux is measured in Watts per square meter (W/m^2). The magnitude of the flux depends on how far from the lightbulb the person is standing, but it does *not* depend on how big the paper is because flux is defined as the intensity per *unit* area.

The fact that flux is measured perpendicular to the direction the wave is traveling is important. Suppose that the person is holding the paper at an angle, rather than perpendicularly, to the light (Figure 10.4b). Although the total area of the paper remains the same, the flux of radiant energy reaching its surface is less because less radiation strikes a given unit area. This simple concept has direct, familiar consequences for Earth's climate. The polar regions are cooler than the tropics because the Sun's rays strike the ground at a higher angle at the poles. Summer temperatures are warmer than winter temperatures because the Sun is higher in the sky during summer. For now, we simply need to understand the concept of flux.

The Inverse-Square Law

Figure 10.4 demonstrates that the flux of radiant energy from a lightbulb depends on how far away the observer (the person holding the paper) is standing. Likewise, the flux of solar energy decreases as distance from the Sun increases; that is why Venus is illuminated more strongly than Earth. The rate at which this *solar flux* decreases with increasing distance is described by a simple relationship. This relationship, called an **inverse-square law,** is expressed mathematically as

$$S = S_0\left(\frac{r_0}{r}\right)^2,$$

where S represents the solar flux at some distance r from the source, and S_0 represents the flux at some reference distance r_0 (Figure 10.5).

The inverse-square law has a straightforward physical interpretation: If we double the distance from the source to the observer, the intensity of the radiation decreases by a factor of $(1/2)^2$, or 1/4. Similarly, if we reduce the distance from the source to the observer by a factor of 3, the radiation intensity increases by a factor of 3^2, or 9.

As an example, consider a hypothetical planet, Planet X, located twice as far from the Sun as is Earth. What would be the solar flux hitting Planet X? Refer to Figure 10.5, and let the Sun be at the center of the two circles. Also, let the inner circle represent Earth's orbit and the outer circle represent the orbit of Planet X. Then r_0 is the average distance from the Earth to the Sun, which is 149,600,000 km, defined as one *astronomical unit* (AU), and S_0 is the solar flux at Earth's orbit, 1370 W/m². (The value of S_0 is determined by satellite measurements.) So according to the inverse-square law, for this example $r = 2$ AU, the solar flux incident at Planet X is

$$S = 1370 \text{ W/m}^2\left(\frac{1 \text{ AU}}{2 \text{ AU}}\right)^2$$
$$= 342.5 \text{ W/m}^2$$

We would have gotten precisely the same answer if we had expressed the distances in kilometers, but the arithmetic would have been harder.

The inverse-square law is of fundamental importance to the study of planetary climates. It allows us to determine quantitatively why Earth's climate differs from that of Venus and Mars. It also plays a crucial role in our understanding of the causes of the glacial–interglacial cycles of the last 3 million years of Earth's history. As we will see later, small variations in the shape of Earth's orbit, combined with the inverse-square relationship between the distance from the Earth to the Sun and solar flux, cause large changes in the climate of the polar regions and in the size and extent of the polar ice sheets.

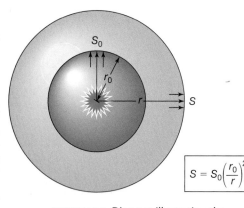

$$S = S_0\left(\frac{r_0}{r}\right)^2$$

FIGURE 10.5 Diagram illustrating the inverse-square law.

10.3 Temperature Scales

To understand climate, which is the prevailing weather patterns of a planet or region over time, we must first understand the concept of temperature. *Temperature* is a measure of the internal heat energy of a substance. Heat energy, in turn, is determined by the average rate of motion of individual molecules in that substance. For a solid, these motions consist of regular vibrations, whereas for a gas or liquid they are just random movements of molecules. The faster the molecules in a substance move, the higher its temperature.

Most areas of the world measure temperature (*T*) by the *Celsius* (formerly, *centigrade*) scale, which is measured in degrees Celsius (°C) and is part of the SI system of units. In the United States, temperature is typically measured in degrees *Fahrenheit* (°F). Scientists, particularly those studying climate, often use the **Kelvin (absolute) temperature scale,** measured in units called *kelvins* (K). (Note that temperatures in the Kelvin scale are given simply as kelvins, not as degrees Kelvin.)

The Celsius temperature scale is defined in terms of the freezing and boiling points of water at sea level (Table 10.1). At sea-level pressure, the freezing point is 0°C, and the boiling point is 100°C. Atmospheric pressure decreases with altitude, as we will see later in the chapter, so it makes a difference where the boiling point is determined. Water boils when its vapor pressure exceeds the overlying atmospheric pressure. Thus, the boiling point decreases with altitude. (This is why it takes longer to hard-boil an egg when you are camping in the mountains. The boiling water is not as hot, so it takes longer to cook the egg.)

The Fahrenheit temperature scale was originally defined on the basis of the temperature of a mixture of snow and table salt (0°F) and the temperature of the human body (about 100°F). Like the Celsius scale, it is defined today in terms of the physical properties of water: The freezing point is 32°F, and the boiling point is 212°F. The following relations allow us to convert temperatures between the Celsius and Fahrenheit scales:

$$T(^{\circ}\text{C}) = \frac{T(^{\circ}\text{F}) - 32}{1.8}$$

$$T(^{\circ}\text{F}) = [T(^{\circ}\text{C}) \times 1.8] + 32$$

Note that converting a temperature *change* from one system of units to the other is easier, because the effect of the different zero points is removed. Thus, a temperature change of 1°C is equal to a change of 1.8°F. Conversely, a change of 1°F is equal to a change of 0.5556 (=1/1.8) °C.

Absolute temperature—that is, temperature on the Kelvin scale—is defined in terms of the heat energy of a substance relative to the energy it would have at a temperature of absolute zero. At *absolute zero,* the molecules of a substance are at rest (or, more precisely, are in their lowest possible energy state). A temperature change of 1 K is equal to a temperature change of 1°C. The zero

TABLE 10.1 Freezing and Boiling Points of Water by Temperature Scale

Temperature Scale	Freezing Point	Boiling Point (at sea level)
Fahrenheit	32°	212°
Celsius	0°	100°
Kelvin (absolute)	273.15	373.15

point of the Kelvin scale is, however, lower than that of the Celsius scale by 273.15°. To convert temperature in degrees Celsius to kelvins, we use the following equation:

$$T(\text{K}) = T(°\text{C}) + 273.15.$$

Thus, a temperature of absolute zero corresponds to a Celsius reading of −273.15°C.

10.4 Blackbody Radiation

In order to fully understand the greenhouse effect, we need one final concept from the world of physics: the concept of blackbody radiation. A *blackbody* is something that emits (or absorbs) electromagnetic radiation with 100% efficiency at all wavelengths. Consider a cast-iron ball (Figure 10.6). At room temperature, the ball looks black because it absorbs most of the light incident on it and gives off little visible radiation of its own. If we heat the ball, however, it begins to glow a dull red. If we heat the ball further, it eventually glows white hot because it radiates at all visible wavelengths. Recall that white light is a mixture of all the colors of the spectrum.

The radiation emitted by a blackbody is called **blackbody radiation.** It has a characteristic wavelength distribution that depends on the body's absolute temperature. This distribution can be described mathematically by a relation called the Planck function. The *Planck function* relates the intensity of radiation from a blackbody to its wavelength, or frequency. When shown graphically, this relation is also known as the *blackbody radiation curve* (Figure 10.7a). The Planck function itself is mathematically complicated and is beyond the scope of our discussion here. We can, however, use this relation to derive two simpler rules that are fundamental to an understanding of climate.

Wien's Law

The first rule derived from the Planck function that will assist us in studying climate is called Wien's law. **Wien's law** states that the flux of radiation emitted by a blackbody reaches its peak value at a wavelength λ_{max}, which depends

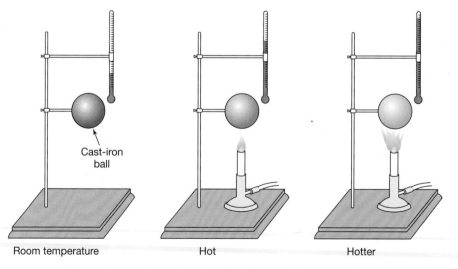

Room temperature   Hot   Hotter

FIGURE 10.6 Change in emitted radiation by a blackbody as it is warmed.

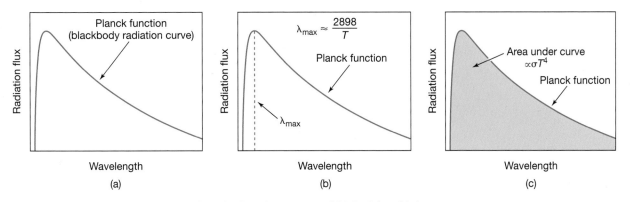

FIGURE 10.7 (a) The Planck function, or blackbody radiation curve; (b) Wien's law; (c) the Stefan–Boltzmann law.

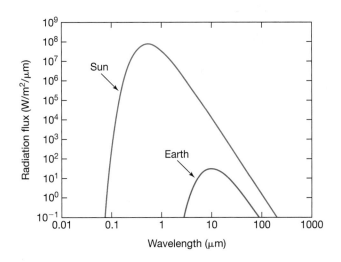

FIGURE 10.8 Blackbody emission curves for the Sun and Earth. The Sun emits more energy per unit area at all wavelengths.

inversely on the body's absolute temperature. According to this rule, hotter bodies emit radiation at shorter wavelengths than do colder bodies. Wien's law may be written as

$$\lambda_{max} \approx \frac{2898}{T},$$

where T is the temperature in Kelvins and λ_{max} is the wavelength of maximum radiation flux in micrometers (Figure 10.7b).

Wien's law allows us to understand why the Sun's radiation peaks in the visible part of the electromagnetic spectrum and why Earth radiates at infrared wavelengths. The Sun emits most of its energy, including visible radiation, from its surface layer, called the **photosphere.** The temperature of the photosphere is about 5780 K. Thus, according to Wien's law, the Sun's radiation flux should maximize at 2898 μm/5780 ≈ 0.5 μm, or 500 nm (Figure 10.8). This is right in the middle of the visible spectrum. (The fact that the solar radiation flux peaks in the visible is no coincidence; our sense of vision presumably evolved as it did to take advantage of the solar spectrum.) Earth, meanwhile, has a surface temperature of about 288 K, so its radiation peaks at 2898 μm/288 ≈ 10 μm—well into the infrared range. In reality, neither Earth nor the Sun is a perfect blackbody, so their emitted radiation flux is not exactly described by the Planck function. Nevertheless, Wien's law is still useful in predicting the wavelength at which most of their radiant energy is emitted.

The Stefan–Boltzmann Law

A second rule derived from the Planck function that will prove useful in climate studies is called the Stefan–Boltzmann law. The **Stefan–Boltzmann law** states that the energy flux emitted by a blackbody is related to the fourth power of the body's absolute temperature:

$$F = \sigma T^4,$$

where T is the temperature in kelvins and σ (the lowercase Greek letter sigma) is a constant with a numerical value of 5.67×10^{-8} W/m^2/K^4. The total energy flux per unit area is proportional to the area under the blackbody radiation curve (Figure 10.7c).

As an example of how the Stefan–Boltzmann law can be applied, consider a hypothetical star that has a surface temperature twice that of the Sun. (We shall use stars rather than planets in this example because the radiation emitted from stars is more nearly approximated as blackbody radiation.) Our Sun has a surface temperature of about 5780 K, so the energy flux per unit area is

$$F_{Sun} = \sigma(5780 \text{ K})^4 \approx 6.3 \times 10^7 \text{ W/m}^2.$$

The other star releases energy at a rate of

$$\begin{aligned} F_{star} &= \sigma(2 \times 5780 \text{ K})^4 \\ &= 2^4 \times \sigma(5780 \text{ K})^4 \\ &= 16 \, F_{Sun}. \end{aligned}$$

Thus, the amount of energy released per unit area per unit time by the hot star is 2^4, or 16, times greater than that released by the Sun. Evidently, the amount of radiation emitted by a blackbody is a very sensitive function of its temperature.

10.5 Planetary Energy Balance

We now have all the tools necessary to analyze Earth's average climate in a quantitative manner. What we need to do next is put them together. The principle that we will apply is that of *energy balance*. To a first approximation, the amount of energy emitted by Earth must equal the amount of energy absorbed. In reality, this cannot be exactly true; if it were, Earth's average surface temperature would never change. However, the average surface temperature is changing—specifically, it is getting warmer. But it is getting warmer precisely because Earth's energy budget is slightly out of balance: The flux of incoming solar energy exceeds the outgoing IR flux by an almost imperceptible amount (a few hundredths of a percent). The imbalance may be caused by the increase in CO_2 and other greenhouse gases in the atmosphere, or it may be caused by natural fluctuations within the climate system. When the climate system eventually reaches *steady state,* that is, when the surface temperature stops changing, the amount of energy going out will exactly equal the amount of energy coming in.

Physically, Earth's surface temperature depends on three factors: (1) the solar flux available at the distance of Earth's orbit, (2) Earth's reflectivity, and (3) the amount of warming provided by the atmosphere (i.e., the greenhouse effect). The solar flux, *S*, as mentioned earlier, is the amount of solar energy reaching the top of Earth's atmosphere. Not all this energy is absorbed, however. About 30% of the incident energy is reflected back to space, mostly by clouds. As we saw in Chapter 2, the reflectivity of a planet is called its *albedo*. It is usually expressed as the fraction of the total incident sunlight that is reflected from the planet as a whole. We shall designate albedo by the letter *A*.

To calculate the magnitude of the third factor, the greenhouse effect, it is convenient to treat Earth as a blackbody even though this is not exactly true. (As we discuss later, the atmosphere radiates and absorbs energy better at some wavelengths than at others because of the presence of gases such as CO_2 and H_2O.) We do this by defining a quantity T_e that represents the **effective radiating temperature** of the planet. This temperature is the temperature that a true blackbody would need to radiate the same amount of energy that Earth radiates. With this definition in place, we can use the Stefan–Boltzmann law to calculate the energy emitted by Earth. By balancing the energy emitted with the energy absorbed, we obtain the following formula (see the Box "A Closer Look: Planetary Energy Balance"):

$$\sigma T_e^4 = \frac{S}{4}(1 - A).$$

This formula expresses the planetary energy balance between outgoing infrared energy and incoming solar energy.

Magnitude of the Greenhouse Effect

What is the significance of the effective radiating temperature? We can think of this quantity as the temperature at the height in the atmosphere from which most of the outgoing infrared radiation derives (see "Critical-Thinking," Problem 4). We can also think of it as the average temperature that Earth's surface would reach if the planet had no atmosphere (assuming that the albedo remained constant). To get a better understanding, let us calculate its value for the present Earth. We can solve the planetary energy balance equation for T_e by dividing both sides of the equation by σ and then taking the fourth root of each side:

$$T_e = \sqrt[4]{\frac{S}{4\sigma}(1 - A)}.$$

If we insert the known values of *S* (1370 W/m²), *A* (30%, or 0.3), and σ (5.67 × 10^{-8} W/m²/K⁴), we get $T_e \approx 255$ K. Thus, Earth's effective radiating temperature is a relatively chilly −18°C, or 0°F.

We saw earlier, however, that the actual mean surface temperature of Earth, T_S, is 288 K, or about 15°C. The difference between the actual surface temperature and the effective radiating temperature is caused by the greenhouse effect of Earth's atmosphere. We can represent this mathematically by letting

$$\Delta T_g = T_s - T_e,$$

where ΔT_g is the magnitude of the greenhouse effect. Thus, $\Delta T_g = 15°C-(-18°C)$ = 33°C.

To place this value in context, we can carry out similar calculations for Venus and Mars from known data of the albedos, surface temperatures, and orbital distances of these planets. (See "Critical-Thinking," Problem 2.) The results show that the solution to the Goldilocks problem posed at the beginning of this chapter is more complicated than we might have guessed. Evidently, a planet's greenhouse

A CLOSER LOOK Planetary Energy Balance

The derivation of the planetary energy balance equation is not difficult, but it does require that we consider the geometry of the Earth–Sun system. The starting point for the derivation is the relation

Energy emitted by Earth = Energy absorbed by Earth.

Let us first calculate the energy emitted by Earth. If we treat Earth as a blackbody with an effective radiating temperature T_e, the Stefan–Boltzmann law tells us that the energy emitted per unit area must be equal to σT_e^4. Earth radiates over its entire surface area, $4\pi R_{Earth}^2$, where R_{Earth} represents Earth's radius (Box Figure 10.1). Thus, the total energy emitted by Earth is

$$\text{Energy emitted} = 4\pi R_{Earth}^2 \times \sigma T_e^4.$$

Now, let us calculate the energy absorbed by Earth. From the Sun, Earth would look like a circle with radius R_{Earth} and area πR_{Earth}^2. Note that it is the area of Earth projected against the Sun's rays that enters here, not half of the surface area of Earth. (Half of Earth's surface area would be $2\pi R_{Earth}^2$, but the Sun's rays do not strike all of this area perpendicularly.) The total energy intercepted must be equal to the product of Earth's projected area and the solar flux (S), or $\pi R_{Earth}^2 S$. The reflected energy is equal to this incident energy times the albedo (A). The difference between these two quantities is the energy absorbed by Earth:

Energy absorbed = Energy intercepted − Energy reflected

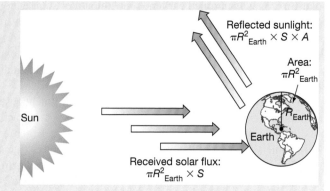

BOX FIGURE 10.1 The amount of sunlight received by and reflected by Earth.

$$= \pi R_{Earth}^2 S - \pi R_{Earth}^2 SA$$
$$= \pi R_{Earth}^2 S(1 - A).$$

All that remains is for us to equate the outgoing and incoming energy. Using the expressions just calculated, we get

$$4\pi R_{Earth}^2 \times \sigma T_e^4 = \pi R_{Earth}^2 S(1 - A).$$

Cancelling out πR_{Earth}^2 on both sides of this equation and dividing both sides by 4, we obtain the desired equation,

$$\sigma T_e^4 = \frac{S}{4}(1 - A).$$

effect is at least as important in determining that planet's surface temperature as is its distance from the Sun.

We can also apply the planetary energy balance equation to the faint young Sun paradox mentioned in Chapter 1. Recall that solar luminosity, and thus S, is estimated to have been 30% lower early in the solar system's history. It is easy to demonstrate that Earth's average surface temperature would have been below the freezing point of water under such circumstances, if the planetary albedo and the atmospheric greenhouse effect had remained unchanged (see "Critical-Thinking," Problem 5). We have already seen, though, that the early Earth had both liquid water and life on its surface. In later chapters, we discuss ways to resolve this apparent paradox.

10.6 Atmospheric Composition and Structure

Atmospheric Composition

To understand the greenhouse effect in more detail, along with other aspects of climate and Earth's radiation budget, we must learn a few fundamental facts about the composition and structure of Earth's atmosphere. Table 10.2 lists the main constituents of Earth's present atmosphere and their relative abundances.

As Table 10.2 indicates, the three most abundant constituents of our atmosphere are nitrogen, oxygen, and argon. Nitrogen is a relatively *inert* (chemically unreactive) gas, but when split into its constituent atoms, it plays an important role in biological cycles. Oxygen, which is highly reactive, is the essential gas that all animals must breathe; it is required by many other life forms as well. Argon is almost completely inert; it is the product of the radioactive decay of potassium, K, in Earth's

THINKING QUANTITATIVELY How the Greenhouse Effect Works: The One-Layer Atmosphere

Although we calculated that Earth's greenhouse effect provides 33°C of surface warming, our method of obtaining this result (by subtracting the calculated effective radiating temperature from the observed mean surface temperature) provides little insight into the physical mechanism that causes the warming. We can remedy this by doing a simple calculation that demonstrates how the greenhouse effect actually works.

Suppose we treat the atmosphere as a single layer of gas and that this gas absorbs (and re-emits) all of the infrared radiation incident on it (Box Figure 10.2). Let us assume that it absorbs and emits infrared radiation equally well at all wave-lengths, so that we can treat it as a blackbody, and that it has an albedo A in the visible spectrum, just like that of the real Earth. What are the temperatures of the gas layer and of the surface beneath it? We will call the layer temperature T_e and the surface temperature T_s, because these quantities are exactly analogous to those discussed in the text.

We can determine the values of T_e and T_s by balancing the energy absorbed and emitted by both the surface and the one-layer atmosphere. Let the amount of sunlight striking the planet be equal to $S/4$ (the globally averaged solar flux). The surface absorbs an amount of sunlight equal to $S/4 \times (1 - A)$, along with a flux of downward infrared radiation from the atmosphere equal to σT_e^4. The atmosphere absorbs an amount of upward infrared radiation from the ground equal to σT_s^4, and it emits infrared radiation in both the upward and downward directions at a rate of σT_e^4. (The real atmosphere also absorbs some of the incoming solar radiation, but we ignore that complication here.) Thus, we can write the overall energy balance in the form of two equations:

For the surface,

$$\sigma T_s^4 = \frac{S}{4}(1 - A) + \sigma T_e^4;$$

for the atmosphere,

$$\sigma T_s^4 = 2\sigma T_e^4.$$

(The factor 2 in the second equation arises because the atmosphere radiates in both the upward and downward directions.) If we now substitute the second equation into the left-hand side of the first equation and substract σT_e^4 from both sides, we obtain

$$\sigma T_e^4 = \frac{S}{4}(1 - A),$$

which is just the familiar energy-balance formula. But dividing the atmospheric energy-balance equation by σ and then taking the fourth root of both sides yields an additional result:

$$T_s = 2^{1/4}\,T_e.$$

Thus, the surface temperature is higher than the one-layer-atmosphere temperature by a factor of the fourth root of 2, or about 1.19. For $T_e = 255$ K, as on Earth at present, we get $T_s = 303$ K, and we calculate a greenhouse effect of

$$\Delta T_g = T_s - T_e = 48 \text{ K}.$$

This is higher than the actual greenhouse effect on Earth by about 15 K.

This example is not meant to be realistic. The real atmosphere is not perfectly absorbing at all infrared wavelengths, so some of the outgoing IR radiation from the surface leaks through to space. This effect tends to make ΔT_g smaller. Conversely, a more-accurate calculation would subdivide the atmosphere into a number of different layers. Including more layers tends to make ΔT_g bigger and is the reason why a thick atmosphere, like that of Venus, can produce a really huge amount of surface warming. The calculation does, however, illustrate the basic nature of the greenhouse effect: By absorbing part of the infrared radiation radiated upward from the surface and re-emitting it in both the upward and downward directions, the atmosphere allows the surface to be warmer than it would be if the atmosphere were not present.

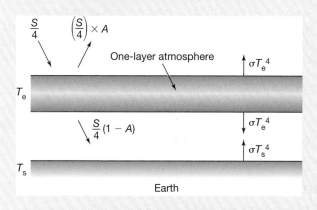

BOX FIGURE 10.2 The greenhouse effect of a one-layer atmosphere.

interior. These three constituents—nitrogen, oxygen, and argon—are not greenhouse gases. In other words, they do not contribute to Earth's greenhouse effect.

Although they appear at the bottom of Table 10.2, water vapor and carbon dioxide are two of the most important atmospheric constituents. Besides being directly used by organisms, they are also strong greenhouse gases. We will soon see what makes a particular gas a greenhouse gas.

TABLE 10.2 Major Constituents of Earth's Atmosphere Today

Name and Chemical Symbol	Concentration (% by volume)
Nitrogen, N_2	78
Oxygen, O_2	21
Argon, Ar	0.9
Water vapor, H_2O	0.00001 (South Pole)–4 (tropics)
Carbon dioxide, CO_2	0.037*

*In 2002

TABLE 10.3 Important Atmospheric Greenhouse Gases

Name and Chemical Symbol	Concentration (ppm by volume)
Water vapor, H_2O	0.1 (South Pole)–40,000 (tropics)
Carbon dioxide, CO_2	370
Methane, CH_4	1.7
Nitrous oxide, N_2O	0.3
Ozone, O_3	0.01 (at the surface)
Freon-11, CCl_3F	0.00026
Freon-12, CCl_2F_2	0.00054

In addition to the major constituents listed in Table 10.2, Earth's atmosphere also contains a number of minor (or "trace") constituents that affect climate. The most important of these are methane, nitrous oxide, ozone, and freons. Their concentrations are generally much lower than those of the major constituents. Despite their low concentrations, these trace gases are important greenhouse gases. Table 10.3 lists the major greenhouse gases. (Note that water vapor and carbon dioxide are repeated here.) It is convenient to keep track of these gases in units of parts per million (ppm), which we defined in Chapter 1. Take a moment to convince yourself that the 0.00001–4% value of water vapor and the 0.037% value of CO_2 given in Table 10.2 are equivalent to the 0.1–40,000 ppm and 370 ppm values of water vapor and of CO_2 given in Table 10.3.

Table 10.3 is by no means a complete list of greenhouse gases. Several other gases affect climate to some extent or are otherwise important in atmospheric chemistry. The gases listed in Table 10.3, however, are the ones that are most important to the modern problem of global warming, and hence they are the ones on which we focus.

Atmospheric Structure

How Atmospheric Pressure Varies with Altitude. Other characteristics of Earth's atmosphere that influence climate and the radiation budget are its pressure and temperature structure. *Pressure* may be defined as the force per unit area exerted by a gas or liquid on some surface with which it is in contact. The pressure exerted by the atmosphere at sea level is defined as one *atmosphere* (atm). A pressure of 1 atm is equivalent to about 15 lb/in^2 in the English system and to 1.013 *bar*, or 1013 *millibars* (mbar), in the metric system. (The pressure unit in the SI system is the *Pascal* (Pa) but this unit is cumbersome in atmospheric work: 1 Pa = 1×10^{-5} bar ≈ 9.9×10^{-6} atm.) An instrument used to measure atmospheric pressure is called a *barometer*, the name of which derives from the metric unit of measure "bar."

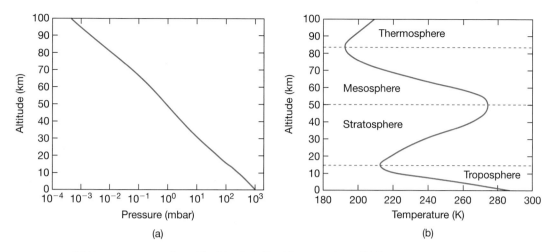

FIGURE 10.9 (a) How pressure varies with altitude in Earth's atmosphere. (b) How temperature varies with altitude in Earth's atmosphere. The different regions of the atmosphere, determined by temperature regimes, are labeled.

At higher levels in the atmosphere, the pressure decreases markedly (Figure 10.9a). This change in pressure is what makes your ears pop in an airplane. (The cabin is pressurized, or the popping would be much worse.) The decrease in altitude follows the **barometric law,** which states that atmospheric pressure decreases by about a factor of 10 for every 16-km increase in altitude. Thus, the pressure is about 0.1 bar at 16 km above the surface, 0.01 bar at 32 km, and so on. In more precise terms, the barometric law says that pressure decreases *exponentially* with altitude. Note from Figure 10.9a that the exponential decrease in pressure appears almost like a straight line when pressure is plotted on a logarithmic scale. The slight deviation from linearity is caused by the variation in temperature with altitude (discussed next). Pressure decreases faster with height in regions where the air is colder.

How Atmospheric Temperature Varies with Altitude. The vertical temperature structure of the atmosphere is more complicated than the vertical pressure structure (Figure 10.9b). This temperature profile is the basis for distinguishing four regions within Earth's atmosphere: the troposphere, the stratosphere, the mesosphere, and the thermosphere. Temperature decreases rapidly with altitude in the lowermost layer of the atmosphere, the **troposphere,** which extends from the surface up to 10–15 km (higher in the tropics, lower near the poles). Immediately above the troposphere is the **stratosphere,** which is located from about 10–15 km to 50 km above the surface and in which temperature increases with altitude. Above the stratosphere, temperature decreases with altitude in the **mesosphere** (from about 50–90 km) and then increases once again in the uppermost layer, the **thermosphere** (above about 90 km). These temperature-based "spheres" overlap with atmospheric layers based on other characteristics. For example, the *ionosphere* (a layer that reflects radio waves) includes parts of both the thermosphere and the mesosphere. The very outermost fringe of the atmosphere, where the gas is so tenuous that collisions between molecules become infrequent, is often termed the *exosphere.*

THE TROPOSPHERE. The atmospheric layers that are most important to climate studies are the two lowermost ones: the troposphere and the stratosphere. The troposphere is where most of the phenomena that we call weather—such as clouds, rain, snow, and storm activity—occur. It differs from the other atmospheric layers in that it is well mixed by convection. **Convection** is a process in which heat energy is transported by the motions of a *fluid* (a liquid or a gas).

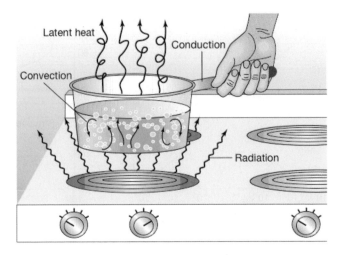

FIGURE 10.10 A pot of water on a stove, illustrating convection. The fluid circulates because it is heated from below. (From R.W. Christopherson, *Geosystems: An Introduction to Physical Geography, 3/e,* 1997. Reprinted by permission of Prentice Hall, Upper Saddle River, N.J.)

Such motions are generated when a fluid in a gravitational field, like that of Earth, is heated from below. A familiar example is the convective motion that occurs when a pot of water is heated on the burner of a stove (Figure 10.10). The warm water at the bottom of the pot is less dense than the cooler water at the top. As a result of this imbalance, the fluid overturns (it circulates, or convects) and will continue to do so as long as the pot is being heated. If the water were heated uniformly or from above, convection would not occur.

We note for completeness that a third mode of heat transfer (in addition to radiation and convection) is **conduction.** Conduction is the transfer of heat energy by direct contact between molecules. The coils of the electric burner shown in Figure 10.10 heat the bottom of the pot by conduction. Conduction plays little role in atmospheric (or oceanic) heat transfer, however, so we will make no further mention of it.

The troposphere is convective because roughly half the incoming sunlight is absorbed by the ground and by the ocean surface. The energy from this light is eventually reradiated to space as IR radiation, but it cannot make its way directly from the surface in this form because IR radiation is absorbed by atmospheric greenhouse gases and by clouds. So, the energy is instead transported by fluid motions until it reaches an altitude where the atmosphere is more transparent to IR radiation. Only then can the heat energy radiate away from Earth.

The upward convection of warm, moist air plays a major role in the global energy balance. Convection of heat in a moist atmosphere is more complicated than that in a dry atmosphere, because water can condense or evaporate. When water is evaporated from the ocean surface or from rivers and lakes, energy is taken up by the resulting vapor. This energy is referred to as the latent heat of vaporization. When the water vapor condenses to form clouds, the same amount of latent heat is released to the atmosphere. In more general terms, **latent heat** is the heat energy released or absorbed during the transition from one phase—gaseous, liquid, or solid—to another.

THE STRATOSPHERE. The stratosphere differs from the troposphere in several respects. The pressure is substantially lower in the stratosphere, in accordance with the barometric law. The two layers differ in composition as well. The stratosphere contains most of Earth's ozone. Stratospheric air is also very dry, containing less than 5 ppm of water vapor on average. Thus, condensation of water vapor does not occur, and so clouds and precipitation are absent. (An exception occurs

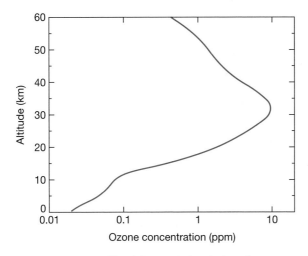

FIGURE 10.11 An approximate profile of the vertical variation of ozone concentration in Earth's atmosphere.

in the polar regions during winter, where tenuous *polar stratospheric clouds* can form. These clouds play a key role in the development of the Antarctic ozone hole. Stratospheric air is not convective and is therefore less well mixed than tropospheric air. Indeed, the name "stratosphere" derives from the word "stratified," which means layered.

THE VERTICAL TEMPERATURE PROFILE. Why does the vertical temperature profile in Figure 10.9b exhibit all those curves? The reason has to do primarily with where the atmosphere is heated—that is, where solar energy is absorbed. The high temperatures near the ground are caused by the absorption of sunlight at Earth's surface, which then heats the atmosphere above it. The high temperatures near 50 km are caused by the absorption of solar UV radiation by ozone. The ozone concentration actually peaks some 20 km lower, in the middle stratosphere (Figure 10.11), but the heating rate is highest in the upper stratosphere because more UV radiation is available at those altitudes. The vertical heating distribution also explains why the stratosphere is not convective: The maximum heating occurs at the top of the layer, so there is no tendency for the air to rise. Above 50 km, both the ozone concentration and the heating rate decline, so the temperature decreases with altitude in the mesosphere. Finally, the temperature rise above 90 km in the thermosphere is caused by the absorption of short-wavelength UV radiation by molecular oxygen, O_2.

10.7 Physical Causes of the Greenhouse Effect

We determined earlier that Earth's greenhouse effect warms the surface by some 33°C compared with the temperature we would expect if there were no atmosphere. This warming has been attributed to the presence of greenhouse gases, especially H_2O and CO_2. Why do some gases contribute to the greenhouse effect whereas others, such as O_2 and N_2, do not?

Molecular Motions and the Greenhouse Gases H_2O and CO_2

The defining property of a greenhouse gas is its ability to absorb or emit infrared radiation. Gas molecules can absorb or emit radiation in the IR range in two different ways. One way is by changing the rate at which the molecules rotate. The

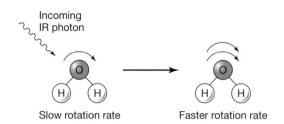

Incoming
IR photon

Slow rotation rate   Faster rotation rate

FIGURE 10.12 The rotation rate of an individual H_2O molecule increases when the molecule absorbs a photon of infrared radiation.

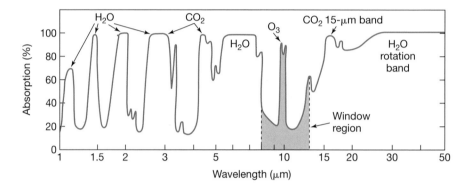

FIGURE 10.13 Percentage of radiation absorbed during vertical passage through the atmosphere. Absorption of 100% means that no radiation penetrates the atmosphere. The nearly complete absorption of radiation longer than 13 μm is caused by absorption by CO_2 and H_2O. Both of these gases also absorb solar radiation in the near infrared (wavelengths between about 0.7 μm and 5 μm). The absorption feature at 9.6 μm is caused by ozone. (From data originally from R. M. Goody and Y. L. Yung, *Atmospheric Radiation, 2nd ed.,* New York: Oxford University Press, 1989, Figure 1.1.)

theory of *quantum mechanics* describes the behavior of matter on a microscopic scale—that is, the size of molecules and smaller. According to this theory, molecules can rotate only at certain discrete frequencies, just as most house fans can operate only at certain speeds. The rotation frequency is the number of revolutions that a molecule completes per second. Consider one photon of an electromagnetic wave that is incident on an individual molecule (Figure 10.12). If the incident wave has just the right frequency (corresponding to the difference between two allowed rotation frequencies), the molecule can absorb the photon. In the process, the molecule's rotation rate increases. Conversely, the rotation rate slows down when the molecule emits a photon.

The frequency (or wavelength) of the radiation that can be absorbed or emitted depends on the molecule's structure. The H_2O molecule is constructed in such a manner that it absorbs IR radiation of wavelengths of about 12 μm and longer. This interaction gives rise to a very strong absorption feature in Earth's atmosphere called the **H_2O rotation band.** It can clearly be seen in Figure 10.13, which shows the percentage of radiation at different wavelengths that is absorbed during vertical passage through the atmosphere. Virtually 100% of infrared radiation longer than 12 μm is absorbed, although some of this absorption is caused by CO_2 (see below). The H_2O rotation band extends all the way into the microwave region of the electromagnetic spectrum (above a wavelength of 1000 μm), which is why a microwave oven is able to heat up anything that contains water.

A second way in which molecules can absorb or emit IR radiation is by changing the amplitude with which they vibrate. Molecules not only rotate, they also vibrate—their constituent atoms move toward and away from each other. Again consider an electromagnetic wave that is incident on a molecule. If the frequency at which the molecule vibrates matches the frequency of the wave, the molecule can absorb a photon and begin to vibrate more vigorously. (Similarly, a vibrating tuning fork will induce vibrations in a second tuning fork if the pitches of the two instruments are the same. The pitch is proportional to the frequency of the sound wave.)

The *triatomic* (three-atom) CO_2 molecule can vibrate in three ways. We need to concern ourselves only with the *bending mode* of vibration (Figure 10.14). This vibration has a frequency that allows the molecule to absorb IR radiation at a wavelength of about 15 μm. It gives rise to a strong absorption feature in Earth's atmosphere called the **15-μm CO_2 band.** The 15-μm CO_2 band overlaps the H_2O rotation band and, hence, is hard to distinguish in Figure 10.13. It is, however, easily seen by satellites that look down at Earth's atmosphere from above. Because it occurs fairly near the peak of Earth's outgoing radiation, this absorption band is particularly important to climate. Earth's surface emits strongly in this wavelength region, but very little of this radiation is able to escape directly to space because it is absorbed by CO_2 molecules in the atmosphere. This is why CO_2 is such an important contributor to the greenhouse effect.

Other Greenhouse Gases

Water vapor and CO_2 are the most important greenhouse gases in Earth's atmosphere, but several other trace gases—notably CH_4, N_2O, O_3, and freons—also contribute to greenhouse warming (Table 10.3). These gases have more of an effect on outgoing radiation than their small concentrations would suggest because they absorb at different wavelengths than do H_2O and CO_2. Freons, for example, have absorption bands within the 8- to 12-μm *window region,* where both H_2O and CO_2 are poor absorbers (see Figure 10.13). Thus, one molecule of Freon-11 contributes much more to the greenhouse effect than does one CO_2 molecule. Ozone also has an absorption band in this region centered at 9.6 μm. Thus, O_3 is a good greenhouse gas as well.

Now, recall that we asked the question, Why are O_2 and N_2 poor absorbers of IR radiation and, thus, do not contribute significantly to the greenhouse effect? We are now ready to answer that question. *Diatomic* (two-atom) molecules can rotate and vibrate just like the more complicated molecules, H_2O and CO_2, discussed earlier (Figure 10.15). The O_2 and N_2 molecules, however, are perfectly symmetric: Both of their constituent atoms are identical. Hence, there is no separation of positive and negative electric charges within the molecule. As noted earlier, an electromagnetic wave actually consists of oscillating electric and magnetic fields. To a first approximation, these fields cannot interact with a totally symmetric molecule; the electromagnetic wave passes by such a molecule without being absorbed. (Note that CO_2 is a symmetric molecule, because the three atoms are, on average, arranged in a line. However, the symmetry is broken when the molecule bends, allowing 15-μm radiation to be absorbed or emitted.)

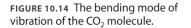

FIGURE 10.14 The bending mode of vibration of the CO_2 molecule.

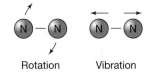

FIGURE 10.15 Rotation and vibration for a diatomic molecule, such as N_2 or O_2.

10.8 Effect of Clouds on the Atmospheric Radiation Budget

Gases are not the only constituents of the atmosphere that affect its radiation balance; that balance is also influenced by the presence of clouds and aerosols. Sulfate aerosols, for example, cooled Earth by about 0.5°C (1°F) for a year or two after the Mt. Pinatubo eruption. The effects of clouds, though, are large and cannot be ignored (Figure 10.16). Unfortunately, these effects cannot always be calculated reliably either, and this leads to significant problems in climate prediction.

FIGURE 10.16 Photo of Earth from space, showing clouds. (From NASA Headquarters.)

(a)   (b)

FIGURE 10.17 Photos of (a) stratus (From Claudia Parks, The Stock Market) and (b) cirrus clouds. (From G.R. Roberts/Nelson Riwaka, Photo Researchers, Inc.)

Types of Clouds

The effect of clouds on Earth's radiation budget is difficult to calculate quantitatively, partly because there are many different types of clouds (Figure 10.17). *Cumulus clouds* are the familiar puffy, white clouds that look like balls of cotton. They are composed of droplets of liquid water and are formed in convective updrafts. *Cumulonimbus clouds* are big, tall cumulus clouds that give rise to thunderstorms. *Stratus clouds* are grey, low-level water clouds that are more or less continuous. They cover much of the eastern United States during winter. *Cirrus clouds* are high, wispy clouds composed of ice crystals rather than liquid water, because the temperature of the upper troposphere is well below the freezing point.

Opposing Climatic Effects of Clouds

Have you ever noticed that cloudy days are relatively cool, yet cloudy nights are relatively warm? That is because clouds affect planetary energy balance in two opposing ways. Clouds cool Earth during the daytime by reflecting incident sunlight back to space. We noted earlier that at present the planetary albedo is about 0.3. A large fraction of this is caused by clouds. In fact, without clouds, Earth's albedo would probably be closer to 0.1. According to the planetary energy balance equation, reducing the albedo from 0.3 to 0.1 would raise the effective radiating temperature of Earth by about 17°C (30°F). The increase in surface temperature on a cloud-free

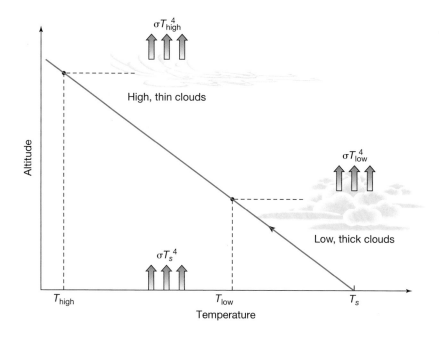

FIGURE 10.18 The different effects of high and low clouds on the atmospheric radiation budget. High, thin clouds are more transparent to incoming sunlight and radiate at a lower temperature than do low, thick clouds. The expressions σT_{high}^4, σT_{low}^4, and σT_s^4 represent the radiation flux at the temperature of high, thin clouds, at the temperature of low, thick clouds, and at the surface temperature, respectively.

Earth would be smaller than this, however, because clouds also absorb and re-emit outgoing infrared radiation and, thus, contribute significantly to the greenhouse effect. This effect dominates at night and helps keep cloudy nights warm.

To complicate matters further, the effect of any particular cloud depends on its height and thickness. Low, thick clouds, such as stratus clouds, generally cool the surface because their primary influence is to reflect incoming solar radiation. High, thin clouds, such as cirrus clouds, tend to warm the surface because they contribute more to the greenhouse effect than to the planetary albedo. The reason for the difference is twofold: First, the elongated ice crystals of which cirrus clouds are composed allow much of the incident solar radiation to pass through but absorb most of the outgoing IR radiation. In contrast, stratus clouds reflect much of the incoming visible radiation, in addition to absorbing radiation at IR wavelengths. Second, cirrus clouds occur higher in the troposphere than do stratus clouds and are therefore colder (Figure 10.18). According to the Stefan–Boltzmann law, cirrus clouds therefore radiate less IR energy to space. Because they absorb the upward-directed IR radiation from the warm surface and reradiate it at a lower temperature, cirrus clouds make a large contribution to the atmospheric greenhouse effect. Lower-lying stratus clouds do this as well, but their radiating temperature is higher and so their contribution to the greenhouse effect is not as large.

Earth's Global Energy Budget

The various factors that we have just discussed can be combined to calculate a global energy budget for Earth, as in Figure 10.19. The incident solar flux in this diagram is normalized to 100 arbitrary "units" of radiation. These 100 units of incoming energy are balanced by 30 units of reflected solar energy (25 reflected by the atmosphere and 5 reflected by the surface) and 70 units of outgoing infrared radiation. About half the incident solar radiation makes it down to the surface; the other half is either reflected or absorbed by the atmosphere. Within the atmosphere, energy is transported by a combination of radiation, convection, and the

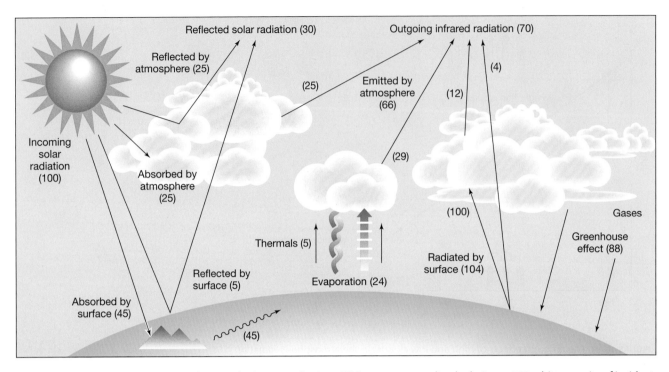

FIGURE 10.19 Earth's globally averaged atmospheric energy budget. All fluxes are normalized relative to 100 arbitrary units of incident radiation. (From S. Schneider, *Climate Modeling,* Scientific American, 256:5, 72–80, 1987.)

latent heat associated with the evaporation and condensation of water vapor. This latter process is a very important one: Roughly half of the solar energy absorbed by the surface (24 out of 45 units) goes directly into evaporating water.

The greenhouse effect is shown here as an additional 88 units of downward-directed infrared radiation. Thus, the total energy flux absorbed by the surface is 133 units (= 45 units of solar radiation + 88 units of IR radiation). This value is almost twice the net amount of energy absorbed by the Earth (70 units). The reason is that infrared radiation is absorbed and re-emitted multiple times within the atmosphere, so the internal fluxes can actually be higher than the net input of energy. *At the top of the atmosphere, however, the net downward solar radiation flux (incoming minus reflected) must equal the outgoing infrared flux.* This statement is the principle of *planetary energy balance.*

10.9 Climate Feedbacks

Climate feedbacks are extremely important because they can either amplify or moderate the radiative effect of changes in greenhouse gas concentrations. Here, we discuss several feedback processes that affect climate on Earth.

The Water Vapor Feedback

One of the most important feedbacks in the climate system involves the concentration of atmospheric water vapor. As noted earlier, water vapor is an excellent absorber of IR radiation and, hence, a good greenhouse gas. Unlike CO_2, however, water vapor is typically close to its *condensation point*—the temperature at which a vapor condenses to form a liquid. If Earth's surface temperature were to decrease for some reason, water vapor would condense out in the form of rain or snow, leaving less water vapor behind in the atmosphere. This reduction in atmospheric water vapor would cause a corresponding decrease in the greenhouse effect, which, in turn, would lower the surface temperature still further. Conversely, an increase in surface temperature would cause an increase in the rate at which water vapor evaporates from the oceans. This would increase the concentration of water vapor in the atmosphere, thereby increasing the greenhouse effect and further warming Earth's surface.

The net result of this interaction between water vapor abundance and Earth's surface temperature is a positive feedback loop that tends to amplify small temperature perturbations (Figure 10.20). This feedback loop can be incorporated in RCMs by assuming a fixed *relative humidity* profile in the troposphere. **Relative humidity** is the concentration of water vapor in an air parcel divided by the concentration that would be present if the air parcel were *saturated* with water vapor (i.e., on the verge of condensation). When such a calculation is performed, the RCM predicts that the equilibrium change in surface temperature for CO_2 doubling, ΔT_{eq}, is about twice that which would have occurred otherwise. Recall that we can write

$$\Delta T_{eq} = \Delta T_0 + \Delta T_f$$

where ΔT_0 is the temperature change with no feedbacks and ΔT_f is the change caused by the feedback. For the problem of CO_2 doubling, $\Delta T_0 = 1.2°C$ (2.2°F), $\Delta T_{eq} \approx 2.4°C$ (4.4°F), so the temperature change caused by the water vapor feedback is approximately 1.2°C. Furthermore, the feedback factor f is given by

$$f = \frac{\Delta T_{eq}}{\Delta T_0} = \frac{2.4°C}{1.2°C} = 2$$

A feedback factor of 2 indicates that this is a strong, positive feedback on the climate system.

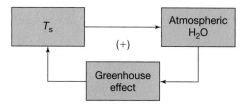

FIGURE 10.20 Systems diagram showing the positive feedback loop that includes atmospheric water vapor.

Snow and Ice Albedo Feedback

A second feedback loop that is expected to have some impact on modern global warming, but is especially important for glacial–interglacial variations, involves albedo changes caused by snow and ice. As Earth's climate cools, the extent of wintertime snow and ice cover increases in temperate regions. On longer time scales, the permanent ice cap in the northern polar regions expands toward the equator, resulting in the periods of glaciation known as the Ice Ages. Snow and ice have a much higher albedo than does land or water. Therefore, increases in snow and ice cover should cause further decreases in surface temperature. The result is a positive feedback loop that tends to amplify induced changes in Earth's surface temperature (Figure 10.21). As snow and ice cover are restricted to middle and high latitudes, modeling this feedback loop quantitatively requires the use of two-dimensional or three-dimensional computer models.

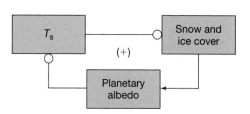

FIGURE 10.21 Systems diagram showing the positive feedback loop that includes snow and ice cover.

The IR Flux/Temperature Feedback

Both of the feedbacks discussed so far are positive. But systems that contain only positive feedback loops are unstable. Does this mean that Earth's climate is unstable? No. Earth's climate system contains a very strong negative feedback that is so basic that it is often overlooked. The feedback loop that stabilizes Earth's climate on short time scales is the relationship between surface temperature and the flux of outgoing IR radiation (Figure 10.22). If Earth's surface temperature were to increase for some reason, the outgoing IR flux from the top of the atmosphere would also increase. But if the outgoing IR flux were to increase, the surface temperature would tend to decrease, because more energy would be lost from the Earth system. This feedback loop might appear to be trivial, but it is not; there are

FIGURE 10.22 Systems diagram illustrating the negative feedback loop between surface temperature and the outgoing flux of infrared radiation. This feedback is the fundamental reason that Earth's climate is stable.

situations in which it can fail. In particular, the positive correlation between surface temperature and the outgoing IR flux can break down if the atmosphere contains a very large amount of water vapor. This, we think, is what happened to our sister planet, Venus, and it led to what is sometimes called a *runaway greenhouse.*

The Uncertain Feedback Caused by Clouds

Another important feedback process in the climate system is that provided by changes in clouds. Unfortunately, this feedback process is not as easy to quantify as the ones just discussed. You already know that clouds can either warm the surface, or cool it, depending on their height. This alone should provide a hint that estimating their feedback effect might be difficult. In addition to this problem, clouds are inherently three-dimensional: they form at some locations and not at others because of the way the winds blow. Keep in mind, though, that cloud feedback is one of the greatest uncertainties in the study of global warming.

In summary, we have now examined Earth's climate system in enough detail to understand how the atmospheric greenhouse effect warms the planet and how the planet's average surface temperature may respond to a human-induced increase in greenhouse gases. But Earth's climate cannot be described by just its average surface temperature. The term "climate" includes many other related factors, such as latitudinal and seasonal temperature gradients, winds, and precipitation. To study these phenomena, we need to broaden our spatial perspective and consider the Earth system from a three-dimensional perspective. The next two chapters describe how the transport of heat from one location to another by the atmosphere and oceans determines these other important features of Earth's global climate.

1. Earth is warmed by the absorption of visible radiation from the Sun and is cooled by the emission of infrared radiation to space.
   a. Much of the infrared radiation emitted by Earth's surface is absorbed and re-emitted by atmospheric gases.
   b. The result is a greenhouse effect that warms the surface by about 33°C. Without this natural greenhouse effect, Earth would be too cold to support life.
2. Only certain atmospheric gases, most importantly H_2O and CO_2, contribute to the greenhouse effect. These gases absorb infrared radiation by changing the rate at which individual molecules rotate or vibrate. Other trace gases, such as freons, can contribute substantially to the greenhouse effect by absorbing radiation at different wavelengths than do H_2O and CO_2.
3. Clouds affect the atmospheric radiation budget both by reflecting incident sunlight and by contributing to the greenhouse effect. Low, thick clouds tend to cool the surface; high, thin clouds tend to warm it.

4. Earth's climate system contains several well-understood feedbacks that play important roles in regulating climate change.
   a. The climate system is stabilized by a strong negative feedback loop between surface temperature and the outgoing infrared flux.
   b. The system is destabilized by a positive feedback loop involving atmospheric water vapor. Because it acts on short time scales, this feedback is likely to play an important role in contemporary global warming. Climate models predict a surface temperature response to CO_2 doubling that is twice that of models in which this feedback is neglected.
   c. The system is also destabilized by a positive feedback loop involving the extent of snow and ice cover due to the effect of albedo.
   d. Clouds may also contribute to climate feedback, but their effect is not well understood.

barometric law
blackbody radiation
conduction
convection
effective radiating temperature
electromagnetic radiation
electromagnetic spectrum
15-μm CO_2 band
flux
frequency
general circulation model

H_2O rotation band
infrared radiation
inverse-square law
Kelvin temperature scale
latent heat
mesosphere
photon
photosphere
radiation
radiative-convective model
relative humidity

Stefan–Boltzmann law
stratosphere
thermosphere
troposphere
ultraviolet radiation
visible radiation
visible spectrum
wavelength
Wien's law

1. How are the wavelength and frequency of an electromagnetic wave related?
2. What is a photon?
3. What physical law describes the manner in which the intensity of sunlight changes as the observer moves away from the Sun?
4. Name two physical laws that apply to blackbody radiation. What do these laws tell us about the nature of the emitted radiation?
5. What is the major contributor to Earth's albedo?
6. What are the three most abundant gases in Earth's atmosphere?
7. List the four layers of Earth's atmosphere. How are they defined?

8. Name three mechanisms by which heat energy can be transferred. Which two are important in Earth's global energy budget?
9. Identify two physical processes by which gases can absorb infrared radiation. Give examples of each process.
10. Why are O_2 and N_2 not greenhouse gases?
11. Describe the different ways in which climate is affected by high and low clouds.
12. Identify two positive feedback loops in Earth's climate system. Why is Earth's climate stable despite these destabilizing, positive feedbacks?

CRITICAL-THINKING PROBLEMS

1. a. Given that a 300-K blackbody radiates its peak energy at a wavelength of about 10 μm, at what wavelength would a 600-K blackbody radiate its peak energy?
    b. If the two bodies in part (a) were the same size, what would be the ratio of the heat emitted by the hotter object to the heat emitted by the colder one?

2. a. Venus and Mars orbit the Sun at average distances of 0.72 AU and 1.52 AU, respectively. What is the solar flux at each planet?
    b. Venus has a planetary albedo of 0.8, and Mars has an albedo of 0.22. Using the answer to part (a), determine the effective radiating temperatures of these planets.
    c. How do the effective radiating temperatures determined in part (b) compare with the value for Earth, and why is this result surprising?
    d. The mean surface temperatures of Venus and Mars are 730 K and 218 K, respectively. Using the answer to part (b), determine the magnitude of the greenhouse effect on each planet.
    e. How do the results of (d) compare with the magnitude of the greenhouse effect on Earth?

3. a. The Sun radiates at an effective temperature of 5780 K and has a radius of about 696,000 km. Remembering that 1 AU = 149,600,000 km, derive the approximate value of the solar flux at Earth's orbit.
    b. Compare your answer with the value given in the text.

4. The tropospheric lapse rate (the rate at which temperature decreases with altitude) is approximately 6°C (11°F) per kilometer. Given that the mean surface temperature of Earth is 288 K and the effective radiating temperature is 255 K, from what altitude does most of the emitted radiation derive?

5. Solar luminosity is estimated to have been 30% lower than today at the time when the solar system formed, 4.6 billion years ago.

    a. If Earth's albedo was the same as it is now ($A = 0.3$), what would have been its effective radiating temperature at that time?
    b. If the magnitude of the greenhouse effect had also remained unchanged ($\Delta T_g = 33$ K), what would Earth's average surface temperature have been? How does this compare with today's value?

6. For atmospheric CO_2 concentrations not too different from the present value, the radiative forcing of CO_2 can be expressed by the formula

$$\Delta F = -6.3 \ln\left(\frac{C}{C_0}\right),$$

where $C_0 = 300$ ppm is the CO_2 concentration near the turn of the 20th century, C is the CO_2 concentration at some other time, and ΔF is the change (in watts per square meter) in the outgoing infrared flux caused by the change in CO_2 concentration. The function $\ln(x)$ denotes the natural logarithm of a given number x. Any scientific calculator has this function key.

    a. By how much would the outgoing infrared flux decrease if the atmospheric CO_2 concentration were increased from 300 ppm to 600 ppm (i.e., if $C = 600$ ppm)?
    b. By how much would surface temperature have to increase in order to bring the radiation budget back into balance in part (a), assuming that the planetary albedo and the amount of water vapor in the atmosphere do not change? (*Hint:* Use the planetary energy balance equation to calculate how much T_e would have to change to balance the radiation budget. Remember that the left-hand side of this equation represents the outgoing infrared flux. The quantity T_s will change by the same amount as T_e if the amount of water vapor is held constant.)

Mathematics Review

Algebra

Using exponents:
$$a^{-x} = \frac{1}{a^x} \qquad a^x a^y = a^{(x+y)} \qquad \frac{a^x}{a^y} = a^{(x-y)} \qquad (a^x)^y = a^{xy}$$

$$a^0 = 1 \qquad a^1 = a \qquad a^{1/n} = \sqrt[n]{a}$$

Fractions:
$$\left(\frac{a}{b}\right)\left(\frac{c}{d}\right) = \frac{ac}{bd} \qquad \frac{a/b}{c/d} = \frac{ad}{bc} \qquad \frac{1}{1/a} = a$$

Logarithms: Natural (base e) logarithms: If $a = e^x$, then $\ln(a) = x \qquad \ln(e^x) = x \qquad e^{\ln(x)} = x$

Base 10 logarithms: If $a = 10^x$, then $\log_{10}(a) = x \qquad \log_{10}(10^x) = x \qquad 10^{\log_{10}(x)} = x$

The following rules hold for both natural and base 10 algorithms:

$$\ln(ab) = \ln(a) + \ln(b) \qquad \ln\left(\frac{a}{b}\right) = \ln(a) - \ln(b) \qquad \ln(a^n) = n\ln(a)$$

The expression $\ln(a + b)$ cannot be simplified.

Linear equations: The graph of the equation $y = ax + b$ is a straight line. a is the slope of the graph. b is the y-intercept.

Proportionality: To say that y is proportional to x, written $y \propto x$, means that $y = ax$, where a is a constant. Proportionality is a special case of linearity. A graph of a proportional relationship is a straight line that passes through the origin. If $y \propto x$, then

$$\frac{y_1}{y_2} = \frac{x_1}{x_2}$$

Slope $a = \dfrac{\text{rise}}{\text{run}} = \dfrac{\Delta y}{\Delta x}$

y-intercept $= b$

Quadratic equation: The quadratic equation $ax^2 + bx + c = 0$ has the two solutions $x = \dfrac{-b \pm \sqrt{b^2 - 4ac}}{2a}$.

Geometry and Trigonometry

Area and volume:

Rectangle
$$A = ab$$

Triangle
$$A = \tfrac{1}{2}ab$$

Circle
$$C = 2\pi r$$
$$A = \pi r^2$$

Rectangular box
$$V = abc$$

Right circular cylinder
$$V = \pi r^2 l$$

Sphere
$$A = 4\pi r^2$$
$$V = \tfrac{4}{3}\pi r^3$$

Arc length and angle: The angle θ in radians is defined as $\theta = s/r$.

The arc length that spans angle θ is $s = r\theta$.

2π rad $= 360°$

Right triangle: Pythagorean theorem $c = \sqrt{a^2 + b^2}$ or $a^2 + b^2 = c^2$

$$\sin\theta = \frac{b}{c} = \frac{\text{far side}}{\text{hypotenuse}} \qquad \theta = \sin^{-1}\left(\frac{b}{c}\right)$$

$$\cos\theta = \frac{a}{c} = \frac{\text{adjacent side}}{\text{hypotenuse}} \qquad \theta = \cos^{-1}\left(\frac{a}{c}\right)$$

$$\tan\theta = \frac{b}{a} = \frac{\text{far side}}{\text{adjacent side}} \qquad \theta = \tan^{-1}\left(\frac{b}{a}\right)$$

In general, if it is known that sine of an angle θ is x, so $x = \sin\theta$, then we can find θ by taking the *inverse sine* of x, denoted $\sin^{-1} x$. Thus $\theta = \sin^{-1} x$. Similar relations apply for cosines and tangents.

General triangle: $\alpha + \beta + \gamma = 180° = \pi$ rad

Identities:

$$\tan\alpha = \frac{\sin\alpha}{\cos\alpha} \qquad\qquad \sin^2\alpha + \cos^2\alpha = 1$$

$$\sin(-\alpha) = -\sin\alpha \qquad\qquad \cos(-\alpha) = \cos\alpha$$

$$\sin(2\alpha) = 2\sin\alpha\cos\alpha \qquad\qquad \cos(2\alpha) = \cos^2\alpha - \sin^2\alpha$$

Expansions and Approximations

Binomial approximation: $(1 + x)^n \approx 1 + nx$ if $x \ll 1$

Small-angle approximation: If $\alpha \ll 1$ rad, then $\sin\alpha \approx \tan\alpha \approx \alpha$ and $\cos\alpha \approx 1$.

The small-angle approximation is excellent for $\alpha < 5°$ (≈ 0.1 rad) and generally acceptable up to $\alpha \approx 10°$.

Answers

Chapter 1

Answers to odd-numbered multiple-choice questions
21. C
23. A
25. B
27. D

Answers to odd-numbered problems
1.

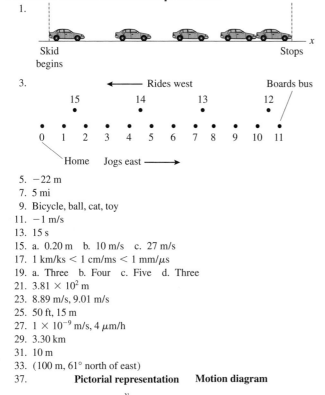

Skid begins   Stops

3.

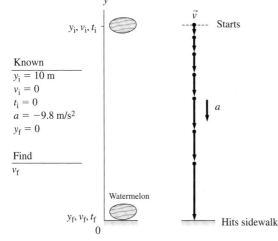

5. -22 m
7. 5 mi
9. Bicycle, ball, cat, toy
11. -1 m/s
13. 15 s
15. a. 0.20 m   b. 10 m/s   c. 27 m/s
17. 1 km/ks $<$ 1 cm/ms $<$ 1 mm/μs
19. a. Three   b. Four   c. Five   d. Three
21. 3.81×10^2 m
23. 8.89 m/s, 9.01 m/s
25. 50 ft, 15 m
27. 1×10^{-9} m/s, 4 μm/h
29. 3.30 km
31. 10 m
33. (100 m, 61° north of east)
37.

Pictorial representation   **Motion diagram**

y

y_i, v_i, t_i $\vec{v}$ --- Starts

Known
$y_i = 10$ m
$v_i = 0$
$t_i = 0$
$a = -9.8$ m/s^2
$y_f = 0$

Find
v_f

a

Watermelon

y_f, v_f, t_f Hits sidewalk
0

41.

Known
$\theta = 20°$
$x_i = 0$ $v_0 = 10$ m/s
$t_i = 0$ $a < 0$
$v_f = 0$

Find
$h = x_f \sin \theta$

Pictorial representation

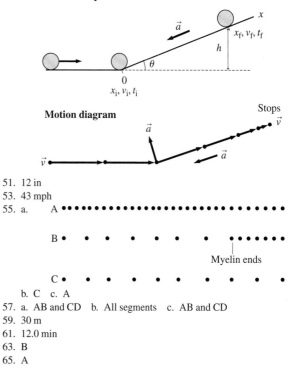

$\vec{a}$ x
x_f, v_f, t_f
h
θ
0
x_i, v_i, t_i

Motion diagram

Stops
$\vec{a}$ $\vec{v}$
$\vec{v}$ $\vec{a}$

51. 12 in
53. 43 mph
55. a.
A ••••••••••••••••••••••••••••

B •   •   •   •   •   ••••••••
                              Myelin ends

C •   •   •   •   •   •   •   •
b. C   c. A
57. a. AB and CD   b. All segments   c. AB and CD
59. 30 m
61. 12.0 min
63. B
65. A

Chapter 2

Answers to odd-numbered multiple-choice questions
17. C
19. D
21. B
23. A
25. D

Answers to odd-numbered problems

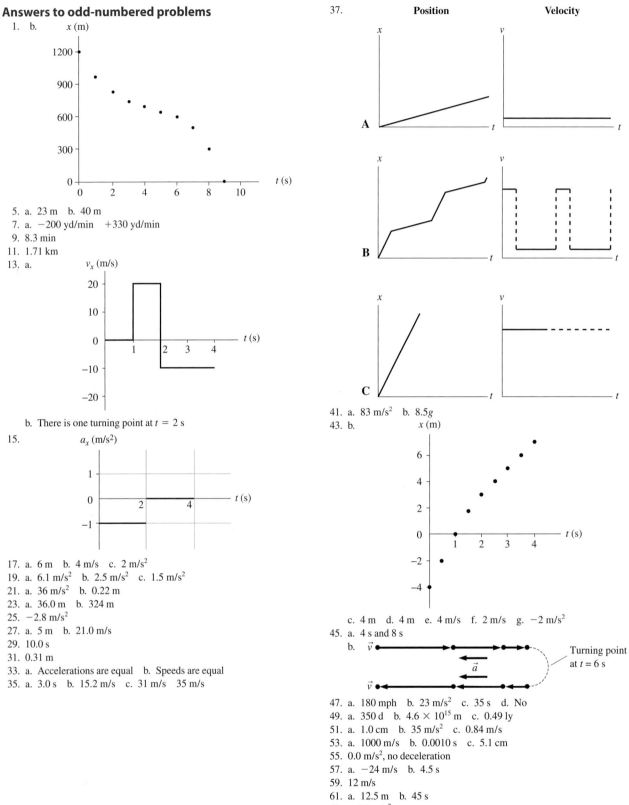

1. b. x (m)

5. a. 23 m   b. 40 m
7. a. -200 yd/min $+330$ yd/min
9. 8.3 min
11. 1.71 km
13. a. v_x (m/s)

   b. There is one turning point at $t = 2$ s
15. a_x (m/s^2)

17. a. 6 m   b. 4 m/s   c. 2 m/s^2
19. a. 6.1 m/s^2 b. 2.5 m/s^2 c. 1.5 m/s^2
21. a. 36 m/s^2 b. 0.22 m
23. a. 36.0 m   b. 324 m
25. -2.8 m/s^2
27. a. 5 m   b. 21.0 m/s
29. 10.0 s
31. 0.31 m
33. a. Accelerations are equal   b. Speeds are equal
35. a. 3.0 s   b. 15.2 m/s   c. 31 m/s   35 m/s

37.   Position   Velocity

41. a. 83 m/s^2 b. 8.5g
43. b. x (m)

   c. 4 m   d. 4 m   e. 4 m/s   f. 2 m/s   g. -2 m/s^2
45. a. 4 s and 8 s
   b.   Turning point at $t = 6$ s

47. a. 180 mph   b. 23 m/s^2 c. 35 s   d. No
49. a. 350 d   b. 4.6×10^{15} m   c. 0.49 ly
51. a. 1.0 cm   b. 35 m/s^2 c. 0.84 m/s
53. a. 1000 m/s   b. 0.0010 s   c. 5.1 cm
55. 0.0 m/s^2, no deceleration
57. a. -24 m/s   b. 4.5 s
59. 12 m/s
61. a. 12.5 m   b. 45 s
63. -1.0 m/s^2
65. a. 4.1 s   b. Both same
67. a. 4.0 s   b. 16 m

69. a. 100 m   b. x (m)

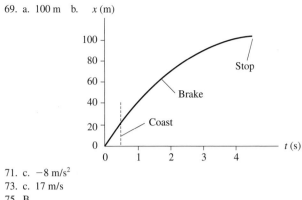

71. c. -8 m/s^2
73. c. 17 m/s
75. B

Chapter 3

Answers to odd-numbered multiple-choice questions
21. C
23. D
25. A
27. B
29. C

Answers to odd-numbered problems
1. First is rear-end; second is head-on
3. People in back can fly forward and injure people in front
5.

7. Weight, tension force by rope
9. Weight, normal force by ground, kinetic friction force by ground
11. Weight, normal force by ground, kinetic friction force by ground
13. $m_1 = 0.08$ kg, $m_3 = 0.50$ kg
15. a. 2.4 m/s^2 b. 0.6 m/s^2
17. a. 16 m/s^2 b. 4 m/s^2 c. 8 m/s^2 d. 32 m/s^2
19. 2.5 m/s^2
21. 0.025 kg
23. a. 25 N   b. 100 N   c. 70 N
25. 0.02 m/s^2
29.

Force identification	**Free-body diagram**

35.

Force identification	**Free-body diagram**

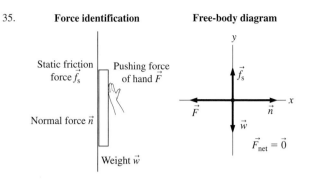

37. The pairs are identified on the diagram.

(i) Earth

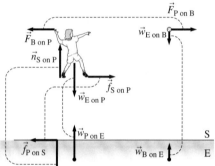

(ii)

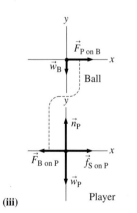

(iii)

39. **Motion diagram**

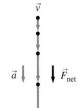

41. **Motion diagram**

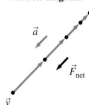

43.

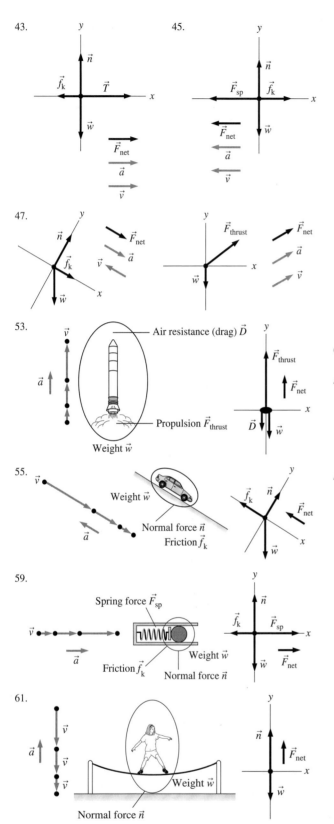

45.

47.

53.

55.

59.

61.

63.

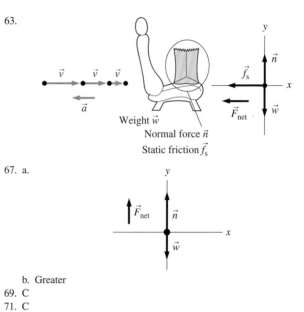

Weight $\vec{w}$
Normal force $\vec{n}$
Static friction $\vec{f}_s$

67. a.

b. Greater
69. C
71. C

Chapter 4

Answers to odd-numbered multiple-choice questions

17. a. C b. D
19. a. C b. B
21. C
23. C
25. D

Answers to selected problems

1. $T_1 = 87$ N $T_2 = 50$ N
3. 110 N each
5. 510 N each
7.

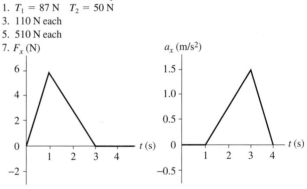

11. $a_x = 1.0$ m/s^2 $a_y = 0.0$ m/s^2
13. a. 0.0 N b. 0.0 N c. 250 N
15. 9800 N toward the rear
17. a. 540 N b. 89 N
19. a. 780 N b. 1600 N
21. a. 780 N b. 1100 N
23. a. 5.9 N b. 5.1 N
25. 0.25
27. 136 m

29. a.   b.

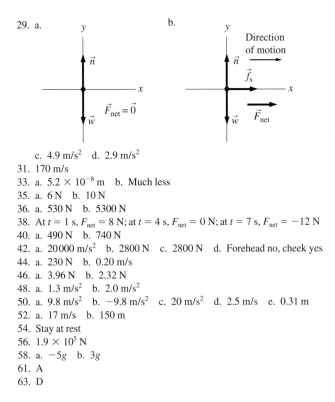

    c. 4.9 m/s^2 d. 2.9 m/s^2
31. 170 m/s
33. a. 5.2×10^{-8} m b. Much less
35. a. 6 N b. 10 N
36. a. 530 N b. 5300 N
38. At $t = 1$ s, $F_{net} = 8$ N; at $t = 4$ s, $F_{net} = 0$ N; at $t = 7$ s, $F_{net} = -12$ N
40. a. 490 N b. 740 N
42. a. 20000 m/s^2 b. 2800 N c. 2800 N d. Forehead no, cheek yes
44. a. 230 N b. 0.20 m/s
46. a. 3.96 N b. 2.32 N
48. a. 1.3 m/s^2 b. 2.0 m/s^2
50. a. 9.8 m/s^2 b. -9.8 m/s^2 c. 20 m/s^2 d. 2.5 m/s e. 0.31 m
52. a. 17 m/s b. 150 m
54. Stay at rest
56. 1.9×10^5 N
58. a. $-5g$ b. $3g$
61. A
63. D

Chapter 5

Answers to selected multiple-choice questions
26. C
28. C
30. C

Answers to selected problems
1. 0 J
3. 12,500 J by the weight, -7920 J by $\vec{T}_1$, -4580 J by $\vec{T}_2$
5. a. 0 J b. 2600 J c. -2600 J
7. The bullet
9. 2
11. 0 J
13. a. 6.8×10^5 J b. 46 m c. No
15. a. 13 m/s b. 14 m/s
17. 31 m/s
19. a. Yes b. 14 m/s
22. 17 m/s
24. a. Potential energy is transformed to kinetic and thermal energy.
    b. 550 J
27. a. 180 J b. 59 W
29. 45 kW

31. a. 30 N b. 45 W
33. 2.0×10^4 W
35. a. 7.7 m/s b. 6.6 m/s
37. 2.3 m/s
39. a. 0.20 kJ b. 98 N c. 2.0 m d. 0.20 kJ
41. 15 m/s
43. 51 cm
45. a. 15 m/s b. They will go hungry.
47. 3.8 m, not dependent on mass
49. a. $\sqrt{\dfrac{(m + M)kd^2}{m^2}}$ b. 200 m/s
    c. 0.9975 kinetic energy transformed to thermal energy
51. 7.9 m/s
53. a. $0.048v_i$ b. 95%
55. a. 100 N b. 0.20 kW c. 1.2 kW
57. 5.5×10^4 L
59. B
61. C
63. A
65. B
67. C

Chapter 6

Answers to even-numbered multiple-choice questions
20. A
22. B
24. C

Answers to odd-numbered problems
1. 8.4×10^5 J
3. 3.3%
5. a. 4.2×10^6 J b. 43 km
7. 230,000 J = 55,000 cal = 55 Cal
9. 1.4 km
11. 710 m
13. a. 200 J b. 16,000 J/day c. 0.0095 donuts/day
15. 0.011 kg
17. a. 1.4×10^6 J b. 1.4×10^6 J
19. a. 190 kJ b. 760 kJ c. 180 Cal d. 140 Cal e. 1200 W

Chapter 7

Answers to odd-numbered problems
1. 830 W
3. 24 W
5. 6.0 W
7. $0.026 \text{ W/(m} \cdot \text{K)}$
9. 2
11. 2100°C

Chapter 8

Answers to odd-numbered multiple-choice questions
23. C
25. C
27. D

Answers to odd-numbered problems
1. 3000 C, 1.9×10^{22}
3. 1.9×10^{20}
5. $0.17 \, \mu A$
7. 13 A
9. 120 C
11. $I_B = 5$ A, $I_C = -2$ A
13. 9.4×10^{18}
15. 12 V
17. 32
19. a. 1   b. 1/2
21. a. $0.087 \, \Omega$ b. $0.0097 \, \Omega$
23. $4100 \, \Omega$
25. 13 mV
27. 3.2 mA
29. a. $2.0 \, \Omega$ b.

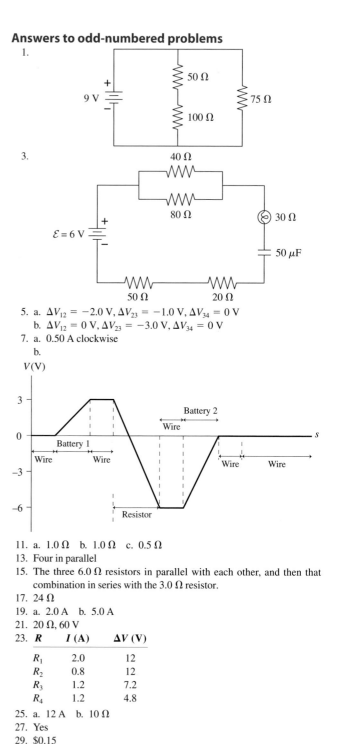

31. a. 200 V/m   b. 100 V/m   c. 0.50 A   d. $480 \, \Omega$
33. More than 15 A
35. 15000 J
37. 23 mA
39. 94 s
41. $42 \, G\Omega$
43. $1800 \, mA \cdot h$
45. $1.4 \, \Omega \cdot m$
47. 1.9 V
49. a. 3.1×10^{14} b. 9.1×10^{5} N/C   c. 0.23 W
51. 0.62 mm
53. Iron
55. 28 cm
57. $8.4 \times 10^{-8} \, \Omega$
59. a. 14 C   b. 27 J
61. a. 0.24 mA   b. 120 mA   c. 30 mW
63. D
65. A

Chapter 9

Answers to selected multiple-choice questions
22. A
24. B
26. B

Answers to odd-numbered problems
1.

3.

5. a. $\Delta V_{12} = -2.0$ V, $\Delta V_{23} = -1.0$ V, $\Delta V_{34} = 0$ V
   b. $\Delta V_{12} = 0$ V, $\Delta V_{23} = -3.0$ V, $\Delta V_{34} = 0$ V
7. a. 0.50 A clockwise
   b.

11. a. $1.0 \, \Omega$ b. $1.0 \, \Omega$ c. $0.5 \, \Omega$
13. Four in parallel
15. The three $6.0 \, \Omega$ resistors in parallel with each other, and then that combination in series with the $3.0 \, \Omega$ resistor.
17. $24 \, \Omega$
19. a. 2.0 A   b. 5.0 A
21. $20 \, \Omega$, 60 V
23.

R	I (A)	ΔV (V)
R_1	2.0	12
R_2	0.8	12
R_3	1.2	7.2
R_4	1.2	4.8

25. a. 12 A   b. $10 \, \Omega$
27. Yes
29. $0.15
31. 19 W
33. a. 1.0 V   b. 1/3
35. 1.2 A

Index

Astronomical Data

Planetary body	Mean distance from sun (m)	Period (years)	Mass (kg)	Mean radius (m)
Sun	—	—	1.99×10^{30}	6.96×10^8
Moon	3.84×10^8*	27.3 days	7.36×10^{22}	1.74×10^6
Mercury	5.79×10^{10}	0.241	3.18×10^{23}	2.43×10^6
Venus	1.08×10^{11}	0.615	4.88×10^{24}	6.06×10^6
Earth	1.50×10^{11}	1.00	5.98×10^{24}	6.37×10^6
Mars	2.28×10^{11}	1.88	6.42×10^{23}	3.37×10^6
Jupiter	7.78×10^{11}	11.9	1.90×10^{27}	6.99×10^7
Saturn	1.43×10^{12}	29.5	5.68×10^{26}	5.85×10^7
Uranus	2.87×10^{12}	84.0	8.68×10^{25}	2.33×10^7
Neptune	4.50×10^{12}	165	1.03×10^{26}	2.21×10^7

*Distance from earth

Typical Coefficients of Friction

Material	Static μ_s	Kinetic μ_k	Rolling μ_r
Rubber on concrete	1.00	0.80	0.02
Steel on steel (dry)	0.80	0.60	0.002
Steel on steel (lubricated)	0.10	0.05	
Wood on wood	0.50	0.20	
Wood on snow	0.12	0.06	
Ice on ice	0.10	0.03	
Synovial joints in the body	0.01	0.003	

Melting/Boiling Temperatures, Heats of Transformation

Substance	T_m (°C)	L_f (J/kg)	T_b (°C)	L_v (J/kg)
Water	0	3.33×10^5	100	22.6×10^5
Nitrogen (N_2)	-210	0.26×10^5	-196	1.99×10^5
Ethyl alcohol	-114	1.09×10^5	78	8.79×10^5
Mercury	-39	0.11×10^5	357	2.96×10^5
Lead	328	0.25×10^5	1750	8.58×10^5

Properties of Materials

Substance	ρ (kg/m³)	c (J/kg · K)	v_{sound} (m/s)
Helium gas (1 atm, 0°C)	0.179		970
Air (1 atm, 0°C)	1.28		331
Air (1 atm, 20°C)	1.20		343
Ethyl alcohol	790	2400	1170
Gasoline	680		
Glycerin	1260		
Mercury	13,600	140	1450
Oil (typical)	900		
Water ice	920	2090	3500
Liquid water	1000	4190	1480
Seawater	1030		1500
Blood	1060		
Muscle	1040	3600	
Fat	920	3000	
Mammalian body	1005	3400	1540
Granite	2750	790	6000
Aluminum	2700	900	5100
Copper	8920	385	
Gold	19,300	129	
Iron	7870	449	
Lead	11,300	128	1200
Diamond	3520	510	12,000